COMPLETE BOOK OF THE WORLD CUP 2006

COMPLETE BOOK OF THE WORLD CUP 2006

CRIS FREDDI

HarperSport

An Imprint of HarperCollins*Publishers*

First published in 2006 by
HarperSport
an imprint of HarperCollins*Publishers*
London

© Cris Freddi 2006

1

A CIP catalogue record for this book is
available from the British Library

ISBN-13   978–0–00–722916–1
ISBN-10   0–00–722916–X

Printed and bound in Singapore by Imago

The HarperCollins website address is
www.harpercollins.co.uk

Contents

Acknowledgements

This book will always be grateful for the contributions of Ron Templeton, Alejandro Rodón, Colin Jose, Carlos Yametti, Héctor Luis Sicco, Tito Ticerán Guerra, Duilio Domingos Martino, José Moretzsohn, Mário Levi Schwartz, Michel Oreggia, Brian Mellowship, Charlie Richards, Rob Smyth, Guy Oliver, David Barber at the FA, Brian Huff and his team at the British Newspaper Library in Colindale, and the HarperSport editorial team of Mike Doggart and Tom Whiting for their faith, patience, and profound football knowledge.

For the 2006 edition, thanks too to Francine Brody Freddi, Toby Austin, Neil Glenn, Julio Macías, Steve Jackson, Peter Raath, Chris Wigginton, Esther Hendriks, Andy Henderson, Olivia Popov-Baertsch at FIFA, Jean Jacques Mouandjo at the Cameroon FA, Nicolas Cornu at the Belgian FA, Thomas Saleteg at the Swedish FA, picture researcher Holley Miles again, Dom Forbes for a great cover design, and above all the utterly indispensable Liam Rigby and his very fine tooth comb.

Introduction to the 2006 edition

The complete book just got more complete.

Except it can't have, can it? Something can't be 'more complete' any more than it can be 'more dead'. Either it's complete or it's not. What's going on?

Let's call it a work in progress. That's the best we can do with the World Cup. It's a strange animal, our premier football competition. Although it began life in 1930, i.e. relatively recently, it's always been rather patchily documented. Some excellent recent work has corrected some of the received wisdom, but even these latest efforts are sprinkled with errors, as are some of FIFA's own Official Reports. A minefield for researchers.

So I've tried to double-check everything, using national sources where possible, e.g. Bulgarian publications and statisticians for Bulgarian line-ups. And where these findings differ from what's already been published, I've added footnotes to that effect. But four years between editions is a long time, and new info keeps coming to light – so some things that once looked cast-iron have had to be cast aside. Sometimes less is more complete.

As always, video's the key. It's come in from 1938 now, and 1974 and 1982 – so nearly every tournament's covered – which is just as well, because a great many written reports bear little resemblance to what's on the screen. So I've avoided re-hashing other people's descriptions of play – except where it's unavoidable. There's no escaping the official book for 1934 (when there's very little coherent film) or newspaper articles for 1930 (when only the Final seems to have been filmed at all, coherently or otherwise) and some of 1950.

The format, meanwhile, stays the same. Descriptions of the individual matches in preference to hundreds of pages of text followed by a great block of statistics. This way the prose and stats should feed off each other, adding context and immediacy. The top line of each report comprises the date of the match, the name of the stadium and city, the number of spectators, and the name and nationality of the referee. At the end of each team line-up, the team manager or coach is listed in italics. This is usually the man in sole charge of team selection and tactics, though sometimes these roles were divided between two or more individuals. Team captains are indicated by the letter C in brackets after their names. The names of substitutes are enclosed in square brackets, followed by the minute in which they came on. Half-time is indicated by the letters HT, full-time by FT (for players who came on just before the start of extra time; those who came on in injury time at the end of a match have a 90 after their name).

Half-time scores (and full-time scores where extra time was played) are shown in brackets, and goal times are in minutes unless specified as seconds.

Players' names

This is the first English publication to include the first name of every player, coach and referee in the World Cup finals. These forenames are mentioned when a player makes his first appearance in a tournament, then excluded from his subsequent matches. I've used initials to differentiate between players with the same surname in a team, including (to save space) Chinese, Koreans, and Middle Eastern players.

Most players are shown by their first names and surnames in the usual European manner, including those commonly known by more than one forename: e.g. Jan Åge Fjørtoft, Jose Luis Lamadrid. Where possible, I've used a player's familiar name or diminutive rather than the formal version of his forename: e.g. Bobby not Robert, Jupp or Sepp not Josef, Enzo or Renzo instead of Lorenzo, Włodek instead of Włodzimierz, Bora instead of Velibor or Borivoje. In most cases the formal name should be obvious (Jack Charlton was christened John, etc), but where this isn't, lack of space sometimes prevents an explanation. For example, the Danny in Danny Blanchflower is a diminutive of Dennis, Ray Wilson was christened Ramon, Sol (Campbell) is short for Sulzeer, Berti Vogts' full name is Hans-Hubert, and the Dutch thankfully shorten their long Latin names, e.g. from Josephus Franciscus Johannes Antonius van Run to 'Sjef'!

Even the use of diminutives isn't something you can do every time. In all countries, some players are known by their formal names (Alessandro Altobelli, Giovanni Lodetti, Giuseppe Bergomi) and some aren't (Sandro Mazzola, Gianni Rivera, Beppe Signori). As a result, we've often had to make a decision, sometimes a compromise, using a formal name where it's more recognisable in this country: Kurt (Hamrin) instead of Kurre, Karl-Erik (Palmér) instead of Kalle, Francisco (Gento) instead of Paco, etc. Bear with it, it's been a difficult juggling act.

A good many players, mainly Brazilian, Spanish, Portuguese, Turkish and North African, were known by their first names. These are shown with their surnames in brackets – Eusébio (Ferreira), Gérson (de Oliveira), etc – and are referred to by just their first names in subsequent matches. Again, this includes players known by two forenames: e.g. Paulo César (Lima), José Augusto (de Almeida). To save space, there's been no attempt to list all the names of, say, the Brazilians (Sócrates had six!) except in a few famous cases: Pelé, Garrincha, Zico and so on. Any player known by a nickname has inverted commas round this, followed by his forename and surname in brackets, e.g. 'Tostão' (Eduardo Gonçalves), 'Jairzinho' (Jair Ventura). The inverted commas disappear in a player's subsequent appearances.

For Spanish names, I've used the Basque spelling where appropriate (e.g. Goikoetxea, Alexanko and Bixente rather than Goicoechea, Alesanco and Vincent). As for translations from other scripts (Cyrillic for Bulgaria and the USSR, Arabic, Hebrew and Greek), I've tried to be consistent but haven't been unduly concerned with matching the versions seen in other publications, especially those from abroad. A Polish book, for instance, writes the name Tsarev as Carew! I've left out accents on the names of players from French-speaking African countries (Kundé, Saïd, etc) because I'm not sure if they would have had those accents in their original languages. This explains the anomaly of Cisse (Senegal) and

Cissé (France) playing against each other in 2002. I've left the accent off the final C in the surname when a player of Yugoslav ancestry appeared for other countries: Buljevic and Utjesenovic for Australia, Lucic and Ibrahimovic for Sweden, etc.

Three final points. Unless otherwise mentioned, players with the same surname are unrelated; I've used the usual English spellings for towns and cities (including Marseilles, Rheims and Hanover), except for Zaragoza (Saragossa seems a tad precious); and the text includes a number of references to 'finals' (as in 'finals matches' and 'finals records'). This refers of course to World Cup finals tournaments, as opposed to qualifying rounds or the finals of any other competition. The word 'Final,' with a capital F, refers to the World Cup Final itself, the deciding match of each tournament and the most important football match in the world.

That's been the bottom line in putting this together: the buzz of covering the greatest sporting show on earth. For all the politics off the field and violence on it, most tournaments have produced enough world-class football to raise the spirits. The World Cup deserves a more complete book. This is the nearest yet.

CMG Freddi
Shepherd's Bush
April 2006

Abbreviations

ALG	Algeria	FRA	France	POR	Portugal
ARG	Argentina	GER	Germany (West	ROM	Romania
AUS	Australia		Germany 1954–90)	RUS	Russia
AUT	Austria	GHA	Ghana	SAF	South Africa
BEL	Belgium	GUA	Guatemala	SAU	Saudi Arabia
BEN	Benin	HKG	Hong Kong	SCO	Scotland
BHR	Bahrain	HOL	Holland	SEN	Senegal
BOL	Bolivia	HUN	Hungary	SNG	Singapore
BRZ	Brazil	IRN	Iran	SPA	Spain
BUL	Bulgaria	ISR	Israel	SVK	Slovakia
CAM	Cameroon	ITA	Italy	SWE	Sweden
CAN	Canada	JAM	Jamaica	SWI	Switzerland
CHI	Chile	JPN	Japan	SYR	Syria
CHN	China	KUW	Kuwait	THA	Thailand
COL	Colombia	LBY	Libya	TRI	Trinidad & Tobago
COS	Costa Rica	MAU	Mauritius	TUN	Tunisia
CZE	Czechoslovakia	MEX	Mexico	TUR	Turkey
DDR	East Germany	MLI	Mali	UAE	United Arab
DEN	Denmark	MOR	Morocco		Emirates
ENG	England	NGA	Nigeria	URU	Uruguay
ECU	Ecuador	NGR	Niger	USA	United States
EGY	Egypt	NIR	Northern Ireland	USR	USSR (Soviet Union)
EIR	Republic of Ireland	NKO	North Korea	VEN	Venezuela
ENG	England	PAR	Paraguay	WAL	Wales
ETH	Ethiopia	PER	Peru	YUG	Yugoslavia
FIN	Finland	POL	Poland	ZAI	Zaire

French for beginners

Prologue

It was a glint in FIFA's eye from the start. When the governing body was formed in 1904, they reserved the exclusive right to organise a world championship – just when there was no real need for one. The Olympics were beginning to produce a universally accepted pecking order, the UK (a.k.a. England amateurs) beating Denmark in the 1908 and 1912 Finals. However, by the time of the 1929 FIFA Congress, football had outgrown the Games, partly because of the spread of professionalism. Time for a trophy of one's own.

Five countries didn't think so – the amateur Scandinavians and Estonia – but the other twenty-five members voted for a tournament to be held within a year. A host country was soon chosen and a stadium built within eight months, including three in the rainy season. Simple when you know it's necessary.

Probably something to do with French flair for getting things done. A Frenchman had inaugurated the modern Olympics, Robert Guérin was the first FIFA president, Jules Rimet one of his successors (1920–54). Henri Delaunay proposed an early World Cup resolution, Abel Lafleur sculpted the first trophy, France played in the first match. Thirty years later, they had a similar influence on the European Cup.

But if the French were the midwives, there was a country that called itself the father of football (acknowledging Britain as the mother), the natural choice for bringing up FIFA's baby.

Home comforts for the first World Cup winners. Back row (l-r): trainer Ernesto Figoli, Gestido, Nasazzi, Ballestrero, Mascheroni, Andrade, Fernández, masseur Luis Greco. Front row (l-r): Dorado, Scarone, Castro (hiding his missing hand), Cea, Iriarte.

1930

1934
1938
1950
1954
1958
1962
1966
1970
1974
1978
1982
1986
1990
1994
1998
2002
2006

New World order

Uruguay **1930**

Almost as soon as they'd voted against the idea of a World Cup, Sweden applied to stage it. Quick learners indeed. Italy applied too, along with Spain and Holland, only for all four to step aside once all the credentials were on the table. Uruguay were clearly the big players.

In some reports it comes across as a surprising decision, as if the game's showpiece had been offered to a Third World shanty town. In fact Montevideo was a thrusting city and port, still surviving the effects of the Wall Street Crash. 1930 was the centenary of Uruguayan independence, and the country's exchequer was buoyant enough to build a grand new stadium and cover the expenses of every country that took part.

The last was surely the clincher as far as FIFA were concerned but seems to have cut little ice with most of Europe. Regular jet travel was still in the future, so the financial guarantees persuaded only four countries to make the ocean voyage. With thirteen taking part, the knockout system had to be replaced by four groups. The real contenders stayed at home: Hungary and Austria, Italy and Germany, Spain – while England and Scotland, as strong as anyone, weren't even eligible, having resigned from FIFA over the question of 'broken time' payments in 1928.

All of which didn't really matter very much. Even against Europe's finest, Uruguay would have been expected to win.

In 1924 they'd played outside South America for the first time, winning the Olympic title in Paris. After thrashing Yugoslavia 7-0 and the hosts 5-1, they outplayed the Swiss 3-0 in the final, their stern defence buttressing some dazzling inter-passing up front. Four years later they won it again.

It wasn't just that they happened to have a strong pool of players. What really separated the leading South American countries from European opposition was a familiarity with tournaments arranged along World Cup lines: several matches played in the space of a month or so. Both continents took part in the Olympics every four years – but Uruguay and the rest were also involved in the Copa América, already staged twelve times since 1910 (fifty years before the European Championship). Ideas on physical preparation and training camps were in advance of anything in most of Europe at the time.

So the hosts were firm favourites, with the only real opposition likely to come from Argentina, who'd taken them to a replay in the Olympic final two years earlier and beaten them 2-0 to win the Copa América in between. The other South American teams were makeweights, Mexico barely that, the United States an unknown quality (polite euphemism). The four European entries weren't particularly good, but at least they were there, and one or two were about to play more than just a bit-part in history.

GROUP 1

Argentina (seeded), Chile, France, Mexico.

13 July 1930 – Pocitos, Montevideo – 4,444 – Domingo Lombardi (URU)

FRANCE   **(3) 4**
Laurent 19, Langiller 40, Maschinot 42, 87

MEXICO   **(0) 1**
Carreño 70

FRANCE Alexis Thépot, Étienne Mattler, Marcel Capelle, Augustin Chantrel, Alexandre Villaplane (c), Edmond Delfour, Marcel Pinel, Lucien Laurent, André Maschinot, Ernest Liberati, Marcel Langiller. *Raoul Caudron.*
MEXICO Oscar Bonfiglio, Rafael Garza Gutiérrez (c), Manuel Rosas, Efraín Amezcua, Alfredo Sánchez, Felipe Rosas, Hilario López, José Ruiz, Dionisio Mejía, Juan Carreño, Luis Pérez. *Juan Luque de Serralonga (SPA).*

France's win against Belgium the previous month had been their first in eleven matches, and they were accustomed to losing heavily against the stronger European sides – but Mexico were even worse. The only country they'd ever beaten was Guatemala, and the one other time they'd dipped their toe in a tournament, they'd lost 7-1 to Spain at the 1928 Olympics.

Still, the match had some history attached. With no qualifying matches necessary, this and the USA-Belgium fixture were the first ever World Cup matches (they kicked off at the same time). Laurent scored the first ever goal, converting Liberati's cross from the right. An injury to Alex Thépot led to Chantrel playing in goal for the last hour, but even with ten men France were too good. Mattler, a big capable full-back, made a goal for Langiller, and Maschinot shot home a pass by Delfour, who doubled as the team's physical trainer. Carreño,

a stumpy Aztec, scored from Mejía's pass, but the Mexicans weren't enjoying the conditions (it had snowed the night before) and the speedy Langiller crossed for Maschinot to finish off what amounted to a training match for tougher things to come. Manuel and Felipe Rosas were the first brothers to play in the World Cup. Carreño, who had scored on his debut in the Olympic defeat by Spain, died of appendicitis when he was only 33. At the other end of the scale, Laurent died at the age of 97 in 2005.

15 July 1930 – Parque Central, Montevideo – 23,409 – Gilberto de Almeida Rêgo (BRZ)

ARGENTINA   **(0) 1**
Monti 81

FRANCE   **(0) 0**

ARGENTINA Ángel Bossio, José Della Torre, Ramón Muttis, Juan Evaristo, Luis Monti, Pedro 'Arico' Suárez, Natalio Perinetti, Francisco Varallo, Manuel (Nolo) Ferreira (c), Roberto Cerro, Marino (Mario) Evaristo. *Francisco Olazar, with Juan José Tramutola.*
FRANCE Thépot, Mattler, Capelle, Chantrel, Villaplane (c), Delfour, Pinel, Laurent, Liberati, Maschinot, Langiller.

In any normal tournament, the next match would have been between the other two teams in the group. Instead the French were made to take on their strongest opposition after only a day's rest. Whimsical days indeed. In the event, they made a brave show of it, resisting for over eighty minutes despite having little luck – or much protection from the referee.

Argentina relied almost totally on pure skill up front, leaving virtually all semblance of defence to their famous centre-half Luisito Monti, a good long passer out to the wings but essentially a destroyer – to say the least. This was the dirtiest great player of his generation. Desperate Dan jaw, no neck, and legs that went right through a man, something they did after only two minutes here: when Laurent had the temerity to try and dribble past him, his ankle was so badly injured that he limped throughout the match and couldn't play in the next. Then Thépot's injury flared up again and France were left with nine fit men for the last seventy minutes.

They nearly survived, partly because Argentina lacked a cutting edge. Ferreira was playing out of position and Cerro, normally so good in the air, was apparently taking medication for his nerves! The late goal came from a free kick that the French defended badly. They didn't put up a wall; instead three defenders stood on the six-yard line, blocking Thépot's view and leaving a gap in the left-hand corner. A straightforward shot by Monti added insult to the injuries he'd inflicted. The Argentinians were also lucky that the referee had to restart the match after blowing the full-time whistle six minutes early with France on the attack. Nevertheless they were the better side, likely to improve as the tournament went on. Especially if they found a genuine striker. Cerro is usually seen misspelt Cherro (the way it's pronounced).

YOUNGEST COACHES

yrs	days			
27	267	Juan José Tramutola	ARG	1930
29	77	György Orth	CHI	1930
30	129	Jaroslav Cejp	CZE	1954
31	210	Octavio Vial	MEX	1950
31	240	Alberto Suppici	URU	1930

Tramutola was Argentina's 'technical director,' with Francisco Olazar as coach.

Cejp was part of a three-man selection committee.

Twelve days later, Suppici became the youngest to win the World Cup. He and Tramutola opposed each other in the Final.

16 July 1930 – Parque Central, Montevideo – 9,249 – Henri Christophe (BEL)

CHILE	**(1) 3**

Vidal 4, 86, M Rosas o.g. 51

MEXICO	**(0) 0**

CHILE Roberto Cortés, Ulises Poirier, Victor Morales, Humberto Elgueta, Guillermo Saavedra, Arturo Torres, Carlos Schneeberger (c), Carlos Vidal, Eberardo Villalobos, Guillermo Subiabre, Tomás Ojeda. *György Orth (HUN)*.
MEXICO Isidoro Sota, R Garza Gutiérrez (c), M Rosas, Amezcua, Sánchez, F Rosas, López, Ruiz, Roberto Gayón, Carreño, Pérez.

In their 42nd international match, Chile kept their first clean sheet, thanks partly to the first World Cup own goal, a Rosas header. Some old sources list the goalscorers as Vidal, Subiabre 2.

19 July 1930 – Centenario, Montevideo – 42,100 – Aníbal Tejada (URU)

CHILE	**(0) 1**

Subiabre 64

FRANCE	**(0) 0**

CHILE Cortés, Ernesto Chaparro, Guillermo Riveros, A Torres, Saavedra, Casimiro Torres, Schneeberger (c), Vidal, Villalobos, Subiabre, Ojeda.
FRANCE Thépot, Mattler, Capelle, Chantrel, Villaplane (c), Delfour, Célestin Delmer, Pinel, Liberati, Émile Veinante, Langiller.

Again France held out determinedly. Ten minutes before half-time, Thépot, a genuine star of the tournament, saved Vidal's penalty, the first awarded in any World Cup match. The French were as dapper as ever, but injuries, tiredness and a reshuffled attack took their toll, and a single headed goal was enough. For Chile, a showdown with Argentina. For France, what else but *la gloire*.

Their captain Alex Villaplane, who was winning his last cap, was later executed for collaborating with the Nazis.

---

19 July 1930 – Centenario, Montevideo – 42,100 – Ulrico Saucedo (BOL)

ARGENTINA   (3) 6
Stábile 8, 17, 80, Zumelzú 10, 55, Varallo 53

MEXICO   (1) 3
M Rosas pen 37, pen 72, Gayón 78

ARGENTINA Bossio (c), Della Torre, Fernando Paternóster, Alberto Chividini, Adolfo Zumelzú, Rodolfo Orlandini, Carlos Peucelle, Guillermo Stábile, Varallo, Atilio Demaría, Carlos Spadaro.
MEXICO Bonfiglio, Francisco Garza Gutiérrez, R Garza Gutiérrez (c), Raymundo Rodríguez, Sánchez, M Rosas, Felipe Olivares, Carreño, Gayón, López, F Rosas.

Part of a double-header, played after the Chile-France match – so four penalties were awarded on the same ground on the same day, all three in this game for handball. Bonfiglio saved Paternóster's kick after 23 minutes and Bossio saved Rosas' second but couldn't keep out the rebound. Mind you, Rosas did well to score at all: the penalty spot was apparently sixteen yards out!

Argentina had found their goal poacher, albeit by accident. With Ferreira back in Buenos Aires taking a law exam (the past is another country, no question), they replaced him with the lean and craggy Stábile, who became the first player to score a hat-trick in the World Cup finals on his international debut, after which he couldn't be left out.

Some modern publications list Zumelzú as captain, but the leading Argentinian statistician disagrees, and Bossio's carrying the pennant in the team photo. Francisco and Rafael Garza Gutiérrez were brothers. The referee was also the manager ('person responsible') of the

Bolivian squad, one of the linesmen (Costel Rădulescu) the manager of Romania. Bonfiglio later became an army general.

---

22 July 1930 – Centenario, Montevideo – 41,459 – John Langenus (BEL)

ARGENTINA   (2) 3
Stábile 12, 14, M Evaristo 51

CHILE   (1) 1
Arellano 15

ARGENTINA Bossio, Della Torre, Paternóster, J Evaristo, Monti, Orlandini, Peucelle, Varallo, Stábile, Ferreira (c), M Evaristo.
CHILE Cortés, Chaparro, Morales, A Torres, Saavedra, C Torres, Juan Aguilera, Vidal, Villalobos, Subiabre (c), Guillermo Arellano.

Again, much as expected. Chile no pushovers, Argentina always likely to qualify, Monti sure to cause mayhem. This time his activities provoked a mass punch-up (photographs show more than thirty officials and police on the pitch). Chile squared the ledger with a foul on Varallo while he was celebrating a goal! Old sources list Subiabre as the Chilean goalscorer. Nine players were winning their last cap for Chile, who didn't play another international till 1935.

GROUP 1

	P	W	D	L	F	A	Pts
Argentina	3	3	0	0	10	4	6
Chile	3	2	0	1	5	3	4
France	3	1	0	2	4	3	2
Mexico	3	0	0	3	4	13	0

Argentina qualified for the semi-finals.

GROUP 2

Bolivia, Brazil (seeded), Yugoslavia.

14 July 1930 – Parque Central, Montevideo – 24,059 – Aníbal Tejada (URU)

YUGOSLAVIA **(2) 2**
Tirnanić 21, Bek 30

BRAZIL **(0) 1**
Preguinho 62

YUGOSLAVIA Milovan Jakšić, Milutin Ivković (c), Dragan Mihajlović, Milorad Arsenijević, Ljubiša Stevanović, Momčilo Đokić, Aleksandar Tirnanić, Blagoje Marjanović, Ivan Bek, Đorđe Vujadinović, Brane Sekulić. *Boško Simonović*.
BRAZIL Joel (de Oliveira), Alfredo Brilhante, 'Itália' (Luis Gervasoni), Hermógenes (Fonseca), Fausto (dos Santos), Fernando (Giudicelli), 'Poly' (Polycarpo Ribeiro), Nilo (Murtinho Braga), Araken (Patuska), 'Preguinho' (João Coelho Netto) (c), Teófilo (Bettencourt). *Píndaro (de Carvalho)*.

On the surface, a surprise result: a so-so European team beating the mighty Brazil – but there was more to it than that. Brazil hadn't played in a full international since 1925 and now fielded ten new caps.

When Joel couldn't hold Sekulić's shot, Tirnanić put in the rebound. Five minutes from the end, he had a goal disallowed. Quick and fit (average age only 21), Yugoslavia had three players good enough to play for French clubs, including one later capped by France under the name Yvan Beck. His goal here was the result of 'a fine individual work'.

After that, Brazil did most of the attacking, scored through the multi-talented Preguinho (basketball, volleyball, water polo), but were frustrated by Jakšić, prominent throughout the tournament, and the huge swarthy Ivković.

17 July 1930 – Parque Central, Montevideo – 18,306 – Francisco Matteucci (URU)

YUGOSLAVIA **(0) 4**
Bek 60, 67, Marjanović 65, Vujadinović 85

BOLIVIA **(0) 0**

YUGOSLAVIA J Jakšić, Ivković (c), Mihajlović, Arsenijević, Stevanović, Đokić, Tirnanić, Marjanović, Bek, Vujadinović, Dragutin Najdanović.
BOLIVIA Jesús Bermúdez, Segundo Durandal, Casiano Chavarría, Juan Jorge Argote, Diógenes Lara, Jorge Luis Valderrama, Gumercindo Gómez, José Bustamante I, Rafael Méndez (c), Mario Alborta, René Fernández. *Ulrico Saucedo*.

Bolivia, playing their only match against European opposition before 1977, made a colourful entrance, each player sporting a letter of the alphabet on the front of his white shirt, forming the words Viva Uruguay. The letter Y wore a black beret, the first letter U a thick white headband.

None of this camouflaged the fact that they were the weakest team in the competition, already established as the whipping boys of the Copa América. Five were making their debuts, and the country had played a grand total of seven internationals, losing the lot.

They might have changed that if they'd had any luck here. Instead they apparently had four goals disallowed, and Gómez broke his leg in a challenge with Ivković. Yugoslavia would have

MOST NEW CAPS IN A TEAM

10	Brazil	1930	v Yugoslavia
10	Argentina	1934	v Sweden
9	Dutch East Indies	1938	v Hungary
8	Brazil	1934	v Spain
7	Peru	1930	v Romania
7	Brazil	1938	v Poland

1934
1938
1950
1954
1958
1962
1966
1970
1974
1978
1982
1986
1990
1994
1998
2002
2006

1930

YOUGEST REFEREES

yrs	days			
27	62	Francisco Matteucci	URU	1930
28	224	Ivan Eklind	SWE	1934
28	281	Mark Shield	AUS	2002
30	40	Peter Mikkelsen	DEN	1990
30	153	Louis Baert	BEL	1934
30	231	José María Codesal	URU	1958
30	262	Ramón Barreto	URU	1970

Later in the tournament, Eklind became the youngest to referee a Final: 28 years 238 days.

been happy with a draw and were happy to wait an hour for the goals to come. Brazil were out.

This and the USA v Paraguay match in Group 4 were played on the same ground on the same day. According to one source, the crowd figure was only 800!

---

20 July 1930 – Centenario, Montevideo – 25,466 – John Balway (FRA)

BRAZIL   **(1) 4**
Moderato 27, 73, Preguinho 57, 83

BOLIVIA   **(0) 0**

BRAZIL Oswaldo Velloso, 'Zé Luiz' (José Luiz de Oliveira), Itália, Hermógenes, Fausto, Fernando, Benedicto (Dantas), 'Russinho' (Moacyr de Siqueira), Carlos de Carvalho Leite, Preguinho (c), Moderato (Visintainer).
BOLIVIA Bermúdez, Durandal, Chavarría, Renato Sáenz, Lara, Valderrama, Eduardo Reyes, Bustamante, Méndez (c), Alborta, Fernández.

With nothing at stake, Brazil sent out another five debutants, one of whom saved Sáenz's penalty with the score still 0-0, leaving Bolivia to wait 64 years for their first goal in the finals. This time Bolivia had no letters on their shirts but berets were worn by three outfield players

on each side. Black footballers were only just beginning to filter into Brazilian national teams, including just one in 1930, the strong centre-half Fausto, who was their best player.

Brazil took the lead when Carvalho Leite hit a post and Moderato put in the rebound, then dominated the second half with their vastly superior technique.

Balway is believed to have been an Englishman living in Paris. The French FA's website calls him Georges Balvay, but this is apparently an error (contemporary French sources spell it Balway and several sources call him John). Sáenz is sometimes seen spelt Sáinz.

GROUP 2

	P	W	D	L	F	A	Pts
Yugoslavia	2	2	0	0	6	1	4
Brazil	2	1	0	1	5	2	2
Bolivia	2	0	0	2	0	8	0

Yugoslavia qualified for the semi-finals.

GROUP 3

Peru, Romania, Uruguay (seeded).

---

14 July 1930 – Pocitos, Montevideo – 300 – Alberto Warnken (CHI)

ROMANIA   **(1) 3**
Deşu 50 sec, Stanciu 74, Kovács 85

PERU   **(0) 1**
Souza Ferreira 63

ROMANIA Ion Lăpuşneanu, Adalbert Steiner, Rudolf Bürger, Ladislau Raffinsky, Alfred Eisenbeisser, Emerich Vogl, Nicolae Kovács, Adalbert Deşu, Rudolf Wetzer (c), Constantin Stanciu, Ştefan Barbu. *Costel Rădulescu.*

PERU Juan Valdivieso, Mario de las Casas, Alberto Soria, Alberto Denegri, Plácido Galindo (c), Domingo García, José María Lavalle, Julio Lores, Alejandro Villanueva, Demetrio Neyra, Luis Souza Ferreira.
Francisco Brú (SPA).
SENT OFF: Galindo 70.

Essentially a curtain-raiser for the entrance of the hosts, the match produced the first World Cup sending-off and the smallest crowd. Although the official figure was 2,549, photographs of the completely empty stands, with very few spectators behind the goals, make 300 look about right.

Peru fielded six new caps, including Valdivieso who conceded a goal in the first minute of his international career, Deşu's 30-yard drive. After that, a series of brawls: Steiner breaking a leg, Galindo sent off by a referee who lost control. Romania then scored twice against ten men.

A respected modern publication mentions Lizandro Nué Rodríguez coming on as substitute for Souza Ferreira after 80 minutes – but the leading Peruvian statistician says this is a definite error. Some British sources still insist on listing the Romanian goalscorers as 'Staucin'

2, Barbu (a bad error) – and the captains as Vogl and de las Casas. Eisenbeisser was commonly known as Fieraru, Kovács as Covaci, Raffinsky also spelt Rafinski. Lores, who later played for Mexico, is misprinted Flores in some reports.

18 July 1930 – Centenario, Montevideo – 57,735 – John Langenus (BEL)

URUGUAY (0) 1
Castro 60
PERU   (0) 0

URUGUAY Enrique Ballestrero, José Nasazzi (c), Domingo Tejera, José Leandro Andrade, Lorenzo Fernández, Álvaro Gestido, Santos Urdinarán, Héctor Castro, Pedro Petrone, Pedro Cea, Santos Iriarte.
Alberto Suppici.
PERU Jorge Pardón, de las Casas, Antonio Maquilón (c), Denegri, Galindo, Eduardo Astengo, Lavalle, Lores, Villanueva, Neyra, Souza Ferreira.

When Uruguay finally made their bow, five days after the first match, in front of the biggest crowd yet, they had an unfinished ground (three tiers in some places, two in others) and a team to match.

1930

1934

1938

1950

1954

1958

1962

1966

1970

1974

1978

1982

1986

1990

1994

1998

2002

2006

SMALLEST CROWDS

300	1930	Romania	v	Peru	Montevideo
2,000	1954	Turkey	v	South Korea	Geneva
2,823	1958	Wales	v	Hungary	Stockholm
3,580	1950	Switzerland	v	Mexico	Pôrto Alegre
4,444	1930	France	v	Mexico	Montevideo

One source says only 1,500 watched Bulgaria v Morocco in 1970. Attendance figures for the Cuba v Romania replay in 1938 vary from 3,993 to 7,536.

Lowest for a Final

45,124	1938	Italy	v	Hungary	Paris

1930

This was the first international played at the new stadium, on the same day as the name of the road leading to it: Avenida 18 Julio, the anniversary of independence. The team was more established than that: eight players had Olympic gold medals and the spine had been there for some time: the 'iron curtain' half-back line, the fearsome Nasazzi at the back, and several of the forwards. But there had been a change in goal, where Andrés Mazali, a star of both Olympic teams, one of the first keepers to patrol his penalty area, had been dropped from the team for breaking curfew. Caught sneaking home for a conjugal visit, he didn't play for Uruguay again. His replacement (misspelt Ballesteros in old sources) wasn't in the same class.

Up front too, things didn't click against Peru. Two of the inside-forward trio were finishers rather than starters: the famous Petrone, so clever at finding space that he was called the first player to play without the ball – and the combative Castro, who'd lost his right hand to an electric saw while working as a carpenter. Petrone was off form, missing chances on a dusty pitch. Pardón made save after save ('*Supermann*' said one German publication), the best from Petrone at point-blank range. When Castro eventually scored, relief was all around.

Despite his sending-off against Romania, Galindo was allowed to play but deprived of the captaincy (some sources say it was given to de las Casas). Seven of the Peruvians weren't capped again, including Pardón who was only 20. Gestido's brother Oscar became president of Uruguay in 1967, dying in office later that year.

---

21 July 1930 – Centenario, Montevideo – 70,022 – Gilberto de Almeida Rêgo (BRZ)

URUGUAY (4) 4
Dorado 7, Scarone 16, Anselmo 30, Cea 35

ROMANIA (0) 0

URUGUAY Ballestrero, Nasazzi (c), Ernesto Mascheroni, Andrade, Fernández, Gestido, Pablo Dorado, Héctor Scarone, Peregrino Anselmo, Cea, Iriarte.
ROMANIA Lăpuşneanu, Iosif Czako, Bürger, Corneliu Robe, Eisenbeisser, Vogl, Kovács, Deşu, Wetzer (c), Raffinsky, Barbu.

Suppici added the last piece to his defence by giving a first cap to the leggy Mascheroni – and above all increased the skill quotient up front, bringing back Anselmo and the crinkly-haired Scarone, who was only six days younger than the manager but looked far older than 31. Less of a finisher by now (this was the last of his 31 goals, still the Uruguay record), he compensated with cleverness and passing skills.

The forward line moved better from the start, playing the one-twos which had so impressed spectators in Europe, Cea scoring after completing one with Anselmo, who suffered from asthma. Dorado, playing on the wrong wing, scored the first with his left foot. In the first half, Romania hadn't been able to cope with the inter-passing and Andrade's all-round strengths; in the second, it's said they didn't have a shot on goal. One way and another, they were the first to know the hosts had re-established themselves as favourites.

Some sources spell Anselmo's first name Pellegrino, but it's Peregrino on the birth certificate.

GROUP 3

	P	W	D	L	F	A	Pts
Uruguay	2	2	0	0	5	0	4
Romania	2	1	0	1	3	5	2
Peru	2	0	0	2	1	4	0

Uruguay qualified for the semi-finals.

GROUP 4

Belgium, Paraguay (seeded), USA (seeded).

13 July 1930 – Parque Central, Montevideo – 18,436 – José Macías (ARG)

USA **(2) 3**
McGhee 41, Florie 44, Patenaude 88

BELGIUM **(0) 0**

USA Jim Douglas, Alec Wood, George Moorhouse, Jim Gallagher, Raphael (Ralph) Tracy, Adelino 'Billy' Gonsalves, Andy Auld, Jim Brown, Bert Patenaude, Tom Florie (c), Bart McGhee. *Robert Millar.*
BELGIUM Arnold Badjou, Theodoor Nouwens, Nic Hoydonckx, Pierre Braine (c), August Hellemans, Jean De Clercq, Louis Versyp, Bernard Voorhoof, Fernand 'Cassis' Adams, Jacques Moeschal, Jan Diddens. *Hector Goetinck.*

No great anticipation here. Belgium were without their best player, the great Raymond Braine, brother of the captain (suspended for opening a cafe!) – and the USA had no form to speak of: seven new caps, no matches for two years, before that an 11-2 thumping by Argentina in the Olympics.

But the Americans were the one real revelation of the tournament. Over the years, legends have grown up about their physiques (the French calling them 'shot putters' etc). They don't look so gargantuan in photographs. Some hefty thighs here and there (Gonsalves, McGhee, Auld) but all quite human really.

They won because they were better, not just brawnier. Although some sources cling to the belief that six of the Americans were British professionals, they had only two English League appearances between them (Moorhouse for Tranmere Rovers). This was a home-grown team – with a surprisingly modern style, breaking out of massed defence with long passes to the wings. Belgium protested about both the first two goals but were well beaten.

Gonsalves' surname was originally spelt in the Portuguese fashion: Gonçalves. Among the American players' clubs: Wieboldt Wonderbolts, Detroit Holley Carburettor, Curry Silver Tops, and the Providence Gold Bugs (previously Providence Clamdiggers). Some old sources credit McGhee with both the first two goals.

17 July 1930 – Parque Central, Montevideo – 18,306 – José Macías (ARG)

USA **(2) 3**
Patenaude 10, 15, 50

PARAGUAY **(0) 0**

USA Douglas, Wood, Moorhouse, Gallagher, Tracy, Gonsalves, Auld, Brown, Patenaude, Florie (c), McGhee.
PARAGUAY Modesto Denis, Quiterio Olmedo, José Luis Miracca, Romilio Etcheverry, Eusebio Díaz, Francisco Aguirre, Lino Nessi, Diógenes Domínguez, Aurelio González, Delfín Benítez Cáceres, Luis Vargas Peña (c). *José Durand Laguna (ARG).*

Even after their performance against Belgium, the Americans' second win was another surprise. Co-seeds Paraguay had finished runners-up in the Copa América, beating a full-strength Uruguay 3-0. Their ball skills were admired by the press, Vargas Peña was a tricky winger, and the 19-year-old Benítez Cáceres was good enough to play for Argentina in 1934.

But here they were hampered by a stiff wind and an injury to Denis. Hesitation cost Nessi a clear shooting chance, and González headed against the bar. The 20-year-old Patenaude scored the first ever World Cup hat-trick. Some sources still credit him with only two goals, but his own team mates maintained that

1930
1934
1938
1950
1954
1958
1962
1966
1970
1974
1978
1982
1986
1990
1994
1998
2002
2006

OLDEST TO SCORE A HAT-TRICK

yrs	days				
29	329	Pedro Cea	URU	1930	v YUG
29	140	Gabriel Batistuta	ARG	1998	v JAM
29	95	Teófilo Cubillas	PER	1978	v IRN
29	43	Pauleta	POR	2002	v POL
28	270	Preben Elkjær	DEN	1986	v URU
28	224	Angelo Schiavio	ITA	1934	v USA
28	43	Max Morlock	GER	1954	v TUR

Cubillas scored two of his goals from penalties.

GROUP 4

	P	W	D	L	F	A	Pts
USA	2	2	0	0	6	0	4
Paraguay	2	1	0	1	1	3	2
Belgium	2	0	0	2	0	4	0

The USA qualified for the semi-finals.

SEMI-FINALS

he scored all three, and two contemporary South American newspapers confirmed it, one even printing diagrams of the goals, all scored from left-wing crosses, the last with a 'violent' shot.

Paraguay's coach was that rarity, a black Argentinian.

---

20 July 1930 – Centenario, Montevideo – 25,466 – Ricardo Vallerino (URU)

PARAGUAY   **(1) 1**
Vargas Peña 40

BELGIUM   **(0) 0**

PARAGUAY Pedro Benítez, Olmedo, Salvador Flores, Santiago Benítez, Díaz, Tranquilino Garcete, Nessi, Gerardo Romero, González, Benítez Cáceres, Vargas Peña (c).
BELGIUM Badjou, Hoydonckx, Rik De Deken, P Braine (c), Hellemans, Moeschal, Versyp, Gérard Delbeke, Nouwens, Adams, Diddens.

Some modern sources put the crowd figure at 9,000, which would seem fair enough for a dead match. But the stadium looks pretty full in photographs.

---

26 July 1930 – Centenario, Montevideo – 72,886 – John Langenus (BEL)

ARGENTINA   **(1) 6**
Monti 20, Scopelli 56, Stábile 69, 87, Peucelle 80, 85

USA   **(0) 1**
Brown 89

ARGENTINA Juan Botasso, Della Torre, Paternóster, J Evaristo, Monti, Orlandini, Peucelle, Alejandro Scopelli, Stábile, Ferreira (c), M Evaristo.
USA Douglas, Wood, Moorhouse, Gallagher, Tracy, Gonsalves, Auld, Brown, Patenaude, Florie (c), McGhee.

The Americans found it harder to close down superior ball players on a much larger pitch (134 yards by 100). In the second half they had to do it without Tracy, who'd severely wrenched a knee – and Douglas injured his leg.

Bossio, who'd kept goal in the group matches, was known as 'the elastic marvel,' which sounds like an ad for a labour-saving appliance but suggests he was a fair keeper (he'd played in the Olympic Final). So why he was dropped isn't clear (there seems to have been no word of an injury) – especially as it meant replacing him with a player winning only his second cap. In the event, Botasso didn't have much to do, but the Final would be a different matter.

The story goes that when the American trainer Jack Coll came onto the pitch, he dropped a bottle of chloroform from his bag and had to be led off in a daze. The US team manager Wilfred Cummings made no mention of this but said the smelling salts temporarily blinded Auld.

The last ten minutes were just as much of a farce, Argentina walking the ball past exhausted opponents. Photos show Stábile leaping to score with a low cross-shot and Douglas face down with the ball just inside his right-hand post. Things might have been a little different if Tracy hadn't begun his unhappy day by missing two chances to open the score.

---

27 July 1930 – Centenario, Montevideo – 79,867 – Gilberto de Almeida Rêgo (BRZ)

URUGUAY (3) 6
Cea 18, 67, 72, Anselmo 20, 31, Iriarte 61

YUGOSLAVIA (1) 1
Vujadinović 4

URUGUAY Ballestrero, Nasazzi (c), Mascheroni, Andrade, Fernández, Gestido, Dorado, Scarone, Anselmo, Cea, Iriarte.
YUGOSLAVIA Jakšić, Ivković (c), Mihajlović, Arsenijević, Stevanović, Đokić, Tirnanić, Marjanović, Bek, Vujadinović, Sekulić.

The same deceptive scoreline. Yugoslavia took an early lead from a cross by Tirnanić, then had a goal controversially disallowed at 2-1 – and legend has it that Uruguay scored their third goal when the ball went out of play and was kicked back on by a policeman in uniform!

Nevertheless, as in the other semi, the right team won. With Nasazzi still giving no change at the back, the forwards cut through the middle at will. The equaliser, in a goalmouth scramble, was put in by the Cea, toothy and skilful (the French player Laurent compared him to Platini); Anselmo scored with a header; Iriarte (who apparently wore canvas boots for comfort) with a powerful low shot. Ultimately the Yugoslavs had little to offer except youthful spirit, though a lasting memory was the performance of Ivković, in every sense massive in defeat. He was killed by the Gestapo in 1943. Old sources credit Sekulić with the opening goal.

FINAL

30 July 1930 – Centenario, Montevideo – 68,346 – John Langenus (BEL)

URUGUAY (1) 4
Dorado 12, Cea 57, Iriarte 68, Castro 89

ARGENTINA (2) 2
Peucelle 20, Stábile 37

URUGUAY Ballestrero, Nasazzi (c), Mascheroni, Andrade, Fernández, Gestido, Dorado, Scarone, Castro, Cea, Iriarte.
ARGENTINA Botasso, Della Torre, Paternóster, J Evaristo, Monti, Suárez, Peucelle, Varallo, Stábile, Ferreira (c), M Evaristo.

If FIFA needed any reassurance about the decision to bring the tournament here, they got it just before the Final. Luis Monti received a death threat.

It proved the match *mattered*. Had it been held in Europe, how many spectators would have been locked out as they were here? Would they have been searched for weapons on the way in? How many European stadia needed a surrounding moat? The ground capacity was reduced for safety reasons.

1930
1934
1938
1950
1954
1958
1962
1966
1970
1974
1978
1982
1986
1990
1994
1998
2002
2006

1930

1934

1938

1950

1954

1958

1962

1966

1970

1974

1978

1982

1986

1990

1994

1998

2002

2006

Additional factors built tension: local derby, impending military dictatorship against Uruguayan coalition. Langenus demanded guarantees of protection and planned a quick escape route to his ship. This isn't something invented by old wives: he later admitted to feeling genuine fear.

On the day of the Final, he was put under extra pressure, both camps wanting to use a ball manufactured in their own country. Langenus ordered each half to be played with a different ball. Dressed in his usual cap and plus-fours, he went out to play the part of gamekeeper.

On a dusty stone-hard pitch, Uruguay scored first. When Scarone's shot was blocked by Paternóster, Castro, back in the team thanks to Anselmo's illness, pushed the loose ball wide to the right, where Dorado came in like a train to shoot under Botasso's body (some say between his legs) and past Juan Evaristo on the line.

Argentina responded with a picture goal. Juan Evaristo, conspicuous by his passing as well as his pale beret, took a return from Monti and found Ferreira, who sent Peucelle away up the right. The winger, one of the most dangerous forwards of his generation, beat Gestido then left Ballestrero standing with a fierce shot high inside his left-hand post.

From this point till half-time, Argentina's emphasis on sheer skill seemed to win all arguments about how to play the game. Think of Brazil in 1982. Then add a decent striker. Monti's long ball drifted over Nasazzi for Stábile to score from close range with Andrade stranded. Nasazzi claimed offside, but the ball had been in the air a long time, and anyway he would wouldn't he. Argentina's flair was more than holding its own. Then half-time came and changed everything.

Crudely put, Uruguay at last began to impose themselves physically. This isn't a euphemism

for fouling; they simply remembered their legendary *garra*, akin to the Welsh *hwyl* and the Finnish *sisu*, a word to be pronounced through clenched teeth.

It's not a hereditary thing. The Germans, say, aren't genetically programmed to make famous comebacks in football matches – but because they've done it in the past, they believe it's there in them. Uruguay believed they were made of sterner stuff than the Argentinians and started acted on it, staying the course better despite a day less to recover from the semi-final.

And suddenly Argentina had no answer. The young Varallo, whose knee injury flared up again, was forced out to the wing, where he was '*complètement neutralisé*' by Mascheroni. Monti, who seems to have taken the death threat to heart, wasn't his usual self (one of the reasons for his move to Italy was the reaction of the Argentinian press). The fight went out of them once and for all when Stábile, of all people, missed a chance to put them 3-1 ahead.

Now Gestido and Fernández were moving up to join the attack. The latter's free kick reached Castro, who found Scarone with his back to goal six yards out. A clever overhead lob took out Della Torre and Paternóster, and Cea pushed a ground shot past Botasso's dive. Ten minutes later, Mascheroni robbed Varallo and brought the ball forward before passing to Iriarte, whose shot from outside the area surprised Botasso, who dived late.

Even then Argentina had their chances. An English source says Stábile hit the bar, and Varallo's shot was cleared 'artistically' by Andrade, the first great black star. In the last minute, Dorado crossed for Castro to beat Della Torre in the air and send a looping header over Botasso's fingertips. Langenus blew the final whistle and made his ship safely, Scarone fell into Castro's arms, eight of the Argentinians were never capped again.

1930

The Evaristos were the first pair of brothers to play in a World Cup Final. The four matches in the tournament constituted Stábile's entire international career. He scored in each of them. Suppici's entire career as Uruguay's coach consisted of these four matches. He's still the youngest (31) to win the World Cup.

Nasazzi doesn't seem to have actually received the World Cup (Rimet handed it to Raúl Jude, president of the Uruguayan FA) but no-one deserved to get his hands on it more. Tall and grim-faced, he's invariably listed at No.2, leading people to talk of his forceful full-back play, whereas in fact he was an early sweeper (already known as a 'broom back'). A natural leader, he was captain in every one of his 41 internationals spread over 13 years. From him, the most influential player of the first

LEADING GOALSCORERS 1930

8	Guillermo Stábile	ARG
5	Pedro Cea	URU
4	Bert Patenaude	USA

World Cup, Uruguay took the determination and drive to turn the Final round, winning the tournament for the same reason they staged it: they wanted it the most.

Naturally the day of the Final was declared a national holiday. Someone died in the celebrations, a mob stoned the Uruguayan embassy in Buenos Aires, and the two FAs broke off relations. It really did matter. Even the Europeans were about to believe it.

1934
1938
1950
1954
1958
1962
1966
1970
1974
1978
1982
1986
1990
1994
1998
2002
2006

The sign of the times. Germany give the Nazi salute before their quarter-final with Sweden.
(l-r) Hohmann, Zielinski, Busch, Kobierski, Siffling, Conen, Lehner, Haringer, Gramlich, Kress, Szepan.

The full Monti

Italy 1934

1930
1938
1950
1954
1958
1962
1966
1970
1974
1978
1982
1986
1990
1994
1998
2002
2006

Having staged the first World Cup in the right place, FIFA now did the opposite. They handed the second tournament to Italy.

Over the years, Mussolini's been portrayed as something of a buffoon, and perhaps he was – but there was nothing very funny about the modern Fascist state, built on one-party rule, brownshirt gangs and informers, state murder and imprisonment without trial. And Mussolini was in power for a decade before Hitler. Naturally the World Cup would be a prime propaganda tool.

Even FIFA must have had reservations: it took them eight meetings to make up their minds. Perhaps they eventually decided that human rights might have to be swept under the carpet for a while, but at least the tournament would run on time.

As for the actual football, again the hosts were expected to win, especially as Italy's coach was one of the great early man-managers and strategists. There had been some bad blood (the Italians called it 'rust') between his centre-half and centre-forward following a league match – so Vittorio Pozzo made them share a room. He needed this kind of no-prisoners centre-half for his system of play, plus a pair of good wingers – and he knew where to find them, helping himself to a number of South American internationals, on the basis that if they could die for Italy (eligible for national service) they could play for Italy.

So in came Filó, capped by Brazil in 1925, and several high-class Argentinians: Demaría who'd played in the 1930 World Cup, Orsi who'd played in the last Olympic final, Guaita on the other wing – and Monti himself, a linchpin at Juventus (four league titles) once his weight problem was sorted. After the tournament, Pozzo picked another 1930 Argentinian, Scopelli, as well as Mascheroni from Uruguay. They were all apparently ineligible, but FIFA turned a blind eye (a German publication uses the word 'collaboration').

There were home-grown stars too, especially the gracile centre-forward Peppino Meazza, whose hat-trick in Hungary had won the Dr Gerő Cup, a forerunner of the European Championship.

Among the opposition, Hungary were improving, using the smooth Sárosi at centre-half as well as centre-forward. Czechoslovakia had Plánička in goal, Nejedlý and the forceful Puč up front, Spain a great goalkeeper in Zamora.

Above all, Austria, managed by the passionate Jewish banker Hugo Meisl, had dominated the early Thirties ('das Wunderteam'), beating Scotland 5-0, Germany 6-0 and 5-0, Switzerland 8-1. Playing the same old Scottish close-passing game as the other Central Europeans, they arrived in Italy without their fine goalkeeper Rudi Hiden, whom Arsenal tried to buy, but still had their share

1930

1934

1938

1950

1954

1958

1962

1966

1970

1974

1978

1982

1986

1990

1994

1998

2002

2006

of world-class players: Smistik the gigantic attacking centre-half, the prolific Schall, two genuinely great forwards in Bican and the slender Sindelar. They were probably just past their peak (Meisl himself thought so) but had recently beaten Italy 4-2 in Turin.

Uruguay, however, stayed away, perhaps in revenge for being snubbed by the main European powers in 1930, or because their team needed rebuilding. Of the other absent friends, England lost in Hungary and Czechoslovakia just before the competition, and Meisl believed they wouldn't have reached the semi-finals.

The tournament had grown too big to be held in a single city – and there were enough entries to warrant a qualifying competition, in which even Italy had to take part, beating the weak Greeks 4-0 in Milan. Elsewhere, the big guns had no trouble with the likes of Luxembourg and the Baltic countries, and the USA had beaten Mexico 4-2 in Rome, all their goals coming from Aldo Donelli, who had an Italian background, was winning his first cap, and also missed a penalty. The problems of a knockout system were there to see: Mexico had travelled 4,000 miles to play a single match, and not even in the competition proper.

The Americans' next game was likely to be rather harder, especially as Il Duce himself, in the words of an Italian book, was 'bestowing the privilege of his presence, which would galvanise the two teams more than any other coefficient.' Should be a cracker.

ROUND 1

Seeded: Argentina, Austria, Brazil, Czechoslovakia, Germany, Holland, Hungary, Italy.

27 May 1934 – Nazionale del PNF, Rome – 25,000 – René Mercet (SWI)

ITALY   **(3) 7**
Schiavio 18, 29, 64, Orsi 20, 69, Ferrari 63, Meazza 90

USA   **(0) 1**
Donelli 57

ITALY Gianpiero Combi, Virginio Rosetta (c), Luigi Allemandi, Mario Pizziolo, Luis Monti, Luigi Bertolini, Amphilóquio 'Anfilogino' Guarisi, Giuseppe Meazza, Angelo Schiavio, Giovanni Ferrari, Raimundo Orsi. *Vittorio Pozzo.*
USA Julius Hjulian, Adolf 'Ed' Czerkiewicz, George Moorhouse (c), Peter Pietras, Adelino 'Billy' Gonsalves, Tom Florie, Francis Ryan, Werner Nilsen, Aldo Donelli, Walter Dick, Bill McLean. *Elmer Schroeder (coach David Gould).*

The full name of the stadium, unsurprisingly, was the Stadio Nazionale del Partito Nazionale Fascista – and there was no shortage of straight-arm salutes before the match (from the referee and linesmen too), while Mussolini sported a natty white sailing cap.

Meazza and Ferrari made goals for Schiavio and Orsi, Guarisi hit the bar, Orsi the angle of post and bar. The USA threw Gonsalves forward at the start of the second half, he forced Combi to a rare save, and Donelli's goal persuaded Napoli to buy him. But Ferrari converted Guarisi's corner, Schiavio headed the fifth (the 100th World Cup goal), Orsi knocked in the rebound when Hjulian punched clear, and Meazza scored a '*bellissimo*' goal. Then more salutes towards Benito's box.

Most sources spell Combi's first name Giampiero, but the *Almanacco Illustrato* insists on Gianpiero. Guarisi was known as 'Filó' in Brazil. Schroeder died a grim and bizarre death in 1953, strangled with the cord of his own window blind.

27 May 1934 – Littorio, Trieste – 8,000 – John Langenus (BEL)

CZECHOSLOVAKIA   **(0) 2**
Puč 48, Nejedlý 65

ROMANIA   **(1) 1**
Dobay 11

CZECHOSLOVAKIA František Plánička (c), Ladislav Ženíšek, Josef Čtyřoký, Josef Košťálek, Stefan Čambal, Rudolf Krčil, František Junek, Josef Silný, Jiří Sobotka, Oldřich Nejedlý, Antonín Puč. *Karel Petrů.*
ROMANIA William Zombory, Emerich Vogl (c), Gheorghe Albu, Vasile Deheleanu, Rudolf Kotormányi, Iosif Moravetz, Silviu Bindea, Nicolae Kovács, Grațian Sepi, Iuliu Bodola, Ștefan Dobay. *Costel Rădulescu, with Josef Uridil (AUT).*

Czechoslovakia were heavy favourites but lucky to get through. Kovács and Sepi, attacking at speed, set up an excellent first goal for Dobay, and Bindea missed an open goal: the turning point.

PLAYED FOR TWO COUNTRIES

Atilio Demaría	1930 ARG	1934 ITA
Luis Monti	1930 ARG	1934 ITA
José Santamaría	1954 URU	1962 SPA
Ferenc Puskás	1954 HUN	1962 SPA
José Altafini	1958 BRZ	1962 ITA

Altafini was known as 'Mazzola' in Brazil.

In the 1990s and 2002, several players appeared for West Germany and the reunified Germany, and for Yugoslavia and Croatia.

Puc, jug-eared and dangerous, remained Czechoslovakia's record goalscorer till the split in 1994. Here he converted Košťálek's free kick, then Sepi missed another glaring chance before Czechoslovakia went ahead with a controversial goal. Deheleanu came off worse in a tackle, the decision went against Romania, Nejedlý scored from Sobotka's pass. Then Plánička made several important saves, especially from Sepi's late thunderbolt.

Many Romanian players of the time had Hungarian ancestry (Kovács and Bodola were capped by both countries), hence names like Kovács, Zombory and Kotormányi, often seen spelt in the Romanian fashion: Covaci, Zombori and Cotormani.

27 May 1934 – Giovanni Berta, Florence – 8,000 – Francesco Mattea (ITA)

GERMANY (1) 5
Kobierski 28, Siffling 47, Conen 67, 70, 86

BELGIUM (2) 2
Voorhoof 32, 44

GERMANY Willi Kress, Sigmund Haringer, Hans Schwartz, Paul Janes, Fritz Szepan (c), Paul Zielinski, Ernst Lehner, Karl Hohmann, Edmund Conen, Otto Siffling, Stanislaus Kobierski. *Otto Nerz.*
BELGIUM André Vandewyer, Philibert Smelinckx, Constant Joacim, Frans Peeraer, Félix Welkenhuysen (c), Jean Claessens, François De Vries, Bernard Voorhoof, Jean Capelle, Laurent Grimmonprez, Albert Heremans. *Hector Goetinck.*

The Nazis had just taken power, and the German team came onto the pitch with a swastika on their flag. Ironically in view of what was to come, their captain was of Polish extraction (original spelling Szczepan).

A versatile player, he was at centre-half today, the Germans one of the very few Continental sides playing with a genuine stopper. Much good it did them before half-

time, even after Kobierski had put them ahead following some slick work by Conen and Siffling. Even without Stanley Vanden Eynde, horribly injured in a qualifying match in Dublin, the Belgian attack swarmed round their penalty area, scoring twice through the fair-haired Voorhoof, his second a header from Claessens' cross.

But the Belgians had exhausted themselves, and Kobierski scored from a free kick, and the 19-year-old Conen from crosses by Kobierski, Zielinski and Hohmann. Conen scored his first two while Claessens was off the field injured, but this was nevertheless a reward for Nerz's homework, many hours spent watching league and cup matches in England.

27 May 1934 – Benito Mussolini, Turin – 15,000 – John van Moorsel (HOL)

AUSTRIA (1) (1) 3
Sindelar 44, Schall 93, Bican 109

FRANCE (1) (1) 2
J Nicolas 18, Verriest pen 115

AUSTRIA Peter Platzer, Franz Cisar, Karl Sesta, Franz Wagner, Josef (Pepi) Smistik (c), Hans Urbanek, Karl Zischek, Josef (Pepi) Bican, Matthias Sindelar, Toni Schall, Rudi Viertl. *Hugo Meisl.*
FRANCE Alexis Thépot (c), Jacques Mairesse, Étienne Mattler, Edmond Delfour, Georges Verriest, Noël Liétaer, Fritz Keller, Joseph Alcazar, Jean Nicolas, Roger Rio, Alfred (Freddy) Aston. *Gaston Barreau (coach George Kimpton (ENG)).*

As in 1930, France gave the second favourites a scare but were unlucky. Nicolas' early head injury forced them to rearrange their forward line three times. Coming back on after treatment, he showed his natural goalscoring ability (seven goals in the two internationals prior to this) by immediately taking advantage of Cisar's blunder from Keller's cross – but it was understandably his last contribution. Platzer had already made an acrobatic save in the first minute.

Even with ten fit men, France held out well in the second half, Mattler playing in the middle to watch Sindelar, who'd equalised from Bican's pass. Schall put Austria ahead from a position that looked clearly offside to everyone (including Schall himself) except the referee; Bican shot the third, high to Thépot's right; and Verriest's penalty, for handball by Wagner, would only have mattered if France had been awarded an earlier one for '*une aggression du terrible arrière Sesta*'. It was the first World Cup match to go to extra time. Kimpton was France's first ever national coach, Rio's son Patrice played in the 1978 finals. Sesta and Sindelar were of Czechoslovak extraction (original spellings Szestak, Matej Šindelár).

27 May 1934 – Luigi Ferraris, Genoa – 30,000 – Alfred Birlem (GER)

SPAIN **(3) 3**
Iraragorri pen 17, Lángara 23, 28

BRAZIL **(0) 1**
Leônidas 52

SPAIN Ricardo Zamora (c), Ciriaco (Errasti), Jacinto Quincoces, Leonardo Cilaurren, José Muguerza, Martín Marculeta, Ramón de Lafuente, José Iraragorri, Isidoro Lángara, Simón Lecue, Guillermo Gorostiza. *Amadeo García de Salazar.*
BRAZIL Roberto Pedrosa, Sílvio Hoffmann, Luiz Luz, Alfredo Tinoco, Martim (Silveira) (c), Heitor Canalli, Luiz M Oliveira, Waldemar de Britto, 'Armandinho' (Armando dos Santos), Leônidas (da Silva), 'Patesko' (Rodolfo Barteczko). *Luiz Vinhaes.*

Again, as in 1930, Brazil scattered the pitch with new caps (a mere eight this time), again there was only one black player in the team (Leônidas), again the black player was their best, knocking in the rebound when Zamora pushed the ball out. But it was too late by then.

Spain scored from a penalty for Martim's handball, a volley from Gorostiza's cross, and after a mix-up between Pedrosa and Luiz Luz. In the second half, Brazil scored, had a goal disallowed on the hour, and missed a penalty (de Britto's nervous kick, on his debut, was saved by Zamora) – but this is deceptive: Spain simply stopped attacking, conserving energy for the second round, employing the bizarre tactic of deliberately giving away corners. Brazil had again looked skilful, but match reports emphasise a lack of cohesion, and they needed more than flashy touches to beat a goalkeeper like Zamora.

27 May 1934 – San Siro, Milan – 35,000 – Ivan Eklind (SWE)

SWITZERLAND **(2) 3**
Kielholz 6, 43, Abegglen 66

HOLLAND **(1) 2**
Smit 29, Vente 69

SWITZERLAND Frank Séchehaye, Severino Minelli (c), Walter Weiler, Albert Guinchard, Fernand Jaccard, Ernst Hufschmid, Willy von Känel, Raymond Passello, Leopold (Poldi) Kielholz, André 'Trello' Abegglen, Giuseppe Bossi. *Heinrich (Henry) Müller.*
HOLLAND Gejus van der Meulen, Mauk Weber, Sjef van Run, Henk Pellikaan, Wim Anderiesen, Gerrit 'Puck' van Heel (c), Frank Wels, Leen Vente, Elisa 'Bep' Bakhuys, Jaap 'Kick' Smit, Joop van Nellen. *Bob Glendenning (ENG).*

Holland had some well-known players, but the Swiss were too quick and determined for them. Kielholz, who played in glasses, scored after Bossi and Abegglen had tiptoed through the tulips, then play was end-to-end for the rest of the first half. Smit scored from van Heel's free kick and a bad bounce took Kielholz's 25-yarder past the keeper.

1930
1934
1938
1950
1954
1958
1962
1966
1970
1974
1978
1982
1986
1990
1994
1998
2002
2006

1934

In the second half, von Känel sprinted away to make a volleyed goal for the bald and skilful Abegglen, one of three international brothers. Holland dominated the last 20 minutes, hitting a post, Vente putting in another free kick – but Switzerland's gritty performance was typical of their performances in pre-war World Cups.

Some publications list Bakhuys' first name as Eberhard, but the main Dutch sources say Elisa – and he was known as Elysée when he played in France.

---

27 May 1934 – Littoriale, Bologna – 19,000 – Eugen Braun (AUT)

SWEDEN　　(1) 3
Jonasson 9, 67, Kroon 80

ARGENTINA　(1) 2
Belis 3, Galateo 50

SWEDEN Anders Rydberg, Nils Axelsson, Sven Andersson, Rune Carlsson, Nils Rosén (c), Ernst Andersson, Gösta Dunker, Ragnar Gustavsson, Sven Jonasson, Tore Keller, Knut Kroon. *József Nagy (HUN).*
ARGENTINA Héctor Luis Freschi, Juan Carlos Pedevilla, Ernesto Belis, José Nehín, Constantino Urbieta Sosa, Arcadio López, Francisco Rúa, Federico Wilde, Alfredo Devincenzi (c), Alberto Galateo, Roberto Irañeta. *Felipe Pascucci (ITA).*

A split in the Argentinian league led to their FA sending over a team of amateurs, of whom only López and the beaky Devincenzi had previously been capped. They provided some dazzling moments, Belis scoring with a 20-yard free-kick, Galateo after a wonderful dribble (he'd earlier beaten five men and missed). But they were overtaken by defensive errors, Jonasson scoring in a scramble then beating a hesitant Freschi to Rosén's long ball. It was Argentina's last World Cup match, and not a distinguished one, until 1957. None of the team won another cap.

LAST CAPS IN A MATCH

11	Argentina	1934	v Spain
11	Dutch East Indies	1938	v Hungary
9	Bolivia	1930	v Brazil
9	Chile	1930	v Argentina
9	Argentina	1982	v Brazil
8	USA	1934	v Italy
8	Uruguay	1974	v Sweden
8	Uruguay	1986	v Argentina

The 1934 crop wasn't one of the richest for Italy to plunder (Devincenzi won a single B cap) – but the Argentinians weren't averse to borrowing foreigners themselves: their coach was Italian and Urbieta Sosa had played against them for Paraguay. One or two sources refer to Carlsson as Karlsson-Wamma, but 'Wamma' was a nickname, and the Swedish FA confirms the spelling Carlsson. Galateo, by then an alcoholic, was murdered by his own son in 1961.

---

27 May 1934 – Giorgio Ascarelli, Naples – 8,000 – Rinaldo Barlassina (ITA)

HUNGARY　(2) 4
Teleki 11, Toldi 31, 61, Vincze 54

EGYPT　　(2) 2
Fawzy 39, 43

HUNGARY Antal Szabó, Gyula Futó, László Sternberg (c), István Palotás, György Szücs, Gyula Lázár, Imre Markos, Jenő Vincze, Pál Teleki, Géza Toldi, Gábor P Szabó. *Ödön Nádas.*
EGYPT Mustafa Kamel Mansour, Ali Khaf, Hamidu (Sharli), Hassan El-Far, Ismail Rafaat, Hassan Raghab, Mohammed Latif, Abdel Rahman Fawzy, 'El-Tetch' (Mahmoud Mokhtar) (c), Mustafa Kamel Taha, Mohammed Hassan Helmy. *Jimmy McRea (SCO).*

Egypt, who'd beaten Hungary 3-0 at the 1924 Olympics, had some skilful players, especially El-Tetch and the young goalkeeper, who apparently broke his nose trying to stop Hungary's fourth goal. The result might have been different if Mokhtar hadn't had a goal mysteriously disallowed after dribbling though and Fawzy hadn't missed an easy chance in the second minute. His two goals didn't quite compensate.

Teleki finished off a 'worthy action in the left-hand sector'; the hefty Toldi ('*Sturmtank*') charged the keeper over the line; Vincze intercepted a weak clearance; and Toldi sprinted in to convert Markos' cross. Victory for the more complete side, who had Sárosi ready to return for the local derby.

One source says Hamidu's last name was Teles, but the Egyptians agree with Sharli (or Charlie!). Another gives the half-time score as 2-1 (Fawzy scoring after 67 minutes). The goal times above come from the official report, and an Egyptian website agrees it was 2-2 at half-time. Teleki had played for Romania back in 1927. The stadium's name was changed soon afterwards because Ascarelli, Napoli's first president, was Jewish.

QUARTER-FINALS

31 May 1934 – San Siro, Milan – 16,000 – Rinaldo Barlassina (ITA)

GERMANY (0) 2
Hohmann 60, 62

SWEDEN (0) 1
Dunker 82

GERMANY Kress, Haringer, Willy Busch, Rudolf Gramlich, Szepan (c), Zielinski, Lehner, Hohmann, Conen, Siffling, Kobierski.

SWEDEN Rydberg, Axelsson, S Andersson, Carlsson, Rosén (c), E Andersson, Dunker, Gustavsson, Jonasson, Keller, Kroon.

The match turned on a weird accident twelve minutes into the second half, a clash of heads forcing Rosén and Ernst Andersson off the pitch. Within five minutes Hohmann put Germany two up, and a goal from one of the shortest players on the pitch came too late.

The tall sinewy Rosén had played a full part in contesting the midfield with his opposite number, the blond all-rounder Szepan. But it had been dull, the Germans earning a reputation for efficiency without flair that stayed with them for decades.

31 May 1934 – Littoriale, Bologna – 14,000 – Francesco Mattea (ITA)

AUSTRIA (1) 2
Horvath 5, Zischek 51

HUNGARY (0) 1
Sárosi pen 62

AUSTRIA Platzer, Cisar, Sesta, Wagner, Smistik, Urbanek, Zischek, Bican, Sindelar, Hans Horvath (c), Viertl.
HUNGARY Szabó, József Vágó, Sternberg (c), Palotás, Szücs, Antal Szalay, Markos, István Avar, György Sárosi, Toldi, Tibor Kemény.
SENT OFF: Markos 63.

The anticipated display of limpid Middle European football turned into another World Cup brawl (there'd already been a few). Whereas Hungary brought back the tall stylish Sárosi to add extra class to their attack, the short and craggy Horvath injected dash and aggression into Austria's. After his opening goal, the game degenerated. Sesta, who'd conceded a penalty in the first round, did it again here, bringing down Kemény. Markos was sent off, Platzer and Wagner received knocks, and an injury to Avar reduced Hungary to nine men for the last 18 minutes.

An unreliable source claims Szabó saved penalties after 52 and 56 minutes, but this seems unlikely and has been impossible to verify. Avar had earlier played for Romania under the name Stefan Auer. Another source lists Vágó's first name as János, an error.

---

31 May 1934 – Giovanni Berta, Florence – 40,000 – Louis Baert (BEL)

ITALY　　　**(1) (1) 1**
Ferrari 45

SPAIN　　　**(1) (1) 1**
Regueiro 31

ITALY Combi (c), Eraldo Monzeglio, Allemandi, Pizziolo, Monti, Armando Castellazzi, Enrique Guaita, Meazza, Schiavio, Ferrari, Orsi.
SPAIN Zamora (c), Ciriaco, Quincoces, Cilaurren, Muguerza, 'Fede' (Federico Sáiz), Lafuente, Iraragorri, Lángara, Luis Regueiro, Gorostiza.

For the only time in their nine pre-war finals matches Italy met a team who played a similar game, ready to trade sweat and studs. Pozzo knew it and made changes.

He'd already left Umberto Caligaris out of the reckoning, after a record 59 caps, allowing the veteran only to carry the flag at the opening ceremony. Against the easy Americans, he'd given a last cap to Rosetta, the other full-back from that famous partnership. Now he recalled the rugged Monzeglio: a signal of intent.

The match was predictably rough and feebly refereed. Baert refused Schiavio a penalty, disallowed a goal by Lafuente, gave Monti all the licence he needed, and above all did nothing to protect Zamora from the attentions of the Italian forwards, especially after the unmarked Regueiro put his whole body into a volley wide of Combi's right hand.

When Spain protected their lead with some full-blooded defending in their own penalty area, Italy seem to have decided a new tactic was needed. Pump in the crosses and pile into the keeper. It worked up to a point. Ferrari equalised from close range while Zamora was being obstructed by Schiavio (who can be seen looking back and using his elbows). And an Italian player's caught on film knocking his cap off with a forearm jab. But the Spanish captain played one of the games of his career, which is saying something.

In England, Zamora was remembered for a miserable display in Spain's 7-1 defeat at Highbury in 1931 – but he was one of the greats, don't doubt it, a brilliant shot-stopper and as brave as anyone in those days of the shoulder charge. In 46 internationals played in an attacking era, he conceded 42 goals. Here, in the only drawn game of the first two finals tournaments, he was treated so badly that he had to miss the replay.

REPLAY

1 June 1934 – Giovanni Berta, Florence – 40,000 – René Mercet (SWI)

ITALY　　　**(1) 1**
Meazza 12

SPAIN　　　**(0) 0**

ITALY Combi (c), Monzeglio, Allemandi, Attilio Ferraris, Monti, Bertolini, Guaita, Meazza, Felice Placido Borel, Atilio Demaría, Orsi.
SPAIN Juan José Nogués, Ramón Zabalo, Quincoces (c), Cilaurren, Muguerza, Lecue, Martín Vantolrá, Regueiro, 'Campanal' (Marcelino González), 'Chacho' (Eduardo González), Crisanto Bosch.

The rematch was held the following day, so both sides had to make changes. Pozzo picked a forward line with three Argentinians and recalled Bertolini and the combative Ferraris. Spain gave Nogués his only cap and feared for their health.

Sources disagree as to whether three or four Spaniards left the field with injuries, Mercet allowing so much latitude that he was suspended by his own federation. Borel had just finished as Serie A's leading scorer for the second successive season, but his slight physique, which earned him the nickname of '*farfallina*' (little butterfly), was out of place in a match like this, and he wasn't capped again despite being only 20.

A year earlier, Chacho had scored a record six goals on his international debut, but the opposing defence was very different here. Meanwhile Italy's usual aggression in the air brought them the only goal, Meazza flinging himself bravely at a corner to head a spectacular goal. The rest was bruises.

Vantolrá's son José played for Mexico in the 1970 finals. Note the difference in the spelling of Ferraris and Demaria's first names.

---

31 May 1934 – Benito Mussolini, Turin – 9,000 – Alois Beranek (AUT)

CZECHOSLOVAKIA　**(1) 3**
Svoboda 23, Sobotka 49, Nejedlý 83

SWITZERLAND　**(1) 2**
Kielholz 18, Jäggi 80

CZECHOSLOVAKIA Plánič" ka (c), Ženíšek, Čtyřoký, Košťálek, Čambal, Krčil, Junek, František Svoboda, Sobotka, Nejedlý, Puč.
SWITZERLAND Séchehaye, Minelli (c), Weiler, Guinchard, Jaccard, Hufschmid, von Känel, Willy Jäggi, Kielholz, Abegglen, Alfred Jaeck.

In steady rain, the Swiss again battled to the wire, but Czechoslovakia were slightly too good. Needing more punch after the display against Romania, they replaced the silky Silný with Svoboda, who equalised from Sobotka's pass and hit a post early in the second half.

Kielholz had opened the scoring from a pass by Jäggi, who scored Switzerland's second with a shot that skidded through the mud. Some old sources wrongly credit Abegglen with the second goal. Not for the last time in the World Cup, he was the best player on the pitch – but Nejedlý again poached the winner, and this time the Czechs deserved it.

SEMI-FINALS

3 June 1934 – Comunale (San Siro), Milan – 45,000 – Ivan Eklind (SWE)

ITALY　**(1) 1**
Guaita 19

AUSTRIA　**(0) 0**

ITALY Combi (c), Monzeglio, Allemandi, Ferraris, Monti, Bertolini, Guaita, Meazza, Schiavio, Ferrari, Orsi.
AUSTRIA Platzer, Cisar, Sesta, Wagner, Smistik (c), Urbanek, Zischek, Bican, Sindelar, Schall, Viertl.

It's said that Austria didn't have a shot on goal in the first forty minutes. If it's true, it's a startling stat: they'd picked just about the strongest forward line in their history, and Italy had played a tough replay only two days earlier.

As in the other semi-final, the two main European schools were in opposition. Reviewing Austria's gentle intricate game, an Italian publication referred to an '*antico dogma*' and a '*dose di narcisismo*'. The Italians seem to have taken almost personal offence at the Viennese habit of trying to walk the ball into the net, an indignation exemplified by the central duel of the match: Sindelar v Monti.

1930
1934
1938
1950
1954
1958
1962
1966
1970
1974
1978
1982
1986
1990
1994
1998
2002
2006

1930

1934

1938

1950

1954

1958

1962

1966

1970

1974

1978

1982

1986

1990

1994

1998

2002

2006

The Austrian was the nearest thing anyone could remember to the old England centre-forward GO Smith. Similar ability to make the play from slightly behind the other forwards, similar paleness and spare physique, in Sindelar's case accentuated by a high forehead and limp smile. *Der Papierene*, the man made of paper. But there was nothing effete about his actual play, which looks sharp and even aggressive on film, like a forerunner of Jürgen Klinsmann. He scored goals too, 27 in 43 internationals, including both in the win over Italy in 1932.

However he was 31 by now, this was the only time he faced Monti in an international (Austria had recently won in Turin without him) – and Monti, untroubled by death threats this time, had decided no more mister nice guy.

Even older than Sindelar but never dependent on pace (his nickname was the rough equivalent of 'Stroller'), he was the most important player in the tournament, a thug but a great one, his long passes turning Austria's full-backs, who couldn't cope with the Argentinian wingers. Meanwhile his other talents pushed Sindelar to the margins, the ghost of a vanished age.

When Milan was hit by a deluge, the hosts were happy to leave pools of water on the pitch to counter the opposition's style of play (shades of West Germany v Poland forty years later). For the third match in a row, they scored just a single goal, yet again in a goalmouth scramble. Years later, Bican remembered Platzer catching the ball and the Italians knocking him over the line from three metres out – but this is just an old man's memory playing tricks. Platzer lost the ball on the ground in Meazza's sliding challenge, and Guaita lunged it over the line when it came back off the near post.

Bican hit a post too (allegedly!), and Combi made good saves from Sesta and Zischek,

but any losing team has moments like these, and anyway Platzer was more often in action. Italy, on a helpfully heavy pitch, bossed it. The only team to keep a clean sheet in the tournament, they did it twice. It was the closest Austria have ever come to reaching the Final.

After scoring 28 goals in 28 internationals, Schall wasn't capped again. Sindelar died in unexplained circumstances in 1939.

---

3 June 1934 – Nazionale del PNF, Rome – 13,000 – Rinaldo Barlassina (ITA)

CZECHOSLOVAKIA	**(1) 3**
Nejedlý 21, 69, 80	
GERMANY	**(0) 1**
Noack 59	

CZECHOSLOVAKIA Plánička (c), Jaroslav Burgr, Čtyřoký, Košťálek, Čambal, Krčil, Junek, Svoboda, Sobotka, Nejedlý, Puč.
GERMANY Kress, Haringer, Busch, Zielinski, Szepan (c), Jakob Bender, Lehner, Siffling, Conen, Rudolf Noack, Kobierski.

The short-passing game was a style doomed to obsolescence, but not just yet. Czechoslovakia were slick up front and Plánička had a much better game than Kress, who was blamed for two of the goals.

Plánička himself made a hash of Noack's shot, but Czechoslovakia had the confidence to keep playing their game – and Nejedlý was in the sort of form a hat-trick suggests.

Similar to Sindelar and Meazza in being graceful but good in the air (he headed two of his goals here), he was one of the great European match-winners. Some old sources credit one of his goals to Krčil, an error he could afford: he scored 28 in 43 internationals. Burgr is no misprint. Nerz was replaced as coach after Germany lost at home to Norway in the 1936 Olympics. In 1945 the Soviets sent him to Sachsenhausen concentration camp, where he died four years later.

3RD-PLACE FINAL

7 June 1934 – Giorgio Ascarelli, Naples – 7,000 – Albino Carraro (ITA)

GERMANY (3) 3
Lehner 24 sec, Conen 29, Lehner 42

AUSTRIA (1) 2
Horvath 30, Sesta 55

GERMANY Hans Jakob, Janes, Busch, Zielinski, Reinhold Münzenberg, Bender, Lehner, Siffling, Conen, Szepan (c), Matthias Heidemann.
AUSTRIA Platzer, Cisar, Sesta, Wagner, Smistik, Urbanek, Zischek, Georg Braun, Bican, Horvath (c), Viertl.

'It is of no purpose and should not exist.' Michel Hidalgo, manager of France, telling it like it is before the 3rd-Place Final of 1982. The biggest anti-climax in the game, unloved but apparently here to stay, someone squeezing every last piece of silver. Perhaps Mussolini needed the gate receipts for his forthcoming African campaign.

Still, at least it was inaugurated with a flourish, Lehner leaping right in front of Platzer to score the fastest World Cup goal till 1962. Conen volleyed just under the bar, Horvath pulled one back from Zischek's cross, but Lehner scored Germany's third with a ground shot.

Soon after half-time, Sesta lined up a free kick thirty yards out. Small and hard, a former wrestler (he and Viertl look like a pair of iffy brothers in team photos), he was the *Wunderteam*'s one concession to the need for combat. Appropriate, in a changing world, that

he should provide its last gesture before it disappeared for ever. Jakob didn't move as the free kick flew past him; it was Sesta's only goal in 44 internationals. Four years later, it wasn't just the Austrian football team that Germany would wipe off the map.

FINAL

10 June 1934 – Nazionale del PNF, Rome – 50,000 – Ivan Eklind (SWE)

ITALY (0) (1) 2
Orsi 81, Schiavio 95

CZECHOSLOVAKIA (0) (1) 1
Puč 71

ITALY Combi (c), Monzeglio, Allemandi, Ferraris, Monti, Bertolini, Guaita, Meazza, Schiavio, Ferrari, Orsi.
CZECHOSLOVAKIA Plánička (c), Ženíšek, Čtyřoký, Košťálek, Čambal, Krčil, Junek, Svoboda, Sobotka, Nejedlý, Puč.

Behind one of the stands in the stadium, in letters standing up over the horizon, ran the exhortation *Acquistate Prodotti Italiani*. Buy Italian.

They weren't even buying Italian tickets. As with Italy's other matches, there were empty spaces in all parts of the ground. Either the Depression was pricing people out or they didn't have much enthusiasm for the event. Either way, not the image the Fascists wanted to project.

Still, there were enough spectators to provide an intimidating atmosphere. There was no moat here as in Montevideo, no running track, so the front row of the crowd came within ten yards of the pitch. And Pozzo spent part of the match squatting next to Plánička's net, presumably for psychological reasons.

1930

1934

1938

1950

1954

1958

1962

1966

1970

1974

1978

1982

1986

1990

1994

1998

2002

2006

Hard to know if it worked. In the only Final with two goalkeeper captains, Plánička was the more prominent, spending most of the video catching aimless high balls unchallenged. With waist-high tackles flying (Bertolini was conspicuous for more than his thick white headband) and forwards struggling to escape defenders on a narrow bumpy pitch, some of the play makes desperate viewing.

With twenty minutes left and tension all around, Ferraris crunched into Puč, who was carried to the sidelines (Pozzo helped, probably eager to see him leave!). A flask of ammonia was waved under his nose, and two minutes later he was breaking Monzeglio's tackle and beating Combi low at the near post. The glorification of drug-taking!

Suddenly Italy fell apart, even in defence. Sobotka hit a post and Nejedlý shot over the bar. The parallels with Sindelar were uncanny. Both frail, both bullied by Monti and the gang. They even looked vaguely similar. Nejedlý's missed chance was Czechoslovakia's last. Three minutes later, Italy were level.

Orsi is the Italian for 'bears'. No-one had a less appropriate name. Sleek-haired and very slim, he was a brilliant dribbler but 32 years old by now, drifting in and out of matches. With time running out, he curled the ball in from the edge of the area. Plánička may have been at fault, though his reach probably had more to do with it (typical of the time, he was only 5′ 8). The ball drifted high to his right as Pozzo jumped for joy behind the net.

At the end of normal time, Pozzo effectively decided the match, telling Schiavio and Guaita to start switching positions. It may not sound much, but it was more than the other lot could

LEADING GOALSCORERS 1934

5	Oldrich Nejedlý	CZE
4	Edmund Conen	GER
4	Angelo Schiavio	ITA

manage. Petrů was an organiser not a tactician, and anyway his tactics were set in stone: Czechoslovakia were still playing with an attacking centre-half (Čambal), essentially a sixth forward.

When Schiavio hit the winner with a cross-shot, it's said that Meazza got away with handball earlier in the move, though there seems to be no evidence of this on film. Allegedly seen with Mussolini before the Final, the referee was born on the same day as the winning goalscorer.

Pozzo was chaired off the pitch. Allemandi received his winner's medal seven years after having been banned for life after a match-fixing scandal (setting a precedent for Rossi in 1982). The veteran Combi, recalled only because the flamboyant Carlo Ceresoli had broken an arm in training, lifted the Cup and retired from international football, as did Schiavio, a triumph for the hardworking man.

No doubt the Fascists used that in their brochures – but it had been a grim and gloomy tournament. Too many dirty matches, possibly some dirty referees, the touch players stamped out. Visitors who'd come for the football glimpsed the reality of the regime. Brutal, and smug with it. Unsmiling. A heavy military presence. And that was just its centre-half.

The judgment of Paris

1930

1934

1938

1950

1954

1958

1962

1966

1970

1974

1978

1982

1986

1990

1994

1998

2002

2006

France **1938**

The World Cup was coming back to the land of its fathers, but any celebrations were tempered by events elsewhere. Austria, one of the great football powers, wasn't even a country any more, swallowed up by the *Anschluss*. Others were soon to follow, including Czechoslovakia, where the Nazis would soon take the Sudetenland without a peep from the West. There was civil war in Spain. And Italy, now firmly established as Germany's sidekick, were still strong on the football field.

Only Monzeglio and the inside-forwards Meazza and Ferrari remained from the 1934 team. Three others came in from the side which won the 1936 Olympics, and there was only one South American this time, the Uruguayan Andreolo in Monti's place. Above all, the latest centre-forward, Silvio Piola, was the best in Europe.

Czechoslovakia still had Plánička, Nejedlý and Puč. Brazil, as usual, hadn't played for more than a year. Hungary were full of goals, Sárosi scoring seven, no less, in an 8-3 win over Czechoslovakia, who had Plánička in goal.

The other goal came from the 21-year-old Zsengellér, who later scored five in the 11-1 qualifying win over Greece.

Uruguay again didn't turn up. Nor did Argentina, who'd won the Copa América the previous year (with Guaita back from Italy). Meanwhile, a month before the tournament, England had won 6-3 in Germany and 4-2 in France, fielding players like Matthews, Bastin, Drake and Hapgood. Still outside FIFA, they apparently turned down an invitation to take Austria's place.

In October the Austrians had beaten lowly Latvia 2-1 to qualify. On 12 March, German troops crossed the border. On 12 April the Austrian FA announced that it had ceased to exist. The Nazis had been welcomed in by a surprising percentage of the population, keen on the idea of 'Greater Germany' and presumably proud when Austrian players were added to the German squad. Nine in all, but not Matthias Sindelar, who – contrary to the conspiracy theorists – was now simply past it.

The winning team joined by extras from a *Godfather* film. Standing (l-r, players and coach only): Biavati, Pozzo, Piola, Ferrari, Colaussi. Kneeling (l-r): Locatelli, Meazza, Foni, Olivieri, Rava, Andreolo. Receiving Meazza's blessing: Serantoni.

ROUND 1

Seeded: Brazil, Czechoslovakia, France, Germany, Hungary, Italy, Cuba, Sweden.

4 June 1938 – Parc des Princes, Paris – 27,152 – John Langenus (BEL)

SWITZERLAND (1) (1) 1
Abegglen 43

GERMANY (1) (1) 1
Gauchel 29

SWITZERLAND Willy Huber, Severino Minelli (c), August Lehmann, Hermann Springer, Sirio Vernati, Ernest Lörtscher, Lauro Amadò, Eugen Walaschek, Alfred Bickel, André 'Trello' Abegglen, Georges Aeby. *Karl Rappan (AUT).*
GERMANY Rudi Raftl, Paul Janes, Willibald Schmaus, Andreas Kupfer, Hans Mock (c), Albin Kitzinger, Ernst Lehner, Rudi Gellesch, Jupp Gauchel, Willi Hahnemann, Hans Pesser. *Sepp Herberger.*
SENT OFF: Pesser 96.

A folkloric glow has settled on this one over the years. The brave little Swiss holding out against Nazi might. The truth is rather more arithmetical. A week after the 6-3 win in Berlin, England had lost 2-1 in Switzerland, who were trying out an early form of *catenaccio* and were favourites here. Germany had won only one of their last five matches, 2-1 against Luxembourg.

No surprise, then, that their pragmatic manager should seize the chance to pick five Austrian internationals (shades of Pozzo's South Americans): Raftl, Mock, Hahnemann, Schmaus and Pesser, the last getting himself sent off for kicking Minelli. Germany dominated most of the match, and Gauchel ran in to thump the ball through a tackle and up past

Huber's left hand. But a defensive error led to the equaliser, the ball coming back off a German shin for Amadò to cross and the unmarked Abegglen to head high into the net.

Unlike England in Berlin, the Swiss refused to give the Nazi Salute before the match. The teams had five days to prepare for the replay. A leisure pursuit, alright.

REPLAY

9 June 1938 – Parc des Princes, Paris – 20,025 – Ivan Eklind (SWE)

SWITZERLAND (1) 4
Walaschek 42, Bickel 64, Abegglen 75, 78

GERMANY (2) 2
Hahnemann 8, Lörtscher o.g. 22

SWITZERLAND Huber, Minelli (c), Lehmann, Springer, Vernati, Lörtscher, Amadò, Walaschek, Bickel, Abegglen, Aeby.
GERMANY Raftl, Janes, Jakob Streitle, Kupfer, Ludwig Goldbrunner, Stefan Skoumal, Lehner, Josef (Pepi) Stroh, Hahnemann, Fritz Szepan (c), Leopold Neumer.

Herberger added three more capped Austrians – Skoumal, Stroh and Neumer – and brought back the 1934 captain Szepan, but again the mix wasn't quite right (Germany hadn't had a quality schemer for years). They led 2-0, played against ten men for a while – and still lost, to the rest of Europe's glee.

Huber's save pushed the ball out to the German right, and when the cross came in, Hahnemann sidefooted it across a covering defender. Then Neumer's shot hit the far post and went in off Lörtscher's leg. With Aeby stretchered off with an 'intensive bleed wound' to the head and Minelli feeling an injury from the first match, Switzerland looked out of it.

But then Aeby came back on, Walaschek scored with a low shot, and Bickel lobbed the loose ball insolently over the last defender

1930
1934
1938
1950
1954
1958
1962
1966
1970
1974
1978
1982
1986
1990
1994
1998
2002
2006

when Raftl was involved in a three-man aerial duel. Abegglen was hopelessly unmarked again when he touched in a soft cross, and side-stepped two players before shooting high into the net. Germany protested about Walaschek, who didn't receive a Swiss passport till eight days later (his father was Russian), but no-one listened. They didn't play in another finals tournament till 1954, when Herberger would still be in charge.

---

5 June 1938 – Chapou, Toulouse – 6,707 – Giuseppe Scarpi (ITA)

CUBA (1) (2) 3
Socorro 44, 103, Magriña 69

ROMANIA (1) (2) 3
Bindea 35, Barátky 88, Dobay 105

CUBA Benito Carvajales, Jacinto Barquín, Manuel Chorens, Manuel Berges, José Rodríguez, Joaquín Arias, José Antonio Magriña, Tomás Fernández (c), Héctor Socorro, Juan Tuñas, Mario Sosa. *José Tápia*.
ROMANIA Dumitru Pavlovici, Rudolf Bürger, Vasile Chiroiu, Vintilă (Cossini), Gheorghe Rășinaru, Ladislau Raffinsky, Silviu Bindea, Nicolae Kovács (c), Iuliu Barátky, Iuliu Bodola, Ștefan Dobay. *Alexandru Săvulescu, with Costel Rădulescu.*

Cuba's seeding had a purely geographical basis; they arrived with little World Cup pedigree. Bizarrely, they'd had to play Mexico three times in the 1934 qualifiers, losing the lot, and qualified this time only because the Mexicans dropped out. Yet they weren't short of confidence, announcing that they were here 'to win a match or two.'

Romania, who'd also qualified because their opponents (Egypt) withdrew, were surprised by the flair of the Cuban forwards, Socorro, short and squat, equalising from Magriña's cross. The talented Kovács had played in the 1930 and 1934 tournaments. Some sources claim he scored the first goal, and there are various versions of the goal times, Cuban scorers and captain (one source says Rodríguez' brother Ignacio played). The details here are confirmed by the leading Cuban statistician and the press officer at the Romanian FA.

Vintilă was one of the very few Eastern European players known by their first names. Alternative spellings: Rafinski, Baratki. Bodola later played for Hungary (1940–48). One source lists him as captain, but Kovács is confirmed by several others, including a Romanian history of the national team.

REPLAY

9 June 1938 – Chapou, Toulouse – 7,536 – Alfred Birlem (GER)

CUBA (0) 2
Socorro 51, Fernández 57

ROMANIA (1) 1
Dobay 35

CUBA Juan Ayra, Barquín, Chorens, Berges, Rodríguez, Arias, Magriña, Fernández (c), Socorro, Tuñas, Sosa.
ROMANIA Robert Sadowski, Bürger, Iacob Felecan, Andrei Bărbulescu, Rășinaru, Raffinsky, Ion Bogdan, Ioachim Moldoveanu, Barátky, Iuliu Prassler, Dobay (c).

Although Carvajales had been a star of the first match, Cuba replaced him with the stocky little Ayra, who'd saved a penalty against Mexico in 1934 and was their best player now,

CONSECUTIVE WINS		
7	Italy	1934–38
7	Brazil	2002
6	England	1966–70
6	Brazil	1970

'a fantastic acrobat.' Despite being flagged for offside by French linesman Georges Capdeville (who went on to referee the Final), Fernández completed the first World Cup shock. Alternative crowd figure: 3,993.

5 June 1938 – Vélodrome, Rheims – 9,091 – Roger Conrié (FRA)

HUNGARY **(4) 6**
Kohut 14, Toldi 16, Sárosi 25, 88

DUTCH EAST INDIES **(0) 0**
Zsengellér 30, 67

HUNGARY József Háda, Lajos Korányi, Sándor Bíró, Gyula Lázár, József Turay, István Balogh, Ferenc Sas, Gyula Zsengellér, György Sárosi (c), Géza Toldi, Vilmos Kohut. *Károly Dietz (coach Alfréd Schaffer).*
DUTCH EAST INDIES Tan Mo Heng, Frans Hu Kom, Jack Samuels, Achmad Nawir, Frans Meeng (c), Anwar Sutan, Tan Hong Djien, Suvarte Sudarmadji, Hendrikus Zomers, Tjak Pattiwael, Hans Taihuttu. *Jan Mastenbroek (HOL).*

The first real World Cup mismatch. Nine of the Indonesians were winning their first caps, most of them were students, all of them were very small. '*Bien trop petits*', said a French reporter, who also thought their forwards '*très brilliants dribbleurs*' but their defence lacking the rudiments. No marking, too many late tackles. Their captain played in glasses and the goalkeeper brought a fat-faced doll onto

LEADING GOALSCORERS 1938

7	Leônidas	BRZ
5	Gyula Zsengellér	HUN
5	György Sárosi	HUN
5	Silvio Piola	ITA

the pitch, but it couldn't put a hex on the Hungarian inside-forward trio, who looked 'the equal of the Italians' and spent the second half practising their passing.

The Tans were brothers. Zomers is also seen spelt Sommers. The stadium was later renamed the Auguste Delaune.

1938

5 June 1938 – Yves du Manoir, Colombes, Paris – 30,454 – Hans Wüthrich (SWI)

FRANCE **(2) 3**
Veinante 35 sec, Nicolas 11, 69

BELGIUM **(1) 1**
Isemborghs 19

FRANCE Laurent Di Lorto, Héctor Cazenave, Étienne Mattler (c), Jean Bastien, Gusti Jordan, Raoul Diagne, Alfred (Freddy) Aston, Oscar Heisserer, Jean Nicolas, Edmond Delfour, Émile Veinante. *Gaston Barreau.*
BELGIUM Arnold Badjou, Bob Paverick, Corneel Seys, John Van Alphen, Emile Stijnen (c), Alfons De Winter, Charley Van Den Wouwer, Bernard Voorhoof, Hendrik Isemborghs, Raymond Braine, Fernand Buyle. *Jack Butler (ENG).*

The hosts would have been very disappointed if they'd lost this. Nicolas, avoiding injury this time, made the first goal with a shot Badjou couldn't hold, dribbled through for the second, then pivoted to hit Aston's cross first time. Isemborghs scored from Voorhoof's free kick – but the tall Diagne, the first black player to be capped by France, broke up Belgium's attacks in midfield. Butler had won a single England cap in 1924 – against Belgium, the country he later coached to their only win in 20 matches against England (1936).

The stadium, originally known as the Olympique (it hosted the 1924 Games), was renamed after a former rugby international who died in 1928.

5 June 1938 – La Cavée Verte, Le Havre – 10,550 – Lucien Leclercq (FRA)

CZECHOSLOVAKIA   (0) (0) 3
Košťálek 93, Zeman 111, Nejedlý 118

HOLLAND   (0) (0) 0

CZECHOSLOVAKIA František Plánička (c), Jaroslav Burgr, Ferdinand Daučík, Josef Košťálek, Jaroslav Bouček, Vlasta Kopecký, Jan Říha, Vladislav Šimůnek, Josef Zeman, Oldřich Nejedlý, Oldřich Rulc. *Karel Meissner (coach Josef Sedláček).*
HOLLAND Adri van Male, Mauk Weber, Bertus Caldenhove, Bas Paauwe, Wim Anderiesen, Gerrit 'Puck' van Heel (c), Frank Wels, Freek van der Veen, Jaap 'Kick' Smit, Leen Vente, Bertus de Harder. *Bob Glendenning (ENG).*

Czechoslovakia should have had little trouble with a Dutch team deprived of its leading scorer Bep Bakhuys and reduced to ten men by van der Veen's second-half injury. Instead their timing was out and Plánička had to save a header and a fierce shot ('*Bombenschuss*') from the 18-year-old de Harder. Košťálek scored from long range and at last the forwards began to combine well, Nejedlý and Zeman making goals for each other.

5 June 1938 – de la Meinau, Strasbourg – 13,452 – Ivan Eklind (SWE)

BRAZIL   (3) (4) 6
Leônidas 18, 93, 104, Romeu 25, Perácio 44, 71

POLAND   (1) (4) 5
Scherfke pen 23, Wilimowski 53, 59, 89, 118

BRAZIL 'Batatais' (Algisto Lorenzato), Domingos (da Guia), Arthur Machado, 'Zezé Procópio' (José Procópio Mendes) Procópio, Martim (Silveira) (c), 'Afonsinho' (Afonso Guimarães), José Lopes, Romeu (Pellicciari), Leônidas (da Silva), José Perácio, Hércules (de Miranda). *Adhemar Pimenta.*
POLAND Edward Madejski, Władysław Szczepaniak (c), Antoni Gałecki, Wilhelm Góra, Erwin Nyc, Ewald Dytko, Ryszard Piec, Leonard Piatek, Fryderyk Scherfke, Ernest Wilimowski, Gerard Wodarz. *Józef Kałuża.*

Brazil had lost the Copa América play-off to Argentina only in extra-time, but this didn't exactly persuade them to build a settled side. Here they picked their usual crop of new caps (seven), plus Leônidas winning his first since 1934. Poland had just drawn with Switzerland and beaten the Republic of Ireland 6-0, and the 21-year-old Wilimowski was one of the sharpest strikers in Europe.

According to Leônidas, the muddy pitch tore the sole off his boot, whereupon he tried playing in his socks, only for Eklind to make him put his footwear back on. At the other end of the body, Zezé Procópio wore a cap with a pale stripe along the top.

Some of Poland's goals were down to bizarre defending (the penalty was awarded for Domingos' copybook rugby tackle, an astonishing sight), but as always the Brazilian forwards were better. The sturdy little Leônidas stood out for his pencil moustache and determination (though his ball skills, on film, don't quite match up to the legend). Some British sources still credit him with four goals, an error. In the first half, a short angled pass sent him in behind a square static defence to shoot high past the keeper from close range. Romeu, burly and balding, scored in a similar way.

When Perácio headed the third, Poland seemed to be out of it – but Wilimowski scored a second-half hat-trick. His fourth came too late to matter but made him the first player to score as many in a finals match. As far as records show, he was the only player to score four goals for the losing side in any international match. Not content with all their new Austrians, Germany later press-ganged him ('Ernst Willimowski') into scoring thirteen goals for them during the War, which was started by the invasion of his own country.

Piątek is wrongly referred to as Piontek in most sources. Dytko and Nyc were later known as Edward, Piec originally called Richard Pietz. Batatais is Portuguese for 'potatoes'.

---

5 June 1938 – Vélodrome, Marseilles – 18,826 – Alois Beranek (GER)

ITALY   (1) (1) 2
Ferraris 2, Piola 94

NORWAY   (0) (1) 1
Brustad 83

ITALY Aldo Olivieri, Eraldo Monzeglio, Pietro Rava, Pietro Serantoni, Miguel Ángel 'Michele' Andreolo, Ugo Locatelli, Piero Pasinati, Giuseppe Meazza (c), Silvio Piola, Giovanni Ferrari, Pietro Ferraris. *Vittorio Pozzo.*
NORWAY Henry Johansen, Rolf Johannesen, Øivind Holmsen, Kristian Henriksen, Nils Eriksen (c), Rolf Holmberg, Odd Frantzen, Reidar Kvammen, Knut Brynildsen, Magnar Isaksen, Arne Brustad. *Asbjørn Halvorsen.*

The holders took the lead when Johansen couldn't hold a low shot and Ferraris poked it in. But in the Olympic Games two years earlier, Norway had lost only 2-1 to Italy after extra-time, Brustad scoring their equaliser, Italy going on to win the tournament. Surely it couldn't all happen again . . .

For virtually the whole ninety minutes, Italy were on the rack: Piola policed by Eriksen, the Italian wingers marked out of the game, the rangy Brynildsen a menace up front. Brustad, good enough to play for the Rest of Europe against England later in the year, ran through to equalise then had a second goal disallowed for offside. His immediate opponent, the 32-year-old Monzeglio, who seems to have been the first player to appear in a finals match on his birthday, wasn't capped again.

Two players rescued Italy. Rava, tall and rugged (he'd been sent off in his first international), and the acrobatic Olivieri, who made several good-looking saves. When Brynildsen broke through on the right, Olivieri offered

him a gap then stopped the fierce shot, after which Brynildsen shook his hand. Relief – followed by Piola's winner when the experienced Johansen again failed to hold a shot, this time a trundler from Pasinati. A bad first day at the office for the new Italy, some of whom would lose their jobs.

Some English sources still persist in crediting the first goal to Ferrari, a bad error. Beranek, listed as German this time, was yet another Austrian making a guest appearance for the Reich.

Sweden bye (Austria withdrew).

QUARTER-FINALS

12 June 1938 – Fort Carré, Antibes – 6,846 – Gustav Krist (CZE)

SWEDEN   (4) 8
H Andersson 9, 81, 89, Wetterström 22, 37, 44, Keller 80, Nyberg 84

CUBA   (0) 0

SWEDEN Henock Abrahamsson, Ivar Eriksson, Olle Källgren, Erik Almgren, Sven Jacobsson, Kurt Svanström, Arne Nyberg, Sven Jonasson, Harry Andersson, Tore Keller (c), Gustav Wetterström. *József Nagy (HUN).*
CUBA Carvajales, Barquín, Chorens, Berges, Rodríguez, Arias, Pedro Ferrer, Fernández (c), Socorro, Tuñas, Juan Alberto Alonso.

Cuba recalled Carvajales, but the rest of the defence was taken apart. Wetterström, who'd proved himself a rabbit killer by scoring a hat-trick in eleven minutes in the qualifier against Estonia, got another here (hard to know why some sources credit him with four goals; the Swedes never have). Like Stábile in 1930, Andersson scored three on his international debut. Cuba were handicapped by an injury to Arias, who had to go off, and their last chance came and went when Sweden's other new cap Abrahamsson saved a Fernández penalty two minutes before half-time. Cuba left their mark on the tournament but haven't been back since.

---

12 June 1938 – Victor Boucquey, Lille – 14,800 – Rinaldo Barlassina (ITA)

HUNGARY   (1) 2
Sárosi 42, Zsengellér 89

SWITZERLAND   (0) 0

HUNGARY Antal Szabó, Korányi, Bíró, Antal Szalay, Turay, Lázár, Sas, Jenö Vincze, Sárosi (c), Zsengellér, Kohut.
SWITZERLAND Huber, Adolf Stelzer, Lehmann, Springer, Vernati, Lörtscher, Bickel, Abegglen (c), Amadò, Walaschek, Tullio Grassi.

Two hard matches left the Swiss without Minelli and Aeby, and they had little chance once Sárosi had put Hungary ahead with Huber distracted by a heading duel between Lörtscher and Zsengellér, who scored the second from long range. At the other end, Switzerland couldn't get past Korányi and Bíró, the best full-back pairing in the tournament.

---

12 June 1938 – Yves du Manoir, Colombes, Paris – 58,455 – Louis Baert (BEL)

ITALY   (1) 3
Colaussi 9, Piola 52, 72

FRANCE   (1) 1
Heisserer 10

ITALY Olivieri, Alfredo Foni, Rava, Serantoni, Andreolo, Locatelli, Amedeo Biavati, Meazza (c), Piola, Ferrari, Gino Colaussi.
FRANCE Di Lorto, Cazenave, Mattler (c), Bastien, Jordan, Diagne, Aston, Heisserer, Nicolas, Delfour, Veinante.

Pozzo, reading the signs as well as ever, made three important changes. Two new wingers, and Foni in place of Monzeglio, a lion of 1934 but now past his best.

France allegedly paid the penalty for throwing themselves into attack in the second half, allowing Piola too much room – but perhaps it was always on the cards. Jordan had scored against England, but he was an attacking centre-half and his immediate opponent Ted Drake had scored twice. Against Italy, Jordan felt he was having to mark two men in the first half, and suggested a change of tactics during the interval, only for Mattler to veto it. At 32, the captain didn't think this was the right moment to become a man-marker for the first time in his career.

So Piola was free to win the match for Italy. When the giant Mattler lost the ball near his left touchline, Meazza nodded it short to Biavati, whose instant lofted pass was met by Piola's dash across the penalty area followed by a low cross-shot. He scored his other goal with a leaping header from Biavati's cross. Very tall and angular but mobile and confident, he scored 30 goals for Italy in only 34 games and wasn't particular how they went in: the following year he scored against England with his fist. What unleashed him in this World Cup was the arrival of the new wingers, especially the balding new cap Biavati, whose foot-over-the-ball feint was the subject of diagrams. When Piola hit the ball out to the flanks, he now knew he'd get it back. And Ferrari had a tremendous, all-action match, punctuated with feints and flicks.

France had equalised when the ball was left for Heisserer to thrash in a rebound at the near post, but Italy held their shape in front of a hostile crowd. Pozzo clearly believed they played better in adversity: he sent them out in a change strip of Fascist black, a set of red rags to the many Italian anti-Fascists who'd escaped to Paris.

The French, meanwhile, had suffered the worst goalkeeping blunder in any World Cup, more glaring than Pat Bonner's in 1994 or anything by Kazadi of Zaire. Surrounded by defenders on the left-hand corner of the penalty area, Colaussi looped a volley straight at Di Lorto, who hopped up for the easy catch then decided to push it away. Somehow he palmed it sideways, tried to follow it as it fell into the net, crashed into the goalpost, and kicked the ball away in disgust. A genuine masterpiece, and all his own work. Earlier in the season, he'd been '*un véritable rampart*' in the goalless draw with Italy – but after this he didn't play for France again. Nor did the stylish Delfour, whose 41st cap was a national record. The match was played on Veinante's 31st birthday. Foni coached Switzerland in the 1966 finals.

---

12 June 1938 – Municipal Parc Lescure, Bordeaux – 22,021 – Paul von Hertzka (HUN)

BRAZIL (1) (1) 1
Leônidas 30

CZECHOSLOVAKIA (0) (1) 1
Nejedlý pen 65

BRAZIL Walter (de Souza), Domingos, Machado, Zezé Procópio, Martim (c), Afonsinho, Lopes, Romeu, Leônidas, Perácio, Hércules.
CZECHOSLOVAKIA Plánička (c), Burgr, Daučík, Košt'álek, Bouček, Kopecký Říha, Šimůnek, Nejedlý, Josef Ludl, Antonín Puč.
SENT OFF: Zezé Procópio 14, Machado 44, Říha 44.

There had been skirmishes before, even police on the pitch – but here was the first World Cup war, resulting in broken limbs for Plánička (arm) and Nejedlý (leg) which kept them out of the replay. Brazil announced their intentions early, Zezé Procópio getting himself sent off for a wild tackle on Nejedlý, who survived long enough to equalise with a left-footed

SENDINGS-OFF IN A MATCH

3	1938	Brazil	v	Czechoslovakia
3	1954	Brazil	v	Hungary
3	1998	Denmark	v	Saudi Arabia

1938

penalty that puffed the chalk on both the spot and the six-yard line. He and Puč were unfit for the replay and Plánička didn't play for Czechoslovakia again, after a world record 73 caps. The players who stayed on the pitch pushed and shoved each other in front of the referee, there were bodies all over the field, and Leônidas was slowed by a bad foul soon after opening the scoring from what may have been an offside position.

This was the first match played at the new stadium, which was still being used in France 98. Von Hertzka's first name is sometimes seen in its Hungarian version: Pál.

REPLAY

14 June 1938 – Municipal Parc Lescure, Bordeaux – 18,141 – Georges Capdeville (FRA)

BRAZIL (0) 2
Leônidas 57, Roberto 62

CZECHOSLOVAKIA (1) 1
Kopecký 24

BRAZIL Walter, 'Jaú' (Euclydes Barbosa) 'Nariz' (Alvaro Cançado Lopes), Hermínio de Britto, José Augusto Brandão, Argemiro (Pinheiro), Roberto (da Cunha), Luiz M Oliveira, Leônidas (c), 'Tim' (Elba de Pádua Lima), 'Patesko' (Rodolfo Barteczko).
CZECHOSLOVAKIA Karel Burkert, Burgr (c), Daučík, Košt'álek, Bouček, Ludl, Václav Horák, Karel Senecký, Vilém Kreuz, Kopecký, Rulc.

A match awaited with bated breath – but Brazil made nine changes, the Czechoslovakians five,

1930
1934
1938
1950
1954
1958
1962
1966
1970
1974
1978
1982
1986
1990
1994
1998
2002
2006

and that seemed to clear the air. The result turned on Walter's save from Senecký, the ball appearing to cross the line, two minutes before Roberto scored the winner. Czechoslovakia were out, and soon their prime minister would be sitting outside a room as the Allies voted to let Hitler take a slice of his country. Luiz M Oliveira is sometimes referred to as 'Luisinho', but not in Brazil.

SEMI-FINALS

16 June 1938 – Parc des Princes, Paris – 20,155 – Lucien Leclercq (FRA)

HUNGARY (3) 5
Jacobsson o.g. 19, Titkos 37, Zsengellér 39, 85, Sárosi 65

SWEDEN (1) 1
Nyberg 35 sec

HUNGARY Szabó, Korányi, Bíró, Szalay, Turay, Lázár, Sas, Zsengellér, Sárosi (c), Toldi, Pál Titkos.
SWEDEN Abrahamsson, Eriksson, Källgren, Almgren, Jacobsson, Svanström, Wetterström, Keller (c), H Andersson, Jonasson, Nyberg.

Not so much that Sweden were found out, more that the Hungarian attack was irresistible ('*Kombinationsmaschine*'). Nyberg ran clear to score in an immediate counter-attack up the right – but Zsengellér aimed a diving header towards two defenders facing their own goal, and the first of them lifted a leg to knock it past his own keeper.

After that, Sweden had no answer to Hungary's two main strikers, who scored 74 goals in 100 internationals, the inventive Zsengellér a natural finisher, Sárosi one of the great all-round players, a withdrawn centre-forward who scored more often than most of his type.

16 June 1938 – Vélodrome, Marseilles – 33,000 – Hans Wüthrich (SWI)

ITALY (0) 2
Colaussi 55, Meazza pen 60

BRAZIL (0) 1
Romeu 87

ITALY Olivieri, Foni, Rava, Serantoni, Andreolo, Locatelli, Biavati, Meazza (c), Piola, Ferrari, Colaussi.
BRAZIL Walter, Domingos, Machado, Zezé Procópio, Martim (c), Afonsinho, Lopes, Luiz M Oliveira, Romeu, Perácio, Patesko.

Italy, growing into their game, were generally expected to win, but it goes without saying that Brazil were dangerous – at least until Leônidas was left out of the team. Legend has it (as does a contemporary French film) that this was the worst selectorial blunder in any World Cup, Pimenta dropping his star striker to save him for the Final. But that was always stretching belief. The truth is what you'd expect: Leônidas simply hadn't recovered from a bruising quarter-final. Against the world champions and their formidable defence, his absence was always likely to be decisive.

On a threadbare pitch, Italy would have led at half-time but for some '*véritablement extra-ordinaire*' saves by Walter. Eventually Colaussi converted a right-wing cross, then Domingos conceded yet another penalty.

Arguably the best defender in the tournament (admired by Pozzo), big and static but a famous reader of the ball, he took a battering when Piola 'began to work with his elbows'. An exasperated foul led to the penalty. Meazza, visibly slower and clumsier by now (he was a famous night owl), scored high to his left then went to the touchline to change his shorts, whose elastic had snapped as he bent to put the ball on the spot. Coolness itself. This was his 33rd and last goal for Italy, the national record until Riva broke it in 1973. Romeu scored from Perácio's corner after Olivieri saved from Luiz Oliveira, but it was far too late.

3RD-PLACE FINAL

19 June 1938 – Municipal Parc Lescure, Bordeaux – 12,500 – John Langenus (BEL)

BRAZIL **(1) 4**
Romeu 44, Leônidas 63, 74, Perácio 80

SWEDEN **(2) 2**
Jonasson 28, Nyberg 38

BRAZIL Batatais, Domingos, Machado, Zezé Procópio, Brandão, Afonsinho, Roberto, Romeu, Leônidas (c), Perácio, Patesko.
SWEDEN Abrahamsson, Eriksson, Erik Nilsson, Almgren, Arne Linderholm, Svanström (c), Nyberg, Erik Persson, H Andersson, Jonasson, Åke Andersson.

All about Leônidas. Back in the team, appointed captain, scoring twice to finish as the tournament's top scorer, a minor consolation. Jonasson's shot went in off a post and the keeper's body and Sweden held their unlikely lead till half-time, but the interpassing of the Brazilian forwards was too much for them in the end. Twelve minutes from time a foul by Nilsson on Roberto led to a penalty which Patesko put over the bar (deliberately, it's said). Nilsson, one of only two players to take part in the finals before and after the War (along with Bickel of Switzerland), was winning his first cap. 'Lillis' Persson was one of three Erik Perssons capped in the 1930s.

FINAL

19 June 1938 – Yves du Manoir, Colombes, Paris – 45,124 – Georges Capdeville (FRA)

1938

ITALY **(3) 4**
Colaussi 6, 35, Piola 16, 82

HUNGARY **(1) 2**
Titkos 7, Sárosi 69

ITALY Olivieri, Foni, Rava, Serantoni, Andreolo, Locatelli, Biavati, Meazza (c), Piola, Ferrari, Colaussi.
HUNGARY Szabó, Gyula Polgár, Bíró, Szalay, György Szücs, Lázár, Sas, Vincze, Sárosi (c), Zsengellér, Titkos.

Much the same story as in 1934: Italian ramparts keeping out the Danube. But this was a brighter, more athletic Italian team, with the pace and fitness to keep turning defence into attack – and the last thing Hungary needed was the injury that forced them to replace the hard-tackling Korányi with Polgár, who'd first been capped as a forward.

In fact the entire Hungarian defence was barely worthy of the name. When a cross came in from the right, Colaussi was completely unmarked – and that barely begins to describe it: there wasn't a single Hungarian in that half of the penalty area. With goalkeepers still tending to stay on their lines, Colaussi was able to prod home from close range.

An immediate equaliser raised false hopes, a cross from the right finding Titkos, who lashed in a high shot at the near post. Sárosi was being successfully marked by Andreolo – but his real problem was the pace at which Italy played (even by today's standards), rushing his decisions. Only the Hungarian wingers carried any threat, and they didn't see enough of the ball.

And there was always Piola. When Szabó fumbled Ferrari's 20-yarder, he was first to

1930
1934
1938
1950
1954
1958
1962
1966
1970
1974
1978
1982
1986
1990
1994
1998
2002
2006

the rebound, hitting the post with a powerful left-footer. Soon he was tapping a pass to Ferrari, who was seven yards out with only the keeper to beat but moved the ball to the right instead of shooting. Meazza laid it back – and there was no-one tight on Piola when he put an end to the pussyfooting by thumping a right-foot drive high inside the near post. Szabó stayed on his line again as Colaussi walked in the third from the same position as the first, this time with a defender's arm round his waist.

Italy sat back after half-time and used Biavati's pace on the counter. When he broke through, Szabó stood eccentrically upright and let the shot hit his foot. Sárosi turned in a cross from close range, but Piola met Biavati's short low cross with an uncompromising ground shot. Meazza received the trophy with a Fascist salute and not a brylcreemed hair out of place,

and the team were received by Mussolini, bareheaded this time while they wore the sailor hats. Pozzo was the only manager to win the World Cup twice.

How shall we play this game? asked the French football writer Jean Eskenazi. Do we make love, or catch a bus? The Mid-Europeans' technique was known for its finesse, but Pozzo had finally found the right Number 9 to go with his Ferrari.

Italians kept winning in Paris in the summer of '38. The great Gino Bartali finished first in the Tour de France, and even their animals were dominant, Nearco taking the Grand Prix de Paris ahead of the winners of the French and English Derbies. But others would be conquering France soon, and there wouldn't be another World Cup until 1950. Right across Europe, the beasts were taking over.

The weight of shadows

Brazil 1950

1930

1934

1938

1950

1954

1958

1962

1966

1970

1974

1978

1982

1986

1990

1994

1998

2002

2006

The first truly peacetime World Cup in twenty years had its parallels with the previous one. Held in South America, only thirteen teams taking part, a league system, a strong host team.

This time the idea of four mini leagues was in place from the start, presumably because FIFA decided knockout matches were an arbitrary way of deciding the best in the world. To emphasise their thinking, the four group winners would qualify for yet another group, the champions to be decided on points. There was no provision for an actual Final – but one materialised all the same, and perhaps the most eviscerating of all.

Several things had happened in 1949 which seemed sure to affect the result of the tournament. Brazil won the Copa América, also held at home, also on a league basis, with scores of 9-1, 10-1, 5-0, 7-1 and 5-1 (v Uruguay) before thrashing Paraguay 7-0 in the play-off, the inside-forward trio of Zizinho, Ademir and Jair combining to dazzling effect. In Italy, an air crash wiped out the entire Torino squad, the backbone of the national team. Sweden, strong Olympic champions in 1948, lost their best players to Italian clubs.

Of the other South Americans, Uruguay were back in the fold but having a mixed year, and Argentina pulled out yet again. Yugoslavia looked the strongest of the Europeans: Olympic runners-up and packed with world-class players. But the most intriguing entry was from the mother country, taking part for the first time.

The 1950 World Cup came a few years too late for England, who'd lost Frank Swift, Tommy Lawton and the incomparable Raich Carter from their team of the immediate post-war years. But Tom Finney was still there, with Billy Wright and Stan Mortensen and (eventually) Stanley Matthews. At the very least, they were expected to qualify for the final pool.

Places had been left open for the top two teams in the Home Championship, but Scotland decided they'd go as champions or not at all. They lost 1-0 to England at Hampden, where Willie Bauld hit the bar – and stayed behind, a mystery to this day.

France too turned down an invitation, as did Turkey, but neither of them was a strong contender. The Germans, on the other hand, still banned by FIFA, might have been an intriguing entry. Although they hadn't played an international match since 1942, some of their building blocks were already there (Turek, Morlock, the Walter brothers) and would be firmly in place four years later.

Instead of re-drawing the competition after this rash of late withdrawals, the organisers left things as they stood. So while two groups consisted of four teams each, Uruguay had only Bolivia to beat. And there was no zoning, which forced teams in the same group to travel hundreds of miles between cities.

Brazil had built a new stadium, the biggest in history, with twice the capacity of Wembley. On the first day of the tournament, it still wasn't ready. But the Brazilian public didn't mind too much. Their team seemed to be.

The moment when the shadows began to fall. Schiaffino (extreme left) equalises against Brazil, watched by (right of the post) the first Englishman to take part in a World Cup Final.

1930
1934
1938

GROUP 1

Brazil (seeded), Mexico, Switzerland, Yugoslavia.

1950 24 June 1950 – Maracanã, Rio de Janeiro – 81,649 – George Reader (ENG)

1954

BRAZIL   (1) 4
Ademir 31, 79, Jair 65, Baltazar 71

MEXICO   (0) 0

1958

BRAZIL Moacyr Barbosa, Augusto (da Costa) (c), Juvenal (Amarijo), Ely (do Amparo), Danilo (Alvim), 'Bigode' (João Ferreira), 'Maneca' (Manuel Marinho Alves), Ademir (Menezes), 'Baltazar' (Oswaldo da Silva), Jair (Rosa Pinto), Albino Friaça. *Flávio Costa*.
MEXICO Antonio Carbajal, Felipe Zetter, Alfonso Montemayor (c), Rodrigo Ruiz, Mario Ochoa, José Antonio Roca, Carlos Septién, Héctor Ortiz, Horacio Casarín, Mario Pérez snr, Lupe Velázquez. *Octavio Vial*.

1962

1966

1970

1974 Unusual for a stadium's capacity to be halved for an opening ceremony, but it was just as well. Along with the fireworks and 5,000 pigeons, there was a 21-gun salute, which the new edifice, its plaster still drying, didn't like very much. English referee Arthur Ellis and others in the stand 'were peppered with a shower of concrete, fortunately none of it in huge blocks!' Then when Brazil scored, fifteen radio commentators and dozens of reporters ran onto the pitch for on-the-spot interviews (it still happens now).

1978

1982

1986

1990

Reader had the field cleared without fuss and Brazil resumed their bombardment. Carbajal, winning his first cap, was described as '*magnifico*' and Brazil hit the woodwork five times. Mexico gave away six free kicks in the first five minutes, Jair hit a post after six, then Ademir touched the ball past the advancing Carbajal, who began picking smoking fireworks out of his goalmouth.

1994

1998

2002

2006

After half-time, Ademir switched to centre-forward, Baltazar moving to the wing. Friaça, Jair (twice) and Baltazar hit the bar, Jair scored with a cross-shot of 'optimum style,' Baltazar headed in a corner from ten yards out, and Ademir drove in Jair's short pass. All this from a team who hadn't decided on their best forward line.

Mario Pérez was the father of Mario junior (1970) and brother of Luis (1930), who was twenty years older. The Maracanã was known as the Municipal at the time, later as the Mário Filho (it's in the Maracanã district of Rio).

25 June 1950 – Independencia, Belo Horizonte – 7,336 – Giovanni Galeati (ITA)

YUGOSLAVIA   (0) 3
Mitić 58, Tomašević 78, Ognjanov 84

SWITZERLAND   (0) 0

YUGOSLAVIA Srdan Mrkušić, Ivan Horvat, Branko Stanković, Zlatko Čajkovski, Miodrag Jovanović, Predrag Đajić, Tihomir Ognjanov, Rajko Mitić (c), Kosta Tomašević, Stjepan Bobek, Bernard Vukas. *Milorad Arsenijević, with Ljubiša Bročić*.
SWITZERLAND Georges Stuber, André Neury, Roger Bocquet, Gerhard Lusenti, Olivier Eggimann, Roger Quinche, Alfred Bickel (c), Charly Antenen, Jean Tamini, René Bader, Jacky Fatton. *Franco Andreoli etc*.

By now the Swiss had perfected the '*verrou*,' their 'bolt' defence, but can't have been surprised by the result: they'd lost 4-0 at home to Yugoslavia two weeks earlier. Here, after the giant Horvat had defused an early crisis, '*el dominio de Yugoslavia es total*'. Stuber made two brilliant saves from Bobek, who eventually sent Mitić in to score. Tomašević headed the second, and Ognjanov finished off a move involving the entire forward line by knocking in a pass by Jovanović.

This was the first finals match in which floodlights were switched on. It started twenty

BIGGEST CROWDS

205,000	1950	Brazil	v	Uruguay	Rio
152,772	1950	Brazil	v	Spain	Rio
142,429	1950	Brazil	v	Yugoslavia	Rio
138,886	1950	Brazil	v	Sweden	Rio
114,600	1986	Mexico	v	Paraguay	Mexico City
114,580	1986	Mexico	v	Bulgaria	Mexico City
114,580	1986	Argentina	v	England	Mexico City
114,580	1986	Argentina	v	Germany	Mexico City

The true figures for Brazil's matches against Spain, Yugoslavia and Sweden in 1950 may have been considerably higher.

The biggest crowd outside the Maracanã and Azteca was the 98,270 who saw England beat France at Wembley in 1966.

1954

1958

1962

1966

1970

1974

minutes late while corner flags were found and a line of chairs moved from right next to one of the touchlines.

breaking out only when the match had been decided. The penalty was given for a foul on Velázquez.

---

28 June 1950 – Eucaliptos, Pôrto Alegre – 11,078 – Reg Leafe (ENG)

YUGOSLAVIA **(2) 4**
Bobek 19, Ž Čajkovski 23, 51, Tomašević 81

MEXICO **(0) 1**
Ortiz pen 87

YUGOSLAVIA Mrkušić, Horvat (c), Stanković, Z Čajkovski, Jovanović, Đajić, Prvoslav Mihajlović, Mitić, Tomašević, Bobek, Željko Čajkovski.
MEXICO Carbajal, Manuel Gutiérrez, Samuel Cuburu, Gregorio Gómez, Ortiz, Roca, Septién, José Naranjo, Casarín (c), Pérez, Velázquez.

Zlatko Cajkovski, a tenacious halfback, made a goal for his brother, who scored his second with a *'violentissimo'* shot. Bobek drove in Mihajlović's cross and Tomašević scored the fourth with a shot Carbajal couldn't hold. Mexico were on the defensive throughout,

---

28 June 1950 – Pacaembu, São Paulo – 42,032 – Ramón Azón (SPA)

BRAZIL **(2) 2**
Alfredo 3, Baltazar 32

SWITZERLAND **(1) 2**
Fatton 17, 88

BRAZIL Barbosa, Augusto (c), Juvenal, José Carlos Bauer, Rui (Campos), Alfredo Noronha, Alfredo (dos Santos), Maneca, Baltazar, Ademir, Friaça.
SWITZERLAND Stuber, Neury, Bocquet, Lusenti, Eggimann, Quinche, Tamini, Bickel (c), Hans Peter Friedländer, Bader, Fatton.

Flávio Costa, reported as calling Switzerland 'contenders without importance,' brought in a number of players with São Paulo clubs, presumably to please the crowd – who nearly lynched him for it. Alfredo scored with an excellent shot after Ademir's cut-back seemed

1978

1982

1986

1990

1994

1998

2002

2006

1930
1934
1938

1950

1954
1958
1962
1966
1970
1974
1978
1982
1986
1990
1994
1998
2002
2006

to have gone out of play, Baltazar headed in Friaça's cross following a corner, Stuber made a marvellous save from Ademir and was knocked out by a shot from Baltazar – but the Swiss wouldn't lie down.

The dangerous little Fatton sped past Augusto to score their first, then tapped in from three yards after Bickel got away late in the game. The result left Yugoslavia needing only a draw with Brazil to qualify, and the police had to save Costa from indignant fans. One plus for Brazil was the form of the statuesque Bauer, a tremendous all-rounder, who was here to stay.

Chilean linesman Sergio Bustamante was the youngest official in any finals match: 26 years 65 days.

---

1 July 1950 – Maracanã, Rio de Janeiro – 142,429 –
Mervyn Griffiths (WAL)

BRAZIL (1) 2
Ademir 3, Zizinho 69

YUGOSLAVIA (0) 0

BRAZIL Barbosa, Augusto (c), Juvenal, Bauer, Danilo, Bigode, Maneca, 'Zizinho' (Thomaz Soares), Ademir, Jair, 'Chico' (Francisco Aramburu).
YUGOSLAVIA Mrkušić, Horvat, Stankoić, Z Čajkovski (c), Jovanović, Đajić, Vukas, Mitić, Tomašević, Bobek, Ž Čajkovski.

There was an '*extraordinaria tensión*' in Rio before the match, and many thought Costa had blundered again by leaving out Baltazar, so good in the air. But he'd got it right this time, restoring the great inside-forward trio even though Zizinho was still feeling the injury that had kept him out so far ('I didn't have the injection. I was terrified of the needle').

Brazil had a slice of luck to set them on the way. In the changing room before the match,

GAPS BETWEEN MATCHES

yrs	days			
12	13	Fred Bickel	SWI	1938–50
12	8	Wilfried Van Moer	BEL	1970–82
12	6	Erik Nilsson	SWE	1938–50
12	1	Alex Czerniatynski	BEL	1982–94
11	359	Michael Laudrup	DEN	1986–98
11	346	Hernán Medford	COS	1990–02
11	340	Niall Quinn	EIR	1990–02
11	325	Pirri	SPA	1966–78

Mitić (a contemporary source says Zlatko Čajkovski) found out just how unfinished the stadium was, cutting his head on an exposed girder. The referee refused to delay the start, and very soon Ademir was guiding the ball low past Mrkušić's left hand.

Then Mitić (or Čajkovski) joined in and Yugoslavia matched Brazil for skill and opportunities, Tomašević blasting over the bar, Barbosa saving from Mitić. It took half an hour for the referee to order Mrkušić to change his jersey because it was the same colour as Brazil's all-white strip.

Željko Čajkovski missed two chances, and Zizinho allegedly had two goals disallowed before shooting in low from the corner of the six-yard box while Mrkušić stayed on his line. The hosts were through to their appointed place, but by the skin of their opponents' brow.

---

2 July 1950 – Eucaliptos, Pôrto Alegre – 3,580 – Ivan
Eklind (SWE)

SWITZERLAND (2) 2
Bader 12, Antenen 44

MEXICO (0) 1
Casarín 75

SWITZERLAND Adolphe Hug, Neury, Bocquet (c), Lusenti, Eggimann, Quinche, Tamini, Antenen, Friedländer, Bader, Fatton.
MEXICO Carbajal, Gutiérrez, Gómez, Roca, Ortiz, Ochoa, Antonio Flores, Naranjo, Casarín (c), José Luis Borbolla, Velázquez.

In between their goals, Switzerland missed good chances through Bader and Tamini. In the second half, Hug saved twice from Casarín, who finally had his reward with a fierce cross shot. Hug's first name is also seen spelt Adolf. Roca was Mexico's manager in the 1978 finals.

GROUP 1

	P	W	D	L	F	A	Pts
Brazil	3	2	1	0	8	2	5
Yugoslavia	3	2	0	1	7	3	4
Switzerland	3	1	1	1	4	6	3
Mexico	3	0	0	3	2	10	0

Brazil qualified for the final pool.

GROUP 2

Chile, England (seeded), Spain, USA.

25 June 1950 – Maracanã, Rio de Janeiro – 29,703 – Karel van der Meer (HOL)

ENGLAND　(1) 2
Mortensen 39, Mannion 51

CHILE　　(0) 0

ENGLAND Bert Williams, Alf Ramsey, Johnny Aston, Billy Wright (c), Laurie Hughes, Jimmy Dickinson, Tom Finney, Wilf Mannion, Roy Bentley, Stan Mortensen, Jimmy Mullen. *Walter Winterbottom.*
CHILE Sergio Livingstone (c), Arturo Farías, Fernando Roldán, Manuel Álvarez, Miguel Busquets, Hernán Carvallo, Lindorfo Mayanés, Atilio Cremaschi, George Robledo, Manuel Múñoz, Guillermo Díaz. *Alberto Buccicardi.*

This was Chile's first match against European opposition since the 1930 World Cup, and

OLDEST REFEREES

yrs	days			
53	236	George Reader	ENG	1950
51	284	Mário Vianna	BRZ	1954
50	140	Alfred Birlem	GER	1938
50	72	Jack Mowat	SCO	1958
50	34	Antonio Márquez	MEX	1986
50	3	Leo Lemešić	YUG	1958
Linesmen				
52	213	Charles Delasalle	FRA	1950
50	179	Alois Beranek	AUT	1950

Beranek refereed in the 1934 and 1938 finals.

Delasalle never refereed a finals match.

1930
1934
1938
1950
1954
1958
1962
1966
1970
1974
1978
1982
1986
1990
1994
1998
2002
2006

1950

their press called it the most difficult match in their history – but they'd beaten Uruguay in their last match before the tournament and were now reinforced by Robledo, who played for Newcastle United (he scored the only goal of the 1952 FA Cup Final) and was the main danger to England, especially as they had a problem at centre-half.

1954

1958

1962

1966

1970

1974

1978

1982

1986

1990

1994

1998

2002

2006

Two months earlier the classy Neil Franklin had gone to look for El Dorado, or at least a living wage, in Colombia, leaving a gap in defence that wasn't fully filled for four years. Without him, England still beat Portugal 5-3 and Belgium 4-1, but the opposition centre-forwards scored three goals between them and Bill Jones was discarded. Like Robledo, the tall Laurie Hughes would be making his debut.

He did well enough, but the defence were regularly surprised by the trickery of the Chileans, Robledo hitting the post with a free kick, Carvallo hitting the bar. The England forwards were praised for their precision but had trouble with 'the vigorous methods of the Chilean defenders' and the whole team found the humid conditions difficult, taking oxygen at half-time (Billy Wright 'gave it a test but found it of little use').

Mortensen headed in Mullen's cross and Mannion steered a cross neatly inside the post – but no-one was unduly impressed. Wright's ghostwriter again: 'I personally did not feel elated.'

Some sources refer to Robledo as Jorge, but although he was born in Chile he was christened George by his English mother.

25 June 1950 – Durival de Brito, Curitiba – 9,511 – Mário Vianna (BRZ)

SPAIN　　　(0) 3
Igoa 80, Basora 82, Zarra 85

USA　　　(1) 1
Pariani 17

SPAIN Ignacio Eizaguirre (c), Gabriel Alonso, Francisco Antúnez, Mariano Gonzalvo, José Gonzálvo, Antonio Puchades, Estanislao Basora, Rosendo Hernández, 'Zarra' (Telmo Zarraonandía), Silvestre Igoa, Agustin 'Piru' Gainza. *Guillermo Eizaguirre, with Benito Díaz.*
USA Frank Borghi, Harry Keough (c), Joe Maca, Ed McIlvenny, Charlie Colombo, Walter Bahr, Adam Wolanin, Virginio (Gino) Pariani, Joe Gaetjens, John 'Clarkie' Souza, Frank Valicenti ('Wallace'). *Walter Giesler (coach Bill Jeffrey (SCO)).*

The Americans had qualified despite losing 6-0 and 6-2 to Mexico – but showed unsuspected stamina and ball skills here, reinforced by Maca from Belgium, Gaetjens from Haiti, and the Scotsman McIlvenny, who later signed for Man United. Colombo invited comment by playing in gloves. Zarra had a goal disallowed then at last the famous Spanish '*furia*' struck, Igoa with a spectacular header, Basora an 'indefensible' shot, Zarra from close range. For one of the goals, the Americans apparently stopped playing because the ball had gone out of play.

Some English sources still credit John Souza with the goal, but the St Louis Post-Despatch said Pariani 'tallied against Spain with a shot that handcuffed one of the world's greatest goaltenders Eizaguirre' – and the American players agreed. Official sources wrongly list Bob Craddock in place of Wolanin. The Gonzalvos were brothers. Bahr's sons Chris and Matt kicked goals in various Superbowls.

LEADING GOALSCORERS 1950

8	Ademir	BRZ
5	Omar Míguez	URU
4	Estanislao Basora	SPA
4	Chico	BRZ
4	Zarra	SPA
4	Alcide Ghiggia	URU

29 June 1950 – Maracanã, Rio de Janeiro – 19,790 –
Alberto da Gama Malcher (BRZ)

SPAIN   (2) 2
Basora 17, Zarra 30

CHILE   (0) 0

SPAIN Antonio Ramallets, Alonso, José Parra,
M Gonzalvo, J Gonzalvo, Puchades, Basora, Igoa,
Zarra, José Luis Panizo, Gainza (c).
CHILE Livingstone (c), Farías, Roldán, Álvarez,
Busquets, Carvallo, Andrés Prieto, Cremaschi,
Robledo, Múñoz, Díaz.

Spain gave a first cap to Ramallets, who would
remain their No. 1 for ten years and started
with a *'meravigliosa'* save from Cremaschi.
Livingstone saved from Zarra, but then Roldán
gave the ball straight to Basora, who scored
easily, and Zarra blasted the second from
twelve yards. In the second half, he had a goal
disallowed. Easy for the Spanish, who were
suddenly being talked up as genuine threats.
Prieto's brother Ignacio played in the 1966
finals.

29 June 1950 – Independencia, Belo Horizonte –
10,151 – Generoso Dattilo (ITA)

USA   (1) 1
Gaetjens 38

ENGLAND   (0) 0

USA Borghi, Keough, Maca, McIlvenny (c),
Colombo, Bahr, Wallace, Pariani, Gaetjens, J Souza,
Ed Souza.
ENGLAND Williams, Ramsey, Aston, Wright (c),
Hughes, Dickinson, Finney, Mannion, Bentley,
Mortensen, Mullen.

Were the USA really taken so lightly? They did
remarkably well against Spain and lost only
1-0 to a strong English FA XI just before the
tournament. Perhaps people took more notice
of the defeats by Mexico, the 5-0 loss to

Turkish club Bešiktas, and the Americans' own
dismissal of their chances, which now sounds
like a smokescreen.

Recent English reports of the match tend
to be little more than a catalogue of missed
chances, Borghi acrobatics, and eccentric refereeing – almost as if the writers think this
was what *must* have happened. In fact there
was much more cut and thrust than that and
the US goal was much better than we've been
led to believe. The story goes that a mishit
clearance from Bahr went in off Gaetjens ear
(Alf Ramsey said he 'ducked to avoid the
ball') – but Bahr himself was scathing: 'What
would I be doing, clearing the ball near the
England goal?' He admitted his cross may
have started life as a shot, but was adamant
that Gaetjens' contribution was a deliberate,
and brilliant, diving header. 'Joe regularly
scored goals like that in the league.' A photo
shows the ball beating Williams down to
his right.

After half-time England moved Mortensen
to centre-forward and Bentley out to the wing,
but made little headway. Match reports recount
chances missed, but usually the same three:
Mortensen's shot possibly crossing the line,
Mullen's header from Ramsey's free-kick doing
the same, Mortensen breaking through to be
rugby-tackled by the Italian Colombo (puns on
the Italian referee's first name). On the other
side of the ledger, Pariani missed a chance and
forced a good save from Williams, and Ramsey
had to kick the ball off the line near the end.
Wallace: 'If I'd hit the ball harder, he'd never
have touched it.' The balding Clarkie Souza was
man of the match.

The only American reporter at the game
was the immortal Dent McSkimming of the
St Louis Post-Despatch, in Brazil on holiday –
and an editor in London thought the scoreline
was a misprint for 10-1. A remarkable match.
Not quite the great shock it appears, but an

1950

1930
1934
1938
1950
1954
1958
1962
1966
1970
1974
1978
1982
1986
1990
1994
1998
2002
2006

upset all the same – and England were relieved to host Italy v North Korea in 1966.

These colonials were becoming real pests. On the same day, England's cricketers lost at home to the West Indies for the first time. One or two sources claim Borghi saved a penalty from Mortensen (or Mannion), but this comes from an American report which refers to free kicks as penalties. Photographs confirm that the crowd swelled to c.40,000 by the end. Gaetjens, who went back to playing for Haiti in the qualifying stages of the next World Cup, is believed to have been murdered by the Tontons Macoute, Duvalier's vicious secret police, in 1964.

A FIFA letter confirms Maca, McIlvenny and Gaetjens were ineligible to play for the States: 'some alteration of the Regulations of the World Cup will be necessary in order to avoid similar mistakes in the future.' Maca: 'We should never have played.' But it would have been churlish for England to say that.

---

2 July 1950 – Maracanã, Rio de Janeiro – 74,462 – Giovanni Galeati (ITA)

SPAIN (0) 1
Zarra 48

ENGLAND (0) 0

SPAIN Ramallets, Parra, Alonso, M Gonzalvo, J Gonzalvo, Puchades, Basora, Igoa, Zarra, Panizo, Gainza (c).
ENGLAND Williams, Ramsey, Bill Eckersley, Wright (c), Hughes, Dickinson, Stanley Matthews, Mortensen, Jackie Milburn, Eddie Baily, Finney.

Winterbottom – or rather the sole selector Arthur Drewry – at last made changes, bringing in the speedy Milburn, new caps Eckersley and Baily, and Matthews at last. There was some definite improvement – but the England players later complained of continual body-checking and handball, Spain persistently booted the ball into the crowd, and Milburn had a headed goal contentiously disallowed after fourteen minutes. Matthews, who provided the cross, claimed that subsequent photographs 'clearly showed a Spanish defender playing Jackie onside'.

But there were too many excuses on this trip. Spain, who needed only a draw and deserved at least that, had some quality players: Ramallets, Panizo, the two wingers – and Zarra, 'apart from Churchill, the best head in Europe', who scored 20 goals in 20 internationals, including this one which appeared on a Spanish postage stamp in 1997. Gainza beat Ramsey in the air and headed Alonso's long right-wing cross back across goal, and Zarra drove it low past the exposed Williams after escaping from Hughes, who wasn't capped again. Once again the England forwards were criticised as too slow.

The bottom line? A teamsheet that reads like a who's who of the best in the Football League just wasn't good enough away from home. Someone really should have buried the hatchet with FIFA twenty years earlier. Matthews was the oldest player in this tournament (35) and the next.

---

2 July 1950 – Ilha do Retiro, Recife – 8,501 – Mário Gardelli (BRZ)

CHILE (2) 5
Robledo 16, Cremaschi 32, 61, 82, Prieto 54

USA (0) 2
Wallace 47, Maca pen 48

CHILE Livingstone (c), Manuel Machuca, Álvarez, Busquets, Farías, Carlos Rojas, Fernando Riera, Cremaschi, Robledo, Prieto, Carlos Ibáñez.
USA Borghi, Keough, Maca, McIlvenny, Colombo, Bahr (c), Wallace, Pariani, Gaetjens, J Souza, E Souza.

Again Robledo was the best Chilean forward, leading the line and scoring the first goal after Cremaschi had beaten a man. Riera crossed for Cremaschi to sprint in and smash home the second. Immediately after half-time, Wallace scored with a header and Farías conceded a penalty by fouling Gaetjens – but Cremaschi drove in Robledo's pass, Prieto beat Maca and put in a shot Borghi might have saved, and Riera got away again to find Cremaschi, short and moustachioed, right in front of goal.

There's genuine confusion over Cremaschi's hat-trick. Old sources credit him with all three, but various publications say only two, with Riera scoring the other. However, the match report in Santiago's *El Mercurio* says three, and we'll go along with that. Early sources list Múñoz in place of Rojas, an error.

Some publications say John Souza scored the USA's first goal and Pariani took the penalty – but *Soccer News* lists Wallace and Maca (pen) as the scorers, while another American publication refers to Wallace scoring 'a beautiful headed goal.' The USA appointed a different captain for each match: Keough v Spain because he spoke Spanish, McIlvenny v England because he was British, Bahr v Chile 'because he was the real captain'!

GROUP 2

	P	W	D	L	F	A	Pts
Spain	3	3	0	0	6	1	6
England	3	1	0	2	2	2	2
Chile	3	1	0	2	5	6	2
USA	3	1	0	2	4	8	2

Spain qualified for the final pool.

GROUP 3

Italy (seeded), Paraguay, Sweden.

25 June 1950 – Pacaembu, São Paulo – 56,502 – Jean Lutz (SWI)

SWEDEN   **(2) 3**
Jeppson 25, 68, S Andersson 33

ITALY   **(1) 2**
Carapellese 7, Muccinelli 75

SWEDEN Karl Svensson, Lennart Samuelsson, Erik Nilsson (c), Sune Andersson, Knut Nordahl, Ingvar Gärd, Stig Sundkvist, Karl-Erik Palmér, Hans Jeppson, Lennart 'Nacka' Skoglund, Stellan Nilsson. *George Raynor (ENG).*
ITALY Lucidio Sentimenti, Attilio Giovannini, Zeffiro Furiassi, Carlo Annovazzi, Carlo Parola, Augusto Magli, Ermes Muccinelli, Giampiero Boniperti, Gino Cappello, Aldo Campatelli, Riccardo Carapellese (c). *Ferruccio Novo et al.*

Both sides had rebuilt, but Sweden shouldn't have had to. It's true that Milan had signed their great 'Grenoli' inside-forward trio (Gren-Nordahl-Liedholm), but they were kept out of the finals by the Swedish FA's refusal to pick players with foreign clubs. If they'd played, Sweden would have been the Europeans most likely to mount a challenge. As it was, Raynor had another chance to prove his ability to identify new talent – but it remains a case of what might have been.

After the Turin air disaster, Italy travelled by ship, to be met by thousands of Italian expatriates, who made up the bulk of the crowd in a stadium that sported a copy of Michelangelo's statue of David. Home from home – but injury sidelined their main striker Benito Lorenzi

1930
1934
1938

1950

1954

1958

1962

1966

1970

1974

1978

1982

1986

1990

1994

1998

2002

2006

(christened in different times) and there was no love lost among their selectors, who brought in two new caps, including Magli, who wasn't picked again.

The long-nosed Cappello raced past a flying tackle on his way to the right-hand goal line, Carapellese volleying in the square pass – but the warning signs were already there: soon after the start, Palmér had slipped his man to hook a diagonal lob against Sentimenti's right-hand post.

Parola was a genuinely world-class stopper, a master of the overhead clearance kick, but he didn't play for Italy again after Jeppson emerged as 'un angelo sterminatore,' or at least a bony nuisance. And the new midgets at inside-forward (Palmér weighed less than nine stone) were full of feints and dribbles, Raynor having stressed that 'We had to be light-footed.'

After Cappello had missed a clear chance to put Italy 2-0 up, Jeppson pushed a low shot wide of Sentimenti's left hand and Andersson's cross-shot from twenty yards sent a loose ball through a busy penalty area into the bottom left-hand corner. Then Sentimenti couldn't hold Palmér's low shot and Jeppson ran round to lash it in from a yard past goalkeeper and defender.

Muccinelli scored with a cool low shot from a short through-pass inside the area. Very near the end Carapellese drove a left-foot shot against either the bar or the left-hand post (it's not clear on the film), and Muccinelli put the rebound wide of an open goal. But the right team won. Thanks to Raynor, at least it was one.

The first defeat for any World Cup holders put an end to Italy's sequence of seven consecutive wins, still the finals record. Jeppson is the correct spelling, (not, say, Jepsson). Italian clubs promptly signed up virtually the whole Sweden team.

29 June 1950 – Durival de Brito, Curitiba – 7,903 – George Mitchell (SCO)

SWEDEN   (2) 2
Sundkvist 17, Palmér 25

PARAGUAY (1) 2
López 34, López Fretes 74

SWEDEN Svensson, Samuelsson, E Nilsson (c), Andersson, Nordahl, Gärd, Egon Jönsson, Palmér, Jeppson, Skoglund, Sundkvist.
PARAGUAY Marcelino Vargas, 'Gonzalito' (Alberto González), Casiano Céspedes, Manuel Gavilán, Victoriano Leguizámon, Castor Sixto Cantero, Rafael Avalos, Atilio López, Darío Jara Saguier, César López Fretes (c), Leongino Unzain. *Manuel Fleitas Solich.*

Paraguay were the Copa América runners-up, '*rapides et dynamiques*', but the Swedes were better on the ball. They were also lucky that López Fretes missed an 'excellent probability' in the first ten minutes.

After that, Sundkvist scored from Jeppson's pass and Skoglund's long ball was knocked in by Palmér. Atilio López equalised after elegantly beating two men then had a goal disallowed for handball, and López Fretes scored from Jara's centre, the ball going in just under the bar.

Jönsson was a different player from Egon Johnsson (they'd played in different qualifying matches against the Republic of Ireland). Another Rafael Avalos played for Mexico in the 1954 finals.

HOLDERS ELIMINATED AT GROUP STAGE

1950	Italy
1966	Brazil
2002	France

Uruguay didn't defend the title in 1934.

2 July 1950 – Pacaembu, São Paulo – 25,811 – Arthur Ellis (ENG)

ITALY   (1) 2
Carapellese 12, Pandolfini 62

PARAGUAY (0) 0

ITALY Bepi Moro, Ivano Blason, Furiassi, Osvaldo Fattori, Leandro Remondini, Giacomo Mari, Muccinelli, Egisto Pandolfini, Amedeo Amadei, Cappello, Carapellese (c).
PARAGUAY Vargas, Gonzalito, Céspedes, Gavilán, Leguizámon, Cantero, Avalos, López, Jara Saguier, López Fretes (c), Unzain.

Italy, who were in a decline that would last the decade, included another three new caps, including Remondini (who was also winning his last) and Pandolfini, who volleyed in Carapellese's left-wing cross.

An Italian TV commentator called this a demonstration of 'the authentic Italian game . . . impetuous but controlled, gladiatorial as well as exquisitely technical' – just when it didn't matter. Amadei's run up the right ended with a cross which Carapellese forced in at the right-hand post, a defender kicking the ball into the roof of the net as he tried to clear. At the other end, Moro was able to 'work without orgasm.' As you do.

GROUP 3

	P	W	D	L	F	A	Pts
Sweden	2	1	1	0	5	4	3
Italy	2	1	0	1	4	3	2
Paraguay	2	0	1	1	1	4	1

Sweden qualified for the final pool.

The group was reduced to three teams by the withdrawal of India. Legend has it that they pulled out because FIFA insisted they had to wear boots!

Seven Paraguayans were winning their last caps. As with Biavati in 1938 (but not Carrizo in 1958), Amedeo is the correct spelling (not Amadeo).

GROUP 4

1950

Bolivia, Uruguay (seeded).

2 July 1950 – Independencia, Belo Horizonte – 5,284 – George Reader (ENG)

URUGUAY   (4) 8
Míguez 14, 40, 51, Vidal 18, Schiaffino 17, 53, Pérez 83, Ghiggia 87

BOLIVIA   (0) 0

URUGUAY Roque Máspoli, Matías González, Eusebio Tejera, Juan Carlos González, Obdulio Varela (c), Víctor Rodríguez Andrade, Alcide Ghiggia, Julio Pérez, Omar Míguez, Juan Schiaffino, Ernesto Vidal.
Juan López.
BOLIVIA Eduardo Gutiérrez, Alberto de Achá, José Bustamante II (c), Antonio Grecco, Antonio Valencia, Leonardo Ferrel, Celestino Algarañáz, Víctor Ugarte, Roberto Caparelli, Benigno Gutiérrez, Benjamin Maldonado. *Mario Pretto (ITA).*

Bolivia made some confident noises beforehand, but once Uruguay had scored their first goal, it turned into an embarrassment on a dustbowl. Bolivia, as bad as in 1930, had just lost 5-0 to Chile, and Uruguay unveiled some tremendous players: Máspoli in goal, Varela the veteran attacking centre-half; Andrade, nephew of the great 1930 player; Schiaffino and Ghiggia both skinny and brilliant.

Míguez met Varela's cross with a '*potente impacto,*' Vidal finished off a three-man move, Schiaffino scored the third and sent Míguez dashing in for the fourth, and Bolivia were handicapped by an injury to Caparelli, a naturalised Argentinian. In the second half Míguez

1930
1934
1938
1950
1954
1958
1962
1966
1970
1974
1978
1982
1986
1990
1994
1998
2002
2006

put in Ghiggia's pass, Schiaffino shot just inside a post, Pérez dribbled the keeper, and Ghiggia surprised Gutiérrez from long range. By staying at home, Scotland missed out on a victory over one of these teams and a lesson from the other.

Some old publications list the scorers as Schiaffino 4, Míguez 2, Vidal, Ghiggia, one even crediting Schiaffino with five – but all reliable sources, including the leading Uruguayan historian, say he scored only two.

GROUP 4

	P	W	D	L	F	A	Pts
Uruguay	1	1	0	0	8	0	2
Bolivia	1	0	0	1	0	8	0

Uruguay qualified for the final pool.

The number of teams in the group was halved by the withdrawal of Scotland, Turkey, and various countries invited to replace them.

FINAL POOL

Brazil, Spain, Sweden, Uruguay.

9 July 1950 – Pacaembu, São Paulo – 44,802 – Mervyn Griffiths (WAL)

URUGUAY   (1) 2
Ghiggia 27, Varela 72

SPAIN   (2) 2
Basora 39, 41

URUGUAY Máspoli, M González, Tejera, JC González, Varela (c), Rodríguez Andrade, Ghiggia, Pérez, Míguez, Schiaffino, Vidal.

SPAIN Ramallets, Alonso, Parra, M Gonzalvo, J Gonzalvo, Puchades, Basora, Igoa, Zarra, Luis Molowny, Gainza (c).

Spain's rough-house tactics suddenly met their match. Andrade was compact and aggressive, Matías González dominated the rugged Zarra, Varela had the physique as well as the face of a bouncer. Ghiggia, coming into tremendous form, sprinted in for the first goal, but Basora headed in Igoa's chip then converted a good pass from Molowny, and Uruguay were only saved when Varela came upfield and beat 'various adversaries' before scoring. A tough game, and two Uruguayans had to miss the next one.

9 July 1950 – Maracanã, Rio de Janeiro – 138,886 – Arthur Ellis (ENG)

BRAZIL   (3) 7
Ademir 17, 37, 51, 59, Chico 39, 87, Maneca 85

SWEDEN   (0) 1
Andersson pen 67

BRAZIL Barbosa, Augusto (c), Juvenal, Bauer, Danilo, Bigode, Maneca, Zizinho, Ademir, Jair, Chico.
SWEDEN Svensson, Samuelsson, E Nilsson (c), Andersson, Nordahl, Gärd, Sundkvist, Palmér, Jeppson, Skoglund, S Nilsson.

After the uncertainties of the group matches, Brazil cut loose. It's tempting to wonder about the Swedish defence, but no-one else did this to them. Nilsson, Nordahl and the goalkeeper were international class, Gärd 'a great getter and tremendous fighter.' They'd simply never met inside-forwards of this standard before, and nor had anyone else.

All three had slim physiques and pencil moustaches, Jair a centre parting, Ademir blue eyes and a Jimmy Hill chin, Zizinho a strong resemblance to Little Richard. Their ball control and inter-passing were beyond anything seen in Europe at the time, and nobody was scoring goals like Ademir.

Tall and elegant, if slightly stiff-legged, he scored the best that referee Ellis had ever seen, a bicycle kick after flipping the ball up with his other foot. One source says he trapped the ball between his ankles and jumped over the keeper! If TV had been there (and if it's true), we wouldn't be talking about Pelé. Sweden's reply, a penalty awarded for handball by Juvenal, looks like a prize for turning up.

Ademir scored one of his goals by running onto a first-time through-ball and flicking a half-volley wide of the advancing keeper, another by dummying to play a one-two before turning at speed and spearing a left-footer just inside the near post. He was good in the air too, happy to mix it with the beleaguered Svensson. Maneca converted Jair's pass from three yards out and a fierce high shot made it Chico time near the end. There might have been more if Brazil hadn't played exhibition football in the last half-hour.

---

13 July 1950 – Pacaembu, São Paulo – 7,987 – Giovanni Galeati (ITA)

URUGUAY   (1) 3
Ghiggia 39, Míguez 77, 84

SWEDEN   (2) 2
Palmér 4, Sundkvist 41

URUGUAY Aníbal Paz, M González, Tejera, Schubert Gambetta, Varela (c), Rodríguez Andrade, Ghiggia, Pérez, Míguez, Schiaffino, Vidal.
SWEDEN Svensson, Samuelsson, E Nilsson (c), Andersson, Gunnar Johansson, Gärd, Jönsson, Bror Mellberg, Jeppson, Palmér, Sundkvist.

Máspoli and Juan Carlos González, injured against Spain, had to be replaced by Paz and the portly Gambetta, and Pérez had barely recovered. But Sweden's harder schedule caught up with them, some of the Uruguayan tackling was barely legal (Jönsson had to go off for treatment), and although Palmér and the blond Skoglund were lionised by the South American press (the former described as a '*gran figura*' for such a tiny man), Raynor later claimed they were 'good in ordinary internationals but not so good in World Cup matches.'

Nevertheless one of them gave Sweden an early lead. After four minutes of the game against Italy, Palmér had had a goal disallowed. After the same time here, he controlled a long free kick from the right that sailed over Jeppson, and stretched to shoot high across the keeper (who should perhaps have come off his line) into the top right-hand corner.

Ghiggia had a goal disallowed for Andrade's foul on Palmér, then ran through a vacant midfield to volley a long cross-shot just under the bar to Svensson's right. One report says it took a deflection off Johansson, but the film's inconclusive.

Sweden immediately regained the lead when Paz this time did come out, only to drop a very high cross under pressure from Jeppson, leaving Sundkvist to lift a left-footed volley past the last two defenders. Like Varela, Paz made his international debut in 1939; after this display, he wasn't capped again. Luckily for Uruguay, the sturdy Míguez twice thumped in a loose ball, the second after Svensson badly spilled a long cross from the right. Just enough to make Uruguay's last match a live one.

Gambetta wasn't the only Uruguayan with musical parents. Beethoven Javier played against England in 1977.

1950

1954

1958

1962

1966

1970

1974

1978

1982

1986

1990

1994

1998

2002

2006

13 July 1950 – Maracanã, Rio de Janeiro – 152,772 – Reg Leafe (ENG)

BRAZIL   (3) 6
Parra o.g. 15, Jair 21, Chico 29, 55, Ademir 57, Zizinho 74

SPAIN   (0) 1
Igoa 70

BRAZIL Barbosa, Augusto (c), Juvenal, Bauer, Danilo, Bigode, Friaça, Zizinho, Ademir, Jair, Chico.
SPAIN Ramallets, Alonso, Parra, M Gonzalvo, J Gonzalvo, Puchades, Basora, Igoa, Zarra, Panizo, Gainza (c).

One newspaper described Panizo as 'a remarkable strategist capable of highlighting the bad marking of the Brazilian defenders.' There were germs of truth in that, but any vulnerability in the Brazilian defence was camouflaged by their attack, which was unstoppable by now, inflicting a scoreline like this on a team which had beaten England. Zizinho thought Spain were a good side, 'but when you looked at them out on the pitch they were white with fear.'

With good reason. In the space of three minutes Ramallets saved from Chico and Zizinho but could only get a hand to a screaming low twenty-yarder from Jair, who'd been allowed a clear run from halfway, the ball going in off the bar. By then Spain were already a goal down.

There used to be genuine confusion as to how many Ademir scored in this match, affecting his total as tournament top scorer. Old English publications said none at all, more recent publications plump for two, especially as the referee credited him with the first – but this was clearly an own goal. Ademir's shot was on target, but he didn't catch it cleanly, falling back in his follow-through. If it had simply hit the defender on its way in, there would have been a case for crediting it to Ademir – but Parra lifted his leg and caught the ball with his thigh, sending Ramallets the wrong way. All informed sources (including three from Brazil) rightly credit Ademir with one goal in this match and eight in total.

After Chico had smashed in a loose ball for the third (and then been hit by an object from the celebrating crowd!), Brazil protected their lead with a mixture of keep-ball and harsh tackling, the stocky little Bigode fouling Basora, Bauer clattering Panizo, Danilo leaving Zarra in need of attention. After half-time Chico was presented with an open goal after Ademir had beaten a man on the right-hand goal line, and Zizinho's short pass made the fifth for Ademir, whose name litters match reports. Finally, Zizinho survived a tackle and smashed a volley low past Ramallets, who was left on his knees.

Meanwhile Zarra hit the bar and Igoa scored the best goal of the game, left unmarked to meet a cross from the right with a gymnastic volley. Small consolation, as was the fact that it could have been worse: the acrobatics of Ramallets had kept the score down to the merely humbling.

---

16 July 1950 – Pacaembu, São Paulo – 11,227 – Karel van der Meer (HOL)

SWEDEN   (2) 3
Sundkvist 15, Mellberg 34, Palmér 79

SPAIN   (0) 1
Zarra 82

SWEDEN Svensson, Samuelsson, E Nilsson (c), Andersson, Johansson, Gärd, Jönsson, Mellberg, Ingvar Rydell, Palmér, Sundkvist.
SPAIN Eizaguirre, Vicente Asensi, Parra, Alonso, Alfonso Silva, Puchades, Basora, Hernández, Zarra (c), Panizo, José Juncosa.

Spain couldn't get up for it, Sweden were already there. Sundkvist darted onto a marvellous pass from Palmér, Mellberg got the second when

Eizaguirre was stranded outside his area, and Palmér shot the third. Basora and Zarra inter-passed through a packed defence to score. Raynor, who'd again worked minor miracles, even beat the Spanish officials at billiards!

---

16 July 1950 – Maracanã, Rio de Janeiro – 205,000 – George Reader (ENG)

URUGUAY   (0) 2
Schiaffino 66, Ghiggia 79

BRAZIL   (0) 1
Friaça 47

URUGUAY Máspoli, M González, Tejera, Gambetta, Varela (c), Rodríguez Andrade, Ghiggia, Pérez, Míguez, Schiaffino, Rubén Morán.
BRAZIL Barbosa, Augusto (c), Juvenal, Bauer, Danilo, Bigode, Friaça, Zizinho, Ademir, Jair, Chico.

Brazil, in front of the biggest crowd ever to watch a football match, needing only a draw, were overwhelming favourites – but there were signs and omens.

Uruguay, in an up-and-down season, had played Brazil three times, all in São Paulo or Rio, winning the first 4-3 before losing only 3-2 and 1-0. A year earlier, Brazil had gone into their last match needing just a draw to win the Copa América – and lost 2-1 to Paraguay before wreaking revenge in the play-off. This time there would be no second chances.

Thoroughly overshadowed by the great trio up front, the Brazilian defenders were adequate enough, especially the athletic Juvenal – but their 'diagonal' formation left their wing-halves with no cover if the opposition wingers broke through. It simply hadn't mattered till now: you could afford to concede a goal through a weakness in your system if its strengths were scoring six and seven at the other end.

Against Uruguay, Brazil threatened to match those earlier scores (they had thirty shots at goal) but were frustrated by a wall of defenders.

Every one of the Brazilian forwards was shadowed, the mighty Varela staying back to help Tejera mark Ademir – and Máspoli played the game of his life.

After some typical interplay with Zizinho, Ademir's shot thumped into Máspoli, who then saved Ademir's 'impeccable' header and Chico's shot from Ademir's pass. The first goal didn't arrive till after half-time. With the Uruguayan defence drawn to the left, Ademir's reverse pass sent Friaça clear on the right. He held off Andrade and scored with a bobbling cross-shot that Máspoli might have stopped. Pandemonium. Friaça had picked an interesting time to score his only goal for Brazil.

Jair later said that there was 'a collective drop in pressure once we had taken the lead' – but it's also true that the goal came too late to persuade Uruguay they were sacrificial lambs, rather than the men who'd played Brazil to a standstill three times in May. They'd recovered from a goal down against Spain and Sweden – and had been unlucky not to open the score here, a low shot from Míguez hitting Barbosa's left-hand post. Now Varela began to emerge from defence, and above all their outside-right had the Indian sign over Bigode.

Moustachioed and beaky, so thin he made footballs look like medicine balls, Ghiggia nevertheless had the classic tools of speed and elusiveness – and only one man to beat. Taking a pass from Varela, he dragged Bigode tight to

FINAL POOL

	P	W	D	L	F	A	Pts
Uruguay	3	2	1	0	7	5	5
Brazil	3	2	0	1	14	4	4
Sweden	3	1	0	2	6	11	2
Spain	3	0	1	2	4	11	1

1930
1934
1938
1950
1954
1958
1962
1966
1970
1974
1978
1982
1986
1990
1994
1998
2002
2006

1930

1934

1938

1950

1954

1958

1962

1966

1970

1974

1978

1982

1986

1990

1994

1998

2002

2006

the touchline, swayed over the ball, then scooted past on the outside before crossing low to the near post. As Juvenal's tackle came in, Schiaffino said he aimed at the far post but swept the ball high past Barbosa's left hand instead. 'Silence in the Maracanã,' said Brazil's coach Flávio Costa, 'which terrorised our players.' Soon afterwards, Ghiggia repeated the move, but this time Schiaffino shot wide.

It's obvious with hindsight that someone should have done something to protect the hapless Bigode, especially once Brazil were in the lead. According to their coach, Juvenal 'just wasn't giving cover on the marking of Ghiggia . . . he hid from the game.' But blaming individual players is the last resort of a coach who hasn't got his preparation right – and anyway defence wasn't Brazil's strength. They went on going forward, Jair forcing yet another save from Máspoli, Andrade tackling Friaça close in – but the unsung Pérez played a one-two with Ghiggia that cut out Bigode, and the winger was away to angle his run towards the near post. With the defence struggling to get across and Barbosa staying on his line, presumably expecting another centre, Ghiggia sent a bouncing bomb under the keeper's hands, which got a faint touch.

Máspoli went on making saves, one at the near post from Jair, another from Chico's toe-poke – and Ademir put a volley high over the bar. When Máspoli was challenged under a high cross, he turned away in triumph after dropping it. One of his team mates was first to the loose ball again – and the final whistle had gone.

Bigode didn't play for Brazil again, Danilo was reported to have attempted suicide, one or two spectators were apparently more successful. A great *pesadumbre* fell over Rio, a despondency, a weight of shadows ('a tragedy, a funeral,' said Schiaffino, 'a horrible sight to witness'). 'I can never forget that match,' said Flávio Costa. 'The people will never let me.' Ademir would be remembered far longer than Gambetta or Tejera – but Uruguay still hadn't lost a World Cup match, and the trophy still hadn't been won by the more skilful side. And we think we invented defensive football.

For years, many Brazilians blamed the black members of the team (they might as well have blamed them for being the three whose names began with a B) while conveniently ignoring the impact of Uruguay's Andrade, who was also black. Thirteen years later, Barbosa was offered the goalposts as a souvenir. He took them home, invited his neighbours to a barbecue, and ceremonially torched them.

Morán was the only player to win his first cap in a World Cup decider. The official crowd figure was 173,850. For once there's little doubt it was on the low side.

The limping major

Switzerland 1954

1930

1934

1938

1950

1954

1958

1962

1966

1970

1974

1978

1982

1986

1990

1994

1998

2002

2006

FIFA retained the mini-league system but couldn't resist a little tinkering. Instead of each team playing all the others in the group, two were seeded and would play only the two non-seeds – and any matches drawn after ninety minutes would go to extra-time. Arbitrary and confusing.

Still, at least it was the first really representative World Cup – just at a time when it didn't seem necessary. No tournament has had a stronger favourite. The Hungarians were coming.

The statistics were impressive in themselves. Beaten only by a Moscow XI in their last 30 matches, they were the reigning Olympic and Dr Gerő Cup champions. But it was the sheer number of goals they scored (121 in those 30 games), and the way they scored them, that delighted and terrified the football world. They crushed even the good teams – Czechoslovakia 5-0 and 5-1, Italy 3-0, Sweden 6-0 – and their Wembley masterclass made them the first foreign country to win in England. Even that famous 6-3 scoreline doesn't tell the whole story: they led 6-2 before coasting the last half-hour. Later that season, in their last match before the World Cup, they inflicted England's record defeat, by the inhuman score of 7-1.

They brought with them genuine tactical innovations – the deep-lying centre-forward, so hard to mark; the near-post crosses later copied by Ron Greenwood; a system based on moving triangles – and some of the best players in the world: Grosics in goal, the smooth Bozsik in midfield, Hidegkuti the centre-forward, Czibor on the wing, and the great front men – Kocsis so marvellous in the air, the incomparable Puskás – who scored 159 international goals between them. Switzerland wasn't a big enough stage.

No-one else seemed to come close, though Uruguay and Yugoslavia had several of their 1950 players and some skilful reinforcements. Brazil, their great forward trio gone, were over-compensating for their defensive frailties last time. Austria, supplanted as the best team in Europe, were in decline. West Germany had only just been allowed back into FIFA.

Meanwhile Scotland deigned to take part this time but had just been well beaten at home by a shell-shocked England. Nothing had prepared them for what was coming.

The expressions say it all as Puskás congratulates Fritz Walter after the Final.

GROUP 1

Brazil (seeded), France (seeded), Mexico, Yugoslavia.

16 June 1954 – Olympique de la Pontaise, Lausanne – 16,000 – Mervyn Griffiths (WAL)

YUGOSLAVIA   (1) 1
Milutinović 14

FRANCE   (0) 0

YUGOSLAVIA Vladimir Beara, Branko Stanković, Tomislav Crnković, Zlatko Čajkovski, Ivan Horvat, Vujadin Boškov, Milos Milutinović, Rajko Mitić, Bernard Vukas, Stjepan Bobek (c), Branko Zebec. *Aleksandar Tirnanić et al.*
FRANCE François Remetter, Lazare Gianessi, Raymond Kaelbel, Bob Jonquet (c), Jean-Jacques Marcel, Armand Penverne, René Dereuddre, Léon Glovacki, Raymond Kopaszewski (Kopa), André Strappe, Jean Vincent. *Gaston Barreau et al (coach Pierre Pibarot).*

Hard to understand why France were seeded. They'd lost 3-1 to Yugoslavia earlier in the season and their opponents had some world-class new boys: Boškov, the balletic Beara, the versatile Zebec. The 21-year-old Milutinović scored from close range after a short pass left him unmarked, then hit an overhead kick which Remetter tipped over the bar. Zebec wasted an '*oportunidad magnífica*' after going round the keeper. Meanwhile Glovacki missed chances in '*le match le plus désastreux de sa carrière*'.

Jonquet broke his nose six minutes from the end and Beara injured a hand. Yugoslavia had won each of their four qualifying matches 1-0 and beaten England by the same score just before the tournament. Here their defence coped easily with France's short-passing game. Milutinović's brother Bora later coached five different countries in the finals.

16 June 1954 – Parc des Sports des Charmilles, Geneva – 13,000 – Paul Wyssling (SWI)

BRAZIL   (4) 5
Baltazar 24, Didi 29, Pinga 34, 43, Julinho 69

MEXICO   (0) 0

BRAZIL Carlos Castilho, Djalma Santos, Nílton Santos, José Carlos Bauer (c), João Carlos Pinheiro, 'Brandãozinho' (Antenor Lucas), 'Julinho' (Júlio Botelho), 'Didi' (Waldir Pereira), 'Baltazar' (Oswaldo da Silva), 'Pinga' (José Lázaro Robles), Francisco Rodrigues. *Alfredo 'Zezé' Moreira.*
MEXICO Salvador Mota, Narciso López, Juan Gómez González, Raúl Cárdenas, Jorge Romo, Rafael Avalos, Alfredo Torres, José Naranjo (c), José Luis Lamadrid, Tomás Balcázar, Raúl 'Pina' Arellano. *Antonio López Herranz (SPA).*

After the dismay of Rio, Brazil had tilted the weight of their team towards the back, keeping the mighty Bauer and introducing a stern stopper (Pinheiro) and two great fullbacks. There was still class up front – the playmaker Didi, Julinho on the right wing – and some more pencil moustaches.

Again the Mexicans were purely sacrificial. Baltazar, who'd scored against them in 1950, did it with his right foot this time, Didi curled one of his speciality free kicks just inside the foot of a post, Pinga scored with a header and drove in a rebound. Mota, winning his only cap, made a marvellous save from Julinho, who later beat two men (one with a drag-back) before scoring with a low cross-shot that went in off a post. Not that Zezé Moreira was unduly impressed. The match, he said, 'showed our weak points'!

One source says Avalos' first name was Narciso, but there seems to be confusion with López. The official programme, the main Mexican football magazine, a history of the Mexican national team, and the leading French statisticians all confirm Rafael Avalos. Mota's brother Antonio, also a goalkeeper, was in the 1962 and 1970 squads but didn't play.

1930
1934
1938
1950
1958
1962
1966
1970
1974
1978
1982
1986
1990
1994
1998
2002
2006

1954

19 June 1954 – Parc des Sports des Charmilles, Geneva – 19,000 – Manuel Asensi (SPA)

FRANCE (1) 3
Vincent 19, Cárdenas o.g. 46, Kopa pen 88

MEXICO (0) 2
Lamadrid 54, Balcázar 85

FRANCE Remetter, Gianessi, Roger Marche (c), Kaelbel, Marcel, Abderrahman Mahjoub, Abdelaziz Ben Tifour, Dereuddre, Kopa, Strappe, Vincent.
MEXICO Antonio Carbajal, López, Romo, Saturnino Martínez, Cárdenas, Avalos, Torres, Naranjo (c), Lamadrid, Balcázar, Arellano.

Both teams had to win and hope Brazil and Yugoslavia didn't draw. Vincent ran in from the left before virtually toe-poking the ball across Carbajal, then Dereuddre's cross-cum-shot from the right was turned in by Cárdenas at the near post. Lamadrid ran through to push the ball past the keeper as he came out, and Balcázar scored a scrappy second with a low shot from near the edge of the area. Romo conceded a penalty by throwing himself in the path of a shot from Vincent: the ball hit his ribs then appeared to touch his arms as it settled under his body.

19 June 1954 – Olympique de la Pontaise, Lausanne – 25,000 – Charlie Faultless (SCO)

BRAZIL (0) (1) 1
Didi 69

YUGOSLAVIA (0) (1) 1
Zebec 48

BRAZIL Castilho, D Santos, N Santos, Bauer (c), Pinheiro, Brandãozinho, Julinho, Didi, Baltazar, Pinga, Rodrigues.
YUGOSLAVIA Beara, Stanković, Crnković, Čajkovski, Horvat, Boškov, Milutinović, Mitić (c), Zebec, Vukas, Dionizije Dvornić.

As in the 1950 match between the two, some high-class skills were on view. Both sides

OLDEST COACHES

yrs	days			
70	194	Gaston Barreau	FRA	1954
70	130	Cesare Maldini	ITA	2002
67	202	Guy Thys	BEL	1990
67	122	Tim	PER	1982
66	337	Mário Zagallo	BRZ	1998
65	74	Sepp Herberger	GER	1962

Barreau was one of the selectors, not a coach as such.

Maldini also coached at the 1998 finals (66 years 126 days).

Tim (Elba de Pádua Lima) played for Brazil in the 1938 finals.

missed chances before Zebec took a pass in yards of space and beat a man before scoring with a low cross-shot from outside the penalty area. Brazil deservedly equalised when Nílton Santos found Didi, who turned inside the defensive cover before shooting. Čajkovski went off injured in extra-time, in which Brazil dominated the first half, Yugoslavia the second, forcing Castilho to make three good saves. Wyssling apart (above), has there ever been a better name for a referee?

GROUP 1

	P	W	D	L	F	A	Pts
Brazil	2	1	1	0	6	1	3
Yugoslavia	2	1	1	0	2	1	3
France	2	1	0	1	3	3	2
Mexico	2	0	0	2	2	8	0

Brazil and Yugoslavia qualified for the quarter-finals.

GROUP 2

Hungary (seeded), Turkey (seeded), South Korea, West Germany.

17 June 1954 – Hardturm, Zürich – 13,000 – Raymond Vincenti (FRA)

HUNGARY   **(4) 9**
Puskás 11, 89, Lantos 17, Kocsis 24, 35, 49, Czibor 58, Palotás 77, 84

SOUTH KOREA   **(0) 0**

HUNGARY Gyula Grosics, Jenő Buzánszky, Mihály Lantos, József Bozsik, Gyula Lóránt, Ferenc Szojka, László Budai, Sándor Kocsis, Péter Palotás, Ferenc Puskás (c), Zoltán Czibor. *Gusztáv Sebes (coach Gyula Mándi)*.
SOUTH KOREA Hong Duk-Yung, Park Kyu-Chong, Kang Chang-Gi, Min Byung-Dae (c), Park Yae-Seung, Chu Yung-Kwang, Chung Nam-Sik, Park Il-Kap, Sung Nak-Woon, Woo Sang-Kwon, Choi Chung-Min. *Kim Yung-Sik*.

The biggest mismatch in any finals tournament. The most dominant team of all time against the absolute minnows, who were almost glad Hungary scored so many goals: Puskás said it allowed them to have a rest before each kick-off! 'They were very weak and had had no training,' and were soon exhausted by chasing Hungary's quick-passing game.

Amazingly, the Koreans should have taken the lead, Sung Nak-Woon missing a very early chance made by Woo Sang-Kwon. But soon Czibor hit the bar and the ball came back off a defender into the path of Puskás, the player expected to make the tournament his own. Lantos fired in a typical free kick, then Kocsis chipped the ball over Hong and scored his second with a spectacular volley. When Palotás scored the seventh from Budai's pass, the

BIGGEST WINS

9-0	Hungary	1954	v South Korea
9-0	Yugoslavia	1974	v Zaire
10-1	Hungary	1982	v El Salvador
8-0	Sweden	1938	v Cuba
8-0	Uruguay	1950	v Bolivia
8-0	Germany	2002	v Saudi Arabia

1954

37-year-old Chung sat down exhausted, whereupon Buzánszky gave him a leg massage. Mercy all round from the Hungarians: they could probably have matched the 12-0 scoreline inflicted by Sweden on a united Korea (with Hong in goal) at the 1948 Olympics.

17 June 1954 – Wankdorf, Berne – 28,000 – José da Costa (POR)

WEST GERMANY   **(1) 4**
Schäfer 12, Klodt 51, O Walter 60, Morlock 84

TURKEY   **(1) 1**
Suat 3

WEST GERMANY Toni Turek, Fritz Laband, Werner Kohlmeyer, Horst Eckel, Jupp Posipal, Karl Mai, Bernhard Klodt, Max Morlock, Ottmar Walter, Fritz Walter (c), Hans Schäfer. *Sepp Herberger*.
TURKEY Turgay Şeren (c), Ridvan Bolatli, Basri Dirimlili, Mustafa Ertan, Çetin Zeybek, Rober Eryol, Erol Keskin, Suat Mamat, Feridun Bugeker, Burhan Sargun, Lefter Küçükandonyadis. *Sandro Puppo (ITA)*.

Looking back, seeding the Turks seems laughable, but they'd qualified ahead of Spain (albeit on the toss of a coin after a play-off) – and the Germans were something of an unknown quantity. They had a famous midfield general in Fritz Walter, but he was a veteran by now (first capped in 1940) and Turek was even older. It was no great surprise when Suat gave Turkey an early lead. He beat two men, let the ball run on too far inside the German penalty area, then got in his shot before the tackle, the ball going in under Turek as he dived too late.

But Posipal, 'the German crack,' held the defence together and the attack was fit and smart. Schäfer ran onto a through-pass and shot across Turgay, who came off his line too late and didn't dive (he made partial amends with a tremendous save from Morlock). Klodt's strong shot went in low at the near post, and Ottmar Walter headed the third into an open net after a cross went over Turgay, then helped set up Morlock. The referee raised a jeer by accidentally barging one of the Turkish forwards off the ball.

Most Turkish players are known by their first names. Oh, and an attention to detail that contributed to ultimate success? West Germany were apparently the first team to use screw-in studs in a finals match.

---

20 June 1954 – Sankt Jakob, Basle – 53,000 – Bill Ling (ENG)

HUNGARY (3) 8
Kocsis 3, 21, 69, 79, Puskás 17, Hidegkuti 52, 55, Tóth 75

WEST GERMANY (1) 3
Pfaff 25, Rahn 78, Herrmann 84

HUNGARY Grosics, Buzánszky, Lantos, Bozsik, Lóránt, József Zakariás, József Tóth I, Kocsis, Nándor Hidegkuti, Puskás (c), Czibor.
WEST GERMANY Heinz Kwiatkowski, Hans Bauer, Kohlmeyer, Posipal, Werner Liebrich, Paul Mebus, Helmut Rahn, Eckel, F Walter (c), Alfred Pfaff, Richard Herrmann.

What do we make of this? Received wisdom now has it that the wily Herberger sent out a skeleton team, concealing his best side while learning all about Hungary's, confident Germany would beat Turkey in the play-off. But why would he deliberately expose his

players to an extra match, and what about the effect on their confidence? Being unconcerned about the result is one thing, but eight goals? According to Fritz Walter, Herberger fielded reserves to play for the draw that would have earned automatic qualification – and Eckel said 'We wanted to look good against Hungary, but the 8-3 defeat was very depressing for us.'

The truth is, throughout their history Hungarian national teams had invariably been ruthless against lesser opposition. This one, for instance, beat Albania 12-0, Finland 8-0 and Poland 6-0, not to mention England. And West Germany were hampered by an injury to Mebus, who limped on the right wing and wasn't capped again.

Kocsis thrashed the ball in high at the near post after Kwiatkowski had dropped a corner under pressure from his own defender; Puskás pushed the ball under the keeper from close range, then set up Kocsis with a gentle through-pass. Pfaff touched the ball delicately wide of Grosics before Kocsis hit the bar with a header; Hidegkuti hit a ground shot past the keeper and a defender on the line, then walked the ball past Kohlmeyer before shooting home; Kocsis tiptoed unchallenged into the penalty area to push the ball wide of the keeper, and hit his fourth under Kwiatkowski in a crowded area; Tóth beat Eckel before driving the ball in high at the near post; Grosics came out all the way to the corner flag, where Rahn beat him before coming back past one defender and chipping the ball over another on the goal line (a sign of things to come from Rahn, but too late here). Finally two Germans walked the ball in with Grosics again absent on the edge of the area.

But the really significant moment was a challenge on Puskás by Liebrich, who was brought in for this match and changed places with Posipal during it. In a book published the following year, Puskás claimed he received 'a

HAT-TRICKS

2	Sándor Kocsis	HUN	1954
2	Just Fontaine	FRA	1958
2	Gerd Müller	GER	1970
2	Gabriel Batistuta	ARG	1994–98

Müller scored from a penalty in one match, Batistuta in both.

vicious kick on the back of my ankle . . . when I was no longer playing the ball.' His tone changed in later years ('I can't imagine it was deliberate') and Hidegkuti called it 'a correct tackle, and quite accepted in football . . . You can see it in the films of the game . . . He was just trying to tackle Puskás, who strained his ankle.' Hungary scored their last three goals without him, but the injury kept him out of the next two matches and mattered enormously in the one after that.

---

20 June 1954 – Parc des Sports des Charmilles, Geneva – 2,000 – Esteban Marino (URU)

TURKEY　　　(4) 7
Suat 10, 28, Lefter 24, Burhan 36, 64, 70, Erol 76

SOUTH KOREA　(0) 0

TURKEY Turgay (c), Ridvan, Basri, Mustafa, Çetin, Rober, Erol, Suat, Necmi Onarici, Lefter, Burhan.
SOUTH KOREA Hong, Park KC (c), Kang, Han Chang-Hwa, Lee Chong-Kap, Kim Ji-Sung, Choi Yung-Keun, Lee Soo-Nam, Lee Ki-Joo, Woo, Chung Kook-Chin.

The Koreans, now captained by a man in glasses, really were cannon fodder, but with the play-off coming up the cannons needed it. Suat drove in the first goal from six yards after a cut-back on the left. Lefter met a clearing header with a marvellous left-footed volley from nearly

25 yards. Suat ran in to push home a square pass from a few yards out. Burhan slammed in the fourth left-footed with defenders at his heels, cracked in his second from equally close range after avoiding two defenders, then drove in a cross-shot from the right after two square passes across the box. Erol took a pass from the left and performed an exaggerated turn before shooting low across the keeper. Somewhere in all that, Suat had a goal disallowed. The times of some of the goals are disputed; these come from a Turkish almanac.

PLAY-OFF

23 June 1954 – Hardturm, Zürich – 17,000 – Raymond Vincenti (FRA)

WEST GERMANY　(3) 7
O Walter 7, Schäfer 12, 79, Morlock 31, 62, 77, F Walter 63

TURKEY　　　　(1) 2
Mustafa 17, Lefter 82

WEST GERMANY Turek, Laband, Bauer, Eckel, Posipal, Mai, Klodt, Morlock, O Walter, F Walter (c), Schäfer.
TURKEY Sükrü Ersoy, Ridvan, Basri, Naci Erdem, Çetin, Rober, Erol, Lefter (c), Necmi, Mustafa, Coşkun Taş.

If Herberger's strategy really did point to this match, he was proved right. It helped his cause that Çetin went off injured and Turkey had to replace their '*phantastischen*' goalkeeper Turgay with Sükrü, who had a poor match. Again they made a game of it in the first half. Mustafa

LEADING GOALSCORERS 1954

11	Sándor Kocsis	HUN
6	Josef Hügi	SWI
6	Erich Probst	AUT
6	Max Morlock	GER

1930
1934
1938
1950

1954

1958
1962
1966
1970
1974
1978
1982
1986
1990
1994
1998
2002
2006

1954

1958
1962
1966
1970
1974
1978
1982
1986
1990
1994
1998
2002
2006

headed in a cross from the left, Turek getting his hand to the ball. Before that, Schäfer's run to the left-hand goal line presented Ottmar Walter with an open goal. Then Suat ran clear in the inside-left channel before shooting in low at the near post. Morlock restored the two-goal lead by running onto a knockdown to volley across the keeper with the outside of his foot from close range. When he bundled in the fourth in a scramble, the match was over.

Schäfer cut the ball back to present Ottmar Walter with an open goal; Schäfer sprinted clear before shooting in low at the near post; Morlock ran onto a knockdown to get between two defenders and volley across the keeper from close range; Fritz Walter gently pushed in the fifth from a square pass with the keeper slow to dive across; Morlock clipped in another square pass from the left with Sükrü again making little effort to get across; and Morlock knocked in the seventh from close range right in front of the keeper.

Lefter, regarded as Turkey's best ever player, was unmarked in front of goal when he trapped a cross from the left and pushed it past the exposed Turek – but it only made up the numbers. West Germany's attack, prompted by Fritz Walter, had looked increasingly impressive. Not bad for a team who'd qualified by beating Norway and The Saar.

GROUP 2

	P	W	D	L	F	A	Pts
Hungary	2	2	0	0	17	3	4
West Germany	2	1	0	1	7	9	2
Turkey	2	1	0	1	8	4	2
South Korea	2	0	0	2	0	16	0

West Germany and Turkey played off to join Hungary in the quarter-finals.

GROUP 3

Austria (seeded), Uruguay (seeded), Czechoslovakia, Scotland.

16 June 1954 – Hardturm, Zürich – 25,000 – Laurent Franken (BEL)

AUSTRIA   (1) 1
Probst 32

SCOTLAND (0) 0

AUSTRIA Kurt Schmied, Gerhard Hanappi, Ernst Happel, Leopold Barschandt, Ernst Ocwirk (c), Karl Koller, Robert Körner, Walter Schleger, Robert Dienst, Erich Probst, Alfred Körner. *Walter Nausch.*
SCOTLAND Fred Martin, Willie Cunningham (c), Jock Aird, Tommy Docherty, Jimmy Davidson, Doug Cowie, John Mackenzie, Willie Fernie, Neil Mochan, Allan Brown, Willie Ormond. *Andy Beattie.*

Scotland made their bow with their first ever team manager but a dearth of class players. No Billy Steel, no Bobby Johnstone or Bobby Evans, no natural captain once big George Young was left out. Faced with group matches against the world champions and one of the strongest teams in Europe, they'd tuned up by playing Norway and Finland.

As it happened, they gave Austria a real contest. Ormond forced a save from Schmied after only thirty seconds and was stopped by Koller's last-ditch tackle, Mochan might have had a penalty after pushing the ball between Happel's legs and being obstructed as he went round him.

But Austria had some exceptional players: Happel himself, Hanappi who could play anywhere, the great Ocwirk. When Alfred Körner beat Aird yet again, the balding Probst took the ball off his toes to score. Ocwirk and Brown came to blows in the second half. The

Körners were brothers. A different Willie Cunningham played for Northern Ireland in the 1958 finals.

---

16 June 1954 – Wankdorf, Berne – 20,000 – Arthur Ellis (ENG)

URUGUAY (0) 2
Míguez 71, Schiaffino 84

CZECHOSLOVAKIA (0) 0

URUGUAY Roque Máspoli, José Santamaría, William Martínez, Víctor Rodríguez Andrade, Obdulio Varela (c), Luis Cruz, Julio César Abbadíe, Javier Ambrois, Omar Míguez, Juan Schiaffino, Carlos Borges. *Juan López.*
CZECHOSLOVAKIA Theodor Reimann, Frantisek Šafránek, Jirí Hledík, Ladislav Novák (c), Jirí Trnka, Jan Hertl, Ladislav Hlaváček, Ota Hemele, Ladislav Kačáni, Emil Pažický, Jirí Pešek. *Karel Borhy, Jaroslav Cejp et al.*

If anything, the holders had an even stronger team than in 1950, Ghiggia had gone to Italy, but Abbadíe and Borges were explosive replacements. Santamaría, later a defensive pillar at Real Madrid, played for Spain in the 1962 finals.

Nevertheless Uruguay had trouble with the heavy pitch and a Czech defence in which Hledík and Reimann had excellent games. Eventually Míguez scored from Varela's pass and Schiaffino curled in a free kick. Santamaría had to make a saving tackle from the stocky Hlaváček, but Uruguay were generally in charge, against a rather anonymous team.

---

19 June 1954 – Sankt Jakob, Basle – 34,000 – Vincenzo Orlandini (ITA)

URUGUAY (2) 7
Borges 17, 48, 58, Míguez 31, 82, Abbadíe 55, 87

SCOTLAND (0) 0

URUGUAY Máspoli, Santamaría, Martínez, Rodríguez Andrade, Varela (c), Cruz, Abbadíe, Ambrois, Míguez, Schiaffino, Borges.
SCOTLAND Martin, Cunningham (c), Aird, Docherty, Davidson, Cowie, Mackenzie, Fernie, Mochan, Brown, Ormond.

Any chance Scotland had of living up to their captain's bravado ('What's to stop us beating Uruguay?') probably disappeared when Andy Beattie resigned as manager after the Austria match – but it wouldn't have made much difference if he'd stayed: Scotland couldn't cope with the Uruguayan wingers, especially on such a hot day.

Abbadíe beat Aird and rolled the ball across the face of the goal for Borges to hold off a man and beat another before shooting high and fiercely past Martin. Schiaffino, rather overshadowed by Ghiggia and the defence four years earlier, was now the complete inside-forward: speed, vision, a fierce shot for someone so emaciated. According to Docherty, poor Cunningham developed 'a sunburned tongue' trying to contain him. He drew two defenders to set Míguez free in front of Martin, who seemed to get a touch to the shot.

In the second half, Máspoli almost fumbled a low shot into his own net, but Borges ran in to score before a tackle could come in, then beat a man before shooting from close range on the left. Abbadíe, stocky and elusive, twice ran clear on Martin from the right, scoring first with a cross-shot then by going round the keeper. Scottish embarrassment was completed in the last minute when Mackenzie shot feebly into Máspoli's hands from only a few yards out. The scale of this record defeat should have taught a few lessons in preparation and team selection, but four years later they still hadn't been learned.

1954

1930
1934
1938
1950

1954

1958
1962
1966
1970
1974
1978
1982
1986
1990
1994
1998
2002
2006

19 June 1954 – Hardturm, Zürich – 26,000 – Vasa Stefanović (YUG)

AUSTRIA　　　　　**(4) 5**
Stojaspal 2, 65, Probst 4, 21, 24

CZECHOSLOVAKIA (0) 0

AUSTRIA Schmied, Hanappi, Happel, Barschandt, Ocwirk (c), Koller, R Körner, Theo Wagner, Ernst Stojaspal, Probst, A Körner.
CZECHOSLOVAKIA Imrich Stacho, Šafránek, Svatopluk Pluskal, Novák (c), Trnka, Hertl, Hlaváček, Hemele, Kačáni, Pažický, Tadeás Kraus.

Those early goals settled it, of course. Stojaspal scored a very good first goal, an instant volleyed lob over the keeper from Ocwirk's long ball. Probst scored his first with an unexceptional ground shot from the edge of the area, his second with a low cross-shot from close range, and his third with a high shot over the keeper's dive, the last two with his left foot. Stojaspal ran onto a long pass to make it five. It wasn't till the 55th minute that Schmied had to make a meaningful save, from Hlaváček.

The Körners had been impressive on the wings, but Ocwirk was again Austria's best player. Tall, dark and snub-nosed, operating from penalty area to penalty area (inevitably nicknamed 'Clockwork' in England), he was the last great attacking centre-half.

GROUP 3

	P	W	D	L	F	A	Pts
Uruguay	2	2	0	0	9	0	4
Austria	2	2	0	0	6	0	4
Czechoslovakia	2	0	0	2	0	7	0
Scotland	2	0	0	2	0	8	0

Uruguay and Austria qualified for the quarterfinals.

GROUP 4

England (seeded), Italy (seeded), Belgium, Switzerland.

17 June 1954 – Sankt Jakob, Basle – 14,000 – Emil Schmetzer (GER)

BELGIUM　　(1) (3) 4
Anoul 4, 74, Coppens 77, Dickinson o.g. 93

ENGLAND　　(2) (3) 4
Broadis 25, 62, Lofthouse 37, 91

BELGIUM Léopold Gernaey, Marcel Dries, Fons Van Brandt, Constant Huysmans, Louis Carré, Vic Mees, Jef Mermans (c), Denis Houf, Rik Coppens, Pol Anoul, Pieter 'Jeng' Vanden Bosch. *Dugald (Dug) Livingstone (SCO)*.
ENGLAND Gil Merrick, Ron Staniforth, Roger Byrne, Billy Wright (c), Syd Owen, Jimmy Dickinson, Stanley Matthews, Ivan Broadis, Nat Lofthouse, Tommy Taylor, Tom Finney. *Walter Winterbottom*.

The trauma of Budapest was less than a month behind them, but at least England had never had any trouble with the Belgians, whom they'd beaten 5-2, 4-1 and 5-0 since the War. Here Belgium managed a very early goal, the bustling Anoul scoring after a scramble in the penalty area, but were overhauled soon enough. Broadis squeezed in the equaliser before colliding with the onrushing Gernaey, then Lofthouse jerked himself at a cross from Taylor and headed in. In the second half Broadis hit Matthews' deflected cross so hard it bent the keeper's wrist on the way in. And Gernaey had to make 'some really brilliant saves'.

This was Matthews' first match against Belgium since 1947, when he'd made all five of England's goals. Now he pulled their defence inside out, preposterously quick and supple for a man of 39. But England still hadn't solved their old problem at centre-half, where Owen was now limping. Anoul ran past him to pull a goal back, then Merrick failed to hold a shot by the fiery Coppens.

In extra-time, Broadis' cross and Taylor's dummy set up Lofthouse for a 'crushing drive' that went in off the far post – but Dickinson headed in a Dries free kick 'when no-one was anywhere near him.' As in darkest 1950, England were left needing to win their last group match to be sure of qualifying.

Broadis allowed himself to be known as Ivor (the Cold War was at its iciest).

---

17 June 1954 – Olympique de la Pontaise, Lausanne – 43,000 – Mário Vianna (BRZ)

SWITZERLAND **(1) 2**
Ballaman 18, Hügi 78

ITALY **(1) 1**
Boniperti 44

SWITZERLAND Eugène Parlier, André Neury, Roger Bocquet (c), Willy Kernen, Marcel Flückiger, Charles Casali, Robert Ballaman, Roger Vonlanthen, Josef Hügi, Eugen Meier, Jacky Fatton. *Karl Rappan (AUT)*.
ITALY Giorgio Ghezzi, Guido Vincenzi, Giovanni Giacomazzi, Maino Neri, Omero Tognon, Fulvio Nesti, Ermes Muccinelli, Giampiero Boniperti (c), Carlo Galli, Egisto Pandolfini, Benito Lorenzi. *Lajos Czeizler (HUN) etc.*

Lorenzi was fit this time, and Italy deserved to be seeded – but again there were problems behind the scenes. They dominated possession in the first half but went behind when Fatton's cross from the left was met by Ballaman's powerful header that dipped across the keeper from twelve yards out. As always, the Swiss were defensive but good on the break.

Italy equalised from a left-wing cross that fell loose in a crowded penalty area. Boniperti, who spent a decade not quite living up to a golden boy tag, lunged in to score despite an ankle swollen by Flückiger's tackle. Play became rough as both teams realised the balding Vianna was a bulldog without a bite. Lorenzi put in a rebound from close range only to be given offside, a decision that looks correct enough on the film. Vianna had to push Italian players off with his hands and needed police protection from Lorenzi after the match.

Parlier pushed a shot onto the base of a post before Switzerland scored the winner when Giacomazzi's back-header fell to Hügi, who scored with a low cross-shot.

---

20 June 1954 – Comunale (Cornaredo), Lugano – 26,000 – Erich Steiner (AUT)

ITALY **(1) 4**
Pandolfini pen 41, Galli 48, Frignani 58, Lorenzi 78

BELGIUM **(0) 1**
Anoul 81

ITALY Ghezzi, Ardico Magnini, Giacomazzi, Neri, Tognon, Nesti, Lorenzi, Pandolfini (c), Galli, Gino Cappello, Amleto Frignani.
BELGIUM Gernaey, Dries, Carré, Van Brandt, Huysmans, Mees, Mermans (c), Anoul, Coppens, Hippolyte Vanden Bosch, P Vanden Bosch.

Italy expected a harder time than this. Lorenzi, one of the personalities of the tournament, dummied his man on the left and crossed for Galli to score with a superb diving header. Frignani lobbed the ball in when Galli's pitiful ground shot was appallingly fumbled by Gernaey, then hit a corner which was glanced on by Galli for Lorenzi to score with a teasing header. Dries had fouled Frignani to concede the penalty, which Pandolfini hit hard and almost straight as Gernaey moved to his right. Anoul got in a low cross-shot before the tackle came in.

1954

1930
1934
1938
1950
1958
1962
1966
1970
1974
1978
1982
1986
1990
1994
1998
2002
2006

The dramatic improvement may have had something to do with the selection of a Hamlet (Frignani) as well as a Homer (Tognon). Hippolyte and Pieter Vanden Bosch were brothers.

Carré was winning his 39th consecutive cap on the way to becoming the first player from any country to win 50 in a row.

1954

20 June 1954 – Wankdorf, Berne – 43,500 – István Zsolt (HUN)

ENGLAND (1) 2
Mullen 44, Wilshaw 70

SWITZERLAND (0) 0

ENGLAND Merrick, Staniforth, Byrne, Bill McGarry, Wright (c), Dickinson, Finney, Broadis, Taylor, Dennis Wilshaw, Jimmy Mullen.
SWITZERLAND Parlier, Neury, Kernen, Olivier Eggimann, Bocquet (c), Heinz Bigler, Charly Antenen, Vonlanthen, Meier, Ballaman, Fatton.

When Matthews pulled out with a bruised toe and Lofthouse with a throat infection, it looked as if somebody was trying to tell England something. But the various injuries cleared the deck a little. Taylor, unhappy in a double centre-forward formation, was now a single centre-forward of growing promise – and Mullen was an experienced winger. Above all, the solution to the centre-half problem had been there all along.

Billy Wright was one of the icons of post-war English football – but a very average wing-half. Now, at the age of 30, in his 60th international, he finally knew his place, staying in it for another five years despite being only 5' 8.

At the other end, with England in dire need of a goal, Taylor headed the ball on, Mullen darted past his fullback, went round Parlier, and never played for England again. No surprise there. Wilshaw's goal was just as good, a

dribble past three players after he 'suddenly remembered his bodyswerve.' But Staniforth had to clear off the line from Ballaman (the ball seemed to cross the line), Fatton had a goal disallowed, and Vonlanthen might have had a penalty. England needed Matthews' toe to heal quickly: the reigning champions were lying in wait.

PLAY-OFF

23 June 1954 – Sankt Jakob, Basle – 30,000 – Mervyn Griffiths (WAL)

SWITZERLAND (1) 4
Hügi 14, 85, Ballaman 48, Fatton 89

ITALY (0) 1
Nesti 67

SWITZERLAND Parlier, Neury, Bocquet (c), Kernen, Eggimann, Casali, Antenen, Vonlanthen, Hügi, Ballaman, Fatton.
ITALY Giovanni Viola, Magnini, Giacomazzi, Giacomo Mari, Tognon, Nesti, Muccinelli, Pandolfini (c), Lorenzi, Armando Segato, Frignani.

It wasn't a defeat, said an Italian paper, it was a disaster. No excuses possible.

Early on, Italy looked over-confident but were probably just tired, allowing Switzerland to dictate from the moment Hügi was sent clear in the inside-left channel to hit a low shot past Viola's right hand. For the second match in a row, Lorenzi had a shot blocked on the line by a defender, then his powerful shot was superbly saved by Parlier. Soon after half-time, new cap Viola tipped a dangerous header over the bar but couldn't stop Ballaman driving in the corner from five yards out.

Muccinelli's backheel was kicked away by a defender, Nesti showing good reactions to get in a header when the ball flew hard straight at him. But Vonlanthen was running the midfield by then, going past the keeper to set up an open goal for Fatton, who had made the third goal with a square pass met by another low shot from Hügi.

Four of the Italians, including Lorenzi, weren't capped again. The squad later complained of boredom at the training camp in Vevey, but that comes with the territory. Pozzo could have told them that, and he was still around to ask.

GROUP 4

	P	W	D	L	F	A	Pts
England	2	1	1	0	6	4	3
Italy	2	1	0	1	5	3	2
Switzerland	2	1	0	1	2	3	2
Belgium	2	0	1	1	5	8	1

Italy and Switzerland played off to join England in the quarter-finals.

QUARTER-FINALS

Not content with the complications they'd arranged for the group matches, FIFA had decided on a free draw for the knockout stage, leaving the possibility of the group winners playing each other in the quarter-finals instead of being rewarded with matches against the runners-up. And the two strongest teams could well meet in the semi-finals.

26 June 1954 – Sankt Jakob, Basle – 28,000 – Erich Steiner (AUT)

URUGUAY (2) 4
Borges 5, Varela 38, Schiaffino 47, Ambrois 79

ENGLAND (1) 2
Lofthouse 15, Finney 66

URUGUAY Máspoli, Santamaría, Martínez, Rodríguez Andrade, Varela (c), Cruz, Abbadíe, Ambrois, Míguez, Schiaffino, Borges.
ENGLAND Merrick, Staniforth, Byrne, McGarry, Wright (c), Dickinson, Matthews, Broadis, Lofthouse, Wilshaw, Finney.

Better go through the Uruguayan goals first, because Merrick was at fault with the last three and has generally been blamed for England's defeat (actually the Uruguayan manager said '*Gil Merrick estuvo magnifico,*' which is stretching it a bit). He couldn't do anything about the first. Borges' cut-back from the left-hand goal line was mishit by one team mate and missed by another's attempted backheel flick – so Borges came off the goal line to smash the ball in.

Uruguay went ahead for the second time when Dickinson headed away a free kick and Varela returned it with a high curling shot from twenty yards which Merrick might have reached. Schiaffino 'rolled a slowish simple-looking shot … Merrick seemed to turn his back and fall down facing his own goal.' Then, perhaps unsighted, he didn't get down to cover Ambrois' optimistic cross-shot.

But pointing the finger at goalkeepers is an old excuse. England played their best World Cup match so far – and it wasn't good enough to beat a team which ended the match with eight fit men after injuries to Andrade (bandaged thigh), Abbadíe and Varela. There had also been pre-match worries over Borges, Schiaffino and Míguez! And if Matthews hit a stanchion in the side netting, then Ambrois hit the bar. Uruguay were a great team and England didn't do badly to lose 4-2.

They equalised when Wilshaw's reverse pass was put away by Lofthouse's left-footed cross-shot. Then Máspoli saved 'miraculously' from Lofthouse at close range. England's second goal was poked in by Finney after Máspoli had saved from Lofthouse, his follow-up going between Varela's legs and past another defender on the line. But the second and third Uruguayan goals came from free kicks conceded by Byrne, who couldn't cope with Abbadíe; Finney, discouraged by Andrade's strong tackling, was a big-occasion flop yet again; and England fell into individualistic play in the second half, which played into the Uruguayans' hands. And the average age of the team was over 30. As Schiaffino said, if they could find some younger players . . .

Their oldest was still their best, and the match programme knew what it was doing when it listed him as St Matthews. Schiaffino was just as influential, dropping back into defence when the injuries began, and playing as well as ever. Two prodigious footballers.

Further down the scale, Merrick wasn't capped again after a season in which he conceded thirty goals in ten matches.

---

26 June 1954 – Olympique de la Pontaise, Lausanne – 32,000 – Charlie Faultless (SCO)

AUSTRIA   (5) 7
Wagner 25, 28, 54, A Körner 26, 34, Ocwirk 32, Probst 77

SWITZERLAND   (4) 5
Ballaman 16, 36, Hügi 17, 18, 60

AUSTRIA Schmied, Hanappi, Happel, Barschandt, Ocwirk (c), Koller, R Körner, Wagner, Stojaspal, Probst, A Körner.
SWITZERLAND Parlier, Neury, Bocquet (c), Kernen, Eggimann, Casali, Antenen, Vonlanthen, Hügi, Ballaman, Fatton.

Whatever happened to the Swiss bolt? The Austrians thrust it aside with short passes, slowing down the play – but only after conceding those three goals in three minutes. An amazing scoreline, unthinkable nowadays – though it

would have been even more eye-catching if Robert Körner hadn't missed a penalty three minutes before half-time!

Ballaman cracked in a high shot from twenty yards; Hügi held off a defender and shot round him past an unsighted keeper for the second, then drove a low right-wing cross high into the net for the third; Wagner took a return pass from one of the Körners to score with a low ground shot which the keeper should probably have reached; Alfred Körner struck a fine goal with the outside of his left foot from out on the right, curling the ball in off the far post; Wagner scored with a low cross-shot; Ocwirk rolled a first-time ground shot across the keeper; Körner forced the ball in after a fumble by the keeper; Ballaman converted a low cross from the right; and Robert Körner put the penalty wide of the post to the keeper's right.

At half-time Schmied and Bocquet received medical attention for sunstroke, then Wagner slid in his third from the corner of the six-yard box. Hügi's 20-yarder swung away from the keeper who should still have saved it instead of just getting a hand to it; and finally Probst chipped the ball over the diving keeper from the left-hand edge of the six-yard area.

With six minutes left, Neury made another saving tackle when Stojaspal seemed sure to score. As if it mattered by then!

GOALS IN A MATCH					
12	1954	Austria	7	Switzerland	5
11	1938	Brazil	6	Poland	5
11	1954	Hungary	8	W Germany	3
11	1982	Hungary	10	El Salvador	1
10	1958	France	7	Paraguay	3

MATCHES WON FROM THREE GOALS DOWN

1954	Austria	v	Switzerland	7-5
1966	Portugal	v	North Korea	5-3

27 June 1954 – Parc des Sports des Charmilles, Geneva – 17,000 – István Zsolt (HUN)

WEST GERMANY   (1) 2
Horvat o.g. 9, Rahn 86

YUGOSLAVIA   (0) 0

WEST GERMANY Turek, Laband, Kohlmeyer, Eckel, Liebrich, Mai, Rahn, Morlock, O Walter, F Walter (c), Schäfer.
YUGOSLAVIA Beara, Stanković, Crnkovcić, Čajkovski, Horvat, Boškov, Milutinović, Bobek, Mitić (c), Vukas, Zebec.

After Horvat had headed a German header over his own goalkeeper, Yugoslavia's chronic goalscoring problem finally caught up with them: six in eight matches. Mitić beat Liebrich and forced a save from Turek, and the unmarked Milutinović shot just over. But Rahn made his first major contribution to the tournament. Very big but superb on the ball, he left Crnković needing attention after trying to tackle him, then apparently beat six men (really?) in one of his dribbles only for Horvat to kick off the line.

GOALS IN A TOURNAMENT

27	Hungary	1954
25	West Germany	1954
23	France	1958

Hungary played five matches, West Germany and France six.

He sealed the match with a long run up the right, holding off the last defender before volleying a bouncing ball across Beara, whose mobility was affected by a leg injury.

27 June 1954 – Wankdorf, Berne – 40,000 – Arthur Ellis (ENG)

HUNGARY   (2) 4
Hidegkuti 4, Kocsis 7, 88, Lantos pen 61

BRAZIL   (1) 2
D Santos pen 18, Julinho 66

HUNGARY Grosics, Buzánszky, Lantos, Bozsik (c), Lóránt, Zakariás, J Tóth I, Kocsis, Hidegkuti, Czibor, Mihály Tóth.
BRAZIL Castilho, D Santos, N Santos, Bauer (c), Pinheiro, Brandãozinho, Julinho, Didi, Humberto (Tozzi), 'Índio' (Aloísio da Luz), 'Maurinho' (Mauro Raphael).
SENT OFF: Bozsik 71, N Santos 71, Humberto 79.

From the first World Cup to be televised, the first video nasty. It's been blamed on a clash of cultures and so on – but it was probably simpler than that. Hungary, for all their goals and brilliance, had some rather basic defenders (Lóránt a standard stopper, Lantos very big for a fullback) and strong characters. Likewise Brazil. And with so much at stake, combustion was always possible. Ellis had to send someone off in an international for the first time. History's generally been kind to him, but he surely lost control here.

Brazil brought in three new forwards – but it was the defence that gave Hungary their flying start, Pinheiro trying to dribble out of his area and losing the ball to Hidegkuti, who blasted a shot from ten yards. Castilho made a wonderful save, then rushed across the goalmouth to block another shot – but was unlucky that the ball ran loose for Hidegkuti to smash high past the Santos fullbacks at the near post. Then he replaced his shorts, ripped by a Brazilian, and

1930

1934

1938

1950

1954

1958

1962

1966

1970

1974

1978

1982

1986

1990

1994

1998

2002

2006

crossed for Kocsis to score the second with a typically powerful header at the far post with no defenders anywhere near him.

Djalma Santos had already had to clear off the line. By the time he converted a penalty for a foul by Buzánszky on Índio, the match was becoming increasingly rough. Ellis broke up a fracas in midfield, József Tóth went off injured, and the mood darkened further when Ellis gave a penalty for a foul on Kocsis that no-one else seemed to notice. There's nothing on the video, in which Kocsis looks as bemused as anyone.

Bauer brought down Bozsik, who needed treatment and came back infuriated. A suave midfield general, one of the all-time greats, no-one knew he had a dander, let alone one that could get up. Yet here he was, sent off with Nílton Santos amid allegations of racial abuse. Czibor was chased by Djalma Santos, someone to be avoided in dark alleys; József Tóth was 'a helpless passenger' by the end; Hidegkuti pushed Índio to the ground and stamped on his calves; and the police had to order photographers off the pitch when Didi exacted revenge!

Julinho lightened things briefly with a fine goal, stepping inside a defender and slicing a drive across Grosics into the far side of the net. A rather forgotten figure by now, superseded by Garrincha, he looked an unlikely footballer, hollow-cheeked and very slim, but he was one of Brazil's best, which means something. This was his last international for five years; recalled against England, he scored within two minutes.

Didi and Maurinho hit a post, then Humberto was sent off for jumping on Kocsis ('one tremendous leap'), who scored Hungary's fourth with a rising drive from outside the area that Castilho should probably have saved.

As the teams left the pitch, a free-for-all broke out, a photographer attacking the police. At least two separate sources say Puskás split Pinheiro's head open with a bottle. In the Hungarian changing room, the lights suddenly went out and some retaliatory glass came flying in. When order was restored ten minutes later, a doctor was ministering to one of the Tóths and there was bad blood everywhere. A classic of its kind.

Mihály Tóth had played for Romania in 1946.

SEMI-FINALS

30 June 1954 – Sankt Jakob, Basle – 57,000 – Vincenzo Orlandini (ITA)

WEST GERMANY (1) 6
Schäfer 31, Morlock 47, F Walter pen 56, pen 65, O Walter 62, 88

AUSTRIA   (0) 1
Probst 52

WEST GERMANY Turek, Posipal, Kohlmeyer, Eckel, Liebrich, Mai, Rahn, Morlock, O Walter, F Walter (c), Schäfer.
AUSTRIA Walter Zeman, Hanappi, Happel, Schleger, Ocwirk (c), Koller, R Körner, Wagner, Stojaspal, Probst, A Körner.

Schmied hadn't recovered from his sunstroke, but it didn't seem to matter. Zeman, whose international career lasted from 1945 to 1960, was one of the best goalkeepers in Europe.

Unfortunately he chose the wrong day to have his worst match for Austria, slow to get down for shots, a headless chicken in the second half. Things might have been different if the prolific Probst hadn't missed two early chances, the first made by Ocwirk.

West Germany took the lead when Fritz Walter appeared on the right wing and Schäfer hit his cross firmly past Zeman from six yards. Later Morlock headed in his corner. Turek gifted Probst a goal by dropping his first shot, but Happel brought down Schäfer in the area and the Germans ran away with it after that, their forwards pouring through a halfback line doomed to keep going forward. When it came after all these years, the demolition of the Viennese school wasn't pretty. The underrated Ottmar Walter knocked in 'the loveliest back-header' then headed the sixth into an empty net after Schäfer got to the ball before Zeman on the right. Fritz Walter converted his second penalty after a foul on a player 'not identified in the tumult.' Even the Hungarians would be sitting up and taking notice.

---

30 June 1954 – Olympique de la Pontaise, Lausanne – 45,000 – Mervyn Griffiths (WAL)

HUNGARY (1) (2) 4
Czibor 12, Hidegkuti 47, Kocsis 109, 116

URUGUAY (0) (2) 2
Hohberg 76, 87

HUNGARY Grosics, Buzánszky, Lantos, Bozsik (c), Lóránt, Zakariás, Budai, Kocsis, Palotás, Hidegkuti, Czibor.
URUGUAY Máspoli, Santamaría, Martínez (c), Rodríguez Andrade, Néstor Carballo, Cruz, Rafael Souto, Ambrois, Schiaffino, Juan Eduardo Hohberg, Borges.

An outstanding candidate for greatest international match of all time, it might have been really quite good if both teams had been at full strength. Hungary had shown there was life after Puskás, but Uruguay were without Varela (whose great international career was over), Abbadíe and Míguez.

The Hungarians tried to take advantage with all-out attack, Palotás forcing a save from Máspoli, Hidegkuti and Bozsik shooting just wide. They were gifted the lead by Máspoli, who should have saved Czibor's mishit cross-shot rather than just getting his hand to it.

Uruguay's first real chance didn't come till the 39th minute, when Schiaffino went round Grosics but couldn't keep his balance. Then Budai beat Cruz and crossed for Hidegkuti to score with a marvellous diving header right under the keeper's nose. Máspoli, a hero of 1950 but now 36 and looking rather heavy, was slow to get across.

It looked all over, especially as Uruguay were hampered by the wet conditions (they beat Scotland and England in sunshine) – but true to the history they'd made for themselves, they came back into it. Hohberg, their naturalised Argentinian, scored with a low cross-shot after being put clear by a short ball from Schiaffino. With time running out, the latter beat two men and put Hohberg through again, to bundle in the rebound after Grosics saved his first shot.

In extra-time Hohberg was in again but this time hit a post. Two minutes later the unheralded Budai made another goal, crossing for Kocsis to head in. By now Schiaffino and Andrade were feeling their earlier injuries, and Kocsis headed the fourth from Bozsik's centre. A fitting end to one of the greatest games.

It's doubtful if anyone ever headed a ball like Sándor Kocsis, certainly no-one else who stood only 5′ 9. Quite slim with it, he had a neck so thick it looked deformed – and TV footage confirms the power of those headers, some from around the penalty spot – so it wasn't just the stuff of legend. Almost as good on the ground, he scored 75 goals in only 68 matches before the 1956 revolution cut short his international career. He scored in ten consecutive games for Hungary (1951–52) but not in the Olympic Final. Now he'd scored 13 in the last five with only the Final to come.

Souto is sometimes referred to by his first name Ángel, but usually as Rafael.

1930
1934
1938
1950
1954
1958
1962
1966
1970
1974
1978
1982
1986
1990
1994
1998
2002
2006

3RD-PLACE FINAL

3 July 1954 – Hardturm, Zürich – 32,000 – Paul Wyssling (SWI)

AUSTRIA   (1) 3
Stojaspal pen 15, Cruz o.g. 59, Ocwirk 78

URUGUAY   (1) 1
Hohberg 21

AUSTRIA Schmied, Hanappi, Walter Kollmann, Barschandt, Ocwirk (c), Koller, R Körner, Wagner, Dienst, Stojaspal, Probst.
URUGUAY Máspoli, Santamaría, Martínez (c), Rodríguez Andrade, Carballo, Cruz, Abbadíe, Hohberg, Omar Méndez, Schiaffino, Borges.

In the 100th World Cup finals match, Stojaspal thumped in a penalty for a foul by Martínez on Dienst; and Körner's shot was deflected in at the near post by the head of Cruz, who'd kicked lumps out of Finney in Montevideo the previous year. As always, Schiaffino and Ocwirk were the best on view, the former dribbling through before setting up Hohberg for the equaliser, then beating the whole defence and shooting wide. Ocwirk, a reminder of an era that was gone forever, shot into the corner of the net with Máspoli standing still and claiming offside.

FINAL

4 July 1954 – Wankdorf, Berne – 62,472 – Bill Ling (ENG)

WEST GERMANY   (2) 3
Morlock 10, Rahn 19, 85

HUNGARY   (2) 2
Puskás 6, Czibor 8

WEST GERMANY Turek, Posipal, Kohlmeyer, Eckel, Liebrich, Mai, Rahn, Morlock, O Walter, F Walter (c), Schäfer.
HUNGARY Grosics, Buzánszky, Lantos, Bozsik, Lóránt, Zakariás, Czibor, Kocsis, Hidegkuti, Puskás (c), M Tóth.

In the days leading up, all the talk was of Puskás, who surely couldn't be brought back now. He's only half fit, they said (he often was), he looks rather thick round the middle (ditto), the team has shown it doesn't need him (hm).

He was also the most extravagantly talented and inspirational player of his day, famously one-footed but with a left foot that juggled the soap in the showers at Real Madrid. The nickname Galloping Major, which refers to his ersatz rank in the army, doesn't paint the right picture. Hungary were always better with him than without.

So he came back and things immediately happened around him. Bozsik sent Kocsis into the German penalty area, the shot hit Liebrich and rebounded to the left, and Puskás beat Turek with a low cross-shot. Two minutes later, Bozsik tried to find Kocsis, Kohlmeyer's back pass put Turek in trouble, Czibor kicked it in. What was that score in the group match?

West Germany were saved by their unity (six players from Kaiserslautern) and instant comeback. Zakariás, facing his own goal, lunged to reach a low cross from the left but could only knock it back towards his own goal (no blame attached) – and Morlock slid in to divert it low past Grosics' right hand. Then Fritz Walter took a corner, Grosics could only flap the ball sideways under Schäfer's challenge, and Rahn stabbed a half-volley past Buzánszky and Lantos on the line.

The rest of the match is usually described as a Hungarian onslaught, kept at bay by Turek and slices of luck. But Hungary were at last facing opponents who weren't intimidated by them. Eckel followed Hidegkuti even when he dropped back (something England hadn't thought of) and although the centre-forward hit the post with a snap shot, he wasn't his usual influential self. Mai stayed close to Kocsis, whose header clipped the top of the bar but was similarly blotted out. Tóth's shot was cleared off the line by Kohlmeyer, but Rahn was always dangerous on the wings and West Germany were on the attack at the end.

There were subsequent rumblings about drug-taking, especially when some of the German team went down with jaundice – but it's more likely that Hungary's hard matches with the South Americans caught up with them. With five minutes left, Schäfer shoved Bozsik off the ball and crossed, Lantos headed away under pressure and the ball reached the unmarked Rahn, who took it away from Lantos to the left before shooting low and left-footed past Grosics' right hand.

In the dying minutes Puskás ran through the inside-left channel to slide the ball under Turek, only for Mervyn Griffiths, the authoritarian, high-profile Welsh linesman, to leave

**WON TOURNAMENT AFTER
LOSING A MATCH**

1954	West Germany
1974	West Germany
1978	Argentina

his mark on the match as he was perhaps always likely to do. Offside. For ever. Years later, Ottmar Walter claimed Puskás 'was standing three yards offside' – and the film's inconclusive. Thirty seconds from the end, Czibor put everything into a shot, but Turek, admirably agile for a man of 35, turned it away.

It was the end of Hungary's virtual invincibility. They had strong claims to that unwanted title: best team never to win the World Cup. Seven years later, Czibor again played for the hot favourites (Barcelona) in a major final (the European Cup) on the same ground, again he scored in a 3-2 defeat. But this was worse, the end of the world.

1930
1934
1938
1950
1954
1958
1962
1966
1970
1974
1978
1982
1986
1990
1994
1998
2002
2006

Achieving everything by the time you're 17 is all too much for Pelé, who leans on the experienced Gylmar in the company of Djalma Santos (left) and Didi. Orlando (right) has his own way of showing his feelings.

Teenage kicks

Sweden 1958

1930

1934

1938

1950

1954

1958

1962

1966

1970

1974

1978

1982

1986

1990

1994

1998

2002

2006

For the first time since 1934, no outright favourite – and no certainty that a great team was going to emerge.

The hosts had as good a chance as anyone once they recalled Raynor as coach and broke with tradition by picking players with Italian clubs. Liedholm, Skoglund, Hamrin and Gustavsson were some of the greatest players of all time. But it was an elderly team (Gren 37, Liedholm 35, Svensson 32) and home support might not be enough.

The 1956 revolution, crushed by Moscow, deprived Hungary of Puskás, Kocsis and Czibor, while Hidegkuti and Bozsik were past their best. The Soviets themselves, entering for the first time, were Olympic champions and had the famous Yashin in goal. West Germany had Rahn and Schäfer, a dynamic young centre-forward in Seeler and two new heavies in Erhardt and Szymaniak, but were still relying on Fritz Walter, now 37, as playmaker.

Brazil had an unsatisfactory European tour in 1956 and their two qualifying games against Peru ended 1-1 and 1-0, but their new 4–4–2 formation was still being bedded down. Uruguay were out, beaten 5-0 in Paraguay. Argentina, back at long last, had won the 1957 Copa América with some scintillating football, scoring 25 goals in six matches – but yet again the Italians had swooped, taking away their brilliant inside forward trio of Sivori-Maschio-Angelillo, all later capped by Italy. It was

another reserve forward line that came to Sweden.

For the first and only time, all four Home countries were there, three of them affected by the Munich air crash which killed so many of the Man United squad and cost Scotland their part-time manager Matt Busby, who was badly injured.

Northern Ireland had beaten an Italian team which returned to its old ruse of picking South Americans, in this case Schiaffino and Ghiggia, no less, the latter getting himself sent off in Belfast. The Munich disaster deprived the Irish of their fine centre-half Jackie Blanchflower, their captain's brother.

Wales, eliminated by Czechoslovakia, were given a second chance when FIFA decided that Israel, blacklisted then as now by the Asian countries, couldn't be allowed to take part without playing any qualifying matches. Wales came out of the hat, won both legs 2-0, and persuaded the Italian FA to release their best-known player, giant John Charles, at the eleventh hour.

England lost three players in the air crash, none of them easily replaced: left-back Roger Byrne, Tommy Taylor up front, and the strapping young midfielder Duncan Edwards. Without them, they lost 5-0 in Belgrade to a team which hit the bar and had three goals disallowed. Things looked bleak, especially as their group included two of the fancied teams. But for Munich, England would have been one of them.

GROUP 1

Argentina, Czechoslovakia, Northern Ireland, West Germany. [No seeds.]

8 June 1958 – Malmö Stadion, Malmö – 31,156 – Reg Leafe (ENG)

WEST GERMANY   (2) 3
Rahn 32, 79, Seeler 42

ARGENTINA   (1) 1
Corbatta 3

WEST GERMANY Fritz Herkenrath, Georg Stollenwerk, Erich Juskowiak, Horst Eckel, Herbert Erhardt, Horst Szymaniak, Helmut Rahn, Fritz Walter, Uwe Seeler, Alfred Schmidt, Hans Schäfer (c). *Sepp Herberger.*
ARGENTINA Amadeo Carrizo, Pedro Dellacha (c), Federico Vairo, Francisco Lombardo, Néstor Rossi, José Varacka, Oreste Corbatta, Eliseo Prado, Norberto Menéndez, Alfredo Rojas, Osvaldo Cruz. *Guillermo Stábile.*

The South American champions gave the holders an early scare, little Corbatta sprinting clear on the right wing to whip in a high shot at the near post. But their non-existent marking allowed Rahn to steal the show. Recalled when Herberger persuaded him to lose weight by reducing his lager intake, he carried on where he left off last time by scoring twice, with his left foot from 25 yards and his right foot from 20, a heavily sliced ground shot that made Carrizo look foolish and spoiled Dellacha's 32nd birthday. Seeler scored the second by sliding in at the far post to put in a mishit shot. The new German defence lost nothing in comparison with 1954. The crowd figure, also listed as 30,953, is still the stadium record.

8 June 1958 – Örjans Vall, Halmstad – 10,647 – Fritz Seipelt (AUT)

NORTHERN IRELAND   (1) 1
Cush 21

CZECHOSLOVAKIA   (0) 0

NORTHERN IRELAND Harry Gregg, Dick Keith, Alf McMichael, Danny Blanchflower (c), Willie Cunningham, Bertie Peacock, Billy Bingham, Wilbur Cush, Derek Dougan, Jimmy McIlroy, Peter McParland. *Peter Doherty.*
CZECHOSLOVAKIA Bretislav Dolejší, Gustav Mráz, Ladislav Novák (c), Svatopluk Pluskal, Jiří Čadek, Josef Masopust, Václav Hovorka, Milan Dvořák, Jaroslav Borovička, Jan Hertl, Tadeás Kraus. *Karel Kolský.*

Regarded as a surprise, then and now – but there was a similar number of quality players on each side. An injury to Billy Simpson led to a first cap for the tall 20-year-old Dougan, but the winning header came from a man several inches shorter, after McParland's short corner was crossed in by McIlroy. Cunningham did well as a makeshift centre-half.

11 June 1958 – Örjans Vall, Halmstad – 14,174 – Sten Ahlner (SWE)

ARGENTINA   (1) 3
Corbatta pen 37, Menéndez 56, Avio 60

NORTHERN IRELAND   (1) 1
McParland 4

ARGENTINA Carrizo, Dellacha (c), Vairo, Lombardo, Rossi, Varacka, Corbatta, Ludovico Avio, Menéndez, Ángel Labruna, Norberto Boggio.
NORTHERN IRELAND Gregg, Keith, McMichael, Blanchflower (c), Cunningham, Peacock, Bingham, Cush, Fay Coyle, McIlroy, McParland.

Now this *was* a surprise. For their only match against Northern Ireland so far, Argentina brought back the 39-year-old Labruna, once a genuinely great player. They were heard whistling and singing before the match, which they eventually dominated – this after Bingham's cross, from Blanchflower's back-heel, had been headed in by McParland. Menéndez put away a precise pass by Avio, who headed the third, but Keith was unlucky to concede the penalty when a cross by Avio came up off his thigh onto his hand. Ireland should have regained the lead when Cush cleverly stepped over McIlroy's centre only for Coyle to shoot 'dismally wide' from six yards. He 'had a couple of bad misses' and wasn't capped again. By the end, the Argentinians were taking the ball off each other to perform party tricks (both Gregg and McIlroy used the phrase taking the mickey).

11 June 1958 – Olympia, Hälsingborg – 25,000 – Arthur Ellis (ENG)

CZECHOSLOVAKIA (2) 2
Dvořák pen 24, Zikán 42

WEST GERMANY (0) 2
Schäfer 60, Rahn 71

CZECHOSLOVAKIA Dolejší, Mráz, Novák (c), Pluskal, Ján Popluhár, Masopust, Hovorka, Dvořák, Pavol Molnár, Jiří Feureisl, Zdeněk Zikán.
WEST GERMANY Herkenrath, Stollenwerk, Juskowiak, Karl-Heinz Schnellinger, Erhardt, Szymaniak, Rahn, Walter, Seeler, Schäfer (c), Bernhard Klodt.

In a strange group, sometimes well balanced, sometimes the opposite, the Germans made

LEADING GOALSCORERS 1958

13	Just Fontaine	FRA
6	Helmut Rahn	WG
6	Pelé	BRZ

one of their famous comebacks but were grateful for a controversial goal, Schäfer barging Dolejší over the line. The Czechs appealed against the appointment of Ellis for their next match, but were presumably happy enough after it.

15 June 1958 – Malmö Stadion, Malmö – 21,990 – Joaquim de Campos (POR)

NORTHERN IRELAND (1) 2
McParland 18, 60

WEST GERMANY (1) 2
Rahn 20, Seeler 78

1958

NORTHERN IRELAND Gregg, Keith, McMichael, Blanchflower (c), Cunningham, Peacock, Bingham, Cush, Tommy Casey, McIlroy, McParland.
WEST GERMANY Herkenrath, Stollenwerk, Juskowiak, Eckel, Erhardt, Szymaniak, Rahn, Walter, Seeler, Schäfer (c), Klodt.

Everything, here and in Hälsingborg, pointed to the Irish going out – but they played their best game of the tournament, Gregg making 'half a dozen fabulous saves' despite hobbling throughout the match (his fullbacks took the goal kicks). They went ahead when Cush challenged the goalkeeper, the ball went loose to the right, and McIlroy's cross reached the unmarked McParland. Rahn, showing a full range of skills for such a powerhouse, hit a beautiful chip over Gregg for the equaliser, McParland volleyed in after Bingham headed on Cush's corner, and Seeler at last got through with a massive 25-yarder. Even then, Ireland almost won it, McParland heading onto the top of the bar from Cunningham's free kick. All honours even.

These were the first matches ever played by Northern Ireland against the three countries in their group.

15 June 1958 – Olympia, Hälsingborg – 16,418 –
Arthur Ellis (ENG)

CZECHOSLOVAKIA   (3) 6
Dvořák 8, Zikán 17, 39, Feureisl 68,
Hovorka 81, 89

ARGENTINA   (0) 1
Corbatta pen 64

CZECHOSLOVAKIA Dolejší, Mráz, Novák (c),
Dvořák, Popluhár, Masopust, Hovorka, Molnár,
Feureisl, Borovička, Zikán.
ARGENTINA Carrizo, Dellacha (c), Vairo, Lombardo,
Rossi, Varacka, Corbatta, Avio, Menéndez,
Labruna, Cruz.

Argentina were expected to win, but their slow
ancient game was taken apart by pace and
movement. Dvořák scored with a cross-shot
from outside the area, then two terrible defensive errors presented the ball to Zikán, who
also clipped in the third when Carrizo fumbled
a gentle shot. Hovorka went round Carrizo for
his first, then put away a low cross which cut
out the keeper and defender. The defeat,
Argentina's worst ever, put an end to Stabile's
reign as manager, which had lasted since 1941.
Six of his last team weren't capped again.

PLAY-OFF

17 June 1958 – Malmö Stadion, Malmö – 6,196 –
Maurice Guigue (FRA)

NORTHERN IRELAND   (1) (1) 2
McParland 44, 97

CZECHOSLOVAKIA   (1) (1) 1
Zikán 18

NORTHERN IRELAND Norman Uprichard, Keith,
McMichael, Blanchflower (c), Cunningham, Peacock,
Bingham, Cush, Jackie Scott, McIlroy, McParland.
CZECHOSLOVAKIA Dolejší, Mráz, Novák (c), Titus
Buberník, Popluhár, Masopust, Dvořák, Molnár,
Feureisl, Borovička, Zikán.
SENT OFF: Buberník 100.

CONSECUTIVE DEFEATS

9	Mexico	1930–58
7	Switzerland	1954–66
6	El Salvador	1970–82

El Salvador have lost every game they've played.

More heroics. The Irish had beaten this side
before, but not with so many players injured:
Gregg and Casey out, Uprichard breaking a
bone in his left hand, Peacock and Cush limping. And there was another new cap (Scott) at
centre-forward. They went a goal down when
Borovicka nudged Keith off the ball, the ball
bounced in the area, and Zikán headed in –
but McParland equalised at an important time,
driving the ball in after Cush had three shots
blocked.

In an extra-time the eight fit men could
have done without, Blanchflower curled a cross
just beyond the keeper to be volleyed home by
McParland, the unexpected bombardier (the
goals in this tournament were his first for
Ireland since the two on his debut in 1954).
Buberník was sent off on his international
debut for spitting at the referee and Scott had a
goal disallowed near the end. Just about
Northern Ireland's finest hour. Or two.

GROUP 1

	P	W	D	L	F	A	Pts
West Germany	3	1	2	0	7	5	4
Czechoslovakia	3	1	1	1	8	4	3
Northern Ireland	3	1	1	1	4	5	3
Argentina	3	1	0	2	5	10	2

*Czechoslovakia and Northern Ireland played off
to join West Germany in the quarter-finals.*

GROUP 2

France, Paraguay, Scotland, Yugoslavia. [No seeds.]

8 June 1958 – Idrottsparken, Norrköping – 16,518 – Juan Gardeazábal (SPA)

FRANCE **(2) 7**
Fontaine 24, 30, 68, Piantoni 51, Wisnieski 62, Kopa 70, Vincent 84

PARAGUAY **(2) 3**
Amarilla 20, pen 43, Romero 50

FRANCE François Remetter, Raymond Kaelbel, André Lerond, Armand Penverne, Bob Jonquet (c), Jean-Jacques Marcel, Maryan Wisnieski, Raymond Kopaszewski (Kopa), Just Fontaine, Roger Piantoni, Jean Vincent. *Paul Nicolas, Albert Batteux, et al.*
PARAGUAY Ramón Mayeregger, Edelmiro Arévalo, Juan Vicente Lezcano, Agustin Miranda, Ignacio Achucarro, Salvador Villalba, Juan Bautista Agüero (c), José Parodi, Jorgelino Romero, Cayetano Ré, Florencio Amarilla. *Aurelio González.*

France had scored a few goals in qualifying – 6-3, 8-3, 5-1 – but no-one expected anything like this, against the team who'd thumped Uruguay and led 3-2 here. Amarilla cracked a left-footed free kick through a broken wall, and Romero put Paraguay back in front after holding off a challenge – but Fontaine twice ran onto through-balls to score, Piantoni equalised with a glorious lob-volley across the keeper, and Wisnieski converted a free kick by Kopa, who made the seventh for Vincent and scored the sixth with his knee! Kopa was wasted on the wing at Real Madrid, and Fontaine had to play as a lone striker because René Bliard was injured – but their partnership was about to become legendary. The original spelling of Wisnieski was Wisniewski, but the French had a real problem with that second W.

8 June 1958 – Arosvallen, Västerås – 9,591 – Paul Wyssling (SWI)

SCOTLAND **(0) 1**
Murray 47

YUGOSLAVIA **(1) 1**
Petaković 6

SCOTLAND Tommy Younger (c), Eric Caldow, John Hewie, Eddie Turnbull, Bobby Evans, Doug Cowie, Graham Leggat, Jimmy Murray, Jackie Mudie, Bobby Collins, Stewart Imlach. *Selection committee.*
YUGOSLAVIA Vladimir Beara, Vasilije Šijaković, Tomislav Crnković, Dobrosav Krstić, Branko Zebec (c), Vujadin Boškov, Aleksandar Petaković, Todor Veselinović, Milos Milutinović, Dragoslav Šekularac, Zdravko Rajkov. *Aleksandar Tirnanić.*

Against expectations, Scotland recovered from an early goal by the player who'd scored a hat-trick against England. A clever feint by Veselinović fooled Cowie, and Petaković had time to pick his spot low in the far corner past a 'somewhat slow' Younger. Petaković looked likely to destroy Hewie, but didn't see enough of the ball. And the cultured Boškov never took a grip on the midfield, so 'the Scots were allowed many mistakes.' They were also quick to realise that Beara was uncomfortable when challenged under the high ball. Murray beat him to Turnbull's cross from the right and headed in, the pair of them left lying on the ground facing the ball in the corner of the net. Mudie was unlucky to have a goal disallowed when the ball went in off him after Beara had simply dropped it – but Veselinović hit a post near the end.

Collins, stubby and skilful, was Scotland's best player – once he'd sorted out a few things in the playground. A 'ridiculously tolerant' referee allowed him to retaliate at length after Šekularac had hit him in the mouth. Evans and the skilful Milutinović came out even in a rather more decorous duel.

1930
1934
1938
1950
1954

1958

1962
1966
1970
1974
1978
1982
1986
1990
1994
1998
2002
2006

11 June 1958 – Idrottsparken, Norrköping – 11,665 – Vincenzo Orlandini (ITA)

PARAGUAY   (2) 3
Agüero 3, Ré 44, Parodi 74

SCOTLAND   (1) 2
Mudie 32, Collins 76

PARAGUAY Samuel Aguilar, Arévalo, Eligio Echagüe, Villalba, Lezcano, Achucarro, Agüero (c), Parodi, Romero, Ré, Amarilla.
SCOTLAND Younger (c), Alex Parker, Caldow, Turnbull, Evans, Cowie, Leggat, Collins, Mudie, Archie Robertson, Willie Fernie.

This time someone got it badly wrong beforehand. Two of the Scottish squad, Robertson and Tommy Docherty, were sent to watch Paraguay play, reporting back that they were 'rough and fit and good.' Despite this, Scotland left out the combative likes of Mackay, Baird and Docherty himself and picked a forward line made up of the slim and the small, 'thrust aside much too easily by unscrupulous opponents'. The 35-year-old Turnbull didn't last the pace this time, and Younger's uncertainty contributed to all three goals and the end of his international career.

Evans did his best at the back, but a miskick by Parker allowed Agüero in to shoot 'not particularly fast' past Younger. Mudie, who 'finished a crippled player', equalised after a move involving Collins and Leggat – but an 'even worse blunder' by Parker allowed Amarilla to shoot and Ré to knock the ball in off the goalkeeper and a post. Finally Younger, under pressure from two opponents, dropped a corner and Parodi put away the loose ball. Collins' fine long-range drive (the 500th goal scored in the finals) held out some hope, but in the last minute Leggat and Mudie missed an open goal between them.

11 June 1958 – Arosvallen, Västerås – 12,217 – Mervyn Griffiths (WAL)

YUGOSLAVIA   (1) 3
Petaković 16, Veselinović 63, 87

FRANCE   (1) 2
Fontaine 4, 85

YUGOSLAVIA Beara, Novak Tomić, Crnković, Krstić, Zebec (c), Boškov, Petaković, Veselinović, Milutinović, Šekularac, Rajkov.
FRANCE Remetter, Kaelbel, Roger Marche (c), Penverne, Jonquet, Lerond, Wisnieski, Kopa, Fontaine, Piantoni, Vincent.

Again there was no stopping Fontaine, who lashed in Piantoni's cross from the left and delicately lobbed Beara – but the French gave all their opponents a chance. Petaković flicked in a ground shot after a corner, a defensive error let Veselinović in for his first, and he ran in to lunge home the winner, leaving France needing at least a draw with Scotland to qualify.

15 June 1958 – Tunavallen, Eskilstuna – 13,103 – Martin Macko (CZE)

YUGOSLAVIA   (2) 3
Ognjanović 12, Veselinović 28, Rajkov 73

PARAGUAY   (1) 3
Parodi 20, Agüero 51, Romero 80

YUGOSLAVIA Beara, Tomić, Crnković, Krstić, Zebec (c), Boškov, Petaković, Veselinović, Rade Ognjanović, Šekularac, Rajkov.
PARAGUAY Aguilar, Arévalo, Echagüe, Villalba, Lezcano, Achucarro, Agüero (c), Parodi, Romero, Ré, Amarilla.

A win would have put Paraguay through, and again they scored three goals – but their defence was caught too square too often. Ognjanović put a left-wing cross into an empty net, Veselinović drove in low from twenty yards, and the long-range shot that eliminated them was badly missed by Aguilar. For Paraguay, Parodi lived up to his name by scoring without meaning to, the ball hitting his leg as he fell, Agüero was tenacious after his first attempt was blocked by Beara, and Romero poked a shot in off a post. End to end, but what a way to run a railroad.

---

15 June 1958 – Eyravallen, Örebro – 13,554 – Juan Brozzi (ARG)

FRANCE **(2) 2**
Kopa 22, Fontaine 45

SCOTLAND **(0) 1**
Baird 65

FRANCE Claude Abbes, Kaelbel, Lerond, Penverne, Jonquet (c), Marcel, Wisnieski, Kopa, Fontaine, Piantoni, Vincent.
SCOTLAND Bill Brown, Caldow, Hewie, Turnbull, Evans (c), Dave Mackay, Collins, Murray, Mudie, Sammy Baird, Imlach.

At last Scotland picked the right team: Mackay and Baird alongside the pugnacious red-haired Evans, Brown winning his first cap after being Younger's reserve for the previous 24 matches. And they had the chance to equalise when Hewie, their tall South African fullback, smacked a penalty against the post immediately after Kopa's goal. But Fontaine hit the bar twice as well as scoring from a long ball and

GROUP 2

	P	W	D	L	F	A	Pts
France	3	2	0	1	11	7	4
Yugoslavia	3	1	2	0	7	6	4
Paraguay	3	1	1	1	9	12	3
Scotland	3	0	1	2	4	6	1

France and Yugoslavia qualified for the quarter-finals.

cutting the ball back for Kopa to sidefoot home. Baird replied with a good early shot from a straightforward through-pass, but again Scotland simply hadn't been good enough – and wouldn't be back in the finals for another sixteen years.

GROUP 3

Hungary, Mexico, Sweden, Wales. [No seeds.]

1958

---

8 June 1958 – Råsunda, Solna, Stockholm – 34,107 – Nikolai Latyshev (USR)

SWEDEN **(1) 3**
Simonsson 16, 64, Liedholm pen 57

MEXICO **(0) 0**

SWEDEN Karl Svensson, Orvar Bergmark, Sven Axbom, Nils Liedholm (c), Bengt 'Julle' Gustavsson, Sigvard Parling, Kurt Hamrin, Bror Mellberg, Agne Simonsson, Gunnar Gren, Lennart 'Nacka' Skoglund. *George Raynor (ENG)*.
MEXICO Antonio Carbajal (c), Jesús del Muro, José Villegas, Alfonso Portugal, Jorge Romo, Francisco Flores, Alfredo Hernández, Salvador Reyes, Carlos Calderón, Crescencio Gutiérrez, Enrique Sesma. *Antonio López Herranz (SPA), with Ignacio Trelles.*

Sweden's turn to have the Mexicans as an easy opener, though they were lucky that Flores hit a post early on. Hamrin was fouled for the penalty, and Simonsson converted two short crosses from Skoglund, one by lunging ahead of the last defender to prod in a volley, the second coolly with the side of his foot. But Sweden had played at a fearfully slow pace to accommodate their veterans.

Some sources list Hernández as captain, but it's clearly Carbajal on TV.

1930
1934
1938
1950
1954
1958
1962
1966
1970
1974
1978
1982
1986
1990
1994
1998
2002
2006

8 June 1958 – Jernvallen, Sandviken – 15,343 – José María Codesal (URU)

HUNGARY **(1) 1**
Bozsik 4

WALES **(1) 1**
J Charles 26

HUNGARY Gyula Grosics, Sándor Mátrai, László Sárosi, József Bozsik, Ferenc Sipos, Pál Berendi, Károly Sándor, Nándor Hidegkuti (c), Lajos Tichy, Deszõ Bundzsák, Máté Fenyvesi. *Lajos Baróti.*
WALES Jack Kelsey, Stuart Williams, Mel Hopkins, Derrick Sullivan, Mel Charles, Dave Bowen (c), Colin Webster, Terry Medwin, John Charles, Ivor Allchurch, Cliff Jones. *Jimmy Murphy.*

Welsh resources were so thin that they had to use Medwin out of position, and it was just as well for them that Hidegkuti, now 36, had a dismal match. After Bozsik's shot had surprised Kelsey out of the shadows of the stand, John Charles climbed above the defence to head in a corner. But his massive presence was soon reduced by a series of fouls tolerated by the referee, who also denied Allchurch a penalty. Codesal's son Edgardo, representing Mexico, refereed the 1990 Final. John and Mel Charles were brothers.

11 June 1958 – Råsunda, Solna, Stockholm – 15,150 – Leo Lemešić (YUG)

MEXICO **(0) 1**
Belmonte 89

WALES **(1) 1**
Allchurch 32

MEXICO Carbajal (c), del Muro, Miguel Gutiérrez, Raúl Cárdenas, Romo, Flores, Jaime Belmonte, Reyes, Carlos Blanco, Carlos González, Sesma.
WALES Kelsey, Williams, Hopkins, Colin Baker, M Charles, Bowen (c), Webster, Medwin, J Charles, Allchurch, Jones.

In their tenth finals match, Mexico avoided defeat for the first time, but Wales should have wrapped this one up earlier. Their goal came from a mishit shot after Webster's corner, Mexico's from a diving header. The injured Sullivan was replaced by new cap Baker, his understudy at Cardiff City, who had a disappointing match, as did Jones, one of the fastest wingers in world football. Romo cracked a bone in his leg near the end.

The 50-year-old Lemešić was one of that very rare breed, an international footballer (1929–32) turned international referee (see Palotai 1974 and Daina 1986).

12 June 1958 – Råsunda, Solna, Stockholm – 38,850 – Jack Mowat (SCO)

SWEDEN **(1) 2**
Hamrin 34, 55

HUNGARY **(0) 1**
Tichy 76

SWEDEN Svensson, Bergmark, Axbom, Liedholm (c), Gustavsson, Parling, Hamrin, Mellberg, Simonsson, Gren, Skoglund.
HUNGARY Grosics, Mátrai, Sárosi, Ferenc Szojka, Sipos, Berendi, Sándor, Tichy, Bozsik (c), Bundzsák, Fenyvesi.

It's now said that the hosts were rather lucky to win, after a shot by Tichy hit the bar and appeared to cross the line – but Svensson got a touch to it, and replays show the ball landing in front of the line. Besides, Sweden could even afford to miss a penalty, Liedholm shooting wide after 71 minutes. It's true, however, that both of Hamrin's goals were rather fortunate, the first from close range after two defenders had a chance to clear, the other with a lob that may have been put in by a defender's lunge. Tichy, whose physique belied his name, eventually got his goal with a marvellous drive into the top corner.

15 June 1958 – Råsunda, Solna, Stockholm – 30,287 – Lucien Van Nuffel (BEL)

SWEDEN 0

WALES 0

SWEDEN Svensson, Bergmark, Axbom, Reino Börjesson, Gustavsson (c), Parling, Bengt Berndtsson, Arne Selmosson, Henry Källgren, Gösta Löfgren, Skoglund.
WALES Kelsey, Williams, Hopkins, Sullivan, M Charles, Bowen (c), Roy Vernon, Ron Hewitt, J Charles, Allchurch, Jones.

To Hungary's wry indignation, Sweden picked several reserves, including four forwards – but Wales were still lucky to survive. Skoglund missed four good chances and John Charles played too deep, either to avoid Gustavsson, whom he called 'the greatest centre-half I have ever seen,' or to see some of the ball for a change. Kelsey was fast emerging as the best keeper in the competition.

15 June 1958 – Jernvallen, Sandviken – 13,310 – Aarne Eriksson (FIN)

HUNGARY (1) 4
Tichy 19, 46, Sándor 54, Bencsics 60

MEXICO (0) 0

HUNGARY István Ilku, Mátrai, Sárosi, Szojka, Sipos, Antal Kotász, László Budai, József Bencsics, Hidegkuti (c), Tichy, Sándor.
MEXICO Carbajal (c), del Muro, M Gutiérrez, Cárdenas, Guillermo Sepúlveda, Flores, Belmonte, Reyes, Blanco, González, Sesma.

Tichy was obviously getting a taste for it. First he beat a man, fed Sándor on the left and banged in the low cross, then dummied a defender before shooting marvellously across Carbajal from over twenty yards. Sándor blasted in from an indirect free kick inside the penalty area, and it's impossible to be sure

who got the last touch for the fourth, which was a real mess: some call it a González o.g. Hungary were now warm favourites to win the play-off.

PLAY-OFF

17 June 1958 – Råsunda, Solna, Stockholm – 2,823 – Nikolai Latyshev (USR)

WALES (0) 2
Allchurch 55, Medwin 76

HUNGARY (1) 1
Tichy 33

WALES Kelsey, Williams, Hopkins, Sullivan, M Charles, Bowen (c), Medwin, Hewitt, J Charles, Allchurch, Jones.
HUNGARY Grosics, Mátrai, Sárosi, Bozsik (c), Sipos, Kotász, Budai, Bencsics, Bundzsák, Tichy, Fenyvesi.
SENT OFF: Sipos 84.

The day before, Imre Nagy, leader of the 1956 uprising, had been executed, and the match was played to an eerie background of Free Hungarian chanting and banners draped in black. The football, for what it mattered, was suitably sombre, often brutal, the Hungarians continuing their assault on John Charles, with Kotász and Mátrai the chief culprits.

A cross by Budai, unmarked on the right, reached Tichy, unmarked on the left, and his confident volley beat Kelsey low at the near post. The Welsh replied with perhaps the greatest shot ever seen in the World Cup. When John Charles flicked on a pass to the left, the ball drifted high just inside the Hungarian penalty area. Allchurch lost his marker and met the ball with a full swing of his left foot, volleying it high just inside the far post. A picture goal. With the TV cameras right behind it, too.

Grosics, who gave the defender an ear-bashing, had only himself to blame for the winner, hitting a goal kick so slowly that Medwin was able to steal it from Sárosi and

1930
1934
1938
1950
1954
1958
1962
1966
1970
1974
1978
1982
1986
1990
1994
1998
2002
2006

shoot home. Sipos was sent off for hacking down Hewitt, who was stretchered off as the remains of the great Hungarian team made a graceless exit. Wales were in the quarter-finals, but the adventure would surely have to end there: the endless fouling had finally caught up with John Charles.

GROUP 3

	P	W	D	L	F	A	Pts
Sweden	3	2	1	0	5	1	5
Hungary	3	1	1	1	6	3	3
Wales	3	0	3	0	2	2	3
Mexico	3	0	1	2	1	8	1

Hungary and Wales played off to join Sweden in the quarter-finals.

GROUP 4

Austria, Brazil, England, USSR. [No seeds.]

8 June 1958 – Nya Ullevi, Gothenburg – 49,348 – István Zsolt (HUN)

ENGLAND   **(0) 2**
Kevan 66, Finney pen 85

USSR   **(1) 2**
Simonian 13, A Ivanov 56

ENGLAND Colin McDonald, Don Howe, Tommy Banks, Eddie Clamp, Billy Wright (c), Bill Slater, Bryan Douglas, Bobby Robson, Derek Kevan, Johnny Haynes, Tom Finney. *Walter Winterbottom.*
USSR Lev Yashin, Vladimir Kessarev, Boris Kuznetsov, Yuri Voinov, Konstantin Krijevsky, Viktor Tsarev, Aleksandr Ivanov, Valentin Ivanov, Nikita Simonian (c), Sergei Salnikov, Anatoly Ilyin. *Gavril Katchalin.*

Winterbottom picked the same team which had been unlucky to only draw in Moscow three weeks earlier, but they were second best for most of this match. Aleksandr Ivanov, winning his first cap, crossed hard and low from the right, and McDonald could only push the ball out to Simonian. The second goal was started by Kessarev, who came up from the back and found Tsarev in space that should have been occupied by Clamp; a third pass put Aleksandr Ivanov clear. The Soviets protected their lead with some hard tackling on the England wingers.

Vittorio Pozzo is alleged to have described a goal by Kevan, the big rawboned England centre-forward, as having been 'scored with the outside of his head' – but they all count, none more so than the one coming up. Wright's long straightforward free kick was touched on by Douglas and put in by the outside of Kevan's head, leaving the great goalkeeper in mid-air with legs splayed. Equally undignified was Yashin's reaction to the penalty, throwing his cap at the referee. The kick, awarded for a collision between Voinov and Haynes, was tucked just inside a post, but it was Finney's last contribution before an injured ankle forced him out of the tournament. Robson had a goal disallowed for a challenge on Yashin, but England were happy with the draw.

8 June 1958 – Rimnersvallen, Uddevalla – 17,778 – Maurice Guigue (FRA)

BRAZIL   **(1) 3**
Mazzola 37, 85, N Santos 50

AUSTRIA   **(0) 0**

BRAZIL Gylmar (dos Santos), Nílton de Sordi, Nílton Santos, Dino Sani, Hideraldo Bellini (c), Orlando (Peçanha), Joel (Martins), 'Didi' (Waldir Pereira), 'Mazzola' (José Altafini), 'Dida' (Edivaldo Alves), Mário Zagallo. *Vicente Feola.*

AUSTRIA Rudi Szanwald, Paul Halla, Franz Swoboda, Gerhard Hanappi (c), Ernst Happel, Karl Koller, Walter Horak, Helmut Senekowitsch, Hans Buzek, Alfred Körner, Walter Schleger. *Josef Argauer, with Josef Molzer.*

Despite the scoreline, Feola wasn't happy with his forwards, worried that the 19-year-old Mazzola was more concerned with an impending move to Italy. Nevertheless he scored twice here, including a marvellous full-blooded twenty-yarder from Didi's through-ball. Nílton Santos got the second after winning a tackle and taking a return pass. If the team wasn't quite right, the outclassed Austrians didn't notice.

Mazzola, who went on to play for Italy in the 1962 finals, took his nickname from Valentino Mazzola, who died in the 1949 air crash and whose son Sandro played in three World Cups. The crowd figure is still the record for the stadium, which was built especially for the World Cup.

11 June 1958 – Nya Ullevi, Gothenburg – 40,895 – Albert Dusch (GER)

BRAZIL 0

ENGLAND 0

BRAZIL Gylmar, De Sordi, N Santos, Dino Sani, Bellini (c), Orlando, Joel, Didi, 'Vavá' (Edvaldo Izídio Neto), Mazzola, Zagallo.
ENGLAND McDonald, Howe, Banks, Clamp, Wright (c), Slater, Douglas, Robson, Kevan, Haynes, Alan A'Court.

England approached this in a negative way, but rightly so: Brazil had more ability. The Tottenham coach Bill Nicholson, out here as Winterbottom's assistant, identified Didi as the focal point of the attack and set out to neutralise him.

Didi was 30 by now, but age didn't matter with someone who rarely did anything at speed, loping his way through three World Cups, using that rare gift of finding space without dashing into it. In every match, despite the great players who were to come, he was the team's point of light.

But England played him well, using Slater as a man-marker with Howe and Banks covering Wright against Brazil's double spearhead. It worked, but only just: Mazzola and Vavá hit the woodwork. At the other end Kevan might have had a penalty when he went down in Bellini's challenge. It was the first goalless draw in the finals, and the first time Brazil failed to score in a World Cup match.

11 June 1958 – Ryavallen, Borås – 21,239 – Carl Frederik Jørgensen (DEN)

USSR (1) 2
A Ivanov 15, V Ivanov 62

AUSTRIA (0) 0

USSR Yashin, Kessarev, Kuznetsov, Voinov, Krijevsky, Tsarev, A Ivanov, V Ivanov, Simonian (c), Salnikov, Ilyin.
AUSTRIA Kurt Schmied, Ernst Kozlicek, Karl Stotz, Swoboda, Hanappi (c), Koller, Horak, Paul Kozlicek, Buzek, Körner, Senekowitsch.

Austria dominated the first hour, but young Buzek hit a penalty straight at Yashin when Kessarev fouled Stotz in the 55th minute. The Soviets had taken the lead when Simonian's centre reached Aleksandr Ivanov, who later crossed for his namesake to score the second in a breakaway. The Kozliceks were brothers.

15 June 1958 – Ryavallen, Borås – 15,872 – Jan Bronkhorst (HOL)

AUSTRIA (1) 2
Koller 15, Körner 71

ENGLAND (0) 2
Haynes 56, Kevan 74

1930
1934
1938
1950
1954
1958
1962
1966
1970
1974
1978
1982
1986
1990
1994
1998
2002
2006

AUSTRIA Szanwald, Walter Kollmann, Swoboda, Hanappi (c), Happel, Koller, E Kozlicek, P Kozlicek, Buzek, Körner, Senekowitsch.

ENGLAND McDonald, Howe, Banks, Clamp, Wright (c), Slater, Douglas, Robson, Kevan, Haynes, A'Court.

Having drawn with the strong teams, England were expected to beat the other one, but were unfortunate that Austria's first goals of the tournament were both scored from long range. On another day, Koller's shot might have gone into the crowd instead of the very top corner. Körner's left-footer went in low off a post.

In between, Haynes smashed the ball in from two yards after Szanwald had made an unbelievable hash of A'Court's simple shot. Kevan scored the second from Haynes' angled pass, and Robson had a late goal disallowed when the ball went in off his hand. But again the attack hadn't been up to standard: Haynes and Douglas had just spent a season in the Second Division, and A'Court was no substitute for Finney. The young Bobby Charlton, who'd scored three goals in his first two England matches that year, was again left out.

There used to be serious confusion as to who refereed this match. Some sources mention Aksel Asmussen of Denmark but most agree on Bronkhorst, including the leading Austrian statistician (who quotes 'all Austrian publications') and the Dutch and Danish FAs.

Brazil had brought a psychiatrist with them, João Carvalhães. Feola, thinking of including two new players, asked him what he thought of them. The first, quoth the good doctor, was 'too young, too infantile,' the other so unsophisticated that 'including him in the team would be a disaster.' Feola disagreed and picked them both. They were Pelé and Garrincha. Brazil had found their team.

Zito was another important replacement, a better tackler than Dino Sani – but Garrincha and Pelé made the difference up front. And how. Garrincha nearly broke the near post in the first minute. Pelé hit one in the second, and Vavá shot in Didi's flick in the third. The Soviets used Netto to mark Didi, but he hadn't fully recovered from injury and it didn't work. Vavá stabbed in a loose ball for the second.

Pelé missed two early chances but obviously had all the skills in the world, eerily assured for a boy of 17. No-one has ever been more explosive from a standing start than Garrincha, who flew past defenders on legs that were bent from birth. Vavá, far less skilful than Mazzola, was a hammer up front. Even Yashin had to hold his hands up.

---

15 June 1958 – Nya Ullevi, Gothenburg – 50,928 – Maurice Guigue (FRA)

BRAZIL (1) 2
Vavá 3, 77

USSR (0) 0

BRAZIL Gylmar, De Sordi, N Santos, 'Zito' (José Ely de Miranda), Bellini (c), Orlando, 'Garrincha' (Manoel Francisco dos Santos), Didi, Vavá, 'Pelé' (Édson Arantes do Nascimento), Zagallo.
USSR Yashin, Kessarev, Kuznetsov, Voinov, Krijevsky, Tsarev, A Ivanov, V Ivanov, Simonian, Igor Netto (c), Ilyin.

PLAY-OFF

17 June 1958 – Nya Ullevi, Gothenburg – 23,182 – Albert Dusch (GER)

USSR (0) 1
Ilyin 69

ENGLAND (0) 0

USSR Yashin, Kessarev, Kuznetsov, Voinov, Krijevsky, Tsarev, Herman Apukhtin, V Ivanov, Simonian (c), Yuri Falin, Ilyin.
ENGLAND McDonald, Howe, Banks, Ronnie Clayton, Wright (c), Slater, Peter Brabrook, Peter Broadbent, Kevan, Haynes, A'Court.

TOURNAMENTS AS CAPTAIN

3	Billy Wright	ENG	1950–54–58
3	Ladislav Novák	CZE	1954–58–62
3	Björn Nordqvist	SWE	1970–74–78
3	Diego Maradona	ARG	1986–90–94
3	Carlos Valderrama	COL	1990–94–98
3	Paolo Maldini	ITA	1994–98–02

Winterbottom at last made changes, but they were unexpected. Still no Charlton, but a return for Clayton, whose performance had been 'just too bad to be true' in Belgrade, and first caps for Broadbent and the 20-year-old Brabrook.

In the end, the personnel didn't matter, as England were unluckier than ever. Six minutes before half-time, Broadbent's low cross from the right found two England players unmarked in front of goal. The first, Brabrook, somehow managed to turn it back straight to Yashin. In the second half, he broke through a tackle and galloped in on goal, only for his shot to trundle against a post. Then he ran at the heart of the defence and hit the same part of the same post. Finally, he slammed the ball in after accidentally controlling it with his hand.

Almost inevitably, when the USSR hit a post, the ball went in. McDonald ruined his excellent tournament by hitting a goal kick

GROUP 4

	P	W	D	L	F	A	Pts
Brazil	3	2	1	0	5	0	5
USSR	3	1	1	1	4	4	3
England	3	0	3	0	4	4	3
Austria	3	0	1	2	2	7	1

England and the USSR played off to join Brazil in the quarter-finals.

straight to Falin, the ball eventually reaching the unmarked Ilyin, who scored with a low cross-shot. Tough to bear, but England hadn't looked like contenders. Again.

QUARTER-FINALS

19 June 1958 – Råsunda, Solna, Stockholm – 31,900 – Reg Leafe (ENG)

SWEDEN (0) 2
Hamrin 49, Simonsson 88

USSR (0) 0

SWEDEN Svensson, Bergmark, Axbom, Börjesson, Gustavsson, Parling, Hamrin, Gren, Simonsson, Liedholm (c), Skoglund.
USSR Yashin, Kessarev, Kuznetsov, Voinov, Krijevsky, Tsarev, A Ivanov, V Ivanov, Simonian (c), Salnikov, Ilyin.

Raynor, astute as ever, recognised that England's problems with the USSR stemmed from Voinov's domination of Haynes, their only creative source. So he turned the tables, setting Liedholm to mark the marker. Gren took over the task of making the play, and this time the Soviet luck deserted them. Hamrin broke clear on the right, his attempted square pass came back off a defender, and his header sent the ball spinning in crazily at the near post. Later he made the second for Simonsson. The three teams who won the group play-offs couldn't manage a goal between them two days later.

19 June 1958 – Idrottsparken, Norrköping – 11,800 – Juan Gardeazábal (SPA)

FRANCE (1) 4
Wisnieski 44, Fontaine 56, 64, Piantoni 68

NORTHERN IRELAND (0) 0

1930
1934
1938
1950
1954
1958
1962
1966
1970
1974
1978
1982
1986
1990
1994
1998
2002
2006

FRANCE Abbes, Kaelbel, Lerond, Penverne, Jonquet (c), Marcel, Wisnieski, Kopa, Fontaine, Piantoni, Vincent.
NORTHERN IRELAND Gregg, Keith, McMichael, Blanchflower (c), Cunningham, Cush, Bingham, Casey, Scott, McIlroy, McParland.

A game too far for the walking wounded. The hardworking Peacock was out, Uprichard's broken hand meant Gregg had to play even though he was using a walking stick around the team hotel, and Casey's leg wound re-opened during the match. But the Irish had only their management to blame for the ridiculous travel arrangements that made them spend twelve hours in a coach 48 hours earlier.

They held out almost to half-time, but then Wisnieski ran onto a loose ball on the right and Gregg couldn't rush out in time. The second half wasn't a contest. Fontaine headed in Piantoni's cross then went round a defender and cracked a low shot across Gregg, and Piantoni broke through a tired challenge to score the fourth. The Irish, who'd suffered enough by then, had done themselves very proud. They were the first British team to win two matches in any finals tournament.

19 June 1958 – Nya Ullevi, Gothenburg – 25,923 – Fritz Seipelt (AUT)

BRAZIL   (0) **1**
Pelé 73

WALES   (0) **0**

BRAZIL Gylmar, De Sordi, N Santos, Zito, Bellini (c), Orlando, Garrincha, Didi, Mazzola, Pelé, Zagallo.
WALES Kelsey, Williams, Hopkins, Sullivan, M Charles, Bowen (c), Medwin, Hewitt, Webster, Allchurch, Jones.

John Charles couldn't play and his replacement Webster missed Wales' only chance of the match, hitting the side netting after Jones had beaten De Sordi early on. After that, Kelsey v the Brazilian attack, the courageous keeper beaten only because Pelé's shot was deflected by Williams.

But this makes it sound as if it was going wide until someone stuck a foot out. In fact Pelé had his back to goal when he took Didi's headed pass on his chest, flicked it inside Charles, then let the ball bounce at last before volleying hard from close in. Williams' tackle simply slowed the ball down on its way in. Pelé wasn't lucky, he was brilliant.

Meanwhile Mazzola's marvellous overhead kick from sixteen yards was disallowed for no obvious reason. Fair-haired and quick, sometimes scintillating, he went on to score the goals that won the 1963 European Cup for Milan and a semi-final for Juventus in 1973. But the match against Wales was his last for Brazil, which was a shame because his partnership with Pelé, average age 18, should have been one of the greats.

Garrincha hadn't had it easy against Hopkins, and Kelsey and Bowen had been excellent throughout the tournament – but, unlike the Irish, Wales never found a goalscorer, which led to an excess of caution, which didn't endear them. And of course they were lucky to be there in the first place. These were their very first matches against each of the four countries they played in these finals.

Gylmar's 17th international clean sheet equalled a world record set in 1918. He broke it against England in 1959.

19 June 1958 – Malmö Stadion, Malmö – 20,055 – Paul Wyssling (SWI)

WEST GERMANY   (1) **1**
Rahn 12

YUGOSLAVIA   (0) **0**

WEST GERMANY Herkenrath, Stollenwerk, Juskowiak, Eckel, Erhardt, Szymaniak, Rahn, Walter, Seeler, Schmidt, Schäfer (c).

YUGOSLAVIA Srboljub Krivokuća, Crnković, Šijaković, Boškov, Zebec (c), Krstić, Petaković, Ognjanović, Milutinović, Veselinović, Rajkov.

Rather dull all round, the German minders muffling an attack that missed the promptings of the hot-blooded Šekularac – but at least it was won by a magnificent goal, Rahn beating three men on the right before scoring with a low shot from almost on the goal line. With a winger like that, with defenders like those, anything was possible, especially against their ageing hosts.

SEMI-FINALS

24 June 1958 – Nya Ullevi, Gothenburg – 49,471 – István Zsolt (HUN)

SWEDEN   **(1) 3**
Skoglund 33, Gren 80, Hamrin 87

WEST GERMANY   **(1) 1**
Schäfer 25

SWEDEN Svensson, Bergmark, Axbom, Börjesson, Gustavsson, Parling, Hamrin, Gren, Simonsson, Liedholm (c), Skoglund.
WEST GERMANY Herkenrath, Stollenwerk, Juskowiak, Eckel, Erhardt, Szymaniak, Rahn, Walter, Seeler, Schäfer (c), Hans Cieslarczyk.
SENT OFF: Juskowiak 58.

If the holders planned to overwhelm Sweden with youthful pace and energy, it would have helped if they'd chosen the right studs. Struggling to keep their feet, they nevertheless took the lead with a spectacular goal. Seeler, mobile and relentless, beat a man on the left, chased the ball to the corner flag, and did well to get in any kind of cross. Schäfer met it twelve yards out from the near post. It's unclear on the film whether he hits a half-

YOUNGEST GOALSCORERS

yrs	days				
17	239	Pelé	BRZ	1958	v WAL
18	93	Manuel Rosas	MEX	1930	v ARG
18	190	Michael Owen	ENG	1998	v ROM
18	197	Nicolae Kovács	ROM	1930	v PER
18	231	Dmitri Sychev	RUS	2002	v BEL
18	364	Aleksandar Tirnanić	YUG	1930	v BRZ

Pelé scored in two other matches in 1958, Owen in another in 1998. Both of Rosas' goals were penalties. Sychev scored in the last minute of Russia's last match in the tournament. Tirnanić may have been exactly a year older.

volley or a volley that goes into the ground first, but the effect was what he wanted, the ball flying high past Svensson. The Germans changed their studs at half-time.

Fritz Walter and Gren, born on the same day in 1920, were cancelling each other out, but another veteran sneaked the equaliser. Liedholm clearly used his arm to intercept a German pass, the referee waved his arms like a windmill, and a tackle sent the ball out to Skoglund free on the left. The unexceptional shot went between a defender's legs and across the keeper. In a long international career (1950–64), Skoglund won only eleven caps and scored only this one goal.

The match turned on a crunching tackle by Parling that temporarily forced Walter off the field and ended his international career – and Juskowiak's sending-off for showing his new studs in retaliating against the sly Hamrin.

Everything was running Sweden's way in front of a crowd roused by cheerleaders led by a middle-aged gent with a Swedish flag. Against an undermanned defence, Hamrin had space to come in off the wing and run clean through. Herkenrath made a good save – but when he punched clear with ten minutes left, Gren returned the ball into the top corner from outside the area, his last goal for Sweden and one of the best. Herkenrath could only turn to his right and watch. Finally Hamrin drifted along the right at walking pace as if in a world of his own, then suddenly dashed past two defenders along the goal line and scored at the near post. The kind of individualism he'd shown throughout the competition, it seemed to give Sweden a real chance in the Final.

---

24 June 1958 – Råsunda, Solna, Stockholm – 27,100 – Mervyn Griffiths (WAL)

BRAZIL   (2) 5
Vává 2, Didi 39, Pelé 52, 64, 75

FRANCE   (1) 2
Fontaine 9, Piantoni 82

BRAZIL Gylmar, De Sordi, N Santos, Zito, Bellini (c), Orlando, Garrincha, Didi, Vává, Pelé, Zagallo.
FRANCE Abbes, Kaelbel, Lerond, Penverne, Jonquet (c), Marcel, Wisnieski, Kopa, Fontaine, Piantoni, Vincent.

Goals were never more inevitable, and the first two arrived quickly, showing up the relative weakness at the centre of each defence. First the elegant Jonquet gave the ball straight to Garrincha (a grenade against a trampoline if ever there was one). Jonquet made an excellent saving tackle, but it took him away to the left, which left Vává free in the middle when Didi's cross came over. The volley bored a hole through Abbes.

The equaliser followed a well-worn route, Fontaine taking Kopa's perfect through-pass round Gylmar for the first goal Brazil conceded in the tournament. But after 26 minutes Vává's dreadful foul left Jonquet limping on the wing for the rest of the match.

Brazil would probably have won anyway – France simply leaked too many goals – but they wouldn't have felt safe against Fontaine if the French had remained at full strength. As it was, two minutes after the injury, Didi's low shot found its way in at the far post, and the rest was a mopping-up operation. Zagallo should have been awarded a goal when his shot hit the bar and came down over the line; Pelé tapped in when Abbes dropped Vává's gentle cross; then he slashed in a lucky rebound after Vává missed his kick. He saved the best till last, running onto Didi's pass, lifting it up with his thigh, and volleying low to the keeper's right to complete the last hat-trick by a Brazilian in a finals match. But it was cruel by then, against a depleted team. Piantoni scored a good goal (nutmeg then 20-yard left-footer) – but by then France knew how the Irish felt.

3RD-PLACE FINAL

28 June 1958 – Nya Ullevi, Gothenburg – 32,483 – Juan Brozzi (ARG)

FRANCE   (3) 6
Fontaine 15, 36, 77, 89, Kopa pen 27, Douis 50

WEST GERMANY   (1) 3
Cieslarczyk 17, Rahn 52, Schäfer 83

FRANCE Abbes, Kaelbel, Lerond, Penverne (c), Maurice Lafont, Marcel, Wisnieski, Yvon Douis, Fontaine, Kopa, Vincent.
WEST GERMANY Heinz Kwiatkowski, Stollenwerk, Schnellinger, Erhardt, Heinz Wewers, Szymaniak, Rahn, Hans Sturm, Alfred Kelbassa, Schäfer (c), Cieslarczyk.

With no tackles taking place in midfield, Fontaine only had to stay on his feet to score goals. He knocked in Kopa's cut-back from the

YOUGEST TO SCORE A HAT-TRICK

yrs	days				
17	244	Pelé	BRZ	1958	v FRA
19	197	Edmund Conen	GER	1934	v BEL
20	255	Bert Patenaude	BRZ	1930	v PAR
20	261	Flórián Albert	HUN	1962	v BUL
21	347	Ernest Wilimowski	POL	1938	v BRZ

Wilimowski scored four goals, the last in extra time.

FINAL

29 June 1958 – Råsunda, Solna, Stockholm – 49,737 – Maurice Guigue (FRA)

BRAZIL   (2) 5
Vavá 9, 32, Pelé 55, 90, Zagallo 68

SWEDEN   (1) 2
Liedholm 4, Simonsson 79

BRAZIL Gylmar, Djalma Santos, N Santos, Zito, Bellini (c), Orlando, Garrincha, Didi, Vavá, Pelé, Zagallo.
SWEDEN Svensson, Bergmark, Axbom, Börjesson, Gustavsson, Parling, Hamrin, Gren, Simonsson, Liedholm (c), Skoglund.

right, pivoted to put in a rebound, ran at the defence to shoot from seventeen yards, and sprinted from the halfway line for his fourth. These were easy pickings – but his credentials as a goalscorer stand up to any scrutiny: 30 in 21 internationals before two broken legs ended his career at the age of 28. There were no sweepers around in 1958, so the 4–2–4 defences were regularly caught square – but no-one else scored 13 goals against them. Deadly in front of goal. Especially in front of Kopa.

The latter, about to become European Footballer of the Year, converted a penalty for Erhardt's foul on Wisnieski, and Douis volleyed the fourth. For the Germans, Cieslarczyk turned inside a defender before shooting, Schäfer converted a knock-down from close in, and Rahn scored the best of the lot, selling an exaggerated dummy before cutting back to the goal line and thrashing in a high shot, signing off as only he could. A World Cup giant.

Kwiatkowski had also been in goal against Hungary in 1954, conceding another four goals to another tournament top scorer. They were his only matches in the finals!

As in the match between the two countries in 1950, Raynor hoped for an early goal, confident that the Brazilians would 'panic all over the show.' This time he got it – and they didn't.

Sweden played the ball confidently out of defence and found Simonsson wide on the right. His square pass reached Liedholm just outside the penalty area. Liedholm turned past Orlando, then past Bellini, then shot. His thin legs made the white ball look too big for him, but the ground shot was just firm enough to go past Gylmar's right hand.

GOALS IN A TOURNAMENT

13	Just Fontaine	FRA	1958	
11	Sándor Kocsis	HUN	1954	
10	Gerd Müller	WG	1970	1 pen
9	Eusébio	POR	1966	4 pen
8	Guillermo Stábile	ARG	1930	
8	Ademir	BRZ	1950	

Fontaine scored four goals and Eusébio one in 3rd-Place Finals, i.e. after their teams had been eliminated.

1930
1934
1938
1950
1954
1958
1962
1966
1970
1974
1978
1982
1986
1990
1994
1998
2002
2006

1930
1934
1938
1950
1954
1962
1966
1970
1974
1978
1982
1986
1990
1994
1998
2002
2006

1958

CONSECUTIVE MATCHES SCORING GOALS

6	Just Fontaine	FRA	1958
6	Jairzinho	BRZ	1970
5	Gerd Müller	WG	1970

YOUNGEST PLAYERS IN FINALS

yrs	days			
17	249	Pelé	BRZ	1958
18	201	Giuseppe Bergomi	ITA	1982
19	344	Rubén Morán	URU	1950

BIGGEST WINS IN FINALS

5-2	Brazil	1958	v Sweden
4-1	Brazil	1970	v Italy
3-0	France	1998	v Brazil

But Raynor already had 'the sneaking suspicion the game was already over. Instead of looking dejected, the Brazilians were calling for the ball to restart the game. If that was their attitude, we were heading for trouble.'

They reached it within minutes. Garrincha went past his marker but topped his low cross, which found its way through to Vavá, who lunged in to score from inside the six-yard box. Twenty minutes later, a virtual re-run, Garrincha this time getting the cross right: too fast for Svensson, turned in by Vavá.

Brazil were on top throughout, their game at last the right mix of the athletic and artistic, 1950 and 1954 blended, brushing aside the Swedish veterans, who had wonderful careers and nothing to be ashamed of now (except perhaps some severe short-back-and-sides, either a sign of solidarity or done for a bet). Gren was twenty years older than Pelé and it showed.

In the first half, Pelé hit a post from twenty yards. In the second, he scored a marvellous goal, chesting Nílton Santos' cross past Parling, flipping the ball over Gustavsson with his thigh, and volleying low past the keeper, who had no chance (or, as commentator Kenneth Wolstenholme had it, 'If I were Svensson, I wouldn't worry about that'). Then Zagallo beat Bergmark to the ball and squeezed it in at the near post.

The key, as always, was Didi. Raynor didn't man-mark him, which was probably a mistake, leaving the job to two different players in different parts of the field. Didi simply flitted in and out of those areas, leaving the defenders chasing shadows. 'It was impossible,' said Raynor. 'He was masterful.'

Meanwhile there was no sign of the Swedish wingers. If Raynor was shrewd, Feola was no fool himself. Once he'd identified the main threat, he didn't hesitate for sentimental reasons: out went the luckless De Sordi, in came big Djalma for his first game of the tournament. Ruthless and right.

Near the end, Liedholm came through the middle unchallenged to make a goal for Simonsson, who may have been slightly offside but deserved it nonetheless: a selfless centre-forward of all-round quality. But it was right that Pelé should apply the finishing touch. After backheeling the ball to Zagallo on the left, he trotted towards the centre to get between two defenders and knock a looping header just inside the post as Svensson wrapped himself round it. Modern football, more or less, had arrived, and with it its greatest player.

The sorcerer's apprentice

Chile 1962

This long slim country had a population of less than eight million, only one stadium of any size, and the aftermath of a giant earthquake two years earlier: a third of all buildings were damaged beyond repair. Yet the president of their FA, Carlos Dittborn, argued that they had to have the World Cup '*because* we have nothing.' He died just before the tournament and the stadium in Arica was named after him.

Since 1958 the Brazilian team had broken up then almost completely re-formed. Zagallo had reclaimed his place from the explosive Pepe, Vavá from the chubby-cheeked Coutinho, Pelé's supercharged partner at Santos. Didi was back from two wasted years at Real Madrid. Only the twin stoppers were missing, and even they'd been replaced by names from the past: Zózimo a reserve in 1958, Mauro who'd won his first cap in 1949. The only question mark was one of age: six first choices were over 30. But Pelé was just 21 and firmly established as the best in the world. They were obvious favourites.

The USSR had won all three matches on a tour of South America the previous year but still looked rather functional. Argentina had a new manager and a more defensive style. Yugoslavia, who'd finally struck Olympic gold after losing the previous three Finals, had Šekularac at his best and dangerous strikers in Galić and Jerković. Czechoslovakia's famous half-backs had muscled their way past Scotland in a play-off.

Spain and Italy tried to find instant success by padding their teams with foreigners. Spain picked Martínez from Paraguay, Santamaría from Uruguay, and none other than Puskás, who was now 36 but had just scored another hat-trick in a European Cup final. The great Argentinian Alfredo Di Stéfano was in the squad but apparently injured. Italy had Maschio and Sivori from Argentina and Altafini (of 1958 fame) and Sormani from Brazil, which should have added up to a dazzling forward line.

England had better players than in 1958: Wilson at left-back, Charlton and Greaves up front. In the 1960–61 season they'd beaten Scotland 9-3, Spain 4-2, Italy 3-2 away, and other teams by scores of 5-2, 9-0, 5-1 and 8-0 – but all the play still went through Haynes and the impetus seemed to have gone.

As for the hosts, they had several players of international class or thereabouts, just enough to make them respectable opposition, but only in partnership with the Santiago crowd, one of the stars of the tournament.

FIFA's latest rule change made sense in a competition where time was limited. From now on, teams level on points would be separated by goal average (later goal difference). The days of play-offs were over.

When you become the first player to score in two World Cup Finals, you're entitled to a small celebration. Vavá jumps for joy after his goal against Czechoslovakia.

GROUP 1

Colombia, Uruguay (seeded), USSR, Yugoslavia.

30 May 1962 – Carlos Dittborn, Arica – 7,908 – Andor Dorogi (HUN)

URUGUAY (0) 2
Cubilla 57, Sasía 73

COLOMBIA (1) 1
Zuluaga pen 18

URUGUAY Roberto Sosa, Horacio Troche (c), Emilio Álvarez, Mario Méndez, Néstor Gonçálvez, Eliseo Álvarez, Luis Cubilla, Pedro Rocha, Ronald Langón, José Sasía, Domingo Pérez. *Juan Carlos Corrazzo, Juan López et al.*
COLOMBIA Efraín 'Caimán' Sánchez, Francisco Zuluaga (c), Jaime González, Oscar López, Héctor Echeverry, Jaime Silva, Marcos Coll, Germán Aceros, Marino Klinger, Delio Gamboa, Jairo Arias. *Adolfo Pedernera (ARG).*

Nothing was expected of the Colombians, appearing in the finals for the first time, but they were Uruguay's equals in the first half. Their veteran captain sent the keeper the wrong with a penalty given for handball by Alvarez, and Coll hit a post. Uruguayan frustration led to some harsh tackling which left Zuluaga with three broken ribs and ended his international career. Eventually Cubilla

FINALS SCORING GOALS

2	Vavá	BRZ	1958 & 1962
2	Pelé	BRZ	1958 & 1970
2	Paul Breitner	GER	1974 & 1982

scored with a shot that seemed to surprise Sánchez, who may have expected a cross – and Sasía took a short through-ball in a packed penalty area before scoring from a narrow angle on the right. Eliseo and Emilio Álvarez were brothers.

31 May 1962 – Carlos Dittborn, Arica – 9,622 – Albert Dusch (GER)

USSR (0) 2
V Ivanov 53, Ponedelnik 85

YUGOSLAVIA (0) 0

USSR Lev Yashin, Eduard Dubinsky, Leonid Ostrovsky, Valery Voronin, Anatoly Maslyonkin, Igor Netto (c), Slava Metreveli, Valentin Ivanov, Viktor Ponedelnik, Viktor Kanevsky, Mikhail Meskhi. *Gavril Katchalin.*
YUGOSLAVIA Milutin Šoškić, Vladimir Durković, Fahrudin Jusufi, Željko Matuš, Vladimir Marković, Vladimir Popović, Muhamed Mujić, Dragoslav Šekularac, Dražen Jerković, Milan Galić (c), Josip Skoblar. *Selection committee (coach Milovan Ćirić).*

A repeat of the 1960 European Nations Cup Final, with the same result. Yashin made fine saves from Šekularac (after a typical blazing dribble) and Galić – but the USSR were generally in command. The 22-year-old Jusufi would develop into one of the best left-backs in Europe, but here he fouled the strongly-built Ponedelnik, who hit the bar with the free-kick, Ivanov beating Šoškić to the rebound and heading in. Then Jusufi was left behind by Voronin, whose pass was driven in by Ponedelnik from the edge of the area. Dubinsky was hospitalised with a broken leg after a bad foul by Mujić, who was sent home by his selectors but not sent off by the referee, who lost control to the point of doing nothing when Jerković struck him. One publication lists Mujić as captain – but other sources, including a Yugoslav history of the national team, nominate Galić.

1962

2 June 1962 – Carlos Dittborn, Arica – 8,829 – Karol Galba (CZE)

YUGOSLAVIA　　**(2) 3**
Skoblar pen 26, Galić 30, Jerković 49

URUGUAY　　**(1) 1**
Cabrera 19

YUGOSLAVIA Šoškić, Durković, Jusufi, Petar Radaković, Marković, Popović, Vojislav Melić, Šekularac, Jerković, Galić (c), Skoblar.
URUGUAY Sosa, Troche (c), Em. Álvarez, Méndez, Gonçálvez, El. Álvarez, Rocha, Mario Bergara, Ángel Rubén Cabrera, Sasía, Pérez.
SENT OFF: Popović 71, Cabrera 71.

Uruguay missed a good early chance before Cabrera headed in a cross from the right, and Yugoslavia seemed to be on their way out. But Šekularac began to run the show. Shortish and neat, apparently of gypsy blood, he had great flair and this time kept his temper in check. Jerković, leggy and very tall, was fouled by Emilio Álvarez for the penalty and finished things off with a header from a right-wing cross. When his volley was saved, Galić poached the rebound. But Yugoslavia were lucky that Uruguay hit the bar with a header at 2-1. In a free-for-all provoked by Sasía's late challenge on Šoškić, faces were slapped, Cabrera and Popović sent off, Sasía lucky to stay on.

3 June 1962 – Carlos Dittborn, Arica – 8,040 – João Etzel (BRZ)

COLOMBIA (1) 4
Aceros 22, Coll 68, Rada 71, Klinger 76

USSR　　**(3) 4**
V Ivanov 5, 13, Chislenko 11, Ponedelnik 57

COLOMBIA Sánchez (c), J González, López, Echeverry, Aníbal Alzate, Rolando Serrano, Coll, Aceros, Antonio Rada, Klinger, Héctor González.
USSR Yashin, Givi Chokheli, Ostrovsky, Voronin, Maslyonkin, Netto (c), Igor Chislenko, Ivanov, Ponedelnik, Kanevsky, Meskhi.

Wow. When the USSR took that early 3-0 lead, the Colombians looked a shambles, even their veteran goalkeeper, once one of the world's best. Ivanov's low left-foot shot from twenty yards went under his body and he might have done better with Ivanov's second, an unexceptional ground shot. His defence let him down for the other goal, allowing the ball to run on until Chislenko slid it in. Aceros pulled one back with a good chip from a position that may have been offside, but then Ponedelnik went past Alzate and that was surely that.

Colombia's recovery began with a freak goal. Coll's corner, hit low and poorly to the near post, should have been cleared by Chokheli. Instead he stood aside and ushered it in, to Yashin's almost comical indignation. Rada poked in the third from eight yards, Klinger stabbed in the loose ball after Yashin had dived at his feet, and the Soviets were hanging on at the end. But normal service was about to be resumed.

6 June 1962 – Carlos Dittborn, Arica – 9,973 – Cesare Jonni (ITA)

USSR　　**(1) 2**
Mamikin 38, V Ivanov 89

URUGUAY　　**(0) 1**
Sasía 53

USSR Yashin, Chokheli, Ostrovsky, Voronin, Maslyonkin, Netto (c), Chislenko, Ivanov, Ponedelnik, Aleksei Mamikin, Galimzian Khusainov.
URUGUAY Sosa, Troche (c), Em. Álvarez, Méndez, Gonçálvez, El. Álvarez, Cubilla, Julio César Cortés, Cabrera, Sasía, Pérez.

The USSR's recovery from their Colombian hangover was aided by an injury to Eliseo Álvarez which reduced Uruguay to ten men. Almost immediately the lively little Chislenko beat Pérez to make a volleyed goal for Mamikin, and a strong midfield did the rest, even after Sasía equalised from a loose ball following a free-kick. The referee originally allowed a late goal by Chislenko when the ball passed through a hole in the side netting, after which Ivanov finished off a classic counter-attack.

---

7 June 1962 – Carlos Dittborn, Arica – 7,167 – Juan Carlos Robles (CHI)

YUGOSLAVIA　　　**(2) 5**
Galić 20, 51, Jerković 25, 88, Melić 82

COLOMBIA　　　**(0) 0**

YUGOSLAVIA Šoškić, Durković, Jusufi, Radaković, Marković, Popović, Andrija Anković, Šekularac, Jerković, Galić (c), Melić.
COLOMBIA Sánchez (c), J González, López, Echeverry, Alzate, Serrano, Coll, Aceros, Klinger, Rada, H González.

No surprises this time, Sánchez' long international career ending in a flurry of goals. Galić ran through alone for the first, Jerković shot the second in off a post then missed an easy chance. Some English publications still insist on crediting him with the third goal, headed in by Galić, giving him not only a hat-trick but eventually five goals in the tournament, which would have made him outright leading scorer. All reliable sources, Yugoslavian included,

GROUP 1

	P	W	D	L	F	A	Pts
USSR	3	2	1	0	8	5	5
Yugoslavia	3	2	0	1	8	3	4
Uruguay	3	1	0	2	4	6	2
Colombia	3	0	1	2	5	11	1

USSR and Yugoslavia qualified for the quarter-finals.

credit it to Galić, though admittedly 'with the help of Jerković'. Melić volleyed in an Anković cross, and Jerković's late long-range shot was a 'masterpiece of precision'.

GROUP 2

Chile (seeded), Italy, Switzerland, West Germany.

---

30 May 1962 – Nacional, Santiago – 65,006 – Ken Aston (ENG)

CHILE　　　**(1) 3**
L Sánchez 44, 54, Ramírez 51

SWITZERLAND　　　**(1) 1**
Wüthrich 6

CHILE Misael Escuti, Luis Eyzaguirre, Sergio Navarro (c), Carlos Contreras, Raúl Sánchez, Eladio Rojas, Jaime Ramírez, Jorge Toro, Honorino Landa, Alberto Fouilloux, Leonel Sánchez. *Fernando Riera.*
SWITZERLAND Karl Elsener, Heinz Schneiter, Fritz Morf, André Grobéty, Ely Tacchella, Hans Weber, Charly Antenen (c), Rolf Wüthrich, Norbert Eschmann, Philippe Pottier, Toni Allemann. *Karl Rappan (AUT).*

Switzerland were now expected to be purely sacrificial, but when Toro couldn't control a bad throw by Escuti, Wüthrich shot in from long range. The stadium reverberated with the sound of silence.

Chile's team responded with some grim tackling, a feature of this World Cup. Aston booked Eschmann then Rojas but should have sent both off when they came to blows a few minutes later. With the Swiss staying back in defence, Toro and Rojas were able to drive their team forward. Contreras and Leonel Sánchez hit a post, and Elsener made two fine

1962

saves from Fouilloux. The Swiss couldn't hold out forever, but Chile had some luck in making the breakthrough, Leonel Sánchez's low shot taking a deflection off Morf and wrongfooting the keeper.

Sánchez scored his second after Elsener bravely saved his first shot. When Ramírez had put Chile ahead by clearing up the aftermath of a shot by Landa, the police had to clear spectators off the pitch after the first goal – but it was just enthusiasm spilling over.

31 May 1962 – Nacional, Santiago – 65,440 – Bobby Davidson (SCO)

ITALY 0
WEST GERMANY 0

ITALY Renzo Buffon (c), Giacomo Losi, Enzo Robotti, Sandro Salvadore, Cesare Maldini, Gigi Radice, Giorgio Ferrini, Gianni Rivera, José Altafini, Omar Sivori, Giampaolo Menichelli. *Giovanni Ferrari etc*.
WEST GERMANY Wolfgang Fahrian, Hans Nowak, Karl-Heinz Schnellinger, Willi Schulz, Herbert Erhardt, Horst Szymaniak, Hans Sturm, Helmut Haller, Uwe Seeler, Hans Schäfer (c), Albert Brülls. *Sepp Herberger*.

The inclusion of Schnellinger and Schulz made the Germans more physical than in 1958, if that was possible, especially with Szymaniak and Erhardt still there. Italy's defence was well marshalled by Maldini, father of Paolo (they were Italy's coach and captain in the 1998 finals) – and the willowy 18-year-old Rivera showed glimpses of his promise despite being generally '*cancellato*' by Szymaniak. But an Italian paper referred to a sense of fear – and the South Americans up front were a disappointment, perhaps intimidated by the crowd. Altafini, unable to escape Erhardt, was booked

in his frustration, and Schulz blotted out Sivori – so Fahrian was allowed to keep a clean sheet on his 21st birthday. The real crowd figure was probably nearer 40,000.

2 June 1962 – Nacional, Santiago – 66,057 – Ken Aston (ENG)

CHILE (0) 2
Ramírez 74, Toro 88
ITALY (0) 0

CHILE Escuti, Eyzaguirre, Navarro (c), Contreras, R Sánchez, Rojas, Ramírez, Toro, Landa, Fouilloux, L Sánchez.
ITALY Carlo Mattrel, Mario David, Robotti, Paride Tumburus, Francesco Janich, Salvadore, Bruno Mora (c), Humberto Maschio, Altafini, Ferrini, Menichelli.
SENT OFF: Ferrini 7, David 44.

Italy had been jeered and whistled in their first match, but this was something else. Two Italian journalists, Antonio Ghirelli and Corrado Pizzinelli, had written a series of articles emphasising the poverty of Santiago and the morals of its women. They left the country before the tournament started, so the Italian team had to bear the brunt of local reaction. They later claimed the Chilean players were spitting in their faces from the start.

Reaction wasn't slow in coming. Aston, tall and jug-eared, took no action when Ferrini and Leonel Sánchez kicked each other, but sent off Ferrini for retaliation against Landa. Play was held up for eight minutes until the police shepherded Ferrini away. Soon afterwards, the worst (and worst refereed) moment of the competition, Leonel Sánchez responding to a series of kicks from David by flattening him with a punch right in front of a linesman. When Aston did nothing, David took things into his own hands, getting himself sent off for kicking the same Sánchez in the neck (they later played together with Milan, where 'we became great friends'!).

Toro not only rugby-tackled Mora but held him down so long that Aston had to get down like a wrestling referee to prise them apart. No sending-off for that, or for Toro's raised fists in the last minute, or the punch that broke Maschio's nose (the finger was variously pointed at Sánchez again and Rojas).

Italy, their selectors again at odds, had sent out a remarkably inexperienced team for such a combustible game: two debutants, and the most experienced international (Mora) winning only his 10th cap. They held out until Mattrel punched away a Leonel Sánchez free kick and Ramírez headed over two defenders into the net. Toro's low 25-yarder brought down the curtain on a horror show, the last of the three great World Cup slugfests. The Italian players were later stoned at their training camp. Aston became a senior member of the refereeing committees at the 1966 and 1970 tournaments, but this was the last match he refereed in the finals.

---

3 June 1962 – Nacional, Santiago – 64,922 – Leo Horn (HOL)

WEST GERMANY (1) 2
Brülls 44, Seeler 60

SWITZERLAND (0) 1
Schneiter 75

WEST GERMANY Fahrian, Nowak, Schnellinger, Schulz, Erhardt, Szymaniak, Willi Koslowski, Haller, Seeler, Schäfer (c), Brülls.
SWITZERLAND Elsener, Tacchella, Schneiter, Grobéty, Wüthrich, Weber, Antenen (c), Roger Vonlanthen, Allemann, Eschmann, Richard Dürr.

Switzerland played the prettier football and were unlucky when Szymaniak's sliding tackle broke Eschmann's ankle early in the first half – but they lacked a goalscorer and Germany

were always stronger. When a defender missed his tackle, Brülls collected the ball, turned inside a challenge, and shot low into the far corner. Seeler, who also beat a man to score the second, had earlier hit a post. Schneiter, a composed defender, shot into the roof of the net following a corner, but couldn't stop Herberger taking belated revenge on Rappan, whom he'd opposed in the 1938 finals.

---

6 June 1962 – Nacional, Santiago – 67,224 – Bobby Davidson (SCO)

WEST GERMANY (1) 2
Szymaniak pen 22, Seeler 82

CHILE (0) 0

WEST GERMANY Fahrian, Nowak, Schnellinger, Schulz, Erhardt, Willi Giesemann, Engelbert Kraus, Szymaniak, Seeler, Schäfer (c), Brülls.
CHILE Escuti, Eyzaguirre, Navarro (c), Contreras, R Sánchez, Rojas, Ramírez, Mario Moreno, Landa, Armando Tobar, L Sánchez.

Chile had already qualified and confidence was high, but Germany put a few things in perspective. Dropping Haller and defending all over the pitch, even using Schäfer to mark the dangerous Rojas, they were rarely in danger. Seeler, fantastic in the air for someone so stocky, was elbowed off the ball for the penalty and headed a marvellous second from a cross by Brülls.

---

7 June 1962 – Nacional, Santiago – 59,828 – Nikolai Latyshev (USR)

ITALY (1) 3
Mora 2, Bulgarelli 65, 67

SWITZERLAND (0) 0

ITALY Buffon (c), Losi, Robotti, Salvadore, Maldini, Radice, Mora, Giacomo Bulgarelli, Angelo Sormani, Sivori, Ezio Pascutti.
SWITZERLAND Elsener, Tacchella, Schneiter, Grobéty, Eugen Meier, Weber, Antenen (c), Vonlanthen, Wüthrich, Allemann, Dürr.

1930
1934
1938
1950
1954
1958
1962
1966
1970
1974
1978
1982
1986
1990
1994
1998
2002
2006

1930
1934
1938
1950
1954
1958
1962
1966
1970
1974
1978
1982
1986
1990
1994
1998
2002
2006

GOALS CONCEDED

25	Antonio Carbajal	MEX	1950–62
25	Mohammed Al-Deayea	SAU	1994–02
19	Sepp Maier	GER	1970–78
18	Lev Yashin	USR	1958–66
17	Harald Schumacher	GER	1982–86

Carbajal also played one match in 1966, keeping his only clean sheet in the finals.

Irrelevant but nice enough. Again the Swiss traced some pleasing patterns, but Italy took their chances, despite leaving out Rivera and bringing in two more new caps, Sormani and Bulgarelli. Pascutti, the best forward on the pitch, headed against the bar after seven minutes, then Elsener made a mess of his cross-shot to set up an open goal for Mora. Bulgarelli scored the second with a kind of sliding tackle on the keeper when clean through, then smacked in the third when Pascutti found him unmarked close in. Elsener made 'some remarkable saves' even after an Italian forward had accidentally trodden on his hand. In all three group matches not involving Chile, the attendance figures look like sheer figments (one Italian source puts this one at around 20,000). Of the goalkeepers who didn't concede a goal in World Cup tournaments, only Buffon played in more than one match.

GROUP 2

	P	W	D	L	F	A	Pts
West Germany	3	2	1	0	4	1	5
Chile	3	2	0	1	5	3	4
Italy	3	1	1	1	3	2	3
Switzerland	3	0	0	3	2	8	0

West Germany and Chile qualified for the quarter-finals.

GROUP 3

Brazil (seeded), Czechoslovakia, Mexico, Spain.

30 May 1962 – Municipal ('El Sausalito'), Viña del Mar – 10,484 – Gottfried Dienst (SWI)

BRAZIL   (0) 2
Zagallo 56, Pelé 72

MEXICO   (0) 0

BRAZIL Gylmar (dos Santos), Djalma Santos, Nílton Santos, 'Zito' (José Ely de Miranda), Mauro (Ramos de Oliveira) (c), Zózimo (Alves), 'Garrincha' (Manoel Francisco dos Santos), 'Didi' (Waldir Pereira), 'Vavá' (Edvaldo Izídio Neto), 'Pelé' (Édson Arantes do Nascimento), Mário Zagallo. *Aymoré Moreira.*
MEXICO Antonio Carbajal (c), Jesús del Muro, José Villegas, Raúl Cárdenas, Guillermo Sepúlveda, Pedro Nájera, Alfredo del Águila, Salvador Reyes, Héctor Hernández, Antonio Jasso, Isidoro Díaz. *Alejandro Scopelli (ARG), with Ignacio Trelles.*

Yet again Brazil met Mexico in their opening match, but there was more defensive organisation around by now. When the first goal finally came, it owed much to Pelé's tenacity as well as his talent: he beat two men, lost the ball in a tackle, eventually won it back, and crossed for Zagallo to run in and score with a diving header.

The second goal was all Pelé's own work. Walking the ball along the right touchline, he nutmegged one player, went past three more, disentangled himself inside in the area, and shot left-footed into the bottom corner. A frightening mixture of skill and power. Especially for someone who was hiding the extent of a groin injury from the team doctor . . .

Moreira, who took over as coach when Feola fell ill, was the brother of Zezé Moreira, who was Brazil's manager in 1954. They're the only brothers to coach teams in the finals.

---

31 May 1962 – Municipal ('El Sausalito'), Viña del Mar – 12,700 – Erich Steiner (AUT)

CZECHOSLOVAKIA (0) 1
Štibrányi 79

SPAIN   (0) 0

CZECHOSLOVAKIA Viliam Schrojf, Jan Lála, Ladislav Novák (c), Svatopluk Pluskal, Ján Popluhár, Josef Masopust, Jozef Štibrányi, Adolf Scherer, Andrej Kvašňák, Jozef Adamec, Josef Jelínek. *Rudolf Vytlačil.*
SPAIN Carmelo (Cedrún), Feliciano Rivilla, Severino Reija, Juan Segarra (c), José Santamaría, Jesús Garay, Luis Del Sol, Ferenc Puskás, Eulogio Martínez, Luis Suárez, Francisco Gento. *Pablo Hernández Coronado (coach Helenio Herrera (ARG)).*

Santamaría and Puskás had played for other countries in the 1954 finals and were still world class – but Czechoslovakia wore them down. Schrojf was the busier keeper early on, saving from Puskás and Suárez and receiving treatment after a full-blooded challenge from Martínez – but eventually the rugged Scherer beat Santamaría and put Štibrányi clear to chip over the diving keeper. Pluskal and the balding Popluhár erected a big solid barrier at the back, and Scherer had a goal disallowed for offside with two minutes left. Herrera had been on Italy's coaching staff in the qualifying rounds. Note the slight spelling differences in the first names of Masopust and Jelínek, Štibrányi and Adamec, and Lála and Popluhár.

---

2 June 1962 – Municipal ('El Sausalito'), Viña del Mar – 14,903 – Pierre Schwinte (FRA)

BRAZIL   0

CZECHOSLOVAKIA 0

BRAZIL Gylmar, D Santos, N Santos, Zito, Mauro (c), Zózimo, Garrincha, Didi, Vavá, Pelé, Zagallo.
CZECHOSLOVAKIA Schrojf, Lála, Novák (c), Pluskal, Popluhár, Masopust, Štibrányi, Scherer, Kvašňák, Adamec, Jelínek.

Early on, Pelé took Garrincha's pass and went through the defence. In trying a shot, he felt something give way in his groin.

Later he remembered the way Popluhár and Lála refused to go into hard tackles while he stood helpless on the wing, 'one of those things I shall always remember with emotion, and one of the finest things that happened in my entire football career.' But it was the last good memory he took from this World Cup; his tournament was over.

---

3 June 1962 – Municipal ('El Sausalito'), Viña del Mar – 11,875 – Branko Tešanić (YUG)

SPAIN   (0) 1
Peiró 89

MEXICO   (0) 0

SPAIN Carmelo, 'Rodri' (Francisco Rodríguez), Sigfrido Gracia, Martín Vergés, Santamaría, 'Pachín' (Enrique Pérez Díaz), Del Sol, Joaquín Peiró, Puskás, Suárez, Gento (c).
MEXICO Carbajal (c), del Muro, Ignacio Jáuregui, Cárdenas, Sepúlveda, Nájera, del Águila, Reyes, H Hernández, Jasso, Díaz.

Hernández missed a couple of late chances but Mexico again spent most of the match in defence and were glad Carbajal had a splendid game, saving from Puskás, Peiró, Vergés – oh well, everybody. Ironic that the goal should come from his failure to hold a shot by Gento, leaving Peiró with an open goal and Carbajal on his knees apparently weeping. An English report on the tournament lists Suárez as captain, but a Spanish history of their national team says Gento.

1930
1934
1938
1950
1954
1958
1962
1966
1970
1974
1978
1982
1986
1990
1994
1998
2002
2006

6 June 1962 – Municipal ('El Sausalito'), Viña del Mar – 18,715 – Sergio Bustamante (CHI)

BRAZIL　　(0) 2
Amarildo 72, 86

SPAIN　　(1) 1
Adelardo 35

BRAZIL Gylmar, D Santos, N Santos, Zito, Mauro (c), Zózimo, Garrincha, Didi, Vavá, Amarildo (Tavares), Zagallo.

SPAIN José Araquistain, Rodri, Gracia, Vergés, Luis María Echeberría, Pachín, Enrique Collar (c), Adelardo (Rodríguez), Puskás, Peiró, Gento.

Looking for extra pace and mobility, Herrera dropped Del Sol, Santamaría and Suárez (but kept the 36-year-old Puskás) and the changes nearly paid off. Adelardo shot into the bottom corner from twenty yards and Spain volleyed wide after Gento, very fast and direct, had sprinted away from an ageing Djalma.

But the talented young Amarildo turned the trick, volleying home Zagallo's centre. His first goal for Brazil was followed by a second, a header after Garrincha at last got it right, beating two men before crossing. Spain had a goal from an overhead kick controversially disallowed – but Brazil had found a replacement for Pelé and looked ready to move up a gear.

It was the end of Puskás' international career, which began in 1945 and was one of the most brilliant of all time, for club and countries. But not quite in the World Cup.

7 June 1962 – Municipal ('El Sausalito'), Viña del Mar – 10,648 – Gottfried Dienst (SWI)

MEXICO　　　(2) 3
Díaz 13, del Águila 30, H Hernández pen 88

CZECHOSLOVAKIA (1) 1
Mašek 15 sec

MEXICO Carbajal (c), del Muro, Jáuregui, Cárdenas, Sepúlveda, Nájera, del Águila, Reyes, H Hernández, Alfredo Hernández, Díaz.

CZECHOSLOVAKIA Schrojf, Lála, Novák (c), Pluskal, Popluhár, Masopust, Štibrányi, Scherer, Kvašňák, Adamec, Václav Mašek.

At the 14th attempt, on their captain's 33rd birthday, Mexico won a finals match for the first time – despite conceding the fastest goal in the competition's history. Mexico kicked off but gave the ball away, Masopust wandered through to set up the blond Mašek on the left, and the shot rolled under Carbajal. All performed in a daze, a kind of slow-motion. But by the end, Czechoslovakia were grateful that they'd already qualified. Díaz swept past two men before blasting the ball in, and del Águila went one better by beating three for the second goal before being fouled for the penalty. Carbajal announced his retirement after the match, having never kept a clean sheet in the finals. Yet.

GROUP 3

	P	W	D	L	F	A	Pts
Brazil	3	2	1	0	4	1	5
Czechoslovakia	3	1	1	1	2	3	3
Mexico	3	1	0	2	3	4	2
Spain	3	1	0	2	2	3	2

Brazil and Czechoslovakia qualified for the quarter-finals.

LEADING GOALSCORERS 1962

4	Flórián Albert	HUN	
4	Valentin Ivanov	USR	
4	Garrincha	BRZ	
4	Leonel Sánchez	CHI	1 pen
4	Dražen Jerković	YUG	
4	Vavá	BRZ	

The actual award, won by Garrincha, was decided by drawing lots.

GROUP 4

Argentina (seeded), Bulgaria, England, Hungary.

30 May 1962 – Braden Copper, Rancagua – 7,134 – Juan Gardeazábal (SPA)

ARGENTINA (1) 1
Facundo 4

BULGARIA (0) 0

ARGENTINA Antonio Roma, Rubén Navarro (c), Silvio Marzolini, Carlos Alberto Sáinz, Federico Sacchi, Raúl Páez, Héctor Facundo, Oscar Rossi, Marcello Pagani, José Sanfilippo, Raúl Belén. *Juan Carlos Lorenzo.*
BULGARIA Georgi Naidenov, Kiril Rakarov (c), Stoyan Kitov, Dimitar Kostov, Ivan Dimitrov, Nikola Kovachev, Todor Diev, Petar Velichkov, Christo Iliev, Dimitar Yakimov, Ivan Kolev. *Georgi Pachedzhiev, with Christo Chakarov.*

Marzolini, an attacking full-back of the highest class, a star in England four years later, showed his ability immediately, sprinting up the left to provide a cross which Pagani touched on to Facundo, who hit it first time. Promising.

But Argentina now had a hard edge, perhaps the result of that 6-1 thrashing in 1958 and certainly instilled by their new coach, who went on to become one of the game's great bogey-men, manager of the Lazio team who attacked Arsenal in the street, Atlético Madrid when they had three men sent off against Celtic, and Boca Juniors when the national team coach refused to include any of their players in the 1978 World Cup. A real scary monster. He would also be Argentina's manager in 1966 . . .

Here he was still learning his trade, but the principle was already established: identify the opposition's main players, then stop them playing. Kolev, who missed two early chances, was cut down time and again, Iliev and Diev

were out injured for the rest of the tournament. They licked their wounds, Lorenzo his lips: Greaves, Charlton and Haynes were next.

31 May 1962 – Braden Copper, Rancagua – 7,938 – Leo Horn (HOL)

HUNGARY (1) 2
Tichy 16, Albert 70

ENGLAND (0) 1
Flowers pen 58

HUNGARY Gyula Grosics (c), Sándor Mátrai, László Sárosi, Ernő Solymosi, Kálmán Mészöly, Ferenc Sipos, Károly Sándor, Gyula Rákosi, Flórián Albert, Lajos Tichy, Máté Fenyvesi. *Lajos Baróti.*
ENGLAND Ron Springett, Jimmy Armfield, Ray Wilson, Bobby Moore, Maurice Norman, Ron Flowers, Bryan Douglas, Jimmy Greaves, Gerry Hitchens, Johnny Haynes (c), Bobby Charlton. *Walter Winterbottom.*

England had given the 21-year-old Moore his first cap eleven days earlier, but he and Flowers were too similar: equally blond, equally defensive, unable to provide the creative help Haynes needed. 1958 all over again. Compare and contrast Hungary's ball-playing halfback Solymosi, or Argentina's Sacchi. The scoreline flattered England.

As the rain came down, Tichy scored a goal reminiscent of his performances in Sweden. Bringing the ball through the inside-left channel, he dummied Moore before thumping the ball high past the keeper's right hand. Springett then saved well from Sándor, and Albert missed from six yards. England were kept out by a packed defence in which the 20-year-old Mészöly was already looking a tremendous player – until Grosics lost the ball in a challenge by Hitchens, and Sárosi did remarkably well to stop Greaves' close-range shot with his hand. Flowers just beat Grosics with the penalty.

1930
1934
1938
1950
1954
1958
1962
1966
1970
1974
1978
1982
1986
1990
1994
1998
2002
2006

But when Flowers slipped on the wet pitch, Albert was clear on goal, taking the ball round Springett, who also lost his footing, and pushing it past the covering Wilson. Not for the first time in a World Cup, England were left needing a big improvement in their second match. This time perhaps they had the players to provide it.

---

2 June 1962 – Braden Copper, Rancagua – 9,794 – Nikolai Latyshev (USR)

ENGLAND   (2) 3
Flowers pen 17, Charlton 42, Greaves 65

ARGENTINA   (0) 1
Sanfilippo 78

ENGLAND Springett, Armfield, Wilson, Moore, Norman, Flowers, Douglas, Greaves, Alan Peacock, Haynes (c), Charlton.
ARGENTINA Roma, Vladislao Cap, Marzolini, Sacchi, Páez, Navarro (c), Antonio Rattin, Juan Carlos Oleniak, Sanfilippo, Rubén Sosa, Belén.

The biters bit. After watching the horror show against Bulgaria, England 'were determined the same thing wasn't going to happen to us.' Winterbottom sent them out to 'bite in,' and the Argentinians began behaving themselves. Charlton went past his man and crossed for the tall new cap Peacock to beat Roma with a header. Navarro handled on the line, and Flowers didn't miss penalties while playing for England.

Charlton was already looking the best outside-left in the competition. When the defence backpedalled, waiting for another dart on the outside, he simply shot with his right foot, all the way along the ground just inside the far post. Greaves put in the loose ball when Roma saved from Douglas, and the much-vaunted Sanfilippo scored from a tight angle but didn't play for Argentina again.

3 June 1962 – Braden Copper, Rancagua – 7,442 – Juan Gardeazábal (SPA)

HUNGARY   (4) 6
Albert 55 sec, 6, 54, Tichy 8, 70, Solymosi 12

BULGARIA   (0) 1
Sokolov 64

HUNGARY István Ilku, Mátrai, Sárosi (c), Solymosi, Mészöly, Sipos, Sándor, János Göröcs, Albert, Tichy, Fenyvesi.
BULGARIA Naidenov, Rakarov (c), Kitov, D Kostov, Dimitrov, Kovachev, Georgi Sokolov, Velichkov, Georgi Asparoukhov, Kolev, Dinko Dermendjiev.

Hungary established themselves as one of the tournament favourites in the first twelve minutes of this one-way traffic, directed by Solymosi and driven home by Albert, who later re-invented himself as a deep-lying centre-forward in the Hidegkuti tradition but was now still the immensely talented striker first capped at 17. He scored the opening goal by cleverly diverting Fenyvesi's corner, the second when Naidenov pushed out a shot by Göröcs, his third when Göröcs ran through to set him up. Naidenov was also at fault with Tichy's first, rushing out and falling over the ball. Tichy went past three men to score the last. Sokolov's twenty-yard consolation beat Ilku, brought in when Grosics damaged a hand. The 19-year-old Sokolov (first capped at 16) suffered from brittle bone disease in later life.

---

6 June 1962 – Braden Copper, Rancagua – 7,945 – Arturo Yamasaki (PER)

ARGENTINA   0
HUNGARY   0

ARGENTINA Rogelio Domínguez, José Manuel Ramos Delgado, Marzolini, Sáinz, Sacchi, Cap, Facundo, Martin Pando (c), Pagani, Oleniak, Alberto González.

HUNGARY Grosics (c), Mátrai, Sárosi, Solymosi, Mészöly, Sipos, Béla Kuharszki, Göröcs, Tichy, Tivadar Monostori, Rákosi.

Hungary, already virtually through, used three reserves up front and stayed on the defensive once Göröcs was forced to hobble through the last hour. Grosics, still slim and agile at 36, made saves from Facundo, Pando and Sáinz, and Argentina were out unless Bulgaria could somehow beat England. Good riddance.

7 June 1962 – Braden Copper, Rancagua – 5,700 – Arthur Blavier (BEL)

BULGARIA 0

ENGLAND 0

BULGARIA Naidenov, Dimitar Dimov, D Kostov, Dobromir Jechev, Dimitrov, Kovachev (c), Aleksandar Kostov, Velichkov, Sokolov, Kolev, Dermendjiev. ENGLAND Springett, Armfield, Wilson, Moore, Norman, Flowers, Douglas, Greaves, Peacock, Haynes (c), Charlton.

There was talk of Bulgaria being happy to see England through at the expense of Lorenzo & Co, but the truth is neither side had the inclination to make anything happen. Greaves went past the keeper but hit the post from a tight angle, Sokolov missed a chance, and Aleksandar Kostov 'completely missed his header in front of an open goal' from Kolev's cross. But these were isolated incidents. Moore: 'We would have a dozen passes at our end then try and hit the ball up to our one forward. He was bound to lose it. So they had a dozen passes down their end. It was one of the worst internationals of all time.' No arguments here.

There used to be all kinds of confusion about the Bulgarian line-up. Some sources still include Asparoukhov in place of Sokolov, but a photo clearly shows the latter's No. 14 shirt (Asparoukhov was No.15).

GROUP 4

	P	W	D	L	F	A	Pts
Hungary	3	2	1	0	8	2	5
England	3	1	1	1	4	3	3
Argentina	3	1	1	1	2	3	3
Bulgaria	3	0	1	2	1	7	1

Hungary and England qualified for the quarter-finals.

QUARTER-FINALS

10 June 1962 – Carlos Dittborn, Arica – 17,268 – Leo Horn (HOL)

CHILE (2) 2
L Sánchez 11, Rojas 28

USSR (1) 1
Chislenko 26

CHILE Escuti, Eyzaguirre, Navarro (c), Contreras, R Sánchez, Rojas, Ramírez, Toro, Landa, Tobar, L Sánchez.
USSR Yashin, Chokheli, Ostrovsky, Voronin, Maslyonkin, Netto (c), Chislenko, Ivanov, Ponedelnik, Mamikin, Meskhi.

Yashin's been blamed for both the Chilean goals, scored from long range, but it's a harsh judgement. It's true that the first, a free kick from wide on his right, surprised him at the near post (the USSR didn't form a wall) but Rojas' low shot was an excellent strike. Yashin later made an amazing one-handed save when Landa was clean through. Chislenko equalised when Escuti stopped Ponedelnik's shot, then Ivanov hit a post, but Chile pulled nine men back in defence and held out, backed by that full-throated crowd.

10 June 1962 – Nacional, Santiago – 63,324 – Arturo Yamasaki (PER)

YUGOSLAVIA   (0) 1
Radaković 85

WEST GERMANY   (0) 0

YUGOSLAVIA Šoškić, Durković, Jusufi, Radaković, Marković, Popović, Vladimir Kovačević, Šekularac, Jerković, Galić (c), Skoblar.
WEST GERMANY Fahrian, Nowak, Schnellinger, Schulz, Erhardt, Giesemann, Brülls, Haller, Seeler, Szymaniak, Schäfer (c).

For the third time in a row, Yugoslavia were faced with West Germany in the quarter-finals, but this time edged through in a fascinating match, full of personal duels with honours even: Šekularac v Szymaniak, Marković v Seeler, both goalkeepers. Seeler hit the post with a low shot after running onto Haller's pass, Schnellinger kicked a shot off the line following a corner, and the only goal came when Galić pulled the ball back after working his way to the goal line. Radaković, his head bandaged after a collision with Seeler, lashed the ball high into the net from twelve yards. It was the end of the canny Herberger's reign as coach, which had begun just before the 1938 finals.

10 June 1962 – Municipal ('El Sausalito'), Viña del Mar – 17,736 – Pierre Schwinte (FRA)

BRAZIL   (1) 3
Garrincha 31, 59, Vavá 53

ENGLAND   (1) 1
Hitchens 38

BRAZIL Gylmar, D Santos, N Santos, Zito, Mauro (c), Zózimo, Garrincha, Didi, Vavá, Amarildo, Zagallo.
ENGLAND Springett, Armfield, Wilson, Moore, Norman, Flowers, Douglas, Greaves, Hitchens, Haynes (c), Charlton.

It was just a matter of time before Garrincha's outrageous individualism paid off. Only Maradona has ever left such a mark on a World Cup quarter-final and semi.

Early on, he beat three men before Haynes tackled him near the goal line. Then, showing an unexpected side of his talent, he got in front of Norman at a Zagallo corner and headed past a stationary Springett and Armfield's desperate dive.

England equalised when Greaves hit the bar with a looping header and Hitchens, back in the side because Peacock had pulled a groin muscle, banged in an instant shot. But the roof fell in on Springett soon after half-time. When Garrincha's free kick blazed through the wall, he bent down and scooped it up for Vavá to head in. Then Garrincha took Amarildo's lay-off just outside the D and curled a marvellous shot into the top corner. A woolly black dog had strayed onto the pitch and avoided capture until Greaves got down on all fours and collared it. But it achieved the rare feat of sidestepping Garrincha.

If England hadn't qualified for the tournament, some might have wondered how this superannuated Brazil (average age of 30) would have fared against the likes of Charlton, Greaves, Moore, Haynes and Wilson. In the event, they emphasised the gulf between the two teams. Like Hitchens, Haynes wasn't capped again. The first £100-a-week man, he was a genuine class act, a fine passer of the ball. But not against World Cup defences.

GOALS IN FINALS

3	Vavá	BRZ	1958 & 1962
3	Geoff Hurst	ENG	1966
3	Pelé	BRZ	1958 & 1970

Pelé hit a post in 1958, Vavá in 1962.

Time for a little humility perhaps. Since before the First World War, England hadn't been as good as they thought they were, and it was beginning to look as if the only way they were going to win this pesky competition was to stage it.

---

10 June 1962 – Braden Copper, Rancagua – 11,690 – Nikolai Latyshev (USR)

CZECHOSLOVAKIA (1) 1
Scherer 13

HUNGARY (0) 0

CZECHOSLOVAKIA Schrojf, Lála, Novák (c), Pluskal, Popluhár, Masopust, Tomáš Pospíchal, Scherer, Josef Kadraba, Kvašňák, Jelínek.
HUNGARY Grosics (c), Mátrai, Sárosi, Solymosi, Mészöly, Sipos, Sándor, Rákosi, Albert, Tichy, Fenyvesi.

Hungary were firm favourites but knocked themselves out on the Czech wall. A patchy pitch didn't help their passing, though Czechoslovakia had little trouble with it when their three half-backs interpassed and Masopust's through-ball cut out three defenders for Scherer to score. Schrojf, shortish and balding, made save after save, from Albert, Sándor, Solymosi and a Sipos thunderbolt. Tichy hit the bar as in 1958, and the utilitarians had won again.

SEMI-FINALS

---

13 June 1962 – Nacional, Santiago – 76,594 – Arturo Yamasaki (PER)

BRAZIL (2) 4
Garrincha 9, 32, Vavá 48, 78

CHILE (1) 2
Toro 42, L Sánchez pen 62

BRAZIL Gylmar, D Santos, N Santos, Zito, Mauro (c), Zózimo, Garrincha, Didi, Vavá, Amarildo, Zagallo.
CHILE Escuti, Eyzaguirre, Manuel Rodríguez, Contreras, R Sánchez, Rojas, Ramírez, Toro (c), Landa, Tobar, L Sánchez.
SENT OFF: Landa 80, Garrincha 84.

Naturally this attracted the biggest attendance of the competition, but Brazil were too old to be affected by a crowd, and Chile were always playing catch-up. The powerful Rojas hit a post early on, but Brazil had an obvious penalty turned down and a goal disallowed for offside (the linesman didn't flag). Soon Zagallo hit a long cross, Vavá missed his overhead kick, and Garrincha cracked the loose ball into the top corner from twenty yards. Right foot, head, now left foot. Pelé wasn't missed.

Later he proved his header against England was no one-off, hammering in another corner by Zagallo, whose lung power and underrated skills were transforming Brazil's 4–4–2 into a virtual 4–3–3. Toro gave Chile hope with a fabulous 25-yard free kick and Zózimo's handball gave away the penalty (he'd done the same at Wembley in 1956) which Leonel Sánchez cracked past a stationary Gylmar. But Vavá headed in a corner and a cross. As the play grew rougher, two players were sent off, Landa for fouling Zito, Garrincha for kicking Rojas. On his way round the pitch, Garrincha had his head cut by a missile from the crowd. Brazil's background team immediately began strenuous negotiations to let the tournament's best player appear in the Final.

---

13 June 1962 – Municipal ('El Sausalito'), Viña del Mar – 5,890 – Gottfried Dienst (SWI)

CZECHOSLOVAKIA (0) 3
Kadraba 48, Scherer 80, pen 84

YUGOSLAVIA (0) 1
Jerković 68

1962

CZECHOSLOVAKIA Schrojf, Lála, Novák (c), Pluskal, Popluhár, Masopust, Pospíchal, Scherer, Kadraba, Kvašňák, Jelínek.

YUGOSLAVIA Šoškić, Durković, Jusufi, Radaković, Marković, Popović, Vasilije Sijaković, Šekularac, Jerković, Galić (c), Skoblar.

In front of another tiny crowd, Czechoslovakia again beat a more skilful side, but again needed Schrojf to do his thing. After Galić had missed two good chances in quick succession, Kadraba headed in a rebound. After 56 minutes Sijaković hit the bar, Skoblar heading the rebound against the same part of the woodwork – then Jerković equalised with a backheader after beating Schrojf to a cross. But if Yugoslavia were unlucky up front, their defence let them down. Scherer was unmarked to push a cross past the onrushing Šoškić, then Marković conceded a penalty by handing the ball a long way from goal. The Czechoslovakians took their chances but were rather worthy winners.

3RD-PLACE FINAL

16 June 1962 – Nacional, Santiago – 66,697 – Juan Gardeazábal (SPA)

CHILE (0) 1
Rojas 89

YUGOSLAVIA (0) 0

CHILE Adán Godoy, Eyzaguirre, Rodríguez, Humberto Cruz, R Sánchez, Rojas, Ramírez, Toro (c), Carlos Campos, Tobar, L Sánchez.
YUGOSLAVIA Šoškić, Durković, Slavko Svinjarević, Radaković, Marković, Popović, Kovačević, Šekularac, Jerković, Galić (c), Skoblar.

In front of spectators like these, no match could be meaningless. It was decided by another long low shot from Rojas, deflecting in

off Marković. Chile's players had grown in stature during the tournament – Rojas and Toro, Raúl Sánchez arguably its best stopper, Eyzaguirre a stylish young right-back, – and nobody begrudged the country its final placing.

FINAL

17 June 1962 – Nacional, Santiago – 68,679 – Nikolai Latyshev (USR)

BRAZIL (1) 3
Amarildo 16, Zito 69, Vavá 78

CZECHOSLOVAKIA (1) 1
Masopust 14

BRAZIL Gylmar, D Santos, N Santos, Zito, Mauro (c), Zózimo, Garrincha, Didi, Vavá, Amarildo, Zagallo.
CZECHOSLOVAKIA Schrojf, Jiří Tichý, Novák (c), Pluskal, Popluhár, Masopust, Pospíchal, Scherer, Kadraba, Kvašňák, Jelínek.

Garrincha was allowed to play – but after putting in an early cross for Vavá to volley against the near post, he made surprisingly little impact, stifled by the veteran Novák and his defence. Still, Brazil had enough firepower elsewhere. As against England, they did just enough to beat a good but not great European side. As in 1958, they won despite conceding an early goal, little Masopust running onto Pospíchal's clever pass to hit a low first-time shot before Zózimo could get to him. If Czechoslovakia, with their muscular defence, could hold the lead for any length of time . . .

Instead, within two minutes Amarildo received a throw-in, shrugged off Kvašňák, beat Pluskal near the left-hand goal line, and shot in at the near post where Schrojf, expecting a cross, had left a wide gap.

The Czech wingers played well after the interval, as did Masopust (who was voted European Footballer of the Year) and the loping Kvašňák – and Czechoslovakia should have had a penalty for a clear handball by Djalma (the video shows him jerking his arm towards the ball as it falls behind him). But they were a pedestrian side, who'd lacked a genuine finisher since Rudolf Kučera was injured before the tournament. And this was Amarildo's day. Zito sent him away on the left with a pass that convulsed Popluhár, Amarildo dummied to cross, cut back onto his right foot, and dinked a cross beyond Schrojf. Zito, short but unmarked, couldn't miss with the header. It was his first international goal for five years.

Schrojf had redeemed himself with several good saves, but the magic was gone. When Brazil won a throw-in near the Czech penalty area, big Djalma came up, held off an opponent by turning his back, then spun and hit a hopeful hanging cross with his left foot. Schrojf came out, overran the ball as it dropped out of the sun, and let it slip out behind him as he fell. Almost as soon as it hit the ground, Vavá knocked it in, grinning like a shark.

It was the end of the international road for Zózimo and two of the greats, Didi and Nílton Santos, the strolling commander and the best left-back of all time. They had just enough left in the tank to survive the first stirrings of the new, more iron-clad football, but they belonged to another time. Nílton saw the change coming: unlike Didi and Zito, he'd shaved off the pencil moustache. Some of the other elders would still be there four years later, with results foreseen by Pelé.

1962

As his shot comes down off the bar in the Final, Geoff Hurst (extreme right) and Willi Schulz lie back and think of Azerbaijan.

The shadow of a doubt

England **1966**

1930

1934

1938

1950

1954

1958

1962

1966

1970

1974

1978

1982

1986

1990

1994

1998

2002

2006

Most certainly, said Alfred Ernest Ramsey, using that phrase of his. Most certainly England will win the World Cup. The man with a legendary aversion to the press had provided them with their juiciest quote. Presumably he'd have taken it back, given the chance. But no, there it was on record, a rod for his own back.

Ramsey knew he hadn't been first choice to replace Winterbottom as manager, but no doubt thought he should have been. None of the other candidates could have achieved what he did in 1961–62, taking little Ipswich Town to the First Division title the season after bringing them out of the Second. Significantly, he achieved it by fitting journeyman players into a system that took the opposition by surprise. The new man had credentials, then – and more power: he only took the job on condition that the selection committee, which had hindered Winterbottom so much, was disbanded. All team decisions would be his, bringing England into the twentieth century.

There was also the little matter of home advantage, and enough good players to fortify Sir Alf's optimism, especially in a very open tournament. Bobby Moore, now the captain, was still making the occasional crass mistake but had matured into probably the best defender in the world – and the rest of the back four was now in place: Ray Wilson still there, George Cohen a robust new right-back, Jack Charlton winning his first cap at 30. Charlton's brother

Bobby had moved into midfield, where he saw more of the ball but didn't quite look the part of playmaker. Greaves recovered well enough from hepatitis to score four goals in a warm-up international.

Just as importantly, Ramsey was in the process of making a revolutionary change to the shape of the team. The first three matches of the season had been a 0-0 draw with Wales, a 3-2 home defeat by Austria (Jimmy Hill: 'England won't win the World Cup. But don't blame Alf. No-one could win it with this lot') and a late 2-1 win over Northern Ireland. So, on a freezing December night in Madrid, Ramsey sent out a team with (gasp) no wingers.

The 2-0 scoreline was a travesty. Spain were lucky to get nil. Their full-backs, looking for someone to mark, were dragged out of position, Alan Ball and two mobile strikers filled the gaps, Moore came up to join the attack. A night when the term 'wingless wonders' wasn't used in derision. Spain's coach José Villalonga: 'They were phenomenal. Far superior in their experiment and in their players.'

This was the match that marked Ramsey as an international coach of the highest rank – yet he wasn't quite ready to act on its findings. A full-back in his playing days, he knew the value of wingers, indeed he went on using them right up to the World Cup quarter-final. It took him a long time to accept there wasn't a stray Garrincha in the country.

1930
1934
1938
1950
1954
1958
1962

1966

1970
1974
1978
1982
1986
1990
1994
1998
2002
2006

While England were winning all four matches on a pre-tournament tour, the other Home Countries were wondering what might have been. Northern Ireland missed out on a play-off by being held to a draw in Albania, and Wales beat the USSR at home but lost in Greece.

Scotland lost 3-0 in Naples after injuries and the refusal of club managers in England (including well-known Scots like Matt Busby and Bill Shankly) had deprived them of a string of international-class players: Law, Baxter, Henderson, McNeill, Bill Brown. A frustrated Jock Stein resigned as manager.

Italy were devastating at home but far less convincing away. West Germany, who'd shown their mettle by winning in Sweden after drawing at home, had Seeler up front, new stars in midfield, and several players from the Borussia Dortmund team which had just beaten Liverpool in the Cup-Winners Cup final. Argentina won the 'Little World Cup' in Brazil, beating the hosts (3-0), England and Portugal, then recalled the dreaded Lorenzo as manager. The Portuguese, heavily reliant on Benfica, had qualified for the first time by putting out the 1962 finalists Czechoslovakia, the only goal in Bratislava scored by Eusébio,

the European Footballer of the Year. The USSR were strong again.

Meanwhile Brazil seemed to believe the Cup was now theirs by right. All they needed was to resuscitate some of the veterans from 1962 and even 1958. So out went the young Carlos Alberto and Djalma Dias, back came Bellini (now 36) and Orlando, in stayed Djalma Santos (37), Gylmar (35), Zito (33) and an injury-prone Garrincha. There were some promising newcomers – Jairzinho, Gérson, Tostão, the 16-year-old Edu – but their time hadn't yet come. As in 1962, Pelé was the one great hope, still very much the best in the world – but there was no Amarildo to act as deputy: he'd been dropped too. 'There is only one way to describe Brazil's 1966 World Cup effort, and that is to openly declare that from the beginning it was a total and unmitigated disaster.' Pelé's words, and England fans wanted to believe them.

In March, the World Cup trophy was stolen from the Stampex exhibition in Westminster. A week later a dog called Pickles discovered it under a hedge in southeast London and its owner handed it in, hoping he wouldn't be the last Englishman to pick it up that summer. Alf had promised as much, so it had to be true. Most certainly.

GROUP 1

England (seeded), France, Mexico, Uruguay.

11 July 1966 – Wembley, London – 87,148 – István Zsolt (HUN)

ENGLAND 0

URUGUAY 0

ENGLAND Gordon Banks, George Cohen, Ray Wilson, Nobby Stiles, Jack Charlton, Bobby Moore (c), Alan Ball, Jimmy Greaves, Bobby Charlton, Roger Hunt, John Connelly. *Alf Ramsey*.
URUGUAY Ladislao Mazurkiewicz, Luis Ubiña, Omar Caetano, Milton Viera, Jorge Manicera, Horacio Troche (c), Julio César Cortés, Néstor Gonçálvez, Héctor Silva, Pedro Rocha, Domingo Pérez. *Ondino Viera*.

If there was any deep optimism beforehand, much of it had drained away by the end of the day's proceedings. Uruguay used Troche as sweeper behind a back four, and everyone else in withdrawn positions, including their two most creative players Rocha and Cortés – a web the England players rarely looked like breaking. When they did, body-checks and knee-high tackles came into play, one of the worst (ironically) committed against Stiles, Ramsey's new guard dog in midfield. Connelly's header dropped onto the top of the bar but he was generally crowded out and the overlapping full-backs channelled into blind alleys. Draw the curtain across.

This was the first of only two examples of a coach picking his son to play in the finals (see Maldini & Son in 1998). Old English sources spell the surname Ubinas, an error. Wembley's official name was the Empire Stadium.

13 July 1966 – Wembley, London – 69,237 – Menachem Ashkenazi (ISR)

FRANCE (0) 1
Hausser 61

MEXICO (0) 1
Borja 48

FRANCE Marcel Aubour, Robert Budzinski, Jean Djorkaeff, Marcel Artelesa (c), Bernard Bosquier, Gabriel De Michele, Joseph Bonnel, Roby Herbin, Néstor Combin, Philippe Gondet, Gérard Hausser. *Henri Guérin*.
MEXICO Ignacio Calderón, Arturo Chaires, Gustavo Peña (c), Gabriel Núñez, Guillermo Hernández, Isidoro Díaz, Salvador Reyes, Magdaleno Mercado, Enrique Borja, Javier Fragoso, Aarón Padilla. *Ignacio Trelles*.

France were proud of their speed, but their ball control and passing were lamentable (the highly touted Combin, playing out of position, was a particular failure) and they never came to terms with Borja, whose 32 goals were a national record until 1997. When Aubour saved his shot, from Padilla's cross, he pushed the loose ball in from close range. France also scored from a rebound, Hausser's ground shot going in off a post, but the only people to take any satisfaction were England and Uruguay.

1966

15 July 1966 – White City, London – 45,662 – Karol Galba (CZE)

URUGUAY (2) 2
Rocha 27, Cortés 32

FRANCE (1) 1
de Bourgoing pen 16

URUGUAY Mazurkiewicz, Ubiña, Caetano, Viera, Manicera, Troche (c), Cortés, Gonçálvez, José Sasía, Rocha, Pérez.
FRANCE Aubour, Djorkaeff, Budzinski, Artelesa (c), Bosquier, Yves Herbet, Bonnel, Héctor de Bourgoing, Jacky Simon, Gondet, Hausser.

1930

1934

1938

1950

1954

1958

1962

Again the French were quick, Herbet taking a return pass at speed and hurtling towards the right-hand goal line, where Manicera pulled him back with a better sense of where the penalty area was than the referee. De Bourgoing, capped by Argentina in 1956–57, made no mistake with the kick but didn't play for France again.

Perhaps this shook the Uruguayans out of their defensive shell. At any rate they took over from then on, missing easy chances after scoring their two goals. First they kept possession interminably until Rocha shot home from the right, then Cortés smashed in a volley from a similar position.

1966

16 July 1966 – Wembley, London – 92,570 – Concetto Lo Bello (ITA)

ENGLAND (1) 2
R Charlton 36, Hunt 76

MEXICO (0) 0

ENGLAND Banks, Cohen, Wilson, Stiles, J Charlton, Moore (c), Terry Paine, Greaves, R Charlton, Hunt, Martin Peters.
MEXICO Calderón, Chaires, Peña (c), Jesús del Muro, Núñez, Hernández, Díaz, Reyes, Ignacio Jáuregui, Borja, Padilla.

It was two hours a-coming but worth the wait. Taking Hunt's pass in the centre circle, Bobby Charlton set off towards the opposite penalty area. With the Mexicans holding off instead of challenging, he swerved to his right with a kind of hitch-kick before hitting one of his patented long shots across the keeper at about chest height. One of the most famous Wembley goals. There was an offside flag up against Greaves at the time, but he wasn't exactly interfering with play!

He had a leading part in the second too, exchanging a series of passes on the left before

1970

1974

1978

1982

1986

1990

1994

1998

2002

2006

sending Greaves in to shoot at Calderón, who could only push the ball straight to Hunt. Better from England, but still room for improvement against these packed defences. When Mexico kicked off at the start of the match, Díaz banged the ball upfield while the rest of the team scuttled towards their own goal, a sign of what football was coming to. Again the solitary winger (Paine) couldn't get into the game, but England were likely to go through.

19 July 1966 – Wembley, London – 61,112 – Bertil Lööw (SWE)

MEXICO 0

URUGUAY 0

MEXICO Antonio Carbajal, Chaires, Peña (c), Núñez, Hernández, Díaz, Mercado, Reyes, Ernesto Cisneros, Borja, Padilla.
URUGUAY Mazurkiewicz, Ubiña, Caetano, Viera, Manicera, Troche (c), Cortés, Goncálvez, Sasía, Rocha, Pérez.

Mexico needed to win by an unlikely two goals to qualify, and never stopped trying

LONGEST PLAYING SPANS

yrs	days			
16	25	Antonio Carbajal	MEX	1950–66
16	17	Hugo Sánchez	MEX	1978–94
16	1	Lothar Matthäus	GER	1982–98
15	363	Giuseppe Bergomi	ITA	1982–98
15	346	Elías Figueroa	CHI	1966–82

Emerson Leão, who kept goal for Brazil in the 1974 and 1978 finals, was also in the squad for 1970 and 1986. If he'd played in both, he could have spanned 16 years 18 days.

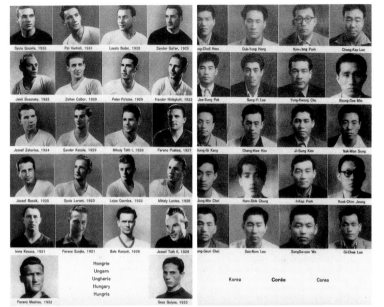

The official poster for the 1950 tournament.

Opposite ends of the talent scale in 1954. The great Hungarians and the not-so-great South Koreans, who lost to them 9–0.

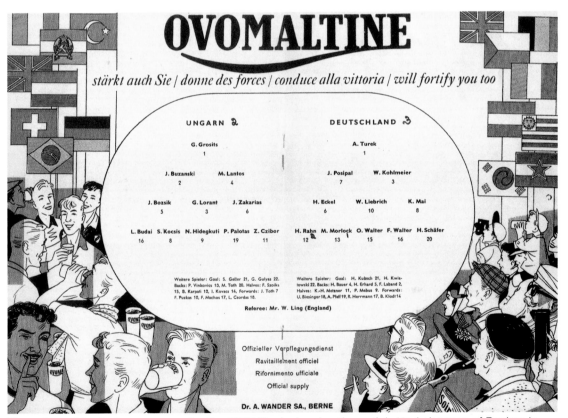

The rather whimsical programme for the 1950 Final, showing the anticipated absence of Puskas in the Hungarian line-up.

Antonio Rattin (third from right) is sent off at Wembley in 1966. The England players are Bobby Charlton (left), Moore (No 6) and Peters.

WHITE CITY STADIUM
LONDON

WORLD CHAMPIONSHIP
1966
Jules Rimet Cup

EIGHTH FINAL

SECRETARY.
THE FOOTBALL ASSOCIATION

FRIDAY JULY 15
KICK-OFF 7.30 p.m.

STANDING ENCLOSURE 7/6

(SEE PLAN & CONDITIONS ON BACK)
TO BE RETAINED

BLOCK
L
STAND
ENTRANCE
12

2897

ENTRANCE
WESTWAY

A ticket for France v Uruguay in 1966, the only World Cup match played at the White City Stadium, which no longer exists. Every group match was an 'eighth final'.

Sir Alf Ramsey, most certainly the top manager in 1966.

A ticket for the 1966
Final, price 50p.

Wembley, 30 July 1966. Wilson struggles to uphold Moore, who has no trouble with the gold statuette, flanked by (left to right) Little Nobby and Big Jack, Banksie, Ballie, Peters, the hidden Hunt, Hurst, Cohen and a tired but happy Bobby Charlton. England – the World Champions.

A ticket for the England v Brazil match of 1970.

Gerson, who scored Brazil's winning goal, looking older and wearier after the 1970 Final.

An advert from 1970. Join a supporters club and meet girls. Yeh, right.

Burgnich looks back in anguish as Pele celebrates his goal in the 1970 Final.

Johan Cruyff had the football world at his feet –
until the 1974 Final.

The Kaiser rules, OK. Franz
Beckenbauer lifts the new trophy
in 1974.

Johan Neeskens blasts home the
first penalty in the 1974 Final.

Kenny Dalglish volleys Scotland's first goal in their surprise win over Holland in 1978.

Teofilo Cubillas of Peru (centre), a star of the 1970 and 1978 tournaments.

A blizzard of tickertape (or paper to that effect), one of the abiding memories of Argentina in 1978.

Angry Algerian fans wave banknotes as Austria and West Germany go through the motions in 1982.

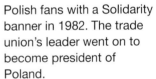

Polish fans with a Solidarity banner in 1982. The trade union's leader went on to become president of Poland.

The price of fame: Diego Maradona faces a crowd of Belgians in 1982.

The first missed penalty in a World Cup Final. Antonio Cabrini shoots wide in 1982.

Claudio Gentile (left) joins in Marco Tardelli's memorable celebration of his winning goal in the 1982 Final.

1930
1934
1938
1950
1954
1958
1962

1966

1970
1974
1978
1982
1986
1990
1994
1998
2002
2006

16 July 1966 – Villa Park, Birmingham – 46,587 – Konstantin Zečević (YUG)

ARGENTINA   0

WEST GERMANY 0

ARGENTINA Roma, Perfumo, Marzolini, Ferreiro, Albrecht, Rattin (c), Solari, González, Artime, Onega, Mas.
WEST GERMANY Tilkowski, Höttges, Schnellinger, Beckenbauer, Schulz, Weber, Brülls, Haller, Seeler (c), Overath, Held.
SENT OFF: Albrecht 66.

The irresistible force met the immovable object, but it was hard to be sure which was which. When the Germans attacked, they were stopped by bodychecks and sly trips followed by practised gestures of innocence. When Argentina ventured upfield, they were hit by tackles they clearly thought were illegal and may well have been: the likes of Schnellinger and Schulz knew how to take man and ball and take them very hard. With so many talented forwards on either side, neither midfield felt free to commit itself to going forward. For Argentina this was a normal state of affairs, but it was odd to see Haller hanging back and Beckenbauer fouling Ferreiro, Overath flattening González.

Eventually, after more than one wild tackle, Albrecht was sent off for kneeing Weber in the groin, which must have been a formidable part of his anatomy: Albrecht was limping as he walked off. Perfumo twice headed against his own bar. The Germans were no angels, but it was Lorenzo's mob who received a warning from FIFA.

19 July 1966 – Hillsborough, Sheffield – 32,127 – Joaquim de Campos (POR)

ARGENTINA   (0) 2
Artime 52, Onega 79

SWITZERLAND   (0) 0

ARGENTINA Roma, Perfumo, Marzolini, Ferreiro, Oscar Calics, Rattin (c), Solari, González, Artime, Onega, Mas.
SWITZERLAND Leo Eichmann, Brodmann (c), Fuhrer, Armbruster, Stierli, Bäni, Kuhn, Gottardi, Künzli, Hosp, Quentin.

Even against clearly inferior opposition, Argentina were still happy to play out a barren first half and wait for the goals. Artime shot in off a post after the Swiss had given the ball away, Onega ran onto a return pass from González and lobbed the keeper as Eichmann and Fuhrer collided (no World War wisecracks required). It was the first time Argentina had qualified for the second phase since 1930 and Switzerland's last appearance in the finals till 1994.

20 July 1966 – Villa Park, Birmingham – 45,187 – Armando Marques (BRZ)

WEST GERMANY (1) 2
Emmerich 39, Seeler 84

SPAIN   (1) 1
Fusté 23

WEST GERMANY Tilkowski, Höttges, Schnellinger, Beckenbauer, Schulz, Weber, Werner Krämer, Held, Seeler (c), Overath, Lothar Emmerich.
SPAIN Iríbar, Sanchís, Reija, Jesús Glaría, Gallego, Zoco (c), Adelardo (Rodríguez), José María Fusté, Amancio, Marcelino (Martínez), Carlos Lapetra.

Spain, needing a win to qualify, seemed to have little chance of achieving it without their three best-known players, Suárez and Del Sol out through injury, Gento dropped for loss of pace. Del Sol wasn't capped again, Suárez not until a valedictory recall in 1972. Yet their team mates took the lead when Fusté ran onto Marcelino's lob.

West Germany woke up after that. They'd added balance to their side by moving Held back inside from the wing, where his left foot had let him down, and bringing in the naturally left-sided Emmerich, his beefy partner at

13 July 1966 – Villa Park, Birmingham – 42,738 – Dimitar Rumenchev (BUL)

ARGENTINA	**(0) 2**
Artime 65, 77	
SPAIN	**(0) 1**
Roma o.g. 71	

ARGENTINA Antonio Roma, Roberto Perfumo, Silvio Marzolini, Roberto Ferreiro, Rafael Albrecht, Antonio Rattin (c), Jorge Solari, Alberto González, Luis Artime, Ermindo Onega, Oscar Mas. *Juan Carlos Lorenzo*.
SPAIN José Ángel Iríbar, Manuel Sanchís snr, Eladio (Silvestre), 'Pirri' (José Martínez), 'Gallego' (Francisco Fernández), Ignacio Zoco, Luis Del Sol, Luis Suárez, José Armando Ufarte, Joaquín Peiró, Francisco Gento (c). *José Villalonga*.

Argentina presented an almost unnerving sight, quite unlike any of their predecessors, almost European with their neat kit, short hair and severe sliding tackles in the rain, many of them directed at Suárez, Inter Milan's delicate playmaker. Contact sport apart, Argentina had as many world-class players as anyone in the tournament: Marzolini and Ferreiro, Onega and the 19-year-old Mas, the 6'3 Rattin a one-man halfback line, Artime a finisher who scored 24 goals in 25 internationals.

Here he converted González' low cross from the right and dragged Onega's pass past a defender before hitting a left-foot shot that drew applause from the St John's Ambulance men on the touchline. Every known source, Spanish and otherwise, credits Spain's equaliser to Pirri, who was winning his first cap – but that's not how it looks on the screen. When a Suárez cross is headed almost straight up in the air, Pirri jumps for it with Roma, but it's clearly the goalkeeper's hand that dunks it in the net like a water polo player. Not the way he'd have chosen to celebrate his 34th birthday. Sanchís' son Manuel junior played in the 1990 finals.

15 July 1966 – Hillsborough, Sheffield – 32,028 – Tofik Bakhramov (USR)

SPAIN	**(0) 2**
Sanchís 57, Amancio 75	
SWITZERLAND	**(1) 1**
Quentin 31	

SPAIN Iríbar, Sanchís, Severino Reija, Pirri, Gallego, Zoco, Del Sol, Suárez, Amancio (Amaro), Peiró, Gento (c).
SWITZERLAND Elsener, Fuhrer, René Brodmann (c), Werner Leimgruber, Kurt Armbruster, Xavier Stierli, Bäni, Jakob (Köbi) Kuhn, Vittore Gottardi, Hosp, René Pierre Quentin.

This already had the look of a scrap between also-rans, and again Switzerland were unlikely to keep pace with the professionals. Nevertheless they took the lead, the reinstated Kuhn sending Gottardi away on the right, Quentin shooting home the cross. But Sanchís had already served warning with a strong run through the middle, and now scored a sensational individual goal, beating man after man before hammering the ball into the roof of the net for his only goal in international football. Short and slight, he'd made his debut in the recent defeat by England, but this was a better day.

Remarkably, Spain's winner was almost as good, Gento going on a long run down the left that recalled his prime, Amancio diving to head in the cross. The Germans, next up, would have taken note.

YOUNGEST GOALKEEPERS

yrs	days			
19	191	Lee Chan-Myung	NKO	1966
19	287	Vincent Enyeama	NGA	2002

17-year-old Walter Brom was in Poland's 1938 squad.

1930
1934
1938
1950
1954
1958
1962
1966
1970
1974
1978
1982
1986
1990
1994
1998
2002
2006

on the pitch after arriving horribly late on Simon ('It was a bad, bad tackle. I got stick and deserved to get stick'). It's said that certain officials wanted him dropped from the team, and only an ultimatum from Ramsey kept him in it. Whatever, he was lucky to have the manager's faith: his tackles had been wild and we don't usually talk about his passing. But at least the back four had again looked impregnable.

It really was the beginning of the end for wingers under Ramsey. Neither Connelly nor Paine was ever capped again, and Callaghan didn't return till 1977, a gap of 11 years 59 days, still the England record.

GROUP 1

	P	W	D	L	F	A	Pts
England	3	2	1	0	4	0	5
Uruguay	3	1	2	0	2	1	4
Mexico	3	0	2	1	1	3	2
France	3	0	1	2	2	5	1

England and Uruguay qualified for the quarter-finals.

GROUP 2

Argentina, Spain, Switzerland, West Germany (seeded).

12 July 1966 – Hillsborough, Sheffield – 36,127 – Hugh Phillips (SCO)

WEST GERMANY   (3) 5
Held 16, Haller 21, pen 77,
Beckenbauer 40, 62

SWITZERLAND   (0) 0

WEST GERMANY Hans Tilkowski, Horst-Dieter Höttges, Karl-Heinz Schnellinger, Franz Beckenbauer, Willi Schulz, Wolfgang Weber, Albert Brülls, Helmut Haller, Uwe Seeler (c), Wolfgang Overath, Sigi Held. *Helmut Schön.*
SWITZERLAND Karl Elsener, André Grobéty, Heinz Schneiter (c), Ely Tacchella, Hansrüdi Fuhrer, Heinz Bäni, Richard Dürr, Karl Odermatt, Fritz Künzli, Robert Hosp, Jean-Claude Schindelholz. *Alfredo Foni (ITA).*

Switzerland had suspended two leading players, Kuhn and Leimgruber, for breaking curfew, but even at full strength wouldn't have been a match for this German team. And it wasn't just a case of brave part-timers being steamrollered by Teutonic power (though there was all of that): West Germany were awesome, and awesomely talented. After Held put in the rebound when Seeler's shot was saved, they scored three of the best goals seen in a single World Cup match, Beckenbauer (twice) and Haller striding through to score with confidence and perfect technique, a masterclass of finishing from midfield. Seeler, at the hub of everything, played a part in all three goals and was fouled for the penalty.

The running from midfield was wonderfully powerful, full of decisions made at speed, Overath distributing with his excellent left foot, Beckenbauer one of the most precocious players in Europe, Haller bulky but full of talent as well as himself. Tilkowski, on his 31st birthday, had little to do.

LEADING GOALSCORERS 1966

9	Eusébio	POR	4 pen
6	Helmut Haller	GER	1 pen
4	Ferenc Bene	HUN	
4	Franz Beckenbauer	GER	
4	Valery Porkujan	USR	
4	Geoff Hurst	ENG	

TOURNAMENTS AS A PLAYER

5	Antonio Carbajal	MEX	1950–54–58–62–66
5	Lothar Matthäus	GER	1982–86–90–94–98
4	Djalma Santos	BRZ	1954–58–62–66
4	Pelé	BRZ	1958–62–66–70
4	Karl-Heinz Schnellinger	GER	1958–62–66–70
4	Uwe Seeler	GER	1958–62–66–70
4	Gianni Rivera	ITA	1962–66–70–74
4	Pedro Rocha	URU	1962–66–70–74
4	Władysław Żmuda	POL	1974–78–82–86
4	Diego Maradona	ARG	1982–86–90–94
4	Franky Van der Elst	BEL	1986–90–94–98
4	Andoni Zubizarreta	SPA	1986–90–94–98
4	Enzo Scifo	BEL	1986–90–94–98
4	Giuseppe Bergomi	ITA	1982–86–90–98
4	Paolo Maldini	ITA	1990–94–98–02
4	Hong Myung-Bo	SKO	1990–94–98–02

to get them, Cisneros hitting a post in the first half, Borja always a threat in the air. In the end, the match mattered most to the 37-year-old Carbajal. Already the first player to take part in four World Cup finals tournaments, he now appeared in a fifth, keeping a clean sheet for the first time. His first and last international matches were in finals tournaments (1950–66). The real crowd figure was probably nearer 35,000. Lööw is no misprint.

---

20 July 1966 – Wembley, London – 98,270 – Arturo Yamasaki (PER)

ENGLAND (1) 2
Hunt 36, 76

FRANCE (0) 0

ENGLAND Banks, Cohen, Wilson, Stiles, J Charlton, Moore (c), Ian Callaghan, Greaves, R Charlton, Hunt, Peters.

FRANCE Aubour, Djorkaeff, Budzinski, Artelesa (c), Bosquier, Herbet, Bonnel, Herbin, Simon, Gondet, Hausser.

Even though the French had to reshuffle their attack after an injury to Herbin after only eight minutes, they gave England another frustrating night, constantly catching Greaves and Hunt offside. In the end the latter celebrated his 28th birthday with two goals, though the second was a gift, Aubour fumbling a header from Callaghan's cross. Earlier, Hunt had put the loose ball in from right next to a goalpost (inevitable cries of offside) after Jack Charlton had headed a cross from Greaves against the base of the other post. England scored their goals at exactly the same times as against Mexico.

Stiles, whose tackle had lamed Herbin early on, had a bad time all round, knocked down by the referee, booked for a foul, lucky to stay

Borussia Dortmund. The latter equalised with a staggering goal, chasing a loose ball to the left-hand goal line and battering it into the roof of the net from an impossible angle. It happened so fast and implausibly that one of the Spaniards cleared the ball upfield like a schoolboy hoping teacher hadn't noticed.

Then Held went back to the left, beat Sanchís, and hit a low cross which Seeler controlled and pushed home. Even under pressure, West Germany had again looked the part.

GROUP 2

	P	W	D	L	F	A	Pts
West Germany	3	2	1	0	7	1	5
Argentina	3	2	1	0	4	1	5
Spain	3	1	0	2	4	5	2
Switzerland	3	0	0	3	1	9	0

West Germany and Argentina qualified for the quarter-finals.

GROUP 3

Brazil (seeded), Bulgaria, Hungary, Portugal.

12 July 1966 – Goodison Park, Liverpool – 47,308 – Kurt Tschenscher (GER)

BRAZIL   **(1) 2**
Pelé 13, Garrincha 63

BULGARIA (0) 0

BRAZIL Gylmar (dos Santos), Djalma Santos, Paulo Henrique (Souza), Denílson (Machado), Hideraldo Luiz Bellini (c), Altair (Gomes), 'Garrincha' (Manoel Francisco dos Santos), Antônio Lima, Alcindo (de Freitas), 'Pelé' (Édson Arantes do Nascimento), 'Jairzinho' (Jair Ventura). *Vicente Feola.*

BULGARIA Georgi Naidenov, Aleksandar Shalamanov, Dimitar Penev, Ivan Vutzov, Boris Gaganelov (c), Stoyan Kitov, Dobromir Jechev, Dinko Dermendjiev, Georgi Asparoukhov, Dimitar Yakimov, Ivan Kolev. *Rudolf Vytlačil (CZE).*

With all his reservations about Brazil's preparation, Pelé set out to win the match on his own, and just about succeeded, even though Bulgaria man-marked him ruthlessly. 'My legs ached as a result of Jechev's constant tripping and kicking.' In the end the referee had to separate them and wag a finger, which is as tough as they ever got in those days. In the debates about footballers from different eras, it's worth remembering the relative protection ball-players get nowadays. Jechev was booked but might have been sent off before half-time today.

Not that Pelé was especially intimidated. He was too well built for a start, a brick powerhouse with genius. How else do you stop that except by fouling? When Bulgaria did it yet again, with only thirteen minutes gone, the great man exacted appropriate revenge. None of the bending and curling commonly associated with Brazilian free kicks; this one (hit with anger?) blazed through the wall and yorked Naidenov. The first goal of the tournament.

Ironically, the free kick had been given away by Yakimov, Bulgaria's most accomplished player. If the team had given him more support, if the talented Asparoukhov had shaken off an ankle injury, who knows what tremors might have been caused in that creaking Brazilian defence? As it was, the 35-year-old Kolev, first capped in 1952, was a peripheral figure.

Until, that is, he committed a rather sheepish foul just outside the area. Garrincha picked himself up and smashed the ball into the top near corner with the outside of his right foot. Those deformed legs, bending in at the knee from the side, looked almost made for shots like this.

Brazil had played well in fits and starts but looked a one-man army. Late in the game, Pelé

1930
1934
1938
1950
1954
1958
1962
1966
1970
1974
1978
1982
1986
1990
1994
1998
2002
2006

CONSECUTIVE MATCHES WITHOUT DEFEAT

13	Brazil	1958–66
12	Italy	1994–02
11	Uruguay	1930–54
11	Brazil	1978–82
11	Germany	1990–94
10	Italy	1982–86

Germany were still West Germany in 1990.

Italy's 12-match sequence includes two defeats on penalties.

put his head down and went on an angled run reminiscent of a famous televised goal by George Best, ending in a shot which Naidenov did well to turn over the bar. Magnificent – but Pelé's legs had taken so much stick that he was rested for the next match ('I think this was another mistake'). Vytlačil's last finals match as coach had also been against Brazil: the 1962 Final.

---

13 July 1966 – Old Trafford, Manchester – 29,886 – Leo Callaghan (WAL)

PORTUGAL (1) 3
José Augusto 2, 65, Torres 88

HUNGARY (0) 1
Bene 60

PORTUGAL Joaquim Carvalho, João Morais, Alexandre Baptista, Vicente (Lucas), Hilário (da Conceição), Jaime Graça, Mário Coluna (c), José Augusto (de Almeida), José Torres, Eusébio (Ferreira), António Simões. *Manuel da Luz Afonso (selector), Otto Glória (BRZ) (coach).*
HUNGARY Antal Szentmihályi, Sándor Mátrai, Benő Káposzta, Kálmán Mészöly, Ferenc Sipos (c), Kálmán Sóvári, Ferenc Bene, István Nagy, Flórián Albert, Gyula Rákosi, János Farkas. *Lajos Baróti.*

Two of the best teams in the tournament, in their contrasting styles, produced a fascinating match and a distorted scoreline. Portugal, marvellous going forward, had a so-so back line. Hungary, with a packed and talented defence, were – well, marvellous going forward. But atrocious goalkeeping and missed chances destroyed them.

Talk beforehand centred round Eusébio and his credentials as the 'European Pelé' (actually the African Pelé: like Coluna, he was born in Mozambique). No-one was disappointed. Showing his intent in the very first minute, he beat Sóvári and Káposzta to force a corner, which Augusto headed in while the 6'4 Torres concentrated defenders' minds.

Hungary, forced to come out at once, dominated the next hour, Albert comfortable in his withdrawn role, Farkas streaming past Vicente, Nagy making the great Coluna lose his rag. But they needed a reciprocal goalkeeping error for their equaliser, Carvalho losing the ball in Albert's challenge to leave Bene with an open goal.

Within five minutes, they were back where they started. Szentmihályi – who, to be fair, had been injured in the very first minute, let an easy cross from Torres bounce off his chest for Augusto to head in again. Mátrai, the masterly grey-haired sweeper, lay on the ground in despair. At the very end Torres headed in Eusébio's corner. By then Szentmihályi was all a-tremble and Hungary were one of those teams who look too good to go down but usually do.

One source gives a crowd figure of 37,311.

---

15 July 1966 – Goodison Park, Liverpool – 51,387 – Ken Dagnall (ENG)

HUNGARY (1) 3
Bene 3, Farkas 64, Mészöly pen 72

BRAZIL (1) 1
Tostão 15

HUNGARY József Gelei, Mátrai, Káposzta, Mészöly, Sipos (c), Gusztáv Szepesi, Bene, Imre Mathesz, Albert, Rákosi, Farkas.
BRAZIL Gylmar, D Santos, Paulo Henrique, Lima, Bellini (c), Altair, Garrincha, Gérson (de Oliveira), Alcindo, 'Tostão' (Eduardo Gonçalves), Jairzinho.

One of the most vivid matches of all time, the subject of regular repeats, it would have been a classic if one side hadn't been so dominant, and you can call them that even though the scores were level for half the match.

Hungary lit the touchpaper early. Sipos pushed the ball out to Bene on the right, the winger jagged inside to stop Altair in his tracks, left him on his backside by beating him on the outside, cut inside Bellini, and scored with a low left-footer inside the near post. A little jewel, and just the start Hungary needed.

Brazil's two goals so far had come from free kicks, as did their third, the ball deflecting through to the 19-year-old Tostão, whose left foot struck it high to Gelei's left. Hungary didn't lose their nerve, and a superb sequence of play nearly put them back in front, Rákosi's crossfield pass was volleyed back by Mathesz then by Mészöly, then Bene played a headed one-two with Albert only for Gylmar to make the save. Seven touches in all, without letting the ball touch the ground.

By now Albert was running the match, socks round his ankles, ball tied to his feet. In the second half, he played Bene in behind the fullback, Farkas volleying the low cross wide of the near post. Bene put his head in his hands, Rákosi remonstrated with all his heart, Farkas snapped back. It looks comical now, but the last thing Hungary needed was another missed chance: as things stood, they were virtually out.

But the same three players produced an almost exact repeat for one of the great World Cup goals. Albert clipped a first-time pass up the right wing. Instead of beating his man, Bene looked up and hit a cross which dropped just above the penalty spot. Farkas, running full pelt, caught it with his instep just above the ground and a fraction behind him. The shot nearly holed the net behind a stationary Gylmar.

Brazil were broken then, missing Pelé like a lost limb. The killer third goal began with a fair but very firm tackle by Szepesi that left Garrincha limping. An inside pass to Albert, who accelerated between two players in midfield and sent the ball out to Bene yet again. He beat Altair and was brought down by Paulo Henrique for the penalty. It was Brazil's first World Cup defeat since 1954, and by the same country.

If Albert was the conductor, Bene was a wonderful second string. Like Albert, he began as a centre-forward first capped at 17, soon scoring all the goals in a 6-0 win over Morocco at the 1964 Olympics. But his size and close control made him perfectly suited to life out on the wing. He scored in every match in these finals, was involved in most of the other goals, and was still playing for Hungary in 1979.

In sad contrast, another brilliant winger wasn't capped again. This was the great Garrincha's 50th and last international, and no-one else has been so indispensable: it was the only time he finished on the losing side.

16 July 1966 – Old Trafford, Manchester – 25,438 – José María Codesal (URU)

PORTUGAL (2) 3
Vutzov o.g. 7, Eusébio 38, Torres 82

BULGARIA (0) 0

PORTUGAL José Pereira, Alberto Festa, Vicente, Hilário, Germano (de Figueiredo), Graça, Coluna (c), José Augusto, Torres, Eusébio, Simões.
BULGARIA Naidenov, Shalamanov, Penev, Vutzov, Gaganelov (c), Jechev, Dermendjiev, Petar Zhekov, Asparoukhov, Yakimov, Aleksandar Kostov.

Much as expected. Torres, very mobile for such a human goalpost, sent in a high cross which Vutzov headed past his own goalkeeper. Torres and Zhekov both hit the bar, then Simões sent Eusébio sprinting in to open his account in the tournament with a low cross-shot that Naidenov touched on its way in. Torres ended the scoring by following Gaganelov's feeble back-pass into the net. Eusébio generally played within himself, happy to test out his long-range shooting. Uncomfortable viewing for Brazil.

The balding Germano, perhaps the greatest central stopper of all time but now 33 and slowed by one cartilage operation too many, was winning his last cap. Common spelling variations: Chalamanov, Jetchev, Jekov.

1966

19 July 1966 – Goodison Park, Liverpool – 58,479 – George McCabe (ENG)

PORTUGAL　(2) 3
Simões 15, Eusébio 24, 85

BRAZIL　　(0) 1
Rildo 71

PORTUGAL Pereira, Morais, Baptista, Vicente, Hilário, Graça, Coluna (c), José Augusto, Torres, Eusébio, Simões.
BRAZIL 'Manga' (Aílton Corrêa), José Maria Fidélis, Hércules Brito, Denílson, Orlando (Peçanha) (c), Rildo (da Costa), Jairzinho, Lima, Walter da Silva, Pelé, 'Paraná' (Adhemir de Barros).

Pelé had to be brought back, but the contest with Eusébio was horribly unequal. Pelé was still injured, and the Portuguese defenders made sure he stayed that way, a wild early tackle cutting his knees from under him without so much as a booking. Before long Morais finished the demolition job with a double foul on the edge of the penalty area. Neither tackle was as horrifying as legend has it, but Pelé hadn't fully recovered and

couldn't withstand this kind of physical confrontation. He was carried off by the team doctor and masseur, taking Brazil's chances with him.

In truth, they hadn't been worth much from the moment their team sheet showed nine changes, including the return of Orlando to mark Eusébio. Pelé thought 'it would have been ridiculous in a junior league. In the World Cup, against one of the strongest teams of the tournament, it was suicidal.'

Manga and the tiny Fidélis had a particularly unhappy time. The goalkeeper, whose pockmarked face earned him the nickname Frankenstein from his kindly peers, looked nervous from the start, and soon Eusébio gave him good reason, beating his man on the left and putting over a near-post cross which Manga was a little unlucky to bat straight onto the head of Simões. The second goal was utterly predictable. Coluna took a free kick deep on the right, Torres soared to head it back from the far post, Eusébio headed almost through Manga, flattening Orlando in the process. Rildo pulled one back with a stern ground shot, but Brazil really needed to win, and Eusébio extinguished their chances with one of the most famous power goals of the World Cup.

After Manga had saved his shot (you could hear the impact from here), he touched the corner short to Simões, whose cross was aimed at Torres as usual. The ball bounced back towards the right, where Eusébio met it with a terrifying shin-high volley that left Manga on his knees. David Coleman: 'Oh my word! Have you ever seen anything like that?' Well actually we had: the shot was from close range and Orlando might have blocked it if he hadn't pulled out of the tackle. Like Garrincha against Hungary, this was his last international and the first in which he finished on the losing side.

That goal was an abiding memory of the tournament, but no more so than the sight of Pelé walking off with a coat round his shoulders and his knee heavily bandaged, vowing never to play in the World Cup again. The whole Brazilian approach had been a monument to complacency. Pelé again: 'I suppose our directors put their faith in the old dictum that "God is a Brazilian," forgetting that God also helps those who help themselves.'

---

20 July 1966 – Old Trafford, Manchester – 24,129 – Roberto Goicoechea (ARG)

HUNGARY   (2) 3
Davidov o.g. 42, Mészöly 44, Bene 53

BULGARIA   (1) 1
Asparoukhov 15

HUNGARY Gelei, Mátrai, Káposzta, Mészöly, Sipos (c), Szepesi, Bene, Mathesz, Albert, Farkas, Rákosi.
BULGARIA Simeon Simeonov, Dimitar Largov, Penev, Vutzov, Gaganelov (c), Jechev, Ivan Davidov, Kolev, Asparoukhov, Yakimov, Nikola Kotkov.

No reprieve for Brazil, although Asparoukhov did give Bulgaria the lead when Gelei ran out in a flap. Earlier Yakimov had hit a post, and it wasn't till half-time that Mészöly hammered a half-volley into the top corner. Bene headed the third, but the goal that eliminated Brazil was an own goal from Davidov (lunging at a cross by Rákosi) in on his international debut. Asparoukhov and Kotkov died in the same car crash in 1971.

GROUP 4

Chile, Italy (seeded), North Korea, USSR.

---

12 July 1966, Ayresome Park, Middlesbrough – 23,006 – Juan Gardeazábal (SPA)

USSR   (2) 3
Malafeyev 30, 88, Banishevsky 31

NORTH KOREA   (0) 0

USSR Anzor Kavazashvili, Vladimir Ponomaryev, Leonid Ostrovsky, Georgy Sichinava, Murtaz Khurtsilava, Albert Shesternev (c), Igor Chislenko, Iosif Sabo, Anatoly Banishevsky, Eduard Malafeyev, Galimzian Khusainov. *Nikolai Morozov.*
NORTH KOREA Lee Chan-Myung, Park Lee-Sup, Shin Yung-Kyoo, Kang Bong-Chil, Lim Zoong-Sun, Im Seung-Hwi, Park Seung-Jin (c), Han Bong-Jin, Park Doo-Ik, Kang Ryong-Woon, Kim Seung-Il. *Myung Rye-Hyun.*

1966

When FIFA refused to guarantee Africa its own qualifier, the entire continent withdrew, as did most of Asia, leaving only two countries to represent two billion people or so. North Korea's 9-2 aggregate win over Australia didn't sow terror among the big names, but many were intrigued by their two years of monastic existence and training in barracks. Fitness, a big failing of the previous Korean team to reach the finals, probably wouldn't be a factor.

Size, however, was. The USSR, big men in any company, looked virtually twice the height

---

GROUP 3

	P	W	D	L	F	A	Pts
Portugal	3	3	0	0	9	2	6
Hungary	3	2	0	1	7	5	4
Brazil	3	1	0	2	4	6	2
Bulgaria	3	0	0	3	1	8	0

Portugal and Hungary qualified for the quarter-finals.

and bulk of the Koreans, none of whom stood higher than 5′8. Some passages of play looked like miss-matched rugby line-outs. The fair-haired Banishevsky made a near-post goal for Malafeyev and headed in Chislenko's free kick, then Malafeyev scored the best of the day, running onto Sabo's chip, chesting down and half-volleying in. For the Koreans, apparently nothing but more hard labour ahead. Sabo was of Hungarian extraction (original spelling József Szabó).

---

13 July 1966 – Roker Park, Sunderland – 27,199 – Gottfried Dienst (SWI)

ITALY	(1) 2
Mazzola 9, Barison 88	
CHILE	**(0) 0**

ITALY Enrico Albertosi, Tarcisio Burgnich, Giacinto Facchetti, Giovanni Lodetti, Roberto Rosato, Sandro Salvadore (c), Marino Perani, Giacomo Bulgarelli, Sandro Mazzola, Gianni Rivera, Paolo Barison. *Edmondo Fabbri.*
CHILE Juan Olivares, Luis Eyzaguirre, Hugo Villanueva, Humberto Cruz, Elías Figueroa, Rubén Marcos, Pedro Araya, Ignacio Prieto, Armando Tobar, Alberto Fouilloux, Leonel Sánchez (c). *Luis Alamos.*

No-one really expected a repeat of the 1962 street fight; there was even a steady drizzle to cool things down. Instead the match was thoroughly tepid, frustratingly so after Italy's upbeat start. The hefty Barison had a shot kicked off the line by a defender before being sent clear by Bulgarelli's perfect pass inside Eyzaguirre. Olivares saved the shot, Mazzola slid in to score.

Mazzola would later move back into mid-field, skilfully but not quite convincingly. For the moment, he was still the wiry and gifted striker who'd helped Inter win two European Cups. Bulgarelli and Rivera were smoothness itself in the middle, Burgnich and Facchetti

already famous fullbacks. But Bulgarelli had to come off for treatment, Rivera was having one of his regular off days, and the whole team seemed obsessed with defence away from home, even against a team reduced to ten men when Tobar went off after an hour.

Eyzaguirre was good enough to have played for the Rest of the World against England in 1963, but Barison's strength troubled him throughout. Right at the end, he made just enough room on the outside to hit a left-footed shot high to the near post. The video suggests a possible deflection off Eyzaguirre; if not, Olivares should have saved it.

But this didn't look like the Italy who'd beaten Bulgaria 6-1, Mexico 5-0 and Argentina 3-0 in June. Still, with two such weak teams in the group, they were surely already through.

---

15 July 1966 – Ayresome Park, Middlesbrough – 13,792 – Ali Kandil (EGY)

CHILE	(1) 1
Marcos pen 27	
NORTH KOREA	**(0) 1**
Park Seung-Jin 88	

CHILE Olivares, Alberto Valentini, Villanueva, Cruz, Figueroa, Marcos, Araya, Prieto, Honorino Landa, Fouilloux, Sánchez (c).
NORTH KOREA Lee Chan-Myung, Park Lee-Sup, Shin Yung-Kyoo, Lim Zoong-Sun, Oh Yoon-Kyung, Park Seung-Jin (c), Im Seung-Hwi, Han Bong-Jin, Park Doo-Ik, Lee Dong-Woon, Kim Seung-Il.

The Koreans were almost unnaturally slim but nimble and young (average age 22) – and their fitness came into its own this time, culminating in Park Seung-Jin's fierce low volley after a defensive header dropped to him on the edge of the box. The Chileans had tried to muscle them out of it but couldn't: Marcos, who thumped in the penalty awarded for a foul by Oh Yoon-Kyung on Araya, was probably the worst offender, booked by the referee and booed by the crowd. A tall spectator in full sailor's costume joined in the celebrations at the end, hugging assorted Koreans, some of whom (probably not for this reason) left the pitch in tears.

---

16 July 1966 – Roker Park, Sunderland – 27,793 – Rudolf Kreitlein (GER)

USSR　　　(0) 1
Chislenko 57

ITALY　　　(0) 0

USSR Lev Yashin, Ponomaryev, Vasily Danilov, Sabo, Khurtsilava, Shesternev (c), Chislenko, Valery Voronin, Banishevsky, Malafeyev, Khusainov.
ITALY Albertosi, Burgnich, Facchetti, Lodetti, Rosato, Salvadore (c), Gianfranco Leoncini, Luigi Meroni, Bulgarelli, Mazzola, Ezio Pascutti.

With both teams apparently certain to qualify, this looked the most obvious draw on the schedule, and neither side took many risks. Here were giants on either side. Facchetti, who stood taller than his goalkeeper, was a fast attacking fullback for Inter but now stayed back to watch Chislenko. Shesternev, similarly broad and wide, was stopper and sweeper in one. He had the better of it today, Chislenko cutting in past Facchetti from the right to score with a tremendous left-footer across Albertosi into the top corner.

Earlier, Mazzola of all people had missed when clean through on goal, but bad memories may have played their part: three years earlier he'd had an important penalty saved by the same keeper.

Towards the end, Bulgarelli slipped Sabo's tackle down the right and crossed for the unmarked Pascutti to get in a powerful header which was blocked by either Yashin or a defender (yet again, the video poses more questions than answers). When the loose ball came back off Pascutti from Danilov's weak clearance, Yashin fell gratefully on the ball. The Italians put their heads in their hands, but the defeat hadn't done their chances any terminal harm: a draw with the Koreans would be enough.

---

19 July 1966 – Ayresome Park, Middlesbrough – 17,829 – Pierre Schwinte (FRA)

NORTH KOREA　　(1) 1
Park Doo-Ik 42

ITALY　　　(0) 0

NORTH KOREA Lee Chan-Myung, Shin Yung-Kyoo, Lim Zoong-Sun, Ha Jung-Won, Oh Yoon-Kyung, Park Seung-Jin (c), Im Seung-Hwi, Han Bong-Jin, Park Doo-Ik, Kim Bong-Hwan, Yang Sung-Kook.
ITALY Albertosi, Spartaco Landini, Facchetti, Romano Fogli, Aristide Guarneri, Francesco Janich, Perani, Bulgarelli (c), Mazzola, Rivera, Barison.

Ferruccio Valcareggi, Fabbri's assistant, was soon to take over as No.1 and lead Italy to the European Championship – which redeemed his reputation somewhat. Sent to watch North Korea's matches, he returned with the opinion that seeing them play was like watching '*una comica di Ridolini*,' a film actor of the 1920s who was Italy's answer to Charlie Chaplin. The Koreans weren't the ones looking like tramps at the end.

Rivera came back, and played well enough – but Italy were a man down for the last hour (people forget this) after Bulgarelli aggravated a knee injury in a late tackle on Park Seung-Jin. Soon afterwards, the famous goal: an Italian clearance was headed back towards their area and Park Doo-Ik let it run into his stride before hitting a ground shot across Albertosi, who might have done better.

1930
1934
1938
1950
1954
1958
1962
1966
1970
1974
1978
1982
1986
1990
1994
1998
2002
2006

Earlier Perani might have scored twice. A diagonal through-ball sent him sprinting clear on the right only to hit his rather average low shot too close to the keeper, who also made an utterly fantastic save from his close-range volley.

North Korea outlasted the ten men in the second half, making a mess of at least two good chances. Fabbri was sacked, Janich, Perani and Barison weren't capped again, and the Italians returned to the traditional reception of tomatoes and other missiles. An astounding result, perhaps the most popular in any World Cup.

Part of Ayresome Park is now someone's front garden, in which lies the bronze cast of the imprint of a football boot, on the spot where Park Doo-Ik hit his shot. He later became a dentist. Quips on a postcard.

1966

20 July 1966 – Roker Park, Sunderland – 16,027 – Jack Adair (NIR)

USSR　　**(1) 2**
Porkujan 29, 87

CHILE　　**(1) 1**
Marcos 33

USSR Kavazashvili, Viktor Getmanov, Aleksei Korneyev, Ostrovsky, Shesternev (c), Valentin Afonin, Slava Metreveli, Voronin, Viktor Serebrianikov, Eduard Markarov, Valery Porkujan.
CHILE Olivares, Valentini, Villanueva, Cruz, Figueroa, Marcos, Araya, Prieto, Landa, Guillermo Yavar, Sánchez (c).

The USSR, already through, sent out their reserves, one of whom stayed in the team after scoring twice on his debut. Porkujan drove in a rebound then lobbed Olivares after the injured Marcos had equalised in a scramble. Chile played with spirit but were worn down by superior ground forces. Story of the tournament.

GROUP 4

	P	W	D	L	F	A	Pts
USSR	3	3	0	0	6	1	6
North Korea	3	1	1	1	2	4	3
Italy	3	1	0	2	2	2	2
Chile	3	0	1	2	2	5	1

The USSR and North Korea qualified for the quarter-finals.

QUARTER-FINALS

23 July 1966 – Wembley, London – 90,584 – Rudolf Kreitlein (GER)

ENGLAND　　**(0) 1**
Hurst 77

ARGENTINA　　**(0) 0**

ENGLAND Banks, Cohen, Wilson, Stiles, J Charlton, Moore (c), Ball, Geoff Hurst, R Charlton, Hunt, Peters.
ARGENTINA Roma, Ferreiro, Marzolini, Albrecht, Rattin (c), Solari, Perfumo, González, Artime, Onega, Mas.
SENT OFF: Rattin 36.

Greaves was one of England's most prolific strikers (44 goals in 57 internationals) but not in the World Cup (one in seven). Again strangely out of sorts, he'd now had his leg gashed open by the French. Ramsey replaced him with Hurst and recalled Ball for his fighting qualities. 'Well, gentlemen, you know the kind of game you have on your hands this afternoon.'

It's hard to get a balanced view on this match. Virtually all the testimony over here comes from the England players and English journalists. The trouble probably grew out of mutual suspicion: Pelé wasn't the only one to hear the rumour ('and I firmly believe it') that

FIFA president Stanley Rous had instructed the referees to go easy on the 'virile' European style of play. Pelé was fouled out of the tournament, an Argentinian sent off against West Germany, and there were dismissals in both the quarter-finals involving South American teams, refereed by a German and an Englishman. Meanwhile Moore & Co had watched Argentina play West Germany and 'We accepted in our guts it was going to be hard. Maybe brutal.'

In the event, Hurst felt as if he'd walked down a dark alley in a strange town: 'At any moment, for no reason, you thought you might be attacked from behind.' Twice, when he was nowhere near the ball, he was kicked in the ankle, each time 'I swung round and there was a ring of blank faces.' Meanwhile Moore himself claimed 'They did tug your hair, spit at you, poke you in the eyes and kick you when the ball was miles away and no-one was looking.' Meanwhile Stiles put his own perspective on things: 'Apart from the violence, I came through with no problems.'

But history is inevitably written by the winners. Most of the aggro here was of the home-grown variety, by Stiles, Cohen, Ball, Hurst, you name it. England beat Argentina 33-19 on the foul count (a point raised in the Commons), and it's pretty clear that Kreitlein simply lost control. Soon after booking Rattin for a painless trip on Bobby Charlton, he sent him off for 'violence of the tongue' – even though he didn't speak Spanish and Rattin knew no German. There's nothing in the video to support the sending-off – so it's no surprise that all hell broke loose.

Rattin refused to go. His excuse: that he'd merely been asking for an interpreter, which was frankly bizarre (who goes around asking for interpreters during a football match?). Albrecht signalled the rest of the team to go with him. Some of them mobbed Kreitlein

instead. After eight minutes that seemed an eternity, Rattin allowed himself to be led off, tried to sit on the touchlines, was talked out of it by the police, and took the scenic route back to the changing room, stopping from time to time to observe the play, villain of the piece over here, martyr back home. A shame, because he'd been the hub of the side, tall and unhurried, always finding a team mate with his passes – and their chances were naturally reduced without him, though it took England a fearfully long time to make the extra man tell.

The violence didn't end with Rattin's departure. Hurst hurt Ferreiro with a high tackle, Jack Charlton came up for a corner and was barged from behind by Albrecht while in mid air, a really dangerous challenge. Eventually, after Roma had made a solid save from Hurst, England scored a very good goal. From wide on the left, Peters hit a kind of brisk lob which left Roma in two minds, and Hurst came in to glance his header across the keeper and inside the far post. A small boy ran on to offer congratulations and had his ear clipped (boo hiss) by Mas.

In the aftermath, while Kreitlein was being escorted off the pitch by the police and Ken Aston (who knew the feeling), Ramsey forcibly stopped Cohen from exchanging shirts with González (who promptly went off and swapped with Wilson!). Later Sir Alf made his notorious speech comparing the Argentinian team to animals, which many felt was unfair to animals. Somehow, in all the mayhem, even Bobby Charlton was booked.

Lorenzo moved on to ply his trade in Europe, and Argentinian clubs began to wreak havoc in the World Club Cup. Against Estudiantes two years later, for example, Stiles was sent off and Bobby Charlton had his shin cut to the bone. Jimmy Johnstone had to wash the spittle out of his hair against Racing, Cruyff's ankle was

1966

severely damaged by Independiente, and three Estudiantes players were jailed by their own president! Sir Alf, for a period of about eight years, was right about the animals – but his own boys had helped to breed them.

23 July 1966 – Hillsborough, Sheffield – 40,007 – Jim Finney (ENG)

WEST GERMANY   (1) 4

Haller 11, 84, Beckenbauer 70, Seeler 77

URUGUAY   (0) 0

WEST GERMANY Tilkowski, Höttges, Schnellinger, Beckenbauer, Schulz, Weber, Held, Haller, Seeler (c), Overath, Emmerich.
URUGUAY Mazurkiewicz, Ubiña, Caetano, Héctor Salvá, Manicera, Troche (c), Cortés, Gonçálvez, Silva, Rocha, Pérez.
SENT OFF: Troche 50, Silva 55.

Meanwhile a carbon copy was emerging further north. Again there were two schools of violence and ways of reacting to it, again the South Americans felt aggrieved. While the German tackles were going right through people, whenever they themselves were challenged they rolled around as if in mortal agony, only to rise from the dead seconds after the free kick had been awarded. Haller was the best at this, and when he flukily diverted Held's shot to open the scoring, Uruguay must have felt there was no justice, certainly not from an English referee who'd waved play on when Schnellinger clearly handled the ball under his own crossbar.

Even so, some of the Uruguayan habits weren't whiter than white. Troche was sent off for kicking Emmerich in the stomach, slapping Seeler's face as he left. Silva, a dead ringer for Uri Geller with a similar influence on football matches, kicked Schulz as Tilkowski collected the ball, then kicked the ball as Tilkowski held it on the ground, and finally joined forces with Caetano for a violent double kick at Haller,

grinding his studs in the German's leg as he received treatment. Another police escort was required.

A goal down with only nine men, Uruguay left great gaps at the back. Beckenbauer repeated one of his runs against Switzerland, taking Seeler's return pass round the keeper. Emmerich charged up the left in oceans of space before passing inside to Held; his square pass went behind Seeler, who calmly re-gathered it before blasting into the top corner from eighteen yards. Cue pitch invasion by fan with German flag and *lederhosen*. Finally Manicera's slip let Haller take Seeler's return chip and push it past the exposed keeper. Merciless, and all adding to the South Americans' sense of grievance – though it would have been interesting to hear them explain away the fact that Haller passed blood that night after having his testicles squeezed during the match, and that Cortés was banned for six internationals after kicking the referee.

23 July 1966 – Goodison Park, Liverpool – 40,248 – Menachem Ashkenazi (ISR)

PORTUGAL   (2) 5

Eusébio 26, pen 43, 57, pen 60, José Augusto 80

NORTH KOREA   (3) 3

Park Seung-Jin 55 sec, Lee Dong-Woon 20, Yang Sung-Kook 24

PORTUGAL Pereira, Morais, Baptista, Graça, Vicente, Hilário, José Augusto, Coluna (c), Torres, Eusébio, Simões.
NORTH KOREA Lee Chan-Myung, Shin Yung-Kyoo, Lim Zoong-Sun, Ha Jung-Won, Oh Yoon-Kyung, Park Seung-Jin (c), Im Seung-Hwi, Han Bong-Jin, Park Doo-Ik, Lee Dong-Woon, Yang Sung-Kook.

A unique match. Certainly no other had such a gobsmacking start. Whereas Brazil had seemed petrified of the Portuguese attack, the Koreans attacked the Portuguese defence, which was weaker. Logical, really.

They were a goal up in less than a minute. Han Bong-Jin rolled the ball square from the right and Park Seung-Jin struck it cleanly with the outside of his left foot into the top left-hand corner. Then Han Bong-Jin's cross from the right went all the way through to Yang Sung-Kook on the left-hand goal line; his instant cross was palmed into the path of Lee Dong-Woon by Pereira. The crowd had just started chanting 'We want three' when they got it. Park Doo-Ik's shot fell to Yang Sung-Kook, who kept his cool to take it round a defender and leave Pereira standing with a ground shot. Portuguese and crowd alike were rubbing their eyes.

Common consensus has it that North Korea lost the match by maintaining all-out attack instead of protecting their lead, but there's too much condescension in that. They were always going to be under threat as soon as Eusébio got into his stride. First he cracked home José Augusto's through-ball then hit both penalties hard to the keeper's right, the first when Torres was fouled by a man half his height, the other when his own forceful run down the left was ended by a sliding tackle. His other goal was similar to his first, shooting without breaking stride. He made the fifth too, his corner being headed back across goal by the inevitable Torres for José Augusto to head in unopposed. It was Eusébio's match, but he had to share it with some of the little people.

HUNGARY Gelei, Mátrai, Káposzta, Mészöly, Sipos (c), Szepesi, Bene, Nagy, Albert, Farkas, Rákosi.

Hungary appeared to have everything necessary for success in the modern game. Massed defence, fast-breaking midfield, slick forwards. But the Soviets simply brutalised them.

Close-marking Bene, Albert and Farkas, thumping home their tackles, they also took advantage of defensive slips, especially an early goalkeeping blunder. Porkujan took a short corner on the left and hit the return low to the near post, where Gelei gathered it comfortably, then let it loose behind him. Chislenko got to it before Banishevsky. Gelei, turning out to be no better than Szentmihályi, knelt and wrung his hand, which wasn't the part his team mates had in mind. Then Khusainov's free kick from the left reached Porkujan absurdly unmarked at the far post.

Mészöly, pushed forward in the second half, burst through a tackle to set up a goal for Bene, but Rákosi missed the ball completely from three yards out, and Yashin, still an acrobat at 36, dived to save a Sipos free kick. Hungary's defeat was everyone's loss, but the USSR got through on sheer strength. Of mind too.

SEMI-FINALS

23 July 1966 – Roker Park, Sunderland – 22,103 – Juan Gardeazábal (SPA)

USSR **(1) 2**
Chislenko 5, Porkujan 48

HUNGARY **(0) 1**
Bene 58

USSR Yashin, Ponomaryev, Danilov, Voronin, Shesternev (c), Sabo, Khusainov, Chislenko, Banishevsky, Malafeyev, Porkujan.

25 July 1966, Goodison Park, Liverpool – 38,273 – Concetto Lo Bello (ITA)

WEST GERMANY **(1) 2**
Haller 43, Beckenbauer 68

USSR **(0) 1**
Porkujan 87

WEST GERMANY Tilkowski, Friedel Lutz, Schnellinger, Beckenbauer, Schulz, Weber, Held, Haller, Seeler (c), Overath, Emmerich.

1966

USSR Yashin, Ponomaryev, Shesternev (c), Danilov, Voronin, Sabo, Khusainov, Chislenko, Banishevsky, Malafeyev, Porkujan.
SENT OFF: Chislenko 44.

If you liked your meat raw, this was the place to be, with one side built like bull calves and the other more hammer than sickle. It came down to who had more men standing at the end.

Germany were ahead on that count almost at once, Sabo twisting an ankle trying to foul Beckenbauer and needing a painkilling injection at half-time. Near the end of the first half, Schnellinger went into a typical tackle on Chislenko, who was about half his size and weight. He took ball and man, leaving Chislenko clutching his ankle, then showed the other side of his game by running power-fully upfield before hitting a pass to the right-hand side of the penalty area, where it was met by Haller's diagonal run and strong shot. Immediately after the kick-off, a limping Chislenko lost the ball to Held and gave him a clip on the back of the ankle. By the standards of this tournament, it was an innocuous foul, but Lo Bello sent him off.

Beckenbauer scored the second by drifting outside a pack of players on the edge of the area before shooting left-footed just inside the left-hand post. Yashin, who stood and watched, was either unsighted or thought the ball was going wide. Porkujan scored when Tilkowski dropped the ball under pressure from Malafeyev, and Banishevsky headed over the bar – but even on an off day the Germans had shown what they were made of, and Chislenko knew what that felt like.

There was some disappointment that England didn't play their semi-final up here, but it was always in the rules of the competition that they'd stay at Wembley if they won their group.

26 July 1966 – Wembley, London – 94,493 – Pierre Schwinte (FRA)

ENGLAND   (1) 2
R Charlton 30, 79

PORTUGAL (0) 1
Eusébio pen 82

ENGLAND Banks, Cohen, Wilson, Stiles, J Charlton, Moore (c), Ball, Hurst, R Charlton, Hunt, Peters.
PORTUGAL Pereira, Festa, Baptista, Graça, José Carlos (da Silva), Hilário, José Augusto, Coluna (c), Torres, Eusébio, Simões.

Of all the teams in the tournament, Portugal had perhaps the most identifiable strengths and weaknesses. There were five Benfica players in the team, the entire forward line. The defence was drawn from four other clubs and played like strangers. If the great Germano and Costa Pereira hadn't been past their prime, things might have been different. Instead Portugal had to make do with José Carlos and José Pereira (no relation, no comparison). Bobby Moore looked forward to it 'the way many League clubs thought about playing West Ham: it would be a good game but not a hard fight, and we would probably win in the end.'

The Portuguese were almost preposterously genteel. No-one to mark Bobby Charlton, no fouls in the first twenty minutes. They'd even dropped Vicente and Morais, who'd kicked pieces out of Pelé. When Charlton scored his second goal, José Augusto shook his hand. Nothing wrong with that, but not something Stiles would have done.

Moore again: 'Eusébio didn't have the stomach for Nobby Stiles,' which seems to be the prevailing view over the years but must be too simplistic by half. Stiles didn't man-mark Eusébio and hardly ever fouled him. The England defence simply retreated rather than diving in and playing to his strengths. As for Eusébio's implied lack of courage, we're back to the question of different eras of refereeing. In the European Cup Final two years later, Stiles bodychecked Eusébio three times in quick succession without so much as a booking. Only one of them would have been a star today.

England's opening goal stemmed from a long pass by Wilson into the path of Hunt, who cleverly touched the ball one side of José Carlos and ran round the other. Pereira rushed out, made a sliding tackle instead of diving at Hunt's feet, and the ball reached Bobby Charlton, who sidefooted it back between goalkeeper and defender into the net.

The other full-back and front runner laid the groundwork for his second goal, Hurst chasing Cohen's long ball to the right-hand goal line. José Carlos should have won the ball but lost it, and Hurst rolled it back for Charlton to smash in one of the famous England goals. He hit the ball quite low but so hard it appeared to hit a pocket of air and rise sharply; in fact (heresy, this) it took a slight deflection.

Portugal didn't give up. If Eusébio was being tamed and Simões getting little change out of Cohen, Coluna was still a force in midfield, built like a welterweight but with all the skills, and not even Big Jack could conquer Mount Torres. Simões, forced to switch wings, hit a high ball to the far post, Banks came out and missed it, Torres headed in, Jack Charlton handled. Eusébio thumped his penalty in the usual place, which annoyed Banks, who'd intended to dive that way but then saw various team mates reminding him of it: 'for some reason they kept pointing me in that direction ... Coluna went and whispered in Eusébio's ear, enough to convince me he was going to change the direction of his kick. I could have cried.' It was the first goal England had conceded in seven matches, still the national record.

There was still time for Torres to beat Charlton in the air again and knock the ball down for Simões to nudge it wide as Banks rushed out. The earlier error was a rare one for Banks, rapidly proving himself Yashin's successor; he showed it at the death here, making an excellent save when Coluna sidestepped a tackle and put everything into a shot just under the bar. The chance had been set up by Eusébio, lest we forget him, but it was Bobby Charlton's day.

3RD-PLACE FINAL

28 July 1966 – Wembley, London – 87,696 – Ken Dagnall (ENG)

1966

PORTUGAL (1) 2
Eusébio pen 13, Torres 88

USSR   (1) 1
Malafeyev 44

PORTUGAL Pereira, Festa, Baptista, Graça, José Carlos, Hilário, José Augusto, Coluna (c), Torres, Eusébio, Simões.
USSR Yashin (c), Ponomaryev, Korneyev, Sichinava, Khurtsilava, Danilov, Serebrianikov, Voronin, Banishevsky, Malafeyev, Metreveli.

Portugal were the better side and people wanted them to win, but it was dull as well as pointless. Khurtsilava, terrified of Torres, committed an unnecessary handball for the penalty, Pereira fumbled Metreveli's long shot for Malafeyev to put in the rebound, and we were spared extra time when Torres won the ball in the air for the thousandth time and José Augusto chipped it back to him. The volley was touched gently past Yashin, whose days came quietly to an end. The actual attendance was probably nearer 70,000.

1930
1934
1938
1950
1954
1958
1962
1970
1974
1978
1982
1986
1990
1994
1998
2002
2006

FINAL

30 July 1966 – Wembley, London – 93,802 – Gottfried Dienst (SWI)

ENGLAND   **(1) (2) 4**
Hurst 19, 100, 119, Peters 78

WEST GERMANY   **(1) (2) 2**
Haller 13, Weber 89

ENGLAND Banks, Cohen, Wilson, Stiles, J Charlton, Moore (c), Ball, Hurst, R Charlton, Hunt, Peters.
WEST GERMANY Tilkowski, Höttges, Schnellinger, Beckenbauer, Schulz, Weber, Held, Haller, Seeler (c), Overath, Emmerich.

As with Puskás in 1954, the whispers began: was Greaves coming back? It was never a straight choice between him and Hunt, who'd been his partner at the start ('A lot of people still say it was me who took Jimmy's place, but it was Geoff Hurst'). Hurst had scored the winner in the quarter-final and made the winner in the semi. Greaves had barely recovered. No contest in Ramsey's mind.

If Greaves' absence left England short of charm, they were nevertheless the only team to make West Germany change their game plan. Bobby Charlton's performance against Portugal persuaded Schön to put a man on him. His midfield didn't have a natural marker, so Beckenbauer would have to do. Do well enough, too – he and Charlton cancelled each other out – but the loss was probably Germany's. If Schön really wanted a minder, he had Klaus-Dieter Sieloff in his squad. All he had to do was drop Emmerich.

After that freakish goal against Spain, the big winger had done very little and looked clumsy on the ball, out of place in a passing team. But this had been Emmerich's big season, especially in the Cup-Winners Cup: six

goals in one match, two in each leg to knock the holders West Ham out of the semi-final. That hammer of a left foot helped him to 115 goals in 183 *Bundesliga* games. Schön decided he needed a matchwinner more than a ball winner and picked an unchanged front five.

It made the better start, on a pitch greased by rain, aided by an England error or three. From out on the left, Held hit a deep cross towards the far post, Banks shouted for Wilson to let it go, Wilson 'seemed to think I was shouting a warning' and went up too early for the header, knocking it down too close to goal. Haller reached back to collect it and shot, none too hard, along the ground past Jack Charlton and Banks ('we left it to each other'). England were already clinging to omens: in every World Cup Final since the War, the side who scored first had lost the match.

Moore later said that Haller 'shouldn't be the sort of player who scores against us and certainly isn't the class of player to win a World Cup Final' – but that's a comment with a lot of baggage. Haller was everything the English loved to hate about German footballers: strutting, snub-nosed and blond, an actor when he was fouled, a first name of Helmut. He was also a world-class player who helped Bologna and Juventus win the Italian league. Why did he deserve a goal in a World Cup Final any less than Hurst or Peters?

Perhaps fuelled by this indignation, Moore came up a long way on the left until Overath brought him down. Taking the free kick before the referee's whistle, he clipped it in to coincide with Hurst's perfect run and downward header. Another West Ham goal.

For the next hour, something of a stand-off punctuated with sporadic shots from behind the barricades: both defences were in control, England superbly marshalled by Moore, Germany coagulating around Schulz, the underrated Höttges hitting his tackles hard.

Eventually Ball took a corner on the right, the ball reached Hurst on the edge of the area, he shot, optimistically and badly, a lunging block by Höttges sent the ball ballooning behind him, and Peters beat Jack Charlton to it on the way down. 'No I didn't feel cheated, I'm glad the bugger never came to me because I'd have kicked it over the bar.' Peters drove it in from seven yards past Tilkowski and Schnellinger, who both ended up sitting on the goal line.

That seemed to be the end of it. The England players believed they should have been able to hold out for twelve minutes, and would have done so if the referee hadn't awarded a free kick against Jack Charlton for leaning on Held, who may have been making a back for him. Emmerich, scenting last-minute redemption, hit the free kick hard, there were assorted ricochets, and Moore appealed for handball by Schnellinger. Banks later maintained that 'There's no way it was deliberate', which was true enough, given that the ball hit Schnellinger in the back of the ribcage. It finally squeezed out to the right, where Weber scooped it over Wilson's leg and Banks' hands. Extra time in a Final for the first time since 1934.

England must have been crushed, but according to Moore 'Alf was unbelievably good,' making his 'you've won it once, now go and win it again' speech with very little time for rehearsal. In extra time Ball set about obeying the instruction. He was up against Schnellinger ('and there's no way that was your birthday') but simply ran the big man ragged. Chasing a long pass from Stiles out to the right-hand corner flag, he hit it first time. Hurst got in front of some shoddy marking by Schulz to control the ball and crash it against the underside of the bar. When it bounced down, Hunt appealed instead of following in ('I wouldn't have got to the ball') and Weber headed it over the bar for a corner. But the referee went to his linesman Tofik Bakhramov, who was in no position and perhaps simply agreed with what Dienst told him. The England players have watched the ball hit the line. They think it's all over. It is now. The linesman says so.

It's still the most controversial moment in any World Cup Final, mainly because it simply wasn't a goal. There's no discussion about it (though there's been some): the film shows the ball landing on the middle of the line, and photographs prove that when the ball meets its shadow, the whole thing clearly isn't over the line.

That was the beginning of the end for this strong and talented German team. In the last minute, Moore chested down a cross in his penalty area, drove Big Jack mad by not kicking it into Neasden, and hit a cool long pass to Hurst just inside the opposition half. He ran on, puffed his cheeks in that way of his, and smashed his shot high inside the near post. He was the only player to score three goals in a World Cup Final, though he needed extra-time and a little help to do it. He scored with his head and each foot. At the other end of the triumph-and-disaster chart, Emmerich wasn't capped again.

At the final whistle, Jack Charlton knelt with his face in his hands. When Stiles jumped on Cohen, the latter's reaction was variously reported as 'it looked like copulation' and 'like being kissed by a piece of liver' (Stiles' dental plate got caught in Cohen's teeth!). The immaculate Moore was about to be voted player of the tournament. And Ramsey sat impassively on the bench while the world jumped around him, basking in being proved right. London could now start calling itself the capital of the world: Swinging Sixties, Jagger and Richards, Norbert Peter Stiles. But if God was now an Englishman, the old devil with the flag was Azerbaijani. The main football ground in Baku is the Tofik Bakhramov Stadium.

The pinnacle of the greatest career. After the Final, some local headgear costs Pelé the shirt off his back.

1930

1934

1938

1950

1954

1958

1962

1966

The height of brilliance: 7,000 feet

Mexico 1970

1970

1974

1978

1982

1986

1990

1994

1998

2002

2006

In the four years between World Cups, Ramsey's England lost just four out of 35 matches, only against very good teams and never by more than one goal. But there were ten draws in that time, and some very dreary performances; England were difficult to beat but just as hard to watch. Still, this may be carping too much: the squad for Mexico looked as good as in 1966. Banks, Moore, Ball, Hurst, Peters and the Charltons were still there, and Stiles had been replaced by Mullery, who was better on the ball and almost as spiky without it. There was a dynamic new winger in Lee and a good crop of attacking fullbacks, increasingly necessary in a wingless team. Preparation had included several matches at altitude, and there was no shortage of confidence. Moore: 'We believed we had the best squad in England's history. We believed we were going to win it again.'

But they weren't the favourites. Brazil had done enough, admittedly in a weak qualifying group, to serve notice that 1966 was firmly behind them, winning all six matches and scoring 23 goals, including ten from Tostão, whose promise was now being fulfilled in a rich partnership with a rejuvenated Pelé, who scored six himself. Carlos Alberto, Gérson and Jairzinho were coming into their prime, and there was some bright new blood in

Clodoaldo and Rivelino. They even picked the right manager. Twice.

João Saldanha, a journalist, had been such a vehement critic of the national team that eventually the patience of the powers-that-be snapped and he was made national coach! What sounds like something done for a bet, a disaster, was an instant success. Saldanha built the team round the Santos club, kept the same squad throughout, and they cut a swathe through the qualifying matches.

Soon, however, his famously short fuse began getting in the way. Pelé said that 'whenever we saw a group in one corner of the pitch, we knew João had invited someone there to settle things with fists.' But it wasn't the fists that provided the last straw; Saldanha was discovered at the house of a particularly vociferous critic – brandishing a revolver! Zagallo, infinitely calmer, a star of 1958 and 1962, took the squad to Mexico.

Intriguingly, a year earlier Brazil had recovered from 1-0 down to score two late goals against England at home, a scoring sequence that gave hope to both camps, who were drawn in the same World Cup group.

Elsewhere, West Germany added the great goalscoring talents of Gerd Müller to their squad but scraped through 3-2 against Scotland. Italy, who'd recovered from their Korean trauma to win the European Championship, looked strong in qualifying, Luigi Riva scoring seven of their ten goals. Argentina, more violent than ever, were eliminated by Peru despite almost unlimited injury time in the deciding match. The USSR put out a Northern Ireland team denied the services of George Best. And Mexico's position as hosts allowed another Central American country to take part, El Salvador qualifying after three matches with neighbouring Honduras which sparked off a war that had more to do with immigration than football (presumably). Three thousand people died.

Another two hundred had been shot dead two years earlier, when armed police opened fire on peaceful demonstrators before the Olympics held in Mexico City. FIFA turned a blind eye, to that and to the enormous problems of heat and altitude which had left European competitors needing oxygen at the Games. In fact they added to them by arranging matches at noon to accommodate European television schedules. While FIFA fiddled, players burned, losing ten pounds in fluid during a single game or being sent home with heatstroke. The tournament produced some exhilarating football, and one of the great forward lines, but the price, in human terms, was a rip off.

GROUP 1

Belgium, El Salvador, Mexico, USSR. [No seeds.]

31 May 1970 – Azteca, Mexico City – 107,160 – Kurt Tschenscher (GER)

MEXICO	0
USSR	0

MEXICO Ignacio Calderón, Gustavo Peña (c), Mario Pérez jnr, Guillermo Hernández, Horacio López, José Vantolrá, Javier Guzmán, Héctor Pulido, Mario Velarde [Antonio Munguía 67], Javier Valdivia, Javier Fragoso. *Raúl Cárdenas.*
USSR Anzor Kavazashvili, Vladimir Kaplichny, Evgeny Lovchev, Gennady Logofet, Albert Shesternev (c), Kakhi Asatiani, Vladimir Muntian, Viktor Serebrianikov [Anatoly Puzach HT], Anatoly Byshovets, Gennady Evriuzhikin, Givi Nodia [Vitaly Khmelnitsky 66]. *Gavril Katchalin.*

As grim a start as everyone feared (altitude and heated tackles), but one with pleasing repercussions. Some blamed Tschenscher for booking five players, but the referees had been given strict instructions and were clearly going to follow them; dirty play was never a feature of the tournament. López missed a couple of chances, but the football in this game was secondary. Puzach was the first substitute to come on in a finals match.

3 June 1970 – Azteca, Mexico City – 92,205 – Andrei Rădulescu (ROM)

BELGIUM	**(1) 3**
Van Moer 8, 54, Lambert pen 79	
EL SALVADOR	**(0) 0**

BELGIUM Christian Piot, Georges Heylens, Jean Thissen, Nico Dewalque, Jean Dockx, Léon Semmeling, Wilfried Van Moer, Johan Devrindt, Paul Van Himst (c), Wilfried Puis, Raoul Lambert [Odilon Polleunis 81]. *Raymond Goethals.*
EL SALVADOR Raúl Magaña, Roberto Rivas, Salvador Mariona (c), Saturnino Osorio, Mauricio Manzano [Santiago Cortéz 67], Antonio Quintanilla, Jorge Vásquez, Salvador Cabezas, Mauricio 'Pipo' Rodríguez [Genaro Sermeño 79], Ramón Martínez, Ernesto Aparicio. *Hernán Carrasco (CHI).*

El Salvador were as weak as predicted and Belgium should have scored more. But the famous Van Himst had a terrible time in the thin air, missing easy chances, and only little Van Moer stood out, hammering the first goal from thirty yards and converting a cross from Semmeling, who was fouled for the penalty. Aparicio wasted a good chance when clean through. The actual crowd figure may have been as low as 30,000.

1970

6 June 1970 – Azteca, Mexico City – 95,261 – Rudi Scheurer (SWI)

USSR	**(1) 4**
Byshovets 14, 63, Asatiani 57, Khmelnitsky 75	
BELGIUM	**(0) 1**
Lambert 86	

USSR Kavazashvili, Kaplichny [Lovchev 43], Valentin Afonin, Revaz Dzodzuashvili [Nikolai Kiselev 65], Murtaz Khurtsilava, Shesternev (c), Asatiani, Muntian, Evriuzhikin, Byshovets, Khmelnitsky.
BELGIUM Piot, Heylens, Thissen, Dewalque, Dockx, Léon Jeck, Semmeling, Van Moer, Van Himst (c), Puis, Lambert.

Billed as an exciting Belgian forward line against the plodding Soviets, the match was turned on its head when Kavazashvili saved a header from Van Moer, who hit the bar from the rebound. The USSR immediately went down the other end and scored the first of their four tremendous goals, Byshovets hammering

1930
1934
1938
1950
1954
1958
1962
1966
1970
1974
1978
1982
1986
1990
1994
1998
2002
2006

home from thirty yards. Despite the conditions, Goethals didn't use any substitutes as the deficit mounted. Asatiani turned Heylens and shot in off the far post. Shesternev, massively impassable as ever, intercepted a pass and fed Byshovets, who cut inside Jeck and Dockx and scored with a screaming left-footed drive. Khmelnitsky's subterranean header from Evriuzhikin's dinked cross made it four, and Lambert's goal, after Van Moer hit a post, went almost unnoticed. Overwhelming.

---

7 June 1970 – Azteca, Mexico City – 103,058 – Ali Kandil (EGY)

MEXICO	(1) 4
Valdivia 44, 47, Fragoso 58, Basaguren 83

EL SALVADOR	(0) 0

MEXICO Calderón, Peña (c), Pérez, Munguía, Enrique Borja [López HT, Juan Ignacio Basaguren 75], Aarón Padilla, Vantolrá, Guzmán, José Luis González, Valdivia, Fragoso.
EL SALVADOR Magaña, Rivas, Mariona (c), Osorio, Cortéz [Mario Monge 66], Quintanilla, Rodríguez, Vásquez, Martínez, Cabezas, Aparicio [Sergio Méndez 56].

Mexico were so poor that the minnows would have held out into the second half but for a mighty refereeing controversy. El Salvador, who thought Kandil had awarded them a throw or a free kick, stood still as he waved away their protests when Mexico took the kick, Padilla crossed, Borja missed an open goal but Valdivia didn't.

Pandemonium. The Salvadoreans surrounded Kandil, turning their backs so he could see their numbers to book them, jostling Bermudan linesman Keith Dunstan, kicking the ball into the crowd. In the second half, they did little except try and kick as many Mexicans as possible, conceding goals to Valdivia (a cross shot after beating a man),

Fragoso (from a López header) and Basaguren, the first substitute to score in a World Cup tournament. TV replays of the main incident are inconclusive (El Salvador may simply have misunderstood) but Kandil never refereed another finals match.

---

10 June 1970 – Azteca, Mexico City – 89,979 – Rafael Hormazábal (CHI)

USSR	(0) 2
Byshovets 51, 73

EL SALVADOR	(0) 0

USSR Kavazashvili, Shesternev (c), Dzodzuashvili, Khurtsilava, Afonin, Serebrianikov, Kiselev [Asatiani 79], Muntian, Puzach [Evriuzhikin HT], Byshovets, Khmelnitsky.
EL SALVADOR Magaña, Rivas, Mariona (c), Osorio, Cabezas [Aparicio 79], Vásquez, Monge, Jaime Portillo, Rodríguez [Sermeño 85], Guillermo Castro, Méndez.

Yet again El Salvador did their best, especially their eccentric goalkeeper, but the chunky and sure-footed Byshovets put away a through-pass from Serebrianikov and shot the second after Muntian had beaten three men. Rodríguez missed a golden chance and El Salvador would have to wait twelve years for their first goal in the finals. Many were disappointed that the Soviets hadn't given a game to Yashin, in the squad at the age of 40.

The real crowd figure was nearer 25,000! Asatiani was shot dead by a hitman at his home in Georgia in 2002.

---

11 June 1970 – Azteca, Mexico City – 108,192 – Norberto Ángel Coerezza (ARG)

MEXICO	(1) 1
Peña pen 15

BELGIUM	(0) 0

MEXICO Calderón, Peña (c), Vantolrá, Guzmán, Pérez, Pulido, González, Munguía, Valdivia (Basaguren HT], Fragoso, Padilla.
BELGIUM Piot, Heylens, Thissen, Dewalque, Dockx, Jeck, Semmeling, Polleunis [Devrindt 65], Van Moer, Van Himst (c), Puis.

Another match in the Azteca, another slice of helpful refereeing. Van Moer mistimed a clearance, Jeck kicked it away, and Valdivia fell over his leg. Penalty, followed by the time-honoured scene of players mobbing the referee, who threw an air punch to fend them off. Valdivia hit a post and Mexico were in the next round for the first time. Hardly surprising with twelve men.

GROUP 1

	P	W	D	L	F	A	Pts
USSR	3	2	1	0	6	1	5
Mexico	3	2	1	0	5	0	5
Belgium	3	1	0	2	4	5	2
El Salvador	3	0	0	3	0	9	0

The USSR and Mexico qualified for the quarterfinals.

GROUP 2

Israel, Italy, Sweden, Uruguay. [No seeds.]

2 June 1970, Cuauhtémoc, Puebla – 20,654 – Bobby Davidson (SCO)

URUGUAY (1) 2
Maneiro 22, Mújica 51

ISRAEL   (0) 0

URUGUAY Ladislao Mazurkiewicz, Atilio Ancheta, Juan Mújica, Julio Montero Castillo, Roberto Matosas, Luis Ubiña, Luis Cubilla, Pedro Rocha (c) [Julio César Cortés 13], Víctor Espárrago, Ildo Maneiro, Julio Losada. *Juan Eduardo Hohberg.*
ISRAEL Yitzak Visoker, Yeshayahu Schwager, David Primo, Daniel Rom [Yohanan Vollach 57], Zvi Rosen, Shmuel Rosenthal, Gyora Spiegel, Mordechai Spiegler (c), Yitzak Shum, Yoshua Feygenbaum, Rachamin Talbi [Shraga Bar HT]. *Emmanuel Schaeffer.*

If any team was equipped to handle Mexican conditions it was probably Uruguay, compact and cautious, doing only just enough – an approach cemented by the leg injury which put their stylish playmaker Rocha out of the tournament. They were still far too good for the Israeli amateurs. Mújica overlapped on the left and put in a basic cross which bounced in front of a hesitant Visoker for Maneiro to dart in and head home. Mújica scored the second himself, driving in the rebound when Visoker saved from Maneiro. Cubilla, tubby but tricky, one of the characters of the tournament, shot against the bar. Spiegler, who later interested West Ham, was Israel's best player.

Rom's original name was Szmulewicz (or Schmolwitch), Vollach's is also written Wallach. Espárrago is Spanish for 'asparagus'.

3 June 1970 – Luis Gutiérrez Dosal, Toluca – 13,433 – Jack Taylor (ENG)

ITALY   (1) 1
Domenghini 11

SWEDEN   (0) 0

ITALY Enrico Albertosi, Tarcisio Burgnich, Giacinto Facchetti (c), Mario Bertini, Comunardo Niccolai [Roberto Rosato 37], Pierluigi Cera, Angelo Domenghini, Sandro Mazzola, Roberto Boninsegna, Giancarlo 'Picchio' De Sisti, Luigi Riva. *Ferruccio Valcareggi.*

SWEDEN Ronnie Hellström, Jan V Olsson, Kurt Axelsson, Bo Larsson [Göran Nicklasson 77], Roland Grip, Björn Nordqvist (c), Tommy Svensson, Ove Grahn, Ove Kindvall, Claes Cronqvist, Leif Eriksson [Inge Ejderstedt 57]. *Orvar Bergmark.*

Toluca lies 8,744 feet above sea level, the highest in the competition – and both teams felt it, notably Riva and Kindvall, who'd scored 13 goals between them in the qualifying rounds. But if Riva had difficulties with the altitude, the Swedish defence had an equally hard time with him. Lean and craggy, with rough edges to his play, he impressed with his acceleration and ability to get in a shot from unpromising positions: in the first few minutes, he turned the ball against a post with his thigh. All he needed was luck.

Italy had some early on. Domenghini pushed a corner on the left to Facchetti, took the return, and shot from outside the area. Hellström, going down at his near post, tried to cup the ball to his chest but let it in under his body. He went on to become Sweden's best ever keeper, a star of the 1974 and 1978 finals, but this was his last match in Mexico.

A different Jan Olsson played in the 1974 tournament. This was Italy's first win over Sweden since 1912, and by the same score. The stadium was commonly known as '*La Bombonera,*' the chocolate box. Picchio is Italian for 'woodpecker'.

6 June 1970 – Cuauhtémoc, Puebla – 29,968 – Rudi Glöckner (DDR)

ITALY 0

URUGUAY 0

ITALY Albertosi, Burgnich, Facchetti (c), Bertini, Rosato, Cera, Domenghini [Giuseppe Furino HT], Mazzola, Boninsegna, De Sisti, Riva.
URUGUAY Mazurkiewicz, Ubiña (c), Mújica, Montero Castillo, Ancheta, Matosas, Cubilla, Cortés, Espárrago, Maneiro, Rubén Bareño [Oscar Zubía 70].

Probably the most predictable of all goalless draws. Cubilla went round Facchetti, Riva sprinted clear of Ancheta to hit the side netting. That's all, folks. The one talking point was Rivera's continued absence, this time even from the subs' bench. The Mazzola-Rivera question occupies minds to this day. It's a little surprising that they couldn't be accommodated in the same midfield, though it's not easy to see who could have been left out. Valcareggi would soon arrive at a solution, but even that wasn't wholly convincing.

7 June 1970 – Luis Gutiérrez Dosal, Toluca – 9,624 – Seyoum Tarekegn (ETH)

ISRAEL (0) 1
Spiegler 57
SWEDEN (0) 1
Turesson 54

ISRAEL Visoker, Bar, Primo, Vollach [Aaron Shuruk 60], Rosen, Schwager, Rosenthal, Shum, Spiegler (c), Spiegel, Feygenbaum.
SWEDEN Sven-Gunnar Larsson, Axelsson, Hans Selander, Grip, Svensson (c), B Larsson, Kindvall, Örjan Persson (Sten Pålsson 75], Tom Nordahl, Tom Turesson, JV Olsson.

Kindvall played better against inferior opposition but was still struggling for breath. At his best he was one of Europe's sharpest strikers: a month earlier, he'd scored the winner for Feyenoord against Celtic in the European Cup final – but here he received some savage treatment from Bar, among others. Meanwhile the Israelis complained to the referee when Schwager was flattened by a punch. Selander's cross from the right was sidefooted in by Turesson, but Israel's spirit compensated for their shortcomings, and they equalised when Larsson was shocked by Spiegler's explosive long-range shot.

Nordahl's uncle Knut played in the 1950 finals. His father Gunnar and another uncle Bertil were also capped by Sweden.

10 June 1970 – Cuauhtémoc, Puebla – 18,163 – Heinrich 'Henry' Landauer (USA)

SWEDEN   **(0) 1**
Grahn 89

URUGUAY   **(0) 0**

SWEDEN SG Larsson, Axelsson, Selander, Nordqvist (c), Grip, Svensson, B Larsson, Nicklasson [Grahn 84], Eriksson, Kindvall [Turesson 57], Persson.
URUGUAY Mazurkiewicz, Ancheta, Matosas, Ubiña (c), Montero Castillo, Mújica, Cortés, Maneiro, Zubía, Espárrago [Dagoberto Fontes 60], Losada.

There was a breath of scandal before the match, a rumour that the original referee de Moraes had asked for money to favour Uruguay. FIFA investigated, decided he had no case to answer, switched him to the Israel-Italy match, and waved away Uruguayan counter-claims about a plot to discredit them. Meanwhile, back in the real world . . .

Sweden needed to win by two goals, and the Uruguayans weren't remotely unhappy to lose by one, though they might have been stirred out of mass defence if Eriksson's first-minute shot had gone in instead of hitting a post. Young Ancheta again looked a fine centre-half and Mazurkiewicz made a good save from Kindvall. Eventually, too late, Grahn headed in Persson's cross. Would the Uruguayan coach have enjoyed being a spectator at his team's matches? It wasn't his business, he said, to think like the crowd. This from the man who'd scored twice in the great Hungary-Uruguay match of 1954.

11 June 1970 – Luis Gutiérrez Dosal, Toluca – 9,860 – Aírton Vieira de Moraes (BRZ)

ISRAEL   **0**

ITALY   **0**

ISRAEL Visoker, Bar, Primo, Schwager, Rosenthal, Rosen, Menachem Bello, Shum, Spiegler (c), Spiegel, Feygenbaum [Rom HT].
ITALY Albertosi, Burgnich, Facchetti (c), Bertini, Rosato, Cera, Domenghini [Gianni Rivera HT], Mazzola, Boninsegna, De Sisti, Riva.

It looks embarrassing on paper (it wasn't much better on the pitch) but the favourites came close several times: a headed goal disallowed, a penalty appeal turned down, De Sisti's fierce left-footer from outside the area hitting the left-hand post. Visoker made some important saves and Riva pulled a cross-shot horribly wide when clean through on the left as Italy qualified from a finals group for the first time. Rivera came on as substitute, but if this was the answer, the question seemed to need re-phrasing. He had a very quiet second half.

1970

GROUP 2

	P	W	D	L	F	A	Pts
Italy	3	1	2	0	1	0	4
Uruguay	3	1	1	1	2	1	3
Sweden	3	1	1	1	2	2	3
Israel	3	0	2	1	1	3	1

Italy and Uruguay qualified for the quarter-finals. Italy set a record by winning their group despite scoring only a single goal.

1930
1934
1938
1950
1954
1958
1962
1966
1970
1974
1978
1982
1986
1990
1994
1998
2002
2006

GROUP 3

Brazil, Czechoslovakia, England, Romania. [No seeds.]

To retain the trophy, England would have to overcome some unnecessary and bizarre obstacles. Which is one way of introducing the Bogotá Affair.

On 18 May, England were in Colombia to play the first of two warm-up matches at altitude. In the foyer of the Tequendama hotel, Moore and Bobby Charlton wandered into the *Fuego Verde* (Green Fire) jewellery shop to kill time. When they left, they were accused of stealing a bracelet. Ramsey smoothed things over, England beat Colombia 4-0 and flew on to play in Ecuador. Their return flight included a stopover back in Bogotá, in fact at the same hotel. Returning to the scene of someone's crime.

To cut the sordid story short, Moore was held for four days before a judge decided there was insufficient evidence for a trial. Álvaro Suárez, the witness who was suddenly unearthed while England were in Ecuador, turned out to be a jewellery dealer not an innocent passer-by (touring teams in Colombia had been subjected to this kind of thing for years). Moore's chief accuser, shop assistant Clara Padilla, fled to the USA, and shop owner Danilo Rojas (who'd asked for £6,000 damages for a £600 bracelet) had to close down. The case wasn't officially dropped for another five years, during which Moore had to endure jibes in the street and the feeling that if he walked into a jewellery shop 'I have to keep my hands behind my back and point with my nose.' The affair underlined his dignity under pressure and only added to people's admiration, but he and the England

camp could have done without it. Mind you, according to Nobby Stiles they'd chosen the right victim: 'If it had been me in that shop, they'd have hung me without a trial!'

Other pressures stemmed from Ramsey's prickliness in press conferences, giving the impression of a Little Englander mentality. The result: an unfriendly press, plus Mexican fans encamped round the team hotel night after night, sounding their car horns and banging on the bodywork. And of course a hostile crowd at every match – but this England team had been there seen that; they could handle it. Especially their ice man of a captain.

---

2 June 1970 – Jalisco, Guadalajara – 50,560 – Vital Loraux (BEL)

ENGLAND (0) 1
Hurst 64

ROMANIA (0) 0

ENGLAND Gordon Banks, Keith Newton [Tommy Wright 52], Terry Cooper, Alan Mullery, Brian Labone, Bobby Moore (c), Francis Lee [Peter Osgood 77], Alan Ball, Bobby Charlton, Geoff Hurst, Martin Peters. *Alf Ramsey.*
ROMANIA Stere Adamache, Lajos Szátmári 'Sătmăreanu', Mihai Mocanu, Ion Dumitru, Nicolae Lupescu, Cornel Dinu, Radu Nunweiller, Emerich Dembrowski, Gheorghe Tataru [Alexandru Neagu 74], Florea Dumitrache, Mircea Lucescu (c). *Angelo Niculescu.*

The creative midfielder Nicolae Dobrin was out of the tournament with heatstroke, but Romania would probably have been just as defensive if he'd played. They nearly took a very early lead, Cooper standing and watching as Dembrowski prodded the ball just wide from Dumitrache's cross – but Lee soon hit the bar with a header.

The Romanian tackling became vicious and then some. Dumitru didn't hold back but Mocanu was something else. First he kicked

Newton's knee so badly he had to go off, then he took Lee's legs, then went after Newton's replacement Wright ('I thought my leg had snapped, my eyes watered like they've never done before'). Lee felt 'he must have created a new tackle, leaving identical bootprints on each knee.' Any one of those fouls would have earned a red card today, but Loraux didn't even book him. The debutant Tataru tried hard but Dumitrache, who'd scored in the 1-1 draw at Wembley in 1969 and boasted he'd get another two here, was still feeling an ankle injury.

England scored when Ball's cross from the right clipped Lee's head on its way to Hurst, who turned past Sătmăreanu and shot left-footed ('he told me later he topped it'), the ball going between Adamache's legs. England's 'slow sodium' pills had seen them through the worst, and Alan Ball enjoyed reminding Dumitrache about his two goals.

Szátmári, who had Hungarian ancestry, was sometimes known as Ludovic, a Romanian version of his first name. Similarly, Dembrowski is often seen spelt Dembrovschi.

---

3 June 1970 – Jalisco, Guadalajara – 52,897 – Ramón Barreto (URU)

BRAZIL   **(1) 4**
Rivelino 24, Pelé 59, Jairzinho 64, 82

CZECHOSLOVAKIA   **(1) 1**
Petráš 11

BRAZIL Félix (Mielli), Carlos Alberto (Torres) (c), Everaldo (Marques), Clodoaldo (Tavares), Hércules Brito, Wilson Piazza [José Fontana 88], 'Jairzinho' (Jair Ventura), Gérson (de Oliveira) [Paulo César (Lima) 73], 'Tostão' (Eduardo Gonçalves), 'Pelé' (Édson Arantes do Nascimento), Roberto Rivelino. *Mário Zagallo*.
CZECHOSLOVAKIA Ivo Viktor, Karol Dobiaš, Alexander Horváth (c), Václav Migas, Vladimír Hagara, Ivan Hrdlička [Andrej Kvašňák HT], Ladislav Kuna, Frantisek Veselý [Bohumil Veselý 75], Ladislav Petráš, Jozef Adamec, Karol Jokl. *Jozef Marko*.

Doubts as well as excitement surrounded the entry of the Brazilians. Had Tostão fully recovered from an operation on a detached retina? Would the late change of manager affect morale? Could Gérson at last influence matches away from home (he'd been invisible in 1966)?

The problems in defence were still there. Clodoaldo held on too long and lost the ball to Petráš, a blond firebrand in only his second international (he'd been sent off in the first!). After stop-starting to confuse Brito, Petráš dragged the ball past him and clipped it past Félix for a splendid individual goal. Soon afterwards, Adamec should have done something with Carlos Alberto's bad pass.

But Brazil had already served notice. Rivelino, bristling with talent, sold an exaggerated dummy before firing in a low cross which deflected off a defender and was put over an open goal by Pelé of all people. Then Rivelino went one better, his left foot aiming a cobra of a free kick straight at Jairzinho on the end of the wall. When Jairzinho got out of the way, Viktor did well to touch the shot on its way in.

On the stroke of half-time, Pelé's sudden shot from inside his own half drifted just wide of the right-hand post, one of the seminal World Cup moments. They're all trying it nowadays, the Beckhams even succeed at times, but it took the master to mark their card.

As Czechoslovakia began to tire, Brazil went ahead with another marvellous goal. Gérson, whose left foot was the equal of Rivelino's, hit a perfect aerial ball which dropped *just* over Hagara for Pelé to chest down and push the volley across the keeper. Then another Gérson pass was in the air long enough for Jairzinho to look offside as he ran on. Flipping the ball over the onrushing Viktor, he slammed it into the empty net.

Before that, Czechoslovakia had missed their one big chance. The tall Kvašňák had done well in the 1962 Final but was now a ghost at the feast. When Hagara's cross reached him five yards out, he blasted it over the bar. Jairzinho completed the scoring with a superb individual goal, resisting two sliding tackles in that inelegant but oddly skilful way of his before finishing with a low cross-shot.

David Coleman's rather triumphal comment about Brazil, made immediately after they went a goal down, turned out to be right ('All we ever knew about them has come true') but not in the way he meant – and Alan Ball's confidence ('We'll beat these') was looking positively unnatural. Paulo César is now known as 'Paulo César Caju' in Brazil.

1970

6 June 1970 – Jalisco, Guadalajara – 56,818 – Diego de Leo (MEX)

ROMANIA (0) 2
Neagu 53, Dumitrache pen 78

CZECHOSLOVAKIA (1) 1
Petráš 3

ROMANIA Adamache, Sătmăreanu, Mocanu, Dumitru [László Gergely 81], Lupescu, Dinu, Neagu, Dembrowski, Nunweiller, Dumitrache, Lucescu (c) [Tataru 69].
CZECHOSLOVAKIA Alex Vencel, Dobiaš, Horváth (c), Migas, Ján Zlocha, Kuna, Kvašňák, B Veselý, Josef Jurkanin [Adamec HT], Petráš, Jokl [F Veselý 74]

Again Petráš scored an early goal, a sharp header from Bohumil Veselý's cross, again Czechoslovakia faded badly in the second half. Neagu beat Migas before shooting the equaliser and was fouled by Zlocha for the penalty. Kvašňák wasn't capped again.

Gergely, of Hungarian extraction, was usually known by the 'official' version of his names: Vasile Ghergheli.

7 June 1970 – Jalisco, Guadalajara – 70,950 – Avraham Klein (ISR)

BRAZIL (0) 1
Jairzinho 62

ENGLAND (0) 0

BRAZIL Félix, Carlos Alberto (c), Everaldo, Clodoaldo, Brito, Piazza, Jairzinho, Paulo César, Tostão [Roberto (Miranda) 68], Pelé, Rivelino.
ENGLAND Banks, Wright, Cooper, Mullery, Labone, Moore (c), Lee [Jeff Astle 64], Ball, R Charlton [Colin Bell 64], Hurst, Peters.

For England fans, there was the nagging feeling that they were hanging in there a little, against better players – but that doesn't prevent it being one of the great matches. The same few incidents have been shown so often that we know them by heart, and it's never enough.

First up: That Save. Carlos Alberto hit a brilliant pass that skidded low inside then outside Cooper into the path of the galloping Jairzinho, who stumbled to the England goal line and got in a cross just before the ball went out of play. At the far post, Pelé outjumped Wright to head down and surely in, only for Banks to dive to his right and fingertip the ball over the bar. In our heart of hearts we think the unthinkable, that it wasn't *that* great (Banks: 'I'm sure I've equalled that save in League games') but it certainly kept England in the match, and Tostão thought it was pretty good: he spent several seconds with his hands up in disbelief.

LEADING GOALSCORERS 1970

10	Gerd Müller	GER	1 pen
7	Jairzinho	BRZ	
5	Teófilo Cubillas	PER	

1930
1934
1938
1950
1954
1958
1962
1966
1974
1978
1982
1986
1990
1994
1998
2002
2006

Mullery, confident enough to leave Pelé alone for a while, chipped a pass out to the right-hand corner flag, where Wright put over an equally good cross. Hurst jumped and missed but barged his man, and Lee came in at speed. He intended a volley, caught his studs in the long grass, and connected with a flying header that brought an unexpectedly good save from the dreadful Félix. Looking for a loose ball, Lee caught the goalkeeper and was booked.

All over the pitch, people were having excellent games, none more so than Moore, showing no ill effects from heat, altitude or Colombian shysters. One copybook tackle took the ball off Jairzinho's toes in the penalty area when the slightest mistiming would have brought a penalty. When Jairzinho repeated his trick of joining the wall at a Rivelino free kick, Moore solved the puzzle by standing behind him. The kick seared through, he stopped it and brought the ball upfield. You almost wished he *had* filched that bracelet: it might have proved he was human.

On the hour, Tostão's work-rate and awareness brought the only goal. When his first shot on the edge of the area was blocked by Labone, he chased back ten yards to regather, took a return pass from Paulo César, elbowed Ball in the face, took a rebound from Moore's shins, beat Wright, and finally (phew) crossed from the left in the general direction of the penalty spot. Unfortunately for England, Pelé was there to trap it and push it short to his right all in one movement, taking out two defenders. Jairzinho, unmarked because Cooper had come inside to see to Pelé, hammered the ball across Banks from six yards. England were back there in numbers and did nothing wrong, but Brazil still got through. The difference between the teams.

But England came desperately close. Moore's perfect tackle on Jairzinho led to Cooper's long cross from the left, which was hilariously mis-kicked by Everaldo deep in his own area, the ball squirting straight to Astle, so good in the air but less so on the deck. With the same left foot that had scored a screaming winner in an FA Cup final, he hit the ball firmly but past the far post, one of the famous misses. Then Ball, picking his spot, was unlucky to clip the top of the bar. England deserved a draw but no more, and Brazil were without their midfield general Gérson – but if defeat is ever glorious, this was it.

---

10 June 1970 – Jalisco, Guadalajara – 50,804 – Ferdinand Marschall (AUT)

BRAZIL   **(2) 3**
Pelé 19, 66, Jairzinho 21

ROMANIA   **(1) 2**
Dumitrache 33, Dembrowski 82

1970

BRAZIL Félix, Carlos Alberto (c), Everaldo [Marco Antônio (Feliciano) 56], Piazza, Brito, Fontana, Jairzinho, Clodoaldo ['Edu' (Eduardo) Américo 73], Tostão, Pelé, Paulo César.
ROMANIA Adamache [Răducanu (Necula) 28], Sătmăreanu, Mocanu, Dumitru, Lupescu, Dinu, Neagu, Dembrowski, Nunweiller, Dumitrache [Tataru 71], Lucescu (c).

There was a preposterous rumour that Brazil might deliberately lose to make qualification more difficult for England. Instead they played some of the best football of the tournament. Pelé slashed a free kick low round the wall for the first goal and toe-poked the third, and Jairzinho scored at the near post after Paulo César beat Sătmăreanu. For Romania, Dumitrache stabbed in a rebound after an attempted dribble went wrong, and Dembrowski headed in Sătmăreanu's cross. Like Vintilă Cossini in 1938, Răducanu was known by his first name.

1930
1934
1938
1950
1954
1958
1962
1966
1970
1974
1978
1982
1986
1990
1994
1998
2002
2006

11 June 1970 – Jalisco, Guadalajara – 49,292 – Roger Machin (FRA)

ENGLAND   **(0) 1**
Clarke pen 48

CZECHOSLOVAKIA   **(0) 0**

ENGLAND Banks, Newton, Cooper, Mullery, Jack Charlton, Moore (c), Bell, R Charlton [Ball 65], Astle [Peter Osgood 60], Allan Clarke, Peters.
CZECHOSLOVAKIA Viktor (c), Dobiaš, Vladimír Hrivnák, Migas, Hagara, Kuna, Ján Čapkovič [Jokl 70], Jaroslav Pollák, Adamec, Petráš, F Veselý.

As usual, the crowd gave England the bird, with some justification this time: a very poor performance to mark Bobby Charlton's 105th cap, which equalled Billy Wright's world record. His brother, now 35, and Astle weren't capped again. Dobiaš hit the bar from long range and England were given a goal by the referee, when Kuna tangled with Bell and fell on the ball with his hand. Clarke, typically cool in the heat, scored on his England debut. It was his wife's birthday, their wedding anniversary, and the anniversary of his transfer from Fulham to Leicester! The real crowd figure was probably nearer 35,000.

GROUP 3

	P	W	D	L	F	A	Pts
Brazil	3	3	0	0	8	3	6
England	3	2	0	1	2	1	4
Romania	3	1	0	2	4	5	2
Czechoslovakia	3	0	0	3	2	7	0

Brazil and England qualified for the quarter-finals.

GROUP 4

Bulgaria, Morocco, Peru, West Germany. [No seeds.]

2 June 1970 – Guanajuato, León – 13,765 – Antonio Sbardella (ITA)

PERU   **(0) 3**
Gallardo 51, Chumpitáz 56, Cubillas 74

BULGARIA   **(1) 2**
Dermendjiev 13, Bonev 49

PERU Luis Rubiños, Eloy Campos [Javier González 27], Nicolas Fuentes, Roberto Challe, Orlando De la Torre, Héctor Chumpitáz (c), Julio Baylón [Hugo Sotil 50], Ramón Mifflin, Pedro 'Perico' León, Teófilo Cubillas, Alberto Gallardo. *'Didi' (Waldir Pereira) (BRZ).*
BULGARIA Simeon Simeonov, Aleksandar Shalamanov, Stefan Aladjov, Ivan Davidov, Dimitar Penev, Ivan Dimitrov (c), Dinko Dermendjiev, Christo Bonev [Georgi Asparoukhov 83], Petar Zhekov, Dimitar Yakimov, Georgi Popov [Dimitar Marashliev 59]. *Stefan Bozhkov.*

Before the match, both sides observed a minute's silence for the victims of Peru's recent earthquake – then Bulgaria caught their opponents cold with a clever free kick. Dermendjiev ran past the left-hand side of the Peruvian wall, the ball went to the other side and was touched into his path by a team mate, he drove in the first goal of the tournament on his 29th birthday. Peru missed chances through some wild shooting, especially by Gallardo, then Bulgaria made the most of another free kick. Bonev, lean and all-purpose, scored a record 47 goals for Bulgaria, but this was just about the softest, his kick full of spin but straight at Rubiños, who fumbled it in.

Peru had no choice but to keep attacking, and eventually one of Gallardo's thunderbolts crashed in off the bar. Then three Peruvians stood in the end of the wall at a free kick; Chumpitáz shot straight at them and scored with a ground shot when they stepped aside. Finally Cubillas played a one-two with Mifflin before beating a man and shooting an excellent winner. Peru, rampant by now, had two other goals disallowed.

An indispensable piece of information: León was the only man to play a finals match in a town whose name matched his surname.

---

3 June 1970 – Guanajuato, León – 12,942 – Laurens van Ravens (HOL)

WEST GERMANY   **(0) 2**
Seeler 56, Müller 78

MOROCCO   **(1) 1**
Houmane 22

WEST GERMANY Sepp Maier, Berti Vogts, Horst-Dieter Höttges [Hannes Löhr 75], Franz Beckenbauer, Klaus Fichtel, Willi Schulz, Helmut Haller [Jürgen Grabowski HT], Uwe Seeler (c), Gerd Müller, Wolfgang Overath, Sigi Held. *Helmut Schön.*
MOROCCO Allal Ben Kassou, Abdullah Lamrani, Boujemaa Benkhrif, Kacem Slimani, Moulay Driss Khanoussi, Mohammed Maaroufi, Said Ghandi, Mouhoub Ghazouani [Abdelkader El-Khyati 55], Driss Bamous (c) [Ahmed Faras 70], Houmane Jarir, Mohammed El-Filali. *Blagoje Vidinić (YUG).*

How would Schön accommodate Seeler and Müller in the same team? By simply withdrawing Seeler into midfield, where he showed what an adaptable player he was, one of the World Cup's most redoubtable figures. Before the partnership began to flourish, West Germany were threatened with one of the great shock results. Morocco had qualified under a French coach called Cluseau, but there was nothing comical about their efforts in the finals. Houmane knocked in a bad defensive header by Höttges, and Allal had a fine game in goal, but eventually Seeler scored in a scramble and

Müller put in the rebound when Seeler's leaping header looped onto the bar. Some of the Moroccans were known by their first names.

---

6 June 1970 – Guanajuato, León – 13,537 – Tofik Bakhramov (USR)

PERU   **(0) 3**
Cubillas 65, 76, Challe 69

MOROCCO **(0) 0**

PERU Rubiños, Pedro González, Fuentes, Challe, De la Torre, Chumpitáz (c), Sotil, Mifflin [Luis Cruzado 55], León, Cubillas, Gallardo [Osvaldo Ramírez 75].
MOROCCO Allal, Lamrani, Boujemaa [Jilali Fadili 65], Slimani, Moulay Driss, Maaroufi, El-Filali, Said [Ahmed Allaoui 80], Bamous (c), Ghazouani, Houmane.

Allal again played well, and León missed chances throughout, including two '*magníficas oportunidades*' in the first few minutes and a shot against the bar from five yards out – so the scoreline was kept within bounds. Cubillas smashed a loose ball into an empty net from very close range, and Allal got a touch to his strong shot for the third, after Sotil had beaten assorted defenders. Challe ran into the penalty area before smashing the ball past the keeper, and Sotil had a late goal disallowed for a foul by Ramírez on Lamrani. Estimates of the real crowd figure range from 4,000 to 7,000.

---

7 June 1970 – Guanajuato, León – 12,710 – José María Ortiz de Mendíbil (SPA)

WEST GERMANY   **(2) 5**
Libuda 19, Müller 27, 52 pen, 88, Seeler 69

BULGARIA   **(1) 2**
Nikodimov 12, Kolev 89

WEST GERMANY Maier, Vogts, Höttges, Beckenbauer [Wolfgang Weber 73], Fichtel, Karl-Heinz Schnellinger, Reinhard Libuda, Seeler (c), Müller, Overath, Löhr [Grabowski 58].

1930
1934
1938
1950
1954
1958
1962
1966
1970
1974
1978
1982
1986
1990
1994
1998
2002
2006

BULGARIA Simeonov, Milko Gaydarski, Dobromir Jechev, Penev, Boris Gaganelov (c) [Shalamanov 57], Todor Kolev, Bonev, Asparoukh Nikodimov, Dermendjiev [Vasil Mitkov HT], Asparoukhov, Marashliev.

Again West Germany conceded an early goal, again Bulgaria scored from a free kick, again the result was the same for both sides. Schön brought in Libuda, a snaky winger who'd scored the goal that knocked out Scotland, and he dominated the match, especially the Bulgarian captain, who wasn't capped again. First he beat Gaganelov to Seeler's through-pass and jabbed a low cross into the six-yard area, where Simeonov let it slip under him and just over the line. Libuda's credited with the goal, but it was clearly an o.g. Next he scuttled through a gap, slipped, got up and dribbled Nikodimov to make an easy volleyed goal for Müller. Then Gaganelov fouled him for the penalty. Seeler arrived at the far post to meet a low cross from Müller, who headed the fifth from a free kick, excellent in the air for someone so short and swarthy. Kolev's brother Ivan played in the 1962 and 1966 finals.

10 June 1970 – Guanajuato, León – 17,875 – Abel Aguilar (MEX)

WEST GERMANY (3) 3
Müller 19, 26, 38

PERU (1) 1
Cubillas 44

WEST GERMANY Maier, Vogts, Höttges [Bernd Patzke HT], Beckenbauer, Fichtel, Schnellinger, Libuda [Grabowski 74], Seeler (c), Müller, Overath, Löhr.
PERU Rubiños, P González, Fuentes, Challe [Cruzado 70], De la Torre, Chumpitáz (c), Sotil, Mifflin, León [Ramírez 51], Cubillas, Gallardo.

Again Schön got it right, planning to stop Peru playing their little one-twos and to hit them with high crosses from the wings. One from Libuda, deep on the right, floated over a defender's head for Müller to chest down and push home. Then Löhr beat González on the left and his low centre to the near post was knocked in by Müller's left foot. Finally Seeler's cross from the right was put in with a cleverly placed looping header. Cubillas scored with a deflected free kick, but the Peruvian defence had been shown up (Müller found yards of space for all three of his goals) and would now have to face the full glare of Brazil.

11 June 1970 – Guanajuato, León – 12,299 – António Saldanha (POR)

BULGARIA (1) 1
Jechev 39

MOROCCO (0) 1
Ghazouani 59

BULGARIA Stoyan Yordanov, Jechev, Shalamanov (c), Penev [Dimitrov 42], Gaydarski, Nikodimov, Kolev, Yakimov [Bonev 62], Asparoukhov, Popov, Mitkov.
MOROCCO Mohammed Hazzaz, Fadili, Moulay Driss, Slimani, Boujemaa, Maaroufi, Bamous (c) [Mustafa Choukri HT], Said, Allaoui [Faras 73], El-Filali, Ghazouani.

Meaningless except for the teams involved. It appeared to be Bulgaria's best chance of winning a finals match for the first time, but they'd lost 3-0 in Morocco the previous year, and although they'd trained at altitude they hadn't bargained for the fact that León was the hottest venue in the tournament; so Morocco became the first African country to avoid defeat in the finals. Mitkov hit a post before taking the free kick from which Jechev made it 1-0 (his only goal in 73 internationals) – but Ghazouani equalised with a 'suave toque'. Estimates of the real crowd figure include 4,000 and even 1,500.

GROUP 4

	P	W	D	L	F	A	Pts
West Germany	3	3	0	0	10	4	6
Peru	3	2	0	1	7	5	4
Bulgaria	3	0	1	2	5	9	1
Morocco	3	0	1	2	2	6	1

West Germany and Peru qualified for the quarter-finals.

QUARTER-FINALS

14 June 1970 – Azteca, Mexico City – 96,085 – Laurens van Ravens (HOL)

URUGUAY (0) (0) 1
Espárrago 117

USSR (0) (0) 0

URUGUAY Mazurkiewicz, Ancheta, Matosas, Montero Castillo, Ubiña (c), Mújica, Cubilla, Cortés, Maneiro, Julio César Morales [Alberto Gómez 96], Fontes [Espárrago 103].
USSR Kavazashvili, Shesternev (c), Dzodzuashvili, Kaplichny, Khurtsilava [Logofet 83], Afonin, Asatiani [Kiselev 71], Muntian, Byshovets, Evriuzhikin, Khmelnitskiy.

In a dreary, rough match (seventy fouls), Uruguay stopped Byshovets by fair means and otherwise, and won because they kept playing to the end. Ancheta, up for one final attack, glanced a header towards the Soviet goal line on the left, Afonin shielded it with his body, only for Cubilla to steal it between his legs from behind and dig up a near-post cross which beat Kavazashvili and was headed in by Espárrago. The USSR surrounded the referee, but TV replays show conclusively that the ball

didn't go out of play. One source puts the attendance at around 45,000.

14 June 1970 – Luis Gutiérrez Dosal, Toluca – 26,851 – Rudi Scheurer (SWI)

ITALY (1) 4
Guzmán o.g. 25, Riva 63, 76, Rivera 70

MEXICO (1) 1
González 13

ITALY Albertosi, Burgnich, Facchetti (c), Bertini, Rosato, Cera, Domenghini [Sergio Gori 84], Mazzola [Rivera HT], Boninsegna, De Sisti, Riva.
MEXICO Calderón, Peña (c), Vantolrá, Guzmán, Pérez, Pulido, González [Borja 67], Munguía [Isidoro Díaz 59], Valdivia, Fragoso, Padilla.

Mexico's goal was a good one, Fragoso coolly flicking the ball sideways to his right, González slicing the ball low past Albertosi – but there were no refereeing handouts this time and Italy were soon in control. Rivera's arrival led to a

TOURNAMENTS AS GOALSCORER

4	Uwe Seeler	GER	1958–62–66–70
4	Pelé	BRZ	1958–62–66–70
3	Joe Jordan	SCO	1974–78–82
3	Grzegorz Lato	POL	1974–78–82
3	Andrzej Szarmach	POL	1974–78–82
3	Dominique Rocheteau	FRA	1978–82–86
3	Michel Platini	FRA	1978–82–86
3	Julio Salinas	SPA	1986–90–94
3	Diego Maradona	ARG	1982–86–94
3	Rudi Völler	GER	1986–90–94
3	Lothar Matthäus	GER	1986–90–94
3	Roberto Baggio	ITA	1990–94–98
3	Jürgen Klinsmann	GER	1990–94–98
3	Gabriel Batistuta	ARG	1994–98–02
3	Fernando Hierro	SPA	1994–98–02

1930
1934
1938
1950
1954
1958
1962
1966
1970
1974
1978
1982
1986
1990
1994
1998
2002
2006

1930
1934
1938
1950
1954
1958
1962
1966

1970

1974
1978
1982
1986
1990
1994
1998
2002
2006

more attacking approach, which unleashed Riva at last. Early sources credit the own goal (from Domenghini's low drive) to Guzmán, and in this case they're right. Some Italian publications cite Peña, but it's clearly No.14 on the replay (Peña, the No.3 wearing the captain's armband, is nowhere near the ball). Rivera came on again at half-time and this time formed a matchwinning partnership with Riva, who'd stayed upbeat despite his lack of goals.

His first of the tournament came from his famous left foot, a low cross-shot that Calderón should have reached. His second was prodded in off Guzmán's heel after his first shot had been saved. In between, Rivera had gone round the keeper and assorted shots had been blocked before Rivera regained possession and came inside a defender to shoot under Calderón at the near post. The Mazzola-Rivera *staffetta* (relay) seemed to be here to stay.

---

14 June 1970 – Jalisco, Guadalajara – 54,233 – Vital Loraux (BEL)

BRAZIL　　**(2) 4**
Rivelino 11, Tostão 15, 52, Jairzinho 75

PERU　　**(1) 2**
Gallardo 27, Cubillas 69

BRAZIL Félix, Carlos Alberto (c), Marco Antônio, Clodoaldo, Brito, Piazza, Jairzinho [Roberto 80], Gérson [Paulo César 67], Tostão, Pelé, Rivelino.
PERU Rubiños, Campos, Fuentes, Challe, José Fernández, Chumpitáz (c), Baylón [Sotil 53], Mifflin, León [Eladio Reyes 61], Cubillas, Gallardo.

Gérson was back and Peru's fate was sealed, their tactic of marking space absurdly vulnerable against a front line as mobile and intelligent as Brazil's. And goals were always likely against the two worst keepers in the tournament.

Pelé hit a post early on then crossed from the right. Campos slipped and chested the ball straight to Tostão, who immediately pushed it

to Rivelino, whose shot went in off the bottom of the far post. Next Tostão took a short corner on the left, ran round a defender to get to the goal line, and hit Rivelino's return pass straight at Campos, who let it in at the near post as Fernández put his face in his hands.

Peru kept trying. Gallardo, tall and powerful, beat Carlos Alberto down the left and hit his shot at Félix, who returned Campos' compliment by letting the ball in off his thigh. But the Peruvian defenders, in their white shirts with a red sash across the chest, were standing around like so many Red Stripe cans. After Rubiños had fumbled Pelé's shot onto a post, Jairzinho put Pelé clear on the right, a defender deflected his gentle cross over the diving Rubiños into the path of Tostão, who knocked it in then put his hand over one ear to cut out the roar of the crowd. Cubillas met a clearance with a low volley from the edge of the area, but Jairzinho went past the hapless Rubiños to score the fourth.

The two coaches, Zagallo and Didi, had played on the winning team in the Finals of 1958 and 1962.

---

14 June 1970 – Guanajuato, Léon – 23,357 – Ángel Norberto Coerezza (ARG)

WEST GERMANY　　**(0) (2) 3**
Beckenbauer 67, Seeler 82, Müller 109

ENGLAND　　**(1) (2) 2**
Mullery 32, Peters 50

WEST GERMANY Maier, Vogts, Höttges [Schulz HT], Beckenbauer, Fichtel, Schnellinger, Libuda [Grabowski 57], Seeler (c), Müller, Overath, Löhr.
ENGLAND Peter Bonetti, Newton, Cooper, Mullery, Labone, Moore (c), Lee, Ball, R Charlton [Bell 69], Hurst, Peters [Norman Hunter 80].

At the last moment, Banks went down with food poisoning ('Montezuma's Revenge') but his replacement came highly recommended. Bonetti had just played brilliantly to help

Chelsea win the FA Cup final, and in his six England appearances he'd been on the winning side every time while conceding just a single goal. Here in León, he was hardly needed in a first hour that belied both teams' form in the tournament so far, England at last looking every inch the world champions.

Their first goal was started and finished by the impressive Mullery. After exchanging passes with Lee, he found Newton overlapping on the right, ran for the return at the near post ('I kept expecting to be clattered any second') and scooped it high past Maier. It was the only goal he scored in 35 internationals, but an exceptional one. Early in the second half Newton put in another cross, this time to the far post, where Peters made his only contribution to the tournament by forcing the ball in off Maier's dive. That was enough for some English journalists to shout '*Auf Wiedersehen*' at the German supporters. They were right, but not in the way anyone expected.

As well as coming forward on the left, Cooper had done a complete job by shutting out Libuda, but the substitute Grabowski was fresh and dangerous. And West Germany were let back in by a goal that according to Moore 'cut into our confidence at the back.' Beckenbauer beat Mullery on the right-hand corner of the England area and shot immediately; the ball seemed to surprise Bonetti for pace and went in under his body. Bonetti made partial amends with a save after Müller had muscled his way past Newton on the right – but, as Moore said, 'From that moment it was one-way traffic towards our goal, a total turnabout.'

Seeler's equaliser owed something to luck. His back-header was aimed towards Müller (if it was aimed at all) but drifted over Bonetti. And England should have gone 3-1 up when Hurst met Bell's right-wing cross with a brave diving header that crept just wide as Lee waited for it to come back off the far post. But Ramsey's dependence on wing-backs was beginning to count against him. In extra-time Grabowski went past a tiring Cooper to the goal line, his high cross was headed back from beyond the far post by Löhr, and Müller at last came to life by getting behind Labone to volley home while in mid-air. Again, Bonetti might have done better.

British prime minister Harold Wilson blamed the result for his defeat in the General Election, and he may not have been joking. Ramsey was later criticised for the timing for his substitutions, but they made sense enough, and in Germany it's seen as a glorious comeback, not something England threw away. But those guys had all the luck: after Müller's goal, Lee beat Schnellinger and pulled the ball back for Hurst, whose goal was mysteriously disallowed by the dreaded Coerezza. A tough way to go for Moore, the heroic Hurst, the exhausted underrated Newton, who didn't play for England again. Nor did Labone, Charlton or the unhappy Bonetti, forever remembered for this one overcrowded hour.

SEMI-FINALS

17 June 1970 – Jalisco, Guadalajara – 51,261- José María Ortiz de Mendíbil (SPA)

BRAZIL **(1) 3**
Clodoaldo 44, Jairzinho 69, Rivelino 89

URUGUAY **(1) 1**
Cubilla 17

BRAZIL Félix, Carlos Alberto (c), Everaldo, Clodoaldo, Brito, Piazza, Jairzinho, Gérson, Tostão, Pelé, Rivelino. URUGUAY Mazurkiewicz, Ancheta, Matosas, Montero Castillo, Ubiña (c), Mújica, Cubilla, Cortés, Maneiro [Espárrago 74], Morales, Fontes.

1930
1934
1938
1950
1954
1958
1962
1966
1970
1974
1978
1982
1986
1990
1994
1998
2002
2006

Perhaps Brazil were still carrying scars from 1950. At any rate they needed a half-time rocket from Zagallo to raise their game. They fell behind to a ludicrous goal, Brito giving the ball straight to Morales, whose chip found Cubilla running into the penalty area on the right. He controlled the ball on his thigh before lifting it across the six-yard box, where Félix let it bounce inside the far post then knelt in despair.

Brazil struggled for the rest of the half but their equaliser arrived at the right time and was beautifully made and finished. Clodoaldo knocked a short ball to Tostão on the left wing then sprinted for the return pass, which he thrashed first time past the keeper's right hand. The other goals also took a while coming but were almost as good. Pelé's touch to Tostão was followed by a pass out to Jairzinho, who cleverly beat Matosas before scoring with a low cross-shot. Finally Pelé rolled the ball back for Rivelino's left foot to do the rest, though Mazurkiewicz bravely got a touch.

Uruguay's impressive run might have been even more successful (and certainly less defensive) if Rocha hadn't been injured – but the better team won here. They still had time for the most imaginative move in any World Cup, Pelé sprinting onto an angled through-ball from Tostão and dummying past Mazurkiewicz, beating a world-class goalkeeper without actually touching the ball. The shot rolled just past the far post, which was just as well: if it had gone in, they'd have had to close the sport down. There'd have been nothing left to aim for.

---

17 June 1970 – Azteca, Mexico City – 102,444 – Arturo Yamasaki (MEX)

ITALY (1) (1) 4
Boninsegna 8, Burgnich 98, Riva 104, Rivera 111

WEST GERMANY (0) (1) 3
Schnellinger 90, Müller 94, 110

ITALY Albertosi, Burgnich, Facchetti (c), Bertini, Rosato [Fabrizio Poletti FT], Cera, Domenghini Mazzola [Rivera HT], Boninsegna, De Sisti, Riva.
WEST GERMANY Maier, Vogts, Patzke [Held 65], Beckenbauer, Schnellinger, Schulz, Grabowski, Seeler (c), Müller, Overath, Löhr [Libuda 51].

A match that rose to the heights despite itself, though the conditions had something to do with it: they weren't made for extra time.

After the willing Boninsegna had despatched a rebound from the edge of the area, Italy set out their stall to hold out. Overath hit the bar with a mighty left-footer and Albertosi recovered to kick clear from Müller after his attempted clearance hit Grabowski and rebounded as far as the goal line. Eventually, in injury time, Grabowski held off two tackles on the left and crossed for Schnellinger to arrive unmarked and leap at the ball with feet splayed, volleying in with his right. Cue the great thirty-minute rollercoaster.

Italy's downhill spiral continued when Poletti ran back towards his own goal and chested the ball towards Albertosi, Müller getting in to touch the ball just over the line. But the game never stopped swinging both ways. Rivera had been bypassed in the urgency of the game, he now chipped in a free kick without a run-up but hit it too far. What Held was doing in his own area isn't clear, especially as it brought his marker back with him. He let the ball bounce off him straight to Burgnich, who banged the ball in with his left foot to score his second and last goal in an eventual 66 internationals.

Riva beat Schnellinger with an exaggerated turn and scored with a confident low cross-shot. Seeler climbed to head on a corner, the ball barely brushed Müller's head, and Rivera seemed to usher it past, only to see it bounce in. He wrapped himself round the post as Albertosi held his hands out in supplication.

But Rivera redeemed himself soon enough. Straight from the kick-off Boninsegna beat the veteran Schulz on the left and Rivera met his low cross with excruciating calmness, sidefooting the ball into the middle of the goal as Maier was forced to dash to his left. With Beckenbauer's arm in a sling and everyone's chest heaving, Italy held out till the end. Top coaches called it a basketball match, and it wasn't a compliment – but fans have always disagreed. It's recently been voted the best World Cup match of all time. Yamasaki represented Peru when he refereed in the 1962 and 1966 tournaments.

3RD-PLACE FINAL

20 June 1970 – Azteca, Mexico City – 104,403 – Antonio Sbardella (ITA)

WEST GERMANY   (1) 1
Overath 26

URUGUAY   (0) 0

WEST GERMANY Horst Wolter, Vogts, Schnellinger [Max Lorenz HT], Patzke, Fichtel, Weber, Libuda [Löhr 73], Seeler (c), Müller, Overath, Held.
URUGUAY Mazurkiewicz, Ancheta, Matosas, Montero Castillo, Ubiña (c), Mújica, Cubilla, Cortés, Maneiro [Rodolfo Sandoval 67], Morales, Fontes [Espárrago HT].

Müller needed three goals to equal Fontaine's 13 in a tournament, but it was never very likely. In fact this was the only game in the competition, including six qualifiers, in which he failed to score. Meanwhile, freed from competitive tensions, Uruguay came out to attack but had no luck. Overath scored with a low shot after Müller laid the ball back, and Seeler hit the bar – but Uruguay might have had three or four. Wolter, in a nervy last international, made a tremendous save from

Ancheta's late header. The real attendance figure has been variously estimated as 32,000 and 85,000!

FINAL

21 June 1970 – Azteca, Mexico City – 107,412 – Rudi Glöckner (DDR)

BRAZIL   (1) 4
Pelé 18, Gérson 66, Jairzinho 71, Carlos Alberto 86

ITALY   (1) 1
Boninsegna 37

BRAZIL Félix, Carlos Alberto (c), Everaldo, Clodoaldo, Brito, Piazza, Jairzinho, Gérson, Tostão, Pelé, Rivelino.
ITALY Albertosi, Burgnich, Facchetti (c), Bertini [Antonio Juliano 74], Rosato, Cera, Domenghini Mazzola, Boninsegna [Rivera 84], De Sisti, Riva.

Italy seemed to start where they left off in the semi-final. Riva took Mazzola's inside pass on the right wing and showed iffy control but great self-belief and shooting power, forcing Félix to tip over from 25 yards. But defence was still the Italian womb, and they retreated immediately and in numbers, Brazil coming forward just as naturally.

From a throw-in on the left, Rivelino hooked over a volleyed cross, Pelé beat Burgnich easily in the air and headed down and in at the far post: Brazil's 100th goal in the finals. Italy were allowed back in by yet another of the slapdash goals Brazil gave away in this tournament, Clodoaldo attempting a lazy backheel, Boninsegna charging it down, Félix coming out much too soon. Boninsegna held off Brito's challenge and the ball ran free towards the left, where Riva was waiting but stood aside for Boninsegna to turn the ball into an empty net. However, the Brazilian menace was always there. Pelé had a goal disallowed only because the referee had blown for half-time, and Rivelino (with his right foot of all things) thrashed a free kick against the bar.

When Brazil's second goal finally arrived, it was very well struck but owed a little to luck. Jairzinho, who looks big and strong on the screen, now found a full-back he couldn't brush aside: Facchetti, who positively dwarfed him, had an excellent match, showing all his concentration and surprising speed. Here he tackled Jairzinho only for the ball to go straight to Gérson, who stepped away from a challenge and scored with a crisp cross-shot just before another tackle came in, the ball beating Albertosi to his left. Within minutes, Gérson hit another of his tremendous long crosses deep to the right-hand side of the Italian penalty area. Pelé was marked by Burgnich, one of the great defensive right-backs but never likely to match him in the air. Pelé headed across goal, for once Facchetti gave Jairzinho too much room, and the winger miskicked the ball in from close range. He emulated Ghiggia (1950) by scoring in every round of a World Cup tournament including the Final.

For some reason Italy didn't man-mark Gérson and had no contingency plan when he began to turn the screw, which he did only in the second half, giving the Italians no chance to change things at half-time. His patience, as well as that remarkable left foot, was probably the determining factor in the Final.

This time Rivera didn't come on at half-time, mainly because Mazzola was playing too well, with great courage as well as intimate control. When Rivera did arrive, it was a ludicrous sop: six minutes, with the match already lost. Meanwhile Juliano, the first substitute in a Final, did little.

The last, celebratory goal showed all the Brazilian skills. Clodoaldo held off several

WORLD CUP WINNER AS PLAYER AND COACH

Mário Zagallo	BRZ	1958–62	1970
Franz Beckenbauer	GER	1974	1990

Beckenbauer, the captain in 1974, was also a losing finalist as a player (1966) and coach (1986).

Italian players deep in his half before feeding Jairzinho on the left. He rushed inside but again Facchetti wouldn't let him pass, so the ball was transferred to Pelé, who repeated the simple square passes which had killed off England and Uruguay. This time Carlos Alberto came charging up on the right and the ball bobbled at the last second, sitting up for the shot which crashed low past Albertosi's right hand. The president's goal, they called it, because the president of Brazil, General Emilio Garrastazu Médici, had predicted they'd score four. A reminder that one of the reasons for the removal of Saldanha as coach had been his political opinions, and that winning the World Cup did Brazil's brutal military government no harm.

But what a front five. The equal of the 1958 forwards. Whether they would have succeeded in a tournament held in a different climate is a debatable point, whether it's important is another. Gérson's lack of fitness (it's said he smoked two packs a day) had been exposed in 1966, and that defence and goalkeeper would have been under greater pressure if the European teams had been able to play their natural game. But the other side of the coin includes the intelligence and economy of Tostão, Pelé's Indian summer, all those dazzling goals. Was that worth some burning Bulgarian lungs, some exhausted Belgians and Englishmen? A definite maybe.

Orange is not the only fruit

West Germany **1974**

1930
1934
1938
1950
1954
1958
1962
1966
1970

1974

1978
1982
1986
1990
1994
1998
2002
2006

Brazil lost the World Cup almost as soon as they regained it. The Jules Rimet Trophy, theirs to keep after winning it for the third time, was stolen and never seen again. Their 1970 team melted away too, Pelé retiring too early at 31 and three important players dropping out injured: Carlos Alberto, Clodoaldo and especially Tostão, whose eye problem had resurfaced. In their absence, Zagallo put together a far more physical side, in the belief that the old skills wouldn't survive against European athleticism.

No-one seemed to epitomise this more than the hosts and favourites, who'd won the 1972 European Championship with some masterly all-round football, outclassing England at Wembley before winning the final 3-0 at a canter. Three of the team finished 1-2-3 in the European Footballer of the Year poll and there were world-class players in every department: Maier in goal, Vogts and the new discovery Breitner at fullback; the incomparable Beckenbauer, now the world's first great attacking sweeper; the imperious blond Netzer in midfield; Müller ever more unstoppable up front. Several of the squad came from Bayern Munich, who'd recently won the European Cup for the first time. The most intriguing match of an easy first round group would be a first meeting with neighbours East Germany.

Italy were as defensive as ever and apparently even more impregnable: Zoff had just completed 12 consecutive internationals without conceding a goal. But they were an ageing team, short of goalscoring power. England were out, after a frantic emotional night against the Poles at Wembley, but Scotland were back for the first time since 1958, good in parts but lacking a genuine midfield general. Holland still hadn't harnessed the brilliance of their Ajax players, who'd just been beaten in the European Cup after winning it three years in a row. Only a very late goal in Norway sent them through at the expense of Belgium, against whom they'd played two goalless draws.

The USSR, required to play off against Chile, were disqualified for refusing to appear in the National Stadium in Santiago, which had been used as a concentration camp for political prisoners after Salvador Allende's elected government had been overthrown by Augusto Pinochet's military coup, backed by the CIA. Chile kicked off against non-existent opponents (shades of Scotland v Estonia in the 1998 qualifiers) and put the ball into an empty net. The Soviet protest might have attracted more sympathy if they'd refused to play Chile before the first leg instead of waiting till they'd been held 0-0 at home.

Yet again FIFA couldn't leave well alone. Although the format of the last three tournaments had been generally acceptable, they insisted on trying to give the event more of the appearance of a league and making the successful teams play an extra match, as if that would give the winners more credibility as world champions. All it succeeded in doing was tiring the players even more and depriving spectators of two knockout rounds. All for a few dollars more.

Franz Beckenbauer spent the Final looking over his shoulder, but Johan Cruijff finished behind him.

1930
1934
1938
1950
1954
1958
1962
1966
1970
1974
1978
1982
1986
1990
1994
1998
2002
2006

GROUP 1

Australia, Chile, East Germany, West Germany (seeded).

14 June 1974 – Olympia, West Berlin – 83,168 – Dogan Babaçan (TUR)

WEST GERMANY   **(1) 1**
Breitner 18

CHILE   **(0) 0**

WEST GERMANY Sepp Maier, Berti Vogts, Paul Breitner, Bernd Cullmann, Georg Schwarzenbeck, Franz Beckenbauer (c), Jürgen Grabowski, Uli Hoeness, Gerd Müller, Wolfgang Overath [Bernd Hölzenbein 75], Jupp Heynckes. *Helmut Schön.*
CHILE Leopoldo Vallejos, Rolando García, Alberto Quintano, Antonio Arias, Elías Figueroa, Juan Rodríguez [Alfonso Lara 83], Carlos Caszely, Francisco Valdéz (c) [Leonardo Véliz 76], Sergio Ahumada, Carlos Reinoso, Guillermo Páez. *Luis Alamos.*
SENT OFF: Caszely 67.

The term Total Football, coined during this tournament, wasn't used to describe West Germany's play – but their opening goal fitted the description. A confident passing movement ended with the bushy-haired Breitner, a Marxist with Harpo tendencies, hitting a 30-yard cross-shot which Vallejos finger-tipped into the top corner. A left-back scoring with his right foot from inside-right. After that: delusion. Netzer, after injury and a poor season with Real Madrid, was badly missed, and the team were whistled off at the end – although some of that was due to the 'merciless' tackling of the Chileans, culminating in the dismissal of the skilful Caszely for a foul on his marker Vogts. The local riot police dealt in their usual fashion with any spectators demonstrating against the military regime in Chile.

14 June 1974 – Volkspark, Hamburg – 18,180 – Youssou Ndiaye (SEN)

EAST GERMANY   **(0) 2**
Curran o.g. 58, Streich 72

AUSTRALIA   **(0) 0**

EAST GERMANY Jürgen Croy, Bernd Bransch (c), Gerd Kische, Konrad Weise, Siegmar Wätzlich, Jürgen Pommerenke, Harald Irmscher, Jürgen Sparwasser, Wolfram Löwe [Martin Hoffmann 55], Joachim Streich, Eberhard Vogel. *Georg Buschner.*
AUSTRALIA Jack Reilly, Dragan 'Doug' Utjesenovic, Peter Wilson (c), Manfred Schaefer, Col Curran, Ray Richards, Jimmy Rooney, Jimmy Mackay, Johnny Warren, Adrian Alston, Branko Buljevic. *Zvonimir 'Rale' Rasić (YUG).*

East Germany were rugged and defensive, grouping round their captain, a sweeper who always stayed back. Australia, willing but limited, couldn't stretch them. Sparwasser, tall and good on the ball, was sent clear on the left to knock the ball under the keeper, Curran rushing back to crash in an own goal just before the ball hit the inside of the far post. When Vogel broke clear on the left again, his cross beat a defensive diving header for the dynamic blond Streich to hit a half-volley as he fell; the ball flashed across a stationary goalkeeper and just under the bar, almost too good a goal for a match like this.

18 June 1974 – Volkspark, Hamburg – 52,000 – Mahmoud Mustafa Kamel (EGY)

WEST GERMANY   **(2) 3**
Overath 12, Cullmann 34, Müller 53

AUSTRALIA   **(0) 0**

WEST GERMANY Maier, Vogts, Breitner, Cullmann [Herbert Wimmer 68], Schwarzenbeck, Beckenbauer (c), Grabowski, Hoeness, Müller, Overath, Heynckes [Hölzenbein HT].
AUSTRALIA Reilly, Utjesenovic, Wilson (c), Schaefer, Curran, Richards, Rooney, Mackay, Ernie Campbell [Attila Abonyi HT], Alston, Buljevic [Peter Ollerton 62].

Overath's famous left-foot found the top corner from 25 yards, and Cullmann and Müller scored with their heads – but the mix still wasn't right and Abonyi hit a post.

---

18 June 1974 – Olympia, West Berlin – 27,000 – Aurelio Angonese (ITA)

CHILE	(0) 1
Ahumada 69	
EAST GERMANY	(0) 1
Hoffmann 55	

CHILE Vallejos, García, Quintano, Arias, Figueroa, Páez, Valdéz (c) [Guillermo Yavar HT], Reinoso, Jorge Socías [Rogelio Farías 67], Ahumada, Véliz.
EAST GERMANY Croy, Kische, Bransch (c), Weise, Wätzlich, Irmscher, Wolfgang Seguin [Hans-Jürgen Kreische 73], Sparwasser, Hoffmann, Streich, Vogel [Peter Ducke 30].

With that severe defence, East Germany looked safe once García's third foul in five minutes had led to a free kick taken by Ducke and forcefully headed in by the 19-year-old Hoffmann, who hit the woodwork in the last four minutes, as did Kreische. But Chile didn't deserve to lose. Croy had to save a soft chip from Reinoso, whose low cross was put in neatly by Ahumada. Figueroa, who 'superbly marshalled the side', hit a post after 73 minutes and Véliz shot straight at Croy. East Germany still needed only a draw in their next match, but since that was against their hosts and neighbours, they suddenly looked vulnerable.

22 June 1974 – Volkspark, Hamburg – 58,900 – Ramón Barreto (URU)

EAST GERMANY	(0) 1
Sparwasser 77	
WEST GERMANY	(0) 0

EAST GERMANY Croy, Lothar Kurbjuweit, Bransch (c), Weise, Wätzlich, Reinhard Lauck, Kreische, Irmscher [Erich Hamann 65], Sparwasser, Kische, Hoffmann.
WEST GERMANY Maier, Vogts, Breitner, Cullmann, Schwarzenbeck [Horst-Dieter Höttges 68], Beckenbauer (c), Grabowski, Hoeness, Müller, Overath [Günter Netzer 69], Heinz Flohe.

The East put up more of a wall than ever but broke dangerously from the back. Although Müller hit a post, Kreische missed an open goal from a short left-wing cross, then Sparwasser chased a long ball into the D, cleverly headed the ball away from Schwarzenbeck, sold Maier half a dummy, and drove high into the net. Croy was surrounded by photographers at the end, but East Germany had condemned themselves to the harder second-round group.

Beckenbauer felt that in many ways 'our football has stagnated' and the team that won Euro 72 'was a far superior outfit in all departments.' In a poignant reminder of that side, Netzer appeared for just 20 minutes in the finals, an influential player reduced to a footnote. Another one: this was the only official international match ever played between the two Germanys.

---

22 June 1974 – Olympia, West Berlin – 16,100 – Jafar Namdar (IRN)

AUSTRALIA	0
CHILE	0

AUSTRALIA Reilly, Utjesenovic, Wilson (c), Schaefer, Curran [Harry Williams 82], Richards, Rooney, Mackay, Abonyi, Alston [Ollerton 65], Buljevic.

1974

1930

1934

1938

1950

1954

1958

1962

1966

1970

1974

1978

1982

1986

1990

1994

1998

2002

2006

CHILE Vallejos, García, Quintano, Arias, Figueroa, Páez, Valdéz (c) [Farías 57], Reinoso, Caszely, Ahumada, Véliz [Yavar 72]. SENT OFF: Richards 83.

The right result between two unexceptional teams. Chile drew two matches and lost the other by a single goal but were very unimpressive. The next time they reached the finals, eight years later, Pinochet would still be in power, after murdering and 'disappearing' thousands of his own people.

GROUP 1

	P	W	D	L	F	A	Pts
East Germany	3	2	1	0	4	1	5
West Germany	3	2	0	1	4	1	4
Chile	3	0	2	1	1	2	2
Australia	3	0	1	2	0	5	1

East Germany and West Germany qualified for the second round.

GROUP 2

Brazil (seeded), Scotland, Yugoslavia, Zaire.

13 June 1974 – Waldstadion, Frankfurt – 61,500 – Rudi Scheurer (SWI)

BRAZIL	0
YUGOSLAVIA	0

BRAZIL Émerson Leão, 'Nelinho' (Manoel Rezende), 'Marinho Chagas' (Francisco das Chagas Marinho), Wilson Piazza (c), Luís Pereira, Mário (Marinho) Peres, Valdomiro (Vaz), 'Jairzinho' (Jair Ventura), 'Leivinha' (João Leiva), Roberto Rivelino, Paulo César (Lima). *Mário Zagallo.*

YUGOSLAVIA Enver Marić, Ivan Buljan, Drazen Mužinić, Enver Hadžiabdić, Josip Katalinski, Vladislav Bogićević, Ilija Petković, Branko Oblak, Jovan Aćimović, Ivo Šurjak, Dragan Džajić (c). *Miljan Miljanić et al.*

Zagallo's apprehensive approach brought its first result, another opening match with no goals – though in fact both teams made chances, Brazil only in the first half. Marić saved from Valdomiro and Marinho Chagas, Leão with his legs after the talented Aćimović had cleverly beaten a man, and Oblak hit the post with a header towards the end. A shortage of quality led to Jairzinho playing in the middle up front, where he was unrecognisable, and not just for his new afro. English sources refer to Marinho Peres as Mario Marinho, which means nothing in Brazil.

14 June 1974 – Westfalen, Dortmund – 25,800 – Gerd Schulenburg (GER)

SCOTLAND	**(2) 2**
Lorimer 26, Jordan 34	
ZAIRE	**(0) 0**

SCOTLAND David Harvey, William 'Sandy' Jardine, Danny McGrain, Davie Hay, Jim Holton, John Blackley, Kenny Dalglish [Tommy Hutchison 75], Billy Bremner (c), Joe Jordan, Denis Law, Peter Lorimer. *Willie Ormond.*
ZAIRE Kazadi Mwamba, Mwepu Ilunga, Mukombo Mwanza, Bwanga Tshimen, Lobilo Boba, Kilasu Masamba, Mayanga Maku [Kembo Uba Kembo 64], Mana Mambwene, Ndaye Mulamba, Kidumu Mantantu (c) [Kibonge Mafu 75], Kakoko Etepe. *Blagoje Vidinić (YUG).*

Easy as expected for Scotland, but they didn't make enough of the opportunity. Zaire showed some skilful touches but were all over the place at the back, leaving Jordan spectacularly unmarked when he headed Bremner's free kick straight at Kazadi, who stood transfixed and let the ball in under his armpit.

Earlier a long cross from the left had found the usual target at the far post, Jordan's header floating square towards Lorimer, whose famous right foot sent a typically thunderous volley high to Kazadi's left. The two goals seemed to satisfy the Scots, who spent too much time passing the ball around in midfield. Law, once a great player but now 34, was a forlorn figure in his last international.

The Zaire players were known by their first names. Bwanga and Kazadi were cousins. Vidinić had coached Morocco in the 1970 finals.

18 June 1974 – Waldstadion, Frankfurt – 60,000 – Arie van Gemert (HOL)

BRAZIL	0
SCOTLAND	0

BRAZIL Leão, Nelinho, Marinho Chagas, Piazza (c), Pereira, Marinho Peres, Jairzinho, 'Mirandinha' (Sebastião Miranda), Leivinha [Paulo César Carpegiani 65], Rivelino, Paulo César.
SCOTLAND Harvey, Jardine, McGrain, Hay, Holton, Martin Buchan, Willie Morgan, Bremner (c), Dalglish, Jordan, Lorimer.

It's now been rewritten as Scotland's braveheart draw with the world champions, Bremner unlucky to see the ball rebound off his shins just past the post – but these were two pedestrian teams and goalless was about right. Jairzinho moved back to the right wing, but the Mirandinha-Leivinha partnership was cumbersome and Paulo César an enormous let-down. At least the defence was much better than in 1970: Leão consistent in goal, Pereira a dominating stopper, the blond Marinho Chagas a glamorous attacking left-back. Leivinha hit the bar from an early Nelinho

corner; Leão saved a long shot from the impressive Hay; and Rivelino and Bremner had their expected testy battle in midfield. Zagallo was probably satisfied as well as relieved, but it made difficult viewing.

18 June 1974 – Parkstadion, Gelsenkirchen – 30,500 – Omar Delgado (COL)

YUGOSLAVIA	(6) 9
Bajević 8, 30, 81, Džajić 14, Šurjak 18, Katalinski 22, Bogićević 35, Oblak 61, Petković 65	
ZAIRE	(0) 0

YUGOSLAVIA Marić, Buljan, Hadžiabdić, Katalinski, Bogićević, Petković, Oblak, Aćimović, Šurjak, Dušan Bajević, Džajić (c).
ZAIRE Kazadi [Tubilandu Dimbi 21], Mwepu, Mukombo, Bwanga, Lobilo, Kilasu, Ndaye, Mana, Kembo, Kidumu (c), Kakoko [Mayanga HT].
SENT OFF: Ndaye 23.

Yugoslavia's skilful forwards put Scotland's performance in perspective, partly because Zaire's players were despondent at not receiving some promised bonuses and just went through the motions. Bajević, a rabbit killer who'd once scored five against Venezuela, started the slaughter with a simple header as the defence stood and ball-watched. Džajić curled in a free kick and Šurjak shot in on the turn. Vidinić took off Kazadi as soon as he'd conceded more goals in 18 minutes than in 90 against the Scots. His substitute's first task was to pick the ball out of the net, put there by Katalinski with two other Yugoslavs in the six-yard box; Ndaye was sent off for protesting too much. Bogićević headed the fifth over the keeper and a defender and Oblak's free kick was badly fumbled by Tubilandu, who conceded more goals, pro rata, than any other finals goalkeeper. Yugoslavia's seven scorers in one match set another record.

1930
1934
1938
1950
1954
1958
1962
1966
1970
1974
1978
1982
1986
1990
1994
1998
2002
2006

22 June 1974 – Waldstadion, Frankfurt – 54,000 – Alfonso Archundia (MEX)

SCOTLAND	(0) 1
Jordan 88	

YUGOSLAVIA	(0) 1
Karasi 81	

YUGOSLAVIA Marić, Buljan, Hadžiabdić, Oblak, Katalinski, Bogićević, Petković, Aćimović, Šurjak, Bajević [Stanislav Karasi 70], Džajić (c).
SCOTLAND Harvey, Jardine, McGrain, Hay, Holton, Buchan, Morgan, Bremner (c), Dalglish [Hutchison 65], Jordan, Lorimer.

Karasi headed in a cross from Džajić, who'd wandered to the right wing and turned inside – and Jordan's goal came too late: volleyed in at the far post after the long-legged Hutchison had beaten his man and crossed low from the left. He should have been in the team from the start, in place of the dreadfully disappointing Dalglish ('I was frightened to try things in case they didn't come off'). Meanwhile the sight of the red-haired Bremner, essentially a ball winner, taking the ball from his goalkeeper showed how little was coming from the midfield. Scotland were the only unbeaten team in the tournament and the first ever to be eliminated without losing a match, but there are lies, damned lies and statistics.

22 June 1974 – Parkstadion, Gelsenkirchen – 35,000 – Nicolae Rainea (ROM)

BRAZIL	(1) 3
Jairzinho 12, Rivelino 66, Valdomiro 79	

ZAIRE	(0) 0

BRAZIL Leão, Nelinho, Marinho Chagas, Piazza (c) [Mirandinha 59], Pereira, Marinho Peres, 'Edu' (Eduardo Américo), Jairzinho, Leivinha [Valdomiro 10], Rivelino, Carpegiani.

ZAIRE Kazadi, Mwepu, Mukombo, Bwanga, Lobilo, Kibonge, Tshinabu Kamunda [Kembo 62], Mana, Ntumba Kalala, Kidumu (c) [Kilasu 61], Mayanga.

At last Brazil scored some goals, but the first was scrappy (Jairzinho's low volley when the ball came back off Pereira's shoulder), and the second took its time. When it arrived it was wasted on a team like Zaire, Jairzinho laying the ball back for Rivelino to hit it so hard that it rebounded yards out off the netting. But the third goal, which sent them through, was a joke. Valdomiro hit a low cross-cum-shot from almost on the right-hand goal line, Kazadi fumbling it in at the near post as he tried to clutch it to his chest. Earlier he'd made a very good one-handed save from Pereira, no consolation to him or the Scots. Mwepu was booked for charging out of the wall at a free kick and kicking the ball away – but it was probably something he'd seen the professionals do. It was about the only thing Zaire learned from their embarrassing three games, which were used to denigrate black African football for years.

GROUP 2

	P	W	D	L	F	A	Pts
Yugoslavia	3	1	2	0	10	1	4
Brazil	3	1	2	0	3	0	4
Scotland	3	1	2	0	3	1	4
Zaire	3	0	0	3	0	14	0

Yugoslavia and Brazil qualified for the second round.

GROUP 3

Bulgaria, Holland, Sweden, Uruguay (seeded).

15 June 1974 – Niedersachsen, Hanover – 53,700 – Károly Palotai (HUN)

HOLLAND   (1) 2
Rep 9, 86

URUGUAY   (0) 0

HOLLAND Jan Jongbloed, Wim Suurbier, Ruud Krol, Wim Jansen, Wim Rijsbergen, Arie Haan, Johan Neeskens, Wim van Hanegem, Johnny Rep, Johan Cruijff (c), Rob Rensenbrink. *Rinus Michels*.
URUGUAY Ladislao Mazurkiewicz, Baudilio Jáuregui, Juan Masnik (c), Pablo Forlán, Ricardo Pavoni, Víctor Espárrago, Julio Montero Castillo, Pedro Rocha, Luis Cubilla [Denis Milar 64], Fernando Morena, Walter Mantegazza. *Roberto Porta*.
SENT OFF: Montero Castillo 69.

Rocha was back, Cubilla still there at 34, Morena the most prolific scorer in Uruguayan club history – but it didn't add up to much against the almost casually brilliant Dutch, who looked disinterested at times but won very easily against a brutal and discredited team. Montero Castillo, swarthy and side-burned, was sent off for kicking Rensenbrink, but others might have gone with him. Forlán, for instance, kicked Neeskens as he went in for a header.

The fair-haired Rep outjumped his marker to head in a right-wing cross and casually used the outside of his right foot to beat a defender on the line after van Hanegem's flick had sent Rensenbrink through on the left to draw the goalkeeper. In between, Jansen hit a post. The quicksilver Cruijff was well established as the greatest attacking player of his generation.

Forlán's son Diego scored in the 2002 finals. Palotai had played for Hungary in the 1964 Olympics. And Cruijff is the correct spelling, not Cruyff, which was something invented to help foreigners with the pronunciation. The great man himself confirms it!

15 June 1974 – Rheinstadion, Düsseldorf – 22,500 – Édison Pérez (PER)

BULGARIA   0

SWEDEN   0

BULGARIA Rumensho Goranov, Zonyo Vasiliev, Kiril Ivkov, Stefan Velichkov, Bojil Kolev, Dimitar Penev, Voin Voinov [Atanas Mikhailov 73], Christo Bonev (c), Georgi Denev, Pavel Panov [Mladen Vasiliev 75], Asparoukh Nikodimov. *Christo Mladenov*.
SWEDEN Ronnie Hellström, Jan O Olsson, Kent Karlsson, Bo Larsson (c), Björn Andersson, Ove Grahn, Staffan Tapper, Ove Kindvall [Benno Magnusson 73], Ralf Edström, Conny Torstensson, Roland Sandberg. *Georg 'Åby' Ericsson*.

Sweden were very defensive, despite having Kindvall and the 6'4 Edström up front. Bonev did his best but there was little happening in front of him, although Denev hit the bar early on.

19 June 1974 – Westfalen, Dortmund – 52,500 – Werner Winsemann (CAN)

HOLLAND   0

SWEDEN   0

HOLLAND Jongbloed, Suurbier, Krol, Jansen, Rijsbergen, Haan, Neeskens, van Hanegem [Theo de Jong 73], Cruijff (c), Rep, Piet Keizer.
SWEDEN Hellström, JO Olsson [Roland Grip 75], Andersson, Karlsson, Björn Nordqvist, Larsson (c), Inge Ejderstedt, Tapper [Örjan Persson 61], Edström, Grahn, Sandberg.

1930
1934
1938
1950
1954
1958
1962
1966
1970

1974

1978
1982
1986
1990
1994
1998
2002
2006

Same again from the Swedes, but Holland were perfectly happy to go along with it, taking their cue from Ajax, whose great European Cup record was sprinkled with 0-0 draws. Here they made light of the loss of Barry Hulshoff, their big bearded stopper, moving Haan back to join the impressive young Rijsbergen. In May they'd replaced their injured first-choice goalkeeper with the 33-year-old Jongbloed whose only previous cap had been as a substitute eleven years earlier. The slow-moving beetle-browed van Hanegem was a marvellous playmaker, the brilliant veteran Keizer used as a reserve.

---

19 June 1974 – Niedersachsen, Hanover – 13,400 – Jack Taylor (ENG)

BULGARIA   (0) 1
Bonev 75

URUGUAY   (0) 1
Pavoni 87

BULGARIA Goranov, Velichkov, Ivkov, Kolev, Z Vasiliev, Penev, Voinov, Bonev (c), Denev, Panov, Nikodimov [Mikhailov 59].
URUGUAY Mazurkiewicz (c), Jáuregui, Forlán, Pavoni, Espárrago, Morena, Rocha, Luis Garisto [Masnik 73], Mantegazza [Alberto Cardaccio 62], Milar, Romeo Corbo.

A rough match between two poor teams. Mikhailov came close with a good shot, but again Bonev was a one-man attack, converting Voinov's cross with an agile volley. The veteran Pavoni missed a good chance before equalising with a long-range shot that Goranov should

have saved, and Morena had a goal disallowed with three minutes left.

---

23 June 1974 – Westfalen, Dortmund – 52,100 – Tony Boskovic (AUS)

HOLLAND   (2) 4
Neeskens pen 5, pen 44, Rep 71, De Jong 88

BULGARIA   (0) 1
Krol o.g. 78

HOLLAND Jongbloed, Suurbier, Krol, Jansen, Rijsbergen, Haan, Neeskens [Theo de Jong 78], van Hanegem [Rinus Israël HT], Cruijff (c), Rep, Rensenbrink.
BULGARIA Stefan Staykov, Velichkov, Ivkov, Z Vasiliev, Penev, Ivan Stoyanov [Mikhailov HT], Bonev (c), Kolev, Voinov, Panov [Krasimir Borisov 55], Denev.

It was as if Holland came to life just because they decided to, swarming round the Bulgarian goal. Both the penalties were indisputable, for crude fouls on Cruijff and Jansen. Neeskens, who took both kicks with tremendous power, also hit a post. Vasiliev's header back across his own penalty area was met by Rep's fierce instinctive volley, and de Jong's diving header finished off a centre by Cruijff, who'd again been kingly throughout. Krol turned a cross past Jongbloed but it was the merest blip.

It was about now that people started talking about Total Football, every player able to attack and defend with equal facility. It wasn't strictly accurate (impossible to imagine Krol and van Hanegem interchanging positions, or Rijsbergen and Cruijff) but you got the gist. This was a game never quite seen before among national teams, introduced by the same coach who'd led Ajax to their first European title. The defenders weren't just hard (something Zagallo seems to have misunderstood) but good on the ball. And the team was more than attractively functional: Cruijff's much-televised piece of genius against Sweden, beating a man tight to the left-hand

LEADING GOALSCORERS 1974

7	Grzegorz Lato	POL	
5	Andrzej Szarmach	POL	
5	Johan Neeskens	HOL	3 pen

goal line by turning the ball behind his own leg, was the undying image of the tournament.

---

23 June 1974 – Rheinstadion, Düsseldorf – 28,300 – Erich Linemayr (AUT)

SWEDEN   (0) 3
Edström 46, 77, Sandberg 74

URUGUAY   (0) 0

SWEDEN Hellström, Andersson, Grip, Karlsson, Nordqvist, Larsson (c), Grahn, Kindvall [Torstensson 76], Edström, Magnusson [Thomas Ahlström 60], Sandberg.
URUGUAY Mazurkiewicz (c), Jáuregui, Forlán, Pavoni, Garisto [Masnik HT], Espárrago, Morena, Rocha, Mantegazza, Milar, Corbo [Cubilla 43].

The Swedes kept their heads down for yet another 45 minutes, then peeked over the ramparts and this time saw nothing threatening. Straight from the second kick-off, Edström was left unmarked at the far post to flip the ball up and score with a crushing left-foot volley. Sandberg ran round a defender's back to score off the base of a post then turned a somersault in delight, and Hellström put his 1970 experience behind him with an excellent first half. Sweden, growing in stature, were deservedly through. Uruguay didn't reach the finals for another twelve years and eight of this team weren't capped again. Nobody missed them.

GROUP 3

	P	W	D	L	F	A	Pts
Holland	3	2	1	0	6	1	5
Sweden	3	1	2	0	3	0	4
Bulgaria	3	0	2	1	2	5	2
Uruguay	3	0	1	2	1	6	1

Holland and Sweden qualified for the second round.

GROUP 4

Argentina, Haiti, Italy (seeded), Poland.

---

15 June 1974 – Olympia, Munich – 51,100 – Vicente Llobregat (VEN)

ITALY   (0) 3
Rivera 52, Auguste o.g. 64, Anastasi 78

HAITI   (0) 1
Sanon 46

ITALY Dino Zoff, Luciano Spinosi, Giacinto Facchetti (c), Romeo Benetti, Francesco Morini, Tarcisio Burgnich, Fabio Capello, Sandro Mazzola, Giorgio Chinaglia [Pietro Anastasi 69], Gianni Rivera, Luigi Riva. *Ferruccio Valcareggi.*
HAITI Henri Francillon, Pierre Bayonne, Arsène Auguste, Guy François, Wilner Nazaire (c), Ernst Jean-Joseph, Philippe Vorbe, Eddy Antoine, Emmanuel Sanon, Jean-Claude Désir, Guy Saint-Vil [Claude Barthélemy HT]. *Antoine Tassy.*

Before the match, the Haitian camp had been playing up their 'secret weapon', voodoo, and for nearly an hour it didn't seem tongue-in-cheek. Italy had virtually all the play but were dreadful up front: Riva past his best, Chinaglia heavy-footed and overrated. Sanon took Vorbe's instant through-ball, sprinted inside Spinosi, who tried to pull him back, then went round Zoff. Haiti had reached the finals only because the qualifying tournament was held at home, and they'd won the decisive match 2-1 after Trinidad had four goals disallowed in front of Duvallier and his thugs. Now, of all teams, they were the ones to end Zoff's run of 1,143 minutes without conceding a goal, still the world record.

Italy camped round the Haitian penalty area and scored all three goals against a packed defence. Mazzola, sharp as ever, beat a man on

1930
1934
1938
1950
1954
1958
1962
1966
1970
1974
1978
1982
1986
1990
1994
1998
2002
2006

1930
1934
1938
1950
1954
1958
1962
1966
1970
1974
1978
1982
1986
1990
1994
1998
2002
2006

the right-hand touchline, Chinaglia's control let him down, but a defender's tackle presented the ball to Rivera, who hit a seriously hard shot high across the keeper from near the penalty spot. Then Benetti's unexceptional low shot was turned in at the near post by Auguste, leaving the wrong-footed Francillon to slap the ground in frustration. Finally a defender missed his diving header, and although Riva couldn't control the ball it ran on to Anastasi, whose shot beat Francillon at the near post.

Italy had made very heavy weather of a simple task. Chinaglia missed an easy chance then gestured dismissively to the bench when he was substituted, adding to the disquiet in the camp. Jean-Joseph was the first player to fail a drugs test in a finals tournament. Whether he took anything deliberately still isn't clear, but that didn't stop Haitian officials beating him up at the team hotel before sending him home to face Baby Doc and his gentle friends. He survived to play in the qualifying rounds of the next two World Cups.

15 June 1974 – Neckar, Stuttgart – 31,500 – Clive Thomas (WAL)

POLAND	**(2) 3**
Lato 7, 62, Szarmach 8	

ARGENTINA	**(0) 2**
Heredia 60, Babington 66	

POLAND Jan Tomaszewski, Antoni Szymanowski, Adam Musiał, Zygmunt Maszczyk, Jerzy Gorgoń, Władyslaw Żmuda, Grzegorz Lato, Henryk Kasperczak, Andrzej Szarmach [Jan Domarski 70], Kazimierz Deyna (c), Robert Gadocha [Leslaw Ćmikiewicz 85]. *Kazimierz Górski, with Jacek Gmoch*. ARGENTINA Daniel Carnevali, Roberto Perfumo (c), Enrique Wolff, Ramón Heredia, Francisco Sá, Ángel Bargas [Roberto Telch 67], Rubén Ayala, Carlos Babington, Mario Kempes, Miguel Ángel Brindisi [René Houseman HT], Agustín Balbuena. *Vladislao Cap*.

Górski had promised that Poland would play 'offensive football,' which raised a grim smile among those who remembered Poland's brutality in their home qualifiers against England and Wales. But here they were a pleasant surprise. Włodek Lubański's injury against England led them to adopt West Germany's successful system of two fast wingers and a single central striker, too much for an Argentinian team infinitely less violent, and formidable, than in recent World Cups.

It wasn't helped by an appalling start. Carnevali was slightly baulked by his own defender but should still have caught Gadocha's left-wing corner instead of dropping it straight in front of Lato, who then made the second by picking up a shocking Argentinian pass and finding the sharp new centre-forward Szarmach, whose long hair, moustache and nose gave him the look of Vlad the Impaler. After running clear of the defence, he dug a low left-footer over the onrushing Carnevali. He later hit a post.

Heredia finished a slick move with an excellent curling right-footer after cutting inside a defender on the left – but Carnevali, one of the worst goalkeepers in the tournament, undid the good work by throwing the ball the width of his penalty area for Lato to run on and shoot past him. Babington sent the ball trickling over the line after four other shots had been blocked, but Poland suddenly looked an exciting and dangerous side.

19 June 1974 – Neckar, Stuttgart – 68,900 – Pavel Kasakov (USR)

ARGENTINA	**(1) 1**
Houseman 20	

ITALY	**(1) 1**
Perfumo o.g. 35	

ITALY Zoff, Spinosi, Facchetti (c), Benetti, Morini [Giuseppe Wilson 66], Burgnich, Capello, Mazzola, Anastasi, Rivera [Franco Causio 66], Riva.

ARGENTINA Carnevali, Wolff [Rubén Glaría 64], Sá, Telch, Heredia, Perfumo (c), Ayala, Babington, Héctor Yazalde [Enrique Chazarreta 78], Houseman, Kempes.

Argentina really were lightweight; they should have beaten this lumpen Italian side. They did score the goal of the tournament, the dynamic little Houseman running onto Babington's tremendous crossfield ball to volley high across Zoff's left shoulder – but the own goal, Perfumo turning the ball in after Benetti had chested it too far forward, seemed to inhibit them. Italy were now likely to qualify but again looked very poor, Burgnich incongruous as a 35-year-old sweeper, Rivera on his last legs.

19 June 1974 – Olympia, Munich – 25,400 – Govindasamy Suppiah (SNG)

POLAND (5) 7
Lato 17, 87, Deyna 18, Szarmach 30, 34, 50, Gorgoń 31

HAITI (0) 0

POLAND Tomaszewski, Szymanowski, Musiał [Zbigniew Gut 71], Maszczyk [Ćmikiewicz 65], Gorgoń, Żmuda, Lato, Kasperczak, Szarmach, Deyna (c), Gadocha.
HAITI Francillon, Bayonne, Auguste, Vorbe, Nazaire (c), Antoine, Fritz André [Barthélemy 37], François, Roger Saint-Vil [Serge Racine HT], Désir, Sanon.

Like Zaire in their second match, Haiti were shown up by the most talented forwards in the group. In April they'd beaten a Poland second string at home – but here André missed the ball *clamorosamente* to leave Lato clear in front of the keeper, and the Haitian defence stood and watched as Deyna and Szarmach headed in corners by Gadocha, who also hit a post and had a header kicked off the line. Even the gigantic blond Gorgoń (only the Killer brothers of Argentina had a better name

for a central defender) thumped in a free kick. Lato drew the defence to make the fifth for Szarmach, who headed the next from a Gadocha cross and headed the ball on for Lato to run through for the final goal.

Francillon had problems knowing when to leave his line, but his bravery helped keep the score below double figures and he was later signed by 1860 Munich. Saint-Vil's brother Guy played against Italy and Argentina.

23 June 1974 – Olympia, Munich – 24,000 – Pablo Sánchez Ibáñez (SPA)

ARGENTINA (2) 4
Yazalde 15, 68, Houseman 18, Ayala 55

HAITI (0) 1
Sanon 63

ARGENTINA Carnevali, Wolff, Heredia, Perfumo (c), Sá, Telch, Ayala, Babington, Yazalde, Kempes [Balbuena 52], Houseman [Brindisi 57].
HAITI Francillon, Serge Ducoste, Bayonne, Vorbe, Désir, Antoine, G Saint-Vil [Fritz Léandre 52], Racine, Nazaire (c) [Joseph-Marion Léandre 25], Sanon, Wilfried Louis.

Argentina, who needed to win by three goals and hope Italy lost, fulfilled their part of the equation but had a slight scare when Sanon scored another good goal, hitting a powerful left-footer from the edge of the area after Carnevali had saved from Antoine. Yazalde restored the necessary advantage, clearing up *una situación confusa* by putting away another rebound. Earlier he'd opened the scoring in much the same way, forcing a good save from Francillon and beating Kempes to the loose ball. Then he was sent away by Babington to set up an easy goal for Houseman, and Wolff's driven free kick was touched in by Ayala. Francillon (who'd saved magnificently from Ayala), Sanon and Vorbe were the only

1930
1934
1938
1950
1954
1958
1962
1966
1970
1974
1978
1982
1986
1990
1994
1998
2002
2006

Haitians not to look out of their depth, the Léandres the only brothers to come on as substitutes in the same finals match.

---

23 June 1974 – Neckar, Stuttgart – 68,900 – Hans-Joachim Weyland (GER)

POLAND (2) 2
Szarmach 38, Deyna 44

ITALY (0) 1
Capello 85

POLAND Tomaszewski, Szymanowski, Musiał, Maszczyk, Gorgoń, Żmuda, Lato, Kasperczak, Szarmach [Ćmikiewicz 77], Deyna (c), Gadocha.
ITALY Zoff, Spinosi, Facchetti (c), Benetti, Morini, Burgnich [Wilson 31], Causio, Capello, Chinaglia [Roberto Boninsegna HT], Mazzola, Anastasi.

Italy needed only a draw and might well have got it if there'd been any justice early on. Straight from the kick-off, Tomaszewski missed a right-wing cross and Anastasi would have turned the ball into the empty net if Szymanowski hadn't taken his legs from behind. No penalty.

After that, the modern athleticism of the Poles showed up Italy's old-fashioned defensiveness. Without needing to, they scored two excellent goals, Szarmach's head and Deyna's fierce right foot converting shallow crosses from the right by Kasperczak, Deyna's able lieutenant in midfield. Several sources, Italian as well as Polish, claim the Poles were offered bribes on the pitch, but they weren't having any of it.

Italy hit a post, Tomaszewski made a fine save, and Capello chested Causio's chip past the last defender before volleying in – but it was too late by then. Chinaglia had another bad match and only the great Mazzola, still fit and determined, sold himself dearly. Like Burgnich, Riva and Rivera, he didn't play for Italy again.

GROUP 4

	P	W	D	L	F	A	Pts
Poland	3	3	0	0	12	3	6
Argentina	3	1	1	1	7	5	3
Italy	3	1	1	1	5	4	3
Haiti	3	0	0	3	2	14	0

Poland and Argentina qualified for the second round.

2ND ROUND

Argentina, Brazil, East Germany, Holland.

GROUP A

---

26 June 1974 – Niedersachsen, Hanover – 58,463 – Clive Thomas (WAL)

BRAZIL (0) 1
Rivelino 60

EAST GERMANY (0) 0

BRAZIL Leão, 'Zé Maria' (José Maria Rodrigues), Marinho Chagas, Carpegiani, Pereira, Marinho Peres (c), Valdomiro, Paulo César, Jairzinho, Rivelino, Dirceu (Guimarães).
EAST GERMANY Croy, Kurbjuweit, Bransch (c), Weise, Wätzlich, Lauck [Löwe 64], Sparwasser, Hamann [Irmscher HT], Streich, Kische, Hoffmann.

A match between two harsh teams was decided by yet another fearsome Rivelino free kick. The East Germans, who apparently hadn't watched replays of Mexico 70, allowed Jairzinho to stand in the middle of their wall. He ducked when Rivelino aimed at him, and the ball skimmed through the gap and in low to Croy's left. The powerful Zé María did well, but East Germany offered little up front.

---

26 June 1974 – Parkstadion, Gelsenkirchen – 55,348 – Bobby Davidson (SCO)

HOLLAND   (2) 4
Cruijff 11, 90, Krol 25, Rep 73

ARGENTINA   (0) 0

HOLLAND Jongbloed, Suurbier [Israël 84], Krol, Jansen, Rijsbergen, Haan, Neeskens, van Hanegem, Rep, Cruijff (c), Rensenbrink.
ARGENTINA Carnevali, Wolff [Glaría HT], Heredia, Perfumo (c), Sá, Telch, Ayala, Balbuena, Yazalde, Carlos Squeo, Houseman [Kempes HT].

Having developed a taste for translating their superiority into goals, the Dutch scored when they felt like it, keeping their feet in a rain-soaked second half. Cruijff went round the keeper for the first and put in the fourth from a tight angle after Carnevali made a good save. Krol's ferocious shot pinballed through a packed area, Rep headed in Cruijff's pinpoint cross, and Neeskens had a goal narrowly disallowed. What really made itself felt, especially

MATCHES ON THE WINNING SIDE

15	Franz Beckenbauer	GER	1966–74
15	Wolfgang Overath	GER	1966–74
15	Lothar Matthäus	GER	1982–98
14	Paolo Maldini	ITA	1990–02
13	Uwe Seeler	GER	1958–70

Beckenbauer played in 18 matches, Overath 19, Matthäus 25. Matthäus' total excludes two drawn matches won on penalties.

on some of the Argentinians, was Holland's severity in the tackle. The first goal followed Rijsbergen's brusque challenge from behind on Yazalde, and Wolff was left writhing on the touchline by a tackle of incredible power from Krol, whose blend of skill and ruthlessness epitomised the whole team. The future looked orange.

---

30 June 1974 – Parkstadion, Gelsenkirchen – 67,148 – Rudi Scheurer (SWI)

HOLLAND   (1) 2
Neeskens 7, Rensenbrink 59

EAST GERMANY   (0) 0

HOLLAND Jongbloed, Suurbier, Krol, Jansen, Rijsbergen, Haan, Neeskens, van Hanegem, Rep, Cruijff (c), Rensenbrink.
EAST GERMANY Croy, Kurbjuweit, Pommerenke, Rüdiger Schnuphase, Bransch (c), Weise, Kische, Lauck [Kreische 64], Löwe [Ducke 54], Sparwasser, Hoffmann.

Back to taking it easy. After scoring the early goal that gave them command, the Dutch played their version of keep-ball while always looking a threat. Neeskens' fierce drive left Croy standing, and Rensenbrink, slightly underrated at the time, scored with a low cross-shot. Cruijff was yet again the dominant personality; it's only a slight exaggeration to say he put Holland on the map. Born in tough circumstances, he knew the value of hard currency (known as 'the Money Wolf' as well as 'Nose') and as a cigarette smoker he was in the Gérson class.

---

30 June 1974 – Niedersachsen, Hanover – 38,000 – Vital Loraux (BEL)

BRAZIL   (1) 2
Rivelino 32, Jairzinho 49

ARGENTINA   (1) 1
Brindisi 35

1974

BRAZIL Leão, Zé Maria, Marinho Chagas, Carpegiani, Pereira, Marinho Peres (c), Valdomiro, Paulo César, Jairzinho, Rivelino, Dirceu.

ARGENTINA Carnevali, Glaría, Heredia, Bargas, Sá [Jorge Carrascosa HT], Brindisi (c), Ayala, Squeo, Babington, Balbuena, Kempes [Houseman HT].

They used to be giants; now it was substandard and untidy – though the goals were good. Rivelino unleashed a low drive from twenty yards, the last of his six goals in World Cup finals: no-one scored so many with such power in one foot. Brindisi curled a free kick in off the bar, and Zé María won the ball and crossed for Jairzinho to head into an empty net. But it's unlikely the Dutch were quaking in their boots.

3 July 1974 – Parkstadion, Gelsenkirchen – 53,054 – Jack Taylor (ENG)

ARGENTINA (1) 1
Houseman 20

EAST GERMANY (1) 1
Streich 14

ARGENTINA Ubaldo Fillol, Wolff (c), Heredia, Bargas, Carrascosa, Brindisi, Ayala, Telch, Kempes, Babington, Houseman.
EAST GERMANY Croy, Kurbjuweit, Bransch (c), Pommerenke, Weise, Schnuphase, Löwe [Vogel 66], Streich [Ducke 81], Sparwasser, Kische, Hoffmann.

Argentina at last dropped Carnevali, giving a first cap to Fillol, an important member of their 1978 side, and played their part in a scrappy match of no consequence. Kische marked Ayala out of the game, and the goals were scored by the best forward on each side, Streich building up to a very impressive total of 55, which remained easily the East German record to the end. Here he headed in a cross after Weise had escaped up the right wing. Houseman, who volleyed in the equaliser after Kempes had beaten two men, left thoughts of

what might have been if the defence had matched his talents and those of Babington and the speedy Ayala, or if the 19-year-old Kempes had lived up to his billing. He, at least, would have another chance four years later.

3 July 1974 – Westfalen, Dortmund – 52,500 – Kurt Tschenscher (GER)

HOLLAND (0) 2
Neeskens 50, Cruijff 65

BRAZIL (0) 0

HOLLAND Jongbloed, Suurbier, Krol, Jansen, Rijsbergen, Haan, Neeskens [Israël 84], van Hanegem, Rep, Cruijff (c), Rensenbrink [De Jong 67].
BRAZIL Leão, Zé Maria, Marinho Chagas, Carpegiani, Pereira, Marinho Peres (c), Valdomiro, Paulo César [Mirandinha 61], Jairzinho, Rivelino, Dirceu.
SENT OFF: Pereira 84.

Holland were expected to stroll it, but no Brazilian team is completely without flair, and they should have taken an early lead when Paulo César shot past the far post. A reasonable reserve in 1970 but dreadful here, he had the misfortune to be touted as the first 'new Pelé.' Jairzinho also missed an early chance, but Leão had to make a fantastic close-range save when Zé María let a cross bounce off him straight to Cruijff.

As in all their previous matches, Holland didn't turn the other cheek. The runs of Marinho Chagas were halted by late tackle after late tackle, and even Rep elbowed Rivelino in the face. Neeskens, as good as any player in the tournament according to Alf Ramsey, was talented but provocative. When Marinho Peres knocked him cold, his reward was a shin gashed from knee to ankle. When Pereira had enough and hacked him down spectacularly from behind, he was sent off. But the match had been decided by then.

Van Hanegem sent a quickly-taken free kick up to Neeskens, who scooped Cruijff's return cross over Leão, two attackers taking out three defenders. Then Krol overlapped on the left, Cruijff volleyed in unchallenged from close range, and Holland stood in the place that Brazil had recently occupied. Some sources list Pereira as captain, but Marinho Peres is wearing the armband on the video.

GROUP A

	P	W	D	L	F	A	Pts
Holland	3	3	0	0	8	0	6
Brazil	3	2	0	1	3	3	4
East Germany	3	0	1	2	1	4	1
Argentina	3	0	1	2	2	7	1

Holland qualified for the Final, Brazil for the 3rd-Place Final.

GROUP B

Poland, Sweden, West Germany, Yugoslavia.

26 June 1974 – Rheinstadion, Düsseldorf – 66,085 – Armando Marques (BRZ)

WEST GERMANY **(1) 2**
Breitner 39, Müller 82

YUGOSLAVIA **(0) 0**

WEST GERMANY Maier, Vogts, Breitner, Rainer Bonhof, Schwarzenbeck, Beckenbauer (c), Hölzenbein [Flohe 78], Wimmer [Hoeness 73], Müller, Overath, Dieter Herzog.
YUGOSLAVIA Marić, Buljan, Hadžiabdić, Mužinić, Katalinski, Oblak [Jure Jerković 84], Danilo Popivoda, Aćimović, Šurjak, Karasi, Džajić (c) [Petković 84].

The hosts were kickstarted by another Breitner long-range special, but this time were far more convincing. There was talk of Schön allowing a cabal led by Beckenbauer to pick the team, but if it was true it didn't do any harm. The strong-running Bonhof galvanised the midfield, as did the return of Hoeness, the star of the European Cup Final replay five weeks earlier. Here he took another good pass from Overath, reached the goal-line, and pulled back a cross; West Germany's lone striker went for it with one foot and put it in with the other as he fell backwards: a classic Müller goal. Behind him, Beckenbauer was also back to his imperious best ('*Der Kaiser*').

GOALS

14	Gerd Müller	GER	1970–74	1 pen
13	Just Fontaine	FRA	1958	
12	Pelé	BRZ	1958–70	
11	Sándor Kocsis	HUN	1954	
11	Jürgen Klinsmann	GER	1990–98	
11	Ronaldo	BRZ	1998–02	1 pen
10	Helmut Rahn	GER	1954–58	
10	Teófilo Cubillas	PER	1970–78	2 pen
10	Grzegorz Lato	POL	1974–82	
10	Gary Lineker	ENG	1986–90	2 pen
10	Gabriel Batistuta	ARG	1994–02	4 pen

FIFA credit Ronaldo with 12, including a blatant own goal by Costa Rica in 2002.

Other British Isles countries

5	Peter McParland	NIR	1958	
3	Robbie Keane	EIR	2002	1 pen
4	Joe Jordan	SCO	1974–82	
2	Ivor Allchurch	WAL	1958	

1974

1930
1934
1938
1950
1954
1958
1962
1966
1970
1978
1982
1986
1990
1994
1998
2002
2006

26 June 1974 – Neckar, Stuttgart – 43,755 – Ramón Barreto (URU)

POLAND **(1) 1**
Lato 43

SWEDEN **(0) 0**

POLAND Tomaszewski, Szymanowski, Gut, Maszczyk, Gorgoń, Żmuda, Lato, Kasperczak, Szarmach [Kazimierz Kmiecik 60], Deyna (c), Gadocha.
SWEDEN Hellström, Karlsson, Grip, Nordqvist, Andersson [Jörgen Augustsson 60], Grahn, Tapper [Ahlström 80], Larsson (c), Edström, Torstensson, Sandberg.

Poland, riding high after their group matches, found the Swedish defence a tougher proposition. Gadocha's corner was headed back by Szarmach for Lato to head in on the bounce, but Deyna wasn't allowed to take control in midfield and Tomaszewski had to save Tapper's penalty after 63 minutes to preserve the win.

1974

30 June 1974 – Waldstadion, Frankfurt – 53,200 – Rudi Glöckner (DDR)

POLAND **(1) 2**
Deyna pen 24, Lato 62

YUGOSLAVIA **(1) 1**
Karasi 43

POLAND Tomaszewski, Szymanowski, Musiał, Maszczyk, Gorgoń, Żmuda, Lato, Kasperczak, Szarmach [Ćmikiewicz 57], Deyna (c) [Domarski 81], Gadocha.
YUGOSLAVIA Marić, Buljan, Hadžiabdić, Katalinski, Bogićević, Oblak [Jerković 16], Petković [Vladimir Petrović 81], Aćimović (c), Bajević, Šurjak, Karasi.

Again the Poles were fortunate to get both points, beneficiaries of a penalty awarded when Karasi gave Szarmach a little kick on the calf. He made up for it by taking a through-pass, dummying Tomaszewski, and shooting

high into the net – but Lato, as sharp in the area as he was quick on the wing, again headed in a Gadocha corner. Yugoslavia, without Džajić, were as disappointing as ever.

30 June 1974 – Rheinstadion, Düsseldorf – 67,861 – Pavel Kasakov (USR)

WEST GERMANY **(0) 4**
Overath 51, Bonhof 52, Grabowski 76, Hoeness pen 89

SWEDEN **(1) 2**
Edström 24, Sandberg 53

WEST GERMANY Maier, Vogts, Breitner, Bonhof, Schwarzenbeck, Beckenbauer (c), Hölzenbein [Flohe 83], Hoeness, Müller, Overath, Herzog [Grabowski 64].
SWEDEN Hellström, JO Olsson, Augustsson, Karlsson, Nordqvist, Larsson (c) [Ejderstedt 32], Torstensson, Tapper, Edström, Grahn, Sandberg.

Probably the match of the tournament. A win would leave West Germany needing only a draw from their last match; anything less would hand the advantage to Poland. And in the first half, less was what they had to make do with. Sweden, keeping their defensive shape, took the lead with another left-footed volley from Edström, this one a wonderful shot that dipped and bent and chewed gum at the same time.

But the loss of Bo Larsson made itself felt when Beckenbauer began streaming out from the back, forcing a good save from the excellent Hellström. As the rain came down, West Germany equalised with that rarity, an Overath right-foot shot, then Bonhof's ground shot went in off both posts. Sweden didn't lie down, Sandberg collecting a misplaced header from Schwarzenbeck and driving low across Maier from the left – but the hosts had more ammunition. The ball was worked determinedly across the Swedish penalty area for

Grabowski to shoot home, and Ejderstedt brought down Müller for the penalty. A close thing against gutsy opposition, but West Germany had never stopped running and deserved the win.

The attendance figure (a sell-out) refers to tickets sold, but there were definite gaps in the crowd.

---

3 July 1974 – Waldstadion, Frankfurt – 61,249 – Erich Linemayr (AUT)

WEST GERMANY   (0) 1
Müller 76

POLAND   (0) 0

WEST GERMANY Maier, Vogts, Breitner, Bonhof, Schwarzenbeck, Beckenbauer (c), Grabowski, Hoeness, Müller, Overath, Hölzenbein.
POLAND Tomaszewski, Szymanowski, Musiał, Maszczyk [Kmiecik 80], Gorgoń, Żmuda, Lato, Kasperczak [Ćmikiewicz 80], Domarski, Deyna (c), Gadocha.

The rain kept on falling, like manna for the hosts. Parts of the pitch were waterlogged, the players could barely move the ball ten yards, and the match probably shouldn't have been played. Certainly Poland thought so: conditions underfoot cancelled out their speed on the flanks.

Even so, even in marshland, their wingers were always dangerous. Maier made excellent saves from Lato's free kick, from Gadocha and Lato after Beckenbauer had completely missed a clearance kick, and from Domarski, whose goal had knocked out England but who wasn't an adequate replacement for the injured Szarmach.

After 53 minutes Hölzenbein, known as a notorious diver in the *Bundesliga*, flew over Żmuda's sliding tackle, but Hoeness had his

MATCHES IN A TOURNAMENT AS SUBSTITUTE

6	Leslaw Ćmikiewicz	POL	1974
6	Denílson	BRZ	1998
5	Denílson	BRZ	2002

These were Ćmikiewicz's only finals matches.

Denílson started one match in 1998 and none in 2002.

penalty saved by Tomaszewski. Then, as the rain stopped, a loose ball reached Müller, the last player any defence should have left unmarked near a penalty spot. Poland were hard done by but had stopped looking like a team to contest the Final. West Germany had begun to show some of the form needed to withstand the Dutch, though few expected them to do it.

1974

---

3 July 1974 – Rheinstadion, Düsseldorf – 37,700 – Luis Pestarino (ARG)

SWEDEN   (1) 2
Edström 29, Torstensson 85

YUGOSLAVIA   (1) 1
Šurjak 27

SWEDEN Hellström, JO Olsson, Augustsson, Karlsson, Nordqvist (c), Tapper, Grahn, Persson, Edström, Torstensson, Sandberg.
YUGOSLAVIA Marić, Buljan, Hadžiabdić, Katalinski, Bogićević, Miroslav Pavlović [Luka Peruzović 77], Petrović [Karasi 67], Jerković, Šurjak, Aćimović, Džajić (c).

The least the Swedes deserved after their contribution to the tournament. Hellström had another fine match, and Sandberg and the towering Edström were involved in both goals. Yugoslavia scored the best of the match, Džajić

1930
1934
1938
1950
1954
1958
1962
1966
1970

1974

1978

1982

1986

1990

1994

1998

2002

2006

'coasting along the left touchline' before dropping a cross onto Šurjak's foot in the six-yard box. But Scotland were the last team not to beat them, which says a few things. The real crowd figure was nearer 10,000.

GROUP B

	P	W	D	L	F	A	Pts
West Germany	3	3	0	0	7	2	6
Poland	3	2	0	1	3	2	4
Sweden	3	1	0	2	4	6	2
Yugoslavia	3	0	0	3	2	6	0

West Germany qualified for the Final, Poland for the 3rd-Place Final.

3RD-PLACE FINAL

6 July 1974 – Olympia, Munich – 74,100 – Aurelio Angonese (ITA)

POLAND	**(0) 1**
Lato 76

BRAZIL	**(0) 0**

POLAND Tomaszewski, Szymanowski, Musiał, Maszczyk, Gorgoń, Zmuda, Lato, Kasperczak [Ćmikiewicz 79], Szarmach [Zdzislaw Kapka 73], Deyna (c), Gadocha.
BRAZIL Leão, Zé Maria, Marinho Chagas, Carpegiani, Alfredo (Mostarda), Marinho Peres (c), Valdomiro, Ademir da Guia [Mirandinha 66], Jairzinho, Rivelino, Dirceu.

Brazil gave a last cap to the fair-haired Ademir da Guia, whose father Domingos had played in the equivalent fixture in 1938, but he was rarely an influence on yet another dull 3rd-Place match. When Lato picked up a pass just inside his own half, Maszczyk pointed the way to goal and Lato outsprinted Alfredo and scuffed the ball past Leão. Soon he was through again, but the goalkeeper saved with his foot. Both teams had found their right level, but Brazil had come down from a different plane. Zagallo was back for the 1998 finals after being re-appointed coach on his 63rd birthday.

FIFA's Official report says both Polish subs came on after 73 minutes, but the leading Polish historians disagree.

FINAL

7 July 1974 – Olympia, Munich – 77,833 – Jack Taylor (ENG)

WEST GERMANY	**(2) 2**
Breitner pen 25, Müller 43

HOLLAND	**(1) 1**
Neeskens pen 2

WEST GERMANY Maier, Vogts, Breitner, Bonhof, Schwarzenbeck, Beckenbauer (c), Grabowski, Hoeness, Müller, Overath, Hölzenbein.
HOLLAND Jongbloed, Suurbier, Krol, Jansen, Rijsbergen [de Jong 68], Haan, Rep, Neeskens, van Hanegem, Cruijff (c), Rensenbrink [René van de Kerkhof HT].

No World Cup Final has had a more sensational opening, or a quicker goal. Held up for several minutes because Taylor noticed the corner flags were missing, it began with a series of passes among the Dutch, simply keeping possession until Cruijff took the ball in the centre circle and ran at Vogts, beating him on the left and being brought down in the area by Hoeness. Penalty, the first in any World Cup Final. Neeskens thrashed it almost straight as Maier dived to his right.

If you believe van Hanegem, Holland lost the match there and then. Half the team wanted to push on and look for a second goal, the rest to play keep-ball and humiliate the Germans. Memories were apparently going back thirty years, when the Nazis imposed systematic starvation on the Dutch to break up a strike. More to the point perhaps, Vogts' marking of Cruijff began to bite. Virtually all of Holland's fifteen goals in the tournament started or finished with their captain, who protested about Vogts' treatment at half-time and was booked. By then Taylor had made a bigger dent in Holland's chances.

As against Poland, Hölzenbein ran into the penalty area from the left and went over an outstretched foot, this time Jansen's. There was something oddly inevitable about it, as if Taylor was always likely to give a second penalty the other way. But this one was far more controversial. On the screen, Hölzenbein dives after the event – but Jansen does seem to catch him, so a penalty wasn't unjustified. However, Taylor doesn't seem to have been sure that any contact was made – in which case he should surely have given the defender the benefit of the doubt. Instead he said he awarded the penalty for intent, because Jansen 'was certainly not going for the ball.' Which means what? He was deliberately trying to give away a penalty in a World Cup Final? After Hoeness' miss against Poland, Breitner took the kick and beat a stationary Jongbloed.

The turning point, if there was one, came when Cruijff broke away, drew Beckenbauer, and gave the ball to Rep on his left. Maier saved the rather unimaginative shot. Almost on half-time, Bonhof's running made its biggest impact, taking him past Haan to the right-hand goal line. When he pulled the ball back, Müller stopped it with an exaggerated action that looked like a miskick, then shot low across Jongbloed (immobile again) as Krol made a desperate attempt to block. It was entirely appropriate that Müller should score his country's 100th goal in the finals: it was his 68th in 62 matches for them, an astounding average in such a defensive era. Like Schiavio in 1934, he retired from international football after scoring the winner in the Final for the host country.

Because winner it already was. Maier, vastly improved since 1970, made another of his marvellous saves from Neeskens' close-range volley, and Holland pressed throughout the second half – but Beckenbauer and Overath kept the play away from them and Cruijff couldn't escape Vogts, who had his most famous match. General disappointment at Holland's defeat, especially as West Germany had no Netzer to compensate – but the hosts had shown there was more than one way to win a football match, and it was only right that Beckenbauer, Overath, Vogts, Grabowski and Müller should have World Cup winners' medals, hard though it was on Krol, Neeskens, van Hanegem and the inimitable Cruijff, who was cut down on the one day Holland, and the football world, wanted to see him blossom.

The 58-year-old Schön was the oldest coach to win the World Cup.

1974

Two faces of Argentina's World Cup. The captain and other ranks.

The last post

Argentina **1978**

1930
1934
1938
1950
1954
1958
1962
1966
1970
1974
1978
1982
1986
1990
1994
1998
2002
2006

It was about time Argentina hosted the main event. They'd applied for it in the past and were one of the major footballing powers, so no-one had many qualms when they were awarded the 1978 tournament. Then a military government seized power and changed the picture.

Not that it persuaded FIFA to move the event to an established democracy. Heaven forbid. But it made a great many people uneasy, especially when the likes of Amnesty International sent documentation on torture and other state atrocities to journalists setting out for Buenos Aires. While the USA were training Argentina's torturers, Britain sold the junta helicopters, jets, frigates and submachine guns with silencers (just the job for the junta's death squads). Meanwhile Henry Kissinger, the Pope, and some English reporters gave their blessings – and the Catholic Church in Argentina compared the coup to the resurrection of Christ.

Even those who could ignore this kind of thing had concerns: the first president of the organising committee, General Actis, was blown up and a policeman died trying to remove another bomb from a press centre. This after the Montoneros, one of the main rebel groups, had promised a ceasefire for the duration of the tournament because it was 'a people's festival.'

Doubts and reservations, however, were swept aside as they invariably are and the junta, deeply in need of a public relations coup, spent the vast sums required to build three new stadia and police the event thoroughly. It passed without much incident off the pitch, but at a cost (more than the 1972 Olympics) in more ways than one.

Of the competing countries, several looked strong in parts. The holders had replaced several of their 1974 team with some talented newcomers but were without Beckenbauer, who'd opted to pick up some easy money in the USA at the end of a wonderful career. Unable to find a replacement, West Germany were using Manni Kaltz, a big attacking right-back, as their sweeper.

If any player was missed even more than the Kaiser, it was Cruijff, who'd simply had enough of life in the goldfish bowl. And van Hanegem dropped out when he couldn't be guaranteed a place in the starting line-up. But Holland retained many of the 1974 side and looked the strongest of the European challengers.

Italy, trying to assimilate the attacking philosophy of a new coach, had beaten an England team with several well-known names (Keegan, Brooking, Channon, Bowles, Emlyn Hughes) but no plan or leadership. Keegan called it 'the worst team ever picked by Don Revie' and the Italian captain Facchetti agreed: 'The worst England team I have ever seen. Disorganised, confused, of only limited ability.' When Revie fled to the financial sanctuary of the desert before the qualifying games were over, Ron

Greenwood stepped in and picked a team which beat Italy 2-0 in the return, but it was too late by then. For the second successive time, England didn't reach the finals.

Brazil, despite a different coach, were just as physical as in 1974. Argentina, like Italy, were trying to go the other way, their coach using two wingers and refusing to pick players from Lorenzo's brutal Boca Juniors. Evolution had been slow (Argentina had a player sent off against both England and Scotland) and results inconclusive (a string of wins over mediocre opposition punctuated by a home defeat by Uruguay), though home advantage would surely count for something.

But it was an open field, and several respected judges, including Rinus Michels and Miljan Miljanic, had a fancy for Scotland, who'd elimi-nated European champions Czechoslovakia. According to Lou Macari, one of the players in the squad, the 3-1 win at Hampden owed more to grit and fight than sound football method – but it was impressive nonetheless, and there seemed to be no shortage of international class: Buchan and Burns at the back, a midfield of Masson the playmaker and Rioch the destroyer who could pass, Jordan to win the ball up front for Dalglish, dribbling left-wingers in John Robertson and the recalled Willie Johnston. Enough to make people believe the voluble new manager when he intimated that Scotland's third match, against Holland, would be to decide who finished top of the group. Before that, only an ageing Peru followed by Iran, who must have been terrified to hear that 'My name is Ally MacLeod and I am a born winner.'

GROUP 1

Argentina (seeded), France, Hungary, Italy.

2 June 1978 – Parque Municipal, Mar del Plata – 42,653 – Nicolae Rainea (ROM)

ITALY **(1) 2**
Rossi 29, Zaccarelli 54

FRANCE **(1) 1**
Lacombe 37 sec

ITALY Dino Zoff (c), Claudio Gentile, Antonio Cabrini, Romeo Benetti, Mauro Bellugi, Gaetano Scirea, Franco Causio, Marco Tardelli, Paolo Rossi, Giancarlo Antognoni [Renato Zaccarelli HT], Roberto Bettega. *Enzo Bearzot.*
FRANCE Jean-Paul Bertrand-Demanes, Gérard Janvion, Max Bossis, Jean-Marc Guillou, Patrice Rio, Marius Trésor (c), Christian Dalger, Henri Michel, Bernard Lacombe [Marc Berdoll 75], Michel Platini, Didier Six [Olivier Rouyer 76]. *Michel Hidalgo.*

Losing the veteran Facchetti had forced the Italians to reorganise their defence, and you'd think the last thing they needed was to concede such a very early goal. Six hared down the left wing to hit a long cross which Lacombe, no giant, headed past Zoff. In fact it turned out to be just the kickstart Bearzot had been looking for. Forced to come out from the start, Italy outplayed a weakened French team. Their goals were both rather odd, the first going in off the bar and various bits of anatomy including Rossi's leg, the second a first-time ground shot with the keeper possibly unsighted. But there was no doubt about the grip established in midfield by Benetti, a famous rottweiler, and the young Tardelli who completely subdued Platini, sometimes fairly. Neither of them was a Neeskens, but as a double act they were scary and good. The

20-year-old Cabrini, winning his first cap, was already adding to Italy's reputation for producing world-class left-backs.

2 June 1978 – Antonio Liberti ('El Monumental'), Buenos Aires – 71,615 – António Garrido (POR)

ARGENTINA **(1) 2**
Luque 14, Bertoni 83

HUNGARY **(1) 1**
Csapó 9

ARGENTINA Ubaldo Fillol, Jorge Olguín, Alberto Tarantini, Américo Gallego, Luis Galván, Daniel Passarella (c), Daniel Valencia [Norberto Alonso 75], Osvaldo Ardiles, Leopoldo Luque, Mario Kempes, René Houseman [Daniel Bertoni 67]. *César Luis Menotti.*
HUNGARY Sándor Gujdár, Péter Török [Gyözö Martos HT], Zoltán Kereki (c), István Kocsis, József Tóth II, Sándor Pintér, Tibor Nyilasi, Sándor Zombori, Károly Csapó, András Törőcsik, László Nagy. *Lajos Baróti.*
SENT OFF: Törőcsik 87, Nyilasi 89.

A snowstorm of blue and white tickertape, descending through the floodlights, welcomed the players onto the pitch, one of the great World Cup visuals. [It was actually toilet paper torn into shreds, but let's not look too closely.]

At first the Argentinian team didn't share the festive mood. This was the toughest of the four groups, and although Hungary had just lost a friendly 4-1 at Wembley they added to Argentina's nervousness with their early goal, Csapó putting in the rebound when Fillol didn't hold Zombori's shot.

The hosts were grateful that Gujdár soon returned the compliment, blocking a Kempes free kick for Luque to force the ball in as the keeper collided with his leg. After that, Hungary were subjected to a series of bodychecks and minor fouls, insignificant on their own but building the frustration. Garrido let most of them go unpunished, though even he had to do

1930
1934
1938
1950
1954
1958
1962
1966
1970
1974

1978

1982
1986
1990
1994
1998
2002
2006

something about Passarella's waist-high kick at Pintér. Ironically it was Hungary's most skilful players who were sent off. Törőcsik, fouled a dozen times without protection, was booked for protesting then sent off for leaving his leg out as Galván ran past. Nyilasi clattered the abrasive Tarantini and walked off with his head held high. Before that, Bertoni had put the ball in the net after Gujdár seemed to have been fouled. Argentina's first appearance had already left a bad taste in the mouth.

6 June 1978 – Parque Municipal, Mar del Plata – 26,533 – Ramón Barreto (URU)

ITALY   (2) 3
Rossi 34, Bettega 35, Benetti 61

HUNGARY (0) 1
A Tóth pen 81

ITALY Zoff (c), Gentile, Cabrini [Antonello Cuccureddu 79], Benetti, Bellugi, Scirea, Causio, Tardelli, Rossi, Antognoni, Bettega [Francesco Graziani 83].
HUNGARY Ferenc Mészáros, Martos, Kocsis, Kereki (c), J Tóth II, Csapó, Pintér, Zombori, László Pusztai, László Fazekas [István Halász HT], Nagy [András Tóth HT].

A single match seemed to have made Italy believe in themselves, and they dominated this one, making light of a pitch that had recently been relaid and now came up in great divots. Facchetti's injury had let in Scirea, who was far better coming forward. Causio was smoothness itself on the right, Rossi a nimble replacement for Graziani. Above all, this was Bettega's match. Suave but forceful in the air, he'd scored four goals in one qualifying match and headed a great one against England. Here he scored another as well as hitting the woodwork three times (it was that kind of tournament for him). Rossi nabbed a poacher's goal when Mészáros couldn't hold Tardelli's low shot, and

Benetti convulsed the keeper from twenty yards. Bellugi's challenge on Csapó gave away a debatable penalty, but by then the match was won and lost.

6 June 1978 – Antonio Liberti ('El Monumental'), Buenos Aires – 71,666 – Jean Dubach (SWI)

ARGENTINA   (1) 2
Passarella pen 45, Luque 73

FRANCE   (0) 1
Platini 60

ARGENTINA Fillol, Olguín, Tarantini, Gallego, Galván, Passarella (c), Valencia [Alonso 61, Oscar Ortiz 70], Ardiles, Luque, Kempes, Houseman.
FRANCE Bertrand-Demanes [Dominique Baratelli 55], Patrick Battiston, Bossis, Dominique Bathenay, Christian Lopez, Trésor (c), Dominique Rocheteau, Michel, Lacombe, Platini, Six.

For drama, tension and atmosphere, the match of the tournament. Kempes hit the post in the first half but the return of Bathenay, Battiston and the tousle-haired Rocheteau made France much more competitive, and many felt they should have won. Platini equalised when Lacombe's lob came back off the bar, Six shot just past the post after running clear, and Argentina's first goal was from a penalty monstrously awarded after the Canadian linesman Werner Winsemann decided the splendid Trésor (his surname means 'treasure') had handled while falling over. An injury to Bertrand-Demanes, crashing his spine against a goalpost, brought in Baratelli, whose first task was to pick the ball out of the net after Luque had scored with a powerful shot from outside the D.

Again poor refereeing had done the hosts no harm, but the force was always with them. Menotti's insistence on a more attacking style didn't mean delicate short passes and clever

LEADING GOALSCORERS 1978

6	Mario Kempes	ARG	
5	Teófilo Cubillas	PER	2 pen
5	Rob Rensenbrink	HOL	4 pen

dribbles: this was ball control at speed, unsettling the opposition with direct running. Even little Ardiles attacked defenders at pace, but the undying memory was of taller men with long black hair (Kempes, Luque, Ortiz) charging like stallions. There was never a more macho team, and only the coolest of teams were likely to resist them. That or a similar referee.

10 June 1978 – Parque Municipal, Mar del Plata – 23,127 – Arnaldo Coelho (BRZ)

FRANCE (3) 3
Lopez 23, Berdoll 38, Rocheteau 42

HUNGARY (1) 1
Zombori 41

FRANCE Dominique Dropsy, Janvion, François Bracci, Jean Petit, Lopez, Trésor (c), Rocheteau [Six 75], Claude Papi [Platini HT], Marc Berdoll, Bathenay, Rouyer.
HUNGARY Gujdár, Martos, László Bálint, Kereki (c), J Tóth II, Nyilasi, Pintér, Zombori, Pusztai, Törőcsik, Nagy [Csapó 73].

Confusion about change strips (black-and-white TV still mattered) led to a delay of forty minutes and France playing in green and white stripes, the colours of local club Kimberley. Lopez and Zombori scored with spectacular long shots, Berdoll's low drive took advantage of a mistake by Kereki, and Rocheteau knocked in Rouyer's short cross from the left. All pleasant enough – and the French reserves had looked skilful – but Platini's Gallic shrug as he came off said it all.

10 June 1978 – Antonio Liberti ('El Monumental'), Buenos Aires – 71,772 – Avraham Klein (ISR)

ITALY (0) 1
Bettega 67

ARGENTINA (0) 0

ITALY Zoff (c), Gentile, Cabrini, Benetti, Bellugi [Cuccureddu 6], Scirea, Causio, Tardelli, Rossi, Antognoni [Zaccarelli 73], Bettega.
ARGENTINA Fillol, Olguín, Tarantini, Gallego, Galván, Passarella (c), Bertoni, Ardiles, Kempes, Valencia, Ortiz [Houseman 73].

Benetti, who could pass as well as terrify, drove Italy to a win that made them look the best team in the qualifying stages – this after they'd chosen to play in this group when Holland were given the fourth seeding spot. Their latest goal was beautifully crafted, Bettega moving in off the left wing and exchanging passes with Antognoni and Rossi before shooting past Fillol as he came out. The two sweepers Scirea and Passarella, born on the same day in 1953, again played superbly in their different styles, and Zoff made two fine saves within a minute. Argentina, whose excesses were kept in check by the best referee in the world, disgracefully stopped him taking charge of any of their remaining matches.

GROUP 1

	P	W	D	L	F	A	Pts
Italy	3	3	0	0	6	2	6
Argentina	3	2	0	1	4	3	4
France	3	1	0	2	5	5	2
Hungary	3	0	0	3	3	8	0

Italy and Argentina qualified for the second round.

1930
1934
1938
1950
1954
1958
1962
1966
1970
1974
1978
1982
1986
1990
1994
1998
2002
2006

1930
1934
1938
1950
1954
1958
1962
1966
1970
1974
1978
1982
1986
1990
1994
1998
2002
2006

GROUP 2

Mexico, Poland, Tunisia, West Germany (seeded).

1 June 1978 – Antonio Liberti ('El Monumental'), Buenos Aires – 67,579 – Ángel Norberto Coerezza (ARG)

POLAND	0
WEST GERMANY	0

POLAND Jan Tomaszewski, Antoni Szymanowski, Henryk Maculewicz, Bohdan Masztaler [Henryk Kasperczak 83], Jerzy Gorgoń, Władysław Żmuda, Grzegorz Lato, Adam Nawałka, Andrzej Szarmach, Kazimierz Deyna (c), Włodek Lubański [Zbigniew Boniek 79]. *Jacek Gmoch*.
WEST GERMANY Sepp Maier, Berti Vogts (c), Herbert Zimmermann, Rainer Bonhof, Rolf Rüssmann, Manni Kaltz, Rüdi Abramczik, Erich Beer, Klaus Fischer, Heinz Flohe, Hansi Müller. *Helmut Schön*.

On another shocking Argentinian pitch, another unappealing opening match. Both sides had declined since 1974. Kaltz was no sweeper, Bonhof no midfield general, Lubański at last played in the World Cup finals but was past his best. Few chances were made and for the fourth time in a row the tournament began with a goalless draw. Schön, proving that the British don't have a monopoly on classic understatement, called it 'a poor game.'

Rüdi has an umlaut here because it's short for Rüdiger, unlike Rudi (short for Rudolf) Völler, etc.

2 June 1978 – Cordiviola, Rosario – 17,396 – John Gordon (SCO)

TUNISIA	(0) 3
Kaabi 55, Ghommidh 80, Dhouib 86	
MEXICO	(1) 1
Vázquez Ayala pen 45	

TUNISIA Mokhtar Naïli, Mokhtar Dhouib, Ali Kaabi, Amar Jebali, Nejib Ghommidh, 'Jendoubi' (Mohsen Labidi), Temime Lahzami (c) [Khemais Labidi 88], 'Agrebi' (Mohammed Ben Rehaien), Mohammed Ali Akid, Tarak Dhiab, Abderraouf Ben Aziza [Slah Karoui 70]. *Abdelmajid Chetali*.
MEXICO José Pilar Reyes, Jesús Martínez, Eduardo Ramos, Alfredo Tena, Arturo Vázquez Ayala (c), Guillermo Mendizábal [Gerardo Lugo 67], Antonio de la Torre, Leonardo Cuéllar, Victor Rangel, Hugo Sánchez, Raúl Isiordia. *José Antonio Roca*.

Tunisia became the first African country to win a finals match, went top of their group, and thoroughly deserved it. Even a dubious penalty, awarded at a critical time for handball by Jebali, didn't faze them. Tarak looked one of the most skilful players in the tournament, and the defenders came up cleverly in attack. Kaabi was given room to hammer the equaliser just inside a post, Ghommidh was unmarked when he scored from a tight angle on the left, and Dhouib also had acres of space when he cut in from the right and scored from close range. Tunisia had exploited Mexico's lack of fitness in the second half, after the first had been played at high speed. According to Roca, 'our supporters overestimated our chances.' Tarak and Temime were known by their first names.

6 June 1978 – Olímpico, Chateau Carreras, Córdoba – 35,258 – Farouk Bouzo (SYR)

WEST GERMANY	(4) 6
D Müller 14, H Müller 29, Rummenigge 38, 71, Flohe 44, 89	
MEXICO	(0) 0

WEST GERMANY Maier, Vogts (c), Bernard Dietz, Bonhof, Rüssmann, Kaltz, Flohe, Dieter Müller, Fischer, H Müller, Karl-Heinz Rummenigge.
MEXICO Pilar Reyes [Pedro Soto 42], Tena, Ramos, Vázquez Ayala (c), Mendizábal, de la Torre, Martínez, Enrique López Zarza [Lugo HT], Sánchez, Cuéllar, Rangel.

For a side with a modicum of World Cup pedigree, Mexico were an embarrassment. After bungling a free kick outside the German penalty area, they allowed Rummenigge to run unchallenged into their own before scoring. The Müllers (no relation to Gerd or each other) scored with a ground shot and a cross shot, Rummenigge from a pull-back, Flohe twice from long range as well as hitting both posts with another shot. Some of the running and shooting was irresistible, but Mexico made the midfield a tackle-free zone and were no sort of yardstick. Dietz's first name is spelt correctly (i.e. not Bernhard).

6 June 1978 – Cordiviola, Rosario – 9,624 – Ángel Martínez (SPA)

POLAND   (1) 1
Lato 42

TUNISIA   (0) 0

POLAND Tomaszewski, Szymanowski, Maculewicz, Kasperczak, Gorgoń, Żmuda, Lato, Nawałka, Szarmach [Andrzej Iwan 59], Deyna (c), Lubański [Boniek 75].
TUNISIA Naïli, Jebali, Dhouib, Kaabi, Khaled Gasmi, Jendoubi, Ghommidh, Temime (c), Agrebi, Tarak, Akid.

Tunisia, showing that their previous result was no fluke, raised their game and were often the better team, Lahzami hitting the bar, Żmuda working overtime on his 24th birthday. But a blunder at the other end decided it, Kaabi missing his kick as the ball dropped over him, the opportunist Lato volleying in.

10 June 1978 – Olímpico, Chateau Carreras, Córdoba – 30,667 – César Orozco (PER)

TUNISIA   0
WEST GERMANY 0

TUNISIA Naïli, Jebali, Dhouib, Kaabi, Gasmi, Jendoubi, Ghommidh, Temime (c), Agrebi, Tarak, Akid [Ben Aziza 82].
WEST GERMANY Maier, Vogts (c), Dietz, Bonhof, Rüssmann, Kaltz, Flohe, D Müller, Fischer, H Müller, Rummenigge.

West Germany would have won but for some fine saves by Naïli (playing in place of the veteran Attouga), especially when Fischer was clean through in the second half – but Tunisia deserved the draw. Again they'd lost little in comparison with a major European team. 'The world has laughed at Africa,' said their manager, 'but now the mockery is over.' The Germans were to agree with that even more wholeheartedly in 1982.

10 June 1978 – Cordiviola, Rosario – 22,651 – Jafar Namdar (IRN)

POLAND   (1) 3
Boniek 42, 83, Deyna 56

MEXICO   (0) 1
Rangel 51

POLAND Tomaszewski, Szymanowski, Masztaler, Gorgoń, Żmuda, Lato, Kasperczak, Boniek, Deyna (c), Wojciech Rudy [Maculewicz 84], Iwan [Lubański 75].
MEXICO Soto, Vázquez Ayala (c), de la Torre, Cristóbal Ortega, Rigoberto Cisneros, Carlos Gómez, Sánchez, Ignacio Flores, Cuéllar, Rangel, Javier Cárdenas [Mendizábal HT].

Even against a demoralised side with little to offer, Poland had to work harder than they would have in 1974, needing two tremendous long shots from Deyna and the new young star Boniek. Cuéllar, with his huge afro and good passing, was again more visible than the two players from whom much had been expected, Rangel (who scored from Ortega's cross) and the 19-year-old Sánchez. Mexico were the most persuasive case yet for the abolition of zonal

1930
1934
1938
1950
1954
1958
1962
1966
1970
1974
1978
1982
1986
1990
1994
1998
2002
2006

1930
1934
1938
1950
1954
1958
1962
1966
1970
1974
1978
1982
1986
1990
1994
1998
2002
2006

qualification, which they were still using to reach the finals 28 years later. Flores' brother Luis played in the 1986 finals.

GROUP 2

	P	W	D	L	F	A	Pts
Poland	3	2	1	0	4	1	5
West Germany	3	1	2	0	6	0	4
Tunisia	3	1	1	1	3	2	3
Mexico	3	0	0	3	2	12	0

Poland and West Germany qualified for the second round.

GROUP 3

Austria, Brazil (seeded), Spain, Sweden.

3 June 1978 – José Amalfitani, Buenos Aires – 40,841 – Károly Palotai (HUN)

AUSTRIA **(1) 2**
Schachner 10, Krankl 79

SPAIN **(1) 1**
Dani 21

AUSTRIA Fritz Koncilia, Robert Sara (c), Gerhard Breitenberger, Josef Hickersberger [Heribert Weber 67], Erich Obermayer, Bruno Pezzey, Walter Schachner [Hans Pirkner 80], Herbert Prohaska, Hans Krankl, Willi Kreuz, Kurt Jara. *Helmut Senekowitsch.*
SPAIN Miguel Ángel (González), Marcelino (Pérez), Jesús de la Cruz, Isidoro San José, 'Migueli' (Miguel Bernardo), 'Pirri' (José Martínez) (c), 'Dani' (Daniel Ruiz Bazán), Julio Cardeñosa [Eugenio Leal HT], Rubén Cano, Juan Manuel Asensi, Carlos Rexach ['Quini' (Enrique Castro) 60]. *Ladislav Kubala (HUN).*

Austria, slight underdogs, opened with a spectacular goal, Schachner running up the right wing, swerving outside his man and beating Miguel Ángel high at his near post. Dani equalised with a low shot that Koncilia should have saved, but the dangerous Krankl (six goals in one of the qualifiers) was quick to sidefoot in a rebound. Austria also hit a post. Weber's first name is correct (i.e. not Herbert).

3 June 1978 – Parque Municipal, Mar del Plata – 38,618 – Clive Thomas (WAL)

BRAZIL **(1) 1**
Reinaldo 45

SWEDEN **(1) 1**
Sjöberg 37

BRAZIL Émerson Leão, Toninho (Dias), 'Edinho' (Edino Nazareth), João Batista, Oscar (Bernardi), João Amaral, 'Gil' (Gilberto Alves) ['Nelinho' (Manoel Rezende) 67], 'Zico' (Arthur Antunes Coimbra), Reinaldo (de Lima), Toninho Cerezo [Dirceu (Guimarães) 80], Roberto Rivelino (c). *Cláudio Coutinho.*
SWEDEN Ronnie Hellström, Hasse Borg, Ingemar Erlandsson, Staffan Tapper, Roy Andersson, Björn Nordqvist (c), Lennart Larsson [Ralf Edström 79], Anders Linderoth, Bo Larsson, Thomas Sjöberg, Benny Wendt. *Georg 'Åby' Ericsson.*

Brazil had shown their current colours in collecting five yellow cards at Wembley, where someone should have been sent off. Here they were less violent but equally uninspired, Rivelino not the force of old, Zico completely off form. The bearded Sjöberg stabbed the ball home when a flick caught the defence square, but Reinaldo equalised after winning the ball from Cerezo's long high cross. The game ended in farcical controversy. When Zico headed in a corner, the goal was disallowed because time had run out – after only eight seconds of injury time. The decision, which looked typical of Thomas, was his last in the finals. Nordqvist's 109th cap broke Bobby Moore's world record.

7 June 1978 – José Amalfitani, Buenos Aires – 41,424 – Charles Corver (HOL)

AUSTRIA **(1) 1**
Krankl pen 44

SWEDEN **(0) 0**

AUSTRIA Koncilia, Sara (c), Breitenberger, Hickersberger, Obermayer, Pezzey, Edi Krieger [Weber 71], Prohaska, Krankl, Kreuz, Jara.
SWEDEN Hellström, Borg, Erlandsson, Tapper [Conny Torstensson 37], Andersson, Nordqvist (c), L Larsson, Linderoth [Edström 60], Sjöberg, B Larsson, Wendt.

Even when Edström came on, Sweden offered little up front and were again grateful to Hellström, who saved everything Krankl threw at him except the penalty, awarded when he was brought down by Nordqvist. Austria, unexpectedly, were already in the second round.

7 June 1978 – Parque Municipal, Mar del Plata – 34,771 – Sergio Gonella (ITA)

BRAZIL **0**

SPAIN **0**

BRAZIL Leão (c), Nelinho [Gil 70], Edinho, Batista, Oscar, Amaral, Zico [Jorge Mendonça 84], Reinaldo, Cerezo, Dirceu, Toninho.
SPAIN Miguel Ángel, Marcelino, Antonio Olmo, San José, Migueli [Antonio Biosca 51], Cardeñosa, 'Uria' (Francisco Javier Álvarez) [Antonio Guzmán 59], Leal, 'Santillana' (Carlos Alonso), Asensi (c), 'Juanito' (Juan Gómez).

Again the appalling Mar del Plata pitch didn't help Brazil's passing game, and Spain really should have won. Santillana, marvellous in the air for a man of medium height, won the ball in a challenge with Leão, only for Cardeñosa to shoot straight at Amaral on the line. The latter, a purely defensive sweeper, was Brazil's best player, but that wasn't saying too much. They played a fullback on the wing (Toninho, on his 30th birthday) in place of the disappointing Gil.

11 June 1978 – José Amalfitani, Buenos Aires – 42,132 – Ferdinand Biwersi (GER)

SPAIN **(0) 1**
Asensi 75

SWEDEN **(0) 0**

SPAIN Miguel Ángel, Marcelino, Olmo [Pirri HT], San José, Biosca, Cardeñosa, Uria, Leal, Asensi (c), Juanito, Santillana.
SWEDEN Hellström, Borg, Erlandsson, Olle Nordin, Andersson, Nordqvist (c), L Larsson, B Larsson, Edström [Wendt 60], Sjöberg [Linderoth 66], Torbjörn Nilsson.

Sweden went out without glory, making little use of Edström's height. Asensi, whose father Vicente played in the 1950 finals, smacked in the only goal from an opening made by Juanito. Too little too late for Spain, who were already looking ahead to 'their' World Cup in four years' time.

11 June 1978 – Parque Municipal, Mar del Plata – 35,221 – Robert Wurtz (FRA)

BRAZIL **(1) 1**
Roberto Dinamite 40

AUSTRIA **(0) 0**

BRAZIL Leão (c), Toninho, José Rodrigues Neto, Batista, Oscar, Amaral, Gil, Cerezo ['Chicão' (Francisco Avanzi) 71], 'Roberto Dinamite' (Roberto de Oliveira), Dirceu, Mendonça [Zico 84].
AUSTRIA Koncilia, Sara (c), Breitenberger, Hickersberger [Weber 61], Obermayer, Pezzey, Krieger [Günther Happich 84], Prohaska, Krankl, Kreuz, Jara.

1978

1930
1934
1938
1950
1954
1958
1962
1966
1970
1974
1978
1982
1986
1990
1994
1998
2002
2006

No Zico, Rivelino or Reinaldo, but a slight improvement from Brazil, albeit against a team that didn't need a result. Dirceu provided some leadership in midfield and Roberto, bigger and stronger than Reinaldo, cracked in Gil's long cross when Pezzey left him badly unmarked. Enough to qualify (a goalless draw would have knocked them out) but not to set any pulses racing, especially in the Argentinian camp.

GROUP 3

	P	W	D	L	F	A	Pts
Austria	3	2	0	1	3	2	4
Brazil	3	1	2	0	2	1	4
Spain	3	1	1	1	2	2	3
Sweden	3	0	1	2	1	3	1

Austria and Brazil qualified for the second round.

GROUP 4

Holland (seeded), Iran, Peru, Scotland.

3 June 1978 – Olímpico, Chateau Carreras, Córdoba – 37,792 – Ulf Eriksson (SWE)

PERU　　　　(1) 3
Cueto 43, Cubillas 70, 76

SCOTLAND　　(1) 1
Jordan 19

PERU Ramón Quiroga, Rodolfo Manzo, Jaime Duarte, José Velásquez, Toribio Díaz, Héctor Chumpitáz (c), Juan José Muñante, César Cueto [Percy Rojas 82], Guillermo La Rosa [Hugo Sotil 62], Teófilo Cubillas, Juan Carlos Oblitas. *Marcos Calderón.*

SCOTLAND Allan Rough, Stuart Kennedy, Martin Buchan, Bruce Rioch (c) [Archie Gemmill 70], Kenny Burns, Tom Forsyth, Kenny Dalglish, Asa Hartford, Joe Jordan, Don Masson [Lou Macari 70], Willie Johnston. *Ally MacLeod.*

Scotland started as they expected to go on, Jordan putting in the loose ball when Rioch's shot was saved – but then the roof fell in on the house Ally built.

There was talk of the 'ageing' Cubillas being past his best – but he was only 29, younger than either Rioch or Masson, who were in poor form with Derby County. Cubillas and Cueto ran the midfield and Peru also had weapons up front: Rinus Michels had warned against their wingers Oblitas and Muñante 'who are two of the fastest and most dangerous in the competition.' Muñante, in fact, was considered so valuable that the Peruvian FA paid his Mexican club an insurance premium to secure his services. Against these two, MacLeod picked Buchan, a composed central defender but too slow for a full-back, and the rookie Kennedy. A shambles. It's said that the sum total of MacLeod's half-time team talk was to urge Rough to kick the ball harder to clear the Peruvian midfield!

MATCHES AS COACH

25	Helmut Schön	GER	1966–78
20	Mário Zagallo	BRZ	1970–98
20	Bora Milutinović	YUG	1986–02
18	Sepp Herberger	GER	1938–62
18	Enzo Bearzot	ITA	1978–86
16	Carlos Alberto Parreira	BRZ	1982–98
15	Lajos Baróti	HUN	1958–78
British Isles countries			
14	Walter Winterbottom	ENG	1950–62

Quiroga made an important fingertip save from a Dalglish lob, but the Peruvian one-twos had their reward when Cueto scored from close in. In the second half, the Scots were thrown a lifeline in the form of a penalty when Cubillas was judged to have brought down Rioch. Masson, whose spot kick had taken Scotland to the finals, hit this one to the same side but Quiroga made a comfortable save. MacLeod took off Masson and Rioch but it was too late. Macari, the smallest player on the pitch, was on the end of the wall when Cubillas caressed a free kick over him with the outside of his foot. That was the clinching goal, a few minutes after he'd hit the winner from even longer range.

MacLeod used the press conference to blame his players rather than his own preparation ('eight of them didn't play') and the Scottish nightmare was compounded when Johnston was sent home for taking a banned substance. The level to which team's standing had fallen was expressed by a Dutch journalist who was told that Burns was the current Footballer of the Year in England: 'You are pulling my trousers.'

Rough's first name is written Alan in most sources, but not on his birth certificate.

---

3 June 1978 – San Martín, Mendoza – 33,431 – Alfonso Archundia (MEX)

HOLLAND (1) 3
Rensenbrink pen 40, 62, pen 78

IRAN (0) 0

HOLLAND Jan Jongbloed, Wim Suurbier, Wim Rijsbergen, Wim Jansen, Ruud Krol (c), Willy van de Kerkhof, Johan Neeskens, Arie Haan, René van de Kerkhof [Dirk 'Dick' Nanninga 71], Johnny Rep, Rob Rensenbrink. *Ernst Happel (AUT)*.
IRAN Nasser Hejazi, Hassan Nazari, Nasrullah Abdollahi, Hossein Kazerani, Andranik Eskandarian,

Ali Parvin (c), Ebrahim Ghasempour, Mohammed Sadeghi, Hassan Naybagha, Hossein Faraki [Hassan Roshan 52], Ghafoor Djahani. *Heshmat Mohajerani.*

As expected, Holland weren't as good as in 1974, but it didn't matter against a defence that gave away too many free kicks and penalties. Rensenbrink, doing his best to put on Cruijff's mantle, sent the keeper the wrong way with both spot kicks and headed in a cross from the right by René van de Kerkhof, who was fouled for the first penalty, Rep for the other. The van de Kerkhofs were twins.

---

7 June 1978 – San Martín, Mendoza – 28,125 – Adolf Prokop (DDR)

HOLLAND 0
PERU 0

HOLLAND Jongbloed, Suurbier, Rijsbergen, Krol (c), Jan Poortvliet, Neeskens [Nanninga 69], Wim Jansen, Haan, W van de Kerkhof, R van de Kerkhof [Rep HT], Rensenbrink.
PERU Quiroga, Manzo, Duarte, Velásquez, Díaz, Chumpitáz (c), Muñante, Cueto, La Rosa [Sotil 62], Cubillas, Oblitas.

1978

As in 1974, the Dutch were happy to play out a goalless draw after winning their first match, using the defensive young Poortvliet in place of Rep. The hardest thing Quiroga had to do was carry the injured Neeskens off the field, for all the world like Michelangelo's *Pietà*.

---

7 June 1978 – Olímpico, Chateau Carreras, Córdoba – 7,938 – Youssou Ndiaye (SEN)

IRAN (0) 1
Danaifar 60

SCOTLAND (1) 1
Eskandarian o.g. 43

IRAN Hejazi, Nazari, Abdollahi, Kazerani, Eskandarian, Parvin (c), Ghasempour, Sadeghi, Iraj Danaifar [Naybagha 89], Faraki [Roshan 83], Djahani.
SCOTLAND Rough, William 'Sandy' Jardine, Willie Donachie, Hartford, Burns, Buchan [Forsyth 57], Macari, Gemmill (c), Dalglish [Joe Harper 73], Jordan, John Robertson.

Scotland's stock crashed even lower, making them the butts of the tournament. Buchan had to go off after having his head cut by Donachie (!) and even their goal was a joke, Eskandarian sticking out a leg after a collision with Jordan. Coming when it did, that should have deflated Iran, but they were well worth their draw, Danaifar holding off Jardine and beating Rough with a low shot at the near post. Dalglish (again) and Robertson were anonymous, but no-one else covered himself in glory. As their bus pulled away after the match, it was serenaded by their own fans singing 'You only want the money.' Back in Britain, the squad was being used to advertise Chrysler cars, a TV ad showing them heading the ball over various vehicles. The prime slot, which must have looked a safe bet, was at half-time in the Iran match. The slogan: 'Both run rings round the opposition.'

11 June 1978 – San Martín, Mendoza – 35,130 – Erich Linemayr (AUT)

SCOTLAND   (1) 3
Dalglish 44, Gemmill pen 46, 68

HOLLAND   (1) 2
Rensenbrink pen 34, Rep 71

SCOTLAND Rough, Kennedy, Donachie, Rioch (c), Forsyth, Buchan, Gemmill, Hartford, Jordan, Graeme Souness, Dalglish.
HOLLAND Jongbloed, Suurbier, Rijsbergen [Piet Wildschut 44], Krol (c), Poortvliet, Neeskens [Jan Boskamp 10], Jansen, Rep, R van de Kerkhof, W van de Kerkhof, Rensenbrink.

A month earlier Souness had made the goal that won Liverpool the European Cup. MacLeod, who admitted he should have played him against Iran, now sent out the midfield line-up that had been crying out to be picked – and suddenly we were reminded that Jekyll and Hyde was written by a Scot. Amazingly, the Jekylls could still qualify: there was just the little matter of beating Holland by three goals. Even with no luck on their side, they came naggingly close.

Rioch headed against the bar, Dalglish had a goal disallowed, and Jordan might have had a penalty, but Holland got one instead when Kennedy fouled Rep. Rensenbrink converted it (the 1,000th goal scored in the finals) and there was less than an hour left.

To their enormous credit Scotland didn't give up. Souness hit a high cross to the far post, where Jordan headed down to the unmarked Dalglish who volleyed nervelessly past Jongbloed's arms and legs. Then Souness was bundled over by Willy K for a penalty. Two goals a minute either side of the interval set up a momentum which Gemmill maintained with one of the best goals in any World Cup. Picking up a loose ball on the right of the Dutch penalty area, he came inside Jansen's lunge, beat Krol on the outside, pushed the ball between Poortvliet's legs, and lifted it over the advancing keeper. One more goal and the impossible would be astounding reality.

But Holland, who'd been going through the motions a little after an early injury to Neeskens, roused themselves to score as if on demand. Running through the middle, Rep hit a long-range shot that faded past Rough's right hand, and there was no way back for Scotland. They'd restored some dignity but added to the frustration at what had gone before.

Masson, Rioch, Macari (banned for speaking his mind), Forsyth and Johnston weren't capped again. Remarkably, the Scottish FA allowed MacLeod to keep his job, but he resigned after one more match. It was the last time anything was expected of Scotland in the World Cup.

---

11 June 1978 – Olímpico, Chateau Carreras, Córdoba – 21,262 – Alojzy Jarguz (POL)

PERU **(3) 4**
Velásquez 2, Cubillas pen 36, pen 39, 79

IRAN **(1) 1**
Roshan 41

PERU Quiroga, Manzo [Germán Leguía 68], Duarte, Velásquez, Díaz, Chumpitáz (c), Muñante, Cueto, La Rosa [Sotil 60], Cubillas, Oblitas.
IRAN Hejazi, Nazari, Abdollahi, Kazerani, Javad Allahvardi, Parvin (c), Ghasempour, Sadeghi, Danaifar, Faraki [Djahani 52], Roshan [Behtash Fariba 66].

Any faint hopes that Iran might do the Scots a favour were extinguished very early, Velásquez heading in Muñante's corner from twelve yards. After that the Iranians fell into their habit of conceding penalties, the first harshly awarded for a shoulder charge on Oblitas, the other when Hejazi brought down Cubillas. Faraki forced a good save from Quiroga and Roshan scored with a low volley, but Cubillas

GROUP 4

	P	W	D	L	F	A	Pts
Peru	3	2	1	0	7	2	5
Holland	3	1	1	1	5	3	3
Scotland	3	1	1	1	5	6	3
Iran	3	0	1	2	2	8	1

Peru and Holland qualified for the second round.

kicked in a rebound for his tenth goal in World Cup finals and the last of his 26 for Peru, still the national record. He was the only player to score five goals in each of two finals tournaments. Peru's passing was again good to watch, but no-one had seriously tested their defence.

2ND ROUND

Austria, Holland, Italy, West Germany.

GROUP A

14 June 1978 – Antonio Liberti ('El Monumental'), Buenos Aires – 67,547 – Dušan Maksimović (YUG)

ITALY **0**

WEST GERMANY **0**

ITALY Zoff (c), Gentile, Cabrini, Benetti, Bellugi, Scirea, Causio, Tardelli, Rossi, Antognoni [Zaccarelli HT], Bettega
WEST GERMANY Maier, Vogts (c), Dietz, Bonhof, Rüssmann, Kaltz, Rummenigge, Zimmermann [Harald Konopka 53], Fischer, Flohe [Beer 68], Bernd Hölzenbein.

With Antognoni outplaying Bonhof, Italy were disappointed not to win. Cabrini, again impressive coming forward, hit the bar with a cross, and Bettega had goalbound shots blocked by Kaltz's heel and Dietz's arm as well as chesting down a cross and poking the ball wide from close in. Fischer seemed to be fouled in the area by Bellugi, but a German win would have been a travesty. Instead Zoff kept his 38th

1930
1934
1938
1950
1954
1958
1962
1966
1970
1974
1978
1982
1986
1990
1994
1998
2002
2006

1930
1934
1938
1950
1954
1958
1962
1966
1970
1974

1978

1982
1986
1990
1994
1998
2002
2006

international clean sheet, breaking the world record set by Gylmar in the 1966 finals.

---

14 June 1978 – Olímpico, Chateau Carreras, Córdoba – 25,059 – John Gordon (SCO)

HOLLAND (3) 5
Brandts 6, Rensenbrink pen 35, Rep 36, 53, W van de Kerkhof 82

AUSTRIA (0) 1
Obermayer 80

HOLLAND Piet Schrijvers, Wildschut, Ernie Brandts [Adri van Kraay 66], Haan, Krol (c), Poortvliet, R van de Kerkhof [Dick Schoenaker 60], Jansen, Rep, W van de Kerkhof, Rensenbrink.
AUSTRIA Koncilia, Sara (c), Breitenberger, Hickersberger, Obermayer, Pezzey, Krieger, Prohaska, Krankl, Kreuz, Jara.

An unexpected and slightly exaggerated score-line, but Holland were certainly on top throughout. The unmarked Brandts, winning his second cap, headed in Haan's free kick, and Jansen was bodychecked by Prohaska for the penalty. Some poor defence let in Rep to lob the third, Rensenbrink presented him with an open goal for the fourth and set up Willy K for the fifth. Even Austria's goal was an embarrassment, Obermayer's almost vertical lob somehow dropping in at the far post. The arrival of the Austrian players' wives raised a few smirks, but it hadn't done the Dutch any harm four years earlier. The two coaches, Happel and Senekowitsch, had played together for Austria in the 1958 finals.

---

18 June 1978 – Olímpico, Chateau Carreras, Córdoba – 40,750 – Ramón Barreto (URU)

HOLLAND (1) 2
Haan 27, R van de Kerkhof 82

WEST GERMANY (1) 2
Abramczik 3, D Müller 70

HOLLAND Schrijvers, Wildschut [Nanninga 79], Brandts, Haan, Krol (c), Poortvliet, Jansen, W van de Kerkhof, R van de Kerkhof, Rep, Rensenbrink.
WEST GERMANY Maier, Vogts (c), Dietz, Bonhof, Rüssmann, Kaltz, Rummenigge, Beer, D Müller, Hölzenbein, Abramczik.
SENT OFF: Nanninga 89.

The champions, shedding their recent poor form, contributed fully to an exciting match. Abramczik scored with a diving header after Schrijvers had saved Bonhof's free kick, and Müller headed in Beer's cross from the left. Haan's thirty-yarder left an unsighted Maier standing, Rep thrashed the ball against the bar, and René K rescued the Dutch by cutting inside Kaltz and swerving the ball round Maier; the giant blond Rüssmann handled the ball on the line but couldn't keep it out. Holland still hadn't beaten West Germany since 1956 but remained top of the group.

Nanninga was the first substitute to be sent off in a finals tournament (for laughing at a refereeing decision). The van de Kerkhofs weren't identical twins but scored their goals in the same minute of different matches.

---

18 June 1978 – Antonio Liberti ('El Monumental'), Buenos Aires – 66,695 – Francis Rion (BEL)

ITALY (1) 1
Rossi 13

AUSTRIA (0) 0

ITALY Zoff (c), Gentile, Cabrini, Benetti, Bellugi [Cuccureddu HT], Scirea, Causio, Tardelli, Rossi, Zaccarelli, Bettega [Graziani 71].
AUSTRIA Koncilia, Sara (c), Heinrich Strasser, Krieger, Hickersberger, Obermayer, Pezzey, Prohaska, Krankl, Kreuz, Schachner [Pirkner 63].

Again Italy should have scored more goals. The one they did get had some skilful beginnings but needed a little help. Rossi backheeled to Causio, Strasser got to the return pass first but let Rossi nick it away from him and score with a low cross-shot. Pezzey made a saving tackle after Graziani had gone round Koncilia, who later saved from Cuccureddu. With three minutes left, Graziani shot wide when Rossi's header sent him clear on the right. The real crowd figure may have been nearer 40,000.

21 June 1978 – Antonio Liberti ('El Monumental'), Buenos Aires – 67,433 – Ángel Martínez (SPA)

HOLLAND **(0) 2**
Brandts 49, Haan 76

ITALY **(1) 1**
Brandts o.g. 19

HOLLAND Schrijvers [Jongbloed 21], Poortvliet, Brandts, Neeskens, Haan, Krol (c), Jansen, W van de Kerkhof, Rep [van Kraay 65], R van de Kerkhof, Rensenbrink.
ITALY Zoff (c), Cuccureddu, Cabrini, Benetti [Graziani 77], Gentile, Scirea, Causio [Claudio Sala HT], Tardelli, Rossi, Zaccarelli, Bettega.

21 June 1978 – Olímpico, Chateau Carreras, Córdoba – 38,318 – Avraham Klein (ISR)

AUSTRIA **(0) 3**
Vogts o.g. 59, Krankl 66, 88

WEST GERMANY **(1) 2**
Rummenigge 19, Hölzenbein 67

AUSTRIA Koncilia, Sara (c), Strasser, Krieger, Hickersberger, Obermayer, Pezzey, Prohaska, Krankl, Kreuz, Schachner [Franz Oberacher 71].
WEST GERMANY Maier, Vogts (c), Dietz, Bonhof, Rüssmann, Kaltz, Rummenigge, Beer [H Müller HT], D Müller [Fischer 60], Hölzenbein, Abramczik.

Even if the other result went their way, West Germany would have to win by four goals to reach the Final. Instead they lost to Austria for the first time since 1931, thanks to an own goal by their captain, the little white terrier who'd kept Cruijff quiet in 1974 but was now playing his 96th and last international. Krankl regained his goal touch when it didn't matter, scoring with a glorious volley and a cool dribble. Rummenigge converted Dieter Müller's pass and Hölzenbein headed in Bonhof's free kick. Schön, in the last match of his great World Cup career, had been making bricks without straw.

Holland needed only a draw but Italy came within two long shots of winning. In the first quarter of an hour, Rossi headed over the bar and Bettega shot wide when clear on the left. Then Benetti sent Bettega through and Brandts came in from behind to knock the ball past Schrijvers, who was injured in the collision. Italy created chances throughout the half, but when Benetti ran his rule down Rensenbrink's leg he was booked for the second time in the tournament, which would keep him out of the Final. Italy's spirit drained away with him.

Even so, it took a ferocious eyes-down twenty-yarder from Brandts, the only player to score for both sides in a finals match, to put Holland in charge. That and some typical tackling: Neeskens should have been sent off for kicking Zaccarelli so hard you could hear the impact on the other side of the ground. But it was hard to feel sympathy for a team that included Benetti and Tardelli in the same midfield. Haan, from preposterously long range, sealed Holland's place in the Final.

Conventional wisdom has it that Italy started the tournament well before running out of steam. In fact they might well have reached the Final (where their opponents

1978

1930
1934
1938
1950
1954
1958
1962
1966
1970
1974
1978
1982
1986
1990
1994
1998
2002
2006

would have been a team they'd already beaten) but for injuries to Antognoni, their young fair-haired playmaker, and the unsung Bellugi, both among the best in Europe.

GROUP A						
	P	W	D	L	F	A	Pts
Holland	3	2	1	0	9	4	5
Italy	3	1	1	1	2	2	3
W Germany	3	0	2	1	4	5	2
Austria	3	1	0	2	4	8	2

Holland qualified for the Final, Italy for the 3rd-Place Final.

GROUP B

Argentina, Brazil, Peru, Poland.

14 June 1978 – San Martín, Mendoza – 31,278 – Nicolae Rainea (ROM)

BRAZIL   **(2) 3**
Dirceu 15, 27, Zico pen 72

PERU   **(0) 0**

BRAZIL Leão (c), Toninho, Rodrigues Neto, Batista, Oscar, Amaral, Cerezo [Chicão 76], Gil [Zico 70], Roberto Dinamite, Dirceu, Mendonça.
PERU Quiroga, Manzo, Duarte, Velásquez, Díaz [José Navarro 11], Chumpitáz (c), Muñante, Cueto, La Rosa, Cubillas, Oblitas [P Rojas HT].

Better from Brazil, but Peru's non-tackling midfield was finally found out, wandering

about in their afroes like extras in a Shaft film. Dirceu scored the first with a long-range free kick to the right of the Peruvian goal, the shot bending so much that it curled back inside the right-hand post. His second was a ground shot fumbled by Quiroga, and Duarte conceded the penalty by tugging Roberto's shirt. Zico, who'd only just come on, made one of his few contributions to the tournament, but it was a cheap shot.

14 June 1978 – Cordiviola, Rosario – 37,091 – Ulf Eriksson (SWE)

ARGENTINA   **(1) 2**
Kempes 16, 72

POLAND   **(0) 0**

ARGENTINA Fillol, Olguín, Tarantini, Gallego, Galván, Passarella (c), Houseman [Ortiz 83], Valencia [Ricardo Villa HT], Ardiles, Kempes, Bertoni.
POLAND Tomaszewski, Szymanowski, Maculewicz, Masztaler [Włodek Mazur 60], Żmuda, Nawałka, Lato, Kasperczak, Szarmach, Deyna (c), Boniek.

With Luque still out injured, Kempes came into his own. The only player Menotti had brought back from Europe, he at last scored in a finals match (his eleventh). His first goal was a classic, a perfectly timed diagonal run to meet Bertoni's left-wing cross with a near-post header, and the second was in the same league, dragging the ball past a defender to shoot low past Tomaszewski. In between, seven minutes before half-time, he made another important contribution, handling on the line to stop Lato's header. Deyna, in his 100th international, hit the penalty too close to Fillol. Ardiles, the dapper playmaker with hair like a black beret, made Kempes' second goal.

18 June 1978 – San Martín, Mendoza – 35,288 – Pat Partridge (ENG)

POLAND **(0) 1**
Szarmach 64

PERU **(0) 0**

POLAND Zygmunt Kukla, Szymanowski, Maculewicz, Masztaler [Kasperczak HT], Gorgoń, Żmuda, Nawałka, Lato, Szarmach, Deyna (c), Boniek [Lubański 86].
PERU Quiroga, Manzo, Duarte, Navarro, Chumpitáz (c), Alfredo Quesada, Muñante [P Rojas HT], Cueto, La Rosa [Sotil 74], Cubillas, Oblitas.

The goal brought back memories (Lato's cross met by Szarmach's diving header) and Deyna hit a post – but the two poorest sides in the group played like it. Quiroga was back in some sort of form but lived up to his nickname of '*El Loco*' by getting himself booked for rugby-tackling Lato near the halfway line.

18 June 1978 – Cordiviola, Rosario – 37,326 – Károly Palotai (HUN)

ARGENTINA **0**

BRAZIL **0**

ARGENTINA Fillol, Olguín, Tarantini, Gallego, Galván, Passarella (c), Bertoni, Ardiles [Villa HT], Luque, Kempes, Ortiz [Alonso 61].
BRAZIL Leão (c), Toninho, Rodrigues Neto [Edinho 36], Batista, Oscar, Amaral, Gil, Chicão, Roberto Dinamite, Dirceu, Mendonça [Zico 68].

The South American version of England v Scotland, except this was serious. Seventeen fouls in the first ten minutes (the restored Luque the first to flash his studs), Edinho lucky not to be sent off. Ardiles, whom John Motson called 'the ferret-faced little man,' looked the coolest player on the pitch – so the Brazilians gashed his ankle to let Villa join in. He was later Ardiles' skilful team mate at Tottenham but

behaved like a bearded version of Benetti here. Both sides had reasons to be fairly satisfied, but it wasn't one for the squeamish.

21 June 1978 – San Martín, Mendoza – 39,586 – Juan Silvagno (CHI)

BRAZIL **(1) 3**
Nelinho 13, Roberto Dinamite 58, 63

POLAND **(1) 1**
Lato 45

BRAZIL Leão (c), Toninho, Nelinho, Batista, Oscar, Amaral, Gil, Zico [Mendonça 7], Roberto Dinamite, Cerezo [Rivelino 75], Dirceu.
POLAND Kukla, Szymanowski, Maculewicz, Kasperczak [Lubański 64], Gorgoń, Żmuda, Nawałka, Lato, Szarmach, Deyna (c), Boniek.

Poland hadn't given up hope of reaching the final, and Lato's goal, exploiting some chaos in the penalty area, gave them a platform for the second half. But Roberto knocked in the rebound after Mendonça hit a post, then repeated the trick, only more so, scoring after the Polish woodwork had been hit three times. Before that, Nelinho's wildly over-optimistic shooting at last had its reward, his free kick searing past Kukla. Dirceu, with his excellent left foot, had another good game. Zico went off injured before he had the chance to disappoint again.

Deyna and Italy's Scirea died in separate car crashes in the space of three days in 1989.

21 June 1978 – Cordiviola, Rosario – 37,326 – Robert Wurtz (FRA)

ARGENTINA **(2) 6**
Kempes 21, 49, Tarantini 43, Luque 50, 72, Houseman 67

PERU **(0) 0**

ARGENTINA Fillol, Olguín, Tarantini, Gallego [Miguel Ángel Oviedo 86], Galván, Passarella (c), Bertoni [Houseman 65], Omar Larrosa, Luque, Kempes, Ortiz.
PERU Quiroga, Manzo, Duarte, Roberto Rojas, Chumpitáz (c), Velásquez [Raúl Gorriti 52], Muñante, Cueto, Quesada, Cubillas, Oblitas.

The match kicked off after Brazil v Poland, so the hosts knew what they had to do: win by three goals while scoring at least four. A tall order, but at least the opposition was the least formidable so far. After the match, Brazilians muttered darkly about bribery and corruption, convinced that Quiroga, a naturalised Argentinian, had helped out the country of his birth – and recent allegations mention Argentinian aid worth £50 million finding its way into the Peruvian economy. But even without this sort of aid, a weak side might still have been overwhelmed by forces beyond their control. And if Peru did agree to sell the match, they went about it rather strangely, Muñante hitting a post early on, Quiroga making some desperate saves.

Kempes, now the man of the hour, went past Manzo to score the first, but the important goal was Tarantini's diving header from a corner. It was the only one he scored in an eventual 61 internationals, but as valuable as it was rare: Argentina could now start believing. Kempes volleyed the third after an exchange of passes in the area, Passarella headed Larrosa's cross back for Luque to fall forward and head in almost on the goal line (not offside), Houseman scored with his first touch, and Luque crashed in the sixth after another inter-passing bout of frightening intensity, small comfort for the death of his brother in a car crash during the tournament. The scoreline stopped Brazil reaching the Final despite remaining unbeaten in every match, but it was somehow the right one, on a remarkable, fervid night.

1978

GROUP B

	P	W	D	L	F	A	Pts
Argentina	3	2	1	0	8	0	5
Brazil	3	2	1	0	6	1	5
Poland	3	1	0	2	2	5	2
Peru	3	0	0	3	0	10	0

Argentina qualified for the Final, Brazil for the 3rd-Place Final.

3RD-PLACE FINAL

24 June 1978 – Antonio Liberti ('El Monumental'), Buenos Aires – 69,659 – Avraham Klein (ISR)

BRAZIL   (0) 2
Nelinho 64, Dirceu 71

ITALY   (1) 1
Causio 38

BRAZIL Leão (c), Nelinho, Rodrigues Neto, Batista, Oscar, Amaral, Gil [Reinaldo HT], Cerezo [Rivelino 64], Roberto Dinamite, Mendonça, Dirceu.
ITALY Zoff (c), Cuccureddu, Cabrini, Patrizio Sala, Gentile, Scirea, Causio, Aldo Maldera, Rossi, Antognoni [C Sala 78], Bettega.

Liberated from the need for points, Brazil were allowed to play like Brazil, which put their earlier efforts into context. Even Rivelino, in his last international, rolled back the years, and Italy matched them in a pleasing match, hitting the woodwork four times. Causio inclined his noble brow to convert Rossi's cross, Nelinho swerved an incredible shot round Zoff from the right-hand corner of the penalty box, and Dirceu volleyed into the same spot, which meant that the last four goals Zoff conceded in the tournament were all from long range. No blame attached. Two sad sights: Klein refereeing this after being scandalously kept out of the Final, and Bettega hitting the woodwork for the fourth time in the tournament. For both teams, a case of what might well have been. The Salas were brothers.

FINAL

25 June 1978 – Antonio Liberti ('El Monumental'), Buenos Aires – 71,483 – Sergio Gonella (ITA)

ARGENTINA   **(1) (1) 3**
Kempes 37, 104, Bertoni 115

HOLLAND   **(0) (1) 1**
Nanninga 82

ARGENTINA Fillol, Olguín, Tarantini, Gallego, Galván, Passarella (c), Bertoni, Ardiles [Larrosa 65], Luque, Kempes, Ortiz [Houseman 74].
HOLLAND Jongbloed, Krol (c), Brandts, Poortvliet, Jansen [Suurbier 72], Haan, R van de Kerkhof, Neeskens, Rep [Nanninga 59], W van de Kerkhof, Rensenbrink.

For the last time in the tournament, Argentina took full advantage of some lamentable refereeing, this time before the match had even started. After keeping the Dutch waiting for almost ten minutes, they suddenly protested about the protective sheath on René K's right forearm. Since he'd been wearing it for the last five matches without objection, a little crude gamesmanship was clearly involved. Worse, Gonella took the complaint seriously, leading van de Kerkhof off by the arm to have it covered with another, useless layer. Both sides now knew what kind of official they were dealing with (he'd been appointed on the casting vote of another Italian), Holland venting their spleen with savage early tackles on Bertoni and Ardiles.

When the game settled down, the Dutch began to exploit Argentina's vulnerability in the air, Rep twice coming close to scoring. First he rose unopposed to Haan's free kick only to head wide (first that miss in the 1974 Final, now this) then he cushioned a dreadful defensive header on his thigh before bringing a marvellous save from Fillol. Argentina would have been lost without him – and without Kempes, who opened the scoring after bursting between two defenders and stabbing the ball under Jongbloed on a carpet of torn toilet tissue. The movement had begun with Ardiles running past two men.

Holland dominated the second half but were frustrated by endless handballs, needless to say unpunished by bookings. In desperation they replaced the hapless Rep with Nanninga, big and direct, who headed the equaliser from René K's right-wing cross. Argentina's defence badly missed the height of Saint-Étienne's Osvaldo Piazza.

In injury time at the end of ninety minutes, the unkindest cut in any World Cup Final. Rensenbrink, running in that hunched way of his, fingers flicking behind him, got to Krol's long free kick deep in the left-hand side of the penalty area and prodded it past Fillol. The ball hit the near post and Holland's last chance was gone. In extra-time, Kempes stormed through again, beating two men. Jongbloed saved at his feet but the ball bounced off Kempes, who prodded it home as two more defenders collided in front of him. Then Bertoni scored gleefully from point-blank range after another cavalry charge and another lucky bounce. Holland were the first country to lose consecutive Finals, each time against the hosts. Tarantini was the only player to appear in a Final without being registered with a club.

The most obscene tableau was saved till the end, Passarella receiving the trophy from the hands of General Jorge Rafael Videla, which

1978

1930

1934

1938

1950

1954

1958

1962

1966

1970

1974

1978

1982

1986

1990

1994

1998

2002

2006

had the blood of thousands on them. The Mothers of the Plaza de Mayo, protesting day after day about the disappearance of their sons, were glad the World Cup had been staged in Argentina, but only because it brought them to the notice of the world. The tournament had been vivid and unforgettable, but then so is an electric cattle prod.

Rossi fixes it

Spain **1982**

1930

1934

1938

1950

1954

1958

1962

1966

1970

1974

1978

1982

1986

1990

1994

1998

2002

2006

Not for the first or last time, FIFA insisted on tampering with the format. Still trying to breed a successful cross between league and cup, they came up with even more of a camel. The top two teams in each group would go into four groups of three, the winners progressing to the semi-finals. Twenty-four countries instead of sixteen, including an increase in the number of finalists from Africa, Asia and Central America.

Of the teams at the other end of the scale, the champions Argentina came with the same coach and many of the same players from 1978, plus one special newcomer, the stocky bushy-haired Maradona, who'd been left out of the 1978 finals only because Menotti thought him too young and vulnerable at 17 (he'd first capped him at 16). Now he looked the world's greatest player since Cruyff or even Pelé, a target for Barcelona and every defender in the tournament.

West Germany, who'd thrown out the old wood, were the European champions and had won all eight qualifiers with a goal tally of 33-3. Rummenigge was now a front player of the highest class, and there were fearsome new defenders in Briegel, Stielike and Karlheinz Förster – but their blond young playmaker Bernd Schuster, the star of the European finals, was out injured.

Italy hadn't looked altogether convincing in qualifying, but at least Rossi was back after serving a suspension of less than two years for his involvement in a major match-fixing scandal. He'd yet to embed himself back in the team, Antognoni had only just recovered from a life-threatening skull fracture, and Bettega and Benetti were gone – but the defence was better than ever and the whole team had been together for four more years. Spain, whose national team rarely matched the success of their club sides, were cursed with unexceptional players just when their time came to host the tournament.

Three of the British Isles countries had qualified and the other two came close. The Republic of Ireland were unfortunate to finish a very close third in a strong group which saw Holland eliminated. Wales beat Czechoslovakia but were undone by a 2-2 draw with Iceland in Swansea, where the floodlights failed. England had made their fans ride a remarkable roller-coaster. Defeats in Romania and Switzerland were followed by a convincing win in Hungary and another defeat, most bonkers of all, in Norway ('Your boys took a helluva beating!'). But Switzerland won in Romania to let them through, after which their first-choice team won six matches in a row – though injuries to Brooking and the talismanic Keegan were a worry.

Northern Ireland, under their benign but pragmatic manager Billy Bingham, who'd played in the 1958 finals, came second in

1930
1934
1938
1950
1954
1958
1962
1966
1970
1974
1978

1982

1986
1990
1994
1998
2002
2006

a group won by Scotland, who'd replaced MacLeod with the unimpeachable figure of Jock Stein. Although the Scots scored only nine goals in eight qualifying games (the Irish scored six), their attack looked better than that and at last there was some organisation at the back.

But they were unlucky with the draw. Originally scheduled to meet Argentina in the opening match, they were moved to another group when FIFA realised there was no guarantee the South American countries would be kept apart. So Scotland found themselves drawn alongside a strong Soviet side and the hot favourites.

Brazil, under a new coach, were looking their old selves again, a very passable impersonation of the 1970 team: thin in defence, explosively brilliant everywhere else. They'd beaten England at Wembley, and in their last match before the finals thrashed the Republic of Ireland 7-0. The 'beautiful game' was back, and the rest of the field would be hoping to admire it at a distance for as long as possible.

So now you're going to believe us, we're going to win the Cup. After Paolo Rossi's third goal against Brazil, people have to take Italy's chances seriously.

1930
1934
1938
1950
1954
1958
1962
1966
1970
1974
1978
1982
1986
1990
1994
1998
2002
2006

GROUP 1

Cameroon, Italy (seeded), Peru, Poland.

14 June 1982 – Balaidos, Vigo – 22,000 – Michel Vautrot (FRA)

ITALY	0
POLAND	0

ITALY Dino Zoff (c), Claudio Gentile, Antonio Cabrini, Giampiero Marini, Fulvio Collovati, Gaetano Scirea, Bruno Conti, Marco Tardelli, Paolo Rossi, Giancarlo Antognoni, Francesco Graziani. *Enzo Bearzot.*
POLAND Józef Młynarczyk, Stefan Majewski, Paweł Janas, Władysław Żmuda (c), Jan Jałocha, Waldemar Matysik, Zbigniew Boniek, Andrzej Buncol, Grzegorz Lato, Andrzej Iwan [Marek Kusto 72], Włodek Smolarek. *Antoni Piechniczek.*

Now regarded as one of Italy's three substandard performances in the group, it was rather better than that. Some good moves from both sides, though Rossi wasn't quite there yet and Boniek (signed by Juventus and up against six of his future team mates) was playing too deep. Zoff, now 40, had a relatively quiet time in his 100th international.

15 June 1982 – Riazor, La Coruña – 15,000 – Franz Wöhrer (AUT)

CAMEROON	0
PERU	0

CAMEROON Thomas Nkono (c), Michel Kaham, Ephrem Mbom, Elie Onana, René Ndjeya, Ibrahim Aoudou, Emmanuel Kunde, Théophile Abega, Grégoire Mbida, Jacques Nguea [Paul Bahoken 72], Roger Milla [Jean-Pierre Tokoto 89]. *Jean Vincent (FRA).*

PERU Ramón Quiroga, Jaime Duarte, Toribio Díaz (c), Salvador Salguero, Jorge Olaechea, José Velásquez, César Cueto, Teófilo Cubillas [Gerónimo Barbadillo 56], Julio César Uribe, Germán Leguía [Guillermo La Rosa 56], Juan Carlos Oblitas. *'Tim' (Elba de Pádua Lima) (BRZ).*

Uribe had looked one of the best players in the world during the win in Paris six weeks earlier, subtle and intricate – but here he simply didn't show. Cameroon, on the other hand, were a minor revelation. Milla, with his gap-toothed grin and excellent control, was the most charismatic player on the pitch. When he took a return pass from Mbida and shot past Quiroga, the goal was disallowed, to his almost jovial disbelief. His original surname was Miller (some say Müller). Both coaches had played in previous finals: Vincent in 1954 and 1958, the 67-year-old Tim back in 1938.

18 June 1982 – Balaidos, Vigo – 25,000 – Walter Eschweiler (GER)

ITALY	(1)	1
Conti 19		
PERU	(0)	1
Díaz 85		

ITALY Zoff (c), Gentile, Cabrini, Marini, Collovati, Scirea, Conti, Tardelli, Rossi [Franco Causio HT], Antognoni, Graziani.
PERU Quiroga, Duarte, Díaz (c), Salguero, Olaechea, Velásquez, Cueto, Cubillas, Uribe [La Rosa 65], Barbadillo [Leguía 65], Oblitas.

Italy played less well this time but should still have won, against a team now clearly in decline. Conti, a new class act, turned his man and shot in off the bar from long range, but a deflected free kick (Italians call it a Collovati own goal) ended Peru's run of 493 minutes without a goal, a finals record until Bolivia in 1994.

19 June 1982 – Riazor, La Coruña – 12,000 – Alexis Ponnet (BEL)

CAMEROON 0

POLAND 0

CAMEROON Nkono (c), Kaham, Mbom, Onana, Ndjeya, Aoudou, Kunde, Abega, Mbida, Nguea [Tokoto HT], Milla.
POLAND Młynarczyk, Majewski, Janas, Żmuda (c), Jałocha, Andrzej Pałasz [Kusto 66], Boniek, Buncol, Lato, Iwan [Andrzej Szarmach 25], Smolarek.

Again Cameroon deserved the draw, though this time it needn't have been goalless. In the first half, Nkono had to save a fierce free kick from Szarmach and prevent an own goal by Kunde. In the second, several Cameroon players had shots at goal, and Milla should have scored in the last minute when he had only the keeper to beat.

22 June 1982 – Riazor, La Coruña – 16,000 – Mario Rubio Vázquez (MEX)

POLAND (0) 5
Smolarek 56, Lato 59, Boniek 61, Buncol 68, Ciołek 77

PERU (0) 1
La Rosa 83

POLAND Młynarczyk, Majewski, Janas, Żmuda (c), Jałocha [Marek Dziuba 27], Matysik, Janusz Kupcewicz, Buncol, Lato, Boniek, Smolarek [Włodek Ciołek 74].
PERU Quiroga, Duarte, Díaz (c), Salguero, Olaechea, Velásquez, Cueto, Cubillas [Uribe 50], La Rosa, Leguía, Oblitas [Barbadillo 50].

After a first half in keeping with the group so far, Peru left their floodgates open, Kupcewicz capitalising on a mistake by Velásquez to set up Smolarek, who finished a good move with a left-footed drive. Then Boniek headed the ball

on and Quiroga rushed headlong out of goal as in 1978, making it easy for Lato, balder but not much slower, to score his tenth finals goal. Boniek side-footed the third from a well-worked free kick, and the fourth was one of the best team goals of the tournament, Buncol and Boniek interpassing their way through. La Rosa's meaty shot brought him the goal his 1978 performances deserved, but it was a dismal end for Cubillas & Co.

23 June 1982 – Balaidos, Vigo – 17,000 – Bogdan Dochev (BUL)

CAMEROON (0) 1
Mbida 62

ITALY (0) 1
Graziani 61

CAMEROON Nkono (c), Kaham, Mbom, Onana, Ndjeya, Aoudou, Kunde, Abega, Mbida, Tokoto, Milla.
ITALY Zoff (c), Gentile, Cabrini, Tardelli, Collovati, Scirea, Gabriele Oriali, Conti, Rossi, Antognoni, Graziani.

In the last World Cup finals match without substitutes, Italy qualified without glory, by scoring one more goal than Cameroon, who were eliminated without losing a match. When Rossi sent in a good deep cross from the left, the agile Nkono slipped as Graziani's far-post header drifted over him. The Italians didn't have time to enjoy their cushion. Milla knocked the ball in, Aoudou got a slight touch with an attempted glancing header, and Mbida lifted the ball in. Then Zoff had to save from Kaham – but Italy deserved at least a draw: in the first half, Antognoni and Gentile missed clear chances and Nkono touched Collovati's header onto the bar. Cameroon were in the middle of a sequence of six consecutive draws, a world record at the time.

1930
1934
1938
1950
1954
1958
1962
1966
1970
1974
1978
1982
1986
1990
1994
1998
2002
2006

1930
1934
1938
1950
1954
1958
1962
1966
1970
1974
1978

GROUP 1

	P	W	D	L	F	A	Pts
Poland	3	1	2	0	5	1	4
Italy	3	0	3	0	2	2	3
Cameroon	3	0	3	0	1	1	3
Peru	3	0	2	1	2	6	2

Poland and Italy qualified for the second round.

GROUP 2

Algeria, Austria, Chile, West Germany (seeded).

16 June 1982 – Municipal ('El Molinón'), Gijón – 25,000 – Enrique Labó (PER)

ALGERIA (0) 2
Madjer 53, Belloumi 69

WEST GERMANY (0) 1
Rummenigge 67

ALGERIA Mehdi Cerbah, Chaabane Merzekane, Mahmoud Guendouz, Nourredine Kourichi, Faouzi Mansouri, Ali Fergani (c), Mustafa Dahleb, Lakhdar Belloumi, Rabah Madjer [Salah Larbes 88], Djamel Zidane [Tedj Bensaoula 64], Salah Assad. *Rachid Mekhloufi, with Mahiedine Khalef.*
WEST GERMANY Harald Schumacher, Manni Kaltz, Hans-Peter Briegel, Wolfgang Dremmler, Karlheinz Förster, Uli Stielike, Pierre Littbarski, Felix Magath [Klaus Fischer 83], Horst Hrubesch, Paul Breitner, Karl-Heinz Rummenigge (c). *Jupp Derwall.*

1986
1990
1994
1998
2002
2006

So what's so surprising? The win merely maintained Algeria's 100% record against West Germany, whom they'd beaten 2-0 in 1964. Seriously, the European champions were unrecognisable, especially in midfield,

where Breitner, for all his abilities, didn't provide enough creative backup for Magath. Rummenigge wasn't fully fit and Littbarski had a late goal disallowed.

But enough of them. Algeria's big names, two of the best players produced in North Africa, scored their goals. Madjer deflected the ball in after a run and shot by Belloumi, who then pushed Assad's left-wing cross into an empty net as an Algerian commentator spread the scorer's name over about fifty syllables. Rummenigge had equalised with a fierce shot from Magath's pass, but the Germans were already in danger of failing to reach the next stage for the first time since 1938. Embarrassment for Derwall ('We're so strong we'll win without problems'). Note the different ways of writing the first names of Förster and Rummenigge.

17 June 1982 – Carlos Tartiere, Oviedo – 22,000 – Juan Cardellino (URU)

AUSTRIA (1) 1
Schachner 22

CHILE (0) 0

AUSTRIA Fritz Koncilia, Bernd Krauss, Erich Obermayer (c), Josef Degeorgi [Ernst Baumeister 78], Bruno Pezzey, Roland Hattenberger, Reinhold Hintermaier, Herbert Prohaska, Heribert Weber [Gernot Jurtin 80], Hans Krankl, Walter Schachner. *Georg Schmidt.*
CHILE Mario Osbén, Antonio Lizardo Garrido, René Valenzuela, Elías Figueroa (c), Vladimir Bigorra, Eduardo Bonvallet, Rodolfo Dubó, Miguel Ángel Neira [Manuel Rojas 73], Gustavo Moscoso [Miguel Ángel Gamboa 66], Patricio Yáñez, Carlos Caszely. *Luis Santibáñez.*

For the first time, two countries had qualified from most of the European groups, so Austria were here despite losing twice to West Germany. Meanwhile Chile had two wins over the reigning South American champions. But the arithmetic didn't hold up here: Austria were slightly the better side in a drab match. The great Figueroa, a veteran of 1966, was still a force at centre-half, so there was only one goal, Schachner's slow-motion header. Four minutes later, Caszely, who'd been sent off in Chile's first match in 1974, missed a penalty, the only player to achieve this unenviable double in World Cup finals.

---

20 June 1982 – Municipal ('El Molinón'), Gijón – 40,000 – Bruno Galler (SWI)

WEST GERMANY **(1) 4**
Rummenigge 9, 57, 67, Reinders 82

CHILE **(0) 1**
Moscoso 89

WEST GERMANY Schumacher, Kaltz, Briegel, Dremmler, K Förster, Stielike, Littbarski [Uwe Reinders 80], Magath, Hrubesch, Breitner [Lothar Matthäus 61], Rummenigge (c).
CHILE Osbén, Garrido, Valenzuela, Figueroa (c), Bigorra, Bonvallet, Dubó, Mario Soto [Juan Carlos Letelier HT], Moscoso, Gamboa [Neira 67], Yáñez.

More like the Germans we used to know. Breitner, back from international retirement after more than five years, had a better game, and Rummenigge looked every inch the European Footballer of the Year – though he and his team were helped on their way by a goalkeeping error. Littbarski, one of the few successes against Algeria, came inside and Rummenigge almost took the ball off him to hit a shot that went under Osbén's body. Then Rummenigge applied a powerful header to another Littbarski cross, the ball going in off a post after Osbén got a hand to it. Rummenigge completed his hat-trick with a velvety touch from Magath's return pass, then helped Hrubesch make the fourth goal for the

unexceptional Reinders. By the time Moscoso beat Kaltz before scoring, Chile had been out of the tournament for some time.

---

21 June 1982 – Carlos Tartiere, Oviedo – 22,000 – Tony Boskovic (AUS)

AUSTRIA **(0) 2**
Schachner 56, Krankl 67

ALGERIA **(0) 0**

AUSTRIA Koncilia, Krauss, Obermayer (c), Degeorgi, Pezzey, Hattenberger, Hintermaier, Prohaska [Weber 81], Krankl, Baumeister [Kurt Welzl HT], Schachner.
ALGERIA Cerbah, Merzekane, Guendouz, Kourichi, Mansouri, Fergani (c), Dahleb [Djamel Tlemcani 75], Belloumi [Bensaoula 66], Madjer, Zidane, Assad.

Without appearing a dominant force, Austria made Algeria's earlier win look a one-off, shackling the influential Fergani, glad that Belloumi was off form. So was Krankl, but his spectacular left-footer from outside the area was enough to seal the match. Schachner's goal came from a loose ball and he had a shot kicked off the line by the '*gigantesco*' Kourichi as the Algerians lost their first-half momentum.

1982

---

24 June 1982 – Carlos Tartiere, Oviedo – 18,000 – Rómulo Méndez (GUA)

ALGERIA **(3) 3**
Assad 8, 31, Bensaoula 34

CHILE **(0) 2**
Neira pen 60, Letelier 74

ALGERIA Cerbah, Merzekane, Guendouz, Kourichi, Mansouri [Dahleb 73], Fergani (c), Larbes, Bensaoula, Abdelmajid Bourrebou [Hocine Yahi 31], Madjer, Assad.
CHILE Osbén, Mario Galindo, Valenzuela, Figueroa (c), Bigorra, Bonvallet [Soto 38], Dubó, Neira, Moscoso, Yáñez, Caszely [Letelier 54].

1930 1934 1938 1950 1954 1958 1962 1966 1970 1974 1978 1986 1990 1994 1998 2002 2006

Algeria became the first African country to win two matches in the finals but ultimately had only themselves to blame for not reaching the next round. Even without Belloumi, who'd pulled a muscle against Austria, they dominated the first half with their speed. Bensaoula rejected the chance of a shot in favour of feeding the better-placed Assad, who then dribbled through for the second. Bensaoula made it 3-0 from outside the penalty area, and Madjer hit the woodwork twice, once with a 'prodezza balistica'.

But Algeria then conceded two important goals, the first from a penalty for Kourichi's foul on Yánez, the second after a fine run by Letelier that took him round the keeper. The score might have finished as 3-3 (Larbes brought Yánez down in the area) or 4-2 (Assad hit a post). If it had stayed 3-0, only a 4-3 win or better would have saved West Germany. The 35-year-old Figueroa, one of the greatest central defenders of all time, was winning his last cap.

25 June 1982 – Municipal ('El Molinón'), Gijón – 41,000 – Bob Valentine (SCO)

1982

WEST GERMANY (1) 1
Hrubesch 11

AUSTRIA (0) 0

WEST GERMANY Schumacher, Kaltz, Briegel, Dremmler, K Förster, Stielike, Littbarski, Magath, Hrubesch [Fischer 69], Breitner, Rummenigge (c) [Matthäus 67].
AUSTRIA Koncilia, Krauss, Obermayer (c), Degeorgi, Pezzey, Hattenberger, Hintermaier, Prohaska, Weber, Krankl, Schachner.

Scandalous, they said – but there's no evidence that the two teams agreed the result beforehand. Morality aside (as always), why would Austria want to see a strong side like West Germany go through? The truth seems to be that the Germans needed the result, got an early goal (Hrubesch almost inadvertently putting in another Littbarski cross), then Austria didn't want to risk the three-goal defeat that would have eliminated them. Still, it was very hard on Algeria, whose fans waved banknotes through the wire fencing in tearful fury. Penny for their thoughts when West Germany reached the Final.

GROUP 2

	P	W	D	L	F	A	Pts
West Germany	3	2	0	1	6	3	4
Austria	3	2	0	1	3	1	4
Algeria	3	2	0	1	5	5	4
Chile	3	0	0	3	3	8	0

West Germany and Austria qualified for the second round.

GROUP 3

Argentina (seeded), Belgium, El Salvador, Hungary.

13 June 1982 – Camp Nou, Barcelona – 95,000 – Vojtěch Christov (CZE)

BELGIUM (0) 1
Vandenbergh 63

ARGENTINA (0) 0

BELGIUM Jean-Marie Pfaff, Eric Gerets (c), Marc Baecke, Luc Millecamps, Maurits De Schrijver, Guy Vandersmissen, Ludo Coeck, Frankie Vercauteren, Jan Ceulemans, Alex Czerniatynski, Erwin Vandenbergh. *Guy Thys.*

ARGENTINA Ubaldo Fillol, Jorge Olguín, Alberto Tarantini, Américo Gallego, Luis Galván, Daniel Passarella (c), Daniel Bertoni, Osvaldo Ardiles, Mario Kempes, Diego Maradona, Ramón Díaz [Jorge Valdano 63]. *César Luis Menotti.*

Nine of the Argentinian starting line-up had played in 1978, but the blend didn't work against the gritty Belgians, European runners-up two years previously. They held Maradona in check and Vandenbergh converted their best chance – eventually. When Vercauteren's long ball put him clear, he and Fillol went into a strange little dance of hesitation before the shot finally came, the first goal in an opening match for twenty years. Ten minutes later Maradona hit the bar with a free kick – but Argentina's performance was as worrying for them as the result.

British sources usually refer to it as the Nou Camp (like the León stadium in 1986), but Catalans know it as the Camp Nou (pronounced Camp Now).

15 June 1982 – Nuevo Estadio, Elche – 6,000 – Ibrahim Youssef Al-Doy (BHR)

HUNGARY   **(3) 10**
Nyilasi 4, 83, Pölöskei 11, Fazekas 24, 55, Tóth 51, Kiss 69, 73, 77, Szentes 71

EL SALVADOR   **(0) 1**
Ramírez Zapata 65

HUNGARY Ferenc Mészáros, László Bálint, Győző Martos, József Tóth II, Imre Garaba, Sándor Müller [Lázár Szentes 69], Tibor Nyilasi (c), Sándor Sallai, András Törőcsik [László Kiss 57], László Fazekas, Gábor Pölöskei. *Kálmán Mészöly.*
EL SALVADOR Luis Guevara Mora, Mario Castillo, Francisco Jovel, Jaime Rodríguez, Carlos Recinos, José Luis Rugamas [Luis Ramírez Zapata 28], Joaquín Alonso Ventura [Ramón Fagoaga 75], Francisco Hernández, Jorge González, Norberto Huezo (c), José María Rivas. *Mauricio 'Pipo' Rodríguez.*

El Salvador scored their only finals goal – but the exchange rate was extortionate. Hungary racked up a record total, including seven goals in one half, another first. After Törőcsik had somehow failed to dip his bread in, Kiss hit the fastest finals hat-trick and the only one by a substitute.

He scored his first goal with a low shot past two players after he'd been allowed to turn in the box when a corner was hit low to him; his second was a neat lob after being put clear on the left, his third a ground shot in off a covering defender after Guevara Mora had dived to push out a cross. Pölöskei broke a tackle on the left before hitting a curving cross-shot; Tóth beat a defender on the goal line and flicked the ball in at the unmanned near post; Fazekas scored from distance then low at the near post after cutting in from the wing; Szentes scuffed a low cross out from under his feet into an open goal; and Nyilasi was unmarked when he headed the first and last. Most of Hungary's goals came from attacks down the left, while Ramírez Zapata, to wild celebrations, converted Huezo's short through ball from close range.

According to Mészöly, the scoreline gave Hungary half a goal advantage over Argentina; a draw would be enough.

18 June 1982 – José Rico Pérez, Alicante – 32,093 – Belaid Lacarne (ALG)

ARGENTINA   **(2) 4**
Bertoni 27, Maradona 28, 57, Ardiles 61

HUNGARY   **(0) 1**
Pölöskei 76

ARGENTINA Fillol, Olguín, Tarantini [Juan Barbas 51], Gallego, Galván, Passarella (c), Bertoni, Ardiles, Kempes, Maradona, Valdano [Gabriel Calderón 25].
HUNGARY Mészáros, Bálint, J Tóth II, Martos [Fazekas HT], Garaba, József Varga, Nyilasi (c), Sallai, Kiss [Szentes 63], Tibor Rab, Pölöskei.

1930
1934
1938
1950
1954
1958
1962
1966
1970
1974
1978

1982

1986
1990
1994
1998
2002
2006

A one-man *tour de force*. Displaying the right stuff after his frustrations against Belgium, Maradona won the match on his own, all muscular brilliance and strut, like Pelé but angrier. A switch in formation helped, Kempes playing deeper to allow Maradona to stay up front.

Hungary seemed to sense what was coming. Nervous from the start, they might have been four goals down before Bertoni scored when Passarella headed down a Kempes free kick. Then Bertoni's shot hit Mészáros and the rebound was put in by Maradona, who almost got another goalscoring touch soon afterwards. In the second half, he accelerated between two defenders before shooting the third. Finally even Ardiles got in on the act, running from halfway before finding Olguín, whose low shot hit a post and the goalkeeper's head before Ardiles put it in from close range. Pölöskei dummied his way through to score, but it had stopped being a contest by then. Some consolation for a country who'd just lost Port Stanley back to the British.

---

19 June 1982 – Nuevo Estadio, Elche – 6,000 – Malcolm Moffatt (NIR)

BELGIUM (1) 1
Coeck 18

EL SALVADOR (0) 0

BELGIUM Pfaff, Gerets (c), Baecke, L Millecamps, Walter Meeuws, Vandersmissen [François Van der Elst HT], Coeck, Vercauteren, Vandenbergh, Czerniatynski, Ceulemans [Wilfried Van Moer 80].
EL SALVADOR Guevara Mora, Francisco Osorto [Miguel Ángel Díaz HT], Jovel, Rodríguez, Recinos, Fagoaga, Ventura, Ramírez Zapata, González, Huezo (c), Rivas.

It looks a very unlikely scoreline, but even El Salvador didn't concede ten goals every game, and Belgium lacked the width in attack to break down a packed defence. Even their goal was unsatisfactory, the 20-year-old Guevara

Mora making no attempt to reach Coeck's very long shot. Van der Elst, the brother of Leo (1986), was a different player from Franky (1986–98).

---

22 June 1982 – Nuevo Estadio, Elche – 22,000 – Clive White (ENG)

BELGIUM (0) 1
Czerniatynski 76

HUNGARY (1) 1
Varga 27

BELGIUM Pfaff, Gerets (c) [Gérard Plessers 62], L Millecamps, Baecke, Meeuws, Vandersmissen [Van Moer HT], Coeck, Vercauteren, Vandenbergh, Czerniatynski, Ceulemans.
HUNGARY Mészáros, Martos, Attila Kerekes, Garaba, Varga, Müller [Sallai 68], Nyilasi (c), Fazekas, Törőcsik, Kiss [Ferenc Csongrádi 71], Pölöskei.

Hungary picked four strikers, but it was a defender who scored their goal, Varga running into the penalty area to beat Pfaff with a rising left-footer. But Belgium scraped the draw they needed when the rugged Ceulemans broke two tackles on the right before finding Czerniatynski. Hungary, who'd won their qualifying group despite losing twice to England, fell very flat, especially Törőcsik and the style guru Nyilasi, who headed slackly wide near the end.

---

23 June 1982 – José Rico Pérez, Alicante – 18,000 – Luis Barrancos (BOL)

ARGENTINA (1) 2
Passarella pen 23, Bertoni 54

EL SALVADOR (0) 0

ARGENTINA Fillol, Olguín, Tarantini, Gallego, Galván, Passarella (c), Bertoni [Díaz 68], Ardiles, Kempes, Maradona, Calderón [Santiago Santamaría 81].

EL SALVADOR Guevara Mora, Osorto [Díaz 32], Jovel, Rodríguez, Recinos, Fagoaga, Ventura [Mauricio Alfaro 80], Ramírez Zapata, González, Huezo (c), Rivas.

More credit to the minnows, who went behind to a penalty awarded for a challenge by Jovel and what looked like a dive by Calderón, who was no great improvement on Díaz. Passarella scored from the spot for the tenth and last time in international football, a world record before the arrival of Christo Stoichkov. Kempes had hit the bar and Guevara Mora saved Passarella's typically hard-hit free kick. Bertoni cut in to score with his left foot from the edge of the penalty area – but Argentina had hardly looked like world champions and were now in the most difficult second-round group.

GROUP 3

	P	W	D	L	F	A	Pts
Belgium	3	2	1	0	3	1	5
Argentina	3	2	0	1	6	2	4
Hungary	3	1	1	1	12	6	3
El Salvador	3	0	0	3	1	13	0

Belgium and Argentina qualified for the second round.

GROUP 4

Czechoslovakia, England (seeded), France, Kuwait.

16 June 1982 – San Mamés, Bilbao – 44,172 – António Garrido (POR)

ENGLAND   (1) 3
Robson 27 sec, 67, Mariner 83

FRANCE   (1) 1
Soler 25

ENGLAND Peter Shilton, Mick Mills (c), Kenny Sansom [Phil Neal 90], Bryan Robson, Terry Butcher, Phil Thompson, Steve Coppell, Ray Wilkins, Paul Mariner, Trevor Francis, Graham Rix. *Ron Greenwood.*

FRANCE Jean-Luc Ettori, Patrick Battiston, Max Bossis, René Girard, Christian Lopez, Marius Trésor, Dominique Rocheteau [Didier Six 71], Alain Giresse, Jean-François Larios [Jean Tigana 74], Michel Platini (c), Gérard Soler. *Michel Hidalgo.*

Coppell took a throw-in on the right, Butcher's back-header found Robson utterly alone in front of goal, and a gymnastic left-footed volley forced the ball past Ettori. England were back in the World Cup finals for the first time in twelve years, and how. Less than half a minute gone.

But the goal didn't give them the expected momentum. The defence, with Coppell and Rix playing deep on the flanks, was solid enough, but Brooking's injury and Hoddle's absence left them short of a playmaker (Wilkins was already crabbing the ball sideways). Soler, sent clear on the left by Giresse, scored with a smart cross-shot, and France had the better of things for half the match, making light of any dip in morale caused by a liaison between Larios and Mrs Platini.

What saved England was the drive and energy of Robson (at last an English version of Neeskens and Tardelli) and errors in the French defence. When Francis crossed from the right, Robson leapt up to score with an athletic header, but little Ettori had come too

GOALS IN A MATCH (ONE TEAM)

10-1	Hungary	1982	v El Salvador
9-0	Hungary	1954	v South Korea
9-0	Yugoslavia	1974	v Zaire

1930 1934 1938 1950 1954 1958 1962 1966 1970 1974 1978 **1982** 1986 1990 1994 1998 2002 2006

far off his line. Then Trésor, of all people, mis-kicked a shot by Francis to let in Mariner behind him. The jury was still out on both teams.

---

17 June 1982 – José Zorrilla, Valladolid – 12,000 – Benjamin Dwomoh (GHA)

CZECHOSLOVAKIA   **(1) 1**
Panenka pen 21

KUWAIT   **(0) 1**
Al-Dakhil 58

CZECHOSLOVAKIA Zdeněk Hruška, Jozef Barmoš, Ladislav Jurkemik, Jan Fiala, Jozef Kukučka, Jan Berger, Antonín Panenka, Tomás Křiž [Premysl Bičovský 63], Petr Janečka [Vlastimil Petržela 69], Zdeněk Nehoda (c), Ladislav Vízek. *Jozef Vengloš.*
KUWAIT Ahmad Al-Tarabulsi, Naeem Sa'ad Mubarak, Mahboub Jum'ah Mubarak, Abdullah Mayouf, Walid Al-Jasem Mubarak, Abdullah Al-Buloushi, Sa'ad Al-Houti (c), Mohammed Ahmad Karam [Fathi Kamil Marzouq 57], Faisal Al-Dakhil, Jasem Yacoub, Abdul Aziz Al-Anbari. *Carlos Alberto Parreira (BRZ).*

Czechoslovakia, who'd qualified despite winning only half their eight matches, were as drippy as expected: Nehoda losing his sharpness, Panenka more idle than ever. The penalty was awarded for a foul, if that's what it was, by Mayouf on Vízek. Kuwait, convincing winners of the Asia-Oceania group, were busy and confident, their equaliser a beauty, Al-Dakhil's flying long shot clipping the bar on its way in.

---

20 June 1982 – San Mamés, Bilbao – 44,182 – Charles Corver (HOL)

ENGLAND   **(0) 2**
Francis 63, Barmoš o.g. 66

CZECHOSLOVAKIA   **(0) 0**

ENGLAND Shilton, Mills (c), Sansom, Robson [Glenn Hoddle HT], Butcher, Thompson, Coppell, Wilkins, Mariner, Francis, Rix.
CZECHOSLOVAKIA Stanislav Seman [Karel Stromšík 75], Barmoš, Jurkemik, Fiala, Rostislav Vojácek, Libor Radimec, Pavel Chaloupka, Berger, Vízek, Nehoda (c), Janečka [Marián Masný 78].

Again England were solid but uninventive, again they were gifted two goals. Seman dropped a corner straight in front of Francis and wasn't capped again, and Barmoš turned Mariner's attempted through-pass just inside a post. Mariner, who'd scored in each of his previous five internationals, tried to claim it, but there are limits. England were already through, but they'd need more from their midfield against the stronger teams.

---

21 June 1982 – José Zorrilla, Valladolid – 30,043 – Miroslav Stupar (USR)

FRANCE   **(2) 4**
Genghini 31, Platini 43, Six 48, Bossis 89

KUWAIT   **(0) 1**
Al-Buloushi 75

FRANCE Ettori, Manuel Amoros, Bossis, Gérard Janvion [Christian Lopez 59], Trésor, Giresse, Bernard Genghini, Platini (c) [Girard 81], Soler, Bernard Lacombe, Six.
KUWAIT Al-Tarabulsi, Naeem Sa'ad, Mahboub, Mayouf, Al-Jasem [Humoud Al-Shemmari 76], Al-Buloushi, Al-Houti (c), Karam [Fathi Kamil HT], Al-Dakhil, Yacoub, Al-Anbari.

Kuwait may well have fancied their chances, but the French midfield was too talented for them. Genghini curled in a free kick, then Giresse sent Platini clear to celebrate his 27th birthday by pushing the ball past the keeper. Platini's high ball put Six in to chest down and volley in spectacularly from sixteen yards – then, in one of the tournament's memorable moments, Giresse had a goal disallowed. The Kuwaiti defence,

YOUNGEST PLAYERS

yrs	days			
17	41	Norman Whiteside	NIR	1982
17	99	Samuel Eto'o	CAM	1998
17	101	Femi Opabunmi	NGA	2002
17	185	Salomon Olembe	CAM	1998
17	235	Pelé	BRZ	1958
17	244	Bartholomew Ogbeche	NGA	2002
17	353	Rigobert Song	CAM	1994

Some publications claim Samuel Eto'o was 17 when he played for Cameroon in the 1998 finals. All authoritative sources say he was a year older.

hearing a whistle in the crowd, hesitated then protested. Their general manager Sheikh Fahd Al-Sabah, resplendent in his robes, called the players off the pitch. Stupar wrongly disallowed the goal (and another by Al-Anbari) and didn't referee another finals match. Bossis made up for it by scoring from a tight angle at close range.

---

24 June 1982 – José Zorrilla, Valladolid – 28,000 – Paolo Casarin (ITA)

CZECHOSLOVAKIA **(0) 1**
Panenka pen 84

FRANCE **(0) 1**
Six 66

FRANCE Ettori, Amoros, Bossis, Janvion, Trésor, Giresse, Genghini, Platini (c), Soler [Girard 88], Lacombe [Alain Couriol 70], Six.
CZECHOSLOVAKIA Stromšík, Barmoš, Fiala, Vojáček, Radimec, Nehoda (c), Bičovský, František Štambacher, Janečka [Panenka 70], Vízek, Kříž [Masný 31].
SENT OFF: Vízek 87.

In the very last minute, Ettori committed his latest blunder of a miserable tournament and

Amoros had to head off the line. But France deserved the draw they needed against a side who contributed nothing to the competition and went out gracelessly, Vízek getting himself sent off for fouling Soler. When Lacombe's shot was blocked by Stromšík, Six put the ball into an empty net from two yards out. Vízek won another penalty after a challenge by Bossis. Panenka and Masný, important players when Czechoslovakia won the European Championship in 1976, weren't capped again.

---

25 June 1982 – San Mamés, Bilbao – 31,000 – Gilberto Aristizábal (COL)

ENGLAND **(1) 1**
Francis 27

KUWAIT **(0) 0**

ENGLAND Shilton, Neal, Mills (c), Hoddle, Steve Foster, Thompson, Coppell, Wilkins, Mariner, Francis, Rix.
KUWAIT Al-Tarabulsi, Naeem Sa'ad, Mahboub, Mayouf, Al-Jasem [Al-Shemmari 75], Al-Buloushi, Al-Houti (c), Fathi Kamil, Youssef Al-Suwayed, Al-Dakhil, Al-Anbari.

Yes, no problem, though it was just as well that Kuwait weren't an attacking force. Hoddle's

GROUP 4

	P	W	D	L	F	A	Pts
England	3	3	0	0	6	1	6
France	3	1	1	1	6	5	3
Czechoslovakia	3	0	2	1	2	4	2
Kuwait	3	0	1	2	2	6	1

England and France qualified for the second round.

1930
1934
1938
1950
1954
1958
1962
1966
1970
1974
1978
1982
1986
1990
1994
1998
2002
2006

1930

1934

1938

1950

1954

1958

1962

1966

1970

1974

1978

1982

1986

1990

1994

1998

2002

2006

many admirers had to admit he didn't really take his chance, but Francis, who looked sharp in the group matches, scored with a low cross-shot after exchanging passes with Mariner following Shilton's long punt. Al-Houti and the 35-year-old Al-Tarabulsi, both impressive, weren't capped again.

GROUP 5

Honduras, Northern Ireland, Spain (seeded), Yugoslavia.

16 June 1982 – Luis Casanova, Valencia – 49,562 – Arturo Ithurralde (ARG)

HONDURAS	**(1) 1**
Zelaya 8	
SPAIN	**(0) 1**
López Ufarte pen 65	

HONDURAS Julio César Arzú, César Gutiérrez, Jaime Villegas, Anthony Costly, José Fernando Bulnes, Ramón Maradiaga (c), Gilberto (Yearwood), Héctor Zelaya, Prudencio Norales [Carlos Caballero 68], Porfirio Betancourt, José Roberto Figueroa. *'Chelato Ucles' (José de la Paz Herrera).*
SPAIN Luis Arkonada (c), José Camacho, Rafael Gordillo, Joaquín (Alonso) [José Sánchez HT], Miguel Tendillo, José Alexanko, Miguel Alonso, Jesús Zamora, Jesús Satrústegui, Roberto López Ufarte, 'Juanito' (Juan Gómez) [Enrique Saura HT]. *José Santamaría (URU).*

The hosts against the least fancied team in the group: we're allowed to make comparisons with bullrings. But Spain were whistled off at the end.

It's not that they were downright bad (the goalkeeper and defence were among the best in Europe), just lacking any great players up front. Juanito, tricky and hot-tempered, did little, and Satrústegui was no great finisher. Honduras were well organised, took the lead when Zelaya took a return pass and shouldered Joaquín aside, and had chances to double it. Arzú in goal, Costly at centre-half, and Gilberto in midfield were their stars. The penalty was given for a clumsy challenge and what looked like dives by two different players! One English paper had its headline already prepared: Manuel Labour. Norales is the correct spelling (not Morales).

17 June 1982 – Municipal ('La Romareda'), Zaragoza – 18,000 – Erik Fredriksson (SWE)

NORTHERN IRELAND	**0**
YUGOSLAVIA	**0**

NORTHERN IRELAND Pat Jennings, Jimmy Nicholl, Mal Donaghy, David McCreery, Chris Nicholl, John McClelland, Gerry Armstrong, Martin O'Neill (c), Billy Hamilton, Sammy McIlroy, Norman Whiteside. *Billy Bingham.*
YUGOSLAVIA Dragan Pantelić, Nikola Jovanović, Milos Hrstić, Velimir Zajec, Nenad Stojković, Ivan Gudelj, Vladimir Petrović, Edhem Šljivo, Ivo Šurjak (c), Safet Sušić, Zlatko Vujović. *Miljan Miljanić.*

Northern Ireland, in the finals for the first time since 1958, set out their stall for a draw, and achieved it without too much strain, O'Neill and McIlroy were talented and careful in midfield; the pace of McClelland was invaluable alongside Chris Nicholl; and Whiteside, a strongly built 17-year-old, made an impressive debut. Yugoslavia had so many players with clubs abroad that Miljanić hadn't bothered to arrange any friendlies since December, an approach which smacked of exasperation (and didn't work).

20 June 1982 – Luis Casanova, Valencia – 50,000 – Henning Lund Sørensen (DEN)

SPAIN **(1) 2**
Juanito pen 14, Saura 66

YUGOSLAVIA **(1) 1**
Gudelj 10

SPAIN Arkonada (c), Camacho, Gordillo, M Alonso, Tendillo, Alexanko, Sánchez [Saura 63], Zamora, Satrústegui ['Quini' (Enrique Castro) 63], López Ufarte, Juanito.
YUGOSLAVIA Pantelić, Jovanović (Vahid Halilhodžić 74], Zlatko Krmpotić, Stojković, Zajec, Gudelj, Vujović [Milos Šestić 83], Petrović, Sušić, Šljivo, Šurjak (c).

Whatever else Spain were going to lack in this tournament, it wasn't refereeing generosity. Their latest penalty was awarded for a foul on Alonso by Zajec, who was careful to trip his man outside the area, as seen on TV. Even then Spain needed a refereeing top-up, Juanito scoring with the retake after López Ufarte put the original kick wide. Gudelj headed in a Petrović free kick, but Saura scored the winner from a pass by the other substitute Quini. Relief around the stadium, but it was Spain's only win in the tournament.

21 June 1982 – Municipal ('La Romareda'), Zaragoza – 15,000 – Chan Tam-Sun (HKG)

HONDURAS **(0) 1**
Laing 60

NORTHERN IRELAND **(1) 1**
Armstrong 10

HONDURAS Arzú, Gutiérrez, Villegas, Costly, José Luis Cruz, Maradiaga (c), Gilberto, Zelaya, Norales [Tony Laing 58], Betancourt, Figueroa.
NORTHERN IRELAND Jennings, J Nicholl, Donaghy, McCreery, C Nicholl, McClelland, Armstrong, M O'Neill (c) [Patrick Joseph 'Felix' Healy 77], Hamilton, McIlroy, Whiteside [Noel Brotherston 65].

After the alleged responses of the two squads to their opening results, an Italian daily billed the match as the Irish, assiduous in discotheques, versus Honduras, assiduous in church. Yawn.

Bingham, budgeting for four points, expected two of them here, and seemed likely to get them when McIlroy hit the bar with a free kick, Chris Nicholl headed the rebound against the bar, and Armstrong nodded in from less than a yard. But again Honduras showed admirable resilience. The 37-year-old Jennings made a good save from a close-range header but couldn't keep out Laing's ferocious near-post header from the subsequent corner. Healy was the only player to appear in a finals match while with an Irish club (Coleraine).

24 June 1982 – Municipal ('La Romareda'), Zaragoza – 12,000 – Gastón Castro (CHI)

YUGOSLAVIA **(0) 1**
Petrović pen 87

HONDURAS **(0) 0**

YUGOSLAVIA Pantelić, Jovanović [Halilhodžić HT], Krmcotić, Stojković, Zajec, Gudelj, Vujović [Šestić 60], Petrović, Šurjak (c), Sušić, Šljivo.
HONDURAS Arzú, Domingo Drummond, Villegas, Costly, Bulnes, Maradiaga (c), Gilberto, Zelaya, Cruz [Laing 65], Betancourt, Figueroa.
SENT OFF: Gilberto 88.

Really tough on Honduras, who again looked the equal of the Europeans. After missing at least two good chances, they were beaten by another harsh penalty (for a challenge by Villegas on Šestić), and had their best player sent off for an off-the-ball incident. The result left Northern Ireland needing a win or a high-scoring draw against the hosts to survive.

25 June 1982 – Luis Casanova, Valencia – 49,562 –
Héctor Ortiz (PAR)

NORTHERN IRELAND   **(0) 1**
Armstrong 47

SPAIN   **(0) 0**

NORTHERN IRELAND Jennings, J Nicholl, Donaghy,
McCreery, C Nicholl, McClelland, Armstrong, M O'Neill
(c), Hamilton, McIlroy [Tommy Cassidy 50], Whiteside
[Sammy Nelson 73].
SPAIN Arkonada (c), Camacho, Gordillo, M Alonso,
Tendillo, Alexanko, Sánchez, López Ufarte [Ricardo
Gallego 78], Satrústegui [Quini HT], Saura, Juanito.
SENT OFF: Donaghy 61.

Sheer *Boy's Own*. Arguably the best performance by a British team in any World Cup,
admittedly against a substandard team without
its playmaker (Zamora) – but one reinforced
by a referee who hadn't taken charge of an
international for two years. The crowd should
also have been Spain's ally, but Bingham had
gauged its mood: 'Intimidating – but they also
put pressure on their own team.' Northern
Ireland defended coolly but needed a goal,
which they got when Hamilton brushed
Tendillo aside on the way to the right-hand
goal line and pulled the ball back low.
Arkonada, once the best keeper in Europe,
could only palm it straight to Armstrong, who
fired it back under him.

After that, Rorke's Drift – but the Irish had
been well briefed. Stay on your feet when the
ball's in the penalty area, don't give the referee
any excuse outside it. They gave him only one,
a push on Camacho's neck making Donaghy
the first British player to be sent off in a finals
match – this while the Spaniards were hardly
observing the niceties. Jennings, idiosyncratic
and brilliant, cleverly avoided the possibility of
a penalty by flipping the ball over Juanito's
head, and in the end Spain were happy to settle
for a 1-0 defeat: another goal would have eliminated them. Northern Ireland couldn't have
picked a better time, a more vibrant night, to
record their only win over Spain.

GROUP 5

	P	W	D	L	F	A	Pts
Northern Ireland	3	1	2	0	2	1	4
Spain	3	1	1	1	3	3	3
Yugoslavia	3	1	1	1	2	2	3
Honduras	3	0	2	1	2	3	2

*Northern Ireland and Spain qualified for the
second round.*

GROUP 6

Brazil (seeded),
New Zealand, Scotland,
USSR.

14 June 1982 – Ramón Sánchez Pizjuán, Seville –
50,000 – Augusto Lamo Castillo (SPA)

BRAZIL   **(0) 2**
Sócrates 75, Éder 87

USSR   **(1) 1**
Bal 34

BRAZIL Waldir Peres, Leandro (Souza), Leovegildo
Júnior, Paulo Roberto Falcão, Oscar (Bernardi),
'Luizinho' (Luiz Ferreira), Dirceu (Guimarães) [Paulo
Isidoro (de Jesus) HT], Sócrates (de Souza) (c),
'Serginho' (Sérgio Bernardino), 'Zico' (Arthur Antunes
Coimbra), Éder (de Assis). *Telê Santana.*
USSR Renat Dasayev, Tengiz Sulakvelidze, Anatoly
Demyanenko, Sergei Baltacha, Aleksandr Chivadze (c),
Vladimir Bessonov, Andrei Bal, Yuri Gavrilov [Yuri
Susloparov 74], Vitaly Daraselia, Ramaz Shengalia
[Sergei Andreyev 88], Oleg Blokhin. *Konstantin Beskov.*

This USSR side was less than the sum of its parts, all of them international class or better – but it matched the favourites for most of the match and took the lead with a goal which showed that this Brazilian team contained another obligatory ingredient from 1970: a dreadful goalkeeper. The ball was moved left to right across the Brazilian penalty area for Bal to shoot from thirty yards. The balding Waldir had once been voted Brazil's player of the year, but that was back in 1975 and he now stood stiff-legged and let the ball in off his shin. A beauty.

It took Brazil a long time to get back on terms, but it was worth the anxious wait. The Soviets had three attempts at clearing their lines but sent the ball straight to the lanky bearded Sócrates, who sidestepped twice to the right before unleashing a heatseeker into the top left-hand corner. The winner was even better, Paulo Isidoro laying the ball back from the right and Falcão stepping over it for Éder to flip it up and volley in at the near post from long range. Dasayev, perhaps the best keeper in the tournament, didn't move. Flair and shooting power of the highest order. A beautiful game, alright. It was the USSR's only defeat in 36 matches.

---

15 June 1982 – La Rosaleda, Malaga – 22,000 – David Socha (USA)

SCOTLAND   **(3) 5**
Dalglish 18, Wark 30, 33, Robertson 73, Archibald 79

NEW ZEALAND   **(0) 2**
Sumner 54, Wooddin 65

SCOTLAND Allan Rough, Danny McGrain (c), Frank Gray, John Wark, Allan Evans, Alan Hansen, Gordon Strachan, Graeme Souness, Alan Brazil [Steve Archibald 53], Kenny Dalglish [David Narey 83], John Robertson. *Jock Stein*.

NEW ZEALAND Frank Van Hattum, John Hill, Sam Malcolmson [Duncan Cole 77], Bobby Almond [Ricki Herbert 66], Adrian Elrick, Keith Mackay, Allan Boath, Steve Sumner (c), Ken Cresswell, Wynton Rufer, Steve Wooddin. *John Adshead (ENG)*.

As in 1974, Scotland met the whipping boys first and made a meal of it, or at least a messy snack. No problems in the first half, with Strachan brisk and clever on the right. Wark, well-known as a midfield opportunist, headed two goals and Dalglish forced the ball in as he was tackled. But after the break the 19-year-old Rufer sent over a cross, McGrain and the woeful Rough hesitated, and Sumner poked the ball in. Then Wooddin drove in Hill's long ball. Crisis.

Pulse rates were lowered by Robertson's curling free kick and Archibald's header, but the margin wasn't what it might have been, and Brazil were next.

---

18 June 1982 – Benito Villamarín, Seville – 47,379 – Luis Siles (COS)

BRAZIL   **(1) 4**
Zico 33, Oscar 49, Éder 65, Falcão 87

SCOTLAND (1) 1
Narey 18

BRAZIL Waldir Peres, Leandro, Júnior, Toninho Cerezo, Oscar, Luizinho, Falcão, Sócrates (c), Serginho [Paulo Isidoro 82], Zico, Éder.
SCOTLAND Rough, Narey, Gray, Wark, Willie Miller, Hansen, Strachan [Dalglish 65], Souness (c), Archibald, Asa Hartford [Alex McLeish 69], Robertson.

The dropping of Dalglish wasn't a factor (although the heat, even in the evening, may have been). Brazil destroyed Scotland with a style of play that had supposedly vanished for ever. The ball control, movement and angles of passing, all done without apparent effort, were

1930
1934
1938
1950
1954
1958
1962
1966
1970
1974
1978
1982
1986
1990
1994
1998
2002
2006

the stuff of mythical beaches, with apparently no need for defence. If Sócrates was the natural leader, Falcão organised everything, Cerezo fetched and carried (better looking than it sounds) and Zico played well because he was surrounded by similarly gifted players. Three of their goals were out of the top drawer.

Before that, Scotland scored a good one of their own. Souness pitched a long diagonal ball to the right-hand corner of the area and Wark headed into the path of the charging Narey, whose first touch wasn't great but whose second sent the ball screaming into the top near corner for his only international goal.

Zico equalised with a free kick curled in at pace off the top of a post, then Scotland really should have prevented the second, Souness being left to mark the towering Oscar at Júnior's near-post corner. It was his first goal for Brazil, in his 38th international.

The third goal was almost embarrassing, Brazil walking the ball out of defence to set Éder free on the left. His reputation for ferocious shooting went before him, and he put it to good use, hitting a delicate chip as Rough tensed for the thunderbolt.

The last goal, if anything, was even better, a string of passes ending with Sócrates laying the ball back for Falcão to shoot low in off a post from outside the area. No contest, but at least Scotland wouldn't be the last to suffer, and it was in a good cause.

---

19 June 1982 – La Rosaleda, Malaga – 17,000 – Youssef El-Ghoul (LBY)

USSR (1) 3
Gavrilov 25, Blokhin 48, Baltacha 69

NEW ZEALAND (0) 0

USSR Dasayev, Sulakvelidze, Demyanenko, Baltacha, Chivadze (c), Bessonov, Bal, Gavrilov [Sergei Rodionov 79], Daraselia [Khoren Oganesian HT], Shengalia, Blokhin.

NEW ZEALAND Van Hattum, Glenn Dods, Herbert, Boath, Elrick, Mackay, Cole, Sumner (c), Cresswell, Rufer, Wooddin.

Comfortable as expected for the Soviets, although New Zealand were well in the game until an unlucky goal did for them. Van Hattum, preferred to Richard Wilson who'd kept nine consecutive clean sheets in the qualifiers, had a shot covered until it hit one of the Soviet players and gave Gavrilov a simple tap-in. Then Blokhin scored with a low left-footer, missed another chance, and made a run that set up Baltacha's cross-shot for the third.

---

22 June 1982 – La Rosaleda, Malaga – 30,000 – Nicolae Rainea (ROM)

SCOTLAND (1) 2
Jordan 15, Souness 87

USSR (0) 2
Chivadze 60, Shengalia 84

SCOTLAND Rough, Narey, Gray, Wark, Miller, Hansen, Strachan [McGrain 71], Souness (c), Archibald, Joe Jordan [Brazil 71], Robertson.
USSR Dasayev, Sulakvelidze, Demyanenko, Baltacha, Chivadze (c), Bessonov, Bal, Gavrilov, Sergei Borovsky, Shengalia [Andreyev 89], Blokhin.

Needing a win to qualify, Scotland recalled the veteran Jordan, who showed his fangs by giving them a deserved lead thanks to Chivadze's poor control of Narey's long ball. But there was always the feeling that the USSR had too many shots in their locker. Chivadze scored by kicking the ball into the ground after Gavrilov's drive was blocked – but the goal that knocked Scotland out was entirely self-inflicted. Miller and the smooth Hansen collided under a long ball by their right-hand touchline and Shengalia ran on to swerve past a dithering Rough. Souness' late slapshot only emphasised his overall contribution. With his team needing real generalship at the highest level, he didn't deliver. But if Jock Stein deserved a better crop of players, at least this time the exit was dignified.

---

23 June 1982 – Benito Villamarín, Seville – 32,000 – Damir Matovinović (YUG)

BRAZIL   (2) 4
Zico 28, 31, Falcão 55, Serginho 69

NEW ZEALAND   (0) 0

BRAZIL Waldir Peres, Leandro, Júnior, Cerezo, Oscar ['Edinho' (Edino Nazareth) 73], Luizinho, Falcão, Sócrates (c), Serginho [Paulo Isidoro 67], Zico, Éder.
NEW ZEALAND Van Hattum, Dods, Herbert, Almond, Elrick, Mackay, Boath, Sumner (c), Cresswell [Cole 77], Rufer [Brian Turner 77], Wooddin.

Brazil were at half-throttle, so the scoreline was kind. Zico's goals were wasted on a brave but limited team, his first a sweet volley, the second a ground shot, both from right-wing crosses. Falcão ran on and bided his time before scoring at the near post, and even the lumbering Serginho stabbed one in, though it was hard to believe there wasn't a better reserve centre-forward in the whole of Brazil; the injuries to Reinaldo and Careca would probably be felt sooner or later. Meanwhile the All Whites hadn't disgraced themselves in a terribly hard group.

GROUP 6

	P	W	D	L	F	A	Pts
Brazil	3	3	0	0	10	2	6
USSR	3	1	1	1	6	4	3
Scotland	3	1	1	1	8	8	3
New Zealand	3	0	0	3	2	12	0

Brazil and the USSR qualified for the second round.

2ND ROUND

GROUP A

Belgium, Poland, USSR.

---

28 June 1982 – Camp Nou, Barcelona – 30,000 – Luis Siles (COS)

POLAND   (2) 3
Boniek 4, 27, 53

BELGIUM   (0) 0

POLAND Młynarczyk, Dziuba, Majewski, Janas, Żmuda (c), Matysik, Lato, Kupcewicz [Ciołek 82], Buncol, Boniek, Smolarek.
BELGIUM Théo Custers, Michel Renquin, L Millecamps, Meeuws (c), Plessers [Baecke 87], Van Moer [Van der Elst HT], Coeck, Vercauteren, Vandenbergh, Czerniatynski, Ceulemans.

After two poor performances, Boniek had been pushed up front against Peru – and now the move paid off in full. Suddenly here was one of the best strikers in Europe, scoring a marvellously varied hat trick. First he lashed in a square pass from the right by Lato (who was winning his 100th cap), then knocked a header over Custers as he came out, and finally broke through to take the ball round the keeper. Juventus had spent their money well. Vandenbergh hit the bar but Belgium

LEADING GOALSCORERS 1982

6	Paolo Rossi	ITA
5	Karl-Heinz Rummenigge	GER
4	Zbigniew Boniek	POL
4	Zico	BRZ

1930
1934
1938
1950
1954
1958
1962
1966
1970
1974
1982
1986
1990
1994
1998
2002
2006

1930
1934
1938
1950
1954
1958
1962
1966
1970
1974
1978

1982

1986
1990
1994
1998
2002
2006

were disorganised, and the dropping of Pfaff, for misbehaviour, didn't help. His replacement wasn't capped again (yes, Custers' last stand).

---

1 July 1982 – Camp Nou, Barcelona – 25,000 – Michel Vautrot (FRA)

USSR	**(0) 1**
Oganesian 49	
BELGIUM	**(0) 0**

USSR Dasayev, Borovsky, Demyanenko, Baltacha, Chivadze (c), Bessonov, Bal [Daraselia 88], Gavrilov, Oganesian, Shengalia [Rodionov 89], Blokhin.
BELGIUM Jacky Munaron, Renquin, L Millecamps, Meeuws (c), De Schrijver [Marc Millecamps 65], Vandersmissen [Czerniatynski 67], René Verheyen, Coeck, Vandenbergh, Vercauteren, Ceulemans.

Vandenbergh, normally so lethal, missed two good chances, and Belgium were unlucky that Oganesian's mishit volley bounced in. Shengalia, for once, and Blokhin, as usual, had a poor match. Luc and Marc Millecamps were brothers.

---

4 July 1982 – Camp Nou, Barcelona – 45,000 – Bob Valentine (SCO)

| **POLAND** | **0** |
| **USSR** | **0** |

POLAND Młynarczyk, Dziuba, Majewski, Janas, Żmuda (c), Matysik, Kupcewicz [Ciołek 52], Buncol, Lato, Boniek, Smolarek.
USSR Dasayev, Sulakvelidze, Demyanenko, Bessonov, Baltacha, Chivadze (c), Borovsky, Gavrilov [Daraselia 79], Oganesian, Shengalia [Andreyev 58], Blokhin.

Poland needed only a draw and packed the midfield to get it. The main talking point was the way the Spanish police, brutal through-

out the tournament, waded in to remove banners supporting the Polish trade union Solidarity, apparently at the request of Soviet television.

GROUP A						
	P	W	D	L	F	A	Pts
Poland	2	1	1	0	3	0	3
USSR	2	1	1	0	1	0	3
Belgium	2	0	0	2	0	4	0

Poland qualified for the semi-finals.

GROUP B

England, Spain, West Germany.

---

29 June 1982 – Santiago Bernabéu, Madrid – 75,000 – Arnaldo Coelho (BRZ)

| **ENGLAND** | **0** |
| **WEST GERMANY** | **0** |

ENGLAND Shilton, Mills (c), Sansom, Robson, Butcher, Thompson, Coppell, Wilkins, Mariner, Francis [Tony Woodcock 76], Rix.
WEST GERMANY Schumacher, Kaltz, Briegel, Stielike, K Förster, Bernd Förster, Rummenigge (c), Hansi Müller [Fischer 74], Reinders [Littbarski 63], Breitner, Dremmler.

Drab and grim, two well organised sides cancelling each other out. England didn't do much up front and were lucky that Rummenigge's long shot hit the bar in the last few minutes. The only hopes raised were Spanish. The Försters were brothers.

2 July 1982 – Santiago Bernabéu, Madrid – 90,089 – Paolo Casarin (ITA)

WEST GERMANY (0) 2

Littbarski 50, Fischer 76

SPAIN (0) 1

Zamora 83

WEST GERMANY Schumacher, Kaltz, Briegel, B Förster, K Förster, Stielike, Rummenigge (c) [Reinders HT], Breitner, Fischer, Dremmler, Littbarski. SPAIN Arkonada (c), Camacho, Gordillo, M Alonso, Tendillo, Alexanko, Santiago Urkiaga, Juanito [López Ufarte HT], 'Santillana' (Carlos Alonso), Zamora, Quini [Sánchez 65].

The defeat by Northern Ireland had sent Spain into a tougher group than expected, and they now paid for it against a side that at last raised its game, even (especially?) when the injured Rummenigge had to go off. Littbarski's recall made a big difference. Small and tricky, he put in the rebound after Arkonada couldn't hold Dremmler's shot, then turned cleverly on the ball to set up Fischer, who pushed it almost cruelly past a covering defender. Despite Zamora's header, the hosts were eliminated without making a mark.

5 July 1982 – Santiago Bernabéu, Madrid – 65,000 – Alexis Ponnet (BEL)

ENGLAND 0

SPAIN 0

SPAIN Arkonada (c), Camacho, Urkiaga, Gordillo, Tendillo [Antonio Maceda 73], Alexanko, M Alonso, Zamora, Satrústegui, Santillana, Saura [Pedro Uralde 67]. ENGLAND Shilton, Mills (c), Sansom, Robson, Butcher, Thompson, Francis, Wilkins, Mariner, Woodcock [Kevin Keegan 63], Rix [Trevor Brooking 63].

England needed to win while scoring at least two goals, but they'd managed a diminishing number in each match so far, and even the use of three strikers didn't change things. Greenwood had his reservations about Hoddle (and the 1986 finals suggested he may have been right) but surely anything was better than the Wilkins-Rix axis, the latter allegedly kept in by Don Howe, his coach at Arsenal and assistant manager here. Spain allowed Shilton to make a save with two forwards descending on him, but the best chances were missed by the England substitutes, their best players for so long. Brooking turned elegantly inside a man and shot straight at Arkonada, then Keegan put a far post header wide from Robson's cross ('No excuses, I should have buried it'). After a World Cup finals career of 27 minutes, neither was capped again. Nor were Mills and five of the Spaniards. England were out without losing a match but without taking many risks to stay in, as if Greenwood had settled for the quiet life to prepare for his retirement.

GROUP B

	P	W	D	L	F	A	Pts
West Germany	2	1	1	0	2	1	3
England	2	0	2	0	0	0	2
Spain	2	0	1	1	1	2	1

West Germany qualified for the semi-finals.

GROUP C

Argentina, Brazil, Italy.

29 June 1982 – Sarriá, Barcelona – 39,000 – Nicolae Rainea (ROM)

ITALY (0) 2

Tardelli 57, Cabrini 67

ARGENTINA (0) 1

Passarella 83

ITALY Zoff (c), Gentile, Cabrini, Tardelli, Collovati, Scirea, Oriali [Marini 75], Conti, Rossi [Alessandro Altobelli 80], Antognoni, Graziani

ARGENTINA Fillol, Olguín, Tarantini, Gallego, Galván, Passarella (c), Bertoni, Ardiles, Díaz [Calderón 58], Maradona, Kempes [Daniel Valencia 58].

SENT OFF: Gallego 85.

Few gave Italy a chance against the resurgent world champions, but they'd closed ranks after the group matches, refusing to give interviews to their own press, and this seemed to add to team spirit. In the first half Rainea booked five players, including some who complained that he wasn't booking others for violent conduct! The only sending-off was for a late foul on Tardelli, one of the chief perpetrators. Someone kept a TV camera on Gentile, which was a real revelation, showing how he kept Maradona quiet by bumping, pushing and shirt-tugging all afternoon, invariably on the blind side of the referee. There's no protection against this kind of thing, and although Maradona (to his great credit) stuck it out without exploding, his contribution was inevitably diminished. Ardiles too was left with a shirt torn down the front as Italy tightened their grip.

In the second half, they moved on to phase two, bringing their talented defenders upfield to score twice. Tardelli left Fillol doing the splits from Antognoni's pass then Conti set up an open goal for Cabrini, who was confirming his promise of 1978. Maradona and Passarella hit the bar and the latter smacked in a free kick with Zoff complaining that the whistle hadn't gone – but Italy were well worth their win.

Gallego, playing in his 73rd and last international, was sent off for 'a lunatic lunge' at Tardelli. The stadium was demolished in 1997.

---

2 July 1982 – Sarriá, Barcelona – 44,000 – Mario Rubio Vázquez (MEX)

BRAZIL   (1) 3
Zico 12, Serginho 68, Júnior 74

ARGENTINA   (0) 1
Díaz 89

BRAZIL Waldir Peres, Leandro [Edevaldo (de Freitas) 82], Júnior, Falcão, Oscar, Luizinho, Cerezo, Sócrates (c), Serginho, Zico [João Batista 84], Éder.
ARGENTINA Fillol, Olguín, Tarantini, Barbas, Galván, Passarella (c), Bertoni [Santamaría 64], Ardiles, Kempes [Díaz HT], Maradona, Calderón.
SENT OFF: Maradona 87.

Argentina saw their reign come to an undignified end, comprehensively beaten and with their best player sent off – but really there was little they could have done against a side that moved up a level from merely brilliant. All the Brazilian goals were state of the art.

When Éder lined up a 35-yard free kick, nobody scoffed. Sure enough, Fillol could only touch the thunderbolt onto the bar, Zico beating Serginho to the rebound with no defender in sight to protect a stunned Fillol. Then Éder curled the ball inside to Zico, whose perfect pass through the defence sent Falcão clear on the right, and even Serginho couldn't miss the far-post header. The third was the best, Zico again threading the ball through for the skilful Júnior to continue his run and push the ball past Fillol. At the death, Tarantini's vengeful challenge on Batista forced the ball through to Díaz, whose tremendous shot into the top corner didn't compensate for his wretched tournament.

Earlier, almost as soon as he came on, Batista had flattened Barbas, Maradona getting himself sent off for exacting some painful studs-up revenge. Frustrated by Italian fouling and Brazilian brilliance, there was nevertheless no doubt about his great talent, and his time would surely come – which couldn't be said about his team mates, nine of whom weren't capped again.

---

5 July 1982 – Sarriá, Barcelona – 44,000 – Avraham Klein (ISR)

ITALY   **(2) 3**
Rossi 5, 25, 74

BRAZIL   **(1) 2**
Sócrates 12, Falcão 68

ITALY Zoff (c), Gentile, Cabrini, Tardelli [Marini 75], Collovati [Giuseppe Bergomi 34], Scirea, Oriali, Conti, Rossi, Antognoni, Graziani.
BRAZIL Waldir Peres, Leandro, Júnior, Cerezo, Oscar, Luizinho, Falcão, Sócrates (c), Serginho [Paulo Isidoro 69], Zico, Éder.

If Hungary-Uruguay 1954 really was the greatest World Cup match, it now had a rival. Even Italy's improved showing against Argentina hadn't melted the bookmakers' stony hearts, especially as Brazil needed only a draw – but Bearzot's men now played the game of their lives, and it was *just* enough.

A good start helped. Conti, full of confidence after his performances so far, kept possession on the right, avoiding two half-hearted tackles, before swinging the ball across to the left. Cabrini dinked in an excellent outswinger and Rossi was left unmarked by Júnior to score his first goal of the tournament with a neat downward header across the keeper.

Even Italian supporters doubted it could last, and it didn't for long. Zico escaped the murderous Gentile with a marvellous back-heeled turn, then his clever angled ball set Sócrates free on the right. The shot beat Zoff at the near post, puffing the chalk on the goal line. But Cerezo knocked a carefree square pass towards three of his team mates deep in their own half. None of them expected it, Rossi stole

it away to the edge of the area, and shot right through Waldir Peres.

The longer the lead lasted, the more possible an Italian victory became, and Rossi should have made it certain in the second half, after the selfless Graziani had beaten his man on the left and knocked the ball across goal. With only poor old Waldir to beat, Rossi sidefooted the ball wide. Within minutes, it looked as disastrous a miss as expected: Brazil equalised again.

Júnior swerved inside from the left wing and gave the ball to the unmarked Falcão on the right-hand side of the Italian area. Cerezo made another of his brave and powerful runs (Zoff had already saved superbly at his feet), taking out three defenders to leave a gap for Falcão, who visibly took aim before scoring with a left-foot shot which took a faint deflection and left Zoff screaming at his defence. Falcão's face, demented with delight, was one of the images of the tournament.

But this was a day of great Italian resilience. From a corner on the right, the ball fell to Tardelli, whose weak shot turned into a perfect short through-pass for Rossi, who swivelled and shot past Waldir from the six-yard line. Júnior stood around claiming offside when he was the one playing Rossi on.

Brazil kept pressing, but Italy went on making chances, Antognoni having a goal understandably but wrongly disallowed for offside. With two minutes to go, Éder's free kick from the left was met by Oscar's header at the far post, only for Zoff to dive and hold the ball just in front of the line, crucial reflexes from a middle-aged man. The big defender couldn't believe his eyes. You will, Oscar, you will.

Italy had put an end to Brazil's run of 24 unbeaten matches, mainly because their defence, which kept its concentration under extreme pressure, was altogether more talented.

1982

1930
1934
1938
1950
1954
1958
1962
1966
1970
1974
1978
1986
1990
1994
1998
2002
2006

1982

Júnior looked good coming forward but it's hard to remember him making a tackle, and the thought of Waldir, Luizinho and Leandro with World Cup winners' medals was as unappealing as Félix and Everaldo in 1970. Bergomi (impressively cold-blooded for an 18-year-old) and Scirea had been immense – and Antognoni matched the Brazilians for poise. But of course it was Rossi's match.

GROUP C

	P	W	D	L	F	A	Pts
Italy	2	2	0	0	5	3	4
Brazil	2	1	0	1	5	4	2
Argentina	2	0	0	2	2	5	0

Italy qualified for the semi-finals.

GROUP D

Austria, France, Northern Ireland.

28 June 1982 – Vicente Calderón, Madrid – 30,000 – Károly Palotai (HUN)

FRANCE	**(1) 1**

Genghini 39

AUSTRIA	**(0) 0**

FRANCE Ettori, Battiston, Bossis, Janvion, Trésor (c), Giresse, Genghini [Girard 85], Soler, Lacombe [Rocheteau 15], Tigana, Six.
AUSTRIA Koncilia, Krauss, Obermayer (c), Degeorgi [Baumeister HT], Pezzey, Hattenberger, Hintermaier, Prohaska, Kurt Jara [Welzl HT], Krankl, Schachner.

By finishing second to England and winning just one of their first three matches, France found themselves in the easiest second round group and made the most of it. Their win here was more clear-cut than the score suggests. Tigana was a very acceptable deputy for Platini, Genghini hit a post before scoring with a swinging free kick, and Koncilia had to make a string of saves. Prohaska, supposedly the playmaker, played too deep, and Degeorgi crashed into an advertising hoarding. Austria were making an untidy exit.

1 July 1982 – Vicente Calderón, Madrid – 24,000 – Adolf Prokop (DDR)

AUSTRIA	**(0) 2**

Pezzey 53, Hintermaier 67

NORTHERN IRELAND	**(1) 2**

Hamilton 28, 74

AUSTRIA Koncilia, Krauss, Obermayer (c), Pezzey, Johann Pregesbauer [Hintermaier HT], Anton Pichler, Baumeister, Prohaska, Max Hagmayr [Welzl HT], Jurtin, Schachner.
NORTHERN IRELAND Jim Platt, J Nicholl, Nelson, McCreery, C Nicholl, McClelland, Armstrong, M O'Neill (c), Hamilton, McIlroy, Whiteside [Brotherston 67].

The Irish were still riding their cloud, doing great things with a front two that consisted of a Watford reserve (Armstrong) and a Third Division player (Hamilton), supported by a 17-year-old midfielder (Whiteside) with only two League matches behind him. Armstrong, a revelation in Spain (losing weight in the heat apparently helped), made another of his strong runs down the right, outpacing Pregesbauer and Obermayer, and Hamilton headed in the cross. Then the Austrians woke up, Prohaska hitting a post, Pezzey deflecting in Baumeister's shot from the corner that followed. Schachner had a goal dubiously disallowed before Hintermaier put them ahead with a long shot from a free kick. But Jimmy Nicholl beat Koncilia to a loose ball on the right, and Hamilton headed in again. Admirable stuff, but the extreme heat had done Northern Ireland no favours, and they now had to beat France, who were coming into form.

4 July 1982 – Vicente Calderón, Madrid – 30,000 – Alojzy Jarguz (POL)

FRANCE   **(1) 4**
Giresse 33, 80, Rocheteau 46, 68

NORTHERN IRELAND   **(0) 1**
Armstrong 75

FRANCE Ettori, Amoros, Bossis, Tigana, Janvion, Trésor, Giresse, Genghini, Soler [Six 63], Platini (c), Rocheteau [Couriol 83].
NORTHERN IRELAND Jennings, J Nicholl, Donaghy, McCreery [John O'Neill 85], C Nicholl, McClelland, Armstrong, M O'Neill (c), Hamilton, McIlroy, Whiteside.

After 26 minutes, with honours roughly even, Martin O'Neill broke through to score, only for the goal to be wrongly disallowed. With their limited resources, that was the last thing Northern Ireland needed, and the last real chance they had. Giresse, the hardworking star of the French midfield, cracked in Platini's pull-back and headed in Tigana's right-wing cross, small though he was. The revitalised Rocheteau ran from halfway for the second, tricked his way through for the third, and had a shot cleared off the line by Jimmy Nicholl. Armstrong, the best British player in the tournament, drove in the loose ball when Whiteside's cross led to Ettori's latest blunder and some hesitation by Trésor. Death with glory for the Irish, who deserved a kinder scoreline. Had O'Neill's goal been allowed, who knows how this brittle French side would have responded?

GROUP D

	P	W	D	L	F	A	Pts
France	2	2	0	0	5	1	4
Austria	2	0	1	1	2	3	1
Northern Ireland	2	0	1	1	3	6	1

France qualified for the semi-finals.

SEMI-FINALS

8 July 1982 – Camp Nou, Barcelona – 55,000 – Juan Cardellino (URU)

ITALY   **(1) 2**
Rossi 22, 73

POLAND   **(0) 0**

ITALY Zoff (c), Bergomi, Cabrini, Tardelli, Collovati, Scirea, Oriali, Conti, Rossi, Antognoni [Marini 28], Graziani [Altobelli 70].
POLAND Młynarczyk, Dziuba, Majewski, Janas, Żmuda (c), Matysik, Kupcewicz, Buncol, Lato, Ciołek [Pałasz HT], Smolarek [Kusto 77].

The rest of the tournament was largely processional for Italy, especially against a Polish team which had lost Boniek to a pointless booking in the previous match. Although Kupcewicz grazed a post, at the other end Rossi was on a roll. He sidefooted in a half-volley when Tardelli's dive distracted the defence at a free kick, then fell gently forward to head the second after Conti had outpaced two men on the left. Italy's only worry, and it was nothing minor, was the injury that would keep Antognoni out of the Final.

1930
1934
1938
1950
1954
1958
1962
1966
1970
1974
1978

1982

1986
1990
1994
1998
2002
2006

8 July 1982 – Ramón Sánchez Pizjuán, Seville – 71,000 – Charles Corver (HOL)

WEST GERMANY   (1) (1) 3
Littbarski 18, Rummenigge 103, Fischer 108

FRANCE   (1) (1) 3
Platini pen 27, Trésor 93, Giresse 99
West Germany 5-4 pens.

WEST GERMANY Schumacher, Kaltz (c), Briegel [Rummenigge 97], B Förster, K Förster, Stielike, Magath [Hrubesch 73], Breitner, Fischer, Dremmler, Littbarski.
FRANCE Ettori, Amoros, Bossis, Janvion, Trésor, Giresse, Genghini [Battiston 50, Lopez 60], Six, Tigana, Platini (c), Rocheteau
PENALTY SHOOT-OUT: Giresse 1-0, Kaltz 1-1, Amoros 2-1, Breitner 2-2, Rocheteau 3-2, Stielike saved, Six saved, Littbarski 3-3, Platini 4-3, Rummenigge 4-4, Bossis saved, Hrubesch 5-4.

If it didn't equal Italy-Brazil for sustained skill, this more than matched it for drama. France, unrecognisable as the team which had lost to England, played some wonderful stuff through midfield, but West Germany had been dining out on this kind of comeback since 1954. The scoreline was about right, though few were pleased by the result or the method of arriving at it. It was the first World Cup match to end in a penalty shoot-out.

Another penalty had started the French scoring, after Bernd Förster was judged to have pulled back Rocheteau. Before that, Littbarski had hit the bar from long range before putting in the rebound from twenty yards when Ettori got in Fischer's way. In the second half, Battiston ran clear onto Platini's pass and was violently bodychecked by Schumacher's follow-through, probably the worst-looking foul in any World Cup. No free kick, no red card, just concussion and broken teeth for Battiston (Schumacher rather crassly offered to pay to have them capped) who was stretchered off and given oxygen. When people

made the joke about Michael Schumacher being a relative, this is what they meant. A myopic piece of refereeing, by the man who'd allowed Brazil to kick lumps out of England in 1978.

France almost gained revenge in the last minute (Amoros hit the bar) and appeared to have done so in extra time, Trésor hooking in a splendid volley from a deflected cross by Giresse, who drove the third in off a post. But Battiston's injury had forced them to use their second substitute, and there was no-one to chase Rummenigge's fresh legs when they came on, so Schumacher's thuggery helped win the match. Rummenigge touched in Littbarski's short cross at the near post and the veteran Fischer equalised with one of his trademark overhead kicks, two goals in keeping with a marvellous match.

When Stielike missed his penalty in the shoot-out, the hard man fell to his knees in despair, but Schumacher added insult to injury by saving from Six and the outstanding Bossis, and the hulking Hrubesch showed a delicate touch with the last kick. Sad for France and everyone who admired them, but the Germans had contributed fully to a splendid occasion. Mind you, if they were grimly satisfied, so too were the Italians, who now had less to fear.

3RD-PLACE FINAL

10 July 1982 – José Rico Pérez, Alicante – 28,000 – António Garrido (POR)

POLAND   (2) 3
Szarmach 42, Majewski 45, Kupcewicz 47

FRANCE   (1) 2
Girard 14, Couriol 75

POLAND Młynarczyk, Dziuba, Majewski, Janas, Zmuda (c), Matysik [Roman Wójcicki HT], Lato, Kupcewicz, Szarmach, Boniek, Buncol.
FRANCE Jean Castaneda, Amoros, Janvion [Lopez 66], Girard, Philippe Mahut, Trésor (c), Couriol, Tigana [Six 83], Soler, Larios, Bruno Bellone.

Entertaining enough, for what it was worth. The French gave their reserves a run-out, and two of them scored their goals, Girard in off the foot of a post from long range, Couriol sent clear by Tigana. But these only sandwiched Poland's three quick strikes either side of the interval. Szarmach volleyed into the ground and in off the far post, Castaneda missed a corner to give the bearded Majewski a free header, and Kupcewicz scored with a crafty low free kick when Castaneda left too much room at his near post. It was the last international match for Szarmach and Lato, remnants of Poland's best ever team.

FINAL

11 July 1982 – Santiago Bernabéu, Madrid – 90,089 – Arnaldo Coelho (BRZ)

ITALY (0) 3
Rossi 56, Tardelli 68, Altobelli 80

WEST GERMANY (0) 1
Breitner 83

ITALY Zoff (c), Bergomi, Cabrini, Gentile, Oriali, Collovati, Scirea, Tardelli, Conti, Rossi, Graziani [Altobelli 18, Causio 89].
WEST GERMANY Schumacher, Kaltz, Briegel, B Förster, K Förster, Stielike, Littbarski, Dremmler [Hrubesch 62], Breitner, Fischer, Rummenigge (c) [H Müller 70].

Did we say processional? Already without their midfield general, Italy lost their centre-forward almost immediately, missed a penalty, and still

OLDEST PLAYERS IN FINALS

yrs	days			
40	133	Dino Zoff	ITA	1982
37	241	Gunnar Gren	SWE	1958
37	212	Jan Jongbloed	HOL	1978
37	32	Nílton Santos	BRZ	1962
35	264	Nils Liedholm	SWE	1958
35	167	Toni Turek	GER	1954

Liedholm was the oldest to score.

won with plenty to spare. Conti and Tardelli took over the playmaking, and again the quality of their defensive players made a vital difference, contributing to all three goals. The strapping Briegel, a former decathlete, had been seen as the future of the game – but every Italian goal came down his flank and he gave away a penalty after 24 minutes by crudely hauling down Conti. Cabrini, who'd once had a spot kick saved at Highbury, became the first player to miss one in a World Cup Final, scuffing the ball low and wide. But West Germany's name wasn't written on the Cup this time.

Rummenigge still wasn't fully fit (Stielike was furious about it afterwards), so Bearzot let Gentile loose on Littbarski, who disappeared without trace. Meanwhile the mop-haired Collovati sealed his excellent tournament by completely dominating Fischer and preventing an equaliser by stopping Rummenigge from reaching a low ball that had sneaked past Zoff.

At the other end, a quickly taken free kick found Gentile in yards of space on the right, his low cross bounced across the area, where Rossi slid in before Cabrini to head it into an empty net; he'd now scored all of Italy's last six goals. The next began with Conti carrying the ball and Scirea backheeling it to Bergomi deep in the German penalty area then pushing the return pass across to Tardelli, who turned away from a defender before lashing in the cross shot. His celebration, all fists and larynx, was the most vivid in any Final. Altobelli scored the third by calmly going round Schumacher after Conti had escaped up the right again. Breitner's volleyed cross-shot, in his last international, made him only the third player to score in two Finals, but it was the merest coat of gloss. West Germany lost to a European country for the first time since the 1978 finals.

Like Menotti in 1978, Bearzot had been vindicated, though he owed even more to his defenders (there were an awful lot of them) than to Rossi, whose rehabilitation was remarkable. At the start of the tournament, an even greater striker, Denis Law, had been adamant that 'You can't be out of the game for two years and come back in a tournament like the World Cup.' Now the Germans were left wishing there were longer bans for fixing the results of Italian football matches.

The Hand of the Baskervilles

Mexico 1986

At first glance, it looked as if FIFA weren't entirely to blame for revisiting Mexico's heat and altitude (Colombia, the original choice, and Brazil both pulled out) – but the truth was murkier than that. Canada and the USA were both allowed to present their case, but there was strong evidence that the decision had already been taken: one of FIFA's vice-presidents, Guillermo Cañedo, was a leading executive with the Mexican television company Televisa, whose owner Emilio Azcarraga was a personal friend of Havelange. Asked about the prohibitively high ticket prices, Cañedo replied that 'people always have TV.' FIFA president João Havelange said his conscience was clear and 'other people may write or say what they like.' What many wrote and said (even those from Thatcher's Britain) was how shocked they were by the ongoing gulf between Mexico's rich and poor. Havelange had no convincing answers when asked why FIFA simply didn't fill the empty seats with needy children or ban Camel cigarettes as a major sponsor.

As for the altitude, teams were fitter by now and appeared to suffer less distress – but most of the fancied teams had other problems. The holders Italy came with the same coach and several of the same players but had a patchy recent record. France had won all twelve of their matches in 1984, including the European Championship in which Platini scored nine goals in five games. But that was at home; the team had begun to creak a little in the two years since; and there was still no reliable striker.

Maradona was at his peak for Argentina but seemed to lack a quality supporting cast. West Germany had Beckenbauer as manager but no midfield general (the brilliant Schuster was now refusing to play for the national team). Brazil were strong at the back and had Careca up front but were still relying on their 1982 creative players, who were all over 30: Zico, Sócrates, Falcão, Júnior. Mexico, who'd been doing well under their Yugoslav coach, seemed to have been strengthened by the inclusion of Hugo Sánchez, now with Real Madrid – but had lost 3-0 to England a month earlier and would again have to lean heavily on home support.

England had qualified far more comfortably this time, without losing a match. The messianic Bryan Robson had a troublesome shoulder but there was a quick new striker in Gary Lineker, the First Division's leading scorer. High hopes but fingers crossed. Northern Ireland came through from the same group after holding out for a goalless draw at Wembley and showing their usual grit by winning 1-0 in Romania.

Scotland were there yet again, after a long haul tinged with tragedy. Jock Stein, still their

1930

1934

1938

1950

1954

1958

1962

1966

1970

1974

1978

1982

1986

manager, had died of a heart attack while watching the 1-1 draw in Cardiff which sent them through to a play-off with Australia. Then the 0-0 draw in Melbourne owed much to Jim Leighton's form in goal.

Yet again the Scots were unfortunate with the draw for the finals, finding themselves in the 'Group of Death' with West Germany, the exciting Danes (in the finals for the first time) and Uruguay, many people's favourites with their array of world class defenders and Francescoli in midfield.

FIFA had carried out their threat to increase the number of qualifiers to 24, partly to uphold Havelange's old election promises to Africa and Asia, who provided his power base. The second stage mini-leagues were scrapped in favour of a knockout format, a return to the 1970 system but with an extra match. To fit 24 into the 16 needed for the second round, the four third-placed teams with the best records would join the top two in each of six groups. The phrase 'keep it simple' only applied on the pitch. But at least the last matches in each group would kick off at the same time to avoid the bad odour trailed by Argentina-Peru 1978 and Austria-West Germany 1982.

Not everything had changed from the last time the tournament came to Mexico: more than ever, the organisers were kowtowing to the wishes of TV companies. Not only were some kick-offs scheduled for the hottest part of the day, but matches were to end on the dot of full time, to fit in with broadcasting deadlines. Very snug. As in someone's pocket.

Diego's devilish handball. Peter Shilton's fist is inches away from where all Englishmen would have liked to see it.

1930
1934
1938
1950
1954
1958
1962
1966
1970
1974
1978
1982

1986

1990
1994
1998
2002
2006

GROUP A

Argentina, Bulgaria, Italy (seeded), South Korea.

31 May 1986 – Azteca, Mexico City – 95,000 – Erik Fredriksson (SWE)

BULGARIA **(0) 1**
Sirakov 85

ITALY **(1) 1**
Altobelli 43

BULGARIA Borislav Mikhailov, Radoslav Zdravkov, Georgi Dimitrov (c), Nikolai Arabov, Aleksandar Markov, Nasko Sirakov, Anjo Sadkov, Stoicho Mladenov, Zivko Gospodinov [Andrej Zheliaskov 73], Plamen Getov, Bojidar Iskrenov [Kostadin Kostadinov 64]. *Ivan Vutzov.*
ITALY Giovanni Galli, Giuseppe Bergomi, Antonio Cabrini, Fernando De Napoli, Pietro Vierchowod, Gaetano Scirea (c), Bruno Conti [Gianluca Vialli 65], Salvatore Bagni, Giuseppe Galderisi, Antonio Di Gennaro, Alessandro Altobelli. *Enzo Bearzot.*

Calling this the best opening match since 1962 sounds like damning with faint praise, but in fact it was a perfectly adequate contest, which Italy should have won against an unambitious team.

Di Gennaro hit a long free kick from the left, and Altobelli arrived at the far post to push a volley high across the keeper. In the second half, Scirea took a return ball from Altobelli and should have done better than hit the ball straight at Mikhailov. Then heads you don't win: another Di Gennaro free kick was headed across goal for Cabrini to head over an open goal then put his head in his hands. The misses came at a cost: Zdravkov chipped a cross, and Sirakov got up between two defenders to head down and up just inside the post.

2 June 1986 – Olímpico, Mexico City – 40,000 – Victoriano Sánchez Arminio (SPA)

ARGENTINA **(2) 3**
Valdano 6, 46, Ruggeri 18

SOUTH KOREA **(0) 1**
Park CS 73

ARGENTINA Nery Pumpido, Néstor Clausen, José Luis Brown, Oscar Ruggeri, Oscar Garré, Ricardo Giusti, Sergio Batista [Julio Olarticoechea 76], Jorge Burruchaga, Diego Maradona (c), Pedro Pasculli [Carlos Tápia 75], Jorge Valdano. *Carlos Bilardo.*
SOUTH KOREA Oh Yun-Kyo, Park Kyung-Joon, Huh Jung-Moo, Cho Min-Kook, Jung Yong-Hwan, Kim Yong-Se [Byun Byung-Joo HT], Kim Pyung-Suk [Cho Kwang-Rae 22], Kim Joo-Sung, Park Chang-Sun (c), Choi Soon-Ho, Cha Bum-Kun. *Kim Jung-Nam.*

South Korea, back in the finals for the first time since 1954, impressed with their determination and long-range goal, but were never comfortable at the back. Burruchaga hit a post in between Valdano's goals, the first scored with a cross-shot which the keeper flapped at as other players crossed his eyeline, the second an easy chance at the far post when the keeper tipped a cross towards him. Ruggeri hammered in a header, all three goals stemming from Maradona, who was the best player on the pitch despite nursing a long-standing injury which the Koreans tried to aggravate. The first two goals came from free kicks after he was tripped, and the Argentinian press referred to an *'indignación por la violencia Coreana.'*

FIFA's Official Report says Joo Byung-Ok came on as a substitute – but this looks like something lost in translation. Several other sources say this was the same Byun Byung-Joo who played against Bulgaria and Italy.

---

5 June 1986 – Cuauhtémoc, Puebla – 32,000 – Jan Keizer (HOL)

ARGENTINA **(1) 1**
Maradona 33

ITALY **(1) 1**
Altobelli pen 6

ARGENTINA Pumpido, Brown, José Luis Cuciuffo, Ruggeri, Garré, Giusti, Batista [Olarticoechea 59], Burruchaga, Maradona (c), Claudio Borghi [Héctor Enrique 76], Valdano.
ITALY Galli, Bergomi, Cabrini, De Napoli [Beppe Baresi 87], Vierchowod, Scirea (c), Conti [Vialli 64], Bagni, Galderisi, Di Gennaro, Altobelli.

Italy took the lead when Garré was judged to have handled intentionally, but Bilardo had correctly identified Altobelli as Italy's only attacking threat and put Ruggeri on him, with the result that Italy were barely worth the draw, although Conti hit a post in the second half. Maradona was man-marked too, by Bagni, but escaped him and Scirea to push in a volley with that famous left foot. The second half, like so many others in the tournament, degenerated into a rash of bookings.

---

5 June 1986 – Olímpico, Mexico City – 45,000 – Fallaj Al-Shanar (SAU)

BULGARIA **(1) 1**
Getov 11

SOUTH KOREA **(0) 1**
Kim JB 69

BULGARIA Mikhailov, Zdravkov, Dimitrov (c), Arabov, Petar Petrov, Sirakov, Sadkov, Mladenov, Gospodinov, Getov [Zheliaskov 58], Iskrenov [Kostadinov HT].
SOUTH KOREA Oh, Park KJ, Huh, Cho Yung-Jeung, Jung Yong-Hwan, Cho KR [Cho MK 71], Park CS (c), No Soon-Jin [Kim Jong-Boo HT], Kim JS, Byun, Cha.

Bulgaria presumably saw this as their latest great opportunity to win a game in the finals, especially when Getov lobbed the ball in when Oh Yun-Kyo missed a cross. But the Koreans refused to lie down. Kim Joo-Sung and Park Chang-Sun came close, then Cho Kwang-Rae headed the ball forward and Kim Jong-Boo chested down before scuffing a low shot past Mikhailov.

---

10 June 1986 – Cuauhtémoc, Puebla – 20,000 – David Socha (USA)

ITALY **(1) 3**
Altobelli 18, 73, Cho KR o.g. 82

SOUTH KOREA **(0) 2**
Choi 62, Huh 89

ITALY Galli, Vierchowod, Cabrini, De Napoli, Fulvio Collovati, Scirea (c), Conti, Bagni [Baresi 68], Galderisi [Vialli 88], Di Gennaro, Altobelli.
SOUTH KOREA Oh, Cho KR, Park KJ, Huh, Jung, Cho YJ, Kim JS [Chung Jong-Soo HT], Park CS (c), Cha, Byun [Kim JB 70], Choi.

A repeat of the 1966 disaster against North Korea would have knocked Italy out, but they were in no great danger of that, even after the gangling Choi had stepped inside a tackle before thumping an equaliser from the edge of the box. Again the Italian attack relied too much on Altobelli, but it didn't matter this time. He scored his first goal with incredible arrogance in the box, chesting the ball down and dummying to shoot before touching it in;

1930
1934
1938
1950
1954
1958
1962
1966
1970
1974
1978
1982
1986
1990
1994
1998
2002
2006

stabbed in a loose ball for his second; pro-voked Cho Kwang-Rae into handling the ball into his own net as they slid in together; and would have had a hat-trick if he hadn't hit the post with a 26th-minute penalty awarded for a foul by Park Kyung-Joon on Galderisi. Huh Jung-Moo stretched to convert a headed pass by Cha Bum-Kun, Korea's best-known foot-baller, who played in the Bundesliga and had been recalled after more than seven years to play in this tournament. If it hadn't been for that long gap, his caps total would probably still be out in front today. As it was, his 121 was a world record for only another two years. His son Cha Doo-Ri played in the 2002 finals. Baresi's more famous brother Franco played in 1990 and 1994.

---

10 June 1986 – Olímpico, Mexico City – 45,000 – Berny Ulloa (COS)

ARGENTINA   (1) 2
Valdano 3, Burruchaga 79

BULGARIA   (0) 0

ARGENTINA Pumpido, Brown, Cuciuffo, Ruggeri, Garré, Giusti, Batista [Enrique HT], Burruchaga, Maradona (c), Borghi [Olarticoechea HT], Valdano. BULGARIA Mikhailov, Petrov, Dimitrov (c), Zheliaskov, A Markov, Sirakov [Zdravkov 72], Sadkov, Georgi Yordanov, Plamen Markov, Getov, Mladenov [Boycho Velichkov 54].

Bulgaria had seen the results from other groups and knew that a narrow defeat would send them through. They packed their team with midfielders and no forwards, missed two tackles to let Cuciuffo set up Valdano's goalscoring header, left Burruchaga unmarked to head in Maradona's cross from the left – yet still qualified for the first time despite taking only two points from three games.

GROUP A

	P	W	D	L	F	A	Pts
Argentina	3	2	1	0	6	2	5
Italy	3	1	2	0	5	4	4
Bulgaria	3	0	2	1	2	4	2
South Korea	3	0	1	2	4	7	1

Argentina, Italy and Bulgaria qualified for the second round.

GROUP B

Belgium, Iraq, Mexico (seeded), Paraguay.

---

3 June 1986 – Azteca, Mexico City – 110,000 – Carlos Esposito (ARG)

MEXICO   (2) 2
Quirarte 23, Sánchez 39

BELGIUM   (1) 1
Vandenbergh 45

MEXICO Pablo Larios, Mario Trejo, Fernando Quirarte, Félix Cruz Barbosa, Raúl Servín, Javier Aguirre, Tomás Boy (c) [Miguel España 69], Carlos Múñoz, Manuel Negrete, Luis Flores [Francisco Javier Cruz 79], Hugo Sánchez. *Bora Milutinović (YUG)* BELGIUM Jean-Marie Pfaff, Eric Gerets, Franky Van der Elst, Hugo Broos, Michel De Wolf, Enzo Scifo, Frankie Vercauteren, René Vandereycken, Jan Ceulemans (c), Erwin Vandenbergh [Stefan Demol 66], Filip Desmet [Nico Claesen 64]. *Guy Thys.*

The hosts had a better team than in 1970, guided by the tall veteran Boy, whose dead ball kicks led to the two goals. His indirect free kick was met by Quirarte's exemplary header, his left-wing corner glanced on for Sánchez to head in from very close to the far post. Vandenbergh headed in when Larios palmed Gerets' long throw towards him, but Belgium were too defensive for their own good. Like Rossi before him, Gerets had been amnestied after being found guilty in a famous bribery case. Spelling variations: Stéphane De Mol, Philippe De Smet.

4 June 1986 – Luis Gutiérrez Dosal, Toluca – 24,000 – Edwin Picon-Ackong (MAU)

PARAGUAY **(1) 1**
Romero 35

IRAQ **(0) 0**

PARAGUAY Roberto Fernández, Juan Torales, César Zabala, Wladimiro Schettina, Rogelio Delgado (c), Adolfino Cañete, Julio César Romero, Jorge Núñez, Buenaventura Ferreira, Alfredo Mendoza [Jorge Guasch 88], Roberto Cabañas. *Cayetano Ré.*
IRAQ Raad Hammoudi (c), Khalil Allawi, Salim Nadhum, Samir Mahmoud, Ali Shihab, Haris Hassan [Abdulrahim Aufi 67], Ahmed Rhadi Amaiesh, Saïd Hussein, Basil Kourkis Hanna [Qasim Basim 84], Natiq Abidoun, Ghanim Al-Roubai. *Evaristo (de Macedo) (BRZ).*

Iraq were unlucky when Rhadi put the ball in the net just after the half-time whistle had

GOALS WHILE CAPTAIN

6	Karl-Heinz Rummenigge	GER	1982–86
6	Diego Maradona	ARG	1986–94
5	György Sárosi	HUN	1938
5	Uwe Seeler	GER	1966–70
5	Lothar Matthäus	GER	1990–94

Seeler scored in five matches while captain, the others in four each.

gone, but Paraguay were too clever for them. Their star player (nicknamed 'Romerito' in Brazil, where he played for Fluminense) ran onto Cañete's deft pass to lob the keeper. Kourkis is sometimes seen spelt Gorgis.

7 June 1986 – Azteca, Mexico City – 114,600 – George Courtney (ENG)

MEXICO **(1) 1**
Flores 3

PARAGUAY **(0) 1**
Romero 85

MEXICO Larios, Cruz Barbosa, Trejo, Quirarte, Servín, Aguirre, Boy (c) [España 57], Múñoz, Negrete, Flores [FJ Cruz 77], Sánchez.
PARAGUAY Fernández, Torales [Ramón Ángel Hicks 75], Zabala, Schettina, Delgado (c), Cañete, Romero, Núñez, Cabañas, Ferreira, Mendoza [Guasch 62].

A dramatic top and tail. Boy sent Servín down the left, a dive by Sánchez distracted the defence, and Flores brought the cross down before volleying low across the keeper. The next eighty minutes were punctuated by bookings, then Romero scored with a fine header from Cañete's cross and Sánchez won a penalty after going down outside the box, only for his image of returning messiah to be dented when Fernández touched his kick onto a post. The crowd's first disappointment, but both sides were surely through.

8 June 1986 – Luis Gutiérrez Dosal, Toluca – 10,000 – Jesús Díaz Palacio (COL)

BELGIUM **(2) 2**
Scifo 16, Claesen pen 19

IRAQ **(0) 1**
Rhadi 59

1930 1934 1938 1950 1954 1958 1962 1966 1970 1974 1978 1982 **1986** 1990 1994 1998 2002 2006

BELGIUM Pfaff, Gerets, Van der Elst, Demol [Georges Grün 68], De Wolf, Scifo [Leo Clijsters 66], Vercauteren, Vandereycken, Ceulemans (c), Desmet, Claesen.
IRAQ Raad (c), Allawi, Nadhum, Samir Mahmoud, Shihab, Haris Hassan, Al-Roubai, Rhadi, Kourkis, Abidoun, Karim Minshid [Aufi 81].
SENT OFF: Kourkis 52.

Belgium badly needed the win and got it without too much trouble, though Iraq's physical style was again hard to deal with. The 20-year-old playmaker Scifo, who'd turned down Italy to play for Belgium, scored with a cross shot after a strong run and lateral pass by Ceulemans, and Allawi brought down Vercauteren for the penalty. After Kourkis had been sent off for fouling De Wolf, Rhadi controlled Abidoun's prodded pass before shooting low across Pfaff.

Clijsters' daughter Kim won the Wimbledon doubles title in 2003 and the US Open singles title in 2005.

11 June 1986 – Azteca, Mexico City – 103,763 – Zoran Petrović (YUG)

MEXICO   (0) 1
Quirarte 54

IRAQ   (0) 0

MEXICO Larios, Rafael Amador [Alejandro Domínguez 61], Quirarte, Cruz Barbosa, Servín, Aguirre, Boy (c), España, Negrete, Flores, Carlos de los Cobos [FJ Cruz 78].
IRAQ Abdulfattah Jassim, Maad Ibrahim Majid, Khalil Allawi (c), Nadhum, Shihab, Rhadi, Minshid, Abidoun [Aufi 60], Ainid Tweresh [Shakir Hamza 68], Basim, Al-Roubai.

Again the Iraqis offered little more than snapping aggression, but Mexico made hard work of it, scoring from another set piece. The Iraqis allowing a long straightforward free kick to reach Quirarte tight on the right-hand goal line, and his volley beat Jassim at the near post.

Sánchez was suspended after bookings in each of the previous two games.

11 June 1986 – Luis Gutiérrez Dosal, Toluca – 10,000 – Bogdan Dochev (BUL)

BELGIUM   (1) 2
Vercauteren 31, Veyt 59

PARAGUAY   (0) 2
Cabañas 50, 76

BELGIUM Pfaff, Michel Renquin, Grün [Leo Van der Elst 89], Vercauteren, Broos, Patrick Vervoort, Demol, Scifo, Ceulemans (c), Claesen, Danny Veyt.
PARAGUAY Fernández, Torales, Zabala, Guasch, Delgado (c), Núñez, Romero, Cañete, Ferreira, Mendoza [Hicks 67], Cabañas.

Paraguay were already in the second round, the Belgians virtually there with them, so this was mainly for entertainment and experiment, and Belgium's new back line was a considerable improvement. Ceulemans, big and rawboned but always influential, gave the ball to Vercauteren, who tried either a cross or a chip and the ball drifted over the keeper. A back-header by Broos found Cabañas unmarked to volley the equaliser, Vervoort sent Veyt through to clip the ball over the keeper, and Cabañas chested a deflected cross past

GROUP B						
	P	W	D	L	F	A	Pts
Mexico	3	2	1	0	4	2	5
Paraguay	3	1	2	0	4	3	4
Belgium	3	1	1	1	5	5	3
Iraq	3	0	0	3	1	4	0

Mexico, Paraguay and Belgium qualified for the second round.

the last defender before touching in another volley. Scifo scored gloriously from a free kick but hadn't noticed that it was indirect. Five minutes from time, Ré became the first coach to be shown a red card in a finals match.

GROUP C

Canada, France (seeded), Hungary, USSR.

1 June 1986 – Nou Camp, León – 35,748 – Hernán Silva Arce (CHI)

FRANCE (0) 1
Papin 79

CANADA (0) 0

FRANCE Joël Bats, Manuel Amoros, Patrick Battiston, Luis Fernandez, Thierry Tusseau, Max Bossis, Alain Giresse, Jean Tigana, Jean-Pierre Papin, Michel Platini (c), Dominique Rocheteau [Yannick Stopyra 70]. *Henri Michel.*
CANADA Paul Dolan, Bobby Lenarduzzi, Ian Bridge, Paul James [Branko Segota 82], Randy Samuel, Bruce Wilson (c), Randy Ragan, Dave Norman, Mike Sweeney [Jamie Lowery 55], Carl Valentine, Igor Vrablic. *Tony Waiters (ENG).*

France naturally dominated the part-timers, several of whom didn't even have a club – but suffered from their chronic lack of a goalscorer up front. Papin, who eventually headed into an empty net after Stopyra had touched back a long cross by Fernandez, wasn't yet the razor-sharp striker who became European Footballer of the Year. He missed a number of chances and volleyed against the bar after 69 minutes. Fernandez hit a post after 78. Canada, coached by a former England international goalkeeper, had their moments but the lively Vrablic was given little support.

2 June 1986 – Revolución, Irapuato – 16,500 – Luigi Agnolin (ITA)

USSR (3) 6
Yakovenko 2, Aleinikov 3, Belanov pen 24, Yaremchuk 66, Dajka o.g. 75, Rodionov 83

HUNGARY (0) 0

USSR Renat Dasayev, Vladimir Bessonov, Oleg Kuznetsov, Nikolai Larionov, Anatoly Demyanenko (c), Vasily Rats, Pavel Yakovenko [Vadim Yevtushenko 72], Aleksandr Zavarov, Igor Belanov [Sergei Rodionov 69], Sergei Aleinikov, Ivan Yaremchuk. *Valery Lobanovsky.*
HUNGARY Péter Disztl, Sándor Sallai, Antal Róth [Győző Burcsa 13], József Kardos, Zoltán Péter [László Dajka 63], Imre Garaba, Antal Nagy (c), Lajos Détári, József Kiprich, Marton Esterházy, György Bognár. *György Mezey.*

Hungary were without the injured Nyilasi, but his World Cup record was spotty and anyway the USSR were simply too strong, though six goals was an unusual haul for them. They were helped by Mezey taking off a defender after the two early goals, but there was no doubting their stamina in the thin air. Lobanovsky, recently appointed coach, was also the manager at Dynamo Kiev, who'd just run away with the Cup-Winners Cup: nine of that team played here, in place of long-standing stars like Blokhin, Chivadze and Protasov.

Yakovenko hit a loose ball in low at the near post past an unsighted keeper, and Aleinikov's demoralising long shot was the pick of the bunch. Belanov blasted a penalty after he'd been caught by Kardos, then had a shot saved and lashed another over the bar. Yakovenko ran strongly through the midfield, beating two men, before finding the unmarked Yaremchuk, who took the ball round the keeper for the fourth; Dajka's tackle knocked the ball beyond his own keeper after the Soviets had interpassed on the edge of the box; and Yakovenko collected Dasayev's throw-out and beat a man

1930

1934

1938

1950

1954

1958

1962

1966

1970

1974

1978

1982

1986

1990

1994

1998

2002

2006

before sending Aleinikov clean through the middle. When Disztl came out and saved with his feet, Rodionov arrived to jab in the loose ball. The Soviets might have equalled the finals record of seven different goalscorers if Yevtushenko hadn't put a penalty wide soon after coming on.

Dajka's own goal is sometimes credited to Yaremchuk. Larionov, Demyanenko and Yakovenko shared the same birthday.

---

5 June 1986 – Nou Camp, León – 36,540 – Romualdo Arppi (BRZ)

FRANCE   (0) 1
Fernandez 62

USSR   (0) 1
Rats 54

FRANCE Bats, William Ayache, Amoros, Fernandez, Bossis, Battiston, Giresse [Philippe Vercruysse 83], Tigana, Papin [Bruno Bellone 76], Platini (c), Stopyra.
USSR Dasayev, Bessonov, Kuznetsov, Larionov, Demyanenko (c), Rats, Yakovenko [Rodionov 69], Zavarov [Oleg Blokhin 59], Belanov, Aleinikov, Yaremchuk.

A fine match, in which both teams looked real contenders. The USSR's goal was another tremendous long shot (Rats beating Bats launched a few headlines) but Giresse's lob put the sturdy Fernandez through and a draw was the right result. Platini hit the post with a free kick but was plagued with tendonitis.

---

6 June 1986 – Revolución, Irapuato – 13,800 – Jamal Al-Sharif (SYR)

HUNGARY   (1) 2
Esterházy 2, Détári 75

CANADA   (0) 0

HUNGARY József Szendrei, Sallai, Kardos, Garaba, József Varga, Nagy (c) [Dajka 61], Détári, Burcsa [Róth 28], Kiprich, Esterházy, Bognár.
CANADA Tino Lettieri, Lenarduzzi, Bridge, James [Segota 54], Samuel, Wilson (c) [Sweeney 41], Ragan, Norman, Gerry Gray, Valentine, Vrablic.
SENT OFF: Sweeney 86.

Hungary kept their hopes alive without impressing anyone. Their first goal was the result of two deflections, one into the path of Esterházy, the other taking his low shot inside the near post. Then Détári put in the rebound after Lettieri had made a brave save. Canada didn't build on their stubborn performance against France: Wilson had a rough time and was substituted, Vrablic and Segota missed chances, and Sweeney was sent off for a second bookable offence, a 'juego brusco' against Bognár.

---

9 June 1986 – Nou Camp, León – 31,420 – Carlos Alberto da Silva Valente (POR)

FRANCE   (1) 3
Stopyra 30, Tigana 63, Rocheteau 84

HUNGARY   (0) 0

FRANCE Bats, Ayache, Amoros, Fernandez, Bossis, Battiston, Giresse, Tigana, Papin [Rocheteau 61], Platini (c), Stopyra [Jean-Marc Ferreri 71].
HUNGARY Disztl, Sallai, Kardos, Garaba (c), Varga, Róth, Péter Hannich [Nagy HT], Dajka, Détári, Kálmán Kovács [Bognár 66], Esterházy.

In emphasising the gulf between the teams, France could have had more goals, Battiston, Fernandez and Stopyra missing clear chances. Although Détári hit the bar, Hungary looked desperately short on morale. Ayache's cross to the far post was met by Stopyra's powerful header, the third goal was scored with only four touches, Rocheteau sliding in Platini's sideways flick from a Bats clearance – but Tigana's was the best. Exchanging passes with Platini and Rocheteau, he shot in sweetly at the near post. Surprisingly it was his only goal in 52 internationals, but he'd had a hand in a few others.

---

9 June 1986 – Revolución, Irapuato – 14,200 – Idrissa Traore (MLI)

USSR   (0) 2
Blokhin 58, Zavarov 75

CANADA   (0) 0

USSR Viktor Chanov, Andrei Bal, Kuznetsov, Gennady Morozov, Aleksandr Bubnov, Gennady Litovchenko, Aleinikov, Yevtushenko, Rodionov, Oleg Protasov [Belanov 56], Blokhin (c) [Zavarov 61].
CANADA Lettieri, Lenarduzzi, Bridge, James [Segota 64], Samuel, Wilson (c), Ragan, Norman, Gray [George Pakos 69], Valentine, Dale Mitchell.

Blokhin, once fearsomely fast (European Footballer of the Year eleven years earlier), was allowed a romp against the bottom team and suffered an injury in converting Belanov's square pass. Zavarov lobbed the keeper after a headed one-two with Belanov. Canada tried hard for a goal and Mitchell came close with a free kick.

GROUP C

	P	W	D	L	F	A	Pts
USSR	3	2	1	0	9	1	5
France	3	2	1	0	5	1	5
Hungary	3	1	0	2	2	9	2
Canada	3	0	0	3	0	5	0

The USSR and France qualified for the second round.

GROUP D

Algeria, Brazil (seeded), Northern Ireland, Spain.

---

1 June 1986 – Jalisco, Guadalajara – 35,748 – Chris Bambridge (AUS)

BRAZIL   (0) 1
Sócrates 61

SPAIN   (0) 0

BRAZIL Carlos (Gallo), Édson Boaro, 'Branco' (Cláudio Vaz), Elzo (Coelho), Júlio César (da Silva), 'Edinho' (Edino Nazareth) (c), Leovegildo Júnior [Paulo Roberto Falcão 78], 'Alemão' (Ricardo de Brito), Walter Casagrande ['Müller' (Luís Corrêa) 65], Sócrates (de Souza), 'Careca' (Antônio de Oliveira). *Telê Santana.*
SPAIN Andoni Zubizarreta, Tomás (Reñones), Andoni Goikoetxea, Antonio Maceda, José Camacho (c), 'Michel' (Miguel González), Víctor (Muñoz), Francisco (López) [Juan Antonio Señor 81], Julio Salinas, Julio Alberto (Moreno), Emilio Butragueño. *Miguel Muñoz.*

Spain had no luck. Two first-choice players were ill, and TV replays showed the ball crossing the line after their best player Michel hit the bar (an impossibly hard decision for the linesman). When Careca hit the bar nine minutes later, Sócrates headed in from an offside position. Careca was a lithe threat up front, and the back line was excellent: Branco a progressive left back, Júlio César and Edinho the best central defensive pairing in the world. Goikoetxea was a different player from Jon Andoni Goikoetxea who scored in the 1994 finals.

---

3 June 1986 – Tres de Marzo, Guadalajara – 22,000 – Valery Butenko (USR)

ALGERIA   (0) 1
Zidane 59

NORTHERN IRELAND (1) 1
Whiteside 6

1930
1934
1938
1950
1954
1958
1962
1966
1970
1974
1978
1982
1986
1990
1994
1998
2002
2006

ALGERIA Larbi El-Hadi, Abdallah Medjadi, Faouzi Mansouri, Nourredine Kourichi, Mahmoud Guendouz (c), Mohammed Kaci Said, Salah Assad, Halim Ben Mabrouk, Djamel Zidane [Lakhdar Belloumi 72], Karim Maroc, Rabah Madjer [Rachid Harkouk 27]. *Rabah Saadane.*

NORTHERN IRELAND Pat Jennings, Jimmy Nicholl, Mal Donaghy, Nigel Worthington, Alan McDonald, John O'Neill, David McCreery, Steve Penney [Ian Stewart 67], Billy Hamilton, Sammy McIlroy (c), Norman Whiteside [Colin Clarke 81]. *Billy Bingham.*

Two of the surprise teams of 1982 were in obvious decline. Both scored from free kicks, Whiteside getting a big deflection off the wall, Zidane hitting a low shot from thirty yards. Before 1998, Harkouk was the only African player to appear in the finals while playing for an English club (Notts County). Medjadi was known as Liégeon when he played for Monaco.

6 June 1986 – Jalisco, Guadalajara – 47,000 – Rómulo Méndez (GUA)

BRAZIL   (0) 1
Careca 66

ALGERIA   (0) 0

BRAZIL Carlos, Édson Boaro [Falcão 10], Branco, Elzo, Júlio César, Edinho (c), Júnior, Alemão, Sócrates, Careca, Casagrande [Müller 58].
ALGERIA Nasreddine Drid, Medjadi, Mansouri, Fodil Megharia, Guendouz (c), Kaci Said, Assad [Tedj Bensaoula 67], Ben Mabrouk, Djamel Menad, Belloumi [Zidane 75], Madjer.

Edinho had to kick clear when Belloumi's shot beat Carlos, but Drid was the busier keeper, making more than one '*espectacular intervención*'. Julio César hit the bar and Branco hit a post, but the goal was the result of some genuinely dreadful defending. Guendouz miskicked Müller's low cross, then Medjadi's hesitation (an '*infantil error*') let Careca in. Of

some concern was the performance of Sócrates, loping around to no great effect, and the need to use Júnior in midfield.

7 June 1986 – Tres de Marzo, Guadalajara – 28,000 – Horst Brummeier (AUT)

SPAIN   (2) 2
Butragueño 1, Salinas 18

NORTHERN IRELAND   (0) 1
Clarke 46

SPAIN Zubizarreta, Tomás, Goikoetxea, Víctor, Ricardo Gallego, Camacho (c), Michel, Francisco, Rafael Gordillo [Ramón Calderé 53], Salinas [Señor 78], Butragueño.
NORTHERN IRELAND Jennings, Nicholl, Donaghy, Worthington [Hamilton 70], McDonald, O'Neill, McCreery, Penney [Stewart 54], Clarke, McIlroy (c), Whiteside.

The early goals were too much for Northern Ireland to make up. Butragueño scored confidently from Michel's superb through-ball, and the hefty Salinas smacked in a loose ball after McIlroy had given the ball away. The Irish replied with a bizarre goal, Zubizarreta slicing a clearance kick up in the air, Gallego heading the ball back, Clarke heading over the keeper as he slipped. In the second half, Jennings stood up well to save when a square pass put Butragueño clean through. Gordillo's return gave Spain extra quality on the left but only for this one match: a broken leg kept him out of the rest of the tournament. FIFA's Official Report says Hipólito Rincón came on as substitute for Salinas, an error confirmed by the Spanish FA.

12 June 1986 – Tecnológico, Monterrey – 23,980 – Shizuo Takada (JPN)

SPAIN   (1) 3
Calderé 15, 68, Eloy 71

ALGERIA   (0) 0

SPAIN Zubizarreta, Tomás, Goikoetxea, Gallego, Camacho (c), Michel [Señor 61], Víctor, Francisco, Calderé, Salinas, Butragueño [Eloy (Olaya) HT]. ALGERIA Drid [Larbi 18], Mansouri, Megharia, Kourichi, Guendouz (c), Kaci Said, Madjer, Maroc, Harkouk, Belloumi, Zidane [Menad 60].

Drid was injured by Goikoetxea, who'd committed a famously appalling foul on Maradona in a Spanish league match – but the change of goalkeeper made little difference: Algeria were a shadow of their 1982 side, and rough with it. The moustachioed Calderé, a sharp runner on both flanks, converted an intelligent cut-back from Salinas, accepted an open goal when Eloy ran through on the keeper, then was found to have taken the stimulant ephedrine, administered by the local hospital for a gastric complaint. The Spanish federation was fined and the team doctor cautioned, but Calderé escaped a ban. Gallego's cross from the right found two players all alone in front of goal, Salinas standing aside to let Eloy shoot in.

12 June 1986 – Jalisco, Guadalajara – 46,500 – Siegfried Kirschen (DDR)

BRAZIL   (2) 3
Careca 15, 87, Josimar 41

NORTHERN IRELAND   (0) 0

BRAZIL Carlos, Josimar (Pereira), Branco, Elzo, Júlio César, Edinho (c), Júnior, Alemão, Sócrates ['Zico' (Arthur Antunes Coimbra) 67], Careca, Müller [Casagrande 27]. NORTHERN IRELAND Jennings, Nicholl, Donaghy, David Campbell [Gerry Armstrong 70], McDonald, O'Neill, McCreery, Stewart, Clarke, McIlroy (c), Whiteside [Hamilton 67].

All three goals were better than they needed to be against a side who were never a threat. Müller, marked by two players near the right-hand corner flag, drove in a low cross which Careca hammered through Jennings' dive. Josimar, the new cap who'd given Müller the

ball, came up again and steadied himself before cracking a 25-yarder into the top corner, reducing Jennings to a desperate hop. The third has been shown less often but was even better, Careca coming inside from the right to collect Zico's backheel and shoot in low at the near post. Jennings, one of the all-time greats, wasn't disgraced now, saving from Júnior, Careca's volley, and when Casagrande and Branco were clean through. Jennings ended his international career on his 41st birthday after winning 119 caps, a European record.

GROUP D

	P	W	D	L	F	A	Pts
Brazil	3	3	0	0	5	0	6
Spain	3	2	0	1	5	2	4
Northern Ireland	3	0	1	2	2	6	1
Algeria	3	0	1	2	1	5	1

Brazil and Spain qualified for the second round.

GROUP E

Denmark, Scotland, Uruguay, West Germany (seeded).

4 June 1986 – La Corregidora, Querétaro – 30,500 – Vojtěch Christov (CZE)

URUGUAY   (1) 1
Alzamendi 4

WEST GERMANY   (0) 1
Allofs 84

URUGUAY Fernando Álvez, Eduardo Acevedo, Victor Diogo, Miguel Ángel Bossio, José Batista,

1930
1934
1938
1950
1954
1958
1962
1966
1970
1974
1978
1982
1986
1990
1994
1998
2002
2006

1930
1934
1938
1950
1954
1958
1962
1966
1970
1974
1978
1982

1986

1990
1994
1998
2002
2006

Nelson Gutiérrez, Jorge Barrios (c) [Mario Saralegui 55], Antonio Alzamendi [Venancio Ramos 81], Sergio Santín, Jorge da Silva, Enzo Francescoli. *Omar Borras.*
WEST GERMANY Harald Schumacher (c), Klaus Augenthaler, Thomas Berthold, Karlheinz Förster, Hans-Peter Briegel, Andreas Brehme [Pierre Littbarski HT], Lothar Matthäus [Karl-Heinz Rummenigge 73], Felix Magath, Norbert Eder, Rudi Völler, Klaus Allofs. *Franz Beckenbauer.*

Uruguay took an early lead against a team missing the injured Rummenigge and Littbarski. A ludicrously long back-pass by Matthäus sent Alzamendi clear to go round the keeper before hitting the bar with a shot that didn't hit the net but clearly crossed the line. But German teams didn't bend the knee, and the two substitutions gave them more oomph up front, a hopeful header forward falling kindly for Allofs to shoot in low from the left. Late relief for a team who were reluctantly using the tubby Magath as a playmaker.

4 June 1986 – Neza 86, Nezahualcoyotl – 18,000 – Lajos Németh (HUN)

DENMARK (0) 1
Elkjær 57

SCOTLAND (0) 0

DENMARK Troels Rasmussen, Morten Olsen (c), Søren Busk, Ivan Nielsen, Klaus Berggreen, Søren Lerby, Jesper Olsen [Jan Mølby 79], Jens-Jørn Bertelsen, Frank Arnesen [John Sivebæk 75], Preben Elkjær, Michael Laudrup. *Sepp Piontek (GER).*
SCOTLAND Jim Leighton, Richard Gough, Maurice Malpas, Steve Nicol, Robert 'Roy' Aitken, Alex McLeish, Willie Miller, Graeme Souness (c), Gordon Strachan [Eamonn Bannon 75], Charlie Nicholas, Paul Sturrock [Frank McAvennie 61]. *Alex Ferguson.*

Scotland were made to look ordinary by the best team Denmark have ever put out, so strong that the likes of Mølby and Jesper Olsen weren't guaranteed a place. Once the veteran Morten Olsen had taken a grip at the back, the front two began to stretch the Scottish defence: Elkjær with his strong running, Laudrup the most gifted young player in the world. The goal, though, was untidy, Elkjær taking a rebound off Miller's legs before shooting in off a post. Strachan ran his heart out and used the ball well, but Souness was disappointing again, and the much vaunted Nicholas put the ball in the net after a wrong offside decision then was badly fouled by Berggreen.

8 June 1986 – La Corregidora, Querétaro – 25,000 – Ioan Igna (ROM)

WEST GERMANY (1) 2
Völler 22, Allofs 49

SCOTLAND (1) 1
Strachan 17

WEST GERMANY Schumacher (c), Berthold, Briegel [Ditmar Jakobs 62], Matthäus, Förster, Augenthaler, Littbarski [Rummenigge 75], Magath, Eder, Völler, Allofs.
SCOTLAND Leighton, Gough, Nicol [McAvennie 60], Aitken, Malpas, Miller, David Narey, Souness (c), Strachan, Bannon [Davie Cooper 74], Steve Archibald.

Again little Strachan was Scotland's only star, thoroughly deserving his goal, a heavily deflected strike from the right-hand side of the penalty area. Cooper's trickery caused a few problems at the end and Archibald did some intelligent running but had no support. Meanwhile the opportunism of the West German strikers turned the match, each making a goal for the other. Allofs' left-wing cross made an open goal for Völler, who later held back a defender as the ball ran to his partner. Ditmar is the correct spelling in this case (not Dietmar).

8 June 1986 – Neza 86, Nezahualcoyotl – 26,500 – Antonio Márquez (MEX)

DENMARK (2) 6
Elkjær 11, 68, 79, Lerby 41, Laudrup 51, J Olsen 88

URUGUAY (1) 1
Francescoli pen 45

DENMARK Rasmussen, M Olsen (c), Busk, Nielsen, Berggreen, Lerby, Henrik Andersen, Bertelsen [Mølby 56], Arnesen, Elkjær, Laudrup [J Olsen 81].
URUGUAY Álvez, Acevedo (c), Diogo, Bossio, Batista, Gutiérrez, Saralegui, Santín [José Salazar 56], da Silva, Francescoli, Alzamendi [Ramos 57]
SENT OFF: Bossio 19.

Hard to know what to think of this. Denmark were direct and skilful and everything a modern power team should be, but Uruguay were a man short for the last seventy minutes and lost their appetite for a struggle. Laudrup scored the best goal of the six, almost tip-toeing past two defenders and the goalkeeper on the left. Elkjær, jutting-jawed and relentless, scored the first goal with a left-footed cross shot after Laudrup had beaten two men, put in the loose ball after Laudrup had prodded the ball against the keeper, ran from half-way before going round Álvez, and crossed for Lerby and Jesper Olsen to score. Francescoli was fouled by Busk for the penalty, but Uruguay's credentials had taken an enormous blow.

13 June 1986 – Neza 86, Nezahualcoyotl – 20,000 – Joël Quiniou (FRA)

SCOTLAND 0
URUGUAY 0

SCOTLAND Leighton, Gough, Arthur Albiston, Nicol [Cooper 70], Miller (c), Narey, Strachan, Paul McStay, Graeme Sharp, Aitken, Sturrock [Nicholas 70].
URUGUAY Álvez, Acevedo, Gutiérrez, Batista, Diogo, Dario Pereyra, Ramos [Saralegui 70], Santín, Wilmar Cabrera, Barrios (c), Francescoli [Alzamendi 83].
SENT OFF: Batista 55 sec.

The tournament's oddball format meant the Scots would qualify if they beat Uruguay, despite losing their first two matches. But Ferguson picked the weakest Scotland team in recent memory and even a ludicrous early sending-off didn't help them.

Immediately after the kick-off, Batista took Strachan's legs and was sent off by a referee who, some say, took out the red card by mistake (the video suggests a possible lack of conviction, though it's hard to be sure). It was the fastest dismissal in a finals match and cost Batista dear: he wasn't capped again till 1993. But Francescoli, on his own in attack, held the ball up magisterially, and Scotland made few chances against a ruthless defence. The best was missed by Nicol, from Strachan's low cross: only six yards out from an empty net, he somehow prodded it back towards Álvez. Later Scotland had another goal wrongly disallowed for offside, from Strachan's quickly taken free kick.

A sore draw for Scotland, whose FA secretary Ernie Walker told us his team had been playing 'the scum of world football' – but both sides had fouled each other from start to finish. Without winning a match, and after losing one 6-1, Uruguay were through, but yet again Scotland hadn't done enough to be mourned. Someone counted that they'd had seven shots on target in three matches.

1930 1934 1938 1950 1954 1958 1962 1966 1970 1974 1978 1982 **1986** 1990 1994 1998 2002 2006

13 June 1986 – La Corregidora, Querétaro – 28,500 – Alexis Ponnet (BEL)

DENMARK (1) 2
J Olsen pen 43, Eriksen 62
WEST GERMANY (0) 0

DENMARK Lars Høgh, M Olsen (c), Busk, Sivebæk, Andersen, Lerby, Mølby, J Olsen [Allan Simonsen 70], Arnesen, Elkjær, Laudrup [John Eriksen HT].
WEST GERMANY Schumacher (c), Berthold, Förster [Rummenigge 70], Brehme, Matthias Herget, Jakobs, Eder, Matthäus, Völler, Wolfgang Rolff [Littbarski HT], Allofs.
SENT OFF: Arnesen 88.

West Germany created several chances – Høgh making a very good save from Völler, Brehme hitting a post – but Morten Olsen, still a fine attacking sweeper at 36, was tripped by Rolff for the penalty, and Arnesen's low cross was turned in by Eriksen. Arnesen's sending-off, for a kick at Matthäus, would cost Denmark their midfield organiser, but they seemed to have more than enough talent to replace him. Simonsen, the forerunner of this talented team, European Footballer of the Year back in 1977, made a token appearance in the finals.

1986

GROUP E

	P	W	D	L	F	A	Pts
Denmark	3	3	0	0	9	1	6
West Germany	3	1	1	1	3	4	3
Uruguay	3	0	2	1	2	7	2
Scotland	3	0	1	2	1	3	1

Denmark, West Germany and Uruguay qualified for the second round.

GROUP F

England, Morocco, Poland (seeded), Portugal.

2 June 1986 – Universitario, Monterrey – 19,694 – José Luis Martínez Bazán (URU)

MOROCCO 0
POLAND 0

MOROCCO 'Zaki' (Ezaki Badou) (c), Khalifa (Labid), Abdelmajid Lamriss, Mustafa El-Biyaz, Nourredine Bouyahiaoui, Abdelmajid Dolmy, Mustafa El-Haddaoui [Abdelaziz Soulaimani 87], Aziz Bouderbala, 'Krimau' (Abdelkrim Merry), Mohammed Timoumi [Abderrazak Khairi 89], Mustafa Merry. *José Faria (BRZ).*
POLAND Józef Młynarczyk, Marek Ostrowski, Roman Wójcicki, Stefan Majewski, Waldemar Matysik, Dariusz Kubicki [Kazimierz Przybyś HT], Ryszard Komornicki, Andrzej Buncol, Włodek Smolarek, Zbigniew Boniek (c), Dariusz Dziekanowski [Jan Urban 55]. *Antoni Piechniczek.*

The more sophisticated team had the three best players on the pitch and more of the play, but seemed happy with the draw. Yes, Morocco should have done better.

Timoumi, Bouderbala and Krimau were in better form than anyone in the Polish team. Boniek, now 30, was playing deep again, and the highly rated Dziekanowski had to be replaced, his substitute hitting a post near the end. Khairi was on the field for only 27 seconds, a finals record. Krimau and Mustafa Merry were brothers.

3 June 1986 – Tecnológico, Monterrey – 19,998 – Volker Roth (GER)

PORTUGAL (0) 1
Carlos Manuel 75
ENGLAND (0) 0

PORTUGAL Manuel Bento (c), Álvaro (Magalhães), Frederico (Rosa), António J Oliveira, Augusto Inácio, Diamantino (Miranda) [José António (Bargiela) 83], António André, Carlos Manuel (Corrêia), Fernando Gomes [Paulo Futre 71], Jaime Pacheco, António Sousa. *José Torres*.
ENGLAND Peter Shilton, M Gary Stevens, Kenny Sansom, Bryan Robson (c) [Steve Hodge 80], Terry Butcher, Terry Fenwick, Glenn Hoddle, Ray Wilkins, Mark Hateley, Gary Lineker, Chris Waddle [Peter Beardsley 80]. *Bobby Robson*.

England's recent unbeaten run included a good win in the USSR, but they now ran up against a brick wall and lost faith in themselves. Portugal had lost their last warm-up match 3-1 at home, but earlier in the season they'd become the first country to beat the Germans in a World Cup qualifier: 1-0 away with a goal by Carlos Manuel.

England created chances – Lineker shooting wide after stretching for Waddle's deflected cross from the left then chesting down Butcher's long ball and prodding the ball gently past Bento for Oliveira to kick clear – but suddenly the use of a big man (Hateley) served by a winger (Waddle) looked woefully predictable. Portugal attacked so infrequently that their goal probably had something to do with England's loss of concentration. Diamantino beat Sansom on the inside and Stevens went AWOL when Carlos Manuel appeared unmarked at the far post to lift the low cross over Shilton, the first goal he'd conceded in his last five finals matches.

The 20-year-old Futre came on to run at England's defence, and Shilton had to make a good save at his feet when he was clean through. A sobering match, during which someone snapped Carlos Manuel sticking his tongue out at Wilkins, which said it all.

One source lists André as a first name, but the leading Portuguese statisticians and a history of the national team call him António Ferreira André.

---

6 June 1986 – Tecnológico, Monterrey – 20,200 – Gabriel González (PAR)

ENGLAND 0
MOROCCO 0

MOROCCO Zaki (c), Khalifa, Lamriss ['Hcina' (Lahcen Ouadani) 73], El-Biyaz, Bouyahiaoui, Khairi, Dolmy, Bouderbala, Krimau, Timoumi, M Merry [Soulaimani 87].
ENGLAND Shilton, MG Stevens, Sansom, Robson (c) [Hodge 41], Butcher, Fenwick, Hoddle, Wilkins, Hateley [Gary A Stevens 75], Lineker, Waddle.
SENT OFF: Wilkins 42.

Nightmare heaped on nightmare for England, who were fortunate that the opposition were almost pathologically cautious. Against a team that lost its inspirational captain and played with ten men for the last fifty minutes, Morocco kept possession and played for another draw. Put it down to modesty in the face of history, but they risked not going through.

Robson's protective harness couldn't save his shoulder when he fell in the Moroccan penalty area. Led off with his arm in a sling, he seemed to be taking his team's hopes with him. Almost immediately Wilkins was penalised, threw the ball towards the referee, and became the first England player to be sent off in a finals match, for a second bookable offence two minutes after his first. England's reputation and position in the group were lower than anyone could have expected.

---

7 June 1986 – Universitario, Monterrey – 19,915 – Ali Ben Nasser (TUN)

POLAND (0) 1
Smolarek 68
PORTUGAL (0) 0

POLAND Młynarczyk, Ostrowski, Wójcicki, Majewski, Matysik, Urban, Komornicki [Jan Karaś 56], Krzysztof Pawlak, Smolarek [Andrzej Zgutczyński 75], Boniek (c), Dziekanowski.

1930
1934
1938
1950
1954
1958
1962
1966
1970
1974
1978
1982
1986
1990
1994
1998
2002
2006

PORTUGAL Vítor Damas, Álvaro, Frederico, Oliveira, Inácio, Diamantino, André [Jaime Magalhães 73], Carlos Manuel, Gomes (c) [Futre HT], Pacheco, Sousa.

A dose of vice-versa for the Portuguese, dominating possession before conceding a breakaway goal, Smolarek sliding the ball just inside the far post. Futre again caused problems with his ball control at speed and should probably have started the game in place of the tall Gomes, who was prolific only at club level. The 38-year-old Damas had to replace the 37-year-old Bento, who'd broken a leg in training and didn't play for Portugal again.

11 June 1986 – Tres de Marzo, Guadalajara – 18,000 – Alan Snoddy (NIR)

MOROCCO (2) 3
Khairi 18, 27, Krimau 61

PORTUGAL (0) 1
Diamantino 79

MOROCCO Zaki (c), Khalifa, Lamriss [Azzeddine Amanallah 69], El-Biyaz, Bouyahiaoui, Khairi, Dolmy, El-Haddaoui [Soulaimani 71], Bouderbala, Krimau, Timoumi.
PORTUGAL Damas, Álvaro [Rui Águas 55], Frederico, Oliveira, Inácio, J Magalhães, Carlos Manuel, Gomes (c), Futre, Pacheco, Sousa [Diamantino 65].

When Morocco decided to come out of their shell, they did it in style, becoming the first African country not only to qualify from a finals group but to win it. Khairi drove in a loose ball from outside the area after Portugal had given the ball away, then met Khalifa's first-time cross with an instant ground shot, Timoumi's cross sent Krimau in to volley across Damas, and Morocco could afford to leave Diamantino unmarked near the end. Portugal's win over England seemed a long time ago.

11 June 1986 – Universitario, Monterrey – 22,600 – André Daina (SWI)

ENGLAND (3) 3
Lineker 9, 14, 34

POLAND (0) 0

ENGLAND Shilton (c), MG Stevens, Sansom, Peter Reid, Butcher, Fenwick, Trevor Steven, Hoddle, Lineker [Kerry Dixon 84], Beardsley [Waddle 75], Hodge.
POLAND Młynarczyk, Ostrowski, Majewski, Matysik [Buncol HT], Wójcicki, Pawlak, Urban, Komornicki [Karaś 23], Smolarek, Boniek (c), Dziekanowski.

Amazingly a draw would still be enough for England to qualify, but in the event they suddenly woke up and played a swaggering first half. It's said that Bobby Robson gave in to player power, but if so he was only doing what Schön had done in the '70s, and anyway the players got it right. They dropped the winger and target man, stationed Steven and Hodge wide in midfield, and played Beardsley just behind Lineker, who used the extra space to score a hat trick that saved everyone's bacon and uplifted a whole country.

All three goals came down the Polish right. Lineker took a square pass and moved the ball to the other wing then forced himself in front of Majewski to scoop in Steven's low cross. Beardsley, lying deep with his back to goal, hit a perfect first-time ball out to the left, where Hodge put in a long cross which Lineker met at full tilt. In the previous two matches, his half-volley would probably have gone into the stands; here it flew just under the bar. There was a similar rub of the green in the third goal, but again Lineker took it well, turning to half-volley into the roof of the net after Mlynarczyk, normally so reliable, had dropped an easy corner. Hodge had a goal disallowed for offside and Lineker volleyed wide in the second half, but let's not be greedy. It was the end of England's four consecutive finals matches without a goal. At the 32nd attempt, they'd won one by more than two goals.

Daina had played international football in the mid-1960s.

GROUP F

	P	W	D	L	F	A	Pts
Morocco	3	1	2	0	3	1	4
England	3	1	1	1	3	1	3
Poland	3	1	1	1	1	3	3
Portugal	3	1	0	2	2	4	2

Morocco, England and Poland qualified for the second round.

2ND ROUND

15 June 1986 – Azteca, Mexico City – 114,580 – Romualdo Arppi (BRZ)

MEXICO   (1) 2
Negrete 34, Servín 61

BULGARIA   (0) 0

MEXICO Larios, Amador, Quirarte, Cruz Barbosa, Servín, Muñoz, España, Negrete, Aguirre, Boy (c) [De los Cobos 79], Sánchez.
BULGARIA Mikhailov, Zdravkov, Arabov, Petrov, Dimitrov (c), Sadkov, Yordanov, Gospodinov, Getov [Sirakov 59], Kostadinov, Atanas Pashev [Iskrenov 70].

Bulgaria were heavily criticised for adding nothing to the tournament – but perhaps, as in 1970, they simply couldn't cope with Mexican conditions. Negrete scored with an acrobatic volley after a volleyed return pass from Aguirre, and Servín headed in a near-post

corner – but Mexico couldn't have asked for more compliant opposition.

15 June 1986 – Camp Nou, León – 32,277 – Erik Fredriksson (SWE)

BELGIUM   (0) (2) 4
Scifo 54, Ceulemans 77, Demol 102, Claesen 108

USSR   (1) (2) 3
Belanov 27, 69, pen 111

BELGIUM Pfaff, Gerets [L Van der Elst 112], Grün [Clijsters 99], Renquin, Vervoort, Demol, Scifo, Vercauteren, Ceulemans (c), Claesen, Veyt.
USSR Dasayev, Bessonov, Kuznetsov, Bal, Demyanenko (c), Rats, Yakovenko [Yevtushenko 78], Zavarov [Rodionov 71], Belanov, Aleinikov, Yaremchuk.

The USSR, their fitness again making light of the conditions, dominated entire periods of play and took the lead when Belanov swerved to his right and hit a twenty-yard cross-shot that careered through the thin air and went in off the top of the post. Small and wiry, he had a tremendous match, a very good tournament, and a successful year at club level, and that shot sealed his selection as European Footballer of the Year. He later restored the lead by drilling Zavarov's cross across Pfaff after Ceulemans had lost possession.

But the Belgians, unimpressive till now, gave the Soviet defence endless trouble with high crosses. When Vercauteren sent one in from the left, Scifo brought it down before knocking it home, and Demol's simple long ball found Ceulemans totally unmarked to chest down and beat Dasayev with a cross-shot. Gerets' cross was met by Demol's emphatic header, and Claesen volleyed in when Clijsters headed on, but yet again the Soviet marking had been non-existent.

Pfaff got a touch to the penalty after Belanov was judged to have been fouled in mid-air, and

1930
1934
1938
1950
1954
1958
1962
1966
1970
1974
1978
1982
1986
1990
1994
1998
2002
2006

1930
1934
1938
1950
1954
1958
1962
1966
1970
1974
1978
1982
1986
1990
1994
1998
2002
2006

Rodionov's marvellous shot hit the angle of post and bar. The USSR's elimination was the tournament's loss, but it was hard to begrudge Belgium their win.

---

16 June 1986 – Jalisco, Guadalajara – 45,000 – Volker Roth (GER)

BRAZIL **(1) 4**
Sócrates pen 29, Josimar 56, Edinho 78, Careca pen 83

POLAND **(0) 0**

BRAZIL Carlos, Josimar, Branco, Elzo, Júlio César, Edinho (c), Júnior, Alemão, Careca, Sócrates [Zico 69], Müller [Silas (do Prado) 73].
POLAND Młynarczyk, Przybyś [Jan Furtok 59], Wójcicki, Majewski, Ostrowski, Ryszard Tarasiewicz [Władysław Żmuda 83], Boniek (c), Karaś, Urban, Smolarek, Dziekanowski.

Poland were inferior but desperately unlucky. Don't look at the scoreline, think of Dziekanowski's chip hitting the post and a huge long shot from Karas coming back off the bar, both with the score still 0-0. After that, a triumph for skill. Careca was barged in the penalty area, Sócrates taking the kick without a run-up. Josimar improved on his goal against the Irish by stepping through three tackles on the right before lashing the ball high past the keeper from a tight angle. He scored in each of his first two internationals, rare for a full-back.

Edinho, so hot-headed in 1978 but now the ideal central defender, scored the third by running the length of the field to pick up Careca's backheel and beat a defender and the keeper with a single turn. The fourth goal also came from a long-range break-out, Mlynarczyk bringing down Zico, sent clear by Careca, whose spot kick hit a post and crept in near the other one. Awesome in the end by Brazil. Żmuda was brought on purely to equal Seeler's total of 21 finals matches, a record at the time.

16 June 1986 – Cuauhtémoc, Puebla – 26,000, Luigi Agnolin (ITA)

ARGENTINA **(1) 1**
Pasculli 41

URUGUAY **(0) 0**

ARGENTINA Pumpido, Brown, Cuciuffo, Ruggeri, Garré, Giusti, Batista [Olarticoechea 85], Burruchaga, Maradona (c), Pasculli, Valdano.
URUGUAY Álvez, Bossio, Gutiérrez, Acevedo [Rubén Paz 60], Eliseo Rivero, Barrios (c), Pereyra, Santín, Cabrera [da Silva HT], Ramos, Francescoli.

Having received a fine and a warning from FIFA, Uruguay couldn't subject Maradona to the kind of tackling they wanted, leaving him free to dominate the match. All the sharper for losing half a stone in training, he was still a meaty 11 stone spread over 5'6, three inches shorter than Pelé. Hard to believe this was the same player who'd had two such unhappy years with Barcelona, a victim of hepatitis in the first and a career-threatening foul in the next. The injury was still affecting him here: one of his boots was larger than the other.

Despite that, he skipped past tackles and made chances for Pasculli and Valdano, hit the bar with a free kick, and had a goal disallowed. Ironically he wasn't directly involved in the goal, Acevedo's hesitant touch giving the ball straight to the unmarked Pasculli. After the first World Cup match between the two countries since the 1930 Final, eight of the Uruguayans weren't capped again (shades of 1974) as their famous past began to look increasingly distant.

---

17 June 1986 – Olímpico, Mexico City – 71,449 – Carlos Esposito (ARG)

FRANCE **(1) 2**
Platini 15, Stopyra 57

ITALY **(0) 0**

FRANCE Bats, Ayache, Amoros, Fernandez [Tusseau 73], Bossis, Battiston, Giresse, Tigana, Stopyra, Platini (c) [Ferreri 84], Rocheteau.
ITALY Galli, Bergomi, Cabrini, De Napoli, Vierchowod, Scirea (c), Conti, Bagni, Altobelli, Baresi [Di Gennaro HT], Galderisi [Vialli 57].

Italy, who'd been living off Altobelli and recent glories, were found out and well beaten. Rocheteau made both the goals, his clever first-time pass sending Platini through the middle to chip over Galli, who was no replacement for Zoff, and his square pass setting up Stopyra for a low shot from the right. A crew-cut Vialli replaced the anonymous Galderisi, who didn't score a goal in his ten internationals and was one of six Italians (including winners like Conti and Scirea) not to be capped again.

17 June 1986 – Universitario, Monterrey – 19,800 – Zoran Petrović (YUG)

WEST GERMANY   (0) 1
Matthäus 88

MOROCCO   (0) 0

WEST GERMANY Schumacher, Berthold, Briegel, Eder, Jakobs, Förster, Rummenigge (c), Matthäus, Völler [Littbarski HT], Magath, Allofs.
MOROCCO Zaki (c), Khalifa, Lamriss, Hcina, Bouyahiaoui, Khairi, Dolmy, El-Haddaoui, Bouderbala, Krimau, Timoumi.

Morocco's Brazilian coach claimed he was waiting to bring on two fresh attackers in extra time, but Matthäus didn't give him the chance, curling a free kick along the ground past a badly placed wall and just inside the post. Morocco had only themselves to blame. Yet again (it becomes repetitive) they'd looked the better side but were too defensive, especially as they were surely more accustomed to 36° heat than the Germans.

18 June 1986 – Azteca, Mexico City – 98,728 – Jamal Al-Sharif (SYR)

ENGLAND   (1) 3
Lineker 31, 72, Beardsley 56

PARAGUAY (0) 0

ENGLAND Shilton (c), MG Stevens, Sansom, Reid [GA Stevens 57], Butcher, Alvin Martin, Steven, Hoddle, Lineker, Beardsley [Hateley 80], Hodge.
PARAGUAY Fernández, Torales [Guasch 64], Zabala, Schettina, Delgado (c), Núñez, Romero, Cañete, Ferreira, Mendoza, Cabañas.

Paraguay were no pushovers but England expected to win matches by now. After Paraguay had made nothing of an early chance, Hoddle did well and the front two kept their enthusiasm in the face of some brutal tackling. Beardsley, for instance, scored his goal, a rebound when Fernández couldn't hold Butcher's half-volley, while Lineker was off the field after being elbowed in the throat by Delgado. He took his revenge with a low cross-shot from the right. Earlier Hodge had pulled the ball back from the left-hand goal line for Lineker to touch it into an empty net. Lineker's flying volley forced a spectacular save from Fernández. Paraguay might have had a penalty when Cabañas seemed to be pulled back by Martin, but England kept a close watch on Romero and were well worth their win. Not for the first time in Mexico, the official crowd figure looks like something invented to placate the critics.

18 June 1986 – La Corregidora, Querétaro – 38,500 – Jan Keizer (HOL)

SPAIN   (1) 5
Butragueño 43, 57, 79, pen 88,
Goikoetxea pen 68

DENMARK (1) 1
J Olsen pen 32

1930
1934
1938
1950
1954
1958
1962
1966
1970
1974
1978
1982
1986
1990
1994
1998
2002
2006

SPAIN Zubizarreta, Tomás, Camacho (c), Víctor, Goikoetxea, Gallego, Julio Alberto, Calderé, Salinas [Eloy HT], Michel [Francisco 83], Butragueño.
DENMARK Høgh, M Olsen (c), Nielsen, Busk, Andersen [Eriksen 60], Lerby, Bertelsen, Berggreen, J Olsen [Mølby 70], Elkjær, Laudrup.

An incredible turn-round. Denmark took the lead when Berggreen was brought down by Gallego and would have been ahead at half time but for the most traumatising error in their football history. Jesper Olsen dropped back and out to the right to collect a short free kick from Høgh, rolled it around to kill a little time, then knocked it square without looking, straight into the path of Butragueño, who slipped it past Høgh without breaking stride.

The goal cut into Denmark's confidence, and Arnesen wasn't here to lift it. The fair-haired Butragueño, known as '*El Buitre*' (the vulture) headed in Camacho's flick-on at a corner, was found unmarked by Eloy's square ball, and was brought down by Busk and Morten Olsen for the penalties. Easy to blame Jesper O, or some imagined lack of Danish bottle, but it was really just a freak result, and a sad one for the tournament. No disrespect to Spain and Butragueño, but they were unlikely to play like this again.

QUARTER-FINALS

21 June 1986 – Jalisco, Guadalajara – 65,677 – Ioan Igna (ROM)

FRANCE	**(1) (1) 1**
Platini 41	
BRAZIL	**(1) (1) 1**
Careca 17	
France 4-3 pens.	

FRANCE Bats, Amoros, Tusseau, Fernandez, Bossis, Battiston, Giresse [Ferreri 84], Tigana, Stopyra, Platini (c), Rocheteau [Bellone 99].
BRAZIL Carlos, Josimar, Branco, Elzo, Júlio César, Edinho (c), Júnior [Silas FT], Alemão, Sócrates, Careca, Müller [Zico 71].
PENALTY SHOOT-OUT: Sócrates saved, Stopyra 1-0, Alemão 1-1, Amoros 2-1, Zico 2-2, Bellone 3-2, Branco 3-3, Platini missed, Júlio César hit post, Fernandez 4-3.

The match of the round. Müller hit a post, Careca headed against the bar, and Bats had to make some important saves – but France were always in the match, Rocheteau missing an open goal, Stopyra twice coming close. They fell behind to a fine goal, Müller and Júnior drawing the defence by exchanging tight little passes on the right before moving the ball inside to the unmarked Careca, who swept it first time over Bats. The equaliser was less tidy but thoroughly deserved. Giresse sent Rocheteau clear on the right, the low cross deflected off Edinho into the path of Stopyra, who missed his stumbling header under pressure from Carlos. The ball ran on for Platini to prod home at the far post. The only player to appear in a finals match on his birthday more than once (his 31st this time), he celebrated with a goal each time. This was his 41st for France (still the record) and the only one Carlos conceded in his five finals matches.

The crucial moment came in the 73rd minute. Zico's perfect sliced pass sent Branco into the area, where Bats dived at his feet and the referee awarded a penalty. Sócrates and Careca had taken the spot kicks against Poland, but Zico stepped up for this one. In 1978 he'd scored from a penalty within two minutes of coming on as substitute against Peru. Now, in a spookily similar repeat, he took another one, but Bats saved easily to his left. Three minutes from the end of extra time, Platini's through-ball sent Bellone clear to go round Carlos, who brought him down without punishment. The ball went straight down the other end and Sócrates missed an open goal from Careca's low cross. Breathless.

Sócrates, taking the first penalty in the shoot-out, got his come-uppance for his cocky approach against Poland, Bats saving easily to his right. Platini, the world's great dead-ball expert, shot over the bar – but Júlio César hit the left-hand post (Bellone's kick had gone in off the post and the keeper's back) and Brazil were the latest quality side to be eliminated. Sócrates, Zico and Rocheteau weren't capped again. The end of an era.

---

21 June 1986 – Universitario, Monterrey – 44,386 – Jesús Díaz Palacio (COL)

WEST GERMANY   (0) (0) 0

MEXICO   (0) (0) 0
West Germany 4-1 pens.

WEST GERMANY Schumacher, Berthold, Briegel, Eder [Littbarski 115], Brehme, Jakobs, Förster, Rummenigge (c) [Dieter Hoeness 58], Matthäus, Magath, Allofs.
MEXICO Larios, Amador [FJ Cruz 70], Quirarte, Cruz Barbosa, Servín, Muñoz, España, Negrete, Aguirre, Boy (c) [De los Cobos 32], Sánchez.
SENT OFF: Berthold 64, Aguirre 99.
PENALTY SHOOT-OUT: Allofs 1-0, Negrete 1-1, Brehme 2-1, Quirarte saved, Matthäus 3-1, Servín saved, Littbarski 4-1.

West Germany were still uninspired but the hosts couldn't take advantage. Boy was caught by Brehme's crunching tackle, Sánchez had another poor match, and Schumacher made a number of late saves as well as two in the shoot-out. The referee, who didn't look in full control, showed seven yellow cards as well as the two red. Hoeness' more famous brother Uli played in the 1974 Final.

---

22 June 1986 – Azteca, Mexico City – 114,580 – Ali Ben Nasser (TUN)

ARGENTINA   (0) 2
Maradona 51, 55

ENGLAND   (0) 1
Lineker 81

ARGENTINA Pumpido, Cuciuffo, Olarticoechea, Batista, Ruggeri, Brown, Giusti, Enrique, Burruchaga [Tápia 75], Maradona (c), Valdano.
ENGLAND Shilton (c), MG Stevens, Sansom, Reid [Waddle 69], Butcher, Fenwick, Steven [John Barnes 74], Hoddle, Lineker, Beardsley, Hodge.

The most controversial World Cup moment since the over-the-line goal in 1966 – but England were struggling before it happened. Bilardo, always flexible, again varied his tactics to match the opposition's strengths, man-marking Lineker and Beardsley and stationing Giusti wide on the right to block Hodge. This effectively left Argentina without conventional fullbacks – but Robson, not thinking on his feet, didn't bring on a winger till Maradona had done the damage.

When Hodge sliced a clearance kick back towards his own penalty spot, the two captains went for it, Shilton slightly too slow off his line but Maradona still unlikely to get there first. At the last second, he made up for his lack of inches by getting his hand to the ball before Shilton's punch, sending it bouncing into the empty net.

Ben Nasser took his share of the flak, but it happened fast enough to deceive most people in the stadium, and anyway it wasn't the referee who handled the ball. A grubby little moment, with major implications, especially when Maradona scored one of the almighty goals, picking the ball up near halfway and beating four men before dummying Shilton.

1930
1934
1938
1950
1954
1958
1962
1966
1970
1974
1978
1982
1986
1990
1994
1998
2002
2006

1930
1934
1938
1950
1954
1958
1962
1966
1970
1974
1978
1982
1986
1990
1994
1998
2002
2006

Commentator Barry Davies got it exactly right: 'You have to say that's magnificent.'

When Barnes went past two defenders on the left and crossed for Lineker to score with a header, people were suddenly wise after the event: why wasn't he on from the start? Because he hadn't been playing well for England, who'd just won their last two matches 3-0. England were lucky when Tápia hit the base of a post, but then Olarticoechea's head touched the ball away after Lineker couldn't quite reach another left-wing cross by Barnes. Excruciating.

The Hand of God was crucial, of course – but England hadn't had a shot on goal before it, and they had a right to expect more from Glenn Hoddle. Tall and enviably gifted, his ball control and passing among the very best (ask Ardiles), he was a controversial figure since his successful first international in 1979. Fans wanted him in, managers generally preferred Wilkins and McDermott. Now, with Wilkins out and a midfield geared to win him the ball, with Lineker up front, he didn't perform in the heat of the kitchen, the bottom line when discussing his England career. He would have been hoping for much better as manager in France 98.

Oh, and having helped Maradona score the first goal, Hodge got the little monster's shirt at the end, his biggest achievement in international football.

---

22 June 1986 – Cuauhtémoc, Puebla – 45,000 – Siegfried Kirschen (DDR)

BELGIUM　(1) (1) 1
Ceulemans 34

SPAIN　　(0) (1) 1
Señor 84
Belgium 5–4 pens.

BELGIUM Pfaff, Gerets, Renquin, Grün, Vervoort, Demol, Scifo, Vercauteren [L Van der Elst 106], Ceulemans (c), Claesen, Veyt [Broos 83].

SPAIN Zubizarreta, Tomás [Señor HT], 'Chendo' (Miguel Portlan), Gallego, Víctor, Camacho (c), Julio Alberto, Calderé, Salinas [Eloy 63], Michel, Butragueño.
PENALTY SHOOT-OUT: Señor 1-0, Claesen 1-1, Eloy saved, Scifo 1-2, Chendo 2-2, Broos 2-3, Butragueño 3-3, Vervoort 3-4, Víctor 4-4, L Van der Elst 4-5.

More intestinal fortitude from Belgium, who survived the loss of Vandenbergh and Vandereycken, both flown home for surgery. The defence lived dangerously at times but conceded only Señor's desperate twenty-yarder from Víctor's free kick. Salinas missed a good chance but so did Veyt. Ceulemans had put Belgium ahead with a strong falling header from Vercauteren's left-wing cross. Pfaff, unsighted when Spain scored, was back to his best after the nonsense of 1982, saving Eloy's weak kick in the shoot-out.

SEMI-FINALS

---

25 June 1986 – Jalisco, Guadalajara – 47,500 – Luigi Agnolin (ITA)

WEST GERMANY　(1) 2
Brehme 9, Völler 89

FRANCE　　　　(0) 0

WEST GERMANY Schumacher, Brehme, Briegel, Eder, Förster, Jakobs, Rummenigge (c) [Völler 57], Matthäus, Allofs, Magath, Rolff.
FRANCE Bats, Ayache, Amoros, Fernandez, Bossis, Battiston, Giresse [Vercruysse 71], Tigana, Stopyra, Platini (c), Bellone [Daniel Xuereb 66].

The one thing France didn't want, against such rugged opponents, was to concede an early goal, especially one like this. Magath tapped a free kick to Brehme, whose low shot was horribly fumbled by Bats, a hero against Brazil and for the past two seasons. The French naturally came forward, but were handicapped by Platini's tendons, Giresse's age (he wasn't capped again) and the absence of the injury-prone Rocheteau. Bossis shot over an empty goal from six yards and Schumacher, the villain of 1982, turned the knife with his usual quota of saves. In the last minute Völler ran on to lift the ball over Bats before scoring. For the second successive time France had lost in the semi-final to West Germany, who were praised for making the most of what they had. But perhaps if Rocheteau and Platini had been fully fit, France would have done the same.

ning at the heart of a very good defence, taking out three opponents and jagging to his left before hooking the ball past the keeper. Belgium were dogged but had no answer. Credit also to Argentina's midfield, where Burruchaga had emerged as a knowing second-in-command.

3RD-PLACE FINAL

28 June 1986 – Cuauhtémoc, Puebla – 21,500 – George Courtney (ENG)

FRANCE (2) (2) 4
Ferreri 27, Papin 43, Genghini 104, Amoros pen 111

BELGIUM (1) (2) 2
Ceulemans 11, Claesen 73

FRANCE Albert Rust, Michel Bibard, Amoros, Tigana [Tusseau 84], Yvon Le Roux [Bossis 56], Battiston (c), Vercruysse, Bernard Genghini, Papin, Ferreri, Bellone.
BELGIUM Pfaff, Gerets, Renquin [F Van der Elst HT], Vervoort, Grün, Demol, Raymond Mommens, Scifo [L Van der Elst 65], Ceulemans (c), Claesen, Veyt.

25 June 1986 – Azteca, Mexico City – 110,420 – Antonio Márquez (MEX)

ARGENTINA (0) 2
Maradona 51, 63

BELGIUM (0) 0

ARGENTINA Pumpido, Cuciuffo, Olarticoechea, Batista, Ruggeri, Brown, Giusti, Enrique, Burruchaga [Ricardo Bochini 85], Maradona (c), Valdano.
BELGIUM Pfaff, Gerets, Renquin [Desmet 53], Vervoort, Demol, Grün, Scifo, Vercauteren, Ceulemans (c), Claesen, Veyt.

Another one-man show, two more smoking barrels. Both teams saturated the midfield but Belgium, toothless in attack, could only hold out for so long. Valdano had a goal ironically disallowed for handball despite chesting the ball in, then Maradona took over. Running into the penalty area from the right, his mind was made up for him when Pfaff came off his line slightly too soon, to be beaten by a flick of that left foot. The second goal was on a par with his legitimate one against England, run-

In the only 3rd-Place Final to go to extra time, Bellone helped make the first two goals and Genghini scored from Ferreri's lobbed pass. Amoros, winning the 39th of his 82 caps, a national record at the time, picked up his only international goal after Gerets had brought him down. Ceulemans scored at one end after Bellone had missed at the other, and Claesen put in Veyt's cross. The 32-year-old Rust, who may have acquired his name by sitting on the bench so often, was at last given his only cap.

FINAL

29 June 1986 – Azteca, Mexico City – 114,580 –
Romualdo Arppi (BRZ)

ARGENTINA   (1) 3
Brown 23, Valdano 56, Burruchaga 85

WEST GERMANY (0) 2
Rummenigge 74, Völler 82

ARGENTINA Pumpido, Cuciuffo, Olarticoechea,
Enrique, Ruggeri, Brown, Giusti, Batista, Burruchaga
[Marcelo Trobbiani 89], Maradona (c), Valdano.
WEST GERMANY Schumacher, Berthold, Briegel,
Jakobs, Förster, Eder, Matthäus, Brehme, Allofs
[Völler HT], Magath [Hoeness 61], Rummenigge (c).

Beckenbauer, who admitted he didn't have
the players to win the title, put Matthäus on
Maradona, hoped for the best, and might have
got it if he hadn't been undermined by the
sudden fallibility of Schumacher, till then
the best goalkeeper in the competition. After
three consecutive clean sheets, he suddenly
charged out for Burruchaga's free kick and was
stranded in mid-air when Brown headed in.
Urged by his team mates to stay back (according to his autobiography) he allowed Valdano
to run in from the right and push the ball past
his outstretched foot. Then Burruchaga was
clean through, only to be called back for a
non-existent offside.

Still, 2-0 seemed to be enough – but ye of
little faith should have remembered that this
was West Germany, and they do things differently there. Dull side though they were, with
Rummenigge still unfit and Magath invisible
in midfield, they hauled themselves back into
it, releasing Matthäus from his marking duties

SHORTEST FINALS CAREERS

mins					
1	Marcelo Trobbiani	ARG	1986	v GER	
1	Lee Carsley	EIR	2002	v SAU	
2	Khemais Labidi	TUN	1978	v MEX	
2	Miguel Pardeza	SPA	1990	v BEL	
2	Magnus Erlingmark	SWE	1994	v RUS	
2	Petar Mikhtarski	BUL	1994	v MEX	
2	Igor Tudor	CRO	1998	v JPN	
3	Corneliu Papură	ROM	1994	v COL & ARG	
3	Ion Vladoiu	ROM	1994	v SWI	
3	Zé Roberto	BRZ	1998	v DEN	
3	Jamal Sellami	MOR	1998	v SCO	

Vladoiu was sent off after coming as a substitute.

Other British Isles

6	Kerry Dixon	ENG	1986	v POL	
6	Scott Booth	SCO	1998	v MOR	

and scoring twice from Brehme's left-wing corners. The first was helped on by Völler for Rummenigge to slide in and force it home, the second was headed back by Berthold for Völler to get his head bravely in front of Pumpido's palms. Hard for Argentina to defend against these with Brown having cracked a bone in his shoulder.

The Germans felt they lost it there and then. Intoxicated by the comeback, they pressed forward instead of playing for extra time, leaving themselves thin at the back when Maradona threaded an instant pass through to Burruchaga in the inside-right channel. He pushed the ball too far ahead, but again Schumacher was slow off his line, made to look hesitant by a low cross-shot.

Völler's goal was the last by a losing side in a World Cup Final. Seven of the Germans weren't capped again, including Briegel and all-time greats like Förster (who retired from international football at 27) and Rummenigge, the only player to captain the losing team in two Finals. West Germany might have won at least one if he'd been fully fit either time, or if Schuster had played.

Their cause hadn't been helped by Mexico's heat and pollution, which were at least as bad as in 1970. Valdano, who had less reason to complain than most, felt 'It was inhuman. They sold a bad football product to the whole world.'

Most of the whole world didn't notice or care, the unhealthy mix having been camouflaged by the skills of one man, who picked up adequate compensation for the frustrations of 1982. No other World Cup tournament has been so dominated by a single player, with a left foot in the Puskás class and that cheating left hand.

1986

After the semi-final shoot-out, a pile of celebrating Germans is no sight for a grieving Englishman.
Lothar Matthäus sympathises with poor Chris Waddle, but his eyes are already on the prize.

Penalties of fame

Italy **1990**

1930

1934

1938

1950

1954

1958

1962

1966

1970

1974

1978

1982

1986

1990

1994

1998

2002

2006

No-one was unduly surprised when Italy became the first European country to host the World Cup more than once. They'd been the first to stage the European Championship twice (before most countries had held it once) and generally knew their way through the corridors of power. That and a strong national team gave them a serious head start. Azeglio Vicini, Bearzot's successor as coach, had been in charge of the Under-21 team which won the European title in 1986, and brought several of those players into the senior squad. The defence, in which Bergomi was now the captain, had been reinforced by the young Paolo Maldini and another great sweeper in Franco Baresi, conceding only one goal in the last nine games. But there were problems and controversies up front (only two goals in the last seven), where Vicini seemed reluctant to use the talents of Roberto Baggio. Much would depend on Vialli, who'd just scored the goals that had won Sampdoria the Cup-Winners Cup.

Argentina still had several of their 1986 players, again led by Maradona, but had won only one of their last ten matches, 2-1 in Israel. They had to take what comfort they could from their second match being staged on Maradona's home club ground.

West Germany had failed to win the European Championship at home two years earlier but could call on many more talented players than in 1986. Brehme, Matthäus and Völler were reinforced by world-class newcomers like Buchwald, Kohler and the dashing blond Klinsmann, and three of the squad played with Inter in Milan. But Beckenbauer, still the coach, was having to use the veteran chain-smoker Augenthaler as sweeper.

Brazil had a new coach and another strong defence, but no replacements for their old midfield stars. Careca was still there but his obvious partner, the immensely gifted Romário, hadn't played since breaking a leg in March. Winners of the Copa América the previous year and the only team to have beaten Italy this season, they were established as joint second favourites or thereabouts.

Ahead of them in the ratings were the Dutch, back in the finals with a team that lost little in comparison with Cruijff & Co, European champions arriving with a battery of all-time greats. Rijkaard and Ronald Koeman, the dreadlocked Gullit, van Basten the complete centre-forward. Although Gullit had been out for almost a year with injury, they were the big stumbling block in England's group.

Nevertheless England had reasons to be cheerful. After their disastrous European finals (three defeats out of three, including a hat-trick by van Basten), Bobby Robson was allowed to stay on and quickly brought in a great new defensive talent in the lightning quick Des Walker. England qualified without conceding a goal and Lineker had recovered from jaundice,

1930
1934
1938
1950
1954
1958
1962
1966
1970
1974
1978
1982
1986

1990

1994
1998
2002
2006

but they were grateful that Poland hit the bar in injury time at the end of their last match.

The Republic of Ireland, who'd beaten England in Euro 88 and were drawn in the same group again, were coached by Jack Charlton, of 1966 fame, who'd adopted an approach that involved banging the ball towards the corner flags to turn opposition defences. Rarely a pretty sight, it was effective enough to take them to the finals for the first time at the expense of their neighbours from the North. The organisers, fearful of English, Irish and Dutch fans all thrown together, packed them all off to Sardinia and policed them brutally, scenes that were to be repeated, on a reduced scale, at England's qualifying match in Rome seven years later.

Scotland, present for the fifth time in a row, found themselves in the same group as Brazil but fancied their chances against Sweden, who'd twice drawn 0-0 with England in the qualifiers. And manager Andy Roxburgh wasn't alone in thinking 'We have nothing to fear from Costa Rica.'

GROUP A

Austria, Czechoslovakia, Italy (seeded), USA.

9 June 1990 – Olimpico, Rome – 72,303 – José Ramiz Wright (BRZ)

ITALY	**(0) 1**
Schillaci 79

AUSTRIA	**(0) 0**

ITALY Walter Zenga, Giuseppe Bergomi (c), Paolo Maldini, Carlo Ancelotti [Luigi De Agostini HT], Riccardo Ferri, Franco Baresi, Roberto Donadoni, Fernando De Napoli, Andrea Carnevale [Salvatore Schillaci 75], Giuseppe Giannini, Gianluca Vialli. *Azeglio Vicini.*
AUSTRIA Klaus Lindenberger, Kurt Russ, Michael Streiter, Ernst Aigner, Robert Pecl, Peter Schöttel, Peter Artner [Manfred Zsak 62], Manfred Linzmaier [Alfred Hörtnagl 77], Toni Polster (c), Andreas Ogris, Andreas Herzog. *Josef Hickersberger.*

Italy's goalscoring problems graphically illustrated. Attacking rather than counter-attacking, they had almost all the match but Lindenberger made a number of saves, Giannini headed an easy chance wide from a corner, and Carnevale shot over an open goal. The staring eyes of his replacement, who scored his first goal for Italy

OLDEST CAPTAINS

yrs	days			
40	292	Peter Shilton	ENG	1990
40	133	Dino Zoff	ITA	1982
38	293	Jan Heintze	DEN	2002
37	343	Manuel Bento	POR	1986
37	82	Franky Van der Elst	BEL	1998
37	40	Thomas Dooley	USA	1998

with an emphatic header, were to become a feature of the tournament. Vialli, always more of an all-round forward than an out-and-out striker, may have had mixed feelings about providing the cross for the goal.

10 June 1990 – Comunale, Florence – 33,266 – Kurt Röthlisberger (SWI)

CZECHOSLOVAKIA	**(2) 5**
Skuhravý 26, 79, Bílek pen 39, Hašek 51, Luhový 89

USA	**(0) 1**
Caligiuri 60

CZECHOSLOVAKIA Jan Stejskal, Miroslav Kadlec, Ján Kocian, František Straka, Michal Bílek, Ivan Hašek (c), Jozef Chovanec, Luboš Kubík, L'ubomír Moravčík [Vladimír Weiss 83], Tomáš Skuhravý, Ivo Knoflíček [Milan Luhový 76]. *Jozef Vengloš.*
USA Tony Meola, Steve Trittschuh, Mike Windischmann (c), Desmond Armstrong, Paul Caligiuri, John Stollmeyer [Marcelo Balboa 64], Tab Ramos, John Harkes, Eric Wynalda, Peter Vermes, Bruce Murray [Chris Sullivan 78]. *Bob Gansler.*
SENT OFF: Wynalda 52.

After watching the opening match of the tournament, Windischmann was quoted as saying his team were 'the Cameroon of our group,' which raised a few chuckles after this overwhelming defeat. Rodney Marsh was nearer the mark when he said most unfancied teams had a puncher's chance but the USA didn't have a punch. Beaten for pace and power, they kept losing the ball too easily, conceded two penalties, two goals from corners, and had Wynalda sent off for pushing Moravčík, who went down rather easily.

Skuhravý steered in Moravčík's square pass; both penalties were awarded for fouls on Hašek, who headed in a Chovanec corner, as did Skuhravý; and Luhový prodded a loose ball in off a post. Caligiuri did well to break a tackle and take it round the keeper, and Meola made

1990

1930
1934
1938
1950
1954
1958
1962
1966
1970
1974
1978
1982
1986
1990
1994
1998
2002
2006

an easy save when Bílek embarrassed himself by trying to chip his second penalty – but there wasn't much else to relieve the American embarrassment. Note the slight difference in the spelling of Stejskal and Kocian's first names.

The USA had now conceded five goals in each of two consecutive finals matches – 40 years apart.

---

14 June 1990 – Olimpico, Rome – 73,423 – Edgardo Codesal (MEX)

ITALY	**(1) 1**
Giannini 11	
USA	**(0) 0**

ITALY Zenga, Bergomi (c), Maldini, Nicola Berti, Ferri, Baresi, Donadoni, De Napoli, Carnevale [Schillaci 52], Giannini, Vialli.
USA Meola, Jimmy Banks [Stollmeyer 80], Windischmann (c), John Doyle, Armstrong, Balboa, Caligiuri, Harkes, Ramos, Vermes, Murray [Sullivan 82].

Vicini gave the same starting line-up a second chance against the whipping boys, but they struggled again, even after taking an early lead when Vialli's dummy gave Giannini the chance to burst past two men and hit a fierce left-footer. After 33 minutes, Windischmann conceded his second penalty in successive matches when Berti ran into him, but Vialli hit a post (it really wasn't his tournament) – and even the introduction of Schillaci didn't help much. Italy were through to the next round, but minus any dancing in the streets.

---

15 June 1990 – Comunale, Florence – 38,962 – George Smith (SCO)

CZECHOSLOVAKIA	**(1) 1**
Bílek pen 29	
AUSTRIA	**(0) 0**

CZECHOSLOVAKIA Stejskal, Kadlec, Kocian, Václav Němeček, Hašek (c), Moravčík, Chovanec [Július Bielik 30], Bílek, Kubík, Skuhravý, Knoflíček [Weiss 81].
AUSTRIA Lindenberger, Aigner, Pecl, Anton Pfeffer, Russ [Streiter HT], Hörtnagl, Zsak, Schöttel [Ogris HT], Herzog, Polster (c), Gerhard Rodax.

Like the hosts, Czechoslovakia qualified at the earliest opportunity, against a dismal and dirty Austrian team who got little from the vaunted pairing of Polster (who later had the gall to criticise his coach) and Rodax. Pfeffer's back pass let in Chovanec, who had to go off after the foul by Lindenberger that conceded the penalty. Bílek fell over after tucking the kick inside a post.

---

19 June 1990 – Olimpico, Rome – 73,303 – Joël Quiniou (FRA)

ITALY	**(1) 2**
Schillaci 9, Baggio 78	
CZECHOSLOVAKIA	**(0) 0**

ITALY Zenga, Bergomi (c), Maldini, Berti, Ferri, Baresi, Donadoni [De Agostini 51], De Napoli [Pietro Vierchowod 66], Schillaci, Giannini, Roberto Baggio.
CZECHOSLOVAKIA Stejskal, Kadlec, Vladimír Kinier, Němeček [Bielik HT], Hašek (c), Moravčík, Chovanec, Bílek, Weiss [Stanislav Griga 59], Skuhravý, Knoflíček.

Vicini changed his front two and was rewarded with a much better performance and a special goal, Baggio taking a return pass from Giannini and almost sauntering past two defenders in a long run on goal. Earlier, Giannini's shot had gone straight into the ground and up for Schillaci to head in, but Italy were rather lucky to be staying in Rome for the second round: after 64 minutes Griga had a headed goal wrongly disallowed for offside.

19 June 1990 – Comunale, Florence – 34,857 – Jamal Al-Sharif (SYR)

AUSTRIA   (0) 2
Ogris 49, Rodax 63

USA   (0) 1
Murray 84

AUSTRIA Lindenberger, Artner, Streiter, Aigner, Pecl, Pfeffer, Ogris, Zsak, Polster (c) [Andreas Reisinger HT], Herzog, Rodax [Gerald Glatzmayer 84].
USA Meola, Banks [Wynalda 55], Windischmann (c), Doyle, Armstrong, Balboa, Caligiuri [Brian Bliss 71], Harkes, Ramos, Vermes, Murray.
SENT OFF: Artner 34.

Bad-tempered and bad. Nine bookings and Artner sent off for a dangerous tackle on Vermes. Ogris sprinted from his own half, beating Windischmann for pace, before clipping the ball over Meola, and Streiter's run set up Rodax. Ramos beat Aigner, and Murray's shot went between Lindenberger's knees; it was his ninth goal for the USA, equalling an unimpressive national record. Small consolation for a side whose own World Cup was due in four years' time.

GROUP A

	P	W	D	L	F	A	Pts
Italy	3	3	0	0	4	0	6
Czechoslovakia	3	2	0	1	6	3	4
Austria	3	1	0	2	2	3	2
USA	3	0	0	3	2	8	0

Italy and Czechoslovakia qualified for the second round.

GROUP B

Argentina (seeded), Cameroon, Romania, USSR.

8 June 1990 – Giuseppe Meazza, Milan – 73,780 – Michel Vautrot (FRA)

CAMEROON   (0) 1
Omam Biyick 67

ARGENTINA   (0) 0

CAMEROON Thomas Nkono, Stephen Tataw (c), Bertin Ebwelle, Victor Ndip, Benjamin Massing, Emmanuel Kunde, Cyrille Makanaky [Roger Milla 82], Émile Mbouh, François Omam Biyick, André Kana Biyick, Louis Paul Mfede [Thomas Libiih 65]. *Valery Nepomniachy (USR)*.
ARGENTINA Nery Pumpido, Néstor Fabbri, Roberto Sensini [Gabriel Calderón 69], Juan Simón, Oscar Ruggeri [Claudio Caniggia HT], Néstor Lorenzo, Jorge Burruchaga, Sergio Batista, Abel Balbo, Diego Maradona (c), José Basualdo. *Carlos Bilardo*.
SENT OFF: Kana Biyick 61, Massing 88.

Not quite the sensation it appears, given the teams' recent records, but still a surprise. Cameroon massed in defence and paid Maradona strict attention, though both sendings-off were for fouls on the lively Caniggia, the first when Kana Biyick seemed to catch him accidentally while running behind him, the second after he'd hurdled two other challenges, Massing lunging in so hard his own boot came off. Lorenzo had to kick off the line in the first half, but the only goal was scrappy, Omam Biyick climbing way above Sensini to head down straight at Pumpido, who let the ball in off his leg. Makanaky was denied a goal when Lorenzo squeezed the ball off the line and round a post.

The Biyicks were brothers. Their surname was spelt Biyik on their shirts in France 98 but Biyick (their FA's preference) in USA 94. Sensini

1930 1934 1938 1950 1954 1958 1962 1966 1970 1974 1978 1982 1986 **1990** 1994 1998 2002 2006

is sometimes referred to by another of his first names (Néstor) but the main Argentinian sources call him Roberto. The stadium, renamed after the star of 1934 and 1938, is still sometimes known by its old name of San Siro.

9 June 1990 – San Nicola, Bari – 42,907 – Juan Cardellino (URU)

ROMANIA (1) 2
Lăcătuş 41, pen 55

USSR (0) 0

ROMANIA Silviu Lung (c), Mircea Rednic, Michael Klein, Gheorghe Popescu, Ioan Andone, Ionut Lupescu, Ioan Sabău, Florin Răducioiu [Gavril Balint 80], Marius Lăcătuş [Ilie Dumitrescu 87], Iosif Rotariu, Daniel Timofte. *Emeric Ienei.*
USSR Renat Dasayev (c), Sergei Gorlukovich, Vladimir Bessonov, Vasily Rats, Vagiz Khidiatulin, Oleg Kuznetsov, Sergei Aleinikov, Gennady Litovchenko [Ivan Yaremchuk 66], Oleg Protasov, Aleksandr Zavarov, Igor Dobrovolsky [Aleksandr Borodyuk 71]. *Valery Lobanovsky.*

Even without their playmaker Hagi, Romania had things stacked in their favour. Yakovenko and Alexei Mikhailichenko were out for the duration, Protasov and Zavarov missed early chances, and the penalty was given for a handball which Khidiatulin committed well outside the area. Lăcătuş opened the scoring with a powerful shot at the near post after Sabău sent him clear on the right, and also missed an open goal, while Sabău shot over with only Dasayev to beat. The official crowd figure didn't reflect the acreage of empty seats.

13 June 1990 – San Paolo, Naples – 55,759 – Erik Fredriksson (SWE)

ARGENTINA (1) 2
Troglio 27, Burruchaga 78

USSR (0) 0

ARGENTINA Pumpido [Sergio Goycochea 9], José Serrizuela, Julio Olarticoechea, Simón, Pedro Monzón [Lorenzo 79], Basualdo, Burruchaga, Batista, Pedro Troglio, Maradona (c), Caniggia.
USSR Aleksandr Uvarov, Bessonov, Gorlukovich, Khidiatulin, Kuznetsov (c), Andrei Zygmantovich, Aleinikov, Igor Shalimov, Protasov [Litovchenko 75], Zavarov [Vladimir Lyuty 85], Dobrovolsky.
SENT OFF: Bessonov 47.

Pumpido broke his right leg in a collision with Olarticoechea – but, with respect, it was the USSR who had all the bad luck in this group. The previous year, Maradona had perpetrated another divine handball, earning a penalty (!) in the UEFA Cup Final, which Napoli won. Now, in the same stadium, he palmed away Kuznetsov's flick-on but the referee didn't see it. After that, Troglio headed in Olarticoechea's hanging cross from the left and Burruchaga took advantage of Kuznetsov's blind back pass. Again a red card was shown for a foul on Caniggia (shirt-pulling this time) as the USSR, full of very good players who kept missing chances, became the first side to be eliminated from the tournament.

14 June 1990 – San Nicola, Bari – 38,687 – Hernán Silva Arce (CHI)

CAMEROON (0) 2
Milla 76, 86

ROMANIA (0) 1
Balint 88

CAMEROON Nkono, Tataw (c), Ebwelle, Ndip, Jules Denis Onana, Kunde [Jean-Claude Pagal 70], Makanaky, Mbouh, Omam Biyick, Mfede, Emmanuel Maboang Kessack [Milla 57].
ROMANIA Lung (c), Rednic, Klein, Popescu, Andone, Rotariu, Lăcătuş, Sabău, Răducioiu [Balint 63], Gheorghe Hagi [Dumitrescu 56], Timofte.

Cameroon, again uncomplicated and aggressive, gave the 38-year-old Milla a run-out

1930
1934
1938
1950
1954
1958
1962
1966
1970
1974
1978
1982
1986
1990
1994
1998
2002
2006

LEADING GOALSCORERS 1990

6	Salvatore Schillaci	ITA	1 pen
5	Tomáš Skuhravý	CZE	
4	Michel	SPA	1 pen
4	Roger Milla	CAM	
4	Lothar Matthäus	GER	1 pen
4	Gary Lineker	ENG	2 pen

worthy of the name and he scored two flamboyant goals, barging Andone illegally off the ball for the first, accelerating past the same player before thrashing in the second, each time celebrating with a little dance round the corner post. Brought out of virtual retirement (a club on Réunion in the Indian Ocean), he was the oldest player to score in a finals match, a record he hadn't finished with yet. Lăcătuş hit a post but Cameroon could afford a late strike by Balint, who may have been offside.

---

18 June 1990 – San Paolo, Naples – 52,733 – Carlos Alberto da Silva Valente (POR)

ARGENTINA **(0) 1**
Monzón 61

ROMANIA **(0) 1**
Balint 68

ARGENTINA Goycochea, Serrizuela, Olarticoechea, Simón, Monzón, Basualdo, Burruchaga [Gustavo Dezotti 62], Batista, Troglio [Ricardo Giusti 53], Maradona (c), Caniggia.
ROMANIA Lung (c), Rednic, Klein, Popescu, Andone, Rotariu, Lăcătuş, Sabău [Dorin Mateuţ 81], Balint [Dănuţ Lupu 73], Hagi, Lupescu.

Romania needed a draw to be sure of qualifying and got it when a Lăcătuş cross was headed back and down by Sabău for Balint to head over the covering defender. Monzón had headed Argentina in front from a near-post corner by Maradona, who was overshadowed by Hagi, 'the Maradona of the Carpathians'.

---

18 June 1990 – San Nicola, Bari – 37,307 – José Ramiz Wright (BRZ)

USSR **(2) 4**
Protasov 20, Zygmantovich 29, Zavarov 52, Dobrovolsky 63

CAMEROON **(0) 0**

USSR Uvarov, Gorlukovich, Anatoly Demyanenko (c), Khidiatulin, Kuznetsov, Zygmantovich, Aleinikov, Litovchenko [Yaremchuk 74], Protasov, Shalimov [Zavarov HT], Dobrovolsky.
CAMEROON Nkono, Tataw (c), Ebwelle, Ndip, Onana, Kunde [Milla 35], Makanaky [Pagal 58], Mbouh, Omam Biyick, Kana Biyick, Mfede.

In their sixth finals match, Cameroon suffered their first defeat, and an emphatic one, the USSR showing what they were made of when it was too late, taking their chances at last. Protasov toed in Litovchenko's low cross; Zygmantovich slid in the second after Aleinikov had gone round the keeper and hit the bar; then Nkono got a hand to Zavarov's shot after he'd been put through by Dobrovolsky, the star of the show, whose well-placed header converted a left-wing cross by Gorlukovich.

GROUP B

	P	W	D	L	F	A	Pts
Cameroon	3	2	0	1	3	5	4
Romania	3	1	1	1	4	3	3
Argentina	3	1	1	1	3	2	3
USSR	3	1	0	2	4	4	2

Cameroon, Romania and Argentina qualified for the second round.

GROUP C

Brazil (seeded), Costa Rica, Scotland, Sweden.

10 June 1990 – delle Alpi, Turin – 62,628 – Tullio Lanese (ITA)

BRAZIL   **(1) 2**
Careca 40, 62

SWEDEN   **(0) 1**
Brolin 78

BRAZIL Cláudio Taffarel, 'Jorginho' (Jorge Amorim), 'Branco (Cláudio Vaz), Mauro Galvão, Ricardo Gomes (c), José Carlos Mozer, 'Müller' (Luís Corrêa), 'Dunga' (Carlos Bledorn Verri), 'Careca' (Antônio de Oliveira), 'Alemão' (Ricardo de Brito), Valdo (Cândido) [Silas (do Prado) 85]. *Sebastião Lazaroni.*
SWEDEN Thomas Ravelli, Roland Nilsson, Roger Ljung [Glenn Strömberg 70], Stefan Schwarz, Peter Larsson, Jonas Thern (c), Anders Limpar, Klas Ingesson, Tomas Brolin, Joakim Nilsson, Mats Magnusson [Stefan Pettersson HT]. *Olle Nordin.*

Without hitting any heights, Brazil made efficiency good-looking, if that's possible. Their five-man defence and functional attack were too much for a Swedish team enlivened only by the baby-faced Brolin, who forced a close-range save from a corner and scored with a clean turn and shot. Both the Brazilian goals were well made and crisply taken. Careca, still slim and sharp, ran onto Branco's through-ball and dummied the keeper, then darted behind Larsson to put Müller's low cross into an empty net.

11 June 1990 – Luigi Ferraris, Genoa – 30,867 – Juan Carlos Loustau (ARG)

COSTA RICA   **(0) 1**
Cayasso 49

SCOTLAND   **(0) 0**

COSTA RICA Luis Conejo, Germán Chavarría, José Carlos Chávez, Róger Flores (c), Héctor Marchena, Mauricio Montero, Ronald González, Oscar Ramírez, Juan Cayasso, Róger Gómez, Claudio Jara [Hernán Medford 86]. *Bora Milutinović (YUG).*
SCOTLAND Jim Leighton, Richard Gough [Stewart McKimmie HT], Maurice Malpas, Robert 'Roy' Aitken (c), Alex McLeish, Dave McPherson, Jim Bett [Ally McCoist 74], Paul McStay, Mo Johnston, Stuart McCall, Alan McInally. *Andy Roxburgh.*

If Roxburgh's pre-match quote was memorable, so was a post-match headline: Scotland Plunged Into Cayasso. Milutinović, who'd coached Mexico in the previous finals, made controversial changes to the squad as soon as he took charge, and they paid off. The goal was cleverly worked, Cayasso clipping Jara's backheel in off Leighton. Earlier, Gough headed McStay's free kick over the bar then stooped to head the ball back for Johnston's volley to force a flying save. After the goal, the mediocre McInally headed over the bar and Conejo made a tremendous save when Johnston went for power after controlling McKimmie's long cross from the right.

Costa Rica were the first Central American team to win a World Cup match in Europe, but yet again this looked an ordinary Scotland team.

16 June 1990 – delle Alpi, Turin – 58,007 – Neji Jouini (TUN)

BRAZIL   **(1) 1**
Müller 33

COSTA RICA   **(0) 0**

BRAZIL Taffarel, Jorginho, Branco, Mauro Galvão, Ricardo Gomes (c), Mozer, Müller, Dunga, Careca ['Bebeto' (Roberto Gama) 84], Alemão, Valdo [Silas 86].
COSTA RICA Conejo, Chavarría, Chávez, Flores (c), Montero, González, Ramírez, Marchena, Cayasso [Alexandre Guimarães 78], Gómez, Jara [Roy Myers 71].

Further determined defence by the underdogs, but Brazil should have won by a greater margin. Müller and defender Marchena hit the Costa Rican crossbar, and Conejo made a number of saves. The goal was streaky, Müller's volley going in off Montero, but Brazil were rightly and swiftly through to the next round. The real crowd figure was probably nearer 40,000.

---

16 June 1990 – Luigi Ferraris, Genoa – 31,823 – Carlos Maciel (PAR)

SCOTLAND (1) 2
McCall 10, Johnston pen 82

SWEDEN   (0) 1
Strömberg 87

SCOTLAND Leighton, Craig Levein, Malpas, Aitken (c), McLeish, McPherson, Robert Fleck [McCoist 85], Murdo MacLeod, Johnston, McCall, Gordon Durie [McStay 75].
SWEDEN Ravelli, R Nilsson, Schwarz, Thern, Larsson [Strömberg 75], Glenn Hysén (c), Limpar, Ingesson, Brolin, J Nilsson, Pettersson [Johnny Ekström 63].

Ordinary team or not, Scotland's morale was in better shape than Sweden's, and the team changes helped. McCall slid the ball in from close range after McPherson helped on a corner, and Aitken would have scored if Roland Nilsson hadn't fouled him for the penalty. Schwarz's very deep cross was deftly volleyed in by Strömberg, a distinctive figure with his long fair hair and beard – but the Scots were worthy winners.

---

20 June 1990 – Luigi Ferraris, Genoa – 30,223 – Zoran Petrović (YUG)

COSTA RICA   (0) 2
Flores 74, Medford 87

SWEDEN   (1) 1
Ekström 31

COSTA RICA Conejo, Chavarría [Guimarães 75], Montero, Chávez, Flores (c), González, Ramírez, Marchena, Cayasso, Gómez [Medford 60], Jara.
SWEDEN Ravelli, R Nilsson, Schwarz, Ingesson, Larsson, Hysén (c), Brolin [Mats Gren 34], Strömberg [Leif Engqvist 82], Ekström, J Nilsson, Pettersson.

A disappointing Sweden achieved the unique feat of losing all three group matches by the same score, this time after taking the lead through Ekström, once one of their golden boys, who put in the rebound when Conejo made his latest fine save, this time from a Schwarz free kick. Another free kick, by González out on the right, was skilfully headed in by the veteran Flores, then the lively Medford ran through to shoot low across Ravelli, putting Costa Rica in the next round and Scotland's first match in perspective.

---

20 June 1990 – delle Alpi, Turin – 62,502 – Helmut Kohl (AUT)

BRAZIL   (0) 1
Müller 81

SCOTLAND (0) 0

BRAZIL Taffarel, Jorginho, Branco, Mauro Galvão, Ricardo Gomes (c), Ricardo Rocha, Romário (de Souza) [Müller 65], Dunga, Careca, Alemão, Valdo.
SCOTLAND Leighton, McKimmie, Malpas, Aitken (c), McLeish, McPherson, McStay, MacLeod [Gary Gillespie 38], Johnston, McCall, McCoist [Fleck 78].

Eighty minutes of clock watching, exactly what Scotland wanted, suddenly meant nothing when Alemão, Brazil's driving midfielder, shot firmly but not overpoweringly from the edge of the box. Leighton, an international class keeper for most of the decade, had recently been in poor form with Manchester United, dropped for the FA Cup Final replay. Here he'd made an important save at Romário's feet, but now couldn't hold Alemão's shot, the rebound was

1990

1930
1934
1938
1950
1954
1958
1962
1966
1970
1974
1978
1982
1986
1990
1994
1998
2002
2006

knocked behind him by Gillespie's lunging tackle, and the ball trundled almost to the goal line before Müller squeezed it in from a narrow angle. On another day, in better times, Leighton's error would have gone unpunished. As it was, he was almost rescued in injury time, when Johnston suffered the same agony as against Costa Rica, Taffarel saving almost miraculously from point-blank range. Scotland were out and still hadn't qualified for the second stage after seven attempts. Leighton was left out for more than three years but recovered to become an important member of the squad that reached the 1998 finals.

GROUP C

	P	W	D	L	F	A	Pts
Brazil	3	3	0	0	4	1	6
Costa Rica	3	2	0	1	3	2	4
Scotland	3	1	0	2	2	3	2
Sweden	3	0	0	3	3	6	0

Brazil and Costa Rica qualified for the second round.

GROUP D

1990

Colombia, United Arab Emirates, West Germany (seeded), Yugoslavia.

9 June 1990 – Renato Dall' Ara, Bologna – 30,791 – George Courtney (ENG)

COLOMBIA (0) 2
Redín 50, Valderrama 85

UNITED ARAB EMIRATES (0) 0

COLOMBIA René Higuita, Luis Herrera, Gilardo Gómez, Andrés Escobar, Luis Perea, Gabriel Gómez, Bernardo Redín, Leonel Álvarez, Freddy Rincón, Carlos Valderrama (c), Arnoldo Iguarán [Carlos Enrique Estrada 75]. *Francisco Maturana*.

UAE Mohsen Musabeh Faraj, Eissa Meer Abdulrahman, Ibrahim Meer Abdulrahman [Abdullah Ali Sultan 74], Khalil Ghanem Mubarak, Mohammed Youssef Hussain, Abdulrahman Mohammed Abdullah, Nasser Khamis Mubarak, Ali Thani Juma'a, Adnan Khamis Al-Talyani, Hussain Ghuloum Abbas [Zubair Bakhit Bilal 53], Fahad Khamis Mubarak (c). *Carlos Alberto Parreira (BRZ)*.

Like Kuwait in 1982, also coached by Carlos Alberto, the Emirates came out to compete and play a bit but didn't have the firepower up front; hardly surprising for a country with less than 3,000 registered players. Valderrama, whose bushy yellow dreadlocks made him the most recognisable figure in the tournament, was also Colombia's most important player, and the Emirates knew it, fouling him repeatedly from the start. At the end, he bent a low shot round a defender and just inside the far post. Redín had headed the first goal when the long-haired Álvarez had escaped up the right. The UAE fielded two sets of brothers: Nasser and Fahad Khamis (no relation to Adnan Khamis) and the Meers.

10 June 1990 – Giuseppe Meazza, Milan – 74,765 – Peter Mikkelsen (DEN)

WEST GERMANY (2) 4
Matthäus 28, 63, Klinsmann 39, Völler 69

YUGOSLAVIA (0) 1
Jozić 54

WEST GERMANY Bodo Illgner, Stefan Reuter, Andreas Brehme, Thomas Berthold, Guido Buchwald, Klaus Augenthaler, Thomas Hässler [Pierre Littbarski 74], Uwe Bein [Andreas Möller 74], Rudi Völler, Lothar Matthäus (c), Jürgen Klinsmann. *Franz Beckenbauer*.

YUGOSLAVIA Tomislav Ivković, Faruk Hadžibegić, Mirsad Baljić, Predrag Spasić, Zoran Vulić, Davor Jozić, Dragan Stojković, Safet Sušić [Robert Prosinečki 55], Srećko Katanec, Dejan Savićević [Dragoljub Brnović 55], Zlatko Vujović (c). *Ivica Osim.*

For the first time since 1966, West Germany opened their account with a compelling display of power football. Stojković, Savićević and the 35-year-old Sušić, some of the most extravagantly gifted players of their generation, were simply swept aside. Buchwald, tall and surprisingly skilful but an adhesive marker, blotted out Savićević. Matthäus did the same to Stojković as well as scoring with two ferocious long shots, one with each foot, the first after sidestepping a tackle, the second after hurdling a defender on his way through the middle. The ultimate all-round midfielder.

His team mates were almost as good. 'A much better team than in 1986,' said Beckenbauer, 'very good offence players'. Brehme whipped in a low cross for Klinsmann to score with a spectacular diving header then fired in a shot which Ivković fumbled for Völler to be credited with the fourth without touching the ball. Jozić headed a Stojković free kick in off a post, but the Yugoslavs, and the rest of the competition, were left breathless.

14 June 1990 – Renato Dall' Ara, Bologna – 32,257 – Luigi Agnolin (ITA)

YUGOSLAVIA	**(0) 1**
Jozić 75	

COLOMBIA	**(0) 0**

YUGOSLAVIA Ivković, Vujadin Stanojković, Brnović, Hadžibegić, Jozić, Spasić, Stojković, Sušić, Katanec [Robert Jarni HT], Vujović (c) [Darko Pančev 55], Refik Šabanadžović.

COLOMBIA Higuita, Herrera, Gilardo Gómez, Escobar, Perea, Gabriel Gómez, Redín [Estrada 80], Rincón [Rubén Dario Hernández 69], Iguarán, Valderrama (c), Álvarez.

Against far less formidable opposition, Yugoslavia hauled themselves back into the frame. Stojković chipped the ball up for Jozić, a skilful sweeper, to chest down and shoot into the roof of the net. The bushy-haired Higuita, whose excursions outside upfield recalled Quiroga of 1978 fame, saved Hadžibegić's unexceptional penalty (for a flying handball by Perea) with eleven minutes left.

15 June 1990 – Giuseppe Meazza, Milan – 71,167 – Alexei Spirin (USR)

WEST GERMANY	**(2) 5**
Völler 35, 74, Klinsmann 37, Matthäus 48, Bein 58	

UNITED ARAB EMIRATES	**(0) 1**
Khalid Ismail 47	

WEST GERMANY Illgner, Berthold [Littbarski HT], Brehme, Reuter, Buchwald, Augenthaler, Hässler, Bein, Völler, Matthäus (c), Klinsmann [Karlheinz Riedle 71].

UAE Faraj, Eissa Meer, Ibrahim Meer [Abdulrahman Mohammed Al-Haddad 87], Khalil Ghanem, Mohammed Youssef, Abdulrahman Mohammed (c), Nasser Khamis, Juma'a, Al-Talyani, Ghuloum Abbas, Khalid Ismail [Hassan Mohammed Hussain 82].

Thunder, lightning, sheeting rain – the worst electrical storm to hit northern Italy in years. In these Wagnerian conditions, the men from drier climes felt the full blast. The Germans should have had ten.

With the score still 0-0, their two strikers missed any number of chances, four of them by Völler alone, the most glaring when Matthäus crossed from the right. Faraj saved from

1930
1934
1938
1950
1954
1958
1962
1966
1970
1974
1978
1982
1986
1990
1994
1998
2002
2006

1930

Klinsmann, and Völler lobbed over the bar instead of knocking the ball past the keeper from seven yards. Klinsmann hit a post and eventually took advantage of a slip by Khalil Ghanem to send in a low cross which Völler neatly flicked in from under his feet. Then Reuter's right-wing cross was put in by Klinsmann's downward header. When Hässler let a long ball bounce over his head, Khalid Ismail shot low across Illgner, but there was no comeback against a team like this. A Matthäus half-volley immediately made it 3-1, Bein thumped the ball in high from outside the D, and Völler was again credited with someone else's goal: his header was kept out by Eissa Meer's arm before being kicked in by his brother.

1934

1938

1950

1954

1958

1962

1966

1970

1974

1978

1982

1986

1990

1994

1998

2002

2006

---

19 June 1990 – Giuseppe Meazza, Milan – 72,510 – Alan Snoddy (NIR)

COLOMBIA   **(0) 1**
Rincón 90

WEST GERMANY   **(0) 1**
Littbarski 88

COLOMBIA Higuita, Herrera, Gilardo Gómez, Escobar, Perea, Gabriel Gómez, Luis Alfonso Fajardo, Alvarez, Rincón, Valderrama (c), Estrada.
WEST GERMANY Illgner, Reuter, Hans Pflügler, Berthold, Buchwald, Augenthaler, Hässler [Olaf Thon 87], Bein [Littbarski HT], Völler, Matthäus (c), Klinsmann.

Colombia needed a draw to qualify, fell behind to Littbarski's near-post shot with only two minutes left, then staged an improbable recovery when Rincón ran onto Valderrama's reverse pass to slip the ball between Illgner's legs as he came out. The Colombians won few friends with their play-acting, Valderrama at one point lying face-down for three minutes while the referee left him to it.

---

19 June 1990 – Renato Dall' Ara, Bologna – 27,833 – Shizuo Takada (JPN)

YUGOSLAVIA   **(2) 4**
Sušić 4, Pančev 7, 46, Prosinečki 90

UNITED ARAB EMIRATES   **(1) 1**
Juma'a 20

YUGOSLAVIA Ivković, Stanojković, Brnović, Hadžibegić, Jozić, Spasić, Stojković, Sušić, Pančev, Šabanadžović [Prosinečki 80], Vujović (c) [Vulić 65].
UAE Faraj, Eissa Meer, Ibrahim Meer, Khalil Ghanem, Al-Haddad, Abdulrahman Mohammed (c), Nasser Khamis [Sultan 35], Juma'a [Fahad Khamis HT], Al-Talyani, Ghuloum Abbas, Khalid Ismail.
SENT OFF: Khalil Ghanem 76.

Easy as expected for the revitalised Yugoslavs. Sušić was on the penalty spot when he headed in a cross from Šabanadžović, then an interception by Nasser Khamis knocked the ball square to Pančev, who volleyed in low from the edge of the area. Soon to become the most feared striker in Europe, he banged in a volley when Vujović chested a Stojković cross into his path. The Emirates again pulled it back to 2-1, Ivković getting a glove to Juma'a's header from Ibrahim Meer's cross – but their involvement ended on the wrong note when Khalil Ghanem was sent off for a second bookable offence, a foul on the ubiquitous Pančev. Finally, Eissa Meer lunged to block Prosinečki's volley, and deflected the ball high over the keeper.

GROUP D

	P	W	D	L	F	A	Pts
West Germany	3	2	1	0	10	3	5
Yugoslavia	3	2	0	1	6	5	4
Colombia	3	1	1	1	3	2	3
UAE	3	0	0	3	2	11	0

West Germany, Yugoslavia and Colombia qualified for the second round.

GROUP E

Belgium (seeded), South Korea, Spain, Uruguay.

12 June 1990 – Marc'Antonio Bentegodi, Verona – 32,790 – Vincent Mauro (USA)

BELGIUM   **(0) 2**
Degryse 53, De Wolf 64

SOUTH KOREA   **(0) 0**

BELGIUM Michel Preud'homme, Eric Gerets (c), Michel De Wolf, Leo Clijsters, Stefan Demol, Bruno Versavel, Marc Emmers, Franky Van der Elst, Marc Degryse, Enzo Scifo, Marc Van der Linden [Jan Ceulemans HT]. *Guy Thys*.
SOUTH KOREA Choi In-Yung, Park Kyung-Joon, Gu Sang-Bum, Hong Myung-Bo, Chung Yong-Hwan (c), Choi Kang-Hee, Kim Joo-Sung, Noh Soo-Jin [Lee Tae-Ho 62], Hwang Sun-Hong, Lee Yung-Jin [Cho Min-Kook HT], Choi Soon-Ho. *Lee Hoe-Taik*.

Versavel hit a post after only six minutes, but it took the introduction of Ceulemans, now 33 but still a force, to kindle the Belgians. Degryse, chasing Scifo's volleyed through-ball, hit a stratospheric lob over the keeper, and De Wolf smashed in a high shot from the left. Choi In-Yung had to make several good saves and South Korea rarely troubled Belgium's ageing defence. Degryse is also seen split in two: De Gryse.

13 June 1990 – Friuli, Udine – 35,713 – Helmut Kohl (AUT)

SPAIN   **0**

URUGUAY   **0**

SPAIN Andoni Zubizarreta, 'Chendo' (Miguel Portlan), Manuel Jiménez, Genaro Andrinúa, Manuel Sanchís jnr, Rafael Martín Vázquez, 'Michel' (Miguel González), Roberto (Fernández), Emilio Butragueño (c), Francisco

Villaroya [Alberto Gorriz 80], Manolo (Sánchez) [Rafael (Rafa) Paz 80]. *Luis Suárez*.
URUGUAY Fernando Álvez, José Herrera, Alfonso Domínguez, Nelson Gutiérrez, Hugo De León, José Perdomo, Antonio Alzamendi [Carlos Aguilera 65], Rubén Pereira [Gabriel Correa 65], Enzo Francescoli (c), Rubén Paz, Rubén Sosa. *Oscar Washington Tabárez*.

Uruguay's recent win at Wembley had just ended England's run of 17 matches without defeat, and their coach stressed they were determined to shake off the reputation for dirty play they'd reinforced in 1986. But in its place there was nothing but tedium, from both teams. Zubizarreta touched Alzamendi's shot onto the bar, and Sosa drove a penalty over the top after Villaroya had handled Herrera's header with twenty minutes left. Martín (Vázquez) is part of the surname, not a first name.

17 June 1990 – Marc'Antonio Bentegodi, Verona – 33,759 – Siegfried Kirschen (DDR)

BELGIUM   **(2) 3**
Clijsters 15, Scifo 22, Ceulemans 46

URUGUAY   **(0) 1**
Bengoechea 72

BELGIUM Preud'homme, Gerets, De Wolf, Clijsters [Emmers HT], Georges Grün, Demol, Versavel [Patrick Vervoort 73], Van der Elst, Degryse, Scifo, Ceulemans (c).
URUGUAY Álvez, Herrera, Domínguez, Gutiérrez, De León, Perdomo, Alzamendi [Aguilera HT], Santiago Ostolaza [Pablo Bengoechea 57], Francescoli (c), Paz, Sosa.
SENT OFF: Gerets 36.

1990

Belgium caught the Uruguayans cold (the veteran Clijsters heading in De Wolf's cross, Scifo scoring with a ground shot from over thirty yards) – and Ceulemans' low volley, after running through a great gap in the centre of the defence, helped them survive the sending-off of Gerets for two bookable offences. Bengoechea volleyed De León's cross in off Preud'homme's

1930
1934
1938
1950
1954
1958
1962
1966
1970
1974
1978
1982
1986
1990
1994
1998
2002
2006

leg, but it wasn't enough, and Herrera had his work cut out on his 25th birthday.

---

17 June 1990 – Friuli, Udine – 32,733 – Elias Jácome (ECU)

SPAIN	**(1) 3**
Michel 23, 63, 82	
SOUTH KOREA	**(1) 1**
Hwang BK 43	

SPAIN Zubizarreta, Chendo, Gorriz, Andrinúa, Sanchís, Martín Vázquez, Michel, Roberto [José María Bakero 82], Butragueño (c) [Fernando (Gómez) 78], Villaroya, Julio Salinas.
SOUTH KOREA Choi IY, Park [Chung Jong-Soo 69], Gu, Hong, Yoon Deuk-Yeo, Choi KH, Kim, Hwang Bo-Kwan, Byun, Chung Hae-Won [Noh 52], Choi SH (c).

South Korea tried to kick Spain out of their stride, equalised from long range when a free kick was touched to Hwang Bo-Kwan, but were generally outplayed. Butragueño might have won a penalty, Salinas had a goal controversially disallowed, and Michel scored three classy goals: with a right-footed volley, a right-footed free kick, and a low left-footer after beating two men.

---

21 June 1990 – Marc'Antonio Bentegodi, Verona – 35,950 – Juan Carlos Loustau (ARG)

SPAIN	**(2) 2**
Michel pen 26, Gorriz 38	
BELGIUM	**(1) 1**
Vervoort 29	

SPAIN Zubizarreta, Chendo, Gorriz, Andrinúa, Sanchís, Martín Vázquez, Michel, Roberto, Butragueño (c) [Rafael Alkorta 83], Villaroya, Salinas [Miguel Pardeza 88].
BELGIUM Preud'homme, Lorenzo Staelens [Van der Linden 79], De Wolf, Demol, Philippe Albert, Emmers [Pascal Plovie 31], Vervoort, Van der Elst, Degryse, Scifo, Ceulemans (c).

Michel had another good match, putting away the penalty when Preud'homme fouled Salinas and floating a free kick to the far post for Gorriz to head home. But Belgium deserved a draw: Vervoort's free kick took a deflection on its way through the wall, and for the second match in a row Spain's opponents missed a penalty, Scifo hitting the bar after Staelens was brought down by Gorriz on the hour.

---

21 June 1990 – Friuli, Udine – 29,039 – Tullio Lanese (ITA)

URUGUAY	**(0) 1**
Fonseca 90	
SOUTH KOREA	**(0) 0**

URUGUAY Álvez, Herrera, Domínguez, Gutiérrez, De León, Perdomo, Sergio Martínez, Ostolaza [Aguilera HT], Francescoli (c), Paz, Sosa [Daniel Fonseca 63].
SOUTH KOREA Choi IY, Park, Choi KH, Chung JS, Hong, Yoon, Kim, Hwang BK [Chung HW 78], Byun [Hwang SH 42], Lee Heung-Sil, Choi SH (c).
SENT OFF: Yoon 70.

Uruguay, who needed a win to be sure of qualifying, achieved one in the finals for the first time since 1970 but left it late, the toothy Fonseca heading in a free kick deep into injury time, a goal that added to Scotland's endless World Cup woes by depriving them of a place

GROUP E						
	P	W	D	L	F	A	Pts
Spain	3	2	1	0	5	2	5
Belgium	3	2	0	1	6	3	4
Uruguay	3	1	1	1	2	3	3
South Korea	3	0	0	3	1	6	0

Spain, Belgium and Uruguay qualified for the second round.

in the next round. South Korea committed their usual quota of fouls and had a player sent off for time-wasting. FIFA's Official Report lists Alzamendi in place of Ostolaza, an error.

GROUP F

Egypt, England (seeded), Holland, Republic of Ireland.

11 June 1990 – Renato Sant'Elia, Cagliari – 35,238 – Aron Schmidhuber (GER)

ENGLAND	**(1) 1**
Lineker 9	
REP. IRELAND	**(0) 1**
Sheedy 73	

ENGLAND Peter Shilton, M Gary Stevens, Stuart Pearce, Bryan Robson (c), Terry Butcher, Des Walker, Chris Waddle, Paul Gascoigne, Gary Lineker [Steve Bull 84], Peter Beardsley [Steve McMahon 69], John Barnes. *Bobby Robson.*
REP. IRELAND Pat Bonner, Chris Morris, Steve Staunton, Paul McGrath, Mick McCarthy (c), Kevin Moran, Ray Houghton, Andy Townsend, Tony Cascarino, John Aldridge [Alan McLoughlin 64], Kevin Sheedy. *Jack Charlton (ENG).*

No Football, We're English. The headline in *La Gazzetta dello Sport* got it about right, but they surely meant to include the Republic. Charlton's long ball tactics were no prettier for being predictable, and England fell into the trap of copying them, playing into the hands of Ireland's straightforward stoppers. For an hour, England consoled themselves with the prospect of ending this grim business with a win. Lineker reached Waddle's through-ball, dummied Bonner and chested it past him in the same motion, then chased it into an empty net ahead of McCarthy and Morris. But McMahon let the ball bobble away from him for Sheedy to shoot low past Shilton. Almost immediately, Butcher should have done better than head Waddle's free kick wide of the post. Bryan Robson, carrying yet another injury (a toe this time), wasn't the force of old. Italian statisticians apparently calculated that the ball was in play for only 49 minutes!

England's preparations had been dogged by the kind of press attention their manager had been living with for years. Isabella Ciaravolo, a Sardinian liaison officer, was transferred elsewhere after unsubstantiated reports of extra-curricular activities with some of the England players. After the Ireland match, one of the tabloids, which had been conducting a savage campaign against Bobby Robson, ran the line 'The *Sun* speaks its mind. Bring them home.' Watch this space for developments.

12 June 1990 – Comunale ('La Favorita'), Palermo – 33,288 – Emilio Soriano Aladrén (SPA)

EGYPT	**(0) 1**
Abdelghani pen 82	
HOLLAND	**(0) 1**
Kieft 58	

EGYPT Ahmed Shoubeir, Ibrahim Hassan, Rabbi Yassin, Ahmed Ramzy [Magdi Tolba 70], Hisham Yakan, Hani Ramzy, 'El-Kass' (Ahmed Abdou), Magdi Abdelghani, Gamal Abdelhamid (c) [Adel Abdelrahman 70], Ismail Youssef, Hossam Hassan. *Mahmoud El-Gohary.*
HOLLAND Hans van Breukelen, Berry van Aerle, Adri van Tiggelen, Jan Wouters, Graeme Rutjes, Ronald Koeman, Gerald Vanenburg [Wim Kieft HT], Frank Rijkaard, Marco van Basten, Ruud Gullit (c), Erwin Koeman [Richard Witschge 69]. *Leo Beenhakker.*

1990

Although the unfancied countries had generally given a good account of themselves so far, this was the one match expected to restore the status quo: predictions of 5-0 were the norm. But Gullit wasn't fully fit, van Basten couldn't get into the game, and Egypt were no mugs: they'd recently won 3-1 in Scotland and if van Basten volleyed wastefully over the bar, so did Tolba. It took a typical piece of poaching by Kieft, after Rijkaard dummied van Basten's cross, to put the Dutch ahead (even then Shoubeir almost turned his flick over the bar). But Egypt equalised when Ronald Koeman pulled Hossam's shirt outside the area. Beenhakker, brought in very late in preference to the players' choice Johan Cruijff, suddenly had a huge task on his hands.

The Koemans were brothers. The Hassan twins were each winning their 44th cap. Witschge's brother Rob played in the 1994 finals. The stadium was renamed the Renzo Barbera in 2002.

---

16 June 1990 – Renato Sant'Elia, Cagliari – 35,267 – Zoran Petrović (YUG)

ENGLAND 0

HOLLAND 0

ENGLAND Shilton, Paul Parker, Pearce, Robson (c) [David Platt 64], Butcher, Walker, Mark Wright, Waddle [Bull 58], Gascoigne, Lineker, Barnes.
HOLLAND van Breukelen, van Aerle, van Tiggelen, Wouters, Rijkaard, R Koeman, Witschge, Gullit (c), van Basten, Hans Gillhaus, John van't Schip [Kieft 74].

1990

Once again in a finals tournament, Bobby Robson allegedly submitted to a version of player power, this time installing a so-called sweeper system, i.e. five at the back, more than enough to stifle this incredibly lifeless Dutch team. Parker, small and quick, was a particular success in place of the heavy-footed Stevens. England had the better of things up front too, Gascoigne running at defenders with skill and muscle, Pearce shooting straight in from an indirect free kick, Bull heading wastefully wide from a cross by Lineker, who missed two good

chances. Encouraging, although the earth hadn't quite moved yet.

Shilton, first capped in 1970, kept a clean sheet in his 120th international, which broke Pat Jennings' European record. Van Tiggelen was celebrating his 33rd birthday.

---

17 June 1990 – Comunale ('La Favorita'), Palermo – 33,288 – Marcel Van Langenhove (BEL)

EGYPT   0

REP. IRELAND   0

EGYPT Shoubeir, I Hassan, Yassin (c), H Ramzy, Yakan, Tolba [Taher Abou Zeid 59], Osman Oraby, El-Kass [Abdelhamid 76], Abdelghani, Youssef, H Hassan.
REP. IRELAND Bonner, Morris, Staunton, McGrath, McCarthy (c), Moran, Houghton, Townsend, Cascarino [Niall Quinn 84], Aldridge [McLoughlin 64], Sheedy.

The funniest moment in the World Cup: listening to Jack Charlton, high priest of non-football, accusing the Egyptians of killing the game. Ahmed El-Mokadem, the Egyptian team's sponsor, retorted that 'any match would have to be more beautiful than playing against the Irish'. Shoubeir made a good save from the only real chance of the match, a shot by Houghton. The result left all four teams absolutely equal, raising the possibility of having to toss a coin to decide who qualified. Drawing lots, you might say.

---

21 June 1990 – Renato Sant'Elia, Cagliari – 34,959 – Kurt Röthlisberger (SWI)

ENGLAND   (0) 1
Wright 58

EGYPT   (0) 0

ENGLAND Shilton (c), Parker, Pearce, McMahon, Walker, Wright, Waddle [Platt 87], Gascoigne, Bull [Beardsley 84], Lineker, Barnes.

EGYPT Shoubeir, I Hassan, H Ramzy, Yakan, Yassin, Youssef, Abdelghani, Abdelhamid (c) [Abdelrahman 78], A Ramzy, El-Kass [Tarek Soliman 78], H Hassan.

The only win in the group. Even with Robson injured again and Butcher dropped to make way for an extra attacker, England's defence was rarely threatened by an unadventurous team, allowing Shilton to keep his ninth clean sheet in the finals, a new record. Wright, kept out of the 1986 finals by a broken leg but now the best of the back four, scored his only goal for England by beating the keeper to Gascoigne's free kick and heading it in off Yakan's head. Fine as far as it went, but that seemed to be no further than the next round, especially if Bull stayed in instead of Beardsley.

21 June 1990 – Comunale ('La Favorita'), Palermo – 33,288 – Michel Vautrot (FRA)

HOLLAND (1) 1
Gullit 10

REP. IRELAND (0) 1
Quinn 71

REP. IRELAND Bonner, Morris, Staunton, McGrath, McCarthy (c), Moran, Houghton, Townsend, Quinn, Aldridge [Cascarino 62], Sheedy [Ronnie Whelan 62]. HOLLAND van Breukelen, van Aerle, van Tiggelen, Wouters, Rijkaard, R Koeman, Witschge [Henk Fräser 59], Gullit (c), van Basten, Kieft [John van Loen 79], Gillhaus.

When Gullit stretched to play a one-two with Kieft then accelerated beautifully between two defenders and finished with a ground shot across Bonner, it seemed class was about to come out on top at last. But whatever Ireland lacked, it wasn't heart. Houghton had a goal disallowed, Sheedy shot over the bar with Aldridge better placed, and eventually the Republic scored the kind of goal Big Jack probably fantasised about. Bonner banged a huge

kick downfield, van Aerle's volleyed back pass was badly fumbled by van Breukelen, and the 6'4 Quinn slid in on his stilts to reach the loose ball. Both teams qualified along with England, but it was a group nobody wanted to dwell on.

GROUP F

	P	W	D	L	F	A	Pts
England	3	1	2	0	2	1	4
Rep. Ireland	3	0	3	0	2	2	3
Holland	3	0	3	0	2	2	3
Egypt	3	0	2	1	1	2	2

England, the Republic of Ireland and Holland qualified for the second round. Second and third places were decided by the drawing of lots.

2ND ROUND

23 June 1990 – San Paolo, Naples – 50,026 – Tullio Lanese (ITA)

CAMEROON (0) (0) 2
Milla 106, 109

COLOMBIA (0) (0) 1
Redín 116

CAMEROON Nkono, Tataw (c), Ebwelle, Ndip, Onana, Kana Biyick, Maboang, Mbouh, Omam Biyick, Mfede [Milla 54], Makanaky [Bonaventure Djonkep 70].
COLOMBIA Higuita, Herrera, Gilardo Gómez, Escobar, Perea, Gabriel Gómez [Redín 80], Fajardo [Iguarán 63], Álvarez, Rincón, Valderrama (c), Estrada.

1990

Billed as a colourful clash of styles, the match wended its dreary way through the first ninety minutes, alleviated only by Rincón's shot against the bar. Then in extra time the two biggest characters in the tournament came face to face, and one of them lost out both times. First Higuita left a glaring gap at his near post when Milla broke through, then he indulged in his well-known habit of dribbling the ball upfield. Trying to drag it back with the sole of his foot, he lost it to Milla, who ran on, an evil grin on his face, to put it in the empty net.

Redín scored after exchanging passes with Valderrama on the left, but the goal came too late to stop Cameroon becoming the first African country to reach the quarter-finals. It was also Higuita's last match in the finals: he missed the 1994 tournament after being imprisoned on charges relating to kidnapping. Having scored from three penalties in internationals, he spent the time inside practising free kicks.

---

23 June 1990 – San Nicola, Bari – 47,673 – Siegfried Kirschen (DDR)

CZECHOSLOVAKIA (1) 4
Skuhravý 11, 62, 82, Kubík 77

COSTA RICA (0) 1
González 56

CZECHOSLOVAKIA Stejskal, Kadlec, Bílek, Kocian, Straka, Hašek (c), Moravčík, Chovanec, Skuhravý, Kubík, Knoflíček.
COSTA RICA Hermidio Barrantes, Chavarría [Guimarães 65], Chávez, Flores (c), Montero, Marchena, Marvin Obando [Medford HT], González, Ramírez, Cayasso, Jara.

1990

Barrantes, not as spectacular as Conejo, did nothing very wrong, and the 19-year-old González headed a fine equaliser from Marchena's free kick – but at last someone was taking advantage of Costa Rica's weakness under the high ball. Skuhravý, heavily built and good in the air, scored a hat trick of headers and had a goal disallowed; Kubík curled in

a left-footed free kick; and Moravčík hit the bar. Costa Rica were well beaten but not at all disgraced. The real crowd figure was probably in the region of 15,000!

---

24 June 1990 – delle Alpi, Turin – 61,381 – Joël Quiniou (FRA)

ARGENTINA (0) 1
Caniggia 81

BRAZIL (0) 0

ARGENTINA Goycochea, Basualdo, Ruggeri, Simón, Monzón, Olarticoechea, Burruchaga, Giusti, Caniggia, Maradona (c), Troglio [Calderón 62].
BRAZIL Taffarel, Jorginho, Branco, Mauro Galvão [Silas 84], Ricardo Gomes (c), Ricardo Rocha, Müller, Dunga, Careca, Alemão [Renato (Portaluppi) 84], Valdo.
SENT OFF: Ricardo Gomes 83.

There was the usual post-match guff about a misguided attempt to make the Brazilian team more 'European'. In fact they played some of the best football in the tournament, losing because they missed chances and had no luck. Three players hit a post: Dunga with a header, Alemão with a long shot, Careca when his cross was touched by Goycochea. In the way of these things, Argentina made only one real chance and took it. If Maradona wasn't at his best in this tournament, it was mainly because an inflamed toenail left him with a badly swollen foot. Playing in pain, he attracted defenders like flies and managed to get a pass away with Ricardo Gomes pushing his shoulder down; Caniggia was completely free on his left to take the ball round Taffarel. One moment of inspiration had been enough, but it was very hard on Brazil, whose frustration culminated in the sending-off of their captain for a tackle from behind when Basualdo was clean through. Someone at FIFA calculated that they'd made 56 chances in their four matches, scoring from four of them.

Renato is now known as 'Renato Gaúcho' in Brazil.

---

24 June 1990 – Giuseppe Meazza, Milan – 74,559 – Juan Carlos Loustau (ARG)

WEST GERMANY   (0) 2
Klinsmann 50, Brehme 84

HOLLAND   (0) 1
R Koeman pen 88

WEST GERMANY Illgner, Berthold, Brehme, Buchwald, Jürgen Kohler, Augenthaler, Littbarski, Reuter, Völler, Matthäus (c), Klinsmann [Riedle 78].
HOLLAND van Breukelen, van Aerle [Kieft 67], van Tiggelen, Wouters, Rijkaard, R Koeman, van't Schip, Aron Winter, van Basten, Gullit (c), Witschge [Gillhaus 78].
SENT OFF: Rijkaard 21, Völler 21.

They had to hold this here: it was the Milan derby. Inter's Germans (Brehme, Matthäus and Klinsmann) v Milan's Dutchmen (Rijkaard, van Basten and Gullit), the setting for one of the great individual performances in the World Cup. Rijkaard was booked for a vicious foul on Völler, who was cautioned for complaining that Rijkaard had spat in his hair. When van Breukelen collected the ensuing free kick, Völler pulled out of the challenge, but Rijkaard got involved nevertheless, and both were sent off, Völler unjustly, Rijkaard spitting twice in his face as they left. The look on Völler's face was a picture.

Deprived of his partner, Klinsmann simply rose to the occasion. Explosive and tireless, he volleyed in Buchwald's cross, crashed a shot against the post, ran the whole Dutch defence to distraction, and went off to a standing ovation. Brehme curled in the second goal with his right foot from the left wing. Koeman's penalty, dubiously awarded for Kohler's tackle on van Basten, was no kind of balm for the most disappointing team in any finals tournament.

---

25 June 1990 – Luigi Ferraris, Genoa – 31,818 – José Ramiz Wright (BRZ)

REP. IRELAND   0

ROMANIA   0
Ireland 5-4 pens.

REP. IRELAND Bonner, Morris, Staunton [David O'Leary 94], McGrath, McCarthy (c), Moran, Houghton, Townsend, Quinn, Aldridge [Cascarino 23], Sheedy.
ROMANIA Lung (c), Rednic, Klein, Popescu, Andone, Rotariu, Sabău [Timofte 98], Balint, Răducioiu [Lupu 75], Hagi, Lupescu.
PENALTY SHOOT-OUT: Hagi 1-0, Sheedy 1-1, Lupu 2-1, Houghton 2-2, Rotariu 3-2, Townsend 3-3, Lupescu 4-3, Cascarino 4-4, Timofte saved, O'Leary 4-5.

Romania didn't quite have the quality to break through the predictable blockade, and Bonner easily saved Timofte's nervous little kick in the shoot-out. McGrath was excellent as usual, but there was little else to admire about the Irish except their fans.

---

25 June 1990 – Olimpico, Rome – 73,303 – George Courtney (ENG)

ITALY   (0) 2
Schillaci 65, Serena 83

URUGUAY   (0) 0

ITALY Zenga, Bergomi (c), Maldini, Berti [Aldo Serena 52], Ferri, Baresi, De Agostini, De Napoli, Schillaci, Giannini, Baggio [Vierchowod 79].
URUGUAY Álvez, José Pintos Saldaña, Domínguez, Gutiérrez, De León, Perdomo, Aguilera [Sosa 55], Ostolaza [Alzamendi 79], Fonseca, Francescoli (c), Pereira.

1990

After a defensive first half, Schillaci twice came close but Uruguay missed the best chance of the match, Zenga making a save after De Napoli's misplaced header let Aguilera through.

Soon afterwards Serena nutmegged Gutiérrez to set up Schillaci, who by now was expecting to score every time he touched the ball: here he turned to hoik a left-foot shot over Álvez from outside the area. Serena, on his 30th birthday, sealed the match by outjumping poor Gutiérrez to head in Giannini's free kick.

---

26 June 1990 – Marc'Antonio Bentegodi, Verona – 34,822 – Aron Schmidhuber (GER)

YUGOSLAVIA   **(0) (1) 2**
Stojković 77, 93

SPAIN   **(0) (1) 1**
Salinas 83

YUGOSLAVIA Ivković, Spasić, Brnović, Hadžibegić, Šabanadžović, Jozić, Stojković, Katanec [Vulić 79], Pančev [Savićević 56], Sušić, Vujović (c).
SPAIN Zubizarreta, Chendo, Gorriz, Andrinúa [Jiménez 48], Sanchís, Villaroya, Martín Vázquez, Michel, Roberto, Butragueño (c) [Rafa Paz 79], Salinas.

Spain hit a post twice and scored a deserved equaliser when the hardworking Martín Vázquez seemed to mishit a shot and presented Salinas with an open goal at the far post. But they were undone by two marvellous pieces of finishing from Stojković, who'd been brilliant but frustrating since his debut as an 18-year-old in 1983. Vujović crossed from the left, Katanec headed on, and Stojković shaped to blast the ball first time then trapped it to let a defender slide past, a wonderfully cool piece of skill, before rolling the ball low into the far corner. When Roberto gave away a free kick, Stojković whipped it round the wall and just inside the post. Savićević, later a star at Milan, helped to keep possession till the end.

---

26 June 1990 – Renato Dall' Ara, Bologna – 34,520 – Peter Mikkelsen (DEN)

ENGLAND   **(0) (0) 1**
Platt 119

BELGIUM   **(0) (0) 0**

ENGLAND Shilton, Parker, Pearce, McMahon [Platt 71], Butcher (c), Walker, Wright, Waddle, Gascoigne, Lineker, Barnes [Bull 74].
BELGIUM Preud'homme, Gerets, De Wolf, Demol, Clijsters, Grün, Van der Elst, Scifo, Versavel [Vervoort 107], Degryse [Nico Claesen 65], Ceulemans (c).

A dramatic match might have been settled a lot sooner. England's five-man defence couldn't stop Ceulemans and Scifo hitting a post, and Barnes had a goal wrongly disallowed for offside. Regularly criticised for his England performances, he played his full part here despite being double marked. Belgium's veterans lasted the pace well, but Claesen did little as substitute and wasn't capped again.

Extra time, which England were playing for the first time since the 1970 World Cup, was almost at an end and they seemed to have settled for the penalty shoot-out. But Shilton shouted at them to keep going forward, and the bearded Gerets, still a quality right-back at 36, made his last World Cup gesture by bringing down Gascoigne, who took the free kick himself. As it dropped over Platt's

1990

CLEAN SHEETS			
10	Peter Shilton	ENG	1982–90
8	Sepp Maier	GER	1974–78
8	Emerson Leão	BRZ	1974–78
8	Cláudio Taffarel	BRZ	1990–98
7	Gylmar	BRZ	1958–66
6	Gordon Banks	ENG	1966–70

Shilton's last was his 66th in all internationals, a world record at the time.

right shoulder in a packed penalty area, he swivelled and hooked it across Preud'homme for his first and most important goal for England, who were in the quarter-finals again, and this time with no Maradona to have a hand in things. It was a final bow for the wily 67-year-old Thys.

Meanwhile The *Sun*'s view by now: 'We never seriously doubted England's chances of clawing their way through the World Cup field.' Read on, it gets better.

QUARTER-FINALS

30 June 1990 – Comunale, Florence – 38,971 – Kurt Röthlisberger (SWI)

ARGENTINA	(0) (0) 0	
YUGOSLAVIA	(0) (0) 0	

Argentina 3-2 pens.

ARGENTINA Goycochea, Serrizuela, Olarticoechea [Troglio 55], Simón, Ruggeri, Basualdo, Burruchaga, Giusti, Caniggia, Maradona (c), Calderón [Dezotti 86].
YUGOSLAVIA Ivković, Vulić, Spasić, Brnović, Hadžibegić, Šabanadžović, Jozić, Stojković, Sušić [Savićević 63], Prosinečki, Vujović (c).
SENT OFF: Šabanadžović 31.
PENALTY SHOOT-OUT: Serrizuela 1-0, Stojković hit bar, Burruchaga 2-0, Prosinečki 2-1, Maradona saved, Savićević 2-2, Troglio hit post, Brnović saved, Dezotti 3-2, Hadžibegić saved.

Hot-blooded from start to finish (five Argentinians booked). The skilful Yugoslavs had the better of it until Šabanadžović was sent off for a second bookable offence, the usual one of fouling Maradona. After that, Ruggeri's header dropped onto the bar and Burruchaga had a very late goal controversially disallowed for handball. Most of the real drama, however, was packed into a fluctuating penalty shoot-out.

When Ivković saved Maradona's feeble kick, the Yugoslavs weren't the only ones to rejoice – but Goycochea again proved an important shot stopper. The fair-haired Prosinečki showed a promise he never quite fulfilled.

30 June 1990 – Olimpico, Rome – 73,303 – Carlos Alberto da Silva Valente (POR)

ITALY	(1) 1	
Schillaci 38		
REP. IRELAND	(0) 0	

ITALY Zenga, Bergomi (c), Maldini, De Agostini, Ferri, Baresi, Donadoni, De Napoli, Schillaci, Giannini [Ancelotti 63], Baggio [Serena 71].
REP. IRELAND Bonner, Morris, Staunton, McGrath, McCarthy (c), Moran, Houghton, Townsend, Quinn [Cascarino 53], Aldridge [John Sheridan 78], Sheedy.

Italy expected a tough match and got it, but the result was never really in doubt. Quinn caused occasional problems with his height, but the Irish defence couldn't hold Toto Schillaci, who hit the underside of the bar from thirty yards and had a goal dubiously disallowed for offside as well as scoring the only goal, an instant strike after Baggio beat three men and Donadoni's high shot knocked Bonner off his feet. There was much talk afterwards of the Republic's romantic World Cup adventure, ended by a single goal from the host country – but they scored only two goals in five games, none of which were won, and contributed little to the tournament except defensive organisation. For various reasons, there were sighs of relief when they left it.

1 July 1990 – Giuseppe Meazza, Milan – 73,347 – Helmut Kohl (AUT)

WEST GERMANY	(1) 1	
Matthäus pen 24		
CZECHOSLOVAKIA	(0) 0	

1990

1990

WEST GERMANY Illgner, Berthold, Brehme, Buchwald, Kohler, Augenthaler, Littbarski, Bein [Möller 82], Riedle, Matthäus (c), Klinsmann.
CZECHOSLOVAKIA Stejskal, Kadlec, Bílek [Němeček 68], Kocian, Straka, Hašek (c), Moravčík, Chovanec, Skuhravý, Kubík [Griga 80], Knoflíček.
SENT OFF: Moravčík 70.

Moravčík's ludicrous dismissal, for kicking his boot away in annoyance, did Czechoslovakia's cause no good, but they'd looked intimidated from the start. Hašek (twice) and Bílek cleared off the line, Buchwald missed an open goal, and Riedle might have had a penalty when Stejskal brought him down. Klinsmann did get one, after beating a man and brushing between two others – and if West Germany were less exciting than in the group matches, Czechoslovakia hardly had a shot on goal.

1 July 1990 – San Paolo, Naples – 55,205 – Edgardo Codesal (MEX)

ENGLAND   **(1) (2) 3**
Platt 25, Lineker pen 83, pen 104

CAMEROON   **(0) (2) 2**
Kunde pen 61, Ekeke 65

ENGLAND Shilton, Parker, Pearce, Platt, Butcher (c) [Trevor Steven 74], Walker, Wright, Waddle, Lineker, Gascoigne, Barnes [Beardsley HT].
CAMEROON Nkono, Massing, Ebwelle, Mfede [Eugène Ekeke 62], Tataw (c), Kunde, Libiih, Pagal, Omam Biyick, Makanaky, Maboang [Milla HT].

Something wondrous strange. Emerging from their earlier shell, Cameroon shredded England's massed defence time after time, only to be let down by indiscipline (they were without four first choices through suspension) and poor finishing. In the first half, Libiih missed two opportunities and Shilton rushed out to block a volley when Maboang's dummy sent Omam Biyick clean through. So England were able to hold on

to the lead provided by Platt's downward header from Pearce's left-wing cross.

Then Milla came on and again changed the flow. Unnecessarily fouled by Gascoigne for the penalty, he then delayed his short pass to usher Ekeke through the ruins of the defence and chip the ball beyond Shilton. With Steven at right-back and Wright forced out to the wing with a bandaged head (another Milla contribution), England were in obvious disarray.

But their most important players kept their nerve when it mattered. Wright's sideways flick found Lineker, who either dived in the act of turning a defender or was clipped from behind by another (the video's inconclusive). It was the first penalty England had been awarded in 53 matches, and there were only seven minutes left. In all the pressure, Lineker sent Nkono the wrong way. In extra time he did the same, finding the middle of the net, after Gascoigne's through-ball had sent him clear. When Massing caught Lineker as he rounded the keeper, Nkono was booked for protesting about the penalty, not the way he'd have chosen to end an impressive international career. Lineker missed the chance of a hat-trick by shooting wide after a run and square pass by Gascoigne.

CONSECUTIVE CLEAN SHEETS

5	Walter Zenga	ITA	1990
4	Gylmar	BRZ	1958
4	Gordon Banks	ENG	1966
4	Emerson Leão	BRZ	1974
4	Sepp Maier	GER	1978
4	Emerson Leão	BRZ	1978
4	Peter Shilton	ENG	1982
4	Carlos	BRZ	1986
4	Oliver Kahn	GER	2002

Two of Brazil's most skilful players, Júnior and the beardered Sócrates, celebrate the goal against Spain in 1986.

Time to stop shouldering the responsibility. Bryan Robson goes off injured in the match against Morocco in 1986.

Palm Sunday. Maradona's first goal against England in 1986.

Rudi Voller heads Germany's equaliser in the 1986 Final against Argentina.

Toto Schillaci celebrates his first goal of the 1990 tournamant.

Pat Bonner makes the penalty save that sends the Republic of Ireland into the quarter-finals in 1990.

What's the collective noun for a group of celebrating Cameroonians? Omam Biyick and Roger Milla jump for joy in 1990.

The spitting image of a great player. Frank Rijkaard (left) and an unsuspecting Rudi Völler are sent off in 1990.

Franky Van Der Elst (No 8) watches David Platt volley England's last-minute winner against Belgium in 1990.

Gazza cried all the way to the bank in Italia 90.

Comrades in arms. Brehme (left) and Augenthaler after the goal against England in the 1990 semi-final.

Gary Lineker scored ten goals in the finals, twice as many as any other British player. Here he celebrates the last, against West Germany in 1990.

Spot the goalkeeper and goalscorer as Ray Houghton's long lob sails in for the Republic of Ireland's goal against Italy in 1994.

Houghton turns a somersault after his winning goal against Italy in 1994. Terry Phelan, who never scored for Ireland, wonders how it's done.

Courting the net. Rashidi Yekeni savours his goal for Nigeria against Bulgaria in 1994.

Saïd Owairan goes past Dick Medved on the way to scoring a sensational goal for Saudi Arabia against Belgium in 1994.

The moment when Brazil win the World Cup for a record fourth time. Italy's number of wins remains at three as Roberto Baggio puts his penalty over the bar in the shoot-out following the 1994 Final.

Not a position Ronaldo expected to find himself in. Barthez shows his determination as France leapfrog Brazil in the 1998 Final. Lilian Thuram, the player of the tournament, takes a detached view.

The other side of Beckham's coin. As the red card comes out against Argentina, Veron points the way back to Old Trafford, where they will both be playing in 2001.

Paul Scholes steps aside to let Michael Owen score one of the goals of France 98. The Argentinians in the crowd probably don't see it like that.

There's no parting the red sea. South Korea's fans were one of the features of 2002.

Good understanding between central defenders as Rio Ferdinand helps Sol Campbell celebrate his first goal for England, against Sweden in 2002.

The calvary arrives. An almost biblical scene as Maldini's disciples mourn his exodus.

Oliver Kahn put his body on the line throughout the 2002 finals. Here he keeps Robbie Keane waiting for Ireland's equaliser.

Thanks for the card. Rudi Völler appreciates the selfless booking that kept Michael Ballack out of the 2002 Final.

Ronaldo never looked back after the opening goal of the 2002 Final. Kahn waits for the earth to swallow him up.

Another divine ponytail flops. David Seaman turns to watch Ronaldinho's freak kick in 2002.

African teams had been progressing through successive World Cups one step at a time, and Cameroon were the most convincing so far – but England would have been disappointed if they'd lost to any of their opponents so far. The next were a different matter.

SEMI-FINALS

3 July 1990 – San Paolo, Naples – 59,978 – Michel Vautrot (FRA)

ARGENTINA (0) (1) 1
Caniggia 67

ITALY (1) (1) 1
Schillaci 17
Argentina 4-3 pens.

ARGENTINA Goycochea, Serrizuela, Olarticoechea, Simón, Ruggeri, Basualdo [Batista 98], Burruchaga, Giusti, Caniggia, Maradona (c), Calderón [Troglio HT].
ITALY Zenga, Bergomi (c), Maldini, De Agostini, Ferri, Baresi, Donadoni, De Napoli, Schillaci, Giannini [Baggio 75], Vialli [Serena 70].
SENT OFF: Giusti 109.
PENALTY SHOOT-OUT: Baresi 1-0, Serrizuela 1-1, Baggio 2-1, Burruchaga 2-2, De Agostini 3-2, Olarticoechea 3-3, Donadoni saved, Maradona 4-3, Serena saved.

Argentina showed their intentions from the start, bringing down Vialli, Maldini and De Napoli in the first four minutes. Giusti was sent off for flattening Baggio, and Vautrot had to issue a warning to both captains. Somewhere in all that, Italy took the lead when Giannini headed on for Vialli to volley, Goycochea to save, and the inevitable Schillaci to mishit the rebound in. The Sicilian bricklayer's son, who'd recently spent seven seasons in the second and third divisions, seemed to be rising to his destiny like Rossi in 1982.

But Italy appeared nervous after half-time, relying on their defence to keep yet another clean sheet. Argentina began to make chances. Olarticoechea crossed from the left, Zenga came out when he should have stayed put, and Caniggia got to the ball before him, glancing a back-header inside the far post. It was the first goal Italy had conceded in eleven matches.

Baggio and Serena were brought on but couldn't change the flow. Schillaci was regularly caught offside, and Giusti's sending-off came too late to matter. When Donadoni, gaunt and brilliant, had his penalty saved in the shoot-out, Italy had to hope that Maradona would miss as he'd done in the previous round – but this time there was no mistake and Argentina had sneaked into a second successive Final. Caniggia, their one real striker, wouldn't be with them. After various attempts to handle the ball as it went over his head, he eventually succeeded and picked up his second booking of the tournament, the daftest reason yet for missing a World Cup Final.

For the hosts, nothing but terrible anticlimax – but perhaps it had been in the stars. This was their first match of the tournament outside Rome, they played it on Maradona's home

MINUTES WITHOUT CONCEDING A GOAL

Excluding injury time.

517	Walter Zenga	ITA	1990
500	Peter Shilton	ENG	1982–86
475	Sepp Maier	GER	1974–78
458	Emerson Leão	BRZ	1978
442	Gordon Banks	ENG	1966
427	Oliver Kahn	GER	2002
401	Carlos	BRZ	1986

1930 1934 1938 1950 1954 1958 1962 1966 1970 1974 1978 1982 1986 **1990** 1994 1998 2002 2006

ground, it was the 17th international staged in Naples, Schillaci scored after 17 minutes, and Donadoni was wearing No. 17. Seventeen is the Italian equivalent of unlucky thirteen. Some things just aren't meant to be.

---

4 July 1990 – delle Alpi, Turin – 62,628 – José Ramiz Wright (BRZ)

WEST GERMANY   (0) (1) 1
Brehme 59

ENGLAND   (0) (1) 1
Lineker 80
West Germany 4-3 pens.

WEST GERMANY Illgner, Berthold, Brehme, Matthäus (c), Kohler, Augenthaler, Buchwald, Hässler [Reuter 68], Völler [Riedle 38], Thon, Klinsmann.
ENGLAND Shilton, Parker, Pearce, Platt, Butcher (c) [Steven 70], Walker, Wright, Beardsley, Lineker, Gascoigne, Waddle.
PENALTY SHOOT-OUT: Lineker 1-0, Brehme 1-1, Beardsley 2-1, Matthäus 2-2, Platt 3-2, Riedle 3-3, Pearce saved, Thon 4-3, Waddle shot over.

An epic. England looked secure at the back, Wright playing with a padded bandage over his left eye, but West Germany's performance was their least convincing of the tournament, especially after Völler, back after suspension, suffered a shin injury. Hässler and Thon were brought in to take some of the load off Matthäus, who was on a yellow card – but England had the better of the first half, Waddle's shot from just inside the German half being touched onto the bar by Illgner.

The first goal was unexpected and fluky, the ball hitting Parker's leg and ballooning over Shilton. Brehme had now scored from free kicks in successive semi-finals, but with considerable help each time. England looked on their way out, but suddenly three German defenders were confused by Parker's long cross from the right, and Kohler let it come off his

leg straight to Lineker, who flicked it away with his thigh and shot low across the keeper with his left foot. For the first time in any World Cup, a country would play extra time in three consecutive matches.

It was this additional half hour that raised the match to its present status. Waddle and Buchwald hit the same post; Shilton saved from Matthäus and Klinsmann, who volleyed weakly wide with his left foot when unmarked; Platt had a headed goal rightly disallowed for offside; and Gascoigne's late tackle on Berthold earned him a booking that would keep him out of the Final if England reached it. Gazza had given away a penalty against Cameroon, and this challenge was astoundingly pointless: Berthold was out on the touchline and no threat to anyone. As Bobby Robson said, 'daft azza brush'.

The penalty shoot-out, the first England had been involved in, was as feverish as they come. West Germany's experience in this lottery was probably decisive: the first country to take part in three World Cup shoot-outs, they've won them all (and we all know about the rematch in Euro 96). Here the normally reliable Pearce hit Illgner's leg and Waddle blazed high into the night sky, images we've had to relive time and again, along with that of

MOST PENALTY SHOOT-OUTS

3	West Germany	1982, 1986, 1990
3	Argentina	1990 (2), 1998
3	France	1982, 1986, 1998
3	Italy	1990, 1994, 1998
3	Brazil	1986, 1994, 1998

West Germany and Argentina won all three, Italy lost all three. The only player to take a kick in each of three shoot-outs was Italy's Roberto Baggio, who scored with his first and third but famously missed in the 1994 Final.

Gascoigne wiping his tears with his shirt, the sight that allegedly started the current football craze (it even appeared on a stamp issued by Bhutan), so it was doubly irritating.

Just a thought here. Dave Beasant was in the squad. Much taller than Shilton, nine years younger, and a well-known shot stopper. Two years earlier, his penalty save in the final had won Wimbledon the FA Cup. Imagine the criticism if Robson had sent him on in the last minute of extra time and England had still lost the shoot-out. Yes but maybe it was the kind of imaginative thinking England needed. Instead Shilton waited till every kick was taken before moving, leaving him less time to stop them, a questionable tactic for a 40-year-old who'd saved only one penalty out of 15 for England.

West Germany set records by reaching the Final for the sixth time and the third in a row. They were (whisper it) a better team than England – but not necessarily on this fraught night, which ended in tears, and not just those of a clown.

A harmless match came to some sort of life when Baggio caught Shilton rolling the ball on the ground, stole it away, took Schillaci's return pass in an offside position, and came inside two defenders to score. A red nose for England's veteran keeper in his last international. Platt, one of the finds of the tournament, headed a crisp equaliser from a cross by the nimble Dorigo, but Parker was judged to have brought down Schillaci, whose penalty made him the tournament's leading scorer. Like England's Fair Play award, it was little consolation. Italy were third after winning six matches and drawing the other, Argentina finished higher after winning two and losing two. If that's fair, FIFA's a banana.

Berti had a headed goal wrongly disallowed in the last minute, and our tabloid friends turned full circle in one of their leaders: 'Around Gazza and his young gang we can build a team to rule the world. Four years on, remember you read it first in the *Sun*.' How could we forget? England didn't qualify for the 1994 finals.

3RD-PLACE FINAL

FINAL

7 July 1990 – San Nicola, Bari – 51,426 – Joël Quiniou (FRA)

| **ITALY** | **(0) 2** |
Baggio 71, Schillaci pen 85

| **ENGLAND** | **(0) 1** |
Platt 81

ITALY Zenga, Bergomi (c), Maldini, Ancelotti, Vierchowod, Baresi, Ciro Ferrara, Giannini [Ferri 90], Schillaci, Baggio, De Agostini [Berti 67].
ENGLAND Shilton (c), MG Stevens, Tony Dorigo, McMahon [Waddle 72], Walker, Parker, Wright [Neil Webb 72], Steven, Lineker, Platt, Beardsley.

8 July 1990 – Olimpico, Rome – 73,603 – Edgardo Codesal (MEX)

| **WEST GERMANY** | **(0) 1** |
Brehme pen 84

| **ARGENTINA** | **(0) 0** |

1990

WEST GERMANY Illgner, Berthold [Reuter 73], Brehme, Buchwald, Kohler, Augenthaler, Hässler, Matthäus (c), Littbarski, Völler, Klinsmann.
ARGENTINA Goycochea, Simón, Sensini, Basualdo, Serrizuela, Ruggeri [Monzón HT], Burruchaga [Calderón 53], Troglio, Lorenzo, Maradona (c), Dezotti.
SENT OFF: Monzón 64, Dezotti 86.

1930

1934

1938

1950

1954

1958

1962

1966

1970

1974

1978

1982

1986

1990

1994

1998

2002

2006

Because it's a World Cup Final, we're expected to give it due respect with a full report, blow by blow. But the heart's not in it.

Argentina, with four players suspended, would have forced extra-time again if the unimpressive Codesal hadn't given a penalty when Völler went down in a tackle by Sensini. Matthäus, suffering a painful ankle, left the kick to Brehme, whose low shot edged past Goycochea. The two sendings-off, the first in a Final, were almost expected: Monzón for a spectacular foul on Klinsmann, Dezotti for grabbing Kohler by the throat. Maradona, man-marked out of it by Buchwald, who towered over him, shed tears in Gazzaesque quantities. A sight for sore English eyes.

West Germany, in their last World Cup as a separate nation, were the first team to keep a clean sheet in a Final. They were worthy enough winners but scored only a single goal in each of their last three matches: two from the penalty spot, the other (in a match decided on penalties) with a deflected free kick. The total of 16 red cards was a finals record at the time; the goals-per-game average of 2.21 is still the lowest. With the possible exceptions of 1962 and the only other time Italy were the hosts, it was the worst before 2002.

The long drought

USA 1994

1930

1934

1938

1950

1954

1958

1962

1966

1970

1974

1978

1982

1986

1990

1994

1998

2002

2006

If FIFA hoped that awarding the World Cup to the land of the dollar would at last crack the supposedly lucrative United States market, it was a triumph of hope over experience. But at least the infrastructure wasn't bad. What visitors were likely to see were matches played in well-appointed stadia, with excellent transport facilities, catering services and communications, an experienced and minimal police presence, and the highest average crowds in World Cup history. If the price was allowing a mediocre USA team free entry, it was worth every cent.

Of the stronger countries, a reunified Germany had a new coach but rather too many old players, though Klinsmann was in his pomp and Sammer a powerful recruit from East Germany. Brazil were without four regular central defenders but others simply stepped off the conveyor belt, and Romário had just scored 30 times in 33 league games for Barcelona as well as the two goals that sent Brazil through at Uruguay's expense. Italy, who'd rather staggered over the finishing line, were still strong at the back but again in search of a reliable goalscorer.

A talented French team (Papin, Cantona, Ginola) stayed at home after losing their last two home games to very late goals, the first against Israel, the second in the very last minute, thanks to a misjudgment by Ginola. Nothing much was expected of their conquerors Bulgaria.

Argentina had gone 31 matches without losing, a world record at the time, which included winning the Copa América twice in a row – but a 5-0 home defeat by Colombia made them recall the 33-year-old Maradona to help them squeeze through in a play-off, beating Australia with an deflected goal. Colombia, still led by Valderrama, with Asprilla a new threat in attack, were naturally included among the favourites.

So too, for the first time, were a team from Africa. Nigeria had just won the African Nations Cup with a blend of skill and raw power that people had been expecting from the continent for years. Yekini, Okocha, Amunike and Amokachi were expected to become big names in the forthcoming month.

Certainly more so than Aizlewood, McKimmie or Carlton Palmer. For the first time since they entered the World Cup, none of the four United Kingdom countries reached the finals. Scotland, Wales and Northern Ireland all finished fourth in their groups, while England's five wins included four against Turkey and San Marino. Their new manager Graham Taylor picked some shocking players as well as 'a pig's arse of a team' (his words, everyone's opinion) against Norway, who won 2-0. So did Holland, in the decisive match, thanks to a referee who should have sent Ronald Koeman off for a professional foul but let him stay on to open the scoring with a free kick. In Taylor's last match in charge, England conceded a goal in the first nine seconds against San Marino, which said it all.

The Republic of Ireland were there again, still playing the same way under Jack Charlton but qualifying on goal difference and unlikely to figure at the sharp end of the tournament, especially as it was being played in fearful heat and humidity (FIFA again scheduled some noonday kick-offs). Nigeria, we were allowed to suppose, would be rather less apprehensive.

After twenty years as president, Havelange was still showing who was boss, banning Pelé from the opening ceremony for daring to criticise the head of the Brazilian FA, Ricardo Teixeira, who happened to be Havelange's son-in-law. Havelange later announced his intention to step down after the 1998 finals. Cue the crocodile tears.

Who's Dopey now? Dunga ends Brazil's long wait, watched by Romário (centre), the best of the other dwarfs.

GROUP A

Colombia, Romania, Switzerland, USA (seeded).

18 June 1994 – Pontiac Silverdome, Detroit – 73,425 – Francisco Lamolina (ARG)

SWITZERLAND	**(1)**	**1**

Bregy 39

USA	**(1)**	**1**

Wynalda 44

SWITZERLAND Marco Pascolo, Marc Hottiger, Dominique Herr, Alain Geiger (c), Yvan Quentin, Christophe Ohrel, Ciriaco Sforza [Thomas Wyss 77], Georges Bregy, Stéphane Chapuisat, Alain Sutter, Thomas Bickel [Néstor Subiat 72]. *Roy Hodgson (ENG).*
USA Tony Meola (c), Cle Kooiman, Paul Caligiuri, Tab Ramos, Alexi Lalas, Marcelo Balboa, Tom Dooley, John Harkes, Mike Sorber, Earnie Stewart [Cobi Jones 80], Eric Wynalda [Roy Wegerle 57]. *Bora Milutinović (YUG).*

Switzerland's first finals match since 1966 was also the first played indoors, which had the players sweating like cheeses. Both goals came from well-taken free kicks, Bregy curling his shot round the wall, Wynalda in off the bar from thirty yards. Dooley and Sutter should have scored, but players were soon beginning to slip and slide on the damp grass, and everyone looked drained by the end.

18 June 1994 – Rose Bowl, Pasadena – 91,865 – Jamal Al-Sharif (SYR)

ROMANIA	**(2)**	**3**

Răducioiu 16, 89, Hagi 34

COLOMBIA	**(1)**	**1**

Valencia 43

ROMANIA Bogdan Stelea, Dan Petrescu, Miodrag Belodedici, Gheorghe Popescu, Daniel Prodan, Gheorghe Mihali, Ionut Lupescu, Dorinel Munteanu,

Florin Răducioiu [Corneliu Papură 89], Gheorghe Hagi (c), Ilie Dumitrescu [Tibor Selymes 67]. *Anghel Iordănescu.*
COLOMBIA Oscar Córdoba, Andrés Escobar, Luis Herrera, Wilson Pérez, Luis Perea, Leonel Álvarez, Carlos Valderrama (c), Gabriel Gómez, Freddy Rincón, Adolfo Valencia, Faustino Asprilla. *Francisco Maturana.*

Romania had only qualified because Paul Bodin hit the crossbar with a penalty in Cardiff, and Colombia were many people's favourites, Pelé included – but the form guide was no help here. Playing six men in midfield to smother Colombia's close-passing game, Romania channelled everything through Hagi, who at last convinced everyone that ten years of hype hadn't been misplaced.

Above all, Romania put away their chances. Răducioiu cut inside two defenders and whipped his shot across Córdoba, then ran clear and resisted the keeper's challenge before lashing the ball into an empty net, each time running onto passes from Hagi, who also scored one of the monster World Cup goals. From out near the left-hand touchline, he fired the ball in at the far post with his left foot. It may have been a fluke (he glanced towards a team mate in the distance) but we'll believe he meant it, because his second glance was at the goal itself, and because we want to. Valencia headed in a corner at the near post, but neither Valderrama nor Asprilla was an influence. Death threats against Gómez reminded people where some of football's money came from in that country.

22 June 1994 – Pontiac Silverdome, Detroit – 61,428 – Neji Jouini (TUN)

SWITZERLAND	**(1)**	**4**

Sutter 16, Chapuisat 53, Knup 66, Bregy 72

ROMANIA	**(1)**	**1**

Hagi 36

SWITZERLAND Pascolo, Hottiger, Herr, Geiger (c), Quentin, Ohrel [Patrick Sylvestre 83], Sforza, Bregy, Adrian Knup, Sutter [Bickel 70], Chapuisat.
ROMANIA Stelea, Petrescu, Belodedici, Popescu, Prodan, Mihali, Lupescu [Basarab Panduru 84], Munteanu, Hagi (c), Dumitrescu [Ion Vlădoiu 70], Răducioiu.
SENT OFF: Vlădoiu 73.

Something of a shock, given the results of the first matches and the half-time score in this one – but perhaps the Swiss were simply acclimatised to the greenhouse effect. The return of Knup, and therefore a more attacking formation, was also a factor. Sutter, his fair hair tied back, cracked the ball in low from the D, but Hagi equalised with an equally good shot from 25 yards. Chapuisat scored in a scramble, Sforza's strong clever run made an open goal for Knup, and Bregy's free kick skimmed a defender's head on its way in (some sources, but not the Swiss, mistakenly credited it to Knup). To complete Romania's disarray, Vlădoiu was sent off within three minutes for showing his studs to Ohrel. It was Switzerland's first win in the finals since 1954.

22 June 1994 – Rose Bowl, Pasadena – 93,194 – Fabio Baldas (ITA)

USA   **(1) 2**
Escobar o.g. 34, Stewart 52

COLOMBIA (0) 1
Valencia 89

USA Meola (c), Fernando Clavijo, Caligiuri, Ramos, Lalas, Balboa, Dooley, Harkes, Sorber, Stewart [Jones 66], Wynalda [Wegerle 61].
COLOMBIA Córdoba, Herrera, Perea, Escobar, Pérez, Valderrama (c), Rincón, Hernán Gaviria, Álvarez, Anthony de Avila [Valencia HT], Asprilla [Iván René Valenciano HT].

When the draw was made, there was every prospect of the host nation being eliminated

at the group stage for the first time – but the USA had few problems with this ghost of a Colombian team. After both sides had hit the post, Escobar turned Harkes' optimistic cross shot into his own net. Then Ramos hit a through-ball, Córdoba rushed out too soon, and Stewart touched it past him and in off the near post. The tall Lalas, whose long red hair and goatee made him as recognisable as Valderrama, had a thumping goal wrongly disallowed for offside. Asprilla was at his irritating worst and had to be substituted, and Valencia's goal, a rebound after a fine save by Meola, couldn't stop the USA winning a finals match for the first time since beating England in 1950. The game had an horrific postscript when Escobar, a slim and talented central defender, was shot dead in Medellín, capital of his country's drug trade, because his own goal had apparently cost someone some money in bets. His killer, Humberto Múñoz, was released in 2005 after serving a quarter of his 43-year sentence.

26 June 1994 – Stanford, Palo Alto – 83,769 – Peter Mikkelsen (DEN)

COLOMBIA   **(1) 2**
Gaviria 44, Lozano 89

SWITZERLAND   (0) 0

COLOMBIA Córdoba, Herrera, Escobar, Alexis Mendoza, Pérez, Valderrama (c), Gaviria [Harold Lozano 78], Rincón, Álvarez, Valencia [de Avila 63], Asprilla.
SWITZERLAND Pascolo, Hottiger, Herr, Geiger (c), Quentin, Ohrel, Sforza, Bregy, Sutter [Marco Grassi 81], Knup [Subiat 81], Chapuisat.

After Pascolo fumbled Gaviria's leaping header, de Avila slipped a shot ball inside to Lozano who beat Herr and scored with a low cross shot. But Switzerland were already through and Colombia already out. Gaviria died when

1994

he was struck by lightning during training in 2002.

26 June 1994 – Rose Bowl, Pasadena – 93,869 – Mario van der Ende (HOL)

ROMANIA   **(1) 1**
Petrescu 17

USA   **(0) 0**

ROMANIA Florian Prunea, Petrescu, Belodedici [Mihali 87], Popescu, Prodan, Selymes, Lupescu,

Munteanu, Hagi (c), Dumitrescu, Răducioiu [Constantin Gâlcă 84].
USA Meola (c), Clavijo, Caligiuri, Ramos [Jones 63],

Lalas, Balboa, Dooley, Harkes, Sorber [Wegerle 74], Stewart, Wynalda.

If the American balloon didn't exactly burst, there was a definite sense of deflation.

Romania, needing at least a draw, were relieved when Harkes hit a post early on. Răducioiu twisted away from a defender before push-

ing a short pass inside Caligiuri for Petrescu to shoot in low at the near post. Florian

(Prunea) and Florin (Răducioiu) are both correct.

GROUP A						
	P	W	D	L	F	A	Pts
Romania	3	2	0	1	5	5	6
Switzerland	3	1	1	1	5	4	4
USA	3	1	1	1	3	3	4
Colombia	3	1	0	2	4	5	3

Romania, Switzerland and USA qualified for the second round.

GROUP B

Brazil (seeded), Cameroon, Russia, Sweden.

19 June 1994 – Rose Bowl, Pasadena – 83,959 – Alberto Tejada Noriega (PER)

CAMEROON   **(1) 2**
Embe 31, FO Biyick 47

SWEDEN   **(1) 2**
Ljung 8, Dahlin 75

CAMEROON Joseph-Antoine Bell, Stephen Tataw (c), Raymond Kalla, Rigobert Song, Hans Agbo, Thomas Libiih, Émile Mbouh, Louis-Paul Mfede [Emmanuel Maboang Kessack 86], Marc Vivien Foe, François Omam Biyick, David Embe [Georges Mouyeme 79]. *Henri Michel (FRA).*
SWEDEN Thomas Ravelli, Roland Nilsson, Roger Ljung, Stefan Schwarz, Patrik Andersson, Joachim Björklund, Klas Ingesson [Kennet Andersson 75], Jonas Thern (c), Jesper Blomqvist [Henrik Larsson 60], Martin Dahlin, Tomas Brolin. *Tommy Svensson.*

Interesting and fun, though neither side looked like title contenders. Ljung, unmarked despite ten Cameroon players in the penalty area, headed in Thern's free kick at the far post. Omam Biyick blocked a clearance on the left before squaring the ball to Embe (fractionally onside), and Omam Biyick himself scored after Patrik Andersson misjudged Song's long free kick. Sweden were saved when the dreadlocked Larsson hit the bar from thirty yards and Dahlin let the ball bounce, chested it down, and half-volleyed past Bell, who was at last getting a game in the finals at the age of 39. Andersson and his brother Daniel were both in the 2002 squad. Foe collapsed and died after a Confederations Cup semi-final in 2003.

20 June 1994 – Stanford, Palo Alto – 81,061 – An-Yan Lim Kee Chong (MAU)

BRAZIL **(1) 2**
Romário 26, Raí pen 53

RUSSIA **(0) 0**

BRAZIL Cláudio Taffarel, 'Jorginho' (Jorge Amorim), Leonardo (Nascimento), Mauro Silva, Ricardo Rocha [Aldair (Nascimento) 74], Márcio Santos, 'Zinho' (Crizam de Oliveira), 'Dunga' (Carlos Bledorn Verri) ['Mazinho' (Iomar do Nascimento) 85], 'Bebeto' (Roberto Gama), Raí (de Souza) (c), Romário (de Souza). *Carlos Alberto Parreira.*
RUSSIA Dmitri Kharin (c), Vladislav Ternavsky, Yuri Nikiforov, Sergei Gorlukovich, Valery Karpin, Andrei Pyatnitsky, Dmitri Radchenko [Aleksandr Borodyuk 77], Dmitri Kuznetsov, Ilya Tsymbalar, Dmitri Khlestov, Sergei Yuran [Oleg Salenko 55]. *Pavel Sadyrin.*

Russia didn't really stand a chance. Earlier in the season, fourteen players had written to the Minister for Sport demanding the sacking of the coach. Instead Sadyrin stayed and seven of the rebels were left out, including vital attacking players like Shalimov, Kanchelskis, Kolyvanov, Kiryakov and Dobrovolsky. Without them, Russia couldn't break down Brazil's strong defence in which Jorginho had been world class for years and Leonardo looked a bright new wing-back. Romário won a push-and-shove with his marker to stab in Bebeto's corner and was fouled by Ternavsky for the penalty, which was converted by Raí, younger brother of Sócrates, the captain in 1982.

24 June 1994 – Stanford, Palo Alto – 83,401 – Arturo Brizio Carter (MEX)

BRAZIL **(1) 3**
Romário 39, Márcio Santos 66, Bebeto 73

CAMEROON **(0) 0**

BRAZIL Taffarel, Jorginho, Leonardo, Mauro Silva, Aldair, Márcio Santos, Zinho [Paulo Sérgio [Silvestre) 75], Dunga, Bebeto, Raí (c) [Müller (Luís Corrêa) 80], Romário.
CAMEROON Bell, Tataw (c), Kalla, Song, Agbo, Libiih, Mbouh, Mfede [Maboang 70], Omam Biyick, Foe, Embe [Roger Milla 65].
SENT OFF: Song 63.

Cameroon's players, who'd threatened to boycott the game unless they were paid bonuses from the qualifying competition, were no match for Brazil's solidity and Romário's neat genius. He out-ran three defenders before toe-poking the ball past a hesitant keeper, and made the third goal with a shot that Bell did well to save, Bebeto turning in the loose ball from a narrow angle. In between, Márcio Santos came in unmarked to score with a plunging header. Cameroon set two World Cup age records: Milla the oldest player (42), Song the youngest to be sent off (17 years 358 days).

24 June 1994 – Pontiac Silverdome, Detroit – 71,528 – Joël Quiniou (FRA)

SWEDEN **(1) 3**
Brolin pen 38, Dahlin 59, 81

RUSSIA **(1) 1**
Salenko pen 4

SWEDEN Ravelli, R Nilsson, Ljung, Schwarz, P Andersson, Björklund [Magnus Erlingmark 88], Ingesson, Thern (c), K Andersson [Larsson 84], Dahlin, Brolin.
RUSSIA Kharin (c), Gorlukovich, Nikiforov, Khlestov, Kuznetsov, Dmitri Popov [Karpin 40], Borodyuk [Dmitri Galyamin 51], Aleksandr Mostovoi, Viktor Onopko, Salenko, Radchenko.
SENT OFF: Gorlukovich 49.

After the exchange of penalties, for fouls by Ljung and Gorlukovich, Dahlin took over. The first black player capped by Sweden, sharp and

1994

athletic, he was lucky to stay on after a violent challenge on Khlestov but won the penalty and scored with two marvellous, very different headers. The second came from a cross by Kennet Andersson, who brought back memories of José Torres with his height and mobility. Russia were on their way out, Gorlukovich going early after a foul on Dahlin, Sadyrin soon to follow.

---

28 June 1994 – Stanford, Palo Alto – 74,914 – Jamal Al-Sharif (SYR)

RUSSIA   **(3) 6**
Salenko 16, 41, pen 44, 73, 75, Radchenko 82

CAMEROON   **(0) 1**
Milla 47

RUSSIA Stanislav Cherchesov, Omari Tetradze, Nikiforov, Ternavsky, Karpin, Tsymbalar, Igor Ledyakov [Vladimir Beschastnykh 77], Khlestov, Onopko (c), Salenko, Igor Korneyev [Radchenko 64].
CAMEROON Jacques Songo'o, Tataw (c), Kalla, Victor Ndip, Agbo, Libiih, André Kana Biyick, Mfede [Milla HT], Foe, Omam Biyick, Embe [Alphonse Tchami 47].

As in 1990, the doomed Russians thrashed Cameroon, who were ageing imitations of that side. Salenko, with the help of a dubious penalty and a goal that looked offside, became the first to score five in a finals match. Two players collided to let him in for the first, his second was an open goal, Tetradze set him up for another, and he went through unchallenged for the fifth as his marker stood and appealed for offside. Radchenko also ran clear to score with a shot that went in off Songo'o. Cameroon's only consolation was an immediate close-range goal by the eternal Milla, marking the end of an extraordinary career.

---

28 June 1994 – Pontiac Silverdome, Detroit – 77,217 – Sándor Puhl (HUN)

BRAZIL   **(0) 1**
Romário 47

SWEDEN   **(1) 1**
K Andersson 23

BRAZIL Taffarel, Jorginho, Leonardo, Mauro Silva [Mazinho HT], Aldair, Márcio Santos, Zinho, Dunga, Bebeto, Raí (c) [Paulo Sérgio 83], Romário.

GOALS IN A MATCH

5	Oleg Salenko	RUS	1994	v CAM	1 pen
4	Ernest Wilimowski	POL	1938	v BRZ	
4	Ademir	BRZ	1950	v SWE	
4	Sándor Kocsis	HUN	1954	v GER	
4	Just Fontaine	FRA	1958	v GER	
4	Eusébio	POR	1966	v NKO	2 pen
4	Emilio Butragueño	SPA	1986	v DEN	1 pen

Wilimowski, Fontaine and Butragueño might have scored five each if they'd take the penalties converted by Fryderyk Scherfke, Raymond Kopa and Andoni Goikoetxea respectively. Butragueño scored from Spain's second penalty in the match.

Leônidas (BRZ) and Gustav Wetterström (SWE), who scored three against Poland and Cuba respectively in 1938, were once credited with four, as was Juan Schiaffino (URU), who scored twice against Bolivia in 1950.

SWEDEN Ravelli, R Nilsson, Ljung, Schwarz [Håkan Mild 75], P Andersson, Pontus Kåmark, Larsson [Blomqvist 62], Thern (c), K Andersson, Ingesson, Brolin.

Kennet Andersson's opener was a superb piece of finishing, a volleyed lob of great touch and control beyond Taffarel. Meanwhile all of Romário's goals in the tournament were scored with a kind of economic brilliance. Here he darted at the centre of the Swedish defence, beating two men through speed and angle of running, before nudging the ball wide of Ravelli. Sweden, improving with every match, deserved the draw but Brazil still looked the strongest team in the competition.

GROUP C

Bolivia, South Korea, Spain, Germany (seeded).

17 June 1994 – Soldier Field, Chicago – 63,117 – Arturo Brizio Carter (MEX)

GERMANY (0) 1
Klinsmann 61
BOLIVIA (0) 0

GERMANY Bodo Illgner, Thomas Berthold, Andreas Brehme, Stefan Effenberg, Jürgen Kohler, Matthias Sammer, Thomas Hässler [Thomas Strunz 82], Lothar Matthäus (c), Karlheinz Riedle [Mario Basler 60], Andreas Möller, Jürgen Klinsmann. *Berti Vogts.*

GROUP B

	P	W	D	L	F	A	Pts
Brazil	3	2	1	0	6	1	7
Sweden	3	1	2	0	6	4	5
Russia	3	1	0	2	7	6	3
Cameroon	3	0	1	2	3	11	1

Brazil and Sweden qualified for the second round.

OLDEST GOALSCORERS

yrs	days				
42	39	Roger Milla	CAM	1994	v RUS
37	236	Gunnar Gren	SWE	1958	v WG
36	279	Obdulio Varela	URU	1954	v ENG
36	64	Tom Finney	ENG	1958	v USR
35	279	John Aldridge	EIR	1994	v MEX
35	264	Nils Liedholm	SWE	1958	v BRZ
35	103	Ricardo Peláez	MEX	1998	v HOL
35	67	Safet Sušić	YUG	1990	v UAE

In 1990, at the age of 38, Milla had been the oldest to score two goals in a match, which he did on two separate occasions.

Liedholm scored another goal earlier in the 1958 finals, Peláez another earlier in 1998.

1930
1934
1938
1950
1954
1958
1962
1966
1970
1974
1978
1982
1986
1990

BOLIVIA Carlos Trucco, Marco Sandy, Miguel Ángel Rimba, Gustavo Quinteros, Luis Cristaldo, Carlos Borja (c), José Melgar, Vladimir Soria, Julio César Baldivieso [Jaime Moreno 65], Erwin Sánchez, William Ramallo [Marco Etcheverry 78]. *Xabier Azkargorta (SPA)*.
SENT OFF: Etcheverry 82.

A tournament that ended with a missed penalty also began with one. As part of the opening ceremony, singer Diana Ross showed that her links with the game were as tenuous as we thought by hooking the ball wide from only a few yards out. The following year, she opened another World Cup, this time the rugby league version at Wembley. She wasn't asked to take a kick at goal.

In Chicago, Germany became the first team to pick up three points for a win, but there was no smooth transition from 1990. Riedle missed chances, the whole team seemed reluctant to mix it physically, and the goal was a mess. A long pass bounced off Hässler, Trucco came out too far, and Klinsmann rolled the ball into an empty net from the edge of the area. Bolivia, who'd qualified for the first time since 1950, might have done better if the long-haired Etcheverry, their great hope, hadn't become involved in some nonsense on the touchline. Playing his first match in six months because of injury, he had a finals career that lasted a grand total of four minutes. Sammer was the first East German to play in the finals since 1974.

1994

1998
2002
2006

17 June 1994 – Cotton Bowl, Dallas – 56,247 – Peter Mikkelsen (DEN)

SOUTH KOREA   (0) 2
Hong 85, Seo 89

SPAIN   (0) 2
Salinas 51, Goikoetxea 56

SOUTH KOREA Choi In-Yung (c), Kim Pan-Keun, Park Jung-Bae, Lee Yung-Jin, Shin Hong-Gi, Hong Myung-Bo, Noh Jung-Yoon [Ha Seok-Ju 72], Kim Joo-Sung [Seo Jung-Won 58], Ko Jeong-Woon, Choi Yung-Il, Hwang Sun-Hong. *Kim Ho*.
SPAIN Santiago Cañizares, Albert Ferrer, 'Sergi' (Sergio Barjuán), Rafael Alkorta, Miguel Ángel Nadal (c), Abelardo (Fernández), Julen Guerrero [José Luis Caminero HT], Jon Andoni Goikoetxea, Julio Salinas [Felipe (Miñambres) 62], Fernando Hierro, Luis Enrique (Martínez). *Javier Clemente*.
SENT OFF: Nadal 25.

Despite losing Nadal for a foul on Ko, Spain established a two-goal lead with a close-range shot and Goikoetxea's header, but the ten men couldn't hold out in extreme heat (43°C) and humidity. The Koreans, fast and incredibly fit, pulled one back with a free kick (the deflection left Cañizares turning his back in disgust) then Seo coolly drilled a shot in low at the near post.

Nadal's nephew Rafael won the 2005 French Open singles title just after his 19th birthday.

21 June 1994 – Soldier Field, Chicago – 63,113 – Ernesto Filippi Cavani (URU)

GERMANY   (0) 1
Klinsmann 48

SPAIN   (1) 1
Goikoetxea 14

GERMANY Illgner, Berthold, Brehme, Matthäus (c), Kohler, Strunz, Effenberg, Hässler, Sammer, Möller [Rudi Völler 61], Klinsmann.
SPAIN Andoni Zubizarreta (c), Ferrer, Sergi, Alkorta, Abelardo, Goikoetxea [José María Bakero 63], Hierro, Salinas, Josep Guardiola [Francisco Camarasa 76], Caminero, Luis Enrique.

Spain had the better of the first half, when Germany left Klinsmann alone up front. He headed Hässler's outswinging free kick down and in, then the arrival of Völler, still sharp at

34, improved the balance, though the Spanish defence did well, the powerful Hierro moving back to sweeper in the manner born. Their goal, though, was laughable. Goikoetxea's cross from the right, no more than eight yards from the goal line, drifted over Illgner and in off the far post.

---

23 June 1994 – Foxboro Stadium, Foxboro – 53,456 – Leslie Mottram (SCO)

BOLIVIA   0

SOUTH KOREA   0

BOLIVIA Trucco, Sandy, Rimba, Quinteros, Cristaldo, Borja (c), Melgar, Soria, Baldivieso, Sánchez, Ramallo [Álvaro Peña 66].
SOUTH KOREA Choi IY (c), Kim PK, Park, Shin, Hong, Lee YJ, Kim JS, Seo [Ha 65], Ko, Noh [Choi YI 71], Hwang.
SENT OFF: Cristaldo 83.

South Korea had high hopes of winning a match in the finals for the first time, Bolivia of scoring their first goal. Neither came to pass in a scrappy match. Again the Koreans never stopped running (even though the referee played eight minutes of injury time) but this time their shooting was also hurried. Cristaldo was controversially sent off for a challenge on Kim Pan-Keun.

---

27 June 1994 – Cotton Bowl, Dallas – 63,998 – Joël Quiniou (FRA)

GERMANY   (3) 3
Klinsmann 12, 37, Riedle 20

SOUTH KOREA   (0) 2
Hwang 52, Hong 63

GERMANY Illgner, Berthold, Brehme, Matthäus (c) [Möller 63], Kohler, Guido Buchwald, Effenberg [Thomas Helmer 74], Hässler, Sammer, Riedle, Klinsmann.

SOUTH KOREA Choi IY (c) [Lee Woon-Jae HT], Choi YI, Hong, Park, Shin, Kim PK, Lee YJ [Chung Jong-Son 39], Ko, Kim JS, Cho Jin-Ho [Seo HT], Hwang.

Once again the heat came to South Korea's aid, but this time not to their rescue. Klinsmann, maintaining his excellent form, flipped up Hässler's low cross, spun round and volleyed in. Then he hit a post for Riedle to thrash in the rebound, and finally chested down another cross before scoring with a shot that Choi In-Yung fumbled in. The change of goalkeepers at half-time came too late, but South Korea bowed out with two fine goals. Park Jung-Bae's pass sent Hwang Sun-Hong streaking clear to cleverly touch the ball past Illgner, then Hong Myung-Bo smashed in a clearance from 25 yards. The match was played on Ko Jeong-Woon's 28th birthday. Effenberg, sent home by Vogts after making a gesture to the crowd, wasn't capped again until after the 1998 finals.

---

27 June 1994 – Soldier Field, Chicago – 63,089 – Rodrigo Badilla (COS)

SPAIN   (1) 3
Guardiola pen 19, Caminero 66, 71

BOLIVIA   (0) 1
Sánchez 67

SPAIN Zubizarreta (c), Ferrer, 'Voro' (Salvador González), Abelardo, Goikoetxea, Caminero, Guardiola [Bakero 67], Felipe [Hierro HT], Sergi, Salinas, Guerrero.
BOLIVIA Trucco, Sandy, Rimba, Juan Manuel Peña, Mauricio Ramos [Moreno HT], Borja (c), Modesto Soruco, Melgar, Soria [Ramiro Castillo 61], Sánchez, Ramallo.

In their sixth finals match, 64 years after the first, Bolivia at last scored their first goal, with the aid of a big deflection. Spain had their luck early on – Ramallo hitting the bar, the penalty controversially awarded – but were much the better side. Caminero scored from a narrow angle after good work by Sergi on the left, then chested down a cross before coolly stubbing it across the keeper. In between, a Spanish defender lunged at Sánchez's fierce 25-yarder and lifted it past Zubizarreta. Castillo was only 29 when he hanged himself in 1997.

GROUP C

	P	W	D	L	F	A	Pts
Germany	3	2	1	0	5	3	7
Spain	3	1	2	0	6	4	5
South Korea	3	0	2	1	4	5	2
Bolivia	3	0	1	2	1	4	1

Germany and Spain qualified for the second round.

GROUP D

Argentina (seeded), Bulgaria, Greece, Nigeria.

21 June 1994 – Foxboro Stadium, Foxboro – 53,486 – Arturo Angeles (USA)

1994

ARGENTINA   (2) 4
Batistuta 2, 44, pen 89, Maradona 60

GREECE   (0) 0

ARGENTINA Luis Islas, Roberto Sensini, Fernando Cáceres, Oscar Ruggeri, José Chamot, Diego Simeone, Fernando Redondo, Gabriel Batistuta, Abel Balbo [Alejandro Mancuso 79], Diego Maradona (c) [Ariel Ortega 82], Claudio Caniggia. *Alfio Basile.*

OLDEST PLAYERS

yrs	days			
42	39	Roger Milla	CAM	1994
41	00	Pat Jennings	NIR	1986
40	292	Peter Shilton	ENG	1990
40	133	Dino Zoff	ITA	1982
39	334	Jim Leighton	SCO	1998
39	260	Ángel Labruna	ARG	1958
39	259	Joseph-Antoine Bell	CAM	1994
39	145	Stanley Matthews	ENG	1954
38	293	Jan Heintze	DEN	2002
38	275	David Seaman	ENG	2002
38	246	Vítor Damas	POR	1986

A member of the Cameroon delegation claimed Milla was 46!

Jennings, Shilton, Zoff, Leighton, Bell, Seaman and Damas were goalkeepers. Matthews set a unique record by being the oldest player in both the 1950 and 1954 tournaments.

GREECE Antonis Minou, Stratos Apostolakis, Thanasis Kolitsidakis, Stelios Manolas, Yannis Kalitzakis, Dimitris Saravakos (c), Nikos Nioplias, Panayotis Tsaluhidis, Nikos Tsiantakis [Spiros Maragos HT], Savas Kofidis, Nikos Machlas [Tasos Mitropoulos 59]. *Alkis Panagoulias.*

Argentina, uncertain about their form, couldn't have asked for an easier start. Greece might not have qualified if the horrors in Bosnia hadn't prompted FIFA to suspend Yugoslavia. They'd recently lost 5-0 at Wembley and the last thing they needed was to concede an early goal. But Batistuta was allowed a long run from deep, his eventual shot slipping past the keeper. Then he dummied a return pass to Chamot before smashing in a spectacular shot from the edge of the area. The penalty was given for accidental handball by Apostolakis. Argentina's best goal involved two one-twos on the edge of the box followed by a flashing left-footer from

Maradona, who celebrated by glaring into a camera lens on the touchline, in your face as always. Suddenly rejuvenated and slimline, he was once again the glue in the team. How did he do it?

---

21 June 1994 – Cotton Bowl, Dallas – 44,932 – Rodrigo Badilla (COS)

NIGERIA **(2) 3**
Yekini 21, Amokachi 43, Amunike 55

BULGARIA **(0) 0**

NIGERIA Peter Rufai (c), Chidi Nwanu, Augustine Eguavoen, Uche Okechukwu, Ben Iroha, Finidi George [Emeka Ezeugo 76], Samson Siasia [Mutiu Adepoju 68], Sunday Oliseh, Rashidi Yekini, Emmanuel Amunike, Daniel Amokachi. *Clemens Westerhof (HOL).*
BULGARIA Borislav Mikhailov (c), Emil Kremenliev, Petar Hubchev, Trifon Ivanov, Tzanko Tzvetanov, Zlatko Yankov, Daniel Borimirov [Ivailo Yordanov 72], Yordan Lechkov [Nasko Sirakov 58], Krasimir Balakov, Emil Kostadinov, Christo Stoichkov. *Dimitar Penev.*

The fiery Stoichkov, banned for life by the Bulgarian FA in 1985 but reprieved a year later, was unlucky to have a goal mysteriously disallowed from a free kick – but Nigeria were 2-0 up by then and fulfilling all expectations. George drove a low cross into the six-yard box, where three team mates were sprinting in on it. Yekini, apparently described as 'a humble and religious stud', got there first and followed the ball into the net, which he grasped in his hands while making joyful faces. George also provided the crosses for the other two goals, Amokachi pushing a defender off the ball then sweeping extravagantly round the keeper, Amunike scoring with a diving header. Like so many in the team, Yekini and Amokachi were great slabs of men but with intricate control. If you'd been told that one of these teams was going to reach the semi-finals, you'd have had no trouble believing it.

CONSECUTIVE MATCHES WITHOUT A WIN

17	Bulgaria	1962–94
14	South Korea	1954–98
13	Mexico	1930–62
13	Chile	1966–98
11	Uruguay	1970–90

The first match South Korea won (in 2002) was the first they played at home.

Chile didn't reach the 2006 finals and will have to wait till at least 2010 before ending their sequence.

---

25 June 1994 – Foxboro Stadium, Foxboro – 54,453 – Bo Karlsson (SWE)

ARGENTINA **(2) 2**
Caniggia 22, 29

NIGERIA **(1) 1**
Siasia 8

ARGENTINA Islas, Sensini [Hernán Díaz 87], Cáceres, Ruggeri, Chamot, Simeone, Maradona (c), Redondo, Balbo [Mancuso 71], Batistuta, Caniggia.
NIGERIA Rufai (c), Nwanu, Eguavoen, Okechukwu, Mike Emenalo, George, Siasia [Adepoju 57], Oliseh [Augustine 'Jay-Jay' Okocha 87], Amunike, Yekini, Amokachi.

The first cracks in the Nigerian massif. They scored another splendid goal, Siasia stepping inside a defender before chipping the ball over Islas as he rushed out to the edge of the penalty area. But they fell asleep at a free kick, which Maradona took quickly and Caniggia curled beyond Rufai. The second goal also followed a free kick, Maradona backheeling the ball for Batistuta to shoot low round the wall, Rufai fumbling the ball for Caniggia to kick it into the roof of the net.

Quite a comeback for Caniggia, whose ban for cocaine use had ended just a month before

1930
1934
1938
1950
1954
1958
1962
1966
1970
1974
1978
1982
1986
1990
1994
1998
2002
2006

1930
1934
1938
1950
1954
1958
1962
1966
1970
1974
1978
1982
1986
1990
1998
2002
2006

the finals – but it wasn't the big drugs story of the tournament. In his eagerness to lose weight quickly, Maradona had employed Ben Johnson (yes, that one) as training advisor and taken a cocktail that included 'five inhibited substances in each urine sample . . . ephedrine and allied substances . . . increasing concentration and physical capacity.' That wasn't the beginning or the end of it, of course. He later admitted he'd been taking cocaine since 1982 (while appearing in an anti-drugs campaign). After testing positive for cocaine in 1991, he was appointed to lead an anti-drugs drive in 1996, then was discovered taking cocaine again in 1997. If he hadn't been caught in Boston, he'd have played more finals matches than anyone else at the time. As it was, his 21 gave him a share in the record. Hero or villain, he was very much the headline player of his generation, impossible to ignore or forget.

Some sources persist in listing Okocha's first name as Austin, but FIFA and Bolton Wanderers confirm Augustine.

MATCHES AS CAPTAIN

16	Diego Maradona	ARG	1986–94
14	Dino Zoff	ITA	1978–82
13	Kaziu Deyna	POL	1974–78
13	Paolo Maldini	ITA	1994–02
12	Ladislav Novák	CZE	1954–62
12	Uwe Seeler	WG	1966–70
12	Daniel Passarella	ARG	1978–82
12	Lothar Matthäus	GER	1990–94

1994

26 June 1994 – Soldier Field, Chicago – 63,160 – Ali Mohammed Bujsaim (UAE)

BULGARIA   (1) 4
Stoichkov pen 5, pen 55, Lechkov 66, Borimirov 89

GREECE   (0) 0

BULGARIA Mikhailov (c), Kremenliev, Hubchev, Ivanov, Tzvetanov [Ilian Kiriakov 76], Lechkov, Yankov, Balakov, Sirakov, Stoichkov, Kostadinov [Borimirov 81].
GREECE Ilias Atmatzidis, Apostolakis (c), Kalitzakis, Vaios Karayannis, Kyriakos Karataidis, Nioplias, Maragos, Minas Hantzidis [Mitropoulos HT], Machlas, Kofidis, Alexis Alexoudis [Vasilis Dimitriadis 57].

No surprise that Bulgaria won a finals match for the first time: Greece were their softest opposition yet. Stoichkov put away two penalties and brought a good save from Atmatzidis with his free kick, Borimirov stabbing in the rebound. Lechkov, the balding general, played a delayed one-two with Kostadinov and ran on to shoot in off a post. As usual, coach Panagoulias had his own succinct account of the proceedings: 'Beaten by that flat-footed poof Ivanov or whatever his name is.' His success in taking Greece to the finals for the first time was already almost forgotten.

30 June 1994 – Cotton Bowl, Dallas – 63,998 – Neji Jouini (TUN)

BULGARIA   (0) 2
Stoichkov 61, Sirakov 89

ARGENTINA   (0) 0

BULGARIA Mikhailov (c), Kremenliev, Hubchev, Ivanov, Tzvetanov, Lechkov [Borimirov 77], Yankov, Balakov, Sirakov, Stoichkov, Kostadinov [Kiriakov 74].
ARGENTINA Islas, Díaz, Cáceres, Ruggeri (c), Chamot, Simeone, Redondo, Leo Rodríguez [Ramón Medina Bello 66], Balbo, Batistuta, Caniggia [Ortega 26].
SENT OFF: Tzvetanov 67.

Like waiting for a bus. It takes 32 years for the first to arrive, then two come along together, this one carrying greater kudos. Maradona's absence had its effect, as did the fact that Argentina were already through. Even after Stoichkov sprinted clear to prod the ball wide of Islas, they were top of the group – until

Sirakov's header from a corner and an even later goal in the other match relegated them to third. Tzvetanov was sent off for bringing down Ortega, his second bookable offence. Mikhailov, who sported a new hair transplant, later owned a wig-making company.

30 June 1994 – Foxboro Stadium, Foxboro – 53,001 – Leslie Mottram (SCO)

NIGERIA **(1) 2**
George 45, Amokachi 90

GREECE **(0) 0**

NIGERIA Rufai, Stephen Keshi (c), Okechukwu, Nwanu, Emenalo, George [Adepoju 83], Siasia, Oliseh, Amunike, Yekini [Okocha 68], Amokachi.
GREECE Christos Karkamanis, Kalitzakis, Karayannis, Alexis Alexiou, Tsaluhidis, Nioplias, Mitropoulos (c) [Tsiantakis 79], Hantzidis, Kofidis, Alekos Alexandris, Machlas [Dimitriadis 79].

George celebrated his goal (a smart chip) by going down on all fours and cocking a leg. Deep into injury time Amokachi wasted a wonderful strike on such a weak team, taking out four defenders before blasting a tremendous right-footer into the top corner, a goal which vaulted Nigeria to the top of the group. The full first name of Alexoudis, Alexandris and Alexiou was Alexandros.

GROUP D

	P	W	D	L	F	A	Pts
Nigeria	3	2	0	1	6	2	6
Bulgaria	3	2	0	1	6	3	6
Argentina	3	2	0	1	6	3	6
Greece	3	0	0	3	0	10	0

Nigeria, Bulgaria and Argentina qualified for the second round.

GROUP E

Republic of Ireland, Italy (seeded), Mexico, Norway.

18 June 1994 – Giants Stadium, East Rutherford – 74,826 – Mario van der Ende (HOL)

REP. IRELAND **(1) 1**
Houghton 12

ITALY **(0) 0**

REP. IRELAND Pat Bonner, Denis Irwin, Terry Phelan, Roy Keane, Phil Babb, Paul McGrath, Ray Houghton [Jason McAteer 67], John Sheridan, Tommy Coyne [John Aldridge 89], Andy Townsend (c), Steve Staunton. *Jack Charlton (ENG)*.
ITALY Gianluca Pagliuca, Mauro Tassotti, Paolo Maldini, Dino Baggio, Alessandro Costacurta, Franco Baresi (c), Roberto Donadoni, Demetrio Albertini, Beppe Signori [Nicola Berti 83], Roberto Baggio, Alberigo Evani [Daniele Massaro HT]. *Arrigo Sacchi.*

Six years earlier Houghton had scored the only goal of another opening group match, crippling England's chances in Euro 88. Here he chested down Baresi's weak header and hooked a long-range volley over Pagliuca. The move had started with a typical Irish mortar bomb, forcing Costacurta into an aerial duel with Coyne.

Sacchi had packed the team with midfielders and stationed little Signori (Serie A's leading scorer for the past two seasons) out on the left. As a result, Italy couldn't find their way through a defence in which Babb was an ideal partner for the 34-year-old McGrath, still a great player despite dodgy knees. Sheridan hit the bar, the Republic avoided defeat against Italy for the first and only time, and Big Jack seemed vindicated again.

1930
1934
1938
1950
1954
1958
1962
1966
1970
1974
1978
1982
1986
1990
1994
1998
2002
2006

19 June 1994 – Robert F Kennedy, Washington DC – 52,359, Sándor Puhl (HUN)

NORWAY   **(0) 1**
Rekdal 85

MEXICO   **(0) 0**

NORWAY Erik Thorstvedt, Alf-Inge Håland, Rune Bratseth (c), Stig Inge Bjørnebye, Erik Mykland [Kjetil Rekdal 77], Øyvind Leonhardsen, Henning Berg, Jahn Ivar Jakobsen [Gunnar Halle HT], Jostein Flo, Lars Bohinen, Jan Åge Fjørtoft. *Egil Olsen.*
MEXICO Jorge Campos, Claudio Suárez, Raúl Gutiérrez [Marcelino Bernal 70], Ignacio Ambriz (c), Ramón Ramírez, Luis García, Joaquín del Olmo, Juan Ramírez, Luis Valdez [Benjamin Galindo HT], Hugo Sánchez, 'Zague' (Luis Alves). *Miguel Mejía Barón.*

Norway had surprisingly finished ahead of Holland and England in qualifying, and their support play and discipline were enough even in these conditions. When Fjørtoft was fouled, the ball ran on to Rekdal, who outpaced Suárez before scoring with a cross shot. Zague, who had a Brazilian father, was sometimes known as 'Zaguinho'. In the last minute his diving header came back off a post, hit his head as he lay on the ground, and was kicked clear by Berg. Jakobsen had his nickname 'Mini' printed on the back of his shirt.

23 June 1994 – Giants Stadium, East Rutherford – 74,624 – Heinz Hellmut Krug (GER)

ITALY   **(0) 1**
D Baggio 69

NORWAY   **(0) 0**

ITALY Pagliuca, Antonio Benarrivo, Maldini, D Baggio, Costacurta, Baresi (c) [Luigi Apolloni 48], Berti, Albertini, Signori, R Baggio [Luca Marchegiani 22], Pierluigi Casiraghi [Massaro 69].
NORWAY Thorstvedt, Håland, Bratseth (c), Bjørnebye, Berg, Mykland [Rekdal 80], Leonhardsen, Sigurd Rushfeldt [Jakobsen HT], Bohinen, Flo, Fjørtoft.
SENT OFF: Pagliuca 21.

A match to enter Italian folklore. When Pagliuca's handball outside the area made him the first goalkeeper ever sent off in the finals, Italy were not only left with ten men for most of the match but took off Roberto Baggio (gasp) to make way for a substitute keeper. Then Baresi was injured and Maldini finished the match limping on the wing, Massaro moving to left-back. Impossible odds.

Norway were subsequently criticised for playing for a point instead of crushing the invalids – but perhaps they were pacing themselves to conserve energy. Italy too would probably have settled for a draw, but Dino Baggio scored with a powerful header after leading the charge to attack Signori's free kick from the left. Bratseth had a goal disallowed with eight minutes left, but the thin blue line deserved to hold out. The referee's second name is no misprint (i.e. not the more common spelling Helmut).

24 June 1994 – Citrus Bowl, Orlando – 61,219 – Kurt Röthlisberger (SWI)

MEXICO   **(1) 2**
L García 43, 66

REP. IRELAND   **(0) 1**
Aldridge 84

MEXICO Campos, Jorge Rodríguez [Gutiérrez 80], Suárez, J Ramírez, del Olmo, Bernal, L García, Ambriz (c), Alberto García Aspe, Carlos Hermosillo [Luis Salvador 80], Zague.
REP. IRELAND Bonner, Irwin, Phelan, Keane, Babb, McGrath, Houghton, Sheridan, Coyne [Aldridge 66], Townsend (c), Staunton [McAteer 65].

In a frying midday sun, Mexico again finished less strongly than the Europeans – but they'd done the damage by then, Luis García scoring with sharp ground shots from the edge of the penalty area. Ireland's two subs (and best players) combined for their goal, McAteer cutting back a good cross from the right for the veteran Aldridge to score. Campos, also capped as an outfield player, wearing a multi-coloured jersey of his own design, was more of a personality than a great goalkeeper. He should have stopped Aldridge's downward header.

Earlier there'd been some fun and games when an official delayed Aldridge's entrance as substitute, provoking strong words from the striker and his manager. Charlton had earlier criticised a decision not to allow players to drink water during matches (it wasn't true: they were simply told to do it on the touchline) and FIFA now lost patience, issuing a one-match ban from the bench and a £10,000 fine. The Official Report (very much in the minority) says Gutiérrez substituted del Olmo.

---

28 June 1994 – Giants Stadium, East Rutherford – 76,322 – José Torres Cadena (COL)

NORWAY   0

REP. IRELAND   0

NORWAY Thorstvedt, Halle [Jakobsen 33], Erland Johnsen, Bratseth (c), Bjørnebye, Flo, Berg, Leonhardsen [Bohinen 67], Gøran Sørloth, Mykland, Rekdal.
REP. IRELAND Bonner, Gary Kelly, Staunton, Keane, Babb, McGrath, McAteer, Houghton, Townsend (c) [Ronnie Whelan 74], Sheridan, Aldridge [David Kelly 64].

Norway's passivity (or problems with the heat) cost them a place in the next round, the only team eliminated with four points. Gary Kelly and Staunton were excellent replacements at full-back, and Charlton used a two-way radio to communicate with his bench. The Republic were in the second round for the second time, but the fires of Orlando were waiting again.

28 June 1994 – Robert F Kennedy, Washington DC – 53,186 – Francisco Lamolina (ARG)

ITALY   (0) 1
Massaro 48

MEXICO   (0) 1
Bernal 58

ITALY Marchegiani, Benarrivo, Apolloni, D Baggio [Donadoni 64], Costacurta, Maldini (c), Berti, Albertini, Casiraghi [Massaro HT], R Baggio, Signori.
MEXICO Campos, Rodríguez, Suárez, J Ramírez, del Olmo, Bernal, L García [Juan Carlos Chávez 80], Ambriz (c), García Aspe, Hermosillo, Zague.

Baresi's absence forced Maldini into the middle but he played as if he'd been there all his life, enjoying his 26th birthday until the ankle flared up again. Massaro, first capped in 1982, scored his only senior international goal after chesting down Albertini's through-ball, but Bernal drove in a ground shot after avoiding Signori's tackle, a goal that moved Mexico from bottom to top and eliminated Norway. Italy had to wait for the result of Russia v Cameroon to be sure they'd qualified.

GROUP E

	P	W	D	L	F	A	Pts
Mexico	3	1	1	1	3	3	4
Rep. Ireland	3	1	1	1	2	2	4
Italy	3	1	1	1	2	2	4
Norway	3	1	1	1	1	1	4

Mexico, the Republic of Ireland and Italy qualified for the second round. Ireland placed second as a result of beating Italy. The only time all four teams finished with the same number of points.

1930
1934
1938
1950
1954
1958
1962
1966
1970
1974
1978
1982
1986
1990
1994
1998
2002
2006

1930
1934
1938
1950
1954
1958
1962
1966
1970
1974
1978
1982
1986
1990
1994
1998
2002
2006

GROUP F

Belgium (seeded), Holland, Morocco, Saudi Arabia.

19 June 1994 – Citrus Bowl, Orlando – 60,790 – José Torres Cadena (COL)

BELGIUM   (1) 1
Degryse 11

MOROCCO   (0) 0

BELGIUM Michel Preud'homme, Georges Grün (c), Michel De Wolf, Rudi Smidts, Lorenzo Staelens, Franky Van der Elst, Marc Degryse, Enzo Scifo, Danny Boffin [Vital Borkelmans 84], Josip Weber, Luc Nilis [Marc Emmers 53]. *Paul Van Himst.*
MOROCCO Khalil Azmi [Zakaria Alaoui 88], Nasser Abdullah, Smahi Triki, Larbi Hababi, Abdelkrim El-Hadrioui, Nourredine Naybet, Mustafa El-Haddaoui (c) [Ahmed Bahja 68], Rachid Azzouzi, Rachid Daoudi, Mustafa Hadji, Mohammed Chaouch [Aziz Samadi 81]. *Abdullah Blinda.*

There was still no getting away from the heat (Van Himst said he was soaking wet 'and I was only sitting on the bench') but Morocco couldn't quite make it count. Chaouch twice hit the bar, the second time via a save by Preud'homme. At the other end Azmi came out for a cross by Nilis but Degryse got his head to it before him. Under a new rule allowing goalkeepers to be replaced, Morocco became the first team to use three substitutes in a finals match.

20 June 1994 – Robert F Kennedy, Washington DC – 52,535 – Manuel Díaz Vega (SPA)

HOLLAND   (0) 2
Jonk 50, Taument 86

SAUDI ARABIA   (1) 1
Amin 19

HOLLAND Ed de Goey, Ulrich van Gobbel, Ronald Koeman (c), Frank de Boer, Wim Jonk, Frank Rijkaard, Marc Overmars [Gaston Taument 57], Jan Wouters, Dennis Bergkamp, Brian Roy [Peter van Vossen 80], Ronald de Boer. *Dick Advocaat.*
SAUDI ARABIA Mohammed Al-Deayea, Abdullah Al-Dossari, Mohammed Al-Khilaiwi, Mohammed Al-Jawad, Ahmed Madani, Fuad Amin, Fahad Al-Bishi, Khalid Al-Muwalid, Talal Jebreen, Majed Abdullah Mohammed (c) [Hamzah Falatah 45], Said Al-Owairan [Hamza Saleh 68]. *Jorge Solari (ARG).*

Holland, not a patch on their 1988 side but skilful as always, were given a fright by a talented and committed side. Saudi Arabia, appearing in the finals for the first time, had ironically sacked their Dutch coach in February (Leo Beenhakker, who'd coached Holland in the 1990 finals) for training them too hard. Here they took the lead through Amin's header from a free kick but obviously hadn't been briefed about Jonk's reputation for long-range shooting. His thirty-yarder swerved past the keeper's left hand. Worse was to follow for Al-Deayea, who came a long way off his line but missed his punch, the cross bouncing behind him for Taument to head in. Solari had played for Argentina in the 1966 finals. The de Boers were twins.

25 June 1994 – Citrus Bowl, Orlando – 62,387 – Renato Marsiglia (BRZ)

BELGIUM   (0) 1
Albert 65

HOLLAND   (0) 0

BELGIUM Preud'homme, Emmers [Dirk Medved 77], Grün (c), De Wolf, Philippe Albert, Borkelmans [Smidts 60], Scifo, Van der Elst, Staelens, Degryse, Weber.
HOLLAND de Goey, Stan Valckx, Koeman (c), F de Boer, Rijkaard, Jonk, Wouters, Taument [Overmars 63], Bergkamp, Roy, R de Boer [Rob Witschge HT].

Albert, a classy attacking defender later signed by Newcastle, shot in off the near post from a corner, and Scifo had a goal disallowed – but Belgium were indebted to the 35-year-old Preud'homme, who gave the goalkeeping performance of the tournament, saving from Koeman, Bergkamp, Rijkaard, you name it, finally touching a shot from Overmars onto the bar in the last minute.

---

25 June 1994 – Giants Stadium, East Rutherford – 72,404 – Philip Don (ENG)

SAUDI ARABIA   **(2) 2**
Al-Jaber pen 8, Amin 45

MOROCCO   **(1) 1**
Chaouch 27

SAUDI ARABIA Al-Deayea, Al-Khilaiwi, Al-Jawad (c), Awad Al-Anazi [Abdullah Zubromawi 29], Madani, Amin, Al-Bishi, Al-Muwalid, Al-Jebreen, Al-Owairan, Sami Al-Jaber [Fahad Al-Ghesheyan 79].
MOROCCO Azmi (c), Abdullah [Abdelsalam Laghrissi 56], Tahar El-Khalej, Triki, Naybet, Azzouzi, El-Hadrioui, Daoudi, Hababi [Hadji 72], Chaouch, Bahja.

In the first finals meeting between two Arab countries, Saudi Arabia became only the second Asian team to win a match, after North Korea in 1966. Naybet fouled Al-Jaber for the penalty, Chaouch was left with a tap-in after some brilliant work by Bahja on the left-hand goal line, foxing four men – but another error by Azmi gave away the winning goal, Amin's long shot bouncing in off his hands.

---

29 June 1994 – Citrus Bowl, Orlando – 60,578 – Alberto Tejada Noriega (PER)

HOLLAND   **(1) 2**
Bergkamp 43, Roy 78

MOROCCO   **(0) 1**
Nader 47

HOLLAND de Goey, Valckx, Koeman (c), F de Boer, Aron Winter, Jonk, Wouters, Witschge, Overmars [Taument 57], Bergkamp, van Vossen [Roy 68].
MOROCCO Alaoui, Samadi, Rachid Neqrouz, Triki, El-Hadrioui, Abdelmajid Bouyboub [Hadji HT], Tahar (c), Azzouzi [Daoudi 62], Hababi, Hassan Nader, Bahja.

Holland got the win they needed to be sure of qualifying, but were again made to work for it, Nader driving in a square pass for the equaliser. Bergkamp, who'd calmly lifted the ball over the keeper for the first goal, swerved past a defender to set up Roy for the winner. In a tight group, Morocco lost all three matches despite playing well, while Holland needed Bergkamp's good form to make up for Koeman's increasing fallibility in defence.

---

29 June 1994 – Robert F Kennedy, Washington DC – 52,959 – Heinz Hellmut Krug (GER)

SAUDI ARABIA   **(1) 1**
Al-Owairan 5

BELGIUM   **(0) 0**

SAUDI ARABIA Al-Deayea, Al-Khilaiwi, Zubromawi, Al-Jawad, Madani, Al-Bishi, Jebreen, Saleh, Majed Abdullah (c) [Al-Muwalid HT], Al-Owairan [Al-Dossari 61], Falatah.
BELGIUM Preud'homme, Medved, Albert, De Wolf, Smidts, Staelens, Van der Elst, Boffin, Scifo (c), Degryse [Nilis 23], Marc Wilmots [Weber 53].

Belgium, expected to stroll through as group winners, had more of the play, but Al-Owairan's goal was worthy of winning any match. Playing with a bandaged wrist, he took a pass well inside his own half, burst between two Belgians, beat another on the outside, a fourth on the inside, then hooked the ball high past Preud'homme. Saudi Arabia were the first Asian country to win

1994

1930
1934
1938
1950
1954
1958
1962
1966
1970
1974
1978
1982
1986
1990
1994
1998
2002
2006

two matches and qualify for the next round. Majed Abdullah, 'the Pelé of the Desert', was winning his last cap. His total of 139, 141 or 147, depending on which source you believe, was a world record at the time.

GROUP F

	P	W	D	L	F	A	Pts
Holland	3	2	0	1	4	3	6
Saudi Arabia	3	2	0	1	4	3	6
Belgium	3	2	0	1	2	1	6
Morocco	3	0	0	3	2	5	0

Holland, Saudi Arabia and Belgium qualified for the second round.

2ND ROUND

2 July 1994 – Soldier Field, Chicago – 60,246 – Kurt Röthlisberger (SWI)

GERMANY   (3) 3
Völler 6, 40, Klinsmann 11

BELGIUM   (1) 2
Grün 8, Albert 89

GERMANY Illgner, Helmer, Matthäus (c) [Brehme HT], Kohler, Berthold, Buchwald, Hässler, Sammer, Martin Wagner, Völler, Klinsmann [Stefan Kuntz 85].
BELGIUM Preud'homme, Grün (c), Albert, De Wolf, Smidts [Boffin 65], Staelens, Van der Elst, Emmers, Scifo, Nilis [Alex Czerniatynski 77], Weber.

This was Belgium's penance for losing to Saudi Arabia, a match with the champions and their famous strikers. Völler scored the first goal by heading the ball on and running through to nick the ball deftly over Preud'homme, who should have stopped the header that made it 3-1. Völler's slick one-two with Klinsmann led to the second goal. Grün stabbed in the equaliser from a free kick and Albert played a one-two before going past Kohler in the penalty area, a definite touch of the Beckenbauers. Germany haven't lost to Belgium since 1954 and were the better side here – but they had a little help: Röthlisberger was sent home after admitting he should have awarded a penalty for a foul by Helmer on Weber.

2 July 1994 – Robert F Kennedy, Washington DC – 53,121 – Mario van der Ende (HOL)

SPAIN   (1) 3
Hierro 15, Luis Enrique 74, Beguiristain pen 87

SWITZERLAND   (0) 0

SPAIN Zubizarreta (c), Alkorta, Ferrer, Camarasa, Nadal, Abelardo, Hierro [Jorge Otero 75], Bakero, Sergi, Goikoetxea [Aitor Beguiristain 60], Luis Enrique.
SWITZERLAND Pascolo, Hottiger, Herr, Geiger (c), Quentin [Jürg Studer 57], Ohrel [Subiat 72], Sforza, Bregy, Bickel, Knup, Chapuisat.

A miserable 26th birthday for Knup as Spain remained unbeaten against Switzerland after eighteen matches going back to 1925. Hierro ran through to score as the Swiss stopped playing, expecting a whistle when Sergi ran back from an offside position. Luis Enrique celebrated his goal with a shirt-over-the-face routine for which Fabrizio Ravanelli took out the patent in England, and Pascolo brought down Ferrer for the penalty. The Swiss badly missed the skills of Sutter, who'd aggravated a serious toe injury when Hodgson picked him for the meaningless last group match. Switzerland have played 22 matches in the finals without keeping a single clean sheet.

3 July 1994 – Cotton Bowl, Dallas – 60,277 – Renato Marsiglia (BRZ)

SWEDEN **(1) 3**
Dahlin 6, K Andersson 51, 88

SAUDI ARABIA **(0) 1**
Al-Ghesheyan 85

SWEDEN Ravelli, R Nilsson, Ljung, Schwarz, P Andersson, Björklund [Kåmark 54], Brolin, Thern (c) [Mild 70], K Andersson, Ingesson, Dahlin.
SAUDI ARABIA Al-Deayea, Zubromawi, Madani, Al-Jawad (c) [Al-Ghesheyan 54], Al-Khilaiwi, Al-Jaber, Amin, Saleh, Al-Owairan, Al-Bishi [Al-Muwalid 62], Falatah.

Thrown into a roasting pan, at noon, against a Middle Eastern team, Sweden drank gallons of water and were always in control, even though the Saudis decorated the match with another excellent goal, Al-Ghesheyan cutting inside from the right and thrashing a high shot inside Ravelli. Once again Dahlin headed in a cross by Kennet Andersson, the star of the front line, who scored with two low shots, the first after holding off a defender, the second in off a post.

3 July 1994 – Rose Bowl, Pasadena – 90,469 – Pierluigi Pairetto (ITA)

ROMANIA **(2) 3**
Dumitrescu 11, 18, Hagi 56

ARGENTINA **(1) 2**
Batistuta pen 16, Balbo 75

ROMANIA Prunea, Petrescu, Prodan, Belodedici, Lupescu, Popescu, Selymes, Munteanu, Hagi (c) [Gâlcă 86], Dumitrescu [Papură 88], Mihali.
ARGENTINA Islas, Sensini [Medina Bello 63], Cáceres, Ruggeri (c), Chamot, José Basualdo, Simeone, Redondo, Ortega, Balbo, Batistuta.

A feast. While Argentina missed Maradona, Romania made up for Răducioiu's suspension by pushing Dumitrescu up front, and he responded with two superb goals. His first was merely a beautifully struck free kick from out on the left, dipping over Islas into the side netting. The second was a gem, Hagi pushing an angled pass between three defenders, Dumitrescu twisting his body to coolly side-foot it in at the near post. Batistuta was awarded a penalty for a challenge by Prodan, and Balbo pulled one back when Prunea badly fumbled Cáceres' low shot – but Romania were full of flair on the break and scored another fine goal to go 3-1 up, Dumitrescu's square pass setting up Hagi to shoot high past Islas. Iordanescu took a gamble by substituting both his goalscorers, but Argentina couldn't force extra time. Ruggeri, a straightforward central defender, was winning his 98th and last cap, a national record at the time.

4 July 1994 – Citrus Bowl, Orlando – 61,355 – Peter Mikkelsen (DEN)

HOLLAND **(2) 2**
Bergkamp 11, Jonk 41

REP. IRELAND **(0) 0**

HOLLAND de Goey, Winter, Valckx, Koeman (c), F de Boer, Rijkaard, Jonk, Witschge [Arthur Numan 78], Overmars, Bergkamp, van Vossen [Roy 69].
REP. IRELAND Bonner, G Kelly, Phelan, Keane, Babb, McGrath, Houghton, Townsend (c), Coyne [Tony Cascarino 73], Sheridan, Staunton [McAteer 62].

1994

A match remembered for Bonner's appalling blunder, but the first goal was almost as bad, Overmars pouncing on Phelan's weak header and sprinting away to set up Bergkamp. Jonk's long-range shot wasn't one of his best, but Bonner let it slip horribly through his hands, which he then used to hold his head. Roy missed two easy chances late on.

1930
1934
1938
1950
1954
1958
1962
1966
1970
1974
1978
1982
1986
1990

1994

1998
2002
2006

Charlton's tactics in the second half are still hard to understand. Two goals down, he continued to use only a single striker, and when he eventually replaced the hardworking Coyne, it was with a blunt instrument like Cascarino instead of Aldridge. And why was the impressive McAteer left on the bench? The Republic have played nine matches in the World Cup finals, winning one and scoring four goals. When the team were given a reception on their return home, the half-empty field suggested that even for their fans it was all wearing a bit thin.

4 July 1994 – Stanford, Palo Alto – 84,147 – Joël Quiniou (FRA)

BRAZIL   (0) 1
Bebeto 74

USA   (0) 0

BRAZIL Taffarel, Jorginho, Leonardo, Mauro Silva, Aldair, Márcio Santos, Mazinho, Dunga (c), Bebeto, Romário, Zinho ['Cafú' (Marcos Evangelista) 68].
USA Meola (c), Clavijo, Caligiuri, Ramos [Wynalda HT], Lalas, Balboa, Dooley, Hugo Pérez [Wegerle 65], Sorber, Jones, Stewart.
SENT OFF: Leonardo 44, Clavijo 87.

Brazil dropped Raí, who'd had a poor season with Paris Saint-Germain, settled for solidity in midfield, and needed it after Leonardo was sent off (and banned for the rest of the tournament) for fracturing Ramos' skull with his elbow. Balboa and Lalas again played well, and the US team had made its contribution to the finals, but Brazil's extra guile told in the end. Romário ran from deep and beat a man before slipping the ball wide to Bebeto, whose shot skidded under Lalas' tackle and just inside the far post. Clavijo, an American sent off on the 4th of July, was the oldest to be dismissed in a finals match: 37 years 162 days. Carlos Alberto Parreira and Milutinovic, the first two coaches to take charge

of three different countries in the finals, did it for the fourth time in 1998.

5 July 1994 – Foxboro Stadium, Foxboro – 54,367 – Arturo Brizio Carter (MEX)

ITALY   (0) (1) 2
R Baggio 88, pen 102

NIGERIA   (1) (1) 1
Amunike 26

ITALY Marchegiani, Roberto Mussi, Benarrivo, Berti [D Baggio HT], Costacurta, Maldini (c), Donadoni, Albertini, Signori [Gianfranco Zola 64], R Baggio, Massaro.
NIGERIA Rufai (c), Eguavoen, Okechukwu, Nwanu, Emenalo, George, Oliseh, Okocha, Yekini, Amunike [Thompson Oliha 56], Amokachi [Adepoju 34].
SENT OFF: Zola 76.

Again everything was stacked against the Italians. A corner bounced off Maldini's shins to set up Amunike's volley for the opening goal, Dino Baggio hit a post, and Zola was controversially sent off after being on the pitch for only twelve minutes on his 28th birthday. There were only two minutes left when Mussi handed off a defender on the right, took a lucky rebound, and set up the finest moment in the competition.

Roberto Baggio was the current European Footballer of the Year and FIFA Player of the Year, yet here he'd been anonymous in two matches and taken off in the other. When Mussi rolled the ball across, it's hard to believe anyone else would have done anything but hit it as hard as possible. Instead Baggio aimed for the absolute bottom corner of the goal, between Massaro and Eguavoen and past Rufai's dive. If he'd missed, they'd have said he didn't even have the bottle to go for his shot, leaving a big minus against his career. In all the pressure, Baggio backed his talent to the end, scored, and resuscitated his and Italy's World Cup.

Courage and class, rewarded with a touch of good fortune: his penalty, for Eguavoen's clumsy challenge on Benarrivo, went in off a post.

Nigeria were an enormous let-down. Stacked with class players, a goal behind in extra time, they kept five or six defenders back against ten men. Perhaps it was time for some more home help. None of the black African countries had employed an African coach in the finals, even though the likes of Charles Gyamfi and Fred Osam Duodu consistently won the African Nations Cup.

5 July 1994 – Giants Stadium, East Rutherford – 71,030 – Jamal Al-Sharif (SYR)

BULGARIA **(1) (1) 1**
Stoichkov 7

MEXICO **(1) (1) 1**
García Aspe pen 18

Bulgaria 3-1 pens.

BULGARIA Mikhailov (c), Kremenliev, Borimirov, Hubchev, Kiriakov, Lechkov, Yordanov, Balakov, Stoichkov, Sirakov [Boncho Genchev 103], Kostadinov [Petar Mikhtarski 118].
MEXICO Campos, Rodríguez, Suárez, J Ramírez, R Ramírez, Bernal, García Aspe, Ambriz (c), L García, Galindo, Zague.
SENT OFF: Kremenliev 50, L García 58.
PENALTY SHOOT-OUT: García Aspe shot over, Balakov saved, Bernal saved, Genchev 0-1, Rodríguez saved, Borimirov 0-2, Suárez 1-2, Lechkov 1-3.

By common consent, a match ruined by the referee. After Stoichkov had sprinted onto Kostadinov's through-ball to thrash it over Campos, Al-Sharif awarded a penalty for a fifty-fifty tussle between Kremenliev and Zague. As well as sending off two players for offences barely worthy of the name, he showed eight yellow cards in a match that was never rough. Bernal lightened things by pulling a stanchion down when he fell into the net after heading the ball off the line (an entire new goal had to be brought out). Bulgaria deserved to go through, if only because Kostadinov hit the post with a free kick. For the second time in a row, 1986 and now this, Mexico were eliminated on penalties.

QUARTER-FINALS

9 July 1994 – Foxboro Stadium, Foxboro – 54,605 – Sándor Puhl (HUN)

ITALY **(1) 2**
D Baggio 26, R Baggio 88

SPAIN **(0) 1**
Caminero 59

ITALY Pagliuca, Tassotti, Benarrivo, D Baggio, Costacurta, Maldini (c), Donadoni, Albertini [Signori HT], Massaro, R Baggio, Antonio Conte [Berti 65].
SPAIN Zubizarreta (c), Ferrer, Sergi [Salinas 59], Alkorta, Nadal, Abelardo, Caminero, Otero, Bakero [Hierro 64], Goikoetxea, Luis Enrique.

Italy's first goal was good (Dino Baggio scoring from well outside the area) and Spain's was lucky (Caminero's shot deflected over Pagliuca) – but it was still another great Italian escape. Spain should have had a penalty when Tassotti elbowed Luis Enrique in the face, and Salinas prodded the ball against Pagliuca when clean through. Italy immediately scored at the other end, Signori accepting a clattering as the price for lifting the ball beyond the last defender, Roberto Baggio swerving past Zubizarreta to score from a tight angle, his low shot going through Abelardo's attempted clearance kick in the goalmouth. Tassotti, not even booked for that elbow, was banned for eight matches, long enough to end his international career.

1994

9 July 1994 – Cotton Bowl, Dallas – 63,998 – Rodrigo Badilla (COS)

BRAZIL　　(0) 3
Romário 52, Bebeto 62, Branco 81

HOLLAND　　(0) 2
Bergkamp 64, Winter 76

BRAZIL Taffarel, Jorginho, 'Branco' (Cláudio Vaz) [Cafú 89], Mauro Silva, Aldair, Márcio Santos, Mazinho [Raí 80], Dunga (c), Bebeto, Romário, Zinho.
HOLLAND de Goey, Winter, Valckx, Wouters, Rijkaard [R de Boer 64], Koeman (c), Jonk, Witschge, Overmars, Bergkamp, van Vossen [Roy 53].

How the Dutch must have wished for one or two better players (the absent Gullit, the injured van Basten) and a different referee. When Bebeto went round de Goey for the second goal, Holland fully expected a whistle as Romário strolled back from an offside position directly in the goalkeeper's line of vision. The two strikers had combined for the first goal, Romário's flashing half-volley meeting Bebeto's cross.

Against a defence that had conceded only one goal in four matches, Holland did tremendously well to get back on level terms. Bergkamp chested the ball past a weak challenge before beating Taffarel, who'd been off form for years and allowed Winter to head in a corner from under his nose. But Brazil had another shot in their locker, a low 25-yard free kick from Branco, the veteran replacing the suspended Leonardo. The ball swerved between Raí and Valckx, who both deliberately avoided it, and went in off the bottom of the post.

Cruel for Holland, but not a patch on Bebeto's goal celebration, the dreaded baby-rocking which later found its way into the English league. Bergkamp had proved he could perform on the big stage, but the once-mighty Koeman wasn't capped again.

10 July 1994 – Giants Stadium, East Rutherford – 72,416 – José Torres Cadena (COL)

BULGARIA　(0) 2
Stoichkov 75, Lechkov 78

GERMANY　(0) 1
Matthäus pen 48

BULGARIA Mikhailov (c), Ivanov, Hubchev, Tzvetanov, Kiriakov, Lechkov, Yankov, Sirakov, Balakov, Stoichkov [Yordanov 84], Kostadinov [Genchev 90].
GERMANY Illgner, Helmer, Matthäus (c), Kohler, Berthold, Buchwald, Hässler [Brehme 83], Möller, Völler, Wagner [Strunz 59], Klinsmann.

In the end experience wasn't enough. Germany, including nine players from the 1990 Final, had an average of 57 previous caps each and took the lead when Lechkov fouled Klinsmann in the area (he remonstrated but Klinsmann impatiently waved him away). For the second successive quarter-final Matthäus scored from the spot, and we waited for German professionalism to do the rest.

But Stoichkov equalised with a sweet free kick and Germany's marking let them down for the winner. When Yankov crossed from the right, only little Hässler was left to challenge Lechkov as his diving header scored the most important goal in Bulgaria's football history. For the second time in the tournament, a player (Matthäus) equalled the record of 21 appearances before being stopped short. It was the end of Völler's glittering international career, sprinkled with successful comebacks, in which he scored 47 goals.

10 July 1994 – Stanford, Palo Alto – 81,715 – Philip Don (ENG)

SWEDEN　　(0) (1) 2
Brolin 79, K Andersson 115

ROMANIA　　(0) (1) 2
Răducioiu 88, 101
Sweden 5-4 pens.

SWEDEN Ravelli, R Nilsson (c), Ljung, Schwarz,
P Andersson, Björklund [Kåmark 83], Brolin, Mild,
K Andersson, Ingesson, Dahlin [Larsson 106].
ROMANIA Prunea, Petrescu, Prodan, Belodedici,
Lupescu, Popescu, Selymes, Munteanu [Panduru 83],
Răducioiu, Hagi (c), Dumitrescu.
SENT OFF: Schwarz 102.
PENALTY SHOOT-OUT: Mild shot over, Răducioiu 0-1,
K Andersson 1-1, Hagi 1-2, Brolin 2-2, Lupescu 2-3,
Ingesson 3-3, Petrescu saved, R Nilsson 4-3,
Dumitrescu 4-4. Sudden death: Larsson 5-4,
Belodedici saved.

Once again Romania played their part in a memorable match, which neither side deserved to lose. Dahlin hit the post with a header in the third minute, Ingesson had a goal disallowed for pushing, and Sweden eventually went ahead with an imaginative free kick. Schwarz ran over the ball, Mild pushed it round the wall, and Brolin sprinted behind it to shoot into the roof of the net.

That seemed to be that, but a deflected free kick found its way to Răducioiu, who celebrated his return from suspension by shooting high into the net. In extra time he scored with a fierce low shot after a dreadful error by Patrick Andersson – but then it was Sweden's turn to score a late equaliser, Kennet Andersson towering over a hesitant Prunea to head in Roland Nilsson's long cross. Ravelli, wild-eyed and still elastic at 34, made two saves in the penalty shoot-out, but it was sad that the second was from Belodedici, one of the great defenders. Applause for Sweden's resilience and skills, but

MATCHES AS REFEREE

8	Joël Quiniou	FRA	1986–94
7	John Langenus	BEL	1930–38
7	Mervyn Griffiths	WAL	1950–58
7	Juan Gardeazábal	SPA	1958–66

Romania's absence would rob the tournament of flair and colour, and make things easier for the eventual winners.

SEMI-FINALS

13 July 1994 – Giants Stadium, East Rutherford –
77,094 – Joël Quiniou (FRA)

ITALY **(2) 2**
R Baggio 20, 25
BULGARIA **(1) 1**
Stoichkov pen 44

ITALY Pagliuca, Mussi, Benarrivo, Berti, Costacurta,
Maldini (c), Donadoni, Albertini, D Baggio [Conte 55],
R Baggio [Signori 70], Casiraghi.
BULGARIA Mikhailov (c), Kiriakov, Hubchev,
Ivanov, Tzvetanov, Lechkov, Yankov, Sirakov,
Balakov, Stoichkov [Genchev 78], Kostadinov
[Yordanov 71].

No luck involved this time. Italy stayed strong throughout and Roberto Baggio scored two exceptional goals, the first a minor classic. Turning his marker in the process of collecting a throw-in on the left, he swerved to the right past another defender, the 'divine ponytail' flapping, before bending his shot round Ivanov and beyond the keeper. John Motson was lost for words and eloquent at the same time: 'Oh, look at that! Just look at that!' Five minutes later Albertini chipped a nicely weighted pass through the inside-right channel for Baggio to hook a low volley across the keeper.

Against that sort of inspiration, Bulgaria could manage only a penalty for a foul on Sirakov by Costacurta, who was later booked for the second time, missing the Final just as he'd missed the European Cup Final in May. The much maligned Sacchi had taken Italy almost all the way but now had to sweat on the

1994

1930
1934
1938
1950
1954
1958
1962
1966
1970
1974
1978
1982
1986
1990
1994
1998
2002
2006

fitness of Roberto Baggio, who'd pulled a hamstring in the second half.

---

13 July 1994 – Rose Bowl, Pasadena – 84,569 – José Torres Cadena (COL)

BRAZIL **(0) 1**
Romário 80

SWEDEN **(0) 0**

BRAZIL Taffarel, Jorginho, Branco, Mauro Silva, Aldair, Márcio Santos, Mazinho [Raí HT], Dunga (c), Bebeto, Romário, Zinho.
SWEDEN Ravelli, R Nilsson, Ljung, Mild, P Andersson, Björklund, Brolin, Thern (c), K Andersson, Ingesson, Dahlin [Stefan Rehn 68].
SENT OFF: Thern 63.

If Romania had won that penalty shoot-out, Brazil would have had some serious counter-attacking threats to cope with. Sweden didn't carry the same kind of threat, despite the talents of Brolin, Dahlin and Kennet Andersson. Tired and listless, they held out only because Zinho and Mazinho missed open goals and Ravelli had a good game. The winner, in the end, was very basic, little Romário getting between two defenders to head Jorginho's long cross just inside a post. Thern, Sweden's playmaker, was sent off for a careless foul on Dunga. After seven matches (a record between any two countries), Sweden have yet to beat Brazil in a finals match.

3RD-PLACE FINAL

---

16 July 1994 – Rose Bowl, Pasadena – 83,716 – Ali Mohammed Bujsaim (UAE)

SWEDEN **(4) 4**
Brolin 8, Mild 30, Larsson 37, K Andersson 39

BULGARIA **(0) 0**

SWEDEN Ravelli, R Nilsson (c), Kåmark, Schwarz, P Andersson, Björklund, Mild, Brolin, K Andersson, Ingesson, Larsson [Anders Limpar 78].
BULGARIA Mikhailov (c) [Plamen Nikolov HT], Kiriakov, Hubchev, Ivanov [Kremenliev 41], Tzvetanov, Lechkov, Yankov, Sirakov [Yordanov HT], Balakov, Stoichkov, Kostadinov.

Jolly but strange, no reflection of what the teams had achieved so far. Ingesson, Sweden's midfield mule, went past Kiriakov, Mikhailov came out too far, and Brolin's downward header bounced in. Mild confidently pushed Brolin's quick free kick past the advancing keeper. Larsson went round Mikhailov and waited for the covering defender to dive past before scoring. Finally Kennet Andersson got his last reward for a skilful and selfless tournament by heading into an empty net. Bulgaria spent the second half trying to set up Stoichkov for the goal that would have made him outright leading scorer. They suffered the biggest defeat in a 3rd-Place Final, but everyone knew they were better than that.

FINAL

---

17 July 1994 – Rose Bowl, Pasadena – 94,194 – Sándor Puhl (HUN)

BRAZIL **0**

ITALY **0**
Brazil 3-2 pens.

BRAZIL Taffarel, Jorginho [Cafú 21], Branco, Mazinho, Aldair, Márcio Santos, Mauro Silva, Dunga (c), Romário, Bebeto, Zinho ['Viola' (Paulo Sérgio Rosa) 105].
ITALY Pagliuca, Mussi [Apolloni 34], Benarrivo, Berti, Maldini, Baresi (c), Donadoni, Albertini, Massaro, R Baggio, D Baggio [Evani 94].
PENALTY SHOOT-OUT: Baresi shot over, Márcio Santos saved, Albertini 1-0, Romário 1-1, Evani 2-1, Branco 2-2, Massaro saved, Dunga 3-2, R Baggio shot over.

Yet again Sacchi had to send out a patched-up team, only more so. Costacurta was suspended, Roberto Baggio still feeling his injury, Mussi hurt early on. Most amazing of all, Baresi was back. Not only had he missed every game since Italy's second, he'd had a knee operation in between! Even McGrath couldn't match that.

Baresi played a monumental game, forcing Romário and Bebeto to forage further back. After Mussi's injury, Maldini simply switched back to the left, where he had an intriguing duel with the pacy Cafú. And the Italian midfield stuck to their task. But there was little happening up front, where Roberto Baggio was literally hamstrung. In a poor match, which the tournament didn't deserve, Brazil made the better chances and more of them. Mazinho should have scored when Pagliuca saved Branco's free kick, Romário missed an open goal, and Pagliuca puffed his cheeks out after fumbling Mauro Silva's shot onto a post. When Italy had their one golden chance, it was too late in the day. A one-two with Massaro gave Roberto Baggio a clear shooting chance, but injury and weariness took their toll and Taffarel made an easy save. The match had been billed as a showdown between Baggio and Romário and they'd both missed in front of goal. But this was the first scoreless World Cup Final and both would have a second chance in the shoot-out.

LEADING GOALSCORERS 1994

6	Oleg Salenko	RUS	1 pen
6	Christo Stoichkov	BUL	3 pen
5	Jürgen Klinsmann	GER	
5	Roberto Baggio	ITA	1 pen
5	Romário	BRZ	
5	Kennet Andersson	SWE	

If this was FIFA's idea of deciding the world champions for the next four years, it was based on the slimmest evidence. About the width of a goalpost. While Italy's two injured totems shot over the bar, Romário put his penalty in off an upright, a reminder of how close the two imposters of success and failure can be: Baggio's penalty against Nigeria had also gone in off a post, and Massaro had scored two goals in that year's European Cup Final. Italy had now lost a World Cup semi-final and Final on penalties. With a fraction more luck, they might have won the Cup twice in a row and five times in all. Instead their opponents became the first team to win it four times, and Italy took no comfort from the Brazilian captain's Italian surname.

Dunga, whose nickname means Dopey, as in the Seven Dwarfs, lifted the trophy on the same ground where he'd played on the losing side in the Olympic Games Final ten years earlier. Carlos Alberto Parreira, after taking two lesser countries to the finals, had won the big one with the big one, but with a team that wouldn't live in the memory.

Several dry spells had come to an end. Brazil, the only country to take part in every finals tournament, won the World Cup for the first time in 24 years, Bulgaria won a match, Bolivia scored a goal. But once again FIFA had sacrificed the tournament to the demands of television, forcing players to play in extreme heat and high humidity. The conditions made recovery all the harder (both semi-finals were won by the teams who had a day's extra rest) and wrecked the Final as a contest and spectacle. When Viola came on and caused havoc, people wondered where Carlos Alberto had been hiding him, but it was just a case of fresh legs. And what was the point of staging indoor matches at the height of summer?

Those who believed Mexico were happy to play the Irish in the midday heat of

1930
1934
1938
1950
1954
1958
1962
1966
1970
1974
1978
1982
1986
1990
1994
1998
2002
2006

1930

1934

1938

1950

1954

1958

1962

1966

1970

1974

1978

1982

1986

1990

1994

1998

2002

2006

Orlando should have listened to their coach Miguel Mejía Barón. 'I would tell those gentlemen of FIFA to take their suits off and play football ... if FIFA were to think about the player, if it were to think more about football and less about business, there would be night games.' Footballers rarely show how much conditions take out of them (except perhaps poor Steve Staunton), so we can persuade ourselves they're not suffering all that much – but some lungs were burning out there. It was vivid, it was indelible, but it wasn't right.

Still, the world's great players keep rising above the machinations of their governing body (who, to be fair, helped by banning the tackle from behind and the pass back to the goalkeeper). There were sparkling goals, some fancy haircuts, and always someone in the news. Those with nothing to prove, except to sections of the press, proved it anyway: Hagi, Stoichkov, Romário, Brolin, Dahlin, Bergkamp, Klinsmann. Defenders too: Babb, Belodedici, Maldini, Philippe Albert, the amazing McGrath, the bionic Baresi. France 98, swollen to 32 teams, had a hard act to follow.

Back force

France **1998**

Having won the World Cup for a record fourth time, Brazil seemed to have the players to make it five. Dunga and Cafú were still there from 1994; Roberto Carlos, a left-back with thighs like jodhpurs, had scored with an astonishing free kick against France the previous year; and Rivaldo provided flair and goals from midfield. Even Romário's absence through injury didn't look so damaging now that the 21-year-old Ronaldo had come into his own. With his control and strength on the ball, the current European Footballer of the Year was generally acknowledged as the best attacking player in the world. A 4-2 defeat in Oslo had ended a world record run of 45 matches without defeat, but it was surely just a blip.

Of the main challengers, Argentina still had the strike power of Batistuta, abetted by the mercurial little Ortega and the generalship of Verón. Holland came with quality defenders, power and touch in midfield, and the ball skills and goals of Bergkamp and Kluivert – but they'd imploded in the finals of Euro 96, losing 4-1 to England and sending Edgar Davids home. We were waiting for the class of '95, who'd won the European Cup for Ajax, to start fulfilling themselves.

The same was still being said of Croatia, who were there for the first time. Jarni, Boban, Prosinečki and Šuker had made a big impression in helping Yugoslavia to win the World Youth Cup back in 1987. This was their last chance to make a genuine mark together at senior level – but the loss of Alen Bokšić appeared to be a major problem up front.

After the break-up of Yugoslavia, a squad bearing that name (essentially Serbia and the odd Montenegrin) would also be there, hoping that the brilliant Dejan Savicevic could recover from injury in time. Spain, the eternal underachievers, still had the powerful presence of Hierro and had found a talented new goalscorer in Raúl – but there were concerns about the selection processes of their stubborn coach Javier Clemente.

Germany were the reigning European champions once again, after reviving memories of Italia 90 by surviving a penalty shoot-out in another semi-final against England. Their European Footballer of the Year from that 1996 campaign, the red-haired sweeper Matthias Sammer, had suffered an injury that ended his international career, and precious few new players had come through – but they nevertheless emerged from a tough qualifying group ahead of Portugal's talented but frustrating 'golden generation'.

England had looked a balanced and attractive team in that Euro 96 tournament, which was held at home – but then immediately dispensed with the services of Terry Venables, apparently because his business interests and court cases weighed more heavily with the FA than his undoubted talent as a coach. Venables

1930
1934
1938
1950
1954
1958
1962
1966
1970
1974
1978
1982
1986
1990
1994
1998
2002
2006

1930
1934
1938
1950
1954
1958
1962
1966
1970
1974
1978
1982
1986
1990
1994

1998

2002
2006

almost made it the finals regardless, coaching Australia to a play-off which they lost on away goals after Iran scored twice late in the second leg in Melbourne.

Glenn Hoddle, his replacement as England manager, came in and picked a motley side who lost 1-0 to Italy at Wembley – but by the time the last qualifying match came round, a goalless draw in Rome was enough. As the finals approached, Hoddle's tetchiness reflected the stress brought on by press coverage of his use of a faith healer, his decision to leave Gascoigne out of the squad (justified by the effects of injury and alcohol), and his doubts as to whether young players like Beckham and Owen were ready.

Italy, forced into a play-off with Russia, won it narrowly. Scotland, with their usual shortage of talent, qualified under their open and rational manager Craig Brown, but only after Andy Herzog's goals for Austria had beaten Sweden 1-0 home and away. Wales and Northern Ireland showed no signs of emerging from their ice age, winning only three matches between them, against San Marino and Albania. The Republic of Ireland did better before losing a play-off to some equally workmanlike Belgians.

Meanwhile, if France were going to make the most of their home advantage, they needed someone to emerge up front like Fontaine in 1958 – or, more plausibly, their midfield to paper over the cracks yet again. But their main man there, Zinedine Zidane, had a spotty record in major events. He'd again failed to lift Juventus in the European Cup Final, finishing on the losing side for the second year running, and had looked tired in the finals of Euro 96. Like England in 1966, the hosts would have to fall back on the best defence in world football.

FIFA, still making changes, made some good ones. A board would be held up near the end of each match to show how much injury time was left – and, more importantly, the tackle from behind was banned at long last. A FIFA study showed that 60% of injuries affected the ankles and Achilles tendons, usually as a result of such challenges. Citing the case of Marco van Basten, whose brilliant career ended before he was 30, the governing body were adamant that 'We don't want to see such a thing happen again.'

Admirable sentiment and necessary change. Perhaps even enough to compensate for the increase in numbers. Thirty-two teams in the same tournament were surely going to be too much of a good thing.

The captain and the defenders who won it for him. Back row (l-r): Blanc, Thuram, Desailly. Front row (l-r): Deschamps, Lizarazu.

1930
1934
1938
1950
1954
1958
1962
1966
1970
1974
1978
1982
1986
1990
1994
1998
2002
2006

GROUP A

Brazil (seeded), Morocco, Norway, Scotland.

10 June 1998 – Stade de France, Saint-Denis, Paris – 80,000 – José María García-Aranda (SPA)

BRAZIL   **(1) 2**
César Sampaio 4, Boyd o.g. 73

SCOTLAND   **(1) 1**
Collins pen 37

BRAZIL Cláudio Taffarel, 'Cafú' (Marcos Evangelista), Roberto Carlos (da Silva), 'Dunga' (Carlos Bledorn Verri) (c), Aldair (Nascimento), 'Júnior Baiano' (Raimundo Ferreira Júnior), César Sampaio, Giovanni (da Silva) [Leonardo (Nascimento) HT], Ronaldo (Nazário de Lima), Rivaldo (Borba Ferreira), 'Bebeto' (Roberto Gama) [Denílson (de Oliveira) 70]. *Mário Zagallo.*
SCOTLAND Jim Leighton, Colin Calderwood, Colin Hendry (c), Tom Boyd, Craig Burley, John Collins, Darren Jackson [Billy McKinlay 78], Paul Lambert, Christian Dailly [Thomas 'Tosh' McKinlay 84], Gordon Durie, Kevin Gallacher. *Craig Brown.*

Faced with Ronaldo and the ghosts of Italia 90, Scotland must have feared the worst – and it was upon them almost immediately. Bebeto's corner from the left went to the near post, where César Sampaio put the ball in with his shoulder, the fastest opening goal in any finals tournament.

But the Scots didn't let the nightmare start destroy them. Leighton played in contact lenses, with thick grease over each eye and his front teeth out – but the old Dracula joke didn't apply: he dropped one easy cross but otherwise redeemed himself after the disaster of 1990, making a smart save from Ronaldo. The veteran Durie was rugged and limited but made some confident runs and could have

done with more support from Gallacher and Collins, though Lambert looked a competent all-round midfielder.

As the Scots regrouped, they were given a controversial penalty when César Sampaio blocked Gallacher off the ball, after which they were very much a match for Brazil, whose assorted left-footers (Roberto Carlos, Leonardo, the hollow-cheeked Rivaldo) did nothing for their balance. The 20-year-old Denílson, who was in the process of breaking the world transfer record, showed some skilful glimpses when he came on, but Brazil made no really good chances in the second half, and Scotland would have been well worth a draw.

They didn't get it because they had the classic bad luck of the underdog. As in 1990, they conceded a late winner against Brazil, but this time Leighton was blameless. Cafú made another of his runs on the right, Leighton blocked his flipped volley, but the ball went in off Boyd's upper arm. Heartbreak.

Left with their usual mountain to climb in the group, Scotland had now played Brazil nine times, drawing two, winning none and scoring only three goals. Ronaldo had been in the 1994 squad as a 17-year-old.

10 June 1998 – de la Mosson, Montpellier – 28,750 – Pirom Un-Prasert (THA)

MOROCCO   **(1) 2**
Hadji 38, Hadda 60

NORWAY   **(1) 2**
Chippo o.g. 45, Eggen 61

MOROCCO Driss Benzekri, Abdelilah Saber, Abdelkrim El-Hadrioui, Tahar El-Khalej [Rachid Azzouzi 90], Nourredine Naybet (c), Youssef Rossi, Mustafa Hadji, Youssef Chippo [Gharib Amzine 78], Abdeljalil Hadda [Ali El-Khattabi 87], Said Chiba, Salaheddine Bassir. *Henri Michel (FRA).*

NORWAY Frode Grodås (c), Henning Berg, Stig-Inge Bjørnebye, Kjetil Rekdal, Ronny Johnsen, Dan Eggen, Håvard Flo [Ståle Solbakken 72], Erik Mykland, Tore André Flo, Øyvind Leonhardsen, Ole Gunnar Solskjær [Vidar Riseth HT]. *Egil Olsen*.

After their quarrelsome performance against England two weeks earlier, Morocco raised some eyebrows with their skill and pep, but goalkeeping uncertainty cost them goals and points. The bearded Hadji, his hair tied back, stood out for his red shoes and extravagant skill. When Tahar's superb volleyed through-ball found him wide on the left, he produced a foot-over-the-ball feint to beat Eggen on the inside, then fired in low across the keeper. Already one of the goals of the tournament.

But then Rekdal took a free kick, Benzekri couldn't claim the ball under Berg's challenge, and Chippo tried to glance it away from goal but only managed to head it into his own net. Back came Morocco with a goal to match their first, volleyed by Hadda after another beautifully weighted pass from Tahar. The pattern of the match was rounded off when Benzekri fumbled another free kick, and Eggen (who'd been embarrassed by both Moroccan goals) headed a second equaliser. Norway weren't exactly an adornment of the tournament, and Hadji's decline in the second half probably had something to do with the broken toe he'd been nursing for some time!

Chippo and Hadji later signed for Coventry City. Michel had previously coached France (1986) and Cameroon (1994) in the finals.

16 June 1998 – Parc Lescure, Bordeaux – 30,236 – László Vágner (HUN)

NORWAY (0) 1
H Flo 46

SCOTLAND (0) 1
Burley 66

NORWAY Grodås (c), Berg [Gunnar Halle 82], Bjørnebye, Solbakken, Eggen, Johnsen, Riseth [Egil Østenstad 72], Rekdal, TA Flo, Roar Strand, H Flo [Jahn Ivar Jakobsen 61].
SCOTLAND Leighton, Calderwood [David Weir 59], Hendry (c), Boyd, Burley, Collins, Jackson [Jackie McNamara 61], Lambert, Dailly, Durie, Gallacher.

Scotland hadn't won since qualifying, Norway hadn't lost for nearly eighteen months, so a draw was as predictable as the quality of the football. Norway, needing a win so as not to rely on a result against Brazil, were almost completely negative in the first half, but Scotland again had no guile or thrust up front. They went behind when Håvard Flo arrived unnoticed at the far post to head in Riseth's low cross from the left – but Weir hit a straightforward long ball, Grodås stayed in no man's land, and Burley lobbed it in.

Norway were in disarray after that. 'If things don't work or we get tired,' said Eggen, 'we do not have an alternative and it looks awful.' No arguments here. Scotland weren't much better, but their fans were different class as always. Ten of them paid £800 to have an Indian meal flown over from Bournemouth.

16 June 1998 – de la Beaujoire-Louis Fonteneau, Nantes – 33,266 – Nikolai Levnikov (RUS)

BRAZIL (2) 3
Ronaldo 8, Rivaldo 45, Bebeto 50

MOROCCO (0) 0

BRAZIL Taffarel, Cafú, Roberto Carlos, Dunga (c), Aldair, Júnior Baiano, César Sampaio ['Doriva' (Dorival Guidoni) 67], Leonardo, Ronaldo, Rivaldo [Denílson 88], Bebeto [Edmundo (Alves) 71].
MOROCCO Benzekri, Saber [Lahcen Abrami 75], El-Hadrioui, Tahar, Naybet (c), Rossi, Hadji, Chippo, Hadda [El Khattabi 89], Chiba [Amzine 75], Bassir.

1930
1934
1938

1950
1954
1958
1962
1966
1970
1974
1978
1982
1986
1990
1994
1998
2002
2006

Having shaken off some cobwebs, Brazil put the Moroccans firmly in their place, in the process becoming the first team to reach the next round. The ball spent a lot of time thumping into Júnior Baiano's torso, which Kevin Keegan saw as 'the sort of chest they used to put gold in to take it overseas. It's huge.' The contest with little Bassir was grotesquely unequal.

Up front, Ronaldo put his marker down on the tournament by pulling away from the last defender to hit a confident low volley from the edge of the area. Rivaldo. whose instant long ball had made the chance, sidefooted the second from a pass by Cafú. Zico, Zagallo's assistant, had wanted his full-backs to do more defending, but Brazil would have had no width without them. Roberto Carlos again flattered to deceive, but Cafú, looking like a miniature version of former Olympic boxing champion Teófilo Stevenson, was a major influence.

Early on, Chiba's studs connected with the area around Ronaldo's groin, ripping his shorts and gashing the inside of his thigh. A wedding tackle, so to speak. But it didn't deter Ronaldo too much: when Saber fell over the ball, he took it away, beat Rossi on the outside, and made an open goal for the disappointing Bebeto. Tahar, on his 30th birthday, was naturally less commanding, and Hadji looked a headless chicken at times – but it was understandable. Pupils have to stand and watch sometimes.

---

23 June 1998 – Geoffroy Guichard, Saint-Étienne – 35,500 – Ali Mohammed Bujsaim (UAE)

MOROCCO (1) 3
Bassir 22, 84, Hadda 47

SCOTLAND (0) 0

MOROCCO Benzekri, Saber [Rossi 72], Naybet, Amzine [Azzouzi 76], Abrami, Tahar, Hadji, Chippo [Jamal Sellami 87], Smahi Triki, Hadda, Bassir.

SCOTLAND Leighton, Weir, Hendry (c), Boyd, McNamara [T McKinlay 54], Lambert, Collins, Burley, Durie [Scott Booth 84], Gallacher, Dailly.
SENT OFF: Burley 53.

Scotland's latest finals exit was the most embarrassing yet. When Tahar's very long ball went over Hendry's head, Bassir hit a massive volley between Leighton and the near post – and that already seemed to be the end of it. At half-time, Alan Hansen suggested that Scotland's best chance was to pile four or five men into the goalkeeper, while Ally McCoist and David Pleat wanted to bring on a big man (Matt Elliott) and hit long balls. The stuff of dinosaurs. Brown, who knew better, didn't make a substitution, aware that there were no options on the bench.

Morocco, nippy and fit, hustled all night and undid Scotland with long balls. From one of these, Hadda outpaced Weir and hit a high half-volley which Leighton got his hands to but could only knock behind him. As he chased back in horror, the ball bounced up into the roof of the net while he entangled himself in it, a humiliation he and the team didn't deserve. When Burley, his hair now dyed yellow, was sent off for a tackle from behind on Bassir, the referee would have done Scotland a mercy if he'd been allowed to stop it on points. Bassir ended the farce by flipping the ball over Boyd and volleying in off Hendry.

Yet again, reaching the finals had been the limit of Scotland's possibilities. Collins, a fitness fanatic with a he-man build, was tidy but simply not a decisive player. No wonder that the Scots lacked penetration up front, a story we're tired of telling. Again they hadn't reached the second stage, again nobody was particularly surprised: their official World Cup song was entitled '*Don't Come Home Too Soon.*'

As for Morocco, the win was surely enough to put them through. Nothing Norway had done so far suggested they had the slightest chance of beating Brazil.

---

23 June 1998 – Vélodrome, Marseilles – 60,000 – Esfandiar Baharmast (USA)

NORWAY (0) 2
TA Flo 82, Rekdal pen 88

BRAZIL (0) 1
Bebeto 77

NORWAY Grodås (c), Berg, Bjørnebye, Leonhardsen, Eggen, Johnsen, Riseth [Jostein Flo 78], Rekdal, TA Flo, Strand [Mykland HT], H Flo [Solskjær 68].
BRAZIL Taffarel, Cafú, Roberto Carlos, Dunga (c), Marcelo Gonçalves, Júnior Baiano, Leonardo, Ronaldo, Rivaldo, Bebeto, Denílson.

Before the kick-off, FIFA allowed a wedding to take place on the pitch, between a Norwegian and a Brazilian – but the harmony ended there. Before Brazil's defeat in Oslo the previous year, Olsen had echoed Alf Ramsey's notorious quote by claiming 'We don't have anything to learn from how Brazil play. They are too badly organised.' Now he was at it again. 'I could coach Brazil better than Zagallo does.' The Brazilian defence was 'as organised as garbage.'

His players put their heart and lungs where his mouth was, especially Tore-André Flo, who produced one of the great individual performances, good enough to overshadow Ronaldo. Júnior Baiano, faced with an opponent he couldn't intimidate physically, was run into the ground. When Denílson was fouled during a run on the left, he got up before the free kick could be awarded and made another open goal for Bebeto. But Flo wouldn't give up. He scored a goal typical of this group by cutting inside Júnior Baiano from the left and driving a low

GOALSCORING SPANS

yrs	days			
12	16	Michael Laudrup	DEN	1986–98
12	6	Uwe Seeler	WG	1958–70
12	3	Diego Maradona	ARG	1982–94
12	2	Pelé	BRZ	1958–70

shot across the keeper, grimacing with the effort. The goal, which put Flo's face on a stamp back home, was voted Norway's all-time favourite footballing moment.

The winning penalty looked very debatable from some angles. Indeed, several British commentators rounded on Tore-André Flo for a dive that cost brave little Morocco a place in the second round. But a Swedish TV camera showed it as it was: a hawk-eyed refereeing decision after some desperate shirt-pulling by a frazzled Júnior Baiano. Rekdal kept his nerve from the spot and Brazil lost a group match in the finals for the first time since 1966.

Norway had now played Brazil three times, winning two and drawing the other. For the first time, three members of one family played in the same finals match: brothers Jostein and Tore-André Flo and their cousin Håvard.

GROUP A

	P	W	D	L	F	A	Pts
Brazil	3	2	0	1	6	3	6
Norway	3	1	2	0	5	4	5
Morocco	3	1	1	1	5	5	4
Scotland	3	0	1	2	2	6	1

Brazil and Norway qualified for the second round.

1998

1930
1934
1938
1950
1954
1958
1962
1966
1970
1974
1978
1982
1986
1990
1994
1998
2002
2006

GROUP B

Austria, Italy (seeded), Cameroon, Chile.

11 June 1998 – Parc Lescure, Bordeaux – 31,800 –
Lucien Bouchardeau (NGR)

CHILE	**(1) 2**
Salas 45, 50

ITALY	**(1) 2**
Vieri 10, R Baggio pen 85

CHILE Nélson Tápia, Ronald Fuentes, Francisco Rojas, Javier Margas [Miguel Ramírez 63], Pedro Reyes, Nélson Parráguez, Clarence Acuña [Fernando Cornejo 81], Moisés Villarroel, Iván Zamorano (c), Fabián Estay [José Luis Sierra 80], Marcelo Salas. *Nélson Acosta (URU).*
ITALY Gianluca Pagliuca, Fabio Cannavaro, Paolo Maldini (c), Dino Baggio, Alessandro Nesta, Alessandro Costacurta, Angelo Di Livio [Enrico Chiesa 61], Roberto Di Matteo [Luigi Di Biagio 57], Christian Vieri [Filippo Inzaghi 71], Demetrio Albertini, Roberto Baggio. *Cesare Maldini.*

Incredible that Italy should have needed a refereeing hand-out to save this match: they utterly dominated the first half. Cesare Maldini was the second coach to pick his son in a finals match (after Viera of Uruguay in 1966) and the first to make him captain. Maldini junior responded by making the opening goal. After intercepting a pass, he hit a perfect long ball that invited Roberto Baggio to touch the ball first time into the path of Vieri, who sidefooted it in. With Cannavaro and Nesta clamping down on the 'Za-Sa' strike-force of Zamorano and Salas, Chile weren't in the match.

Then in injury time Zamorano headed on Estay's corner, and a rebound fell kindly for Salas. who lashed it in. Stocky and beetle-browed, the current South American Footballer of the Year, Salas had recently scored both goals in Chile's 2-0 win at Wembley. Now he out-jumped Cannavaro to head in Acuña's cross, and suddenly Italy were struggling, their counter-attacks held up by a slow Roberto Baggio and the lumbering Vieri. Even so, Baggio nearly created the equaliser before he scored it. When he got round the back of the last defender, Tápia made a vital save, then another when Baggio's sublime little through-ball sent Inzaghi clear. But Italy had run out of ideas with five minutes left.

Despite some newspaper reports, the referee came from Niger not Nigeria. Apparently the fittest in pre-tournament tests, he was never quite in control here, allowing Acuña to stay on the pitch despite poleaxing Roberto Baggio with an elbow. After awarding a penalty when a cross from the same Baggio hit Fuentes' arm, Bouchardeau was sent home early, taking Italy's thanks with him.

There was the little matter of actually taking the kick. After his famous miss in the 1994 Final, Baggio looked small and fragile when put on the spot again, and Tápia got a hand to the penalty. Chile could be forgiven for not agreeing that the draw was a fair result.

11 June 1998 – Municipal, Toulouse – 37,500 –
Epifanio González (PAR)

AUSTRIA	**(0) 1**
Polster 90

CAMEROON	**(0) 1**
Njanka 77

AUSTRIA Michael Konsel, Harald Cerny [Peter Stöger 82], Arnold Wetl, Anton Pfeffer, Peter Schöttel, Wolfgang Feiersinger, Heimo Pfeifenberger [Mario Haas 82], Roman Mählich, Toni Polster (c), Andreas Herzog [Ivica Vastic 82], Dietmar Kühbauer. *Herbert Prohaska.*

CAMEROON Jacques Songo'o, Rigobert Song, Raymond Kalla, Pierre Njanka, Pierre Wome, Didier Angibeaud, Patrick Mboma, Augustine Simo [Salomon Olembe 65], François Omam Biyick (c) [Alphonse Tchami 84], Joseph-Cyrille Ndo, Samuel Ipoua [Joseph-Desiré Job 65]. *Claude Le Roy (FRA)*.

No change from 1990, then. Cameroon, the so-called Indomitable Lions, weren't so much uncaged as untutored: they didn't seem to know how to make a legitimate challenge. Most of their tackles were fouls, mainly painful ones inflicted by big strong men. Just a selection: Njanka's assault on Cerny: Ipoua and Simo leaving their studs in the way of Feiersinger and Pfeifenberger respectively; Wome elbowing Polster; Kalla treading on Herzog's arm. Austria did well to keep their tempers (Feiersinger, in his thin headband, was very impressive in defence) – but they were pedestrian as well as dogged, so there seemed no way back once Cameroon had scored a marvellous individual goal, similar to Hadji's against Norway but better.

Njanka ran a long way up the left, swerved past Feiersinger, stepped inside Schöttel (a dummy with each foot), and fired across the keeper. But somebody up there wouldn't allow Cameroon to get away with it. In injury time (an apt term in a match like this), Pfeffer headed on a corner and Polster took his time before crunching the ball in off the bar. He was 34 now and virtually stationary, his '70's perm didn't get any more fashionable – but some of the poacher's knack was still there: this his 44th goal for Austria, still the national record.

17 June 1998 – Geoffroy Guichard, Saint-Étienne – 30,392 – Gamal El-Ghandour (EGY)

AUSTRIA	(0) 1
Vastic 90	
CHILE	(0) 1
Salas 69	

AUSTRIA Konsel, Cerny [Markus Schopp HT], Wetl, Pfeffer, Schöttel, Feiersinger, Pfeifenberger, Haas [Vastic 73], Polster (c), Mählich, Kühbauer [Herzog HT]. CHILE Tápia, Fuentes, Rojas, Margas, Reyes, Parráguez, Acuña, Villarroel [Cristian Castañeda 67], Zamorano (c), Estay [Sierra 56], Salas.

For the second time in a row, Austria snatched a 1-1 draw with a goal deep into injury time, and again it wasn't clear if they deserved it. Chile, frustrated once again, had more luck on their side this time. When Konsel made a good reflex save from Zamorano's header, Salas caught the rebound with his thigh, and the keeper was judged to have dragged the ball over the line, although it's hard to know how the referee could have been sure when it's unclear in slow-motion replays. Vastic snatched another draw by jagging to his right before curling the ball high beyond Tápia from outside the area. In every sense, a finish out of keeping with a dreadful match.

17 June 1998 – de la Mosson, Montpellier – 35,000 – Eddie Lennie (AUS)

ITALY	(1) 3
Di Biagio 8, Vieri 75, 89	
CAMEROON	(0) 0

ITALY Pagliuca, Costacurta, Maldini (c), D Baggio, Cannavaro, Nesta, Francesco Moriero [Di Livio 83], Albertini [Di Matteo 62], Vieri, R Baggio [Alessandro Del Piero 64], Di Biagio. CAMEROON Songo'o, Ndo, Njanka, Wome, Song, Kalla, Olembe, Mboma [Samuel Eto'o 66], Omam Biyick (c) [Tchami 66], Angibeaud, Ipoua [Job HT]. SENT OFF: Kalla 42.

1998

Italy had to undergo the same full-frontal assault inflicted on Austria, but this time Cameroon had more talented opposition to deal with. Roberto Baggio's good flat cross

1930
1934
1938
1950
1954
1958
1962
1966
1970
1974
1978
1982
1986
1990
1994
1998
2002
2006

from the left was put in by a sharp glancing header that came off Di Biagio's shaved head, one of many in the tournament. His first international goal was also Italy's 100th in the finals.

The gigantic Kalla was sent off for sliding in, studs up, on Di Biagio, and Njanka should have joined him after a foul from behind on Roberto Baggio, who never recovered. According to one Italian paper, Baggio 'absorbed with Christian resignation frightening access to his heels'. Vieri, put clear by Moriero on the right, superbly chipped the keeper to make it 2-0. A rugged handful throughout (one paper called him '*il Rambo versione Italia*'), he had a goal disallowed for offside after Del Piero's sweet dribble, then nudged Wome in the back to get to a loose ball, which he bundled into the ground and up over the keeper. Song, booked for a huge foul on Del Piero, should have been the first player to be sent off twice in World Cup finals, a distinction that wasn't delayed for long. Meanwhile Italy had found the goalscorer they sometimes unearth in World Cup tournaments. For once, Christian had devoured the Lions.

---

23 June 1998 – Stade de France, Saint-Denis, Paris – 75,000 – Paul Durkin (ENG)

ITALY (0) 2
Vieri 48, R Baggio 89

AUSTRIA (0) 1
Herzog pen 90

ITALY Pagliuca, Costacurta, Maldini (c), D Baggio, Cannavaro, Nesta [Giuseppe Bergomi 3], Moriero, Del Piero [R Baggio 72], Vieri [Inzaghi 60], Di Biagio, Gianluca Pessotto.
AUSTRIA Konsel, Wetl, Pfeffer, Schöttel, Feiersinger, Pfeifenberger [Herzog 78], Hannes Reinmayr, Vastic, Polster (c) [Haas 62], Mählich, Kühbauer [Stöger 74].

Third time not lucky. Austria's latest injury-time strike, a penalty awarded for a foul by Costacurta on Reinmayr, didn't change anything. With no need to rush, Italy bided their time before scoring, then Vieri gatecrashed the defence to head in Del Piero's short free kick, and Inzaghi's return pass gave Roberto Baggio a tap-in for the second. The referee allowed too many dangerous tackles, Nesta injuring his knee so badly that didn't play again until December. Bergomi, the teenaged discovery of 1982, had recently been recalled after a gap of seven years. Polster's 94th cap broke the national record set by Gerhard Hanappi in 1962.

---

23 June 1998 – de la Beaujoire-Louis Fonteneau, Nantes – 39,000 – László Vágner (HUN)

CAMEROON (0) 1
Mboma 55

CHILE (1) 1
Sierra 20

CAMEROON Songo'o, Ndo ['Lauren' (Laureano Bisan-Etame Mayer) 82], Njanka, Wome, Song, Marcel Mahouve, Olembe [Angibeaud 68], Mboma, Omam Biyick (c), Michel Pensée Billong, Job [Tchami 72].
CHILE Tápia, Fuentes, Rojas [Ramírez 76], Margas, Reyes, Parráguez, Acuña, Villarroel [Cornejo 70], Zamorano (c), Sierra [Estay 70], Salas.
SENT OFF: Song 51, Lauren 88.

To no-one's surprise, Song had already been booked by the time he took a wild kick at Zamorano to concede the free kick which Sierra curled left-footed into the top corner. But Mboma beat Reyes in the air to head in Omam Biyick's cross, and Cameroon had chances to go ahead, Tápia saving from Omam Biyick and Mboma. Omam Biyick would have become the only African player to score in three finals tournaments if he hadn't had two goals disallowed, the first correctly, the other when Mboma was controversially penalised while jumping to head the ball on. As the irritation spread, Song was sent off for elbowing Salas, Lauren for a wild late tackle on the same player.

Chile weren't blameless (bookings for Rojas, Parráguez and Villarroel kept them out of the match against Brazil) – but they'd reached the next round for only the second time and the first away from home. Cameroon went home to nurse grievances but not to learn how to tackle without maiming: they were just as violent in winning the Olympic gold medal two years later. Lauren's full name has been spotted in a variety of guises (Laurent, Lavriano, shortened to Etame Mayer, etc). The one above comes direct from Arsenal, whom he joined in 2000.

GROUP B

	P	W	D	L	F	A	Pts
Italy	3	2	1	0	7	3	7
Chile	3	0	3	0	4	4	3
Austria	3	0	2	1	3	4	2
Cameroon	3	0	2	1	2	5	2

Italy and Chile qualified for the second round.

GROUP C

Denmark, France (seeded), Saudi Arabia, South Africa.

12 June 1998 – Félix Bollaert, Lens – 38,140 – Javier Castrilli (ARG)

DENMARK   (0) 1
Rieper 68

SAUDI ARABIA   (0) 0

DENMARK Peter Schmeichel, Søren Colding, Michael Schjønberg, Jes Høgh, Marc Rieper, Morten Wieghorst [Allan Nielsen 65], Thomas Helveg, Martin Jørgensen [Per Frandsen 73], Ebbe Sand, Michael Laudrup (c), Brian Laudrup [Jan Heintze 83]. *Bo Johansson (SWE).*
SAUDI ARABIA Mohammed Al-Deayea, Mohammed Al-Khilaiwi, Hussain Sulimani, Abdullah Zubromawi, Mohammed Al-Jahani, Ibrahim Al-Shahrani, Khamis Al-Owairan Al-Dossari, Fuad Amin (c) [Hamzah Saleh 79], Said Al-Owairan [Obeid Al-Dossari 79], Khalid Al-Muwalid, Sami Al-Jaber [Youssef Al-Tuniyan 84]. *Carlos Alberto Parreira (BRZ).*

This was the same Saudi team which had drawn 0-0 at Wembley three weeks earlier, so Denmark didn't expect to have things all their own way. Bigger and stronger, they dominated possession without making many chances. Jørgensen and Nielsen should have scored, and Brian Laudrup's good cross presented the hulking Rieper with a free header in the aftermath of a corner. Said Al-Owairan, who'd scored that brilliant solo goal in 1994, was totally anonymous, Michael Laudrup not much more visible, and the match in general was error-strewn and dull.

Michael Laudrup was winning his 100th cap. He and Brian were brothers, the Al-Owairans cousins. The stadium, which belonged to the club which had just won the French league title for the first time, had a crowd capacity bigger than the entire population of the town.

12 June 1998 – Vélodrome, Marseilles – 55,077 – Márcio Rezende de Freitas (BRZ)

FRANCE   (1) 3
Dugarry 34, Issa o.g. 78, o.g. 90

SOUTH AFRICA   (0) 0

FRANCE Fabien Barthez, Lilian Thuram, Bixente Lizarazu, Emmanuel Petit [Alain Boghossian 73], Marcel Desailly, Laurent Blanc, Thierry Henry, Didier Deschamps (c), Stéphane Guivarc'h [Christophe Dugarry 26], Zinedine Zidane, Youri Djorkaeff [David Trezeguet 82]. *Aimé Jacquet.*

SOUTH AFRICA Hans Vonk, Willem Jackson, David Nyathi, Quinton Fortune, Pierre Issa, Mark Fish, Lucas Radebe (c), Brendan Augustine [Helman Mkhalele 56], Phil Masinga, John 'Shoes' Moshoeu, Benni McCarthy [Shaun Bartlett 88]. *Philippe Troussier (FRA).*

France had beaten South Africa only 2-1 earlier in the season, and Fish and Radebe were respected defenders in England – so any kind of half-time lead was a plus. Wearing a headband rather like a personal stereo, Dugarry got in front of Vonk to head in a Zidane corner.

In the second half, Dugarry had a goal disallowed for offside, then Vonk had Djorkaeff's weak shot covered before Issa, very tall and lean, lunged it past him. Djorkaeff blazed over the bar after a splendid run by Henry, who skipped past Jackson in injury time and chipped low over Vonk. He's credited with the goal, but it was clearly another o.g. by Issa, who stopped the ball just before the line then knocked it in with his trailing foot. He was the only player to score two own goals in a World Cup match, let alone one played on his home club ground!

Making their finals debut against talented hosts, South Africa weren't disgraced, but no-one made a name for himself, including the 20-year-old McCarthy, who discovered that scoring against African defences and small Dutch clubs was rather different from facing Desailly and Thuram. Djorkaeff's father Jean had played in the 1966 finals. Some English sources mistakenly put on an accent or two when writing Trezeguet's name: Trézéguet.

1998

18 June 1998 – Municipal, Toulouse – 36,500 – John Jairo Toro Rendón (COL)

DENMARK	**(1) 1**
Nielsen 13	

SOUTH AFRICA	**(0) 1**
McCarthy 52	

DENMARK Schmeichel, Colding, Schjønberg [Wieghorst 82], Høgh, Rieper, Nielsen, Helveg, Jørgensen, Sand, [Miklós Molnár 58], M Laudrup (c) [Heintze 58], B Laudrup.
SOUTH AFRICA Vonk, Mkhalele, Nyathi [Delron Buckley 88], Fortune, Issa, Fish, Radebe (c), Augustine [Alfred Phiri HT], Bartlett [Masinga 77], Moshoeu, McCarthy.
SENT OFF: Molnár 66, Phiri 68, Wieghorst 84.

South Africa were often wide open at the back, leaving Nielsen unmarked to sidefoot in a volley from another fine cross by Brian Laudrup. But McCarthy showed some of his talent by taking Bartlett's backheel and bursting between two defenders before shooting in off Schmeichel's ankle. By the end, Denmark were happy to settle for a point, especially after Fortune had launched a few puns by hitting the bar from nearly thirty yards in injury time.

There were other close calls, notably when Jørgensen (direct from a corner) and Sand hit a post, and when McCarthy's low cross from the right cut out Schmeichel, only for Mkhalele to miss a completely open goal, one of the great World Cup blunders. But the match was memorable for its three red cards, all shown to substitutes. Earlier in the tournament, perhaps after watching Belgium v Holland or Cameroon v anybody, France's coach Aimé Jacquet had stressed the need for more sendings-off to quell the aggression. Toro Rendón did precisely that, on specific instructions from FIFA, who promptly dropped him from the tournament. He received some appalling knee-jerk stick from the media, but all three red cards were absolutely justified: Molnár for a violent follow-through on Radebe, Phiri for hitting Helveg with his forearm, Wieghorst for a tackle from behind on McCarthy. The referee also did everyone a favour by booking Schmeichel for expressing an opinion too many. If the tournament calmed down after the sparring of the opening rounds, it owed a debt to John Jairo Toro Rendón, cool anti-hero and sacrificial lamb.

---

18 June 1998 – Stade de France, Saint-Denis, Paris – 75,000 – Arturo Brizio Carter (MEX)

FRANCE   **(1) 4**
Henry 36, 77, Trezeguet 67, Lizarazu 84

SAUDI ARABIA   **(0) 0**

FRANCE Barthez, Thuram, Lizarazu, Boghossian, Desailly, Blanc, Henry [Robert Pires 78], Deschamps (c), Dugarry [Trezeguet 29], Zidane, Bernard Diomède [Djorkaeff 58].
SAUDI ARABIA Al-Deayea, Al-Jahani [Ahmed Dukhi Al-Dossari 75], Al-Shahrani, Sulimani, Al-Khilaiwi, Zubromawi, K Al-Owairan, Amin (c), Saleh, S Al-Owairan [Ibrahim Al-Harbi 33, Al-Muwalid 63], Al-Jaber.
SENT OFF: Al-Khilaiwi 18, Zidane 69.

France would surely have won anyway, but the contest was made cruelly unequal by the rather harsh sending-off of Al-Khilaiwi for a late tackle on Lizarazu. Cue seventy minutes of last-ditch Saudi defending, with Zubromawi heroic in the air. Before the match, the organisers had played the Saudi national anthem, then held a minute's silence for a co-president of the organising committee, then played the *Marseillaise*. Some clever crowd control.

Following a terrible miss by Zidane, who volleyed wide with only the keeper in front of him, France scored a very good goal. Zidane's tonsure gave him the look of a heavily built Franciscan friar, but nobody had a lighter touch. Spinning out of a challenge, he flicked a pass that set Lizarazu free on the left, Henry dragging the low cross into an open goal.

Trezeguet missed several half-chances before scoring from the easiest, heading into an empty net when Al-Deayea let Thuram's cross slip out of his gloves behind him. Zidane was sent off for stamping on Amin's rump, allegedly in response to a slur against the Kabyles, his

nomadic Muslim ancestors. A bad slip by Khamis Al-Owairan allowed Henry to run on and push the ball wide of the resigned keeper, but the fourth goal was better, Lizarazu cracking in Djorkaeff's backheel. Saudi Arabia, the first team to be eliminated, crassly sacked Carlos Alberto Parreira after the match, replacing him with their tenth coach in four years. France were through as early as expected, but Zidane's absence from the second round would be a worry.

---

24 June 1998 – Gerland, Lyons – 43,500 – Pierluigi Collina (ITA)

FRANCE   **(1) 2**
Djorkaeff pen 13, Petit 56

DENMARK   **(1) 1**
M Laudrup pen 42

FRANCE Barthez, Christian Karembeu, Vincent Candela, Petit [Boghossian 65], Desailly, Frank Lebœuf, Patrick Vieira, Diomède, Pires [Henry 72], Djorkaeff, Trezeguet [Guivarc'h 85].
DENMARK Schmeichel, Schjønberg, Heintze, Jacob Laursen [Colding HT], Høgh, Rieper, Nielsen, Helveg, Jørgensen [Sand 55], M Laudrup (c), B Laudrup [Stig Tøfting 75].

Both penalties were debatable, Høgh brushing the ball away before catching Trezeguet, Jørgensen leaning into Candela before falling. Petit, his fair hair tied back like Alain Sutter in 1994, scored his first goal for France by hammering the ball in low through a crowded area. Desailly was as massively good as ever, but Denmark again looked a poor side, their attitude exemplified by the substitution of their only world class attacker with Tøfting, a cross between Tintin and a bull terrier. Schmeichel, whose 103rd cap set a new national record, felt 'Our limitations were obvious today' and his coach's tactics 'proved to be incorrect for the second time running. It's no use making

1998

detailed plans to cope with French players who aren't even playing.' Not a particularly memorable 27th birthday for Helveg. Denmark were in the second round too, but that was surely as far as they went.

---

24 June 1998 – Parc Lescure, Bordeaux – 34,500 – Mario Sánchez Yantén (CHI)

SAUDI ARABIA   **(1) 2**
Al-Jaber pen 45, Al-Tuniyan pen 73

SOUTH AFRICA   **(1) 2**
Bartlett 19, pen 90

SAUDI ARABIA Al-Deayea, Al-Jahani, Zubromawi, Sulimani, K Al-Owairan, Saleh, Nawaf Al-Temiyat, Amin, Al-Jaber, Fahad Al-Mehalel [Al-Shahrani 64], Al-Tuniyan (c) [Al-Harbi 81]. *Mohammed Al-Kharashi.*
SOUTH AFRICA Vonk, Jackson [Buckley HT], Nyathi, Issa, Fish, Radebe (c), Mkhalele, Moshoeu, Fortune [Doctor Khumalo 66], Bartlett, McCarthy [Jerry Sikhosana HT].

South Africa were still taking things seriously. They sent Augustine home for nightclubbing (along with another squad member, the aptly-named Naughty Mokoena) and played for the win that gave them a chance of going through. Bartlett shot in at the near post where Al-Deayea had left far too big a gap.

After his two own goals against France, Issa now conceded two penalties, but both were very iffy. Al-Tuniyan jack-knifed through the air at the slightest touch, and Al-Shahrani was involved in a mutual wrestling match. Al-Sulimani conceded the other spot kick by fouling Sikhosana. As if Issa didn't have enough problems, FIFA investigated the possibility that he might have been wearing a listening apparatus, presumably to receive instructions from his coach. It turned out that a photo had caught his necklace flicking up by his ear. Khumalo's complete first names were Theophilus Doctorson.

GROUP C

	P	W	D	L	F	A	Pts
France	3	3	0	0	9	1	9
Denmark	3	1	1	1	3	3	4
South Africa	3	0	2	1	3	6	2
Saudi Arabia	3	0	1	2	2	7	1

France and Denmark qualified for the second round.

GROUP D

Bulgaria, Nigeria, Spain (seeded), Paraguay.

---

12 June 1998 – de la Mosson, Montpellier – 27,650 – Abdul Rahman Al-Zeid (SAU)

BULGARIA 0

PARAGUAY 0

BULGARIA Zdravko Zdravkov, Anatoli Nankov, Ivailo Petkov, Radostin Kishishev, Trifon Ivanov (c), Ivailo Yordanov, Ilian Iliev [Daniel Borimirov 77], Zlatko Yankov, Luboslav Penev [Emil Kostadinov 68], Krasimir Balakov, Christo Stoichkov. *Christo Bonev.*
PARAGUAY José Luis Chilavert (c), Carlos Gamarra, Celso Ayala, Pedro Sarabia, Julio César Enciso, Jorge Campos [Juan Carlos Yegros 78], Roberto Acuña, Carlos Paredes, Miguel Benítez, José Cardozo [César Ramírez 70], Carlos Morales [Denis Caniza 42]. *Paulo César Carpegiani (BRZ).*
SENT OFF: Nankov 88.

Paraguay arrived on the back of four consecutive defeats and no wins since February, and Bulgaria were only shadows of their 1994 side – so excitement was off the menu. Still, no match involving Stoichkov was ever completely uneventful. Angry at not being awarded an early penalty, he squared up to Morales, argued with Ayala after being pushed, argued with Balakov after getting in the way of a pass, and was booked for fouling Benítez. Somewhere in all that, he hit a post.

Even so, he had a rival as personality of the match in the unique figure of Chilavert, who was kind enough to share his philosophy with us: 'In the morning eat like a king, at noon like a prince, at night like a pauper.' From the look of his bared midriff when exchanging shirts, he'd been feasting like an emperor all day – but this was a world class keeper, something usually forgotten in the publicity surrounding his feats at the other end. He scored in four World Cup qualifying tournaments and came close here, his free kick bringing a very good save out of Zdravkov. Nankov was sent off for a second bookable offence, a foul on Yegros. Penev, nephew of 1994 coach Dimitar, had missed that tournament with testicular cancer, the same disease from which Bobby Moore had recovered before the 1966 finals.

---

13 June 1998 – de la Beaujoire-Louis Fonteneau, Nantes – 33,257 – Esfandiar Baharmast (USA)

NIGERIA   (1) 3
Adepoju 24, Lawal 72, Oliseh 77

SPAIN   (1) 2
Hierro 20, Raúl 46

NIGERIA Peter Rufai, Mobi Oparaku [Rashidi Yekini 69], Céléstine Babayaro, Garba Lawal [Godwin Okpara 90], Uche Okechukwu (c), Taribo West, Finidi George, Victor Ikpeba [Tijani Babangida 82], Sunday Oliseh, Augustine 'Jay-Jay' Okocha, Mutiu Adepoju. *Bora Milutinović (YUG)*.
SPAIN Andoni Zubizarreta (c), Albert Ferrer [Guillermo Amor HT], 'Sergi' (Sergio Barjuán), Miguel Ángel Nadal [Alberto Celades 76], Iván Campo, Rafael Alkorta, Fernando Hierro, Luis Enrique (Martínez), Alfonso (Pérez) [Joseba Etxeberría 57], 'Kiko' (Francisco Narváez), Raúl (González).
Javier Clemente.

Hard to remember a match being turned so upside-down by a single goalkeeping error. When Raúl coolly volleyed in Hierro's good long ball, Nigeria seemed already buried, especially as little Okocha had disappeared once Nadal went back into defence. But then Lawal's low cross from the left was palmed into his own net by Zubizarreta, who was winning his 124th cap and appearing in his fourth finals. A French paper dubbed him '*Zubi n'arrêta*', Zubi didn't stop it.

Spain's confidence was turned off like a stopcock, and suddenly everything Nigeria did came off. Hierro's defensive header was lashed in from beyond the penalty area by Oliseh, the unsighted Zubizarreta doing well to get his fingertips to the ball, which went in off the near post. Earlier Hierro's low free kick had bounced in as Rufai stood and watched, and Adepoju headed in Lawal's corner.

Disaster for Spain, success as well as flamboyance from Nigeria. West had dyed his hair green, Oparaku and Okocha orange. West, a black version of The Prodigy singer Keith Flint, told us 'I will still tie ribbons in my hair because it's fun and it's fashionable.' So he was half right.

---

19 June 1998 – Parc des Princes, Paris – 48,500 – Mario Sánchez Yantén (CHI)

NIGERIA   (1) 1
Ikpeba 26

BULGARIA (0) 0

NIGERIA Rufai, Adepoju, Babayaro, Oliseh, Okechukwu (c), West, George [Babangida 85], Ikpeba [Yekini 75], Daniel Amokachi [Nwankwo Kanu 67], Okocha, Lawal.
BULGARIA Zdravkov, Gosho Ginchev, Petkov, Kishishev, Ivanov (c), Marian Christov [Borimirov HT], Iliev [Penev 68], Yankov [Georgi Bachev 85], Kostadinov, Balakov, Stoichkov.

1930
1934
1938
1950
1954
1958
1962
1966
1970
1974
1978
1982
1986
1990
1994
1998
2002
2006

Bulgaria were so appallingly bad that Nigeria could play loosely and still humiliate them. The bearded Ivanov ('Wolfman'), unfit to the point of slapstick, was easily beaten by Ikpeba for the goal, and Stoichkov could only flicker. Four minutes from time, Kostadinov's classy backheel gave him space for a shot that hit the bar, but a draw would have distorted the facts. Milutinovic, in charge of his fourth country at the finals, had now taken them all to the second round.

19 June 1998 – Geoffroy Guichard, St Étienne – 35,300 – Ian McLeod (SAF)

PARAGUAY	0
SPAIN	0

PARAGUAY Chilavert (c), Gamarra, Campos [Paredes HT], Francisco Arce, Ayala, Sarabia, Enciso, Acuña [Yegros 74], Aristides Rojas [Ramírez 83], Caniza, Benítez.
SPAIN Zubizarreta (c), Alkorta, Sergi, Carlos Aguilera, Abelardo (Fernández) [Celades 56], Hierro, Amor, Luis Enrique, Juan Antonio Pizzi [Fernando Morientes 52], Raúl [Kiko 65], Etxeberría.

Spain began nervously and got worse, still apparently crushed by Zubizarreta's calamity against Nigeria – so Paraguay, as defensive as ever, had no trouble achieving another draw. Chilavert again showed he was more than just an eccentric showman by making a brilliant save from Raúl. Pizzi, a disaster in Euro 96,

YOUNGEST CAPTAINS

yrs	days			
21	327	Nwankwo Kanu	NGA	1998
22	33	Turgay Seren	TUR	1954
22	193	Ladislav Novák	CZE	1954
22	222	Harry Keough	USA	1950

seemed to be another of Clemente's stubbornly eccentric selections: he also left out a play-maker (Guerrero) and wouldn't have the impish little Iván de la Peña in the squad.

24 June 1998 – Félix Bollaert, Lens – 41,275 – Mario van der Ende (HOL)

SPAIN	(2) 6

Hierro pen 5, Luis Enrique 18, Morientes 53, 80, Bachev o.g. 88, Kiko 90

BULGARIA	(0) 1

Kostadinov 56

SPAIN Zubizarreta (c), Alkorta, Sergi, Aguilera, Nadal, Hierro, Amor, Luis Enrique [Julen Guerrero 70], Morientes, Alfonso [Kiko 64], Etxeberría [Raúl 51].
BULGARIA Zdravkov, Kishishev, Ivanov (c), Yordanov, Ginchev, Balakov [Marian Christov 59], Nankov [Penev 28], Borimirov, Bachev, Kostadinov, Stoichkov [Iliev HT].

Needing to win and hoping Nigeria did the same against Paraguay, Spain confirmed that it was a tournament too far for this Bulgarian vintage. Luis Enrique was involved in the first three goals: Yordanov gave him the merest shove for the penalty (six spot kicks, all converted, were awarded on the same day), he shot in off the far post from Etxeberría's return pass, then sent Morientes in to score with a cross-shot.

Kostadinov cracked the ball in off the near post from a tight angle – but Morientes took Raúl's volleyed through-ball round the keeper, and Kiko headed a corner against the bar, the ball bouncing off the keeper's back then in off Bachev. Finally Kiko shot between Zdravkov's legs after collecting a long free kick with no defender bothering to go with him. It could have been worse for Bulgaria: Morientes also hit the bar with a header.

Bonev resigned as coach. 'This match', he said, 'shows the true condition of Bulgarian football', which would have to cling to memories of USA 94. A save by Zubizarreta had the crowd chanting his name in his final match for Spain, but there was an eerie silence for the last half-hour as news came through from Paraguay v Nigeria.

---

24 June 1998 – Municipal, Toulouse – 37,500 – Pirom Un-Prasert (THA)

PARAGUAY　　(1) 3
Ayala 53 sec, Benítez 58, Cardozo 86

NIGERIA　　(1) 1
Oruma 10

PARAGUAY Chilavert (c), Arce, Ayala, Caniza [Yegros 55], Gamarra, Sarabia, Benítez [Acuña 68], Enciso, Paredes, Hugo Brizuela [Rojas 78], Cardozo.
NIGERIA Rufai, Augustine Eguavoen, Ben Iroha, Uche Okafor, West, Babangida, Kanu (c), Lawal, Yekini, Oliseh [Okpara HT], Wilson Oruma [George 69].

Just when we were wondering if a team might qualify without scoring a goal, Paraguay got one almost at once. Ayala leaping in front of Rufai to hammer in a header from a free kick. Oliseh's superb through-ball found Babangida, whose square ball was chipped over the diving keeper by Oruma. Chilavert had to make three very good saves – but Paraguay rode it out. Benítez scored powerfully from outside the area, and Cardozo's low cross-shot finished a move which began with Rufai's poor kick-out. Milutinović was criticised, as coaches always

GROUP D

	P	W	D	L	F	A	Pts
Nigeria	3	2	0	1	5	5	6
Paraguay	3	1	2	0	3	1	5
Spain	3	1	1	1	8	4	4
Bulgaria	3	0	1	2	1	7	1

Nigeria and Paraguay qualified for the second round.

are in this situation, for fielding some second-string players and making Paraguay's task easier at the expense of Spain. But he was well within his rights to rest his players. He'd already done his job, Clemente should have done his.

GROUP E

Belgium, Holland (seeded), Mexico, South Korea.

---

13 June 1998 – Gerland, Lyons – 37,588 – Günter Benkö (AUT)

MEXICO　　(0) 3
Peláez 51, Hernández 74, 83

SOUTH KOREA　　(1) 1
Ha 28

MEXICO Jorge Campos, Pavel Pardo, Braulio Luna [Jesús Arellano HT], Jesús Ramírez, Duilio Davino, Claudio Suárez, Raúl Lara, Alberto García Aspe (c) [Marcelino Bernal 71], Luis Hernández, Jaime Ordiales [Ricardo Peláez HT], Cuauhtémoc Blanco.
Manuel Lapuente.
SOUTH KOREA Kim Bjung-Ji, Kim Tae-Yung, Lee Min-Sung, Hong Myung-Bo, Lee Sang-Yoon, Ha Seok-Ju, Kim Doh-Keun [Choi Sung-Yong 60], Yoo Sang-Chul (c), Ko Jong-Soo [Seo Jung-Won 71], Noh Jung-Yoon [Jang Hyung-Seok 55], Kim Do-Hoon.
Cha Bum-Kun.
SENT OFF: Ha 29.

South Korea didn't have time to ride their luck. A minute after his free kick had flicked Davino's head and sent Campos the wrong way, Ha was shown a red card for catching Ramírez from behind, making him only the second goalscorer to be sent off in a finals match, following Garrincha in 1962. Kevin Keegan, who'd tried to excuse Leonardo's elbow in 1994, did the same here, but Ramírez took a long time to recover.

1930 1934 1938 1950 1954 1958 1962 1966 1970 1974 1978 1982 1986 1990 1994 **1998** 2002 2006

The 35-year-old Peláez eventually equalised following a corner, and Hernández killed off the ten men by touching in a volley and converting Blanco's square pass. Top scorer in the 1997 Copa América but very poor here until his two goals, he played with his dyed blond hair tied back in a string, very much like Caniggia who kept him out of the team at Boca Juniors. Blanco, in his red-white-and-green boots (the colours of the Mexican flag), twice grasped the ball between his feet and hopped between two defenders, a move that never quite caught on. It was Mexico's first World Cup win in Europe, but their performance made a mockery of the FIFA rankings which had them at No.4.

did most of the attacking, but two muscular defences were generally in control. Stam, whom Manchester United had just made the most expensive defender of all time, looked a snip at under £11 million – but it was legitimate to wonder if any supplementary assistance was involved: like Davids and Frank de Boer, he tested positive for nandrolone in 2001.

Kluivert, frustrated throughout, was sent off for reacting to assorted 'appalling comments' by barely touching Staelens, who naturally collapsed holding his face. Since Kluivert had once been in court as a result of a fatal car accident and had just been cleared of rape, Staelens had plenty of ammunition.

---

13 June 1998 – Stade de France, Saint-Denis, Paris – 75,000 – Pierluigi Collina (ITA)

BELGIUM   **0**

HOLLAND   **0**

BELGIUM Filip De Wilde, Bertrand Crasson [Eric Deflandre 21], Lorenzo Staelens, Vital Borkelmans, Franky Van der Elst (c), Marc Wilmots, Luis Oliveira [Émile Mpenza 59], Luc Nilis, Philippe Clement, Mike Verstraeten, Danny Boffin. *Georges Leekens.*
HOLLAND Edwin van der Sar, Frank de Boer (c), Arthur Numan, Aron Winter, Ronald de Boer [Wim Jonk 78], Jaap Stam, Philip Cocu, Clarence Seedorf [Boudewijn Zenden 65], Jerrel 'Jimmy Floyd' Hasselbaink [Dennis Bergkamp 65], Patrick Kluivert, Marc Overmars. *Guus Hiddink.*
SENT OFF: Kluivert 80.

A graphic illustration of the change in physique between this era and those before it. Rawboned defenders on both sides, especially the skinheads Stam and Verstraeten, whose knees looked bigger than some of yesterday's thighs. And so many painful illegal tackles. Crasson, who couldn't cope with Overmars, was soon replaced by Deflandre, who fouled the little winger like it was going out of fashion. Holland

---

20 June 1998 – Parc Lescure, Bordeaux – 34,750 – Hugh Dallas (SCO)

BELGIUM   **(1) 2**
Wilmots 43, 48
MEXICO   **(0) 2**
García Aspe pen 56, Blanco 62

BELGIUM De Wilde, Deflandre, Borkelmans, Gordan Vidović, Staelens, Van der Elst (c) [Glen De Boeck 67], Wilmots, Oliveira, Nilis [É Mpenza 77], Enzo Scifo, Danny Boffin [Gert Verheyen 17]
MEXICO Campos, Pardo, Ramírez, Joel Sánchez, Davino, Suárez, Francisco Palencia [Arellano HT], García Aspe (c) [Lara 67], Hernández, Ordiales [Germán Villa 58], Blanco.
SENT OFF: Pardo 28, Verheyen 55.

Belgium didn't enjoy a scorcher of a day in which 100 spectators were treated for heatstroke, but seemed to have weathered it when they took a 2-0 lead against ten men. After Pardo had been sent off for crippling Borkelmans from behind, a corner hit Wilmots in the ribs and bounced in between Campos' legs. The second goal was just as unconvincing. Wilmots, big and heavy like most of his team mates, showed poor control but then nicked the ball past a man, broke a tackle and scuffed the ball past Campos.

Mexico were rescued by a penalty given for Verheyen's red-card foul on Ramírez. With numbers equal again, Arellano's good cross-field pass set Ramírez free on the left, the cross finding Blanco unmarked to volley in at the far post. Mexico still didn't look a quality side but were lively throughout, whereas the Belgians, with their average age of 31 years 304 days, were running on empty by the end.

---

20 June 1998 – Vélodrome, Marseilles – 55,000 – Ryszard Wójcik (POL)

HOLLAND (2) 5
Cocu 37, Overmars 41, Bergkamp 71, van Hooijdonk 79, R de Boer 82

SOUTH KOREA (0) 0

HOLLAND van der Sar, F de Boer (c), Numan [Winston Bogarde 80], Edgar Davids, Winter, R de Boer [Zenden 83], Jonk, Stam, Cocu, Bergkamp [Pierre van Hooijdonk 77], Overmars.
SOUTH KOREA Kim BJ, Choi Yung-Il (c), Lee MS, Hong, Choi SY [Kim TY 52], Seo [Lee Dong-Kook 76], Kim DH [Ko 69], Kim DK, Yoo, Choi Yong-Soo, Lee SY.

Against a team that didn't plan to kick them out of it, Holland predictably cut loose. All their goals were high class. English commentators had just decided that Cocu didn't look comfortable playing up front when he made room for a fierce left-footer that left the keeper standing. Overmars cut inside before cracking the ball in low at the near post. Bergkamp, sharp from the start against a massed defence, scored a fine individual goal, needing a little luck to break a tackle by Lee Min-Sung but cleverly beating Lee Sang-Yoon. Van Hooijdonk headed Overmars' cross past an exposed keeper, and Ronald de Boer turned inside Lee Min-Sung before hitting a heavy volley.

Despite the scoreline, Hong Myung-Bo had another good game in defence – but Holland were simply different class. Numan, a David Bowie lookalike, was very smooth on the left, the 'Pitbull' Davids a well-known midfield enforcer, the de Boers quietly efficient as usual. Cha Bum-Kun became the latest coach to be sacked during the tournament, which seemed harsh after having to face a team like this.

---

25 June 1998 – Geoffroy Guichard, Saint-Étienne – 35,500 – Abdul Rahman Al-Zeid (SAU)

HOLLAND (2) 2
Cocu 4, R de Boer 18

MEXICO (0) 2
Peláez 74, Hernández 90

HOLLAND van der Sar, Michael Reiziger, Numan [Bogarde 71], Davids, Stam, F de Boer (c), R de Boer, Jonk [Winter 71], Cocu, Bergkamp [Hasselbaink 78], Overmars.
MEXICO Campos, Suárez, Sánchez [Peláez 54], Davino, Salvador Carmona, Villa, Ramírez, García Aspe (c), Hernández, Luna [Arellano HT], Blanco.
SENT OFF: Ramírez 89.

For the second time in a row, Mexico drew a match in which they'd been 2-0 down, this time after being outclassed to the point of ridicule. Bergkamp skilfully controlled a high ball before hitting a lob which Cocu met with a low volley across the keeper. Then Ronald de Boer won a header-on and held off three defenders before snapping a cross-shot in off the post. Holland bossed the rest of the half with their simple crisp passing, Mexico making no chances. Overmars should have made it 3-0 and Cocu hit the bar after 50 minutes – but the second half became scrappy, which suited the Mexicans, who were nothing if not game. Peláez's header from a corner bounced between Bogarde and Blanco on its way in. When Blanco had a goal rightly disallowed,

Ramírez was sent off for contesting the decision – but Stam got a simple ball tangled up under his feet to let in Hernández, who toe-poked it under van der Sar to become the only Mexican to score more than two finals goals in total. Unless Belgium could beat South Korea by two goals in a high-scoring match, Mexico were through.

---

25 June 1998 – Parc des Princes, Paris – 48,500 – Márcio Rezende de Freitas (BRZ)

BELGIUM (1) 1
Nilis 6

SOUTH KOREA (0) 1
Yoo 71

BELGIUM Philippe Vande Walle, Borkelmans, Clement [É Mpenza 74], Deflandre, Staelens, Vidovic, Scifo (c) [Van der Elst 65], Nico Van Kerckhoven, Nilis, Oliveira [Mbo Mpenza HT], Wilmots.
SOUTH KOREA Kim BJ, Lee MS, Lee Sang-Hun [Jang 66], Kim TY, Hong, Choi SY [Lee Lim-Saeng HT], Yoo (c), Kim DK [Ko HT], Ha, Choi YS, Seo. *Kim Pyong-Sok*.

Belgium started as they were expected to finish, Nilis scoring with a hard low shot after a corner, and missed any number of chances to double their lead, especially when Nilis, prominent throughout, skilfully turned a man and shot against the bar. But they ran out of puff again, and Yoo Sang-Chul escaped all marking to slide in and volley home Ha Seok-Ju's free kick. The last 15 minutes were a siege, the Koreans throwing their bodies in the way of the ball. So the draw mattered to them, but after 14 finals matches they were still without a win, a sequence they were hoping to end as co-hosts in 2002. Belgium were eliminated without losing a match, but few were sorry to see them go. The Mpenzas were brothers.

GROUP E

	P	W	D	L	F	A	Pts
Holland	3	1	2	0	7	2	5
Mexico	3	1	2	0	7	5	5
Belgium	3	0	3	0	3	3	3
South Korea	3	0	1	2	2	9	1

Holland and Mexico qualified for the second round.

GROUP F

Germany (seeded), Iran, USA, Yugoslavia.

---

14 June 1998 – Geoffroy Guichard, Saint-Étienne – 30,392 – Alberto Tejada Noriega (PER)

YUGOSLAVIA (0) 1
Mihajlović 73

IRAN (0) 0

YUGOSLAVIA Ivica Kralj, Zoran Mirković, Goran Đorović, Slaviša Jokanović, Siniša Mihajlović, Vladimir Jugović, Branko Brnović [Dejan Stanković 51], Željko Petrović, Savo Milošević [Perica Ognjenović 58], Dragan Stojković (c) [Darko Kovačević 68], Predrag Mijatović. *Slobodan Santrač*.
IRAN Nima Nakisa, Mehdi Mahdavikia, Javad Zarincheh, Mehdi Pashazadeh, Mohammed Khakpour, Nader Mohammedkhani (c), Hamid Reza Estili [Ali Reza Mansourian 68], Karim Bagheri, Ali Daei, Khodadad Azizi, Mehrdad Minavand Chal. *Jalal Talebi*.

Đorović hit the bar with a looping header from an early corner, but Yugoslavia were incoherent throughout. Things improved with the departure of Stojković, who was past his best, and the arrival of three substitutes – but they had to rely on an old staple for their goal. The wall was badly positioned for Mihajlović's free kick, and although Mahdavikia made some positive runs up the right, Iran didn't quite belong at this level.

---

15 June 1998 – Parc des Princes, Paris – 43,815 – Said Belqola (MOR)

GERMANY (1) 2
Möller 8, Klinsmann 64

USA (0) 0

GERMANY Andreas Köpke, Jürgen Kohler, Stefan Reuter [Christian Ziege 68], Jens Jeremies, Olaf Thon, Christian Wörns, Thomas Hässler [Dietmar Hamann 49], Andreas Möller [Markus Babbel 90], Jörg Heinrich, Oliver Bierhoff, Jürgen Klinsmann (c). *Berti Vogts.*
USA Kasey Keller, Tom Dooley (c), Eddie Pope, David Régis, Mike Burns [Frankie Hejduk HT], Claudio Reyna, Earnie Stewart, Cobi Jones, Brian Maisonneuve, Chad Deering [Tab Ramos 70], Eric Wynalda [Roy Wegerle 64]. *Steve Sampson.*

A similar story here. The USA, absurdly ranked No.11 by FIFA, were dogged in defence, the promising young Pope sticking gamely to Bierhoff, who looked heavy and wooden – but they were so toothless up front that even Kohler felt free to join in attacks. And they couldn't cope with the German midfield, which rotated splendidly, Möller surging forward time and again. He headed the first goal when Klinsmann outjumped Régis and Pope to nod the ball across.

Sampson had dropped John Harkes from the squad, putting his faith in Reyna's touch. But the long-haired Jeremies emerged as a hard-working find, and Reyna joined the list of players from the minor countries who didn't play up to their reputations: McCarthy, Bagheri, Daei, Badra, etc. When Bierhoff crossed from the right, Klinsmann lost the 37-year-old Dooley before chesting down and

sidefooting a volley across the keeper. The Germans were hard and often late into the tackle, a story of the tournament.

---

21 June 1998 – Félix Bollaert, Lens – 41,275 – Kim Milton Nielsen (DEN)

GERMANY (0) 2
Mihajlović o.g. 73, Bierhoff 79

YUGOSLAVIA (1) 2
Jeremies o.g. 13, Stojković 53

GERMANY Köpke, Kohler, Ziege [Michael Tarnat 66], Jeremies, Thon, Wörns, Hamann [Lothar Matthäus HT], Möller [Ulf Kirsten 58], Heinrich, Bierhoff, Klinsmann (c).
YUGOSLAVIA Kralj, Mihajlović, Slobodan Komljenović, Petrović [Miroslav Stević 74], Đorović, Jokanović, Stojković (c), Stanković [Dejan Govedarica 68], Jugović, Kovačević [Ognjenović 57], Mijatović.

The longest day of the year was another hot one, and Germany's veterans only lasted the pace because Yugoslavia took their foot off the pedal after going two up. They scored their first when Köpke was distracted by Stankovic's run and let a low cross flick his knee on the way behind him. It came back out off the far post, caught Jeremies in the chest, and barely crossed the line. The goal's generally credited to Stanković, who didn't appear to touch it.

Germany were uncertain in goal and central defence, where Thon, a converted midfielder, was usually absent – and they missed Hässler's cleverness in midfield. When Köpke made a horrible mess of Kovačevic's low cross, Stojković put the ball into an empty net. Surely this creaking German team didn't have the quality to add to their history of famous comebacks.

Silly question. Ziege, not fully recovered from injury, wasn't the dynamic influence he'd been in Euro 96 – so his substitution was a vital change. When Tarnat lashed in a long free kick, Mihajlović lifted a leg to send Kralj the

1930
1934
1938
1950
1954
1958
1962
1966
1970
1974
1978
1982
1986
1990
1994
1998
2002
2006

1930
1934
1938
1950
1954
1958
1962
1966
1970
1974
1978
1982
1986
1990
1994
1998
2002
2006

wrong way. Soon afterwards, Bierhoff's back-header from a corner was touched onto the bar by the keeper, but he wasn't kept out for long. The quality of Germany's crosses had been so poor (Klinsmann was constantly furious) that Bierhoff was made to look a blunt instrument again – but there'd never been any doubt about his power in the air: he equalised with an imperious header from a corner.

Matthäus came on to play his 22nd finals match, a new record. It was twenty years to the day since Vogts had won his last cap during the 1978 finals. Four German fans were imprisoned for leaving French policeman Daniel Nivel in a coma after the match, in scenes that were repeated in England's group.

---

21 June 1998 – Gerland, Lyons – 44,000 – Urs Meier (SWI)

IRAN   (1) 2
Estili 40, Mahdavikia 83

USA   (0) 1
McBride 87

IRAN Ahmed Reza Abedzadeh (c), Mahdavikia, Zarincheh [Naim Saadavi 77], Pashazadeh, Khakpour, Mohammedkhani [Mohammed Ali Peyravani 75], Estili, Bagheri, Daei, Azizi [Mansourian 74], Minavand Chal. USA Keller, Hejduk, Dooley (c) [Maisonneuve 82], Pope, Régis, Joe-Max Moore, Reyna, Jones, Brian McBride, Ramos [Stewart 57], Wegerle ['Preki' (Predrag Radosavljević) 57].

If this was the politically charged event we were told to expect, the teams did their best to diffuse it. A joint team photo, gifts exchanged by all 22 players, no hostility in the stadium or on the pitch. The USA hit a post through Reyna (very disappointing again) after 33 minutes and Régis after 73, and McBride scored with a deflected header when Abedzadeh missed a corner – but Iran's counter-attacks were decisive. Zarincheh's skilfully hooked cross was put away by Estili's

dropping header, and the stocky Mahdavikia confirmed the impression he'd made against Yugoslavia. Fast and full of running, he ran clear from halfway to shoot hard across Keller, who did well to get his fingers to the ball. In another breakaway, he made a good save from Daei, whose shot was kicked off the line by Régis. Iran had always seemed to want it more, but both sides reminded a few people that this was just a football match rather than an excuse to praise the Lord and pass the ammunition.

---

25 June 1998 – de la Mosson, Montpellier – 35,500 – Epifanio González (PAR)

GERMANY   (0) 2
Bierhoff 50, Klinsmann 57

IRAN   (0) 0

GERMANY Köpke, Wörns, Tarnat [Ziege 77], Matthäus, Kohler, Thomas Helmer, Thon [Hamann HT], Heinrich, Bierhoff, Hässler [Kirsten 69], Klinsmann (c). IRAN Abedzadeh (c), Mahdavikia, Zarincheh [Sirous Dinmohammedi 70], Pashazadeh, Mohammedkhani, Khakpour, Estili, Bagheri, Daei, Azizi, Minavand Chal.

The Germans came into the match with an average age of 31 years 328 days, a finals record – and 61 caps each, far too experienced for the latest minnows. If Germany didn't have a single really good chance in the first half, Iran didn't make one in the whole match. Bierhoff pounded in another header from Hässler's right-wing cross, then volleyed against the post for Klinsmann to throw himself forward and head into the empty net: his tenth finals goal from his only opportunity of the match. Helmer was rough on Mahdavikia, and Daei looked timid throughout the tournament. He went on to break Puskás' world record and become the first player to score 100 international goals – but only by scoring hat-tricks against Guam, Nepal, Lebanon, Laos and the

Maldives. Matthäus was immaculate when he reverted to sweeper in place of Thon, but the question of age looked likely to resurface against stronger opposition.

---

25 June 1998 – de la Beaujoire – Louis Fonteneau, Nantes – 39,000 – Gamal El-Ghandour (EGY)

YUGOSLAVIA	**(1) 1**	
Komljenović 3		
USA	**(0) 0**	

YUGOSLAVIA Kralj, Petrović, Komljenović, Đorović, Mihajlović, Jokanović, Stojković (c) [Dejan Savićević 62], Stanković [Brnović 54], Jugović, Milošević, Mijatović [Ognjenović 31].
USA Brad Friedel, Hejduk [Wynalda 64], Dooley (c) [Marcelo Balboa 82], Régis, Jones, Maisonneuve, Reyna, Burns, McBride, Moore [Preki 58], Stewart.

Like the Germans, Yugoslavia achieved identical results against the lesser teams. The USA hit a post again, this time through Hejduk's aimless cross after only twenty seconds or so – but once Mihajlović took another free kick, they were already in trouble. The shot went round a poorly placed wall, Friedel pushed it away, and Komljenović headed in gently from a narrow angle. It was all too obvious that Savićević, once the maestro at Milan, wasn't fully fit after injury.

GROUP F

	P	W	D	L	F	A	Pts
Germany	3	2	1	0	6	2	7
Yugoslavia	3	2	1	0	4	2	7
Iran	3	1	0	2	2	4	3
USA	3	0	0	3	1	5	0

Germany and Yugoslavia qualified for the second round.

GROUP G

Colombia, England, Romania (seeded), Tunisia.

---

15 June 1998 – Vélodrome, Marseilles – 54,587 – Masayoshi Okada (JPN)

ENGLAND	**(1) 2**	
Shearer 42, Scholes 89		
TUNISIA	**(0) 0**	

ENGLAND David Seaman, Sol Campbell, Graeme Le Saux, David Batty, Tony Adams, Gareth Southgate, Darren Anderton, Paul Ince, Alan Shearer (c), Teddy Sheringham [Michael Owen 85], Paul Scholes.
Glenn Hoddle.
TUNISIA Chokri El-Ouaer, Sami Trabelsi (c), Mounir Boukadida, Hatem Trabelsi [Tarek Thabet 79], Kaies Ghodbane, Khaled Badra, Adel Sellimi, Sirajeddine Chihi, Skander Souayeh [Zoubeir Baya HT], Clayton (Robeiro), Mehdi Ben Slimane [Imed Ben Younes 64].
Henryk Kasperczak (POL).

For some, this was almost an afterthought to the pre-match violence they came for. The night before, tear gas had been used to break up fights between rival fans. According to a *Guardian* editorial, 'the start of the trouble coincided with the arrival of a double-decker bus, sponsored by the *Sun*, playing the national anthem and handing out bowler hats.' According to the *Independent*, 'It seems that careful cropping was required to ensure that the ruckers sporting *Sun* bowlers were not seen by the paper's readers.' An hour before kick-off, England fans threw bottles at Tunisians. Just before it, some booed the Tunisian national anthem and didn't respect a minute's silence.

The match itself was far less acrimonious (though Sami Trabelsi manhandled Shearer all afternoon), mainly because it wasn't much of a contest. Tunisia looked the weakest and least

1998

ambitious team in the tournament so far, Ben Slimane round as a barrel – so England might have won with more to spare.

Scholes was unmarked when he headed Le Saux's cross straight at the keeper, who later did well to touch Sheringham's dipping volley onto the bar. Eventually Shearer headed Le Saux's free kick past an eccentric dive by the keeper, and Scholes ensured that Gascoigne wasn't missed. England's final ball wasn't too good, so they had to wait till the end for their clinching goal. Ince backheeled to Scholes, whose first instinct was to attempt a one-two 'but my first touch wasn't good enough'. He broke a tackle before whipping the ball inside the post from the edge of the area. Not bad for someone who used an inhaler every day.

There were debates as to whether Hoddle was picking his best available team, but the players had more trouble with the pitch than the opposition. The hard ground, another constant of the tournament, left Shearer and Adams with blistered feet after they'd worn studs instead of ribbed soles.

---

15 June 1998 – Gerland, Lyons – 37,572 – An-Yan Lim Kee Chong (MAU)

ROMANIA   **(1) 1**
Ilie 45

COLOMBIA   **(0) 0**

ROMANIA Bogdan Stelea, Dan Petrescu, Liviu Ciobotariu, Gabriel Popescu [Ovidiu Stânga 68], Iulian Filipescu, Gheorghe Popescu, Dorinel Munteanu, Constantin Gâlca, Viorel Moldovan [Radu Niculescu 85], Gheorghe Hagi (c) [Lucian Marinescu 76], Adrian Ilie. *Anghel Iordănescu.*

COLOMBIA Farid Mondragón, Wilmer Cabrera, Jorge Bermúdez, José Fernando Santa, Ever Palacios, Mauricio Serna, Harold Lozano, Freddy Rincón, Víctor Aristizábal [Adolfo Valencia HT], Carlos Valderrama (c), Faustino Asprilla [Leider Preciado 84]. *Hernán Darío Gómez.*

Colombia had failed to win any of their six internationals since qualifying, partly because they were still using the 36-year-old Valderrama as their orchestrator, and his passes were more unthreatening than ever. Asprilla, who was his usual petulant and provocative self, got little change out of the tall Filipescu and was sent home after making unflattering comments about the coach and not turning up for training. Even his own team didn't miss him.

A rough unsatisfying match was decided by a sumptuous goal. Hagi's backheel touched a defender on its way to Ilie on the left, and he cut outside Serna before showing great technique and confidence in digging the ball over the keeper with his right foot. Like his coach, Aristizábal had received death threats, apparently because someone didn't think he was worth his place in the team! No laughing matter among Colombians, who unfurled a banner with a photo of Andrés Escobar, shot dead for his own goal in 1994.

---

22 June 1998 – de la Mosson, Montpellier – 35,500 – Bernd Heynemann (GER)

COLOMBIA   **(0) 1**
Preciado 83

TUNISIA   **(0) 0**

COLOMBIA Mondragón, Cabrera, Bermúdez, Santa, Palacios, Serna [Jorge Bolano 62], Lozano, Rincón [Aristizábal 57], Valencia [Preciado 57], Valderrama (c), Anthony de Avila.
TUNISIA El-Ouaer, Thabet [Ghodbane 76], S Trabelsi (c), Ferid Chouchane, Clayton, Chihi, Riadh Bouazizi, Souayeh, Baya [Faycal Ben Ahmed 74], Ben Slimane, Sellimi [Ben Younes 68].

On another hot day, with the scoreboard urging spectators to keep drinking water, two non-tackling midfields allowed the opposition a string of chances. Mondragón punched the ball onto Bouazizi's shoulder and against the bar and turned Ben Slimane's header onto a post, Valencia headed Valderrama's corner against another, and de Avila hit one near the end. Valderrama rarely misplaced a pass, but did little damage until he shocked everyone by actually winning the ball. His superb angled through-ball sent Preciado past Trabelsi's desperate lunge for a low shot that El-Ouaer touched on its way in. Kasperczak became the third coach to be sacked before the tournament was over, while Colombia were left hoping that England and Romania didn't play out a draw later in the day.

---

22 June 1998 – Municipal, Toulouse – 37,500 – Marc Batta (FRA)

ROMANIA (0) 2
Moldovan 46, Petrescu 89

ENGLAND (0) 1
Owen 83

ROMANIA Stelea, Petrescu, Ciobotariu, Gab. Popescu, Filipescu, Gh. Popescu, Munteanu, Gâlca, Moldovan [Marius Lăcătuş 86], Hagi (c) [Stânga 73, Marinescu 84], Ilie.
ENGLAND Seaman, Gary Neville, Campbell, Le Saux, Batty, Adams, Anderton, Ince [David Beckham 33], Shearer (c), Sheringham [Owen 73], Scholes.

The crowd seemed to be 90% English, and there was still no escape from the tedious military obsession of Euro 96 (a band here played interminable renditions of the theme from a war film). But at least this time the opposing national anthem was heard in total, respectful silence.

On the pitch, Romania kept the ball so well that England looked uncomfortable in every department. Like Valderrama, Hagi was past his best, but there was no getting away from him. Within the first three minutes, he took his health in his hands by fouling Ince and was booked for tripping Campbell. He moaned at

the referee, shot wildly throughout the first half and did little in the second except stand on the left touchline – and make the opening goal. Wheeling away from Le Saux in receiving a throw-in on the right, he lobbed a cross over Adams for Moldovan to chest down and volley past Seaman. An injury to Southgate had brought in Neville, with his limited experience of playing in a back three. He should have stayed closer to Moldovan, who'd scored only one League goal for Coventry City that season.

In the first half, Ilie had chipped against the bar. In the second, Romania played keep-ball after taking the lead, and England looked unimaginative and overrated. Adams (once quoted as saying he'd had the potential to be another Beckenbauer) was shaky, Scholes and Sheringham invisible, and Filipescu did another good job, this time on Shearer, who was starved of service. But Beckham followed a quiet first half with some good passes in the second. One of them sent Shearer wide to put in a low cross from the right, Scholes turned Gheorghe Popescu, and the 18-year-old Owen got there first to volley in the loose ball.

Both sides would have settled for a draw, but Le Saux suddenly lost the duel with his Chelsea club mate Petrescu, whom he'd nutmegged earlier on. Munteanu's long ball from the left touchline was met by Petrescu's diagonal run into the box, where he chested the ball down and held off Le Saux with an elbow across the windpipe before shooting between Seaman's legs. Both of Romania's goals had been scored by their two players with English clubs.

There was still time for Owen to run forward in injury time and hit the post with a low shot from nearly 25 yards. In Bucharest an estimated 200,000 people came out onto the streets, including groups of teenagers chanting 'One two three, we peed on them.' Now England would be keeping everything crossed for the decider in Lens.

1998

26 June 1998 – Félix Bollaert, Lens – 41,275 – Arturo Brizio Carter (MEX)

ENGLAND   (2) 2
Anderton 20, Beckham 29

COLOMBIA (0) 0

ENGLAND Seaman, Neville, Le Saux, Ince [Batty 82], Campbell, Adams, Anderton [Rob Lee 79], Beckham, Shearer (c), Owen, Scholes [Steve McManaman 73]. COLOMBIA Mondragón, Cabrera, Bermúdez, Palacios, Serna [Hamilton Ricard HT], Antonio Moreno, Lozano, Rincón, Preciado [Valencia HT], Valderrama (c), de Avila [Aristizábal HT].

The usual disquiet before the match. Arrests and riot police. Nerves on it, too. With less than two minutes gone, Seaman hit a goal kick straight to Preciado, who couldn't control it. Colombia stoked the tension by keeping the ball well early on – but England had found their team and were never in danger.

When Moreno, who had a dreadful night, slipped and lost the ball, Owen's cross was headed back to the right by big Bermúdez, and Anderton did the rest. Control, one step, huge volley into the roof of the net at the near post, beating Mondragón by sheer power.

In front of a crowd that made this another virtual home game for England, Anderton was given too much room throughout the first half, with Beckham operating in the middle. Before the match, Mondragón had issued the predictable insult about Beckham being 'one of the Spice Girls' boyfriend'. Now he was beaten by a 30-yard free kick. It became Beckham's trademark in later years, but this was his only goal in his first 38 internationals.

Owen's sheer speed was a weapon in itself, but he often looked raw. Put completely clear by an instant pass from Shearer, he had time to do better than hit the ball straight at the keeper. But England were so comfortable at the back that Campbell felt free to come forward

in a run that took him past three players. Mondragón and Bermúdez had done well, but by now Valderrama was a parody of himself, and not just for his yellow fright wig. No-one made more passes in a career, but most of them were so short they only loaned you the ball. It was his 111th and last international, a record 109 as captain. After the match, he swapped shirts with Beckham – but if it was a mantle being handed over, the Spice Boy should have been disappointed if he didn't improve on it.

26 June 1998 – Stade de France, Saint-Denis, Paris – 80,000 – Eddie Lennie (AUS)

ROMANIA   (0) 1
Moldovan 72

TUNISIA   (1) 1
Souayeh pen 10

ROMANIA Stelea, Petrescu, Cristian Dulca [Gh. Popescu 31], Anton Dobos, Ciobotariu, Gâlca, Munteanu, Ilie Dumitrescu [Moldovan 67], Lăcătuş [Ilie HT], Hagi (c), Marinescu. TUNISIA El-Ouaer (c), S Trabelsi, Boukadida, Chouchane, Baya, Ghodbane [Thabet 83], Bouazizi, Chihi, Souayeh [Ben Younes 90], Sellimi, Ben Slimane [Riadh Jelassi 54]. *Ali Selmi*.

Romania were so light-hearted that the coach and his entire squad dyed their hair yellow, apart from the shaven-headed keeper. But the attitude may have spilled over onto the pitch. With some of their first-choice players rested, they struggled to recover from the early goal, Souayeh's first for Tunisia, a penalty awarded when Dulca brought down Sellimi. Eventually, with first place in the group under threat, Ilie's lob volley took out the keeper, and Chouchane's desperate back-header only reached Moldovan, who volleyed in. Mission accomplished, but a reminder that Romania weren't much more than first among equals.

GROUP G

	P	W	D	L	F	A	Pts
Romania	3	2	1	0	4	2	7
England	3	2	0	1	5	2	6
Colombia	3	1	0	2	1	3	3
Tunisia	3	0	1	2	1	4	1

Romania and England qualified for the second round.

GROUP H

Argentina (seeded), Croatia, Jamaica, Japan.

14 June 1998 – Municipal, Toulouse – 33,400 – Mario van der Ende (HOL)

ARGENTINA   **(1) 1**
Batistuta 28

JAPAN   **(0) 0**

ARGENTINA Carlos Roa, Roberto Sensini [José Chamot 73], Roberto Ayala, Javier Zanetti, Nélson Vivas, Diego Simeone (c), Matías Almeyda, Juan Sebastián Verón, Gabriel Batistuta, Ariel Ortega, Claudio López [Abel Balbo 62]. *Daniel Passarella.*
JAPAN Yoshikatsu Kawaguchi, Masami Ihara (c), Naoki Soma [Takashi Hirano 85], Yutaka Akita, Akira Narahashi, Eisuke Nakanishi, Motohiro Yamaguchi, Hiroshi Nanami, Masashi Nakayama [Wagner Lopes 66], Hidetoshi Nakata, Shoji Jo. *Takeshi Okada.*

Some of the pre-match publicity centred on the 21-year-old Nakata, the current Asian Footballer of the Year, who apparently claimed he was using the tournament as a shop window for a move to Europe. If so, it worked: he was bought by Perugia then Roma and

Parma – though perhaps more in the hope of selling replica shirts in Japan than for any outstanding talent. Here he gave the impression he was slumming it, standing out more for his burnt orange hair than any real penetration. Japan were the first country to have qualified for the finals thanks to a sudden death 'golden goal', but they'd left out their leading goalscorer Kazu Miura and couldn't take their chances against Argentina.

At the other end, against the run of play, the ball broke to Batistuta off Nanami, and he bided his time before chipping it coolly over the diving keeper. Batistuta also headed against a post in each half, a goalscoring threat that was the difference between the teams.

14 June 1998 – Félix Bollaert, Lens – 38,058 – Vítor de Melo Pereira (POR)

CROATIA   **(1) 3**
Stanić 26, Prosinečki 52, Šuker 68

JAMAICA   **(1) 1**
Earle 45

CROATIA Drazen Ladić, Zvonimir Soldo, Robert Jarni, Aljosa Asanović, Igor Štimac, Slaven Bilić, Dario Simić [Goran Vlaović 72], Robert Prosinečki, Davor Šuker, Zvonimir Boban (c), Mario Stanić. *Miroslav Blazević.*
JAMAICA Warren Barrett (c), Frank Sinclair, Ricardo Gardner, Robbie Earle [Andrew Williams 72], Ian Goodison, Onandi Lowe, Peter Cargill [Darryl Powell 69], Fitzroy Simpson, Theodore Whitmore, Deon Burton, Paul Hall [Walter Boyd 81]. *René Simôes (BRZ).*

The most colourful match of the tournament. Jamaica in yellow, Croatia in red and white checks, like tablecloths on a picnic lawn, with fans to match. In a group with three countries making their finals debut, Jamaica probably wished it included Italy, whose coach had complained about having to take part in a play off while weaker countries qualified automatically. He mentioned Jamaica by name.

The injury that kept Alen Bokšić out of the tournament led to Stanić, normally a wing back, playing up front with Šuker. Another main striker, Igor Cvitanović, had been left out of the squad for refusing to do extra laps in training. Even so, Croatia, who'd emerged in Euro 96, were expected to win without much trouble. Jamaica's forwards were so goal-shy that they'd recently set a world record by playing in five consecutive 0-0 draws.

Although Simić headed Earle's header off the line, Štimac shot against the bar and Stanić knocked in the rebound after disentangling the ball from under his legs. Soldo hit the bar soon afterwards, but then the 19-year-old Gardner crossed from the left – and Earle, still recovering from a broken toe, leapt up to head his first international goal at the age of 33. Cue the best half-time in World Cup history.

Croatia regained the lead with either a superb finish or a chunk of luck, a situation similar to Hagi's breathtaking goal against Colombia in 1994. Prosinečki dummied to cross from the left, cut back towards the goal line, and whipped a shot or cross over the keeper and in off Lowe's arm. He was the only player to score for two countries in the finals, though this one had once been part of the other (Yugoslavia in 1990). Almost from the kick-off, Jamaica missed a great chance for a second equaliser, Burton glancing a header wide – so Croatia were able to seal the match when Šuker chested down Stanić's cross and had his shot deflected over Barrett by Gardner. Jamaica were chasing shadows by the end and even their fans were put in the shade by the tablecloths on the terraces. Simões had threatened to resign when the size of his salary was revealed in a country where one in three people was officially classed as poor.

20 June 1998 – de la Beaujoire – Louis Fonteneau, Nantes – 39,000 – Ramesh Ramdhan (TRI)

CROATIA   **(0) 1**
Šuker 76

JAPAN   **(0) 0**

CROATIA Ladić, Soldo, Jarni, Asanović, Štimac [Vlaović HT], Bilić, Simić, Prosinečki [Silvio Marić 66], Šuker (c), Krunoslav Jurčić, Stanić [Igor Tudor 88].
JAPAN Kawaguchi, Ihara (c), Soma, Akita, Narahashi [Hiroaki Morishima 79], Nakanishi, Yamaguchi, Nanami [Lopes 83], Nakayama [Masayuki Okano 61], Nakata, Jo.

A demonstration of the gulf between the haves and the have-nots in this two-tier tournament. Like all the other teams who made up the numbers, Japan were neat and determined but lacked a striker who could operate at this level. In contrast, Šuker's left foot was a constant menace, hitting the bar with a clever volleyed lob and scoring the only goal. Like the Jamaican defence, Japan didn't spot him drifting away from the last man at the far post. The move had begun when Asanović intercepted a pass by Nakata, who was still showboating, wanting too much time on the ball. Croatia had generally looked sluggish but their beefy and experienced central defenders coped easily with Japan's rather unimaginative final ball, and even the grass was cut in squares, as if to match their kit!

---

21 June 1998 – Parc des Princes, Paris – 48,500 – Rune Pedersen (NOR)

ARGENTINA   **(1) 5**
Ortega 31, 54, Batistuta 72, 76, pen 83

JAMAICA   **(0) 0**

ARGENTINA Roa, Sensini [Vivas 24], Chamot, Ayala, Zanetti, Simeone (c) [Héctor Pineda 79], Almeyda, Verón, Batistuta, Ortega, López [Marcelo Gallardo 74].

JAMAICA Barrett (c), Sinclair, Christopher Dawes, Steve Malcolm [Boyd 62], Gardner, Goodison, Powell, Simpson, Whitmore [Earle 73], Burton [Cargill HT], Hall. SENT OFF: Powell 45.

So Cesare Maldini was right about Jamaica after all, although better sides would have struggled to cope with Ortega's buzzing skill. He lifted the ball deftly over Barrett after the referee had got out of the way for Verón to play a one-two with Simeone before making the final pass. When Powell was sent off for a second bookable offence, a foul on Ortega, it was impossible for Jamaica's ten men to hold out in that heat. Ortega clipped the ball over the keeper again after going between two defenders, then set up Batistuta with a neat square flick. All three of Batistuta's goals were scored with almost sadistic power, including a penalty when Dawes levered Ortega (who else?) to the ground. The kick was hit so hard that Barrett could only flinch. The veteran keeper, who looked intimidated whenever Ortega ran in on him or Batistuta lined up a shot, wasn't capped again. Batistuta was the only player to score a hat-trick in more than one finals tournament, each time with the help of a late penalty against the weakest team in the group. Blame was aimed at the Jamaican players with English clubs, but the home-grown crop wilted even more.

---

26 June 1998 – Parc Lescure, Bordeaux – 36,500 – Said Belqola (MOR)

ARGENTINA (1) 1
Pineda 36

CROATIA (0) 0

ARGENTINA Roa, Vivas, Pineda, Ayala, Zanetti [Simeone 67], Pablo Paz, Almeyda, Verón, Batistuta (c), Ortega [López 53], Gallardo [Sergio Berti 81]. CROATIA Ladić, Soldo, Jarni, Asanović, Bilić, Simić, Prosinečki [Štimac 67], Marić [Vlaović HT], Šuker, Boban (c), Stanić.

Both teams had already qualified, so there was skill but no great endeavour. As a result, neither Šuker nor Batistuta had a single half-chance in the whole match. After a first half-hour completely devoid of incident, Ortega's chip set Pineda free to chest the ball down before volleying inside the near post as the keeper came out. Kicks on the ankle, the tournament's favourite foul, were replaced by some enthusiastic shirt-pulling, and there were some quirky self-inflicted wounds: Štimac was the latest player to suffer from blistered feet, and Vlaović injured himself shooting against the bar.

---

26 June 1998 – Gerland, Lyons – 43,500 – Günter Benkö (AUT)

JAMAICA (1) 2
Whitmore 39, 54

JAPAN (0) 1
Nakayama 74

JAMAICA Aaron Lawrence, Sinclair, Gardner, Goodison (c), Malcolm, Dawes, Simpson [Earle 90], Whitmore, Lowe, Hall [Boyd 71], Marcus Gayle [Burton 80]. JAPAN Kawaguchi, Narahashi, Akita, Ihara (c), Soma, Norio Omura [Hirano 59], Nanami [Shinji Ono 79], Nakata, Yamaguchi, Jo [Lopes 59], Nakayama.

In the battle of the makeweights, Gayle headed on a long ball for Whitmore to shoot low past the keeper's right hand. He scored his second by cutting back onto his left foot when Simpson's through-ball set him free on the right. Narahashi side-footed a deep cross against the far post before Soma's long cross was met by a Lopes header which seemed to be aimed at goal but fell square for Nakayama, completely unmarked, to touch into the empty net. Whitmore later found his own level by playing for Hull City, Hall and Lowe for Rushden & Diamonds. Malcolm was only 30

1998

when he died in a car crash a few hours after playing for Jamaica in January 2001. In February 2005, Lowe was cleared of trying to smuggle crack cocaine into the UK.

GROUP H							
	P	W	D	L	F	A	Pts
Argentina	3	3	0	0	7	0	9
Croatia	3	2	0	1	4	2	6
Jamaica	3	1	0	2	3	9	3
Japan	3	0	0	3	1	4	0

Argentina and Croatia qualified for the second round.

2ND ROUND

27 June 1998 – Vélodrome, Marseilles – 60,000 – Bernd Heynemann (GER)

ITALY   (1) 1
Vieri 18

NORWAY   (0) 0

ITALY Pagliuca, Bergomi, Maldini (c), D Baggio, Cannavaro, Costacurta, Moriero [Di Livio 62], Di Biagio, Vieri, Albertini [Pessotto 72], Del Piero [Chiesa 77].
NORWAY Grodås (c), Berg, Bjørnebye, Leonhardsen [Strand 12, Solbakken 39], Eggen, Johnsen, Riseth, Rekdal, TA Flo, Mykland, H Flo [Solskjær 72].

This was the first finals match played under the golden goal rule, but Italy didn't need it. Di Biagio, in charge throughout, hit some excellent passes, including the one that sent Vieri away between two defenders. Stronger on his left foot, he took this chance well with his right, shooting low across the keeper. With the bearded little Mykland having another unproductive match, Italy should have killed the game off earlier, avoiding a scrappy last half-hour. Instead, although Del Piero showed some good touches, his shooting lacked snap. At the other end, Cannavaro played Tore-André Flo well but was grateful for a wonderful save by Pagliuca when Flo for once made his height tell, getting his head to Mykland's cross. Norway's three defeats in the finals have all been by Italy, including this one played in the same stadium as the match between the two countries sixty years earlier.

27 June 1998 – Parc des Princes, Paris – 48,500 – Marc Batta (FRA)

BRAZIL   (3) 4
César Sampaio 11, 26, Ronaldo pen 45, 70

CHILE   (0) 1
Salas 68

BRAZIL Taffarel, Cafú, Roberto Carlos, Dunga (c), Aldair [Gonçalves 77], Júnior Baiano, Leonardo, César Sampaio, Ronaldo, Rivaldo, Bebeto [Denílson 64].
CHILE Tápia, Fuentes, Ramírez [Marcelo Vega HT], Margas, Reyes, Mauricio Aros, Acuña [Luis Musrri 80], Cornejo, Zamorano (c), Sierra [Estay HT], Salas.

Despite the scoreline, the lasting picture was of Zamorano's face as he sang the national anthem. Psyched up from the start, he never stopped challenging in the air or holding the ball up with skill, never letting his head drop, a real Apache. The same went for his team mates, outgunned and out of luck as they were – but they failed to pick up César Sampaio at free kicks. He launched himself into an early header and pushed in a ground shot after a deflection, scoring from the first two chances Brazil made.

Chile had no width and only three attacking players, so there was no way back. Ronaldo hit

1930 1934 1938 1950 1954 1958 1962 1966 1970 1974 1978 1982 1986 1990 1994 **1998** 2002 2006 the post and bar as well as scoring twice. Tápia could have been sent off for bringing him down for the penalty, and he took his second coolly, waiting for the keeper to move before shooting across him. His toothy smile looked like becoming the image of the tournament. A fabulous run by Rivaldo, in which he beat three men before hitting a superb angled pass, ended with Júnior Baiano almost treading on the ball with only the keeper to beat.

Leonardo and Roberto Carlos looked out of place again, but Chile had only a Salas header to console them, after Taffarel had blocked a ball with his chest. In injury time, he saved a free kick to deny Zamorano the goal he deserved. Chile, back in the finals for the first time since 1982, still hadn't won a match in them since 1962, or away from home since 1950.

---

28 June 1998 – Félix Bollaert, Lens – 41,275 – Ali Mohammed Bujsaim (UAE)

FRANCE	**(0) (0) 1**

Blanc 113 *(golden goal)*

PARAGUAY	**(0) (0) 0**

FRANCE Barthez, Thuram, Lizarazu, Petit [Boghossian 70], Desailly, Blanc, Henry [Pires 65], Deschamps (c), Trezeguet, Djorkaeff, Diomède [Guivarc'h 77].
PARAGUAY Chilavert (c), Arce, Ayala, Gamarra, Sarabia, Benítez, Acuña, Enciso, Paredes [Caniza 75], Cardozo [Rojas FT], Campos [Yegros 56].

Reverting to type, Paraguay defended in depth, and did it supremely well, especially Gamarra, who apparently didn't commit a single foul throughout the tournament and ended it as probably the best central defender in the world. Man-for-man marking frustrated the French, who missed Zidane terribly. Deschamps, forced to try and make the play, embarrassed himself, through no great fault of his own. Diomède

wasn't the answer up front, Djorkaeff looked short of confidence, and Petit's thigh problem was yet another injury aggravated by the hard pitches.

So Paraguay were able to hold out into extra time, though they were relieved when Henry hit a post after outstripping the defence. The substitutions led to waves of French attacks, virtually a siege, but no real improvement. Then suddenly Trezeguet's cushioned header was met by Blanc's volley for the first golden goal in any World Cup. Chilavert, totally exposed, still managed to get part of his body in the way of the shot, defiant to the end. Class goalkeeper, leader and gourmet: the personality of the tournament. His opposite number Barthez enjoyed his 27th birthday, but only after the match.

---

28 June 1998 – Stade de France, Saint-Denis, Paris – 79,500 – Urs Meier (SWI)

DENMARK	**(2) 4**

Møller 2, B Laudrup 11, Sand 59, Helveg 76

NIGERIA	**(0) 1**

Babangida 77

DENMARK Schmeichel, Heintze, Colding, Helveg, Rieper, Høgh, Nielsen, Jørgensen, Peter Møller [Sand 59], M Laudrup (c) [Frandsen 84], B Laudrup [Wieghorst 78].
NIGERIA Rufai, Adepoju, Babayaro, Oliseh, Okechukwu (c), West, George, Ikpeba, Kanu [Yekini 65], Okocha, Lawal [Babangida 72].

For the Danes, almost a complete reversal of 1986. Very unimpressive so far, they were expected to lose to a more talented side, but instead exposed Nigeria as the sham they were, a team that made them look like world beaters.

The early goals settled the match. Jørgensen's excellent pass set Michael Laudrup free to flick the ball square towards the hefty Møller, who drove a confident left-footer

1930
1934
1938
1950
1954
1958
1962
1966
1970
1974
1978
1982
1986
1990
1994
1998
2002
2006

inside the near post. Then Møller's meaty free kick went under the jumping Okocha, Rufai blocked it, and Brian Laudrup smacked in the rebound.

After that, one-way traffic towards the Danish goal – but the third goal killed Nigeria off. Again Michael Laudrup was involved, breaking a tackle and scooping the ball forward for Sand to head sideways away from West and half-volley his first international goal less than half a minute after coming on. Then Rufai couldn't hold Jørgensen's shot and the ball found its way to Helveg, who smacked it high into the net. Babangida's volley beat Schmeichel's outstretched foot at the near post, but it was no consolation.

Nigeria had started the tournament with a scandalous request for a minute's silence for their military dictator Sani Abacha, who'd authorised the execution of dissident writer Ken Saro Wiwa as well as squirreling away £1.2 billion of his country's money. They ended it with a capitulation on the pitch that was even worse than in 1994. Rufai wasn't capped again after an international career which began in 1981; Ikpeba had a shocker; and when Oliseh complained of having to run the midfield on his own and described his team mates as 'circus artists', he was surely thinking of Okocha, the media's favourite at the group stage. Twice in the first half, his party tricks foxed Colding – but there was no end product at all. The following year, Okocha's £90,000-a-month wages at Paris Saint-Germain were 'in stark contrast to his poor performances and general apathy on the field', and in the 2000 African Cup of Nations Final he was 'static, never supported colleagues, and obliged Kanu to run himself to a standstill.'

Denmark, grateful for any contributions of this kind, would have been hoping for a few more in the next round, now that Brazil hadn't been able to disguise all their weaknesses against Chile.

29 June 1998 – de la Mosson, Montpellier – 35,000 – Vítor de Melo Pereira (POR)

GERMANY   **(0) 2**
Klinsmann 74, Bierhoff 86

MEXICO   **(0) 1**
Hernández 47

GERMANY Köpke, Wörns, Tarnat, Matthäus, Babbel, Helmer [Ziege 37], Hamann, Heinrich [Möller 58], Bierhoff, Hässler [Kirsten 74], Klinsmann (c).
MEXICO Campos, Pardo, Davino, Suárez, Palencia [Arellano 53], García Aspe (c) [Peláez 86], Lara, Hernández, Villa, Bernal [Carmona HT], Blanco.

Having come from behind in every match so far, Mexico made the mistake of taking the lead for the first time. Hernández, not altogether convincing so far despite his goals, kept marvellously cool in the penalty area to score, working his way round Tarnat and biding his time before jabbing the ball across Köpke.

On yet another hot day, the German midfield lacked flair (Hässler didn't come into it often enough) and missed the drive of Jeremies. Nevertheless they could have a penalty for a late tackle by Suárez on Helmer, and Bierhoff should have done better than head Hässler's cross against the bar. They would have gone 2-0 down but for two vital saves by Köpke, once when Blanco set up an easy chance for Hernández. But in the end noone was too surprised at the traditional comeback, though it owed a lot to poor Lara, who let Bierhoff's back-header squirt out behind him for Klinsmann to slide in and score, then was beaten to a cross by Bierhoff, who put another uncompromising header high into the net. Spirit had taken this lightweight Mexican side as far as it could, but luck was surely going to run out sometime for this superannuated German team.

Like Wieghorst of Denmark, Babbel missed the 2002 finals but was simply glad to be alive after recovering from GBS (Guillain-Barré Syndrome), which paralysed Wieghorst's breathing muscles, forcing him to use a ventilator, and left Babbel unable to walk or talk or close his eyelids.

---

29 June 1998 – Municipal, Toulouse – 37,500 – José María García-Aranda (SPA)

HOLLAND   (1) 2
Bergkamp 37, Davids 90

YUGOSLAVIA   (0) 1
Komljenović 48

HOLLAND van der Sar, Reiziger, Numan, Davids, Stam, F de Boer (c), R de Boer, Seedorf, Cocu, Bergkamp, Overmars.
YUGOSLAVIA Kralj, Mirković, Petrović, Komljenović, Đorović, Mihajlović [Niša Saveljić 78], Jokanović, Stojković (c) [Savićević 57], Mijatović, Jugović, Brnović.

Considering the talent on both sides, Yugoslavia's defensive attitude made this scrappier than it should have been. Mihajlović was impressive throughout, but Frank de Boer's excellent left foot sent a long ball down the inside-left channel, and Bergkamp pushed Mirković to the ground before shooting in at the near post under a goalkeeper who should have done better. Again Stojković was off the pace, although he did make the equaliser. His free kick, curled high to the far post, was met by Komljenović's header from much the same place as his goal against the USA.

The match turned on two incidents soon afterwards, and each time Yugoslavia lost out. First Stam held on to Jugović's shirt to give away a penalty. Six weeks earlier, Mijatović had looked one of the sharpest strikers in Europe when he scored the only goal of the European Cup Final. Here he hardly saw the ball in four matches, so Yugoslavia deprived themselves of a cutting edge up front. When his big

MATCHES SCORING GOALS

10	Jürgen Klinsmann	GER	1990–98
9	Uwe Seeler	GER	1958–70
9	Gerd Müller	GER	1970–74
9	Ronaldo	BRZ	1998–02
8	Helmut Rahn	GER	1954–58
8	Pelé	BRZ	1958–70
8	Jairzinho	BRZ	1970–74
8	Grzegorz Lato	POL	1974–82

chance came, he was probably rusty, blasting the penalty against the bar so hard it made the net shudder. Almost immediately, Bergkamp should have been sent off for pushing Mihajlović over and treading on his ribs. Instead Holland were at full strength when a series of corners led to their very late winner, the ball eventually coming back to Davids whose low left-footer touched Đorović on its way in. A very close thing (again Kralj got a touch) – but the tournament was better off for Holland still being in it.

---

30 June 1998 – Parc Lescure, Bordeaux – 34,700 – Javier Castrilli (ARG)

CROATIA   (1) 1
Šuker pen 45

ROMANIA   (0) 0

CROATIA Ladić, Simić, Jarni, Jurčić, Štimac, Bilić, Stanić [Tudor 82], Vlaović [Petar Krpan 76], Šuker, Boban (c), Asanović.
ROMANIA Stelea, Petrescu [Marinescu 76], Ciobotariu, Gab. Popescu [Niculescu 60], Filipescu, Gh. Popescu, Munteanu, Gâlca, Moldovan, Hagi (c) [Gheorghe Craioveanu 57], Ilie.

1998

The penalty was harshly awarded, after Asanovic had twisted away from Gabriel Popescu, and retaken after Boban encroached

1930
1934
1938
1950
1954
1958
1962
1966
1970
1974
1978
1982
1986
1990
1994
1998
2002
2006

in the D, Šuker hitting it low to the keeper's left each time. He put his fingertips to his neck before taking each kick. Checking his pulse rate, he said ('When it was 120, I knew I could control my nerves') – which is creative to say the least: he didn't have time to take a reading, and if he hadn't been able to keep his nerves in check, what would he have done, ask someone else to take the kick?

After that, like other teams in this round, Romania were exposed for their lack of bite. Croatia were able to sit back in the second half, easily absorbing the little that Hagi had to offer at this stage of his career. Some of the Croatian fans even turned their backs on the action to start their celebrations early.

---

30 June 1998 – Geoffroy Guichard, Saint-Étienne – 35,500 – Kim Milton Nielsen (DEN)

ARGENTINA   (2) (2) 2
Batistuta pen 5, Zanetti 45

ENGLAND   (2) (2) 2
Shearer pen 10, Owen 15
Argentina 4-3 pens.

ARGENTINA Roa, Chamot, Zanetti, Almeyda, Vivas, Ayala, Simeone (c) [Berti 91], Verón, Batistuta [Hernán Crespo 68], Ortega, López [Gallardo 68].
ENGLAND Seaman, Neville, Le Saux [Southgate 71], Ince, Adams, Campbell, Anderton [Batty 97], Beckham, Shearer (c), Owen, Scholes [Paul Merson 78].
SENT OFF: Beckham 47.
PENALTY SHOOT-OUT: Berti 1-0, Shearer 1-1, Crespo saved, Ince saved, Verón 2-1, Merson 2-2, Gallardo 3-2, Owen 3-3, Ayala 4-3, Batty saved.

Given the history between the two countries, it was predictable that both national anthems would be heckled – but it didn't set the tone for a match had something for everyone.

The first half alone was overflowing. Seaman, who conceded the first penalty by arriving late on Simeone, almost kept out Batistuta's kick.

Owen charged into Ayala to earn the equaliser, which put an end to Argentina's run of eight successive clean sheets – then scored the goal that changed his life.

Taking Beckham's pass past Chamot, he outpaced him on his way through to the last defender. Adams was scathing about Ayala's positioning ('square on and flat-footed . . . allowing him to go to his right rather than forcing him left') – but he was understandably wary of Owen's pace by now, and it shouldn't detract too much from the swift swerve and finish, the ball steered high across the keeper.

Seven minutes from half-time, Scholes arrived at speed to meet Shearer's back-header with a low left-footer that went just wide of the far post. A difficult chance that had to be taken instantly, it might have settled the match there and then. Instead, in injury time, Argentina equalised with an expertly-worked free kick. Batistuta ran over the ball, Verón pushed it to the right of the wall, and Zanetti emerged from behind it to pivot and shoot left-footed beyond Seaman.

Pulse rates barely had time to regulate themselves. In the second minute of the second half, Simeone barged Beckham from behind then appeared to tread on him as he lay prone. Beckham responded with a flick of his leg, catching Simeone on the calf. Simeone fell back as if caught in a mantrap, and the referee made the worst of several important mistakes by showing a ridiculously harsh red card.

After his goal against Colombia, Beckham had been photographed in a triumphant pose, engagement ring showing, a moment when he had it all. Now it was time to face the other twin imposter. Vilified throughout the following season, he ended it by winning the Treble of League, FA Cup and European Cup, and the last-gasp free kick that took England to the 2002 finals made him a national hero. But for now his absence pushed the team into all-out defence just when Owen was giving them an option at the other end.

England's rearguard action was one of the bravest and most composed in any World Cup. Campbell, colossal in every sense, headed in from a corner with nine minutes left, only for the goal to be disallowed because Shearer had used an elbow on the keeper's head. Campbell's face was a picture: rapture followed by panic as Argentina charged down the other end and almost scored while England were still celebrating. Campbell didn't score an international goal until his 47th match – but at least it was England's next in the finals.

In extra time, the referee ignored Chamot's unintentional handball as he jumped with Shearer in the penalty area. When Hoddle brought on Batty five minutes later, he seemed to have settled for penalties, a wry irony.

Before that, even with ten men, England might have given themselves a chance to win it. Adams wasn't the only one to wonder if they might have done better to take off Shearer, no longer the scary striker who'd finished as top scorer in the last finals of Euro 96. According to Graham Kelly, the FA chief executive at the time, Shearer had threatened to drop out of the World Cup squad if charges were brought against him after he'd appeared to tread on Leicester City's Neil Lennon. They weren't (Lennon: 'It shows you there are some players who are untouchable') – but someone should have taken Shearer at his word: here in France all he really had to offer was aggression, and that was ultimately a liability.

Following the agonies of 1990 and Euro 96, the penalty shoot-out went the way most England fans feared it would, even after Seaman had saved Argentina's second kick. Ince had been prodigious, especially in extra time ('I love tackling. It's better than sex.') – but didn't have much of a pedigree as a penalty taker. Nor did Batty, only more so: 'It's the first

one I've ever taken in my life.' While England were let down again by this lack of preparation, Argentina won a World Cup shoot-out for the third time out of three, matching West Germany's record.

Others who enjoyed the moment probably included Le Saux's Argentinian wife and the whole of Marseilles, who wouldn't have the English fans back for the quarter-final. Roa, who made two saves in the shoot-out, later retired from football to follow his religion. And yes, Berti came on a minute after the start of extra time.

QUARTER-FINALS

3 July 1998 – Stade de France, Saint-Denis, Paris – 77,000 – Hugh Dallas (SCO)

| **FRANCE** | (0) (0) 0 |
| **ITALY** | (0) (0) 0 |

France 4-3 pens.

FRANCE Barthez, Thuram, Lizarazu, Petit, Desailly, Blanc, Karembeu [Trezeguet 64], Deschamps (c), Guivarc'h [Henry 64], Zidane, Djorkaeff.
ITALY Pagliuca, Bergomi, Maldini (c), D Baggio [Albertini 52], Cannavaro, Costacurta, Moriero, Di Biagio, Vieri, Del Piero [R Baggio 67], Pessotto [Di Livio 90].
PENALTY SHOOT-OUT: Zidane 1-0, R Baggio 1-1, Lizarazu saved, Albertini saved, Trezeguet 2-1, Costacurta 2-2, Henry 3-2, Vieri 3-3, Blanc 4-3, Di Biagio hit bar.

Zidane was back, and the Italians knew all about him from Serie A – so they were even more defensive than usual and France were better going forward. But both sides lacked a finisher against defences like these. Desailly blotted out Vieri, Costacurta and Cannavaro did well, and Maldini was still the best left-back in the world despite competition from Lizarazu and Numan.

Guivarc'h was the latest attempt to solve the problem up front, but his main contribution was an elbow in the face that forced Cannavaro

to wear a net dressing to keep an eye patch in place. Moriero, a skilful wide player, was

another disappointment. Roberto Baggio came close to pilfering a win in extra time when his lob passed just wide of the far post, but he was

only on the pitch because Del Piero had again been a handicap. Once the golden boy of Italian

football, he was the leading scorer in that season's European Cup; perhaps as a result, he

looked leg-weary here. Subsequent injuries set him back, and two unforgivable pieces of finishing cost Italy the Final of Euro 2000.

Djorkaeff was just as bad here, perpetrating a truly terrible miss by shooting weakly wide of

the far post. Rumour had it that Desailly and Deschamps wanted him dropped, and he didn't take part in the shoot-out even though

he was the team's penalty taker ('I was too tired'), leaving the job to two 20-year-olds,

Trezeguet and Henry. As so often in these things, the decisive kick was missed by one of the losing side's best players. Italy set a finals

record by going out on penalties for the third time in a row, leaving Paolo Maldini in despair: 'I have played 19 matches in the finals and lost

only one in normal time, yet I have not won anything.' He hoped to celebrate his 34th

birthday in the last-chance saloon of 2002.

The following day, Deschamps' cousin

Nathalie Tauziat lost in the Wimbledon singles final.

3 July 1998 – de la Beaujoire – Louis Fonteneau, Nantes – 35,500 – Gamal El-Ghandour (EGY)

BRAZIL   **(2) 3**
Bebeto 10, Rivaldo 26, 60

DENMARK   **(1) 2**
Jørgensen 2, B Laudrup 50

BRAZIL Taffarel, Cafú, Roberto Carlos, Dunga (c), Júnior Baiano, Aldair, Leonardo [Émerson (da Rosa) 71], César Sampaio, Ronaldo, Rivaldo ['Zé Roberto' (José Roberto da Silva) 87], Bebeto [Denílson 64].
DENMARK Schmeichel, Heintze, Colding, Helveg [Schjønberg 87], Rieper, Høgh, Nielsen [Tøfting HT], Jørgensen, Møller [Sand 66], M Laudrup (c), B Laudrup.

Again Denmark scored very early on, the Laudrups combining at a free kick to set up Jørgensen's first goal for Denmark – but this time the opposition wasn't as brittle as they might have hoped. Brazil always seemed to have another gear, and although Schmeichel thought 'Ronaldo was a disaster. He lost the ball almost every time he got it', he still made Brazil's first two goals despite suffering from tendonitis. His superb angled pass set Bebeto free to run through the middle and shoot low across Schmeichel, who'd come out as far as the penalty spot.

As with other successful teams in the tournament, both sides stationed a holding player in front of the back four. One of them (Helveg) allowed the other (Dunga) to rob him, and a short pass to Ronaldo was followed by another which put Rivaldo clear to chip the ball over the diving Schmeichel.

Some teams would have lain down, but Denmark kept passing the ball – and Brazil gifted them their second goal. Roberto Carlos again tested everyone's patience with some preposterous long-range free kicks, and his comic rendition of an overhead kick presented the ball to Brian Laudrup, who half-volleyed it into the roof of the net. But the red sea kept parting in the middle, and Rivaldo ran through unchallenged to score from 25 yards. The ground shot was accurate enough to go just inside the far post, but it was a surprise to see Schmeichel beaten this way for the second time in the match.

Even then Denmark didn't give up. An outstanding move involving Helveg, Sand and Rieper nearly brought another equaliser, as did Rieper's last-minute header. If he'd timed his jump slightly better, he might have scored instead of hitting the bar. The Danes had come that close after progressing further than ever before, not with one of their best teams but one that never stopped playing its football. It was the end of Michael Laudrup's often frustrating international career, which had begun on his 18th birthday in 1982 but at least ended in a bright autumn, he and his brother matching the Brazilians for skill.

---

4 July 1998 – Vélodrome, Marseilles – 55,000 – Arturo Brizio Carter (MEX)

HOLLAND   **(1) 2**
Kluivert 12, Bergkamp 89

ARGENTINA   **(1) 1**
López 17

HOLLAND van der Sar, Reiziger, Numan, Davids, Stam, F de Boer (c), R de Boer [Overmars 64], Cocu, Kluivert, Bergkamp, Jonk.
ARGENTINA Roa, Chamot [Balbo 90], Zanetti, Almeyda [Pineda 67], Sensini, Ayala, Simeone (c), Verón, Batistuta, Ortega, López.
SENT OFF: Numan 76, Ortega 87.

Although it wasn't quite regarded as a classic at the time, this was one of the great World Cup matches, full of deluxe ball control and invention. The Dutch dominated possession in the second half but Argentina were always dangerous on the break.

And there was no shortage of incident. Jonk (after less than five minutes), Ortega (from 30 yards) and Batistuta (after cutting inside Frank de Boer) all hit a post. Ortega, otherwise contained by Davids, was about to be shown a yellow card for diving when it changed to red after he brushed van der Sar's chin with his head as he got up (there was that much difference in height). Numan had been sent off for a second bookable offence, a hard late tackle that put Simeone on a stretcher, although it may have looked on the right side of acceptable to some English eyes.

The first Dutch goal was beautifully made and finished. Ronald de Boer swerved past Batistuta and drilled the ball to the left, where Bergkamp fell back in executing a velvety header across goal, ushering Kluivert in to touch the ball across the diving Roa. But Verón was one of the playmakers of the tournament, sinewy and understated, never wasting a ball. From one of his many long passes, López sprang the offside trap, hesitated, then rolled the ball under the keeper's leg for Argentina's 100th finals goal.

López was a constant menace, but Batistuta again couldn't prove he was anything more than a rabbit killer at this level: none of his ten finals goals were scored from open play against strong opposition. Here he got no change from a much improved Stam, so Holland were able to go forward and win the match. If their first goal had been merely superb, the second was one of the all-time greats. Frank de Boer's stretch limo of a pass travelled into the right-hand depths of the penalty area, where Bergkamp brought it down, turned sweetly inside Owen's victim Ayala and volleyed high across the keeper. It was his 36th goal for Holland, breaking the record set by Faas Wilkes in 1961. Bergkamp's celebration against a sea of waving orange was one of the sights of the season, a grander version of scenes at Wimbledon on the same day, when Dutch tennis players Jacco Eltingh and Paul Haarhuis won the men's doubles final.

1930
1934
1938
1950
1954
1958
1962
1966
1970
1974
1978
1982
1986
1990
1994
1998
2002
2006

1930
1934
1938
1950
1954
1958
1962
1966
1970
1974
1978
1982
1986
1990
1994

1998

2002
2006

4 July 1998 – Gerland, Lyons – 39,100 – Rune Pedersen (NOR)

CROATIA   (1) 3
Jarni 45, Vlaović 80, Šuker 85

GERMANY   (0) 0

CROATIA Ladić, Simić, Jarni, Štimac, Soldo, Bilić, Stanić, Vlaović [Marić 83], Šuker, Boban (c), Asanović.
GERMANY Köpke, Wörns, Tarnat, Matthäus, Kohler, Jeremies, Hamann [Olaf Marschall 79], Heinrich, Bierhoff, Hässler [Kirsten 69], Klinsmann (c).
SENT OFF: Wörns 40.

There are limits to how many times you can keep making these comebacks on ageing legs, especially when you're missing a pair. Germany could have done without Wörns' red card for a late tackle on Šuker, but they might have held out for penalties like England against Argentina if they hadn't conceded a goal deep into first-half injury time. Jarni hit a low cross shot from outside the penalty area to score his only goal in an eventual 81 internationals, still the national record – and Germany faced a purgatorial second half.

Jeremies was all willingness and lung power, and his team mates showed great courage. They lacked creativity but also luck: with the score still 1-0, Hamann's fierce deflected shot hit a post. Bierhoff, battered by Simić and Štimac, was nevertheless dominant in the air again – but although Klinsmann didn't miss a goalscoring chance in the tournament, he had only three, and couldn't get into this match, his last for Germany. He finished a superlative career with a winner's medal in the World Cup and European Championship, the Footballer of the Year trophy in England, and 47 international goals – but none of his last eight had been scored against a major footballing country, and there was talk of a falling-out with Möller, whose talent was missed.

Vlaović's low cross-shot from the right was a mirror image of Jarni's goal, and Šuker even scored with his right foot, after cutting inside Heinrich. World Cup greats like Matthäus, Klinsmann, Kohler and Hässler deserved a better ending than this (it was hardly their fault that the new generation wasn't as good) – but the only undignified exit was made by some English journalists, saddoes to a man, who jeered the team after the match, even though the Germans had gone further than England in every World Cup since 1966, a sequence that shows no sign of ending.

SEMI-FINALS

7 July 1998 – Vélodrome, Marseilles – 54,000 – Ali Mohammed Bujsaim (UAE)

BRAZIL   (0) (1) 1
Ronaldo 46

HOLLAND   (0) (1) 1
Kluivert 86
Brazil 4-2 pens.

BRAZIL Taffarel, 'Zé Carlos' (José Carlos de Almeida), Roberto Carlos, Dunga (c), Aldair, Júnior Baiano, Leonardo [Émerson 85], César Sampaio, Ronaldo, Rivaldo, Bebeto [Denílson 69].
HOLLAND van der Sar, Reiziger [Winter 56], Cocu, Jonk [Seedorf 111], Stam, F de Boer (c), R de Boer, Davids, Kluivert, Bergkamp, Zenden [van Hooijdonk 74].
PENALTY SHOOT-OUT: Ronaldo 1-0, F de Boer 1-1, Rivaldo 2-1, Bergkamp 2-2, Emerson 3-2, Cocu saved, Dunga 4-2, R de Boer saved.

REFEREES: SENDINGS-OFF

7	Arturo Brizio Carter	MEX	1994–98
5	Joël Quiniou	FRA	1986–90–94
4	Jamal Al-Sharif	SYR	1986–90–94

Immediately after a cagey first half, Rivaldo's long ball found Ronaldo in the vacant inside-left channel, and the left-foot shot went under van der Sar's legs for a goal that seemed to stop the Dutch in their tracks. They took an age getting back into it, partly because Dunga did another expert covering job, partly because Overmars hadn't recovered from injury, so Roberto Carlos was spared a serious examination against pace. Free to come forward as he liked, he hit some more dreadful crosses and one laughable 40-yard free kick all the way along the ground into the keeper's arms. On the other flank, little Zé Carlos made a bad start to his international career, regularly beaten by Zenden. Hard to understand why Holland didn't attack him more in the second half.

Davids got a toe in from behind when Ronaldo was clean through and a goal looked certain. At the other end, Kluivert should probably have scored when van Hooijdonk's return ball sent him clear – but he eventually got the headed goal he deserved, climbing way above the defence to attack Ronald de Boer's cross, just reward for his class and persistence.

Brazil created the better chances in extra time, two wasted by Roberto Carlos, one saved by Frank de Boer, superb throughout, who made a wonderful saving tackle between Ronaldo's legs. Another of his long passes gave Kluivert a chance, and Stam was an industrial-size Caesar again – but the Dutch probably suspected they needed to settle it before the dreaded shoot-out. They've never won one, even after a Euro 2000 semi-final held at home, so it was no great surprise when Taffarel, winning his 100th cap, saved two of their kicks. Frank de Boer gave his twin an earful for not hitting his shot hard enough, but penalties probably wouldn't have been necessary if Bergkamp had been anywhere near his best.

Instead, kept at bay by a pack of defenders on the edge of the area, he went missing in action, just when Holland needed him most and immediately after his great game three days earlier. His well-known fear of flying, the result of a bumpy flight during the 1994 finals, would have kept him out of the 2002 tournament even if Holland had qualified, so his international career fell just short of the highest peaks. The following season, his missed penalty in an FA Cup semi-final helped Manchester United on the way to their Treble.

---

8 July 1998 – Stade de France, Saint-Denis, Paris – 76,000 – José María García-Aranda (SPA)

FRANCE (0) 2
Thuram 47, 69

CROATIA (0) 1
Šuker 46

FRANCE Barthez, Thuram, Lizarazu, Petit, Desailly, Blanc, Karembeu [Henry 30], Deschamps (c), Guivarc'h [Trezeguet 69], Zidane, Djorkaeff [Lebœuf 75].
CROATIA Ladić, Šimić, Jarni, Štimac, Soldo, Bilić, Stanić [Prosinečki 89], Vlaović, Šuker, Boban (c) [Marić 65], Asanović.
SENT OFF: Blanc 74.

A similar story to the first semi. A banner, attempting a pun that didn't work, urged the

MATCHES

25	Lothar Matthäus	GER	1982–98
23	Paolo Maldini	ITA	1990–02
21	Uwe Seeler	GER	1958–70
21	Władysla Żmuda	POL	1974–86
21	Diego Maradona	ARG	1982–94
20	Grzegorz Lato	POL	1974–82
British Isles			
17	Peter Shilton	ENG	1982–90

1930
1934
1938
1950
1954
1958
1962
1966
1970
1974
1978
1982
1986
1990
1994
1998
2002
2006

1930
1934
1938
1950
1954
1958
1962
1966
1970
1974
1978
1982
1986
1990
1994
1998
2002
2006

French team to *Fête Nous Rever*, make us dream. Both sides accomplished the first part by inducing sleep. But at least one drab half was followed by a feature of the tournament, a goal in the first thirty seconds of the other. Asanović's classy angled pass sent Šuker clear to toe the ball firmly under Barthez, the only goal France conceded in open play in the competition.

If Croatia had been able to hold the lead for any length of time, against a team struggling for goals . . . instead Boban loitered near his own penalty area, giving Thuram time to rob him and take a return pass from Djorkaeff before shooting across Ladić, atonement for having played Šuker onside. Then Thuram edged Jarni off the ball before scoring with his left foot from the corner of the penalty area. Some welcome history was repeating itself for the French. In the European Championships back in 1984, another full-back, Jean-François Domergue, scored his only two goals for France to turn a major semi-final after they'd been a goal down at home. By the end of 2005, these were the only goals Thuram had scored in 110 internationals.

In a poor match, Zidane disappeared in the second half as he tended to do on the big occasion, and Djorkaeff's positive thinking didn't help: 'I know I'm going to score . . . it's a kind of premonition . . . I may have only a couple of chances but I'm going to score.' He didn't; he had another shocker, as did Guivarc'h – and although Trezeguet would go on to score the goal that won Euro 2000, neither he nor Henry were ready yet, so France's chronic striking problem persisted.

The other main talking point was Blanc's stupid sending-off for flicking Bilić on the chin. Bilić disgracefully reacted by collapsing with a hand to his eye, then came up with an even more grotesque apologia: 'I know I held my head as I fell, but I do that even if I have injured my knee.' As Blanc went off, he touched the grass, made the sign of the cross and kissed his fingers. He wouldn't be there to conduct his usual ritual of kissing Barthez's bald head before the Final. Small mercies. Henry escaped a booking despite elbowing Jarni in the head, drawing blood and necessitating a net bandage. As in 1994, both semifinals were won by the teams with an extra day's rest. The organisers got the Final they wanted, but not on a level playing field.

3RD-PLACE FINAL

11 July 1998 – Parc des Princes, Paris – 45,500 – Epifanio González (PAR)

CROATIA   (2) 2
Prosinečki 13, Šuker 36

HOLLAND   (1) 1
Zenden 21

CROATIA Ladić, Soldo, Jarni, Štimac, Bilić, Stanić, Prosinečki [Vlaović 78], Asanović, Šuker, Boban (c) [Tudor 86], Jurčić.
HOLLAND van der Sar, Cocu [Overmars HT], Numan, Jonk, Stam, F de Boer (c), Davids, Kluivert, Seedorf, Bergkamp [van Hooijdonk 58], Zenden.

When Jarni cut in from the left, Prosinečki took his square pass and turned Numan before scoring with a low cross-shot. Zenden held off Jarni in a run inside then hit a convulsive left-footer, and van der Sar was wrong-footed by Šuker's first-time ground shot. Croatia were widely praised for finishing third on their finals debut, but they might have done even better if Bokšić had been there as a support striker. As it was, Šuker picked up the consolation prize of tournament top scorer, thanks to a goal in a match played after his team had been eliminated. Meanwhile Vieri scored five, all from open play, in four matches. The logic's escapable.

FINAL

---

12 July 1998 – Stade de France, Saint-Denis, Paris – 75,000 – Said Belqola (MOR)

FRANCE   (2) 3
Zidane 27, 45, Petit 90

BRAZIL   (0) 0

FRANCE Barthez, Thuram, Lizarazu, Petit, Desailly, Lebœuf, Karembeu [Boghossian 57], Deschamps (c), Guivarc'h [Dugarry 66], Zidane, Djorkaeff [Vieira 75].
BRAZIL Taffarel, Cafú, Roberto Carlos, Dunga (c), Aldair, Júnior Baiano, Leonardo [Denílson HT], César Sampaio [Edmundo 74], Ronaldo, Rivaldo, Bebeto.
SENT OFF: Desailly 67.

The decisive contest within a contest, between Ronaldo and the French back four, simply wasn't one. Theories behind his pre-match collapse ranged from an epileptic fit, through overdoses of painkillers throughout the tournament, to allegations of interference in team affairs by Nike, the Brazilian federation's sponsors. The joke in Brazil was that 'to bear Roberto Carlos in the same room for 53 days was too much for him'. The feisty Edmundo was originally included in the team, only for Ronaldo to arrive at the stadium with less than an hour to spare. The effect on the team's morale was all too obvious.

As a result, France were never in danger, and would have won by an unthinkable margin if they'd taken their chances. Guivarc'h, about to become a bad buy for Newcastle United, should have scored in the first few minutes when sent clear on goal, then sliced the ball high and wide when Cafú's back pass fell short.

His replacement Dugarry also missed when clean through, but his team could afford it by then.

Before the tournament, Roberto Carlos had been arrogance itself in interviews. During it, his crossing was invariably useless, and some of his free kicks were so bad they looked like a time-wasting measure. Here in the Final, he gave France the chance to open the scoring, kicking the flag in frustration after his poor control had conceded a corner. Petit hit it to the near post, where Zidane attacked it like a hammerhead. Another inswinging corner to the near post, this time by Djorkaeff from the left, was met by another downward header by Zidane. Roberto Carlos, covering on the line, could only hold his hands up in surrender.

Both of Zidane's headers were firm and authentic, but they came from dead ball kicks, the most basic situations to defend – and if he was an unlikely bet as the only player to score two headed goals in a World Cup Final, Leonardo wasn't any more obvious as a marker likely to beat him in the air. When the second goal went in, he was otherwise occupied, involved in a collision with Dunga. Brazil's defending was just about the worst ever seen in a Final.

Earlier in the year, Tostão predicted that Júnior Baiano would soon be regarded as the best centre-back in the world – or the worst. He didn't play for Brazil again, though he resurfaced in club football with bans for cocaine use and punching an opponent. Taffarel too wasn't capped again, after winning 101 caps and a World Cup winner's medal without always looking the part.

Juninho Paulista, of Middlesbrough fame, left out of the squad after a serious ankle injury, had to watch the left-footed Leonardo struggle to fill the right-sided midfield position. After the red card that kept him out of the 1994 Final, Leonardo had no chance of doing

1930
1934
1938
1950
1954
1958
1962
1966
1970
1974
1978
1982
1986
1990
1994

1998

2002
2006

1930
1934
1938
1950
1954
1958
1962
1966
1970
1974
1978
1982
1986
1990
1994
1998
2002
2006

himself justice now. With Ronaldo barely there even in body, France could smother the midfield and wait for their chances.

They won the Cup without a goal from their front men in their last five matches, with virtually no contribution from Djorkaeff, and only sporadic interventions from Zidane. They were carried through by the workrate and reliability of Deschamps and Petit in midfield, and above all the best back four of all time.

Zidane was voted European Footballer of the Year, an award that should have embarrassed him. Thuram was the best player in the tournament, with Desailly not far behind (his red card for arriving late on Cafú was just an aberration). Lizarazu, a dead ringer for the singer kd lang, was a motorised all-rounder on the left, the unfortunate Blanc as elegant as ever. They protected Barthez so well that he could get away with being a shot stopper rather than an all-round keeper (his errors at Manchester United were a talking point of the 2001–02 season). In the 27 matches they started together as a back four, they never finished on the losing side. France set a record by winning the trophy while conceding only two goals, one of them a dubious penalty.

In injury time at the end of the Final, Denílson hit the top of the crossbar when Lebœuf gave him too much room – but then Vieira ushered Petit through to slip a cross-shot just inside the far post. Everything Petit touched turned to gold that season. This was France's 1,000th goal in official internationals; he and Vieira won the League and FA Cup with Arsenal; and during an end-of-season holiday he put a ten-franc coin in a slot machine and walked off with £17,000.

In contrast, Belqola died during the 2002 finals at the age of 45 – and the bad times were only just beginning for Ronaldo, who was out injured for two years before the 2002 finals. One or two Frenchmen may also have had mixed feelings about the outcome. Eric Cantona had referred to the captain as a water carrier, Zidane's gofer. Deschamps proved it was still the age of Aquarius by matching Beckenbauer's feat of lifting the World Cup and European Championship. Cantona had enjoyed himself in an English league without many holding players in midfield, but won nothing in Europe.

One of the main benefits of the racial mix in the French squad was the way it stuck in the craw of Jean-Marie Le Pen, leader of the right-wing National Front. Quoted as saying that the World Cup, like the Holocaust, was no more than a historical 'detail', he had to face the fact that it had been won by players born in Guadeloupe, Ghana, New Caledonia, Senegal and French Guiana, or of Algerian, Armenian and Polish stock, as well as Basques and blond Normans. Time to contrive an original response. He'd always recognised, he said, that France could be 'composed of different races and religions' so long as they displayed the proper level of patriotism. Of course he had.

An equally prominent figure was just as unenthusiastic. Régis Fassier, the actor inside the costume of the tournament mascot Footix, a woolly cockerel, didn't receive many invitations to appear at the matches. 'It's sad for the spectators,' he complained, 'and personally I'm pissed off.'

As for the finals as a whole, enlargement didn't lead to any improvement. There were too many matches that smacked of a tournament within a tournament: Jamaica v Japan, Iran v USA, South Africa v Saudi Arabia. We'd had enough of seeing South Korea run all day and Cameroon collect red cards, and some of the successes of 1994 took steps backwards: Nigeria, Romania, Bulgaria, the Saudis. There was the usual quota of eye-catching goals, but also too many defensive teams involved in dreary matches – and it was hard to revel in a competition won by the home team, especially

COACHING SPANS

yrs	days			
28	21	Mário Zagallo	BRZ	1970–98
24	6	Sepp Herberger	WG	1938–62
24	3	Karl Rappan	SWI	1938–62
20	23	Gaston Barreau	FRA	1934–54
20	2	Lajos Baróti	HUN	1958–78

Barreau was a selector, not a coach as such. He was also in charge in 1930 but didn't make the trip to Uruguay.

Herberger was also assistant coach in 1934.

LEADING GOALSCORERS 1998

6	Davor Šuker	CRO	1 pen
5	Christian Vieri	ITA	
5	Gabriel Batistuta	ARG	2 pen

The leading scorers in the last six tournaments had each scored six goals.

one that reinforced its midfield with an extra full-back (Karembeu) in the Final.

The additional African and Asian teams didn't add much to the mix, but then nor did most of the extra Europeans. FIFA no doubt enjoyed the extra revenue – but although the format was based on the much-loved 1970 finals, a place in France 98 was devalued by the fact that twice as many teams were in it.

Still, it takes more than this kind of grumble to stop it being the people's game. In one location, 'about 400 teenagers smashed furniture, television sets and windows . . . at least three people were injured in four hours of battles that followed as guards and 200 riot police tried to restore order.' English and Tunisian fans in Marseilles? No, youths at a detention centre in Thailand after officials stopped them watching Brazil v Morocco on TV. It mattered just as much as in 1930.

1998

Zinedine Zidane holds his head, but his left thigh was rather more important.

The injured party

Japan & South Korea **2002**

When the great overblown circus descended on Asia for the first time, it landed in two different places, almost three. Long after coming up with the painful compromise of splitting the finals between two countries, FIFA were still talking of staging the odd match in North Korea. Fifty years of diplomacy had failed to reconcile the two Koreas, but football could obviously accomplish it in a single World Cup cycle. The usual FIFA hubris.

There might have been a fraction more humility in the air if they'd arrived without their ringmaster. In the month before the finals, the major English broadsheets were reporting on accusations of mismanagement made against FIFA president Sepp Blätter by his own general secretary Michel Zen-Ruffinen, a qualified lawyer. According to Z-R, the claims 'include direct corruption charges . . . I mean corruption through which one or two people had been bought.' His report even suggested 'a lookalike imposter' had impersonated Haiti's delegate at the 1998 FIFA congress when Blätter was elected. Nothing would have surprised us by then.

In April, UEFA president Lennart Johansson had 'called for an investigation into a report that a $100m slush fund had been established to help Sepp Blätter become FIFA president four years ago.' By May, the *Sunday Times* were telling us that allegations were being made from inside FIFA and in the media that Blätter became president as the result of 50,000 bribes [*sic*] and had 'unilaterally halted an audit commission looking into his claims that FIFA lost no more than £22 million when ISL, its marketing partner, collapsed with debts of at least £300 million in 2001. Since then Kirch, the German television company to which Blätter and Havelange sold the rights to this World Cup, has also gone into liquidation.' The same paper listed other allegations by Zen-Ruffinen, including the writing-off of a £6 million loan to CONCACAF, run by FIFA vice-president Jack Warner; the additional £650,000 that went to CONCACAF the following year, under instruction from Blätter and without 'appropriate authorisation'; Blätter's payment of £72,000 to an African official expected to back him in the election; more than £150,000 paid by Blätter, again without authorisation, to his supporters in the Gulf; and a 'questionable' payment of £35,000 to Havelange. Pause for breath.

Zen-Ruffinen presented a 21-page dossier to an emergency meeting of FIFA's executive committee, detailing what he called 'possible criminal acts' during Blätter's four-year term. He gave his boss a week to reply before he presented his file, representing 'just the tip of the iceberg', to the Swiss authorities. Blätter was facing criminal proceedings after 11 members of FIFA's executive committee accused him of corruption.

1930
1934
1938
1950
1954
1958
1962
1966
1970
1974
1978
1982
1986
1990
1994
1998
2002
2006

It couldn't last, of course. Within a week, Blätter's supporters had relieved Zen-Ruffinen of financial control. At the FIFA congress a few days before the finals, Blätter was booed off stage after refusing to allow speeches from anyone who didn't support him – and the accounts were never shown. He was re-elected president two days before the opening match of the finals. Zen-Ruffinen resigned, and nine of the eleven accusers wrote to the Swiss Public Prosecutor saying they were no longer interested in pursuing the case against Blätter, the only exceptions being Antonio Mattarese of Italy and South Korea's Chung Mong-Joon. David Will, the British chairman of the audit committee set up to examine FIFA's finances, had already been suspended. The case against Blätter was finally dropped in November.

Writing in a Chelsea match programme, Ken Bates echoed a few other people's thoughts when he hoped this would be 'the last World Cup under the rotten, corrupt, crooked reign of Blätter . . . even the monkey from Hartlepool would be an improvement.' The *Sunday Times* put the boot in even harder: 'FIFA is now more discredited even than the IOC.'

On the pitch, the circus almost arrived without its most celebrated jugglers. Having lost only one qualifier in the twentieth century, Brazil now lost six, against six different countries, before scraping through on the last day. Despite the presence of Rivaldo and the new star Ronaldinho, not much was expected of them, especially as Ronaldo had only just returned after years of injury following two operations on his right knee.

Elsewhere, the decline of Scotland, Wales and Northern Ireland continued, but the Republic of Ireland qualified by winning a play-off at last – only for Roy Keane, their captain and only world-class player, to leave the squad after a bust-up with his manager after complaining about training facilities.

England, meanwhile, lost their manager Glenn Hoddle when the press picked up on an old remark he'd made about the disabled. The World Cup campaign began with defeat in the last match at the old Wembley, to a goal by Liverpool's Dietmar Hamann which put an abrupt end to Kevin Keegan's confused reign as manager. Then a goalless draw in Helsinki left England five points behind Germany with only two matches played. Enter their first ever foreign coach, Sven-Göran Eriksson, who turned things round immediately, against a series of poor teams but also in Munich the following year, when England conceded an early goal before Michael Owen scored a hat-trick in a 5-1 win that kept Eriksson in credit for years (and made the Liverpool changing room an interesting place). Even then, England needed Beckham's goal from an injury-time free kick in their last match, at home to Greece, to go through. Germany, forced into the play-offs after drawing 0-0 at home to Finland, beat a talented (Shevchenko, Rebrov) but almost suspiciously supine Ukraine.

The number of the beast had gone up to 777, a record number of qualifying matches. Croatia, Denmark, Italy, Spain, Sweden, South Africa and Tunisia qualified without losing a game; and the play-offs provided contrasting fortunes for minnows. Slovenia continued the romantic rise they'd started at Euro 2000 by beating Romania to reach the finals for the first time; and poor Tony Vidmar finished on the losing side in a play-off for the third World Cup in a row as Australia went down to Uruguay. The usual suspects came through from Africa, with the exception of Senegal, who would be making their finals debut at the expense of old hands like Algeria (who beat them 4-0 in Dakar) and Morocco.

Of the absent friends, many were kept out by the rigours of their profession. A list of players who missed the finals through injury would take up a chapter of its own. A representative sample includes England's Steven Gerrard and Gary Neville, Germany's Sebastian Deisler, Joos Valgaeren of Belgium and Celtic, Croatia's leading defender Igor Tudor, Robert Pires and Christian Karembeu of France, Paulo Sousa and Luis Boa Morte of Portugal, and Spain's Josep Guardiola. One or two of the mishaps were self-inflicted, e.g. Spain's goalkeeper Santiago Cañizares slicing a tendon when he caught a bottle of aftershave on his foot to stop it hitting the floor. But the rest came from accidents in the workplace.

Among the whole teams that didn't make it, Holland were likely to be the most sorely missed. At the start of the season, they'd embarrassed England at White Hart Lane, a match in which Ruud van Nistelrooij confirmed what we knew about him and Marc van Bommel looked the best attacking midfielder in Europe. They scored both the goals in a win that left England looking like play-off fodder. And yet, less than three weeks later, Owen & Co had their romp in Munich while the Dutch were losing against ten men in Dublin. Everyone was at a loss.

This left two teams as most people's favourites. Despite the collapse of their economy, Argentina lost only one of their 18 qualifying matches. They had Walter Samuel at the back, Verón and Ortega still in midfield, and Batistuta hungry for a last hurrah. The holders France retained the core of their 1998 side, and Trezeguet had just finished as joint top scorer in Serie A – but there were question marks against the age of their famous back four, Zidane had torn a thigh muscle, and a whisper was seeping out from the training ground: it had been a very long season and there were going to be some tired legs out there . . .

2002

1930
1934
1938
1950
1954
1958
1962
1966
1970
1974
1978
1982
1986
1990
1994
1998
2002
2006

GROUP A

Denmark, France (seeded), Senegal, Uruguay.

31 May 2002 – World Cup Stadium, Seoul – 62,561 –
Ali Mohammed Bujsaim (UAE)

SENEGAL **(1) 1**
Bouba Diop 30

FRANCE **(0) 0**

SENEGAL Tony Sylva, Ferdinand Coly, Omar Daf,
Salif Diao, Pape Malick Diop, Aliou Cisse (c),
Moussa Ndiaye, Pape Bouba Diop, Ousseynou
Diouf, Khalilou Fadiga, Lamine Diatta. *Bruno
Metsu (FRA)*.
FRANCE Fabien Barthez, Lilian Thuram, Bixente
Lizarazu, Emmanuel Petit, Marcel Desailly (c), Frank
Lebœuf, Sylvain Wiltord [Djibril Cissé 81], Patrick
Vieira, David Trezeguet, Youri Djorkaeff [Christophe
Dugarry 60], Thierry Henry. *Roger Lemerre*.

Vieira, playing against the country he was born
in, claimed Senegal would be afraid of France –
but the African first-timers must have taken
comfort in familiarity. They had a French
coach, the whole team played their club football in France (of the opposition, only Lebœuf
was with a French club), and they were up
against a back four with an average age of 32.

When Diouf skinned Lebœuf on the left
and put a low ball across the box, Petit
knocked it back, and the ball hit Barthez before
falling into Bouba Diop's path in front of an
open goal, after which he tossed his shirt on
the ground and danced round it with some of
his team mates.

In a clean game, France pressed throughout,
but without Zidane there was precious little
leadership, and the team's weariness made
them look uninterested. In contrast, Senegal
didn't need to make any substitutions, and

although Diouf was caught offside time and
again, he was a thorough nuisance to the
French defence, who needed midfield protection more than ever and didn't get it this time
from an under-par Petit. Henry hit the bar
in the second half, but Fadiga had done the
same a minute earlier, as Senegal emulated
Cameroon in 1990.

The largest football-only stadium in Asia
cost only £100 million to build (compare with
the new Wembley). Diouf is habitually referred
to as El-Hadji, but this is a title not a forename
(loosely akin to The Right Honourable), given
to those who make a pilgrimage to Mecca.
When Fadiga was falsely accused of stealing a
gold necklace in Taegu, the shop sent him a
pendant as a gift. Bobby Moore would have
enjoyed that.

1 June 2002 – Munsu, Ulsan – 30,157 – Saad Mane
(KUW)

DENMARK (1) 2
Tomasson 44, 83

URUGUAY (0) 1
Rodríguez 47

DENMARK Thomas Sørensen, Thomas Helveg, Jan
Heintze (c) [Niclas Jensen 58], Stig Tøfting, Martin
Laursen, René Henriksen, Dennis Rommedahl, Jon
Dahl Tomasson, Ebbe Sand [Christian Poulsen 88],
Thomas Gravesen, Jesper Grønkjær [Martin
Jørgensen 70]. *Morten Olsen*.
URUGUAY Fabián Carini, Gustavo Méndez, Darío
Rodríguez [Federico Magallanes 87], Gianni Guigou,
Gonzalo Sorondo, Paolo Montero (c), Pablo García,
Gustavo Varela, Sebastián Abreu [Richard Morales 88],
Álvaro Recoba [Mario Regueiro 80], Darío Silva.
Víctor Púa.

Recoba, known as 'El Cino' for oriental features
he simply didn't have, was reported to earn the
highest salary in Serie A. Here he did some
clever things but generally looked as overpaid

as ever, though he came close with a free kick after only eight minutes. Soon afterwards, Sand should have scored instead of heading the ball into the ground and onto the bar, and when Denmark finally scored the goal they deserved, it came from an excellent team move, full of clever angled passes on the left, especially between Grønkjær and Tomasson.

Uruguay equalised against the run of play with one of the all-time great goals. When Henriksen's defensive header from a corner reached García outside the Danish penalty, he kept it up in the air with two touches before knocking it sideways to the left, where Rodríguez ran in and volleyed it in high at the near post. Shades of Ivor Allchurch in 1958.

But Denmark dominated the rest of the half, hitting hard in the tackle and keeping their shape, which was essentially 4–2–4, with Gravesen and Tøfting bald and aggressive in the middle and Rommedahl and Grønkjær fast on the wings. Sand, who'd recovered from testicular cancer in 1998, was employed to batter the door down and let Tomasson in to strike from deep. Recently voted man of the match in the UEFA Cup Final, he scored a winning goal in keeping with the other two in this match, an elegant glancing header in off the bar from Jørgensen's left-wing cross. One in the eye for Newcastle United, where Tomasson had been written off as a failure after being played as an out-and-out striker. With Laursen and Henriksen tall and impressive at the back, and their old-fashioned structure, the Danes looked likely to give other teams some unexpected problems.

---

6 June 2002 – Asiad Main Stadium, Busan – 38,289 –
Felipe Ramos Rizo (MEX)

FRANCE   0

URUGUAY   0

FRANCE Barthez, Thuram, Lizarazu, Petit, Desailly (c), Lebœuf [Vincent Candela 16], Wiltord [Dugarry 90], Vieira, Trezeguet [Cissé 81], Johan Micoud, Henry.
URUGUAY Carini, Alejandro Lembo, García, Rodríguez [Guigou 72], Sorondo, Montero (c), Varela, Marcelo Romero [Gonzalo De los Santos 71], Abreu, Recoba, Silva [Magallañes 60].
SENT OFF: Henry 25.

The holders' task was hard enough without having to attempt it without Henry, who was rightly sent off for sliding in, studs up, on Romero's ankle, a really dangerous challenge. After that, the French conducted a running battle with the spiky little Silva, whose dyed hair gave him the look of a dodgy pensioner: Petit should have been red-carded for blocking and pushing him, and he came close to being sent off himself. Desailly, Recoba and Abreu missed good chances, and Petit hit the outside of a post with a free kick taken left-footed from the right, but Wiltord was beginning to raise questions about his ability at this level. Uruguay didn't use their extra man well, never committing enough players forward, and the only winners were Denmark and Senegal.

---

6 June 2002 – World Cup Stadium, Daegu – 43,500 –
Carlos Batres (GUA)

DENMARK   **(1) 1**
Tomasson pen 16

SENEGAL   **(0) 1**
Diao 52

DENMARK Sørensen, Helveg, Heintze (c), Tøfting, Laursen, Henriksen, Rommedahl [Peter Løvenkrands 89], Tomasson, Sand, Gravesen [Poulsen 62], Grønkjær [Jørgensen 50].
SENEGAL Sylva, Coly, Daf, Diatta, Malick Diop (c), Ndiaye [Henri Camara HT], Pape Sarr [Souleymane Camara HT, Habib Beye 83], Diao, Bouba Diop, Fadiga, Diouf.
SENT OFF: Diao 80.

2002

After seeing Denmark's approach against Uruguay, Senegal came out to match them tackle for tackle, and this wasn't a contest for gentle souls. Fadiga should have been sent off (he won a free kick instead!) for hitting Helveg in the mouth with his forearm, and Sand was booked for a scary sliding foul on Diao, who conceded the penalty by barging Tomasson in the back and was sent off for planting his studs on Henriksen's shin. In between, his slick flick finished off a precise and pacy movement the length of the pitch, after which Denmark seemed happy to conserve energy in the heat (they'd complained about the 3.30 starting time). With their wingers kept in check this time, especially Jørgensen, who got no change out of the dreadlocked Coly, they seemed happy enough with the draw. Senegal perpetrated a string of painful fouls; Gravesen and Tøfting did their Mitchell Brothers impersonation again; and Helveg had a good game but trod a fine line: fouling, squaring up, pulling shirts in his own penalty area. But the 38-year-old Heintze survived the whole 90 minutes, and Denmark could face their last group match with guarded optimism, against some increasingly frantic reigning champions.

11 June 2002 – Munhak, Incheon – 48,100 – Vítor Melo Pereira (POR)

DENMARK   **(1) 2**
Rommedahl 22, Tomasson 67

FRANCE   **(0) 0**

DENMARK Sørensen, Helveg, N Jensen, Tøfting [Brian Steen Nielsen 79], Laursen, Henriksen (c), Rommedahl, Tomasson, Poulsen [Kasper Bøgelund 76], Gravesen, Jørgensen [Grønkjær HT].
FRANCE Barthez, Candela, Lizarazu, Claude Makelele, Desailly (c), Thuram, Dugarry [Cissé 54], Vieira [Micoud 71], Trezeguet, Zinedine Zidane, Wiltord [Djorkaeff 83].

Predictably and desperately, France brought back Zidane, who played with his left thigh strapped and couldn't be expected to make much difference. After Rommedahl arrived unmarked to volley in Tøfting's delicate cross from the right, Denmark concentrated on contesting the midfield. Desailly suffered the indignity of having his shirt pulled by Tomasson, who ran on to put in Grønkjær's left-wing cross, and France became the first defending champions since 1966 to go out before the second stage, and the first to be eliminated without scoring a goal. But they'd had no luck. Desailly and Trezeguet hit the bar in the second half – and their whole tournament might have gone very differently if Trezeguet had scored instead of hitting the top of a post with the score still 0-0 against Senegal.

11 June 2002 – World Cup Stadium, Suwon – 33,681 – Jan Wegereef (HOL)

SENEGAL   **(3) 3**
Fadiga pen 20, PB Diop 26, 38

URUGUAY   **(0) 3**
Morales 46, Forlán 69, Recoba pen 88

SENEGAL Sylva, Coly [Beye 63], Daf, Cisse (c), Diatta, Malick Diop, Bouba Diop, Alassane Ndour [Amdy Faye 76], Fadiga, H Camara [Ndiaye 67], Diouf.
URUGUAY Carini, Lembo, Rodríguez, García, Sorondo [Regueiro 32], Montero (c), Varela, Romero [Morales HT], Abreu [Diego Forlán HT], Recoba, Silva.

Needing only a draw to qualify at Uruguay's expense, Senegal were again aggressive from the start, collecting two yellow cards in the first four minutes. There were eventually 12 bookings in the match, and the penalties were won by preposterous dives from Diouf and Morales – but it wouldn't be remembered for any of that. Needing an unlikely four goals in the second half, Uruguay couldn't have come much closer.

LEADING GOALSCORERS 2002

7	Ronaldo	BRZ	
5	Miroslav Klose	GER	
5	Rivaldo	BRZ	1 pen

FIFA credit Ronaldo with 8 goals, including a blatant own goal by Costa Rica.

Camara made both goals for Diop, one from each flank, with a square pass after breaking a tackle near halfway, and a cross from the right which was touched in on the volley from an offside position – only for Uruguay's half-time substitutions to change everything. Forlán did a passable impression of Uruguay's goal against Denmark by chesting the ball down before volleying superbly from outside the area (he later needed 27 matches and a penalty to score his first goal for Man United). And Morales was a burly handful throughout, scoring within 16 seconds when Sylva saved from Silva, then stealing the late penalty. But it was his missed header in injury time, when Varela's very long low shot was headed up in the air by Diatta, which cost Uruguay a place in the second round. An ironic end to the biggest rollercoaster ride in town.

GROUP A

	P	W	D	L	F	A	Pts
Denmark	3	2	1	0	5	2	7
Senegal	3	1	2	0	5	4	5
Uruguay	3	0	2	1	4	5	2
France	3	0	1	2	0	3	1

Denmark and Senegal qualified for the second round.

GROUP B

Paraguay, Slovenia, South Africa, Spain (seeded).

2 June 2002 – Asiad Main Stadium, Busan – 25,186 – Luboš Michel (SVK)

PARAGUAY   **(1) 2**
Santa Cruz 39, Arce 55

SOUTH AFRICA   **(0) 2**
T Mokoena 63, Fortune pen 90

PARAGUAY Ricardo Tavarelli, Francisco Arce, Julio César Cáceres, Estanislao Struway [Juan Carlos Franco 86], Celso Ayala, Carlos Gamarra (c), Denis Caniza, Guido Alvarenga [Diego Gavilán 66], Roque Santa Cruz, Roberto Acuña, Jorge Campos [Gustavo Moringo 72]. *Cesare Maldini (ITA)*.
SOUTH AFRICA André Arendse, Naughty Mokoena, Cyril Nzama, Bradley Carnell, Lucas Radebe (c), Pierre Issa [MacDonald Mukasi 27], Quinton Fortune, Tebeho Mokoena, Benni McCarthy [George Koumantarakis 78], MacBeth Sibaya, Sibusiso Zuma. *Jomo Sono*.

The president of Paraguay, Luis González Macchi, was quoted as saying South Africa were the worst team in the tournament – and he must have been congratulating himself when Arce curled a free kick in at the near post from wide on the left. Arce was known by a diminutive of his first name, which he wore with his surname on the back of his shirt – so one of the goals of the tournament was scored by a Chiqui Arce. When Arendse missed an earlier Arce free kick, Santa Cruz opened the scoring with a brave header, and Paraguay had no cause to regret leaving out Cardozo in favour of a five-man midfield, especially as McCarthy was invisible against the old firm of Ayala and Gamarra. At the other end, Radebe was winning his 67th cap, a new national record – but this was his first competitive game

1930
1934
1938
1950
1954
1958
1962
1966
1970
1974
1978
1982
1986
1990
1994
1998
2002
2006

in over a year, and Santa Cruz had the beating of him in the air.

But his team were given hope when Struway diverted Tebeho Mokoena's shot past Tavarelli – and, for the second successive finals match, they nicked a 2-2 draw thanks to an injury-time penalty, this one for Tavarelli's unnecessary dive at Zuma's feet. Fortune, first capped in 1998, scored an international goal at last.

The leading South African statistician confirms the other Mokoena was known as Naughty and not by his first name Aaron. Luboš Michel is correct, not Michel Luboš.

---

2 June 2002 – World Cup Stadium, Gwangju – 28,598 – Mohammed Guezzaz (MOR)

SPAIN   **(1) 3**
Raúl 44, Valerón 74, Hierro pen 87

SLOVENIA   **(0) 1**
Cimirotič 82

SPAIN Iker Casillas, Carles Puyol, 'Juanfran' (Juan Francisco García) [Enrique Romero 82], Rubén Baraja, Miguel Ángel Nadal, Fernando Hierro (c), Luis Enrique (Martínez) [Iván Helguera 74], Javi de Pedro, Raúl (González), Juan Carlos Valerón, Diego Tristán [Fernando Morientes 67]. *José Camacho*.
SLOVENIA Marko Simeunovič, Željko Milinovič, Marinko Galič, Aleksandar Knavs, Đoni Novak [Sašo Gajser 77], Aleš Čeh (c), Miran Pavlin, Amir Karič, Milan Osterc [Sebastjan Cimirotič 57], Zlatko Zahovič [Milenko Ačimovič 63], Mladen Rudonja. *Srečko Katanec*.

Spain, an outside bet to win the World Cup as so often, were unconvincing yet again, but too good for an hardworking but unexceptional side. They should have scored long before Luis Enrique battled through the defence and Raúl held the loose ball long enough for Čeh's tackle to slide past, then prodded it between Milinovič's legs past the unsighted keeper.

In the second half, Slovenia were more combative but never really competitive. The performance of Zahovič, their star of Euro 2000, was a continuation of his poor season with Benfica, though perhaps he was just another veteran European struggling in the heat and humidity. Valerón scored his first international goal by sliding in a cross shot after a long centre from de Pedro. Cimirotič, more mobile than the big static Osterc, scored after a one-two with Ačimovič – but Gajser fouled Morientes, and Hierro scored his tenth international penalty.

Long-suffering Spanish fans may have seen an omen in the fact that the last time Spain had won their opening match in the finals (1950) was the only year they reached the last four. Carles (not Carlos) is the correct spelling of Puyol's first name.

---

7 June 2002 – World Cup Stadium, Jeonju – 24,000 – Gamal El-Ghandour (EGY)

SPAIN   **(0) 3**
Morientes 53, 69, Hierro pen 82

PARAGUAY   **(1) 1**
Puyol o.g. 10

SPAIN Casillas, Puyol, Juanfran, Baraja, Nadal, Hierro (c), Luis Enrique [Helguera HT], Valerón ['Xavi' (Xavier Hernández) 85], Tristán [Morientes HT], Raúl, de Pedro.
PARAGUAY José Luis Chilavert (c), Arce, Cáceres, Caniza [Struway 78], Ayala, Gamarra, Carlos Paredes, Gavilán, José Cardozo [Campos 63], Acuña, Santa Cruz.

Even when making a meal of it, Spain were too good for the other teams in this easy group. They fell behind when Casillas pushed Arce's shot onto Puyol's foot – but Paraguay had left their best midfield marker out of the squad (Julio César Enciso, who'd played in 1998) in favour of his club reserve Franco, allegedly because Chilavert hadn't forgiven him for being unavailable to play against Brazil the previous year. As a result, Spain ran through their midfield in the second half. Morientes came on to head in a corner from around the penalty spot, then bundled in the second when Chilavert flapped at de Pedro's cross. Chilavert tried to make amends with a free kick saved by Casillas, but Hierro converted another penalty after Raúl was held while trying to turn Paredes, and Spain were already in the last sixteen.

The official attendance figure was 41,428.

---

8 June 2002 – World Cup Stadium, Daegu – 47,226 – Ángel Sánchez (ARG)

SOUTH AFRICA   (1) 1
Nomvete 4

SLOVENIA   (0) 0

SOUTH AFRICA Arendse, Nzama, Carnell, N Mokoena, Radebe (c), Sibaya, T Mokoena, Fortune [Jabu Pule 84], McCarthy [Koumantarakis 80], Siyabonga Nomvete [Delron Buckley 71], Zuma.
SLOVENIA Simeunovič, Milinovič, Muamer Vugdalič, Knavs [Spasoje Bulajič 60], Novak, A Čeh (c), Ačimovič [Nastja Čeh 60], Pavlin, Karič, Cimirotič [Osterc 41], Rudonja.

A match as poor as everyone expected was settled by an early goal worthy of it. Fortune's free kick from the left found Nomvete unmarked; he missed his attempt at a downward header, and the ball went in off his thigh. With Zahovič back home after allegedly coming to blows with the coach when he was substituted against Spain, the rest of the squad now joined him, bringing about Katanec's resignation. Slovenia laboured in the heat and made no real chances, while McCarthy missed two at the other end. It was only South Africa's second win over European opposition since the end of apartheid.

12 June 2002 – World Cup Stadium, Daejeon – 31,024 – Saad Mane (KUW)

SPAIN   (2) 3
Raúl 4, 56, Mendieta 45

SOUTH AFRICA   (1) 2
McCarthy 31, Radebe 53

SPAIN Casillas, Cristóbal 'Curro' Torres, Helguera, Nadal (c), Romero, Joaquín (Sánchez), Xavi, Gaizka Mendieta, Morientes [Alberto Luque 77], Raúl [Luis Enrique 82], David Albelda [Sergio (González) 52].
SOUTH AFRICA Arendse, Nzama, Carnell, N Mokoena, Radebe (c) [Thabang Molefe 80], Sibaya, T Mokoena, Fortune [Jacob Lekgetho 83], McCarthy, Nomvete [Koumantarakis 74], Zuma.

Needing a draw to qualify, South Africa could have done without another fourth-minute goal, this one at the wrong end thanks to a shocking error by Arendse, who collected an easy through-ball then simply let it slip out for Raúl (who appeared to kick it out of his hands) to wrap up the gift. Spain constantly threatened to add to their lead, pouring through midfield and almost applying the final pass more than once. But a minute after Morientes' strong header had brought a fine reaction save from Arendse, Casillas didn't come out in time as McCarthy stretched to put in Nomvete's header back across goal from Fortune's left-wing cross. However, Spain were finding goals easy to score by now, and Arendse gave them another helping hand by positioning himself directly behind the wall, leaving his left side completely open, as Mendieta hit a low free kick.

South Africa didn't give up, Radebe's heading in a corner – but then Raúl got behind him to head in a right-wing cross. Arendse's fine save denied Luque a goal in the first minute of his international debut, but by then South Africa were already hoping for a favour from Slovenia.

1930
1934
1938
1950
1954
1958
1962
1966
1970
1974
1978
1982
1986
1990
1994
1998
2002
2006

1930
1934
1938
1950
1954
1958
1962
1966
1970
1974
1978
1982
1986
1990
1994
1998
2002
2006

12 June 2002 – Jeju World Cup Stadium, Seogwipo – 30,176 – Felipe Ramos Rizo (MEX)

PARAGUAY   **(0) 3**
Cuevas 65, 84, Campos 73

SLOVENIA   **(1) 1**
Ačimovič 45

PARAGUAY Chilavert (c), Arce, Cáceres, Caniza, Ayala, Gamarra, Paredes, Acuña, Cardozo [Nélson Cuevas 61, Franco 90], Santa Cruz, Alvarenga [Campos 54].
SLOVENIA Mladen Dabanovič, Bulajič, Milinovič, Rajko Tavčar, Novak, A Čeh (c), Pavlin [Rudonja 40], Karič, Cimirotič, Osterc [Senad Tiganj 77], Ačimovič [N Čeh 62]. *Danilo Popivoda.*
SENT OFF: Paredes 22, N Čeh 81.

After Paredes collected two early yellow cards, the remaining ten men had to watch Ačimovič dribble up the right and put in a low cross which went in off Chilavert, who was looking like a furious old Buddha nowadays, as well as something of a liability. With half an hour to go, Paraguay still needed two goals to qualify, which would have been three if Ačimovič hadn't hit the angle of post and crossbar from long range. But the substitutions did the trick. Cuevas hit a low shot inside the near post after cutting in from the right – then, after Gamarra had deflected Osterc's cross onto his own bar, Campos scored with a low cross-shot from the left, after which Slovenia's late substitution wasn't so successful, Nastja Čeh receiving a red card for sliding in, foot high, on Arce, after which Cuevas stepped inside two men before hammering a left-footer into the top corner to put some tasty icing on the celebration cake. Chilavert came as close as he ever would to scoring in the finals, Dabanovič touching his free kick onto the bar.

GROUP B

	P	W	D	L	F	A	Pts
Spain	3	3	0	0	9	4	9
Paraguay	3	1	1	1	6	6	4
South Africa	3	1	1	1	5	5	4
Slovenia	3	0	0	3	2	7	0

Spain and Paraguay qualified for the second round.

GROUP C

Brazil (seeded), China, Costa Rica, Turkey.

3 June 2002 – Munsu, Ulsan – 33,842 – Kim Yung-Joo (SKO)

BRAZIL   **(0) 2**
Ronaldo 50, Rivaldo pen 87

TURKEY   **(1) 1**
Şaş 45

BRAZIL Marcos (Silveira), 'Cafú' (Marcos Evangelista) (c), Roberto Carlos (da Silva), Gilberto Silva, José Roque Júnior, 'Lúcio' (Lucimar da Silva), 'Ronaldinho' (Ronaldo de Assis) [Denílson (de Oliveira) 67], 'Juninho Paulista' (Osvaldo Giroldo Júnior) ['Vampeta' (Marcos Batista) 72], Ronaldo (Nazário Lima) ['Luizão' (Luiz Goulart) 73], Rivaldo (Borba Ferreira), Edmílson (Gomes). *'Felipão' (Luís Felipe Scolari).*
TURKEY Rüstü Reçber, Alpay Özalan, Hakan Ünsal, Bülent Korkmaz [İlhan Mansiz 66], Fatih Akyel, Ümit Özat, Yildiray Bastürk [Ümit Davala 65], Tugay Kerimoğlu [Arif Erdem 88], Hakan Şükür (c), Hasan Şaş, Emre Belözoğlu. *Senol Günes.*
SENT OFF: Alpay 86, Ünsal 90.

Despite Brazil's problems in qualifying, Roberto Carlos was as arrogant as ever: 'we'll need to operate at only 40% to beat Turkey'. Well, that was about the right figure in the first half – and it nearly cost them. Tugay's free kick took a deflection off Gilberto and brushed the top of the bar, and although Rüstü made some important saves, Turkey just about deserved their half-time lead. Bastürk shaped to shoot from the right and instead pitched a superb angled pass to the left, where the unsmiling Şaş took advantage of Cafú's usual absence to meet the bouncing ball and volley his first international goal. Quite a character this, with his shaven head, six-month drug ban, and visible scar from putting his fist through a changing room window.

Brazil then deigned to play at about 70% – enough to dominate the second half. Although Ronaldo's pace was clearly gone for ever, he was still dangerous. His trademark foot-over-the-ball trick had already made a headed chance for Rivaldo; now he stretched to reach the latter's curling cross from the left, volleying it down into the ground and up over the keeper's hand.

Meanwhile Ronaldinho had been living up to the hype. Even toothier than Ronaldo (who was originally known as Ronaldinho himself), his flair and dribbling twanged the Turkish defence. On the hour, Rivaldo had a headed goal ruled out for offside (a superb decision by the linesman), and although Roque Júnior was lucky he wasn't spotted pulling Şükür's shirt in the Brazilian penalty area, Turkey's captain was having a mare. Known as the Bull of the Bosporus (which didn't remotely reflect his style of play), he'd been more of a camel with various Italian clubs and hardly saw the ball here.

Turkey held out until Rüstü spoiled a fine performance with a poor clearance kick straight to Luizão. Alpay, who hadn't played for Aston Villa since December because of a bad ankle injury, was sent off for pulling Luizão's shirt outside the penalty area but not releasing

it until the attacker had fallen in the area. Tough on Turkey, who'd matched Brazil for flair, especially Şaş and his dragbacks. Commercials played on İlhan's surname and the word *amansiz* (merciless); he showed great skill in flipping the ball up behind him to beat Roberto Carlos – and his hair (tied back) was long enough to play for Argentina.

In injury time, the match was polluted by Rivaldo's collapse, holding his face and rolling around on the ground when Hakan Ünsal kicked the ball against his leg. Ünsal was sent off, and Rivaldo, a multi-millionaire, was fined £5,000 – part of FIFA's 'clampdown on simulation'. Scolari's defence of his player was in the Ferguson and Wenger class: 'It was an instinctive defensive reaction. He put his hands over his face to protect himself.' A total scandal, which provoked clashes between Brazilian and Turkish fans after the match, one of the very few examples during the tournament.

---

4 June 2002 – World Cup Stadium, Gwangju – 27,217 – Kyros Vassaras (GRE)

COSTA RICA	**(0) 2**
Gómez 61, Wright 65	
CHINA	**(0) 0**

COSTA RICA Erick Lonnis (c), Luis Marín, Carlos Castro, Harold Wallace [Steven Bryce 70], Mauricio Wright, Gilberto Martínez, Mauricio Solís, Walter Centeño, Paulo César Wanchope [Wilmer López 80], Rolando Fonseca [Hernán Medford 57], Ronald Gómez. *Alexandre Guimarães.*
CHINA Jiang Jin, Wu Chenying, Ma Mingyu (c), Li Weifeng, Fan Zhiyi [Yu Genwei 74], Sun Jihai [Qu Bo 26], Li Tie, Hao Haidong, Li Xiaopeng, Yang Chen [Su Maozhen 66], Xu Yunlong. *Bora Milutinović (YUG).*

The second half was cooler than the first, but we're talking relativity here: 31°C as opposed to 34°C. When a clever short pass from Gómez took out three defenders, the 36-year-old

2002

1930
1934
1938
1950
1954
1958
1962
1966
1970
1974
1978
1982
1986
1990
1994
1998
2002
2006

Medford, a hero of 1990, forced a good block from Xu, and Gómez thumped the loose ball high into the net. Then Gómez received a short corner on the left and twisted back to the goal line; Yang didn't defend that option even though Gómez was completely left-footed, and the near-post cross was met by a glancing header across the keeper by Wright (who had Wrigth on the back of his shirt!). Earlier, Wanchope should have had a penalty when Wu mistimed a challenge and kicked him in the calf. China's heads went down after the

goals (the body language on each side was unmistakable), they had no obvious leadership, no long ball to mix the short passing, and no cutting edge up front. And there was the small matter of Brazil to come.

---

8 June 2002 – Jeju World Cup Stadium, Seogwipo – 36,750 – Anders Frisk (SWE)

BRAZIL   **(3) 4**
Roberto Carlos 15, Rivaldo 32, Ronaldinho pen 44, Ronaldo 55

CHINA   **(0) 0**

BRAZIL Marcos, Cafú (c), Roberto Carlos, Gilberto, Roque Júnior, Lúcio, Juninho Paulista ['Ricardinho' (Ricardo Pozzi) 70], Ânderson Polga, Ronaldo [Edílson (da Silva) 72], Rivaldo, Ronaldinho [Denílson HT].
CHINA Jiang, Wu, Ma (c) [Yang Pu 62], Li WF, Li T, Zhao Junzhe, Du Wei, Li XP, Qi Hong [Shao Jiayi 66], Xu, Hao [Qu 75].

TOURNAMENTS AS COACH

5	Bora Milutinović	YUG	1986–90–94–98–02
4	Sepp Herberger	GER	1938–54–58–62
4	Walter Winterbottom	ENG	1950–54–58–62
4	Helmut Schön	GER	1966–70–74–78
4	Lajos Baróti	HUN	1958–62–66–78
4	Carlos Alberto Parreira	BRZ	1982–90–94–98

Feeding time – in a group full of easy meat. The first bite summed up China's defence: when Roberto Carlos smashed a straight shot past their wall, it was the first time he'd scored direct

COUNTRIES COACHED

5	Bora Milutinović	86 MEX	90 COS	94 USA	98 NGA	02 CHN
4	Carlos Alberto Parreira	82 KUW	90 UAE	94 BRZ	98 SAU	
3	Henri Michel	86 FRA	94 CAM	98 MOR		
2	Rudolf Vytlacil	62 CZE	66 BUL			
2	Blagoje Vidinic	70 MOR	74 ZAI			
2	Cesare Maldini	98 ITA	02 PAR			
2	Hernán Darío Gómez	98 COL	02 ECU			
2	Philippe Troussier	98 SAF	02 JPN			
2	Guus Hiddink	98 HOL	02 SKO			

Michel was also in charge when Tunisia qualified in 2002, but was replaced before the finals.

from a free kick since his classic against France in 1997. The unsighted Jiang was probably grateful he wasn't sighted. Ronaldinho was booked for diving when his shirt was pulled in the Chinese penalty area, and Rivaldo missed an open goal before sliding in front of the keeper to put in a cross by Ronaldinho, who then scored from the spot when Li Weifeng added to the epidemic of shirt-pulling in this competition by dragging Ronaldo back after he'd beaten two men. Cafú made an open goal for Ronaldo, who hardly saw the ball in the first half.

China's players were that rarity in these finals: all still with clubs in their own country – which was the problem. They ran all day, Shao added a little flair, and Zhao hit a post with a fierce shot on the hour, but let's draw the veil. Even Milutinović's alchemy didn't work on this team: this was his fifth finals tournament (a record) and the first in which he failed to reach the next round.

Criticised by his coach for not punching his weight against Brazil, Şükür apparently vowed never to play in a major tournament again (promises, promises) because his team mates were playing for themselves. Early in the second half, he missed two good chances in a minute.

Turkey had just started to lose the midfield when the chunky Emre B rolled the rebound just inside the near post after his first shot had been blocked by Martínez. But again his defence conceded a very late goal, the 20-year-old Parks hitting a left-foot volley after the ball had been lobbed away from Rüstü. who'd had his thigh strapped at half-time. There was enough time for Parks to miss an open goal after going past the keeper, and Emre B to be booked for pushing a member of the Costa Rican coaching staff in his hurry to get the ball back. Haste wasn't enough for Turkey, who now needed a helping hand from the group leaders.

---

9 June 2002 – Munhak, Incheon – 42,299 – Coffi Codjia (BEN)

COSTA RICA **(0) 1**
Parks 86

TURKEY **(0) 1**
Emre B 56

COSTA RICA Lonnis (c), Wallace [Bryce 77], Marín, Castro, Wright, Martínez, López [Winston Parks 77], Solís, Centeño [Medford 66], Wanchope, Gómez.
TURKEY Rüstü, Emre Asik, Fatih, Ergün Penbe, Özat, Davala, Tugay [Arif 87], Bastürk [Nihat Kahveci 79], Şükür (c) [İlhan 75], Şaş, Emre B.

Turkey seemed be on a downer after Brazil, and Costa Rica's tackling didn't help them up. Şaş was stretchered off for a while when his leg was trodden on by Wright, who also used his forearm on the back of Tugay's head. And Asik was booked when Wanchope ran into him.

---

13 June 2002 – World Cup Stadium, Suwon – 38,524 – Gamal El-Ghandour (EGY)

BRAZIL **(3) 5**
Marín o.g. 10, Ronaldo 13, Edmílson 38, Rivaldo 62, Júnior 64

COSTA RICA **(1) 2**
Wanchope 39, Gómez 56

BRAZIL Marcos, Cafú (c), 'Júnior' (Jenílson de Souza), Gilberto, Ânderson Polga, Lúcio, Edmílson, Juninho Paulista [Ricardinho 61], Ronaldo, Rivaldo ['Kakà' (Ricardo Izecson Santos) 72], Edílson [Kléberson (Pereira) 57].
COSTA RICA Lonnis (c), Wallace [Bryce HT], Marín, Castro, Wright, Martínez [Parks 74], López, Solís [Fonseca 65], Wanchope, Centeño, Gómez.

Jolly japes – though not if you were Costa Rican. Needing a draw to qualify, they pulled back to 3-2 and might even have won if they

2002

1930
1934
1938
1950
1954
1958
1962
1966
1970
1974
1978
1982
1986
1990
1994
1998
2002
2006

hadn't missed a whole string of chances and Marcos hadn't made some good saves. Wanchope hit the bar and had a shot kicked off the line by Ânderson Polga, and Gómez should have scored from a corner instead of heading over. Eventually Wanchope's shot went in off Lúcio after he'd exchanged passes with Wright, and Gómez scored with a diving header at the far post.

Brazil missed chances too. Rivaldo volleyed over an empty net and hit a post with a free kick, Ronaldo also hit a post and should have had two penalties. But they also took a few, all five after attacking up the left wing. Ronaldo twisted to shoot in low from a near-post corner; Edmílson applied a kind of half-overhead to a deflected cross; Rivaldo swept in a ball from Júnior, who was presumably named after the 1982 left-back and gave a fair impersonation of that player by running clear, controlling instantly, and shooting inside the near post. FIFA still persist in crediting the own goal to Ronaldo, but it's a joke, completely unacceptable. When Júnior stabbed the ball in low, Ronaldo barely touched it sideways before Marín lunged in to bulldoze it past his own keeper.

Ânderson Polga was known by his forename and surname together, never as just Ânderson or Polga.

---

13 June 2002 – World Cup Stadium, Seoul – 43,605 – Oscar Ruiz (COL)

TURKEY   (2) 3
Şaş 6, Bülent 9, Davala 85

CHINA   (0) 0

TURKEY Rüstü [Ömer Çatkiç 35], Emre A, Fatih, Bülent, Ünsal, Tugay [Tayfur Havutçu 84], Davala, Bastürk [İlhan 70], Şükür (c), Emre B, Şaş.
CHINA Jiang (c), Wu [Shao HT], Yang P, Li WF, Du, Xu, Li T, Zhao, Li XP, Hao [Qu 73], Yang C [Yu 73].
SENT OFF: Shao 59.

The early goals ensured there would be no slip-up against the whipping boys. Şaş thrashed the ball over Jiang after Li Weifeng let the ball bounce off him, and Bülent's looping header was touched in by Şükür after it crossed the line. China were eliminated without scoring a goal, but hit a post again, this time through Yang Chen's massive first-time volley. Shao was shown a straight red for catching Emre B with his studs. Like Germany's Ziege and Mathis of the USA, Davala was sporting one of Beckham's old mohican haircuts; his low volley converted Şaş's long cross from the left. Oh and shock horror: Şükür almost scored, his high header bringing a good save from Jiang.

GROUP C

	P	W	D	L	F	A	Pts
Brazil	3	3	0	0	11	3	9
Turkey	3	1	1	1	5	3	4
Costa Rica	3	1	1	1	5	6	4
China	3	0	0	3	0	9	0

Brazil and Turkey qualified for the second round.

GROUP D

Poland, Portugal, South Korea (seeded), USA.

---

4 June 2002 – Asiad Main Stadium, Busan – 48,760 – Oscar Ruiz (COL)

SOUTH KOREA   (1) 2
Hwang 26, Yoo 53

POLAND   (0) 0

SOUTH KOREA Lee Woon-Jae, Kim Tae-Yung, Kim Nam-Il, Choi Jin-Chul, Yoo Sang-Chul [Lee Chun-Soo 61], Hong Myung-Bo (c), Lee Eul-Yung, Song Chong-Guk, Hwang Sun-Hong [Ahn Jung-Hwan 50], Park Ji-Sung, Seol Ki-Hyeon [Cha Doo-Ri 89]. *Guus Hiddink (HOL)*.
POLAND Jerzy Dudek, Michal Żewłakow, Tomasz Hajto, Piotr Świerczewski, Radoslaw Kałuzny [Marcin Żewłakow 65], Tomasz Wałdoch (c), Jacek Krzynówek, Maciej Zurawski [Paweł Kryszałowicz HT], Emmanuel Olisadebe, Jacek Bąk [Tomasz Kłos 51], Marek Koźmiński. *Jerzy Engel*.

With almost everyone wearing a national team shirt, the whole stadium looked like an oversized red flag, and the hosts were happy to be wrapped in it: without a win from 14 previous finals matches, they needed their home comforts. Poland's big and heavy men were run ragged by their hosts, who were as madcap as ever but more accustomed to the heat.

After Krzynówek shot wide when put clear in the second minute, Poland lost control of midfield, and Hwang, who'd scored in the 1994 finals but didn't play in 1998, got his 50th and last international goal when he was left unmarked to volley in at the near post. Yoo Sang-Chul had a goal disallowed for offside by three players, then Joo Sang-Chul won the ball and beat another man before scoring. Dudek got both hands to the shot and might have saved it, but it was travelling at a fair pace. Meanwhile the Nigeria-born Olisadebe, who'd scored eight goals in qualifying, hardly saw the ball.

Hong was the first player from outside Europe and the Americas to play in four finals tournaments. After the finals, Cha Doo-Ri signed for Bayer Leverkusen, for whom his father Cha Bum-Kun had scored in the 1988 UEFA Cup Final ('I feel more German than Korean'). The Żewłakows were twins. A female Polish fan sued singer Edyta Gorniak for delivering the Polish national anthem too slowly in the stadium, thereby 'putting the players to sleep.' Sadly the case was dismissed.

The official attendance figure was 55,982.

---

5 June 2002 – World Cup Stadium, Suwon – 37,306 – Byron Moreno (ECU)

USA **(3) 3**
O'Brien 4, J Costa o.g. 29, McBride 36

PORTUGAL **(1) 2**
Beto 39, Agoos o.g. 71

USA Brad Friedel, Tony Sanneh, Frankie Hejduk, Pablo Mastroeni, Eddie Pope [Carlos Llamosa 80], Jeff Agoos, Landon Donovan [Joe-Max Moore 75], Earnie Stewart (c) [Cobi Jones HT], Brian McBride, John O'Brien, DaMarcus Beasley. *Bruce Arena*.
PORTUGAL Vítor Baía, 'Beto' (Roberto Seveiro), Rui Jorge (Oliveira) [Paulo Bento 69], 'Petit' (Armando Teixeira), Jorge Costa [Jorge Andrade 73], Fernando Couto (c), 'Figo' (Luís Madeira Caeiro), João V Pinto, 'Pauleta' (Pedro Resendes), Rui Costa ['Nuno Gomes' (Nuno Ribeiro) 80], Sérgio Conceição. *António AR Oliveira*.

After winning the World Youth title in 1989 and 1991, Portugal's 'golden generation' had failed to step up. This and the next Euro finals (held at home) were their last chances. And they seemed to have been given some unexceptional opposition to set them on their way.

Arena spread it around that he couldn't find a weakness in the Portuguese team – but his team found some early on, O'Brien volleying in after Baía saved a header from McBride, whose ability in the air was already apparent. His falling header from Sanneh's right-wing cross made him the first American to score in two separate finals tournaments. And when the ball sailed in at the near post off Jorge Costa's head, even FIFA couldn't credit the goal to Donovan.

With the gum-chewing Rui Costa struggling to make the play, and Figo visibly frustrated by

1930
1934
1938
1950
1954
1958
1962
1966
1970
1974
1978
1982
1986
1990
1994
1998
2002
2006

the service he wasn't getting, Portugal were lucky to get a goal back so quickly, Beto reacting instantly when O'Brien inadvertently kicked his header straight back to him at a corner. The ponytailed Agoos, winning his 131st cap, at last played in a finals match (he missed 1994 through injury and was in the squad in 1998) – and promptly volleyed a spectacular own goal from Pauleta's cross. But the two 20-year-olds Donovan and Beasley ran well with the ball, while Figo (who looked exhausted by half-time) and Conceição did nothing on the wings. It was the first time since 1930 that the USA had won their opening finals match.

Couto was back after a ban for taking nandrolone. There's some doubt about the spelling of Pauleta's surname; we've gone with a recent Portuguese history of the national team. And yes, 'Figo' (the Portuguese for 'fig') is a nickname.

10 June 2002 – World Cup Stadium, Daegu – 60,778 – Urs Meier (SWI)

SOUTH KOREA   (0) 1
Ahn 78

USA   (1) 1
Mathis 24

SOUTH KOREA Lee WJ, Kim TY, Yoo [Choi Yong-Soo 69], Choi JC, Kim NI, Hong (c), Lee EY, Song, Park [Lee CS 38], Hwang [Ahn 56], Seol.
USA Friedel, Sanneh, Hejduk, O'Brien, Pope, Agoos, Donovan, Clint Mathis [Josh Wolff 82], McBride, Claudio Reyna (c), Beasley [Eddie Lewis 75].

The usual Korean all-out pace, but their final ball was poor and the USA's goal seemed to deflate them. Mathis brought the ball down well and hit an excellent low volley when O'Brien's through-ball found him unmarked. Choi Jin-Chul was lucky not to give away a

penalty for pulling Beasley's shirt, and South Korea needed all of Hong's experience at the back. Agoos conceded a penalty by using his forearm on Hwang, who was wearing a bandage over his whole head after cutting his right eye when he headed the back of Hejduk's head. Lee Chun-Soo put the ball on the spot but the kick was taken by Lee Eul-Yung, whose mild shot was saved by Friedel.

In the second half, the USA were content to hold on to their lead, but Reyna couldn't pull any strings with so few forwards attached to them, and eventually South Korea's possession paid off, the lively Ahn heading in a free kick down the middle, controversially awarded for Donovan's tackle on Lee Eul-Yung. Despite all the steel and concrete, you could actually feel the stadium shake.

10 June 2002 – World Cup Stadium, Jeonju – 31,000 – Hugh Dallas (SCO)

PORTUGAL   (1) 4
Pauleta 14, 65, 77, Rui Costa 88

POLAND   (0) 0

PORTUGAL Baía, Bento, Rui Jorge, Petit, J Costa, Couto (c), Figo, Nuno Frechaut [Beto 63], Pauleta, Pinto [R Costa 60], Conceição ['Capucho' (Nuno Gonçalves) 69].
POLAND Dudek, Wałdoch (c), Hajto, Mi. Żewłakow [Tomasz Rząsa 71], Kryszałowicz, Świerczewski, Kałuzny [Arkadiusz Bąk 16], Krzynówek, Olisadebe, Zurawski [Ma. Żewłakow 56], Koźmiński.

The steady rain that fell at the start soon became torrential, but if Poland were grateful for the cooler climate, their big central defenders didn't enjoy the slippery surface. Leaving out Rui Costa, Portugal benefited from Figo's improvement in the second half, after Pauleta had cut inside Hajto and scored at the near post. Poland were unlucky that the hefty Kryszałowicz had a goal disallowed when Baía simply dropped the ball – then Olisadebe, short on determination as well as service, gave the ball away, and Figo's low cross was put in by Pauleta as Koźmiński pulled the top of his shirt. Figo hit a post, Baía saved from Kryszałowicz, and Pauleta completed his hat-trick after cutting inside again. Rui Costa broke away to slide in a right-wing cross from Capucho, then should have made it 5-0 after going round the keeper. Poland could have done with the Polish-born Klose, who was scoring freely for Germany. The first European team to qualify, they were the first to go out.

In the first half, Seol had a goal disallowed when Baía was nudged by Choi Jin-Chul. In the second, Park chested the ball down, flipped it up inside Conceição with his right foot, then volleyed between Baía's legs with his left. In a frantic finish, with the crowd chanting Beethoven's *Ode to Joy*, Nuno Gomes missed an easy chance in front of the keeper, and Ahn might have scored twice on the break. Baía was up for a corner at the death, but it was the end for the golden boys, who went on to lose the Final of Euro 2004.

Xavier, hair and beard dyed like a yellow Neptune, later became the first English Premiership player to be suspended for taking a banned performance-enhancing drug.

---

14 June 2002 – Munhak, Incheon – 50,239 – Ángel Sánchez (ARG)

SOUTH KOREA (0) 1
Park 70

PORTUGAL (0) 0

SENT OFF: JV Pinto 27, Beto 65.
SOUTH KOREA Lee WJ, Kim TY, Kim NI, Choi JC, Yoo, Hong (c), Lee Yong-Pyo, Park, Seol, Song, Ahn [Lee CS 90].
PORTUGAL Baía, Beto, Rui Jorge [Abel Xavier 73], Petit [Nuno Gomes 77], J Costa, Couto (c), Figo, Bento, Pauleta [Andrade 69], Pinto, Conceição.
SENT OFF: JV Pinto 27, Beto 65.

As it turned out, a draw would have been enough for Portugal – but they were handicapped by the red cards, the heat (Couto was taking on water within half-an-hour), and the continuing weariness of Figo, who was marked out of it by Song. João Pinto was shown a straight red for a foul on Park Ji-Sung, and Couto might have gone with him after holding the referee by the face! Beto received a second yellow when he tried to pull out of a tackle but caught Lee Yung-Pyo with his knee.

---

14 June 2002 – World Cup Stadium, Daejeon – 26,482 – Lu Jun (CHN)

POLAND (2) 3
Olisadebe 3, Kryszałowicz 5, Ma. Żewłakow 66

USA (0) 1
Donovan 83

POLAND Radoslaw Majdan, Kłos [Wałdoch 89], Jacek Zieliński (c), Koźmiński, Arkadiusz Głowacki, Cezary Kucharski [Ma. Żewłakow 65], Kryszałowicz, Maciej Murawski, Olisadebe [Paweł Sibik 86], Krzynówek, Zurawski.
USA Friedel, Hejduk, Sanneh, Mathis, Pope, Agoos [Beasley 36], Donovan, O'Brien, McBride [Moore 58], Reyna (c), Stewart [Jones 67].

By the end, the States were waiting anxiously for news from the other match – but Poland's meaningless revival wasn't enough to knock them out. Two goals came from corners: Żewłakow's header and Olisadebe thrashing a bouncing ball in off the bar. Kryszałowicz side-footed a near-post cross, and Donovan (who'd had a goal correctly disallowed for a shoulder charge), volleyed in a Mathis header. Sanneh

2002

tripped the persevering Kryszałowicz, but Friedel blocked Zurawski's spot kick to become only the second goalkeeper (after Tomaszewski in 1974) to save two penalties in a finals tournament. Agoos finished his unfortunate tournament by pulling a leg muscle, which kept him out of the knockout stages. Moore came on to win his 100th and last cap.

GROUP D

	P	W	D	L	F	A	Pts
South Korea	3	2	1	0	4	1	7
USA	3	1	1	1	5	6	4
Portugal	3	1	0	2	6	4	3
Poland	3	1	0	2	3	7	3

South Korea and USA qualified for the second round.

GROUP E

Cameroon, Germany (seeded), Republic of Ireland, Saudi Arabia.

1 June 2002 – Prefectural ('Big Swan'), Niigata – 33,679 – Toru Kamikawa (JPN)

CAMEROON   **(1) 1**
Mboma 39

REP. IRELAND   **(0) 1**
Holland 52

CAMEROON Alioum (Boukar), Bill Tchato, Pierre Wome, Marc-Vivien Foe, Raymond Kalla, Rigobert Song (c), 'Lauren' (Laureano Bisan-Etame Mayer), Salomon Olembe, Patrick Mboma [Patrick Suffo 69], Samuel Eto'o, Geremi (Njitap). *Winfried Schäfer (GER)*.

REP. IRELAND Shay Given, Gary Kelly, Ian Harte [Steven Reid 77], Mark Kinsella, Gary Breen, Steve Staunton (c), Jason McAteer [Steve Finnan HT], Matt Holland, Robbie Keane, Damien Duff, Kevin Kilbane. *Mick McCarthy*.

Ireland clearly missed Roy Keane in the first half, when Kinsella and Holland did very little and Cameroon were much more threatening and incisive, especially Eto'o, who broke through to force a save from Given then made the goal by beating Staunton and prodding the ball square for Mboma.

After the break, the Republic were soon rewarded for a more attacking approach. Geremi should have scored after a mistake by Harte, and in the next minute Holland hit a low drive just inside a post when Kalla's weak header found him on the edge of the area. Stopped in their tracks, Cameroon didn't switch play in the way that had troubled England in a friendly six days earlier, and Song might have conceded a penalty when he kept the ball away from Keane with his chest and arm.

McCarthy had trumpeted the potential of his two strikers ('they could be the stars of the World Cup) – but Duff couldn't get past defenders and Keane was simply useless, constantly dispossessed too easily, until he suddenly hit a post with seven minutes left after another poor clearance by Kalla.

British sources usually refer to Cameroon's goalkeeper as Boukar Alioum, but he had the reverse on the back of his shirt, and the Cameroon FA confirm this order of names (he was known by his forename). One Ireland full-back (Kelly) was an uncle of the other (Harte); they were the only players from different generations to play in the same finals match. McAteer, who'd told McCarthy porkies about his fitness, was replaced at half-time.

1 June 2002 – Sapporo Dome, Sapporo – 32,218 –
Ubaldo Aquino (PAR)

GERMANY   **(4) 8**
Klose 20, 25, 69, Ballack 40, Jancker 45,
Linke 72, Bierhoff 84, Schneider 90

SAUDI ARABIA   **(0) 0**

GERMANY Oliver Kahn (c), Thomas Linke, Christoph
Metzelder, Dietmar Hamann, Carsten Ramelow [Jens
Jeremies HT], Bernd Schneider, Torsten Frings,
Carsten Jancker [Oliver Bierhoff 67], Miroslav Klose
[Oliver Neuville 76], Michael Ballack, Christian Ziege.
Rudi Völler.
SAUDI ARABIA Mohammed Al-Deayea, Redha Tukar,
Abdullah Zubromawi, Mohammed Noor, Sami Al-Jaber
(c), Ahmed Dukhi Al-Dossari, Hussain Sulaimani,
Khamis Al-Owairan Al-Dossari [Ibrahim Al-Shahrani
HT], Abdullah Al-Waked Al-Shahrani, Nawaf Al-Temyat
[Abdulaziz Al-Khathran HT], Al-Hassan Al-Yami
[Abdullah Gaman Al-Dossari 77]. *Nasser Al-Johar.*

Saudi Arabia came with experience (Al-Deayea
winning his 167th cap, Al-Jaber his 144th,
Zubromawi his 120th) and recent home wins
over Uruguay and Senegal – which didn't
shield them from this aerial pounding. Five of
the goals were headed, by Klose (all three),
Ballack and Linke; Jancker, who hadn't scored
a League goal all season, put in Klose's backheel flick; Bierhoff toe-poked the ball in from
25 yards; and Schneider curled in a free kick.
All this after Jancker had had an early goal
wrongly disallowed when Al-Deayea missed a
clearance kick. Noor tried hard in midfield,
but Germany's physique and aggressive running made the Saudis look underfed and
anxious.

Klose, long, rangy and elegant, had scored
two other hat-tricks for Germany that season,
including one in his previous match. An eight-
month-old Canadian boy was refused entry
into the stadium because he didn't have a
ticket.

Some sources refer to AD Al-Dossari and
AJ (Jamaan) Al-Dossari, but they had Dukhi
and Gaman on their shirts in these finals.

5 June 2002 – Prefectural (Kashima), Ibaraki – 35,854 –
Kim Milton Nielsen (DEN)

GERMANY   **(1) 1**
Klose 19

REP. IRELAND   **(0) 1**
Keane 90

GERMANY Kahn (c), Linke, Metzelder, Hamann,
Frings, Ramelow, Schneider [Jeremies 89], Klose
[Marco Bode 85], Jancker [Bierhoff 75], Ballack,
Ziege.
REP. IRELAND Given, Finnan, Harte [Reid 74], Kinsella,
Breen, Staunton (c) [Kenny Cunningham 87], Kelly
[Niall Quinn 73], Holland, Keane, Duff, Kilbane.

Germany were in a slump that showed no sign
of ending as the 2006 finals approached.
They'd lost their European title without much
of a fight and couldn't remember such a dearth
of world-class players. But they were rarely in
any real danger after taking the lead here. Two
of the goals against Saudi Arabia had come
from left-wing crosses by Ballack, who sent in
another one here, Klose getting in front of
Harte to head in from right above the penalty
spot before celebrating with a forward somersault in mid-air.

After that, Keane missed an overhead kick
from close in, Kahn threw himself in front of
Duff's point-blank volley; Given saved from
Hamann; and the hulking Jancker lobbed just
wide when Ballack played him in. But these
were isolated incidents; Germany were happy
to squeeze play between the two penalty areas;
Keane had a running battle with the 21-year-
old Metzelder, a find at left-back, who towered
over him; and the match looked won and
lost by the time Finnan sent in a prehistoric
long ball from the right-back position. Quinn

2002

craned his neck for a back-header, and Keane chested it past Ramelow before blasting it in. Even then Kahn nearly kept it out: the ball went in off his head and the near post. Relief for the Irish, who now only needed to score twice in a finals match for once.

Staunton was winning his 100th cap.

---

6 June 2002 – Saitama Stadium 2002, Saitama – 52,328 – Terje Hauge (NOR)

CAMEROON   (0) 1
Eto'o 65

SAUDI ARABIA   (0) 0

CAMEROON Alioum, Tchato, Wome [Pierre Njanka 84], Foe, Kalla, Song (c), Lauren, Daniel Ngom Kome [Olembe HT], Mboma [Pius Ndiefi 74], Eto'o, Geremi. SAUDI ARABIA Al-Deayea (c), Mohammed Al-Jahani, Tukar, Zubromawi [Gaman 72], Fouzi Al-Shehri, Hussain Sulaimani, Al-Khathran [Noor 86], Al-Waked, I Al-Shahrani, Al-Temyat, Obeid Al-Dossari [Al-Yami 35].

Cameroon were the reigning African and Olympic champions but looked completely out of sorts and almost lost to this fragile Saudi team, who again made puny tackles but this time also a number of chances, Obeid missing a free header after only eight minutes. Lauren had a headed goal disallowed because Eto'o was offside, but Mboma and Eto'o were generally kept at bay as Al-Temyat ran the show. Slim and fragile, recently recovered from a career-threatening knee injury, he'd looked tentative against Germany but seemed to grow in confidence during this match. A superb backheel volley put Obeid clear, and he should have scored at least twice, once after a superb run.

Tchato, already wearing a sticking plaster on his skull after colliding with Kalla against Ireland, went off to have his wrist bandaged after blocking Al-Temyat. Al-Deayea was injured when Eto'o landed on his head, and

didn't do much to stop him scoring after he'd run onto Geremi's long ball. As in 1998, Saudi Arabia were the first team to be eliminated.

---

11 June 2002 – Shizuoka Stadium ('Ecopa'), Shizuoka – 47,085 – Antonio López Nieto (SPA)

GERMANY   (0) 2
Bode 50, Klose 79

CAMEROON   (0) 0

GERMANY Kahn (c), Linke, Metzelder, Hamann, Ramelow, Frings, Schneider [Jeremies 80], Klose [Neuville 84], Jancker [Bode HT], Ballack, Ziege. CAMEROON Alioum, Tchato [Suffo 53], Wome, Foe, Kalla, Song (c), Lauren, Olembe [Ngom Kome 64], Mboma [Job 80], Eto'o, Geremi. SENT OFF: Ramelow 40, Suffo 77.

Cameroon's tackling had been strong but clean in their two previous matches, but they lost their composure towards the end, though some of the bookings were down to the wet surface. Sixteen yellow cards were shown (a finals record), to fourteen different players, eight of them German. The two reds came out for fouls on Eto'o and Ballack. Earlier in the season, Suffo had been sent off two minutes after coming on for Sheffield United in a flammable match with West Brom. Lauren was lucky to stay on after a frightening foul on Hamann, whose second-half performance was decisive.

Olembe broke through early on then virtually passed the ball to Kahn, Song headed wide when left unmarked at a free kick, and Lauren hit the post with a header. Germany took off Jancker's scary shaved head, and his substitute put away Klose's through-ball after Cameroon gave the ball away in midfield. Then Alioum didn't come off his line as Klose went up for Ballack's cross. No-one else has headed five goals in the finals, let alone in one tournament.

PLAYERS BOOKED IN A MATCH

14	2002	Germany (8)	v	Cameroon (6)
12	2002	Senegal (7)	v	Uruguay (3)
9	1990	Austria (5)	v	USA (4)
9	1994	Italy (5)	v	Nigeria (4)
8	1986	Mexico (5)	v	West Germany (3)
8	1994	Bulgaria (4)	v	Greece (4)
8	1994	Spain (4)	v	Switzerland (4)
8	1994	Germany (5)	v	Bulgaria (3)

16 yellow cards were shown in the Germany-Cameroon match: two players were sent off after being booked for a second time.

A tenth player (another Austrian) was sent off in the Austria v USA match.

Two players were sent off in the Mexico v West Germany match, one of whom had previously been booked. Italy also had another player sent off.

Ten cards (three red, seven yellow) were shown in the Denmark v South Africa match of 1998.

11 June 2002 – International, Yokohama – 65,320 – Falla Ndoye (SEN)

REP. IRELAND   **(1) 3**
Keane 7, Breen 61, Duff 87

SAUDI ARABIA   **(0) 0**

REP. IRELAND Given, Finnan, Harte [Quinn HT], Kinsella [Lee Carsley 89], Breen, Staunton (c), Kelly [McAteer 80], Holland, Keane, Duff, Kilbane.
SAUDI ARABIA Al-Deayea (c), Al-Jahani [Dukhi 79], Tukar, Zubromawi [Gaman 68], Al-Shehri, Sulaimani, Al-Temyat, Al-Khathran [Mohammed Al-Shloub 67], Al-Owairan, I Al-Shahrani, Al-Yami.

Even the conditions favoured the Irish. Wind and steady rain instead of the usual breathless oven. Like Turkey against China, they qualified by beating a poor side 3-0. At the 15th attempt, they scored more than one goal in a World Cup or European Championship finals match. Some poor marking allowed Keane to hit a low volley that made him their first player to score twice in any finals.

As the first half went on, Ireland began to lose the midfield, and Holland pulled Sulaimani's shirt in the Irish penalty area. But eventually Breen lunged to volley in Staunton's free kick, which went some way to justifying McCarthy's persistence with him at the expense of the younger and more talented John O'Shea.

Al-Deayea let it be known that he was using the tournament as a showcase for a move to a European club. Now he seemed to think Duff deserved a goal, so he gave him one, fumbling a shot that was hit straight at him. He went on to win 173 caps, and he'd been voted Asian Goalkeeper of the Century, which raised questions about the others. Some really appalling errors led to goals in three World Cups. Against the likes of Bangladesh, Macao, Vietnam and Mongolia, he set a world record all of his own by keeping 70 clean sheets – but it was more appropriate that he equalled Carbajal's total by conceding 25 goals in World Cup finals.

GROUP E

	P	W	D	L	F	A	Pts
Germany	3	2	1	0	11	1	7
Rep. Ireland	3	1	2	0	5	2	5
Cameroon	3	1	1	1	2	3	4
Saudi Arabia	3	0	0	3	0	12	0

Germany and the Republic of Ireland qualified for the second round.

2002

GROUP F

Argentina (seeded), England, Nigeria, Sweden.

2 June 2002 – Prefectural (Kashima), Ibaraki – 34,050 – Gilles Veissière (FRA)

ARGENTINA **(0) 1**
Batistuta 63

NIGERIA **(0) 0**

ARGENTINA Pablo Cavallero, Mauricio Pochettino, Juan Pablo Sorín, Javier Zanetti, Diego Simeone, Diego Placente, Walter Samuel, Ariel Ortega, Gabriel Batistuta [Hernán Crespo 81], Juan Sebastián Verón (c) [Pablo Aimar 78], Claudio López [Cristian 'Kily' González HT]. *Marcelo Bielsa.*
NIGERIA Ike Shoronmu, Efe Sodje [Justice Christopher 73], Céléstine Babayaro, Taribo West, Isaac Okoronkwo, Joseph Yobo, Garba Lawal, Nwankwo Kanu [Pius Ikedia 48], Julius Aghahowa, Augustine 'Jay-Jay' Okocha (c), Bartholomew Ogbeche. *Festus 'Adegboye' Onigbinde.*

Argentina lost their captain when Roberto Ayala pulled a thigh muscle in the warm-up, but were threatening and exciting from the start. Ortega gave Babayaro a hard time, and the young Nigerian attack made no headway against a strong defence. When Okocha beat Sorín (twice) and Verón before bringing a save from Cavallero, it was Nigeria's only shot on target. In comparison, Sodje had just been relegated to the Second Division with Crewe. The first member of the Urhobo tribe to play for Nigeria, he wasn't allowed to wear his trademark bandana here but tied his beard in a small knot.

Like the rest of the defence, he struggled against a persistent Batistuta, especially when Verón took corners from the left. Batistuta kicked the advertising boards after heading

wide with the keeper nowhere, lunged in to scrape a volley wide of an open goal with his studs, and finally arrived beyond the far post to head in from a very tight angle. It was his tenth finals goal at exactly a goal a game; for the third time in a row, he scored his team's opening goal, but this was the last of his 56 for Argentina, a very impressive national record.

Verón had just spent an unhappy first season at Man United, where he'd been made to stand in the corner to accommodate Roy Keane, a waste of a great puppeteer. Here he penned Nigeria in their own half and forced them to concede free kicks and corners as Argentina justified their position as favourites.

Onigbinde was the first black African to coach a black African country in the finals, followed by Jomo Sono of South Africa later the same day. He changed his baptismal name because Festus 'didn't mean anything'. Justice Christopher is correct, not Christopher Justice.

2 June 2002 – Saitama Stadium 2002, Saitama – 62,561 – Carlos Simon (BRZ)

ENGLAND **(1) 1**
Campbell 24

SWEDEN **(0) 1**
Alexandersson 59

ENGLAND David Seaman, Danny Mills, Ashley Cole, Owen Hargreaves, Sol Campbell, Rio Ferdinand, David Beckham (c) [Kieron Dyer 63], Paul Scholes, Michael Owen, Darius Vassell [Joe Cole 74], Emile Heskey. *Sven-Göran Eriksson (SWE).*
SWEDEN Magnus Hedman, Olof Mellberg, Teddy Lucic, Tobias Linderoth, Andreas Jakobsson, Johan Mjällby (c), Niclas Alexandersson, Magnus Svensson [Anders Svensson 56], Marcus Allbäck [Andreas Andersson 80], Henrik Larsson, Fredrik Ljungberg. *Tommy Söderberg & Lars Lagerbäck.*

After a nervous start in which he was booked for a lunging foul on Larsson and missed a tackle that almost let Allbäck in, Campbell applied some balm to an old wound. In an eerily exact copy of his disallowed goal in France 98, he headed his first goal for England, in his 47th game, from Beckham's left-wing corner while Hedman was being baulked by Allbäck, who was preoccupied with holding on to Owen's shirt.

For the rest of the half, Sweden remained totally unthreatening, especially Ljungberg, who was playing in pain from a hip injury, and Larsson, whose 64 league goals in the last two seasons had been scored in Scotland (enough said); when he elbowed Ashley Cole in the face, it was probably to let us know he was on the pitch.

But England fell away completely after half-time, giving one of their very worst performances under Eriksson, which is saying something. They hit long passes up to small strikers against a defence that stayed deep, and put too many balls into fifty-fifty situations, apparently because the coach believed it was better to lose the ball in the last third of the field! Heskey, horribly out of position, was his usual timid self, and Scholes did nothing going forward.

Meanwhile Beckham had been out for eight weeks with a broken foot (the first time most of the population had heard the word 'metatarsal'). Our friends at the *Sun* even printed a shot of his foot, urging readers to put their hands on it and pray. Here he became increasingly invisible in the time he survived, but his removal set Lucic free to come forward, and Seaman had to save his volley when Larsson put him through. It was only a matter of time before Mills chested the ball back, recovered to lunge it away, but sent it only as far as Alexandersson, who made space to his left before thumping a shot high past an unsighted Seaman.

England disintegrated after that, doing even the basics badly. Ashley Cole, a defensive liability

at this stage of his career, miskicked to set up Larsson and headed the ball back into the danger area for Linderoth to shoot over. You could almost forgive the England band for still giving us the theme from *The Great Escape*.

Having a Swedish manager didn't help against Sweden, who'd now gone ten games without defeat against England since 1968 (they added an 11th in 2004); they've never lost a competitive match to England. Linderoth's father Anders played in the 1978 finals. Beckham (white), Ljungberg (red) and Hedman (yellow) wore their hair in coloured crests.

---

7 June 2002 – Kobe Stadium ('Wing'), Kobe – 36,194 – René Ortube (BOL)

SWEDEN   **(1) 2**
Larsson 35, pen 62

NIGERIA   **(1) 1**
Aghahowa 27

SWEDEN Hedman, Mellberg, Lucic, Linderoth, Jakobsson, Mjällby (c), Alexandersson, A Svensson [M Svensson 84], Allbäck [Andersson 64], Larsson, Ljungberg.
NIGERIA Shoronmu, Ifeanyi Udeze, Babayaro [Kanu 66], Yobo, Okoronkwo, West, Okocha (c), Christopher, Aghahowa, Ogbeche [Ikedia 71], John Utaka.

Sweden had failed to win any of their last seven matches and barely survived against a raw Nigerian team who were unlucky to be eliminated. They hit the post twice: with a clearance kick by Lucic that rebounded off Mjällby's shin after Okocha's slippery run, and a low left-footer by Yobo, whose cross had earlier been gloriously headed in by Aghahowa.

But Larsson, the 1994 dreadlocks cut down to the skull by now, scored goals at this level as well as against Motherwell and St Johnstone. Eight in the qualifiers were followed by a swerve inside Okoronkwo and a penalty after

2002

he'd been pulled back by Udeze. Christopher kicked Mjällby's header off the line, Mjällby kicked Utaka's shot off the line, and a draw would have been fairer to everyone.

---

7 June 2002 – Sapporo Dome, Sapporo – 35,927 – Pierluigi Collina (ITA)

ENGLAND   **(1) 1**
Beckham pen 44

ARGENTINA   **(0) 0**

ENGLAND Seaman, Mills, A Cole, Nicky Butt, Campbell, Ferdinand, Beckham (c), Hargreaves [Trevor Sinclair 19], Owen [Wayne Bridge 80], Heskey [Teddy Sheringham 56], Scholes.
ARGENTINA Cavallero, Pochettino, Sorín, Zanetti, Simeone, Placente, Samuel, Ortega, Batistuta [Crespo 60], Verón (c) [Aimar HT], González (López 64).

To no-one's great surprise, Diego Maradona threw his contribution into the cauldron by announcing that 'England are quaking in their boots.' They may have been, too. In his time as coach at Lazio, Eriksson had bought Verón, Simeone, Crespo and López – and there was probably a kind of fearful respect in the decision to station Scholes on the left wing, where he'd probably have been lost as an attacking force. Luckily the move was scuppered as early as the fourth minute, when Hargreaves was injured in a collision with Owen, allowing Sinclair to come in and keep the Argentinian right wing fully occupied.

Revenge for the traumatic elimination of 1998 (perhaps even 1986) was achieved by a very defensive performance but a good one that faced Argentina down in their areas of strength. Of his time at Man United, Verón said 'At times this season I feel like I've been humiliated . . . I have no feelings for the English people.' But he was taken off at half-time when these particular English people didn't allow him to show what

he could still do. Butt was in his element as a holding player, Batistuta got no change out of Campbell and a much-improved Ferdinand, Cole survived against Ortega, and Owen was a handful throughout, hitting a post, shooting wide after rolling Placente, and showing Argentina another of his party pieces by waiting for Pochettino to stick out a leg, then making sure he fell heavily when contact was made. You could see it coming from here.

Simeone and *that* red card had preyed on people's minds for four years, and the bogey-man himself made sure they still did as Beckham prepared to take the penalty, offering a handshake that was turned down but almost worked: the penalty left Cavallero standing but skimmed his left foot. As the teams went off for half-time, Beckham deigned to let Simeone shake his hand.

A frustrated Argentina were reduced to other examples of gamesmanship, targeting players they obviously considered volatile, González pushing Mills in the face and Scholes being abused in the tunnel. It didn't work. On a pitch that slid in on a bed of air, under a roof and in a controlled temperature, England held out to record their first win over Argentina since 1980 and their first against them in the World Cup since 1966. The 38-year-old Seaman had to get down to block Pochettino's header from a corner, but the rest of the team had paid their dues for that. One or two Englishmen were quietly pleased that Simeone's 106th and last international (an Argentinian record) ended with this result against this country.

---

12 June 2002 – Miyagi Stadium, Miyagi – 45,777 – Ali Mohammed Bujsaim (UAE)

ARGENTINA   **(0) 1**
Crespo 88

SWEDEN   **(0) 1**
A Svensson 59

ARGENTINA Cavallero, Pochettino, Sorín [González 63], Zanetti, José Chamot, Samuel, Ortega, Matías Almeyda [Verón 63], Batistuta (c) [Crespo 58], Aimar, López.
SWEDEN Hedman, Mellberg, Lucic, Linderoth, Jakobsson, Mjällby (c), Alexandersson, A Svensson [Mattias Jönsson 68], Allbäck [Andersson HT], Larsson [Zlatan Ibrahimovic 88], M Svensson.

At the end of a match absolutely dripping with tension, the lasting image was of sweaty long hair hanging down in despair, Batistuta ending his international career looking like a crushed Christ. Almeyda and especially Sorín made the 1978 boys look like skinheads, and Placente was probably dropped for tying his in a ponytail.

Argentina made the only chances in the first half, López twice shooting just wide, Sorín coming close with two headers, the first well saved by Hedman. But when Almeyda fouled Anders Svensson, Cavallero could only palm the 30-yard free kick into the side netting. Then Almeyda hammered a cross against his own keeper, and Cavallero tipped Andersson's shot onto a post. When Hedman saved Ortega's penalty, Crespo's follow-up should have been disallowed for encroachment. The 35-year-old Caniggia, an important player in 1990 and 1994 but now in the squad at the expense of the 20-year-old Javier Saviola, was sent off from the bench for abusing the referee, presumably in a language they both understood. Another ponytail bobbing into oblivion.

12 June 2002 – Nagai, Osaka – 44,864 – Brian Hall (USA)

ENGLAND 0

NIGERIA 0

ENGLAND Seaman, Mills, A Cole [Bridge 85], Butt, Campbell, Ferdinand, Beckham (c), Scholes, Owen [Vassell 77], Heskey [Sheringham 69], Sinclair.

NIGERIA Vincent Enyeama, Sodje, Udeze, Christopher, Okoronkwo, Yobo, James Obiora, Benedict Akwuegbu, Aghahowa, Okocha (c), Femi Opabunmi [Ikedia 86].

The afternoon kick-off led to temperatures of 34°C, the hottest conditions Ferdinand had ever played in ('People were burning'), but he played with real authority as a sweeper. England conserved energy by keeping possession and hitting on the break, and the 19-year-old keeper did well to touch Scholes' 30-yard shot onto a post. Aghahowa and Okocha (a clown in 1998 but infinitely more effective this time) were the only stars in a young squad (Ogbeche and Opabunmi were only 17).

The National Electric & Power Authority (NEPA, known to Nigerians as Never Enough Power Anywhere), placed ads in newspapers pleading: 'Please don't take the law into your own hands ... If you go on an orgy of destruction simply because there was a power failure during a match, you will not be helping matters.' The team wasn't successful enough to spark such a reaction – but at least Sodje was allowed to wear his bandana this time.

The spelling Obiorah surfaced in a number of places, but not on his shirt in this match.

GROUP F

	P	W	D	L	F	A	Pts
Sweden	3	1	2	0	4	3	5
England	3	1	2	0	2	1	5
Argentina	3	1	1	1	2	2	4
Nigeria	3	0	1	2	1	3	1

Sweden and England qualified for the second round.

2002

1930
1934
1938
1950
1954
1958
1962
1966
1970
1974
1978
1982
1986
1990
1994
1998
2002
2006

GROUP G

Croatia, Ecuador, Italy (seeded), Mexico.

3 June 2002 – Prefectural ('Big Swan'), Niigata – 32,239 – Lu Jun (CHN)

MEXICO **(0) 1**
Blanco pen 60

CROATIA **(0) 0**

MEXICO Oscar Pérez, Salvador Carmona, Ramón Morales, Gabriel Caballero, Manuel Vidrio, Rafael Márquez (c), Braulio Luna, Sigifredo Mercado, Jared Borgetti [Luis Hernández 68], Gerardo Torrado, Cuauhtémoc Blanco [Francisco Palencia 79]. *Javier Aguirre.*
CROATIA Stipe Pletikosa, Robert Kovač, Robert Jarni, Stjepan Tomas, Josip Šimunić, Boris Živković, Niko Kovač, Zvonimir Soldo, Davor Šuker (c) [Danijel Šarić 64], Robert Prosinečki [Milan Rapaić HT], Alen Bokšić [Mario Stanić 67]. *Mirko Jozić.*
SENT OFF: Živković 59.

A clean contest between two very average teams was decided by its one good move, Borgetti's backheel finding Blanco, who was brought

CONSECUTIVE DRAWS

5	Belgium	1998–02
4	Rep. Ireland	1990
3	Wales	1958
3	England	1958
3	Cameroon	1982
3	Italy	1982
3	Holland	1990
3	Norway	1994–98
3	Chile	1998
3	South Africa	1998–02

down by Živković, whose red card was the only one of either colour in the match. The heat and humidity visibly affected the Croatians: three of their ancient monuments were replaced, and the other, Jarni, had lost his famous speed and couldn't make his forward runs in these climatic conditions. Mexico were their usual lightweight selves, with the bouncy Blanco again impersonating a very good player. Šuker and the chain-smoking Prosinečki weren't capped again. The Kovačs were brothers.

3 June 2002 – Sapporo Dome, Sapporo – 31,081 – Brian Hall (USA)

ITALY **(2) 2**
Vieri 7, 27

ECUADOR **(0) 0**

ITALY Gianluigi Buffon, Christian Panucci, Paolo Maldini (c), Damiano Tommasi, Alessandro Nesta, Fabio Cannavaro, Gianluca Zambrotta, Luigi Di Biagio [Gennaro Gattuso 69], Christian Vieri, Francesco Totti [Alessandro Del Piero 73], Cristiano Doni [Angelo Di Livio 64]. Giovanni Trapattoni.
ECUADOR José Cevallos, Ulises de la Cruz, Iván Hurtado, Alfonso Obregón, Augusto Porozo, Raúl Guerrón, Édison Méndez, Edwin Tenorio [Marlon Ayovi 59], Agustín Delgado, Alex Aguinaga (c) [Carlos Tenorio HT], Cléber Chalá [Nicolás Asencio 85]. *Hernán Darío Gómez (COL).*

In an open World Cup, this was the place to find the dark horses. Italy had the best goalkeeper and defence in the world (Nesta and Cannavaro looking like brothers with their thin black headbands), Totti to make the play, Vieri back after missing Euro 2000, midfield enforcers and quality substitutes galore, and a tempo suited to the conditions. Their first run-out was the most impressive in the opening round of matches.

Cevallos had already dived at Vieri's feet and Cannavaro had been flattened by Edwin Tenorio's punch in the Ecuadorian penalty area by the time Totti's run and cross allowed Vieri to sidefoot the ball imperiously high inside the near post. Di Biagio celebrated his 31st birthday by hitting a long ball for Vieri to brush off Hurtado, shoot against the underside of the keeper's leg, and follow up almost unnecessarily as the rebound bounced towards goal.

That was enough for the Italians, who sat back and counter-attacked in time-honoured fashion. Vieri was left increasingly isolated, but it hardly mattered against such a tame team. Delgado's nine goals made him joint leading scorer in the South American qualifiers, but he'd lost match sharpness by returning to Ecuador from Southampton for knee surgery, and the veteran playmaker Aguinaga couldn't cope with Italy's tackling, which won the ball without conceding free kicks.

Meanwhile it was hard to believe this was Totti's first game for two months because of thigh trouble: in contrast with Beckham's exhaustion against Sweden, he was fit and sharp and at the heart of every attacking move. In the second half, Doni hit the bar with a raised foot (hurting the keeper), but the job had been done by then.

The match was played in an indoor stadium on a retractable pitch floating on a bed of air. Maldini's 71st international as captain broke the national record he shared with Facchetti. Chalá and Delgado were cousins. Spelling variations: Poroso (Porozo on his shirt) and Cléver Chalá.

---

8 June 2002 – Prefectural (Kashima), Ibaraki – 36,472 – Graham Poll (ENG)

CROATIA   **(0) 2**
Olić 73, Rapaić 76

ITALY   **(0) 1**
Vieri 55

CROATIA Pletikosa, R Kovač, Jarni (c), Šimunić, Sarić, Tomas, Rapaić [Dario Šimić 79], N Kovač, Soldo [Jurica Vranjes 62], Davor Vugrinec [Ivica Olić 57], Bokšić.
ITALY Buffon, Panucci, Maldini (c), Tommasi, Nesta [Marco Materazzi 24], Cannavaro, Zambrotta, Cristiano Zanetti, Vieri, Totti, Doni [Filippo Inzaghi 79].

Croatia had been right to shed their veterans and were now brighter and busier – but for most of the match they looked likely to go the same way as Ecuador. After having his left knee bandaged at half-time, Vieri came from well behind his marker to dive and head a goal from Zambrotta's volleyed flick-on, only to be booked for protesting when it was ludicrously disallowed. It didn't matter. Within five minutes, he was hanging in the air to head Doni's cross over the keeper, and that seemed that.

But this time the retreat into defence turned into a siege, allowing Vugrinec, Rapaić and Bokšić to pose problems with their movement. Doni looked lost as Totti's creative assistant, and Maldini didn't go forward at all, leaving Italy with no width on the left. Vieri would have made it 2-0 if he hadn't blazed high and wide when a deflected long ball put him clear – and a minute later Olić came from behind three defenders to touch Jarni's cross across Buffon.

A draw would still have been a useful second prize for Italy, but they packed a season's bad luck into one match. Nesta's early injury brought in Materazzi, who'd once had a very mixed season with Everton but looked the part in Italy's win at Elland Road in March. Here he went to pieces at the end of the match, almost conceding a goal after getting in a tangle with Maldini on the left touchline, and two minutes later, Rapaić's volley spun off his leg and sailed over Buffon.

Italy kept trying to the end. When Totti took a free kick, the ball passed behind the keeper

2002

after hitting the near post, and in injury time Inzaghi was controversially penalised for linking arms with Šimić as Materazzi's 60-yard chip bounced all the way in.

Italy had missed the chance to equal Brazil's record of 13 finals matches without defeat. Instead of qualifying with a game to spare, they were left needing to match Croatia's result five days later, a position they should never have been in.

---

9 June 2002 – Miyagi Stadium, Miyagi – 45,610 – Mourad Daami (TUN)

MEXICO   (1) 2
Borgetti 28, Torrado 56

ECUADOR   (1) 1
Delgado 5

MEXICO Pérez, Jesús Arellano, Morales, Carmona, Vidrio, Márquez (c), Johan Rodríguez [Caballero 87], Blanco [Mercado 90], Borgetti [Hernández 77], Torrado, Luna.
ECUADOR Cevallos, de la Cruz, Porozo, Hurtado (c), Guerrón, Méndez, Obregón [Aguinaga 58], E Tenorio [Ayovi 35], Delgado, Iván Kaviedes [C Tenorio 53], Chalá.

After Pérez had pushed Delgado's header in off bar and post, Ecuador abandoned the midfield, wasting Carlos Tenorio's speed and allowing Torrado to run the game. Hair cropped short like a layer of rock salt, he scored the winner from outside the penalty area. Borgetti, who hit a post in the second half, equalised from Morales' near-post cross, and Mexico were already through.

---

13 June 2002 – Oita Stadium ('Big Eye'), Oita – 39,291 – Carlos Simon (BRZ)

ITALY   (0) 1
Del Piero 85

MEXICO   (1) 1
Borgetti 34

ITALY Buffon, Panucci [Francesco Coco 63], Maldini (c), Tommasi, Nesta, Cannavaro, Zambrotta, Zanetti, Vieri, Totti [Del Piero 78], Inzaghi [Vincenzo Montella 55].
MEXICO Pérez, Arellano, Vidrio, Carmona, Márquez (c), Morales [Rafael García 76], Torrado, Blanco, Borgetti [Palencia 80], Rodríguez [Caballero 76], Luna.

The stress was there for all to see. From the start, Italy were stiff as boards while Mexico went for a stroll. Already enjoying their place in the second round, they kept the ball for an eternity before Borgetti got in front of Maldini to score with a crafty glancing header across the keeper. Maldini had seen the ghost of this goal back in 1990, when Caniggia put the knife into Italy for Argentina. Now Cannavaro made a vital block from Borgetti and kicked off the line when Blanco and the dangerous Arellano interpassed through the defence.

But even though Italy grew visibly desperate, Totti kept on piercing the Mexican defence, his through-passes leading to an early disallowed goal by Inzaghi and bad misses by Inzaghi again and Vieri. Then Montella's lob was also ruled out (also correctly), and Italy began to suspect the gods had picked someone else in the sweepstake.

But they relented long enough for Montella to hook in a volleyed cross that bounced in the

FASTEST GOALS

secs				
11	Hakan Sükür	TUR	2002	v SKO
15	Václav Mašek	CZE	1962	v MEX
24	Ernst Lehner	GER	1934	v AUT
27	Bryan Robson	ENG	1982	v FRA
35	Émile Veinante	FRA	1938	v BEL
35	Arne Nyberg	SWE	1938	v HUN
37	Bernard Lacombe	FRA	1978	v ITA

1930
1934
1938
1950
1954
1958
1962
1966
1970
1974
1978
1982
1986
1990
1994
1998
2002
2006

penalty area, and Del Piero paid off a fraction of the debt he owed from the last European Final by running through (well onside!) to head in. That was the easy bit. Now, after watching Mexico string together 54 consecutive passes, Italy had to wait for news from Yokohama.

13 June 2002 – International, Yokohama – 65,862 – William Mattus (COS)

ECUADOR **(0) 1**
Méndez 48

CROATIA **(0) 0**

ECUADOR Cevallos, de la Cruz, Porozo, Hurtado (c), Guerrón, Méndez, Obregón [Aguinaga 40], C Tenorio [Kaviedes 76], Delgado, Ayovi, Chalá.
CROATIA Pletikosa, Šimunić, Jarni (c), Tomas, Šimić [Vugrinec 52], R Kovač, N Kovač [Vranjes 59], Sarić [Stanić 68], Rapaić, Olić, Bokšić.

If you beat Italy, you should be able to beat the team Italy beat, yes? Not this team of yo-yos. Although Bokšić clipped the outside of a post in the first half, Croatia simply didn't make enough chances, and Ecuador took one well, Méndez volleying in Delgado's knock-down to lower a few Italian pulse rates. By the time Olić's sharp header hit Aguinaga on the line, Croatia needed two goals and were getting ready to kick themselves.

GROUP G

	P	W	D	L	F	A	Pts
Mexico	3	2	1	0	4	2	7
Italy	3	1	1	1	4	3	4
Croatia	3	1	0	2	2	3	3
Ecuador	3	1	0	2	2	4	3

Mexico and Italy qualified for the second round.

The result was a reward for Gómez, who'd ended the racial segregation that saw black, white and indigenous players eating at different tables. He'd once been shot by a hitman allegedly acting for Ecuador's former president Abdalá 'El Loco' Bucaram, whose son had been left out of the Under-20 squad.

GROUP H

Belgium, Japan (seeded), Russia, Tunisia.

4 June 2002 – Saitama Stadium 2002, Saitama – 55,256 – William Mattus (COS)

BELGIUM **(0) 2**
Wilmots 57, Van der Heyden 75

JAPAN **(0) 2**
Suzuki 59, Inamoto 68

BELGIUM Geert De Vlieger, Eric Van Meir, Peter Van der Heyden, Jacky Peeters, Timmy Simons, Yves Vanderhaeghe, Gert Verheyen [Branko Strupar 83], Daniel Van Buyten, Marc Wilmots (c), Johan Walem [Wesley Sonck 70], Bart Goor. *Robert Waseige.*
JAPAN Seigo Narazaki, Naoki Matsuda, Koji Nakata, Kazuyuki Toda, Ryuzo Morioka (c) [Tsuneyasu Miyamoto 72], Takayuki Suzuki [Hiroaki Morishima 69], Daisuke Ichikawa, Junichi Inamoto, Atsushi Yanagisawa, Hidetoshi Nakata, Shinji Ono ['Alex' (Alessandro dos Santos) 64]. *Philippe Troussier (FRA).*

Japan started like their co-hosts, full of running and hasty passes, though it was only a matter of time before Belgium's power in the air paid off, Wilmots scoring with an overhead kick. But Belgium's first defensive error cost them the equaliser. Van der Heyden left a long ball down the middle, and Suzuki stretched to get there before De Vlieger and push it just inside the post. Then Inamoto won the ball,

2002

ran on for a pass, beat Van Meir on the left on the edge of the area, and finished with a strong left-footer as the keeper went down a fraction early.

Belgium were wilting now, but Van der Heyden atoned for his mistake by scoring his first goal for Belgium, running in from deep to touch a volley over Narazaki. In the final minutes, Inamoto had a goal disallowed for his foul on Van der Heyden, and Sonck should have had a penalty for a trip by Koji Nakata. The other Nakata showed some touches of class but was generally disappointing again, though the aggressive Toda made some important tackles.

This was Van Meir's third World Cup finals tournament – and his first game. Miyamoto wore a Lone Ranger mask to protect a broken nose, and several Japanese players dyed their hair for the occasion: Toda red, Matsuda chestnut, Suzuki bronze, Inamoto yellowish bronze, Narazaki reddish brown, Hidetoshi Nakata burnt sienna, Morioka something vaguely pale.

5 June 2002 – Kobe Stadium ('Wing'), Kobe – 30,957 – Peter Prendergast (JAM)

RUSSIA   **(0) 2**
Titov 59, Karpin pen 64

TUNISIA   **(0) 0**

RUSSIA Ruslan Nigmatullin, Andrei Solomatin, Yuri Kovtun, Igor Semshov [Dmitri Khokhlov HT], Viktor Onopko (c), Yuri Nikiforov, Dmitri Karpin, Marat Izmailov [Dmitri Alenichev 78], Yegor Titov, Vladimir Beschastnykh [Dmitri Sychev 55], Ruslan Pimenov. *Oleg Romantsev.*
TUNISIA Ali Boumnijel, Hatem Trabelsi, Hassan Gabsi [Zoubeir Baya 67], Raouf Bouzaiene, Radhi Jaidi, Khaled Badra [Ali Zitouni 84], Adel Sellimi (c) [Imed Mhadhebi 67], Mohammed Mkacher, Ziad Jaziri, Riadh Bouazizi, Slim Ben Achour. *Ammar Souayeh.*

This would have been another case of a big ponderous European team being moved

around by nimble opponents – if Tunisia hadn't been so irritatingly fiddly. They hadn't improved since 1998, and you could see why they'd recently gone seven matches without a goal. Zitouni had only just returned after a long-standing knee injury, and Sellimi was dropped for the next game.

Beschastnykh was disappointing too, and Russia were galvanised by his 18-year-old replacement. Sychev nearly scored with a lob from a tight angle and won the penalty when Jaidi's shoulder got in his way. Boumnijel, playing because Chokri El-Ouaer had retired from international football with back trouble, wasn't first choice at Bastia. A penalty might have been given when he caught Pimenov in the back of the head, and his poor throw-out led to Titov scoring with a low cross shot.

The veterans in central defence, Nikiforov and Onopko, looked as if they might struggle against better teams in these conditions, but they were allowed to amble through this one. Onopko had lost most of his hair in his teens, though some observers enjoyed the fact that he lived near Chernobyl.

9 June 2002 – International, Yokohama – 66,108 – Markus Merk (GER)

JAPAN   **(0) 1**
Inamoto 51

RUSSIA   **(0) 0**

JAPAN Narazaki, Matsuda, K Nakata, Toda, Miyamoto (c), Tomokazu Myojin, Inamoto [Takashi Fukunishi 85], Suzuki [Masashi Nakayama 72], Yanagisawa, H Nakata, Ono [Toshihiro Hattori 75].
RUSSIA Nigmatullin, Solomatin, Kovtun, Alexei Smertin [Beschastnykh 57], Onopko (c), Nikiforov, Karpin, Izmailov [Khokhlov 52], Semshov, Titov, Pimenov [Sychev HT].

Some people in Moscow thought Russia should have come away with at least a draw. Two people were killed there, vehicles were set on fire, and the injured included five Japanese students.

Russia sent some clever short passes into the penalty area, but Japan got bodies in the way and lasted the pace better. Inamoto hadn't played a League match for Arsenal, who probably signed him to sell shirts in Japan and shipped him on to Fulham the following month. But his quick feet and workrate did the trick again here, getting him on the end of Yanagisawa's superb cushioned touch for the only goal.

Solomatin should have had a penalty when Toda grabbed him by the neck – but what really sparked the Moscow mob was a truly terrible miss by Beschastnykh, the national team's record goalscorer. Less than a minute after coming on, he reminded us of Parks' blunder for Costa Rica v Turkey by going beyond the keeper before slicing the ball into the side netting. His recent form had been so bad he'd wished he could 'cut my legs off and throw them away', which might have put ideas in the heads of some shady people back home. An improving Hidetoshi Nakata hit the bar with a handsome long-range shot.

10 June 2002 – Oita Stadium ('Big Eye'), Oita – 37,900 – Mark Shield (AUS)

BELGIUM   **(1) 1**
Wilmots 13

TUNISIA   **(1) 1**
Bouzaiene 17

BELGIUM De Vlieger, Eric Deflandre, Glen De Boeck, Van Buyten, Van der Heyden, Simons [Mbo Mpenza 74], Verheyen [Sonck HT], Vanderhaeghe, Strupar [Sven Vermant HT], Wilmots (c), Goor.

TUNISIA Boumnijel, Trabelsi, Gabsi [Sellimi 67], Bouzaiene, Jaidi, Badra (c), Kaies Ghodbane, Bouazizi, Jaziri [Zitouni 77], Mourad Melki [Baya 88], Ben Achour.

Wilmots volleyed in low from close range when Vanderhaeghe headed the ball back; Bouzaiene's free kick brought his first international goal; Deflandre should have conceded a penalty for a foul on Melki immediately afterwards – then the sticky heat took over again. Belgium became stodgy, the Tunisians slapdash. Strupar was invisible in the first half, Sonck limp throughout. Jaidi was clumsy at times but at least added some height and presence at the back. Ghodbane nearly scored an excellent goal by volleying fractionally wide, and Sonck or Wilmots would have headed in a right-wing cross if they hadn't both gone for it. The 28-year-old Shield was the youngest to referee a finals match since 1934.

14 June 2002 – Nagai, Osaka – 45,213 – Gilles Veissière (FRA)

JAPAN   **(0) 2**
Morishima 48, H Nakata 75

TUNISIA   **(0) 0**

JAPAN Narazaki, Matsuda, K Nakata, Toda, Miyamoto (c), Myojin, Inamoto [Ichikawa HT], Suzuki, Yanagisawa [Morishima HT], H Nakata [Mitsuo Ogasawara 84], Ono.
TUNISIA Boumnijel, Trabelsi, Clayton (Robeiro) [Mhadhebi 61], Bouzaiene [Zitouni 78], Jaidi, Badra (c), Ghodbane, Bouazizi, Jaziri, Melki [Baya HT], Ben Achour.

Even against a timid side, Japan again couldn't score till the second half, by which time even their players were taking on water. Morishima scored when Bouzaiene's sliding tackle sent the ball square across the penalty area; Nakata's diving header hit Boumnijel's heel on its way

2002

1930
1934
1938
1950
1954
1958
1962
1966
1970
1974
1978
1982
1986
1990
1994
1998
2002
2006

between his legs; and Morishima almost scored a great goal when his diving header hit the base of a post. Jaidi did well again, and Zitouni volleyed against the bar near the end – but Trabelsi's runs from right-back were Tunisia's only attacking threat: again Toda was lucky not to give away a penalty for fouling him. Japan qualified as they'd hoped, but they were going to need something more from their strikers before their tournament was out.

---

14 June 2002 – Shizuoka Stadium ('Ecopa'), Shizuoka – 46,640 – Kim Milton Nielsen (DEN)

BELGIUM   (1) 3
Walem 7, Sonck 78, Wilmots 82

RUSSIA   (0) 2
Beschastnykh 52, Sychev 88

BELGIUM De Vlieger, Van Buyten, Peeters, Vanderhaeghe, De Boeck [Van Meir 90], Nico Van Kerckhoven, Verheyen [Simons 78], Wilmots (c), Mpenza [Sonck 70], Walem, Goor.
RUSSIA Nigmatullin, Solomatin, Kovtun, Smertin [Sychev 34], Onopko (c), Nikiforov [Dmitri Sennikov 43], Karpin [Aleksandr Kerzhakov 83], Khokhlov, Beschastnykh, Titov, Alenichev.

Just when it looked as if Belgium were about to draw six finals matches in a row and be eliminated without losing one for the second World Cup in a row, Sonck headed in a corner, which was delayed to allow Simons to come on, then performed a cartwheel followed by an aerial back-flip. Wilmots' shot took a deflection off Onopko, and Sychev's alert run came too late to matter. Earlier Walem had placed a free kick so well it curled inside the side netting, and big Beschastnykh seemed to have made amends by putting in the rebound when De Vlieger saved at Sychev's feet.

Including four matches for the CIS (the renamed USSR), Onopko was winning his 100th cap.

GROUP H

	P	W	D	L	F	A	Pts
Japan	3	2	1	0	5	2	7
Belgium	3	1	2	0	6	5	5
Russia	3	1	0	2	4	4	3
Tunisia	3	0	1	2	1	5	1

Japan and Belgium qualified for the second round.

2ND ROUND

---

15 June 2002 – Jeju World Cup Stadium, Seogwipo – 25,176 – Carlos Batres (GUA)

GERMANY   (0) 1
Neuville 88

PARAGUAY   (0) 0

GERMANY Kahn (c), Linke, Metzelder [Frank Baumann 60], Frings, Marko Rehmer [Sebastian Kehl HT], Ballack, Jeremies, Schneider, Klose, Neuville [Gerald Asamoah 90], Bode.
PARAGUAY Chilavert (c), Arce, Caniza, Struway [Cuevas 90], Ayala, Gamarra, Carlos Bonet [Gavilán 84], Acuña, Cardozo, Santa Cruz [Campos 29], Cáceres.
SENT OFF: Acuña 90.

The match was staged on a rather inaccessible island, hence the small crowd, but a record 87.70% of the population watched on German TV – and were glad of it only at the very end. Both sides were depressingly cautious and kept giving the ball away. An injury to Santa Cruz prevented Paraguay from exploiting the suspensions of Hamann and Ziege, so Kahn kept another clean sheet on his 33rd birthday. Germany put a man on the line when Chilavert sent his final free kick over the bar; Acuña was sent off for elbowing Ballack in the face; and even Ballack joined the orgy of shirt-pulling when he tugged Cáceres in his own penalty area. The watching millions were spared any more tedium when Schneider crossed from the right and Neuville smacked a near-post half-volley across the keeper.

Afterwards, Chilavert was his usual gracious self: 'We lost as national heroes . . . Germany were not superior to us. They were lucky and we were their equals.' Before the start of the next season, he was released by Strasbourg for being overweight and undisciplined.

Asamoah, born in Ghana, the first black player to be capped by the unified Germany, was once advised to give up football because his heart septum was too big. Whenever he played, there was always a defibrillator, a resuscitation device, at the side of the pitch.

but this was closer to 5–95. Faced with a virtual open goal, Ferdinand contrived to head the ball sideways, and Sørensen clutched it to his chest, dropped it, then tried to claw it back. While it was crossing the line, Helveg was adding injury to insult by smacking his head against the advertising boards behind the goal.

Owen turned and scored when Butt's flick was deflected into his path by Gravesen, and thanks to the rain even the goal-shy Heskey dipped his bread in, his shot skidding through Sørensen when Beckham squared the ball after an error by Jensen. We needn't bother with the second half.

Denmark's 13th finals match was the first in which they failed to score. Tøfting spent three months in jail for assaulting the manager of the Café Ketchup in Copenhagen a few days after the match.

---

15 June 2002 – Prefectural ('Big Swan'), Niigata – 40,582 – Markus Merk (GER)

ENGLAND   (3) 3
Sørensen o.g. 5, Owen 22, Heskey 44

DENMARK   (0) 0

DENMARK Sørensen, Helveg [Bøgelund 7], N Jensen, Tøfting [Claus Jensen 58], Laursen, Henriksen (c), Grønkjær, Tomasson, Sand, Gravesen, Rommedahl.
ENGLAND Seaman, Mills, Cole, Butt, Campbell, Ferdinand, Beckham, Scholes [Dyer 49], Heskey [Sheringham 69], Owen [Robbie Fowler HT], Sinclair.

Impressive so far, Denmark must have fancied their chances – which they undermined almost immediately. Laursen's wayward header conceded a left-wing corner which Beckham hit to the far post. In a decision that matched 'Ronaldo's' goal against Costa Rica, FIFA awarded this one to Ferdinand: 'If it is 50–50, then we will go with the attacking player.' Yes

---

16 June 2002 – Oita Stadium ('Big Eye'), Oita – 39,747 – Ubaldo Aquino (PAR)

SENEGAL   (1) (1) 2
H Camara 37, 104 (golden goal)

SWEDEN   (1) (1) 1
Larsson 11

SENEGAL Sylva, Coly, Daf, Diatta, Malick Diop [Beye 65], Cisse (c), Bouba Diop, Pape Thiaw, Faye, H Camara, Diouf.
SWEDEN Hedman, Mellberg, Lucic, Linderoth, Jakobsson, Mjällby (c), Alexandersson [Ibrahimovic 76], A Svensson, Allbäck [Andersson 65], Larsson, M Svensson [Jönson 99].

Sweden's booby prize for winning their group was a match in blazing afternoon heat against African opponents. Once Larsson had headed in a corner, they massed in defence but couldn't stop Camara scoring two exceptional goals, with a ground shot from each foot after beating

2002

1930
1934
1938
1950
1954
1958
1962
1966
1970
1974
1978
1982
1986
1990
1994
1998
2002
2006

a man both times, scuffing the second in off a post. Bouba Diop goal had a goal disallowed for a fractional offside, and Diouf was warned by the referee for diving. The talented Ibrahimovic, very tall and very arrogant, wasted two opportunities in a minute.

The difference between success and a plane home can be cruelly slim at times. Earlier on in extra time, Anders Svensson's fantastic turn opened the way for a ferocious shot against an upright. Then the second post brought equally bad news for Sweden.

---

16 June 2002 – World Cup Stadium, Suwon – 38,926 – Anders Frisk (SWE)

SPAIN (1) (1) 1
Morientes 8

REP. IRELAND (0) (1) 1
Keane pen 89
Spain 3-2 pens.

SPAIN Casillas, Puyol, Juanfran, Baraja, Helguera, Hierro (c), Valerón, Luis Enrique, Morientes [Albelda 72], Raúl [Luque 80], de Pedro [Mendieta 66].
REP. IRELAND Given, Finnan, Harte [David Connolly 82], Kinsella, Breen, Staunton (c) [Cunningham 50], Kelly [Quinn 55], Holland, Keane, Duff, Kilbane.
PENALTY SHOOT-OUT: Keane 1-0, Hierro 1-1, Holland hit bar, Baraja 1-2, Connolly saved, Juanfran shot wide, Kilbane saved, Valerón hit post, Finnan 2-2, Mendieta 2-3.

Once Morientes had beaten Breen in the air and scored with a strong glancing header at the near post, Spain kept plenty of men back in defence, outnumbering the Irish attackers. Helguera, left out of the starting line-up for the first two group matches, bemoaned the fact that 'It's the same with Real Madrid. Every year they cut my head off and I have to prove myself time and again' – but was included in place of the 35-year-old Nadal to counter the pace of Duff and Keane.

Spain used clever angles to move the ball quickly through midfield and were mobile and dangerous up front, Luis Enrique and Raúl having goals disallowed for offside. But Ireland won two penalties in the second half. The first, just after the hour, was a farce, Juanfran collecting a yellow card for barely touching Duff, whose dive won the kick. Perhaps he was simply too exhausted to stand up: he was visibly struggling for breath by now. Harte's dead-ball delivery (his only use at international level) wasn't its usual self in this tournament, and Casillas easily saved his penalty, Kilbane volleying the rebound wide of a virtually empty net.

But Hierro, who'd already got away with pulling Duff's shirt in the Spanish area, tried the same again, almost lifting Quinn's collar over his head – and at last a referee in this tournament spotted it. Keane, who hadn't taken a penalty in 18 months, left Casillas standing from the spot. Injuries left Spain down to ten men in extra time, and they were relieved to win a penalty shoot-out for the first time, Mendieta's winning kick bobbling over Given's leg.

Ireland's only defeat throughout this World Cup had been an irrelevant injury-time loss in Iran, and they were unbeaten against Holland, Portugal, Cameroon, Germany and Spain. If Roy Keane had still been there, they might well have gone even further. In November, the FA of Ireland general secretary Brendan Menton resigned after an independent inquiry endorsed Keane's criticisms. The FAI, it said, had 'no culture of discipline' and had 'learned nothing' from previous World Cups. Brazil's Edmílson echoed Keane's concerns about the hard grounds aggravating injuries: 'The pitches are shit, the balls are shit, everything is shit around here. I have no idea why we came here. Some players are feeling knee pains, others in the ankle.' Brazil changed bases four times 'due to the condition of the pitches.' Keane could be a hot handful at times, on and off the pitch, but it's hard to believe that McCarthy couldn't have found a way to keep him in the squad if he'd wanted to. He resigned in November after defeats in the first two European qualifiers.

---

17 June 2002 – World Cup Stadium, Jeonju – 36,380 – Vítor Melo Pereira (POR)

USA   (1) 2
McBride 8, Donovan 65

MEXICO   (0) 0

USA Friedel, Gregg Berhalter, Mastroeni [Llamosa 90], Lewis, Pope, Sanneh, O'Brien, Wolff [Stewart 59], McBride [Jones 79], Reyna (c), Donovan.
MEXICO Pérez, Arellano, Carmona, Morales [Hernández 28], Vidrio [Mercado HT], Márquez (c), Luna, Torrado [Alberto García Aspe 78], Borgetti, Rodríguez, Blanco.
SENT OFF: Márquez 88.

So now Mexico knew how the Italians felt. Starting a knockout match as favourites, their tension was increased when the USA scored in their first move upfield, McBride's good strike adding to his American firsts by making him their only player to score in three finals matches. After that, already pouring with sweat, Mexico didn't have the pace to unsettle a defence in which Reyna played very well as a wing-back.

Berhalter was astonishingly lucky not to concede a penalty with a really glaring hand-ball – but then a simple direct move ended with Donovan heading in Lewis' cross, and Stewart volleyed against the outside of a post. It was the USA's first clean sheet in the finals since the famous win over England in 1950.

There seemed to be some history between Jones and the Mexican players. García Aspe was booked for a savage sliding foul on him, Márquez (after one bad tackle had gone unpunished) was sent off for a terrifying double whammy, lifting his studs and heading the back of Jones' dreadlocks, after which Mercado went unpunished after driving his studs into Jones' calf then kicking him in the chest! Nothing like losing with dignity.

---

17 June 2002 – Kobe Stadium ('Wing'), Kobe – 40,440 – Peter Prendergast (JAM)

BRAZIL   (0) 2
Rivaldo 67, Ronaldo 87

BELGIUM   (0) 0

BRAZIL Marcos, Cafú (c), Roberto Carlos, Gilberto, Roque Júnior, Lúcio, Juninho Paulista [Denílson 57], Edmílson, Ronaldo, Rivaldo [Ricardinho 90], Ronaldinho [Kléberson 81].
BELGIUM De Vlieger, Peeters [Sonck 73], Van Kerckhoven, Van Buyten, Simons, Verheyen Wilmots (c), Vanderhaeghe, Mpenza, Walem, Goor.

An ageing and cumbersome Belgian team had no flair but also no shortage of heart and teamwork. Even in 95% humidity, they made the Three Rs look eminently human. Ronaldinho did nothing, Rivaldo next to nothing, and when Ronaldo scored in a late break-away, it was virtually the first time he'd touched the ball after half-time. Marcos was busier than De Vlieger, a sharper striker than Mpenza might have tilted the match the other way, and much was made of a disallowed header by Wilmots, an unexpected star of the tournament, though he clearly pushed Roque Júnior in the back before jumping.

Even so, Belgium didn't have much luck. When Rivaldo chested down and turned before volleying from outside the area, the ball

2002

was deflected beyond the keeper by Simons' outstretched studs (not Van Buyten's, as in some sources). A limited team had pushed Brazil hard, and another one was waiting in Shizuoka.

---

18 June 2002 – Miyagi Stadium, Miyagi – 45,666 – Pierluigi Collina (ITA)

TURKEY   **(1) 1**
Davala 12

JAPAN   **(0) 0**

TURKEY Rüstü, Fatih, Ünsal, Ergün, Bülent, Alpay, Davala [Nihat 74], Tugay, Şükür (c), Bastürk [İlhan 89], Şaş [Tayfur 85].
JAPAN Narazaki, Matsuda, K Nakata, Toda, Miyamoto (c), Myojin, Inamoto [Ichikawa HT, Morishima 86], H Nakata, Ono, Alex [Suzuki HT], Akinori Nishizawa.

The humidity was a mere 77% this time, but rain fell on the parade. Active but scatter-brained as ever, Japan conceded a headed goal from a corner then wasted all their possession by misplacing their passes and overhitting cross after cross, making Turkey look better than they were. The Brazil-born Alex almost scored an undeserved equaliser when his free kick hit the top of a post, but Hidetoshi Nakata had another poor one, and Morishima, who'd helped turn the match against Tunisia, came on far too late.

Appendices one and two: Ono had his removed six days later after complaining of stomach pains during the tournament, and this was Nishizawa's first match since an operation in May. On the flight in from Seoul, Rüstü had picked up a head injury by leaving his seat belt off during a period of turbulence, a bigger headache than anything he got from his hosts.

2002

---

18 June 2002 – World Cup Stadium, Daejeon – 38,588 – Byron Moreno (ECU)

SOUTH KOREA   **(0) (1) 2**
Seol 88, Ahn 116 (*golden goal*)

ITALY   **(1) (1) 1**
Vieri 18

SOUTH KOREA Lee WJ, Choi JC, Kim NI [Lee CS 68], Lee YP, Kim TY [Hwang 63], Hong (c) [Cha 83], Yoo, Park, Song, Seol, Ahn.
ITALY Buffon, Panucci, Coco, Tommasi, Mark Iuliano, Maldini (c), Zanetti, Zambrotta [Di Livio 72], Vieri, Totti, Del Piero [Gattuso 61].
SENT OFF: Totti 103.

Ah yes, *schadenfreude* all round. The big bad defensive dinosaurs beaten by the brave little hosts. A repeat of 1966 and all that. Try telling people it wasn't that simple. Alright let's do that.

The opening phase put a damper on even the Koreans' enthusiasm. After only five minutes, Coco pushed Yoo, and Panucci grabbed Seol like a dance partner, but Buffon saved Ahn's penalty. When Totti hit a corner to the near post, Choi grabbed Vieri's shirt and was taken on a sleigh ride through the goal area before the mighty beast scored with a heavyweight header.

Vieri had urged the team to relax when they played; South Korea's rigid system made it easy for them. In every game, their defenders defended, their attackers attacked, their midfielders midfielded. After the penalty, forced to play at Italy's slower tempo, they didn't make a single opening till two minutes from time, and even then only because the enemy opened the gate to their own strongbox. Hwang, winning his 100th cap, scooped the ball in from the right, it went just over Iuliano's head, and a distracted Panucci let it bounce off his thigh and arm for Seol to whack it low past Buffon's left hand.

Italy almost turned the match back on

its head in the very next minute. Tommasi's left-wing cross found Vieri racing in unmarked at the far post, only for the volley to disappear into orbit. He'd had to lunge in for the shot, but it was in front of an open goal. Late in the second half, he'd shot wide of the same post after running clear of the defence. Strong as a rhino, a one-man strike force, Vieri scored nine goals in nine finals matches but will probably be best remembered for this single miss.

In extra time, Italy went down to ten men when their playmaker was debatably sent off. A surprising number of people remain unconvinced by Totti. It's true he was banned from Euro 2004 for spitting, but he'd been superb in Euro 2000 – and in this World Cup, playing for a defensive team and having to pace himself in the heat, he still managed to hit more than his share of defence-splitting passes. Booked for diving against Mexico, he was now sent off for the same offence, if that's what it was. Moreno was vilified in Italy (a holiday resort in Sicily named a row of toilets after him), and it's true he was later suspended for 20 matches after a league match in Ecuador. But he seemed to referee this one well and fairly.

Totti's departure left the team with no creative players to speak of, the over-cautious Trapattoni having replaced Del Piero with his midfield wolverine. When Seol's backheel put Gattuso clear, he could only shoot straight at the keeper. And by now Coco was wearing a crepe bandage holder like a Scrooge nightcap after a clash of heads with Tommasi. Eliminated from the last three World Cups on penalties, Italy were in the ironic position of holding on for another shoot-out when Lee Yong-Pyo hit a high cross from deep on the left.

With Cannavaro and Nesta out, Maldini had moved sideways to give his usual masterclass in central defence. Like Beckenbauer, he was on the losing side in a World Cup Final and a European Championship Final, but without the Kaiser's considerable consolation of also winning both competitions. And he came close to finishing on the winning side for the 15th time in a finals match, equalling the record. His last act of a great but greatly frustrating international career was to jump in vain as Ahn scored with a downward header. Cue explosion of delight from the 1.25 million watching on giant screens in central Seoul. Perugia chairman Luciano Gaucci didn't extend Ahn's loan period because 'I have no intention of paying a salary to someone who has ruined Italian soccer.' It was a joke, of course. Ahn went home because he wasn't good enough against Serie A defences – though he'd had the last laugh on this one.

QUARTER-FINALS

21 June 2002 – Shizuoka Stadium ('Ecopa'), Shizuoka – 47,436 – Felipe Ramos Rizo (MEX)

BRAZIL (1) 2
Rivaldo 45, Ronaldinho 50

ENGLAND (1) 1
Owen 23

BRAZIL Marcos, Cafú (c), Roberto Carlos, Gilberto, Roque Júnior, Lúcio, Edmílson, Kléberson, Ronaldo [Edílson 70], Rivaldo, Ronaldinho.
ENGLAND Seaman, Mills, A Cole [Sheringham 80], Butt, Campbell, Ferdinand, Beckham (c), Scholes, Heskey, Owen [Vassell 79], Sinclair [Dyer 56].
SENT OFF: Ronaldinho 57.

In the end, it didn't matter that Brazil had two days' less rest than England, who didn't score a second-half goal in these finals. In the first, they looked perfectly comfortable after taking

1930
1934
1938
1950
1954
1958
1962
1966
1970
1974
1978
1982
1986
1990
1994
1998
2002
2006

the lead. Heskey hit his forward pass too early, but Lúcio let it bounce off his thigh for Owen to send the keeper the wrong way. Then everything changed in a few manic minutes around half-time.

When the ball went loose on the England right, Beckham was criticised for jumping out of the challenge – but that's being too hard on him. With the ball going out of play, it would have been reckless to risk his fragile foot against the two tackles that came in. Roque Júnior somehow kept the ball in, and when it was moved into the centre Scholes missed his tackle. Ronaldinho's foot-over-the-ball feint took him past Cole, and a pass to the right found Rivaldo, whose left foot sent the ball low across Seaman. There was barely time to kick off.

Ronaldinho's winning free kick has probably been shown to everyone on the planet. Genius, they said. Complete fluke, they said back. Either he was aiming to chip a 6'4" goalkeeper from that range – or, if he was trying a cross, he got it incredibly wrong for such a gifted player. Frankly it looked as if he'd aimed at the near post and hooked his shot too far – and he eventually admitted as much. Beaten by Nayim's famous lob in a European Final, Seaman now had to face a similar demon.

Ronaldinho was soon sent off for a surreptitiously nasty foul, leaving his studs and elbow up for Mills to run into – but Scolari, whose strong-arm approach had been widely criticised in Brazil, liked to practise playing with ten men, to prepare for a red card! England didn't create a single chance against his depleted team, and it's still hard to understand Eriksson's substitutions. While Vassell and Sheringham were unlikely to spread dread through the Brazilian defence, Joe Cole's flair might just have provided the can opener.

An 'unnamed member of Real Madrid's inner circle' later decided Ronaldinho was 'so ugly that he'd sink you as a brand' – so they

bought Beckham instead: 'Just look how handsome he is . . . the whole of Asia has fallen in love with us because of Beckham. Ronaldinho was too ugly to sign.' While Beckham was having a humiliating first season with Real, Ronaldinho was a sensation at Barcelona and helped them win the League title in 2004–05.

England had beaten Argentina in a controlled environment and Denmark in the rain. In their three other matches, they suffered as much as anyone. Eriksson's assistant coach Tord Grip admitted 'We really did struggle in the heat . . . Drinking water is so important but if you're not used to it then even that is not easy . . . I think we were a little burned out.' And you couldn't disagree with him. But that last half-hour against Brazil was like a silent horror film, complete with three lions going out with a whimper.

---

21 June 2002 – Munsu, Ulsan – 37,337 – Hugh Dallas (SCO)

GERMANY (1) 1
Ballack 39
USA (0) 0

GERMANY Kahn (c), Linke, Metzelder, Hamann, Frings, Kehl, Schneider [Jeremies 60], Neuville [Bode 80], Klose [Bierhoff 88], Ballack, Ziege.
USA Friedel, Sanneh, Mastroeni [Stewart 80], Hejduk [Jones 65], Pope, Berhalter, Lewis, O'Brien, McBride [Mathis 58], Reyna (c), Donovan.

This time perhaps the extra two days did matter. The USA began to flag in the second half, and the running of Jones, who was winning his 159th cap and his 50th (a world record) as a substitute, was never a threat to the best teams. In the first half, Kahn had saved from the talented Donovan (twice) and Lewis.

The German players wore black armbands in memory of Fritz Walter, their 1954 captain, who'd died four days earlier. Klose, who played for Walter's club Kaiserslautern, had received cards and gifts from the great man and wanted to score in his memory. Instead one of his headers shook the base of a post, and Ballack got his goal instead, with another header, from Ziege's inswinging free kick.

When Frings stopped Berhalter's shot on the line soon after half-time, the Americans weren't the only ones to cry foul. But Frings had kept his arm by his side, without moving a muscle, so quite rightly no penalty. Thanks to their two world-class players, Germany had once again gone further in the World Cup than England, who were seeing that 5-1 in Munich in a different light.

---

22 June 2002 – World Cup Stadium, Gwangju – 42,114 – Gamal El-Ghandour (EGY)

SOUTH KOREA   (0) (0) 0
SPAIN   (0) (0) 0
South Korea 5-3 pens.

SOUTH KOREA Lee WJ, Choi JC, Hong (c), Kim TY [Hwang 89], Song, Kim NI [Lee EY 32], Yoo [Lee CS 61], Lee YP, Ahn, Park, Seol.
SPAIN Casillas, Puyol, Romero, Helguera [Xavi 93], Nadal, Hierro (c), Joaquín, Valerón [Luis Enrique 80], Morientes, Baraja, de Pedro [Mendieta 70].
PENALTY SHOOT-OUT: Hwang 1-0, Hierro 1-1, Park 2-1, Baraja 2-2, Seol 3-2, Xavi 3-3, Ahn 4-3, Joaquín saved, Hong 5-3.

Back to the drawing board for the two-day theory. South Korea were too fit and fresh to need anything as trivial as rest, and when Lee Woon-Jae came off his line to save Joaquín's penalty, they became the first Asian country to reach the semi-finals, though they could only have done it at home. Having left out Pedro Munitis, who'd made Thuram look mortal in Euro 2000, Spain were short of width on the left and yet again flattered slightly to deceive. But they would still have won if they hadn't had an Italian-size helping of bad luck.

In the second minute of extra time, Morientes had a headed goal disallowed because the linesman decided, quite wrongly, that the ball had gone out of play before Joaquín crossed it. Then Morientes volleyed against the far post, and Spain flew home with their Great Under-achievers trophy still in their baggage. A little undeservedly this time.

---

22 June 2002 – Nagai, Osaka – 44,233 – Oscar Ruiz (COL)

TURKEY   (0) (0) 1
İlhan 94 *(golden goal)*
SENEGAL   (0) (0) 0

TURKEY Rüstü, Fatih, Ergün, Tugay, Alpay, Bülent, Davala, Şaş, Şükür (c) [İlhan 67], Bastürk, Emre B [Arif FT].
SENEGAL Sylva, Coly, Daf, Diatta, Malick Diop, Bouba Diop, Cisse (c), Diao, H Camara, Fadiga, Diouf.

Again the match was lost by the team with a couple of extra days in bed. As against France, Senegal didn't use any substitutes, even when their attacks petered out in the second half. Diouf, later a big disappointment at Liverpool, made the odd run – but the game only went on as long as it did because Şükür gave his worst performance of a miserable tournament. Hesitant every time the ball came near him, he surpassed himself by letting the ball roll under his foot with only the keeper in front of him.

Thankfully Davala crossed from the right at last, and İlhan arrived at the near post to score a goal reminiscent of Germany's against Paraguay by sweeping the ball confidently across Sylva, and bars in Istanbul rang to chants of '*İlhan Mansiz, Hakan Fikirsiz* (clueless)'. Pelé, who'd once claimed that an African

2002

1930
1934
1938
1950
1954
1958
1962
1966
1970
1974
1978
1982
1986
1990
1994
1998
2002
2006

country would win the World Cup by 2000, now tried to cover himself by saying the continent needed a football infrastructure that worked, and FIFA should help provide it. If it happens by the time South Africa host the finals in 2010, start believing in miracles.

SEMI-FINALS

25 June 2002 – World Cup Stadium, Seoul – 65,625 – Urs Meier (SWI)

GERMANY	**(0) 1**
Ballack 75	
SOUTH KOREA	**(0) 0**

GERMANY Kahn (c), Linke, Metzelder, Hamann, Frings, Ramelow, Schneider [Jeremies 85], Neuville [Asamoah 88], Klose [Bierhoff 70], Ballack, Bode.
SOUTH KOREA Lee WJ, Choi JC [Lee Min-Sung 56], Hong (c) [Seol 80], Kim TY, Song, Yoo, Park, Lee YP, Cha, Hwang [Ahn 54], Lee CS.

Another good save by Kahn, another goal by Ballack, not much else to report as Germany reached their seventh World Cup Final with their third 1-0 win in a row. Kim Tae-Yung, wearing a face mask like Japan's Miyamoto, kept Klose in check, and the German defence did the same with Ahn, so the only goal came from the game's one clear chance. When Neuville hit a low cross from the right, the inevitable Ballack ran in to force a save with his right foot then put in the rebound with the other. Two-footed in a world of one-footed professionals, he'd earlier used his left to pick up a yellow card that kept him out of the Final. After the match, Völler congratulated him for a selfless foul in the team cause – but Germany would be a flair-free zone without him. It was

the end of a fun run by South Korea and their crowd – and by Hiddink, who lost a second successive World Cup semi-final.

26 June 2002 – Saitama Stadium 2002, Saitama – 61,058 – Kim Milton Nielsen (DEN)

BRAZIL	**(0) 1**
Ronaldo 49	
TURKEY	**(0) 0**

BRAZIL Marcos, Cafú (c), Roberto Carlos, Gilberto, Roque Júnior, Lúcio, Edmílson, Kléberson [Juliano Belletti 85], Ronaldo [Luizão 68], Rivaldo, Edílson [Denílson 75].
TURKEY Rüstü, Fatih, Ergün, Tugay, Alpay, Bülent, Davala [Mustafa (Muzzy) Izzet 74], Bastürk [Arif 88], Şükür (c), Emre B [İlhan 62], Şaş.

Instead of being up for this, out for revenge after the tough beat in their opening match, Turkey looked intimidated, only pulling their socks up when Ronaldo was taken off. Attacking in waves, Brazil missed several chances to make the game safe, and Rüstü had his second good game against them, saving from Cafú (with his elbow) and Ronaldo (after fumbling Rivaldo's shot), and diving bravely at Edílson's feet – but he should have kept out the shot that won the game. Surrounded by defenders on the left-hand corner of the area, Ronaldo toe-poked the ball across the keeper, who got a big hand to it but couldn't keep it out of the bottom corner. Ronaldo's grin took attention away from his new haircut: a half-moon at the front with nothing behind.

Near the end, Şükür actually connected with the ball, but Marcos had no great problem with his hooked volley. And İlhan missed with a header but otherwise didn't do much against a tenacious defence. Turkey's ninth finals match was the only one in which they failed to score. Eight of the squad were born in Germany – but they didn't get to play against the country of their birth. Brazil had also reached their seventh World Cup Final. Unlike Germany, they'd be playing in it with a full complement.

3RD-PLACE FINAL

29 June 2002 – World Cup Stadium, Daegu – 63,483 – Saad Mane (KUW)

TURKEY   **(3) 3**
Şükür 11 sec, İlhan 12, 32

SOUTH KOREA   **(1) 2**
Lee EY 9, Song 90

TURKEY Rüstü, Fatih, Alpay, Bülent, Ergün, Davala [Okan Buruk 76], Tugay, Bastürk [Tayfur 86], Şükür (c), Emre B [Ünsal 41], İlhan.
SOUTH KOREA Lee WJ, Song, Lee MS, Hong (c) [Kim TY HT], Lee EY [Cha 65], Park, Yoo, Lee YP, Lee CS, Ahn, Seol [Choi Tae-Uk 79].

Typical. After the most miserable month of his career, Şükür put himself in the record books with a goal of no importance. Even then he needed help from İlhan, who robbed Hong to set him up after 10.8 seconds, the fastest goal in any World Cup finals. Having missed a penalty against the USA, Lee Eul-Yong scored his first international goal with a smooth free kick that brushed the top of a post. But while South Korea poured forward in a lively first half, Turkey were dangerous on the break against a defence that was still uncertain. İlhan scored twice after some sweet interpassing with Sükür, who could have done with playing alongside him in the matches that mattered. Bülent elbowed Lee Min-Sung in the throat in the Turkish penalty area, and Ahn had a goal disallowed when Lee Chun-Soo was very offside, before South Korea were allowed the last

word, Song's long shot bouncing in off Cha's left buttock.

A lot was made of Turkey's ascent to world class – but they lost twice, drew with Costa Rica, beat only Senegal and the three Far Eastern countries, and didn't meet any European opposition. If these were the third and fourth best teams in the world, it was a world of FIFA's creation.

Yoo Sang-Chul became one of the five players who won their 100th caps in these finals. Hiddink set an obscure record by coaching two teams in 3rd-Place Finals.

FINAL

30 June 2002 – International, Yokohama – 69,029 – Pierluigi Collina (ITA)

BRAZIL   **(0) 2**
Ronaldo 67, 79

GERMANY   **(0) 0**

BRAZIL Marcos, Cafú (c), Roberto Carlos, Gilberto, Roque Júnior, Lúcio, Kléberson, Edmílson, Ronaldo [Denílson 89], Rivaldo, Ronaldinho [Juninho Paulista 85].
GERMANY Kahn (c), Linke, Metzelder, Jeremies [Asamoah 77], Ramelow, Frings, Schneider, Hamann, Klose [Bierhoff 74], Neuville, Bode [Ziege 84].

Remarkably, this was the first time the World Cup's two most successful countries had ever met in the finals. At almost any other time, it would have been a classic, especially if the 1970 tournament had been held at sea level. Now, while one side had three of the most skilful players in the world, backed by the talented newcomer Kléberson and a solid defence, Völler knew Germany were not only 'not a team that can put other teams up against the wall' but had to play the biggest match of their

1930
1934
1938
1950
1954
1958
1962
1966
1970
1974
1978
1982
1986
1990
1994
1998
2002
2006

1930
1934
1938
1950
1954
1958
1962
1966
1970
1974
1978
1982
1986
1990
1994
1998
2002
2006

lives without their best outfield player. A real catchweight contest.

Despite all their handicaps, his men stayed true to their history by making a fight of it. The first twenty minutes were mainly German attacks and Brazilian fouls, though Klose was booked for elbowing Edmílson in the face. Schneider ran Gilberto Silva ragged and Bode played well against Cafú, while Rivaldo was reduced to performing his old trick of holding his face when Schneider trod on his chest. But the Germans weren't making chances, and just before half-time Kléberson served notice by hitting the bar from outside the area.

Early in the second half, Neuville hit a free kick from somewhere over the horizon but Marcos touched it onto a post. That was Germany's last chance. When Hamann gave the ball away, Rivaldo hit a ground shot from twenty yards.

In the first half, Ronaldo had threatened to match the fiasco of his 1998 Final, missing three very good chances, two of them set up by Ronaldinho. Now he suddenly received help from the most unexpected source. After conceding a single injury-time goal in six matches, Kahn had been voted player of the tournament, and he'd just made another fine save from Gilberto's offside header. Now he went down to Rivaldo's easy shot – then inexplicably patted it against his chest and out again for Ronaldo to push it in. It was Brazil's first goal in a Final since 1970.

Then Rivaldo dummied over Kléberson's cross and Ronaldo stepped in ahead of Asamoah to roll the ball past Kahn's left hand again. Cafú, the only man to play in three World Cup Finals, became the fifth Brazilian captain to hold the trophy, which they'd now won in four different continents.

Skill and flair had overcome gutsy doggedness, but spare a thought for the Bayer Leverkusen quartet of Ramelow, Schneider,

Neuville and Ballack. That season they finished runners-up in the German League, the German Cup, the Champions League and now this. Forgive them if they cast envious glances at their club colleague Lúcio.

People were quick to pat both hosts on the back. The tournament was almost completely free of hooliganism, they said – and it was true. Distance and stringent checks kept most of the bad boys away.

The Korean fans were the best ever, they said – and it was simply patronising, as if no other host crowds had shown any passion. Well the Japanese hadn't, relatively speaking. No matches were staged in Tokyo, and crowds were relatively subdued. Having been Havelange's favourites to host the party, they'd had the concept of sharing foisted on them – and relations with South Korea weren't especially cordial. 'Why don't the Japanese don't eat with spoons?' asked South Korea's FIFA vice-president Chung Mong-Joon. 'Because the Koreans never taught them how.' Chung won the right to call the tournament Korea/Japan not Japan/Korea (one comes first in French), and these things obviously matter.

Forget all that, they said. Look at the football. At least you had to admire both hosts for being fit and fast. But it's easy to stay keen if you don't play sixty or seventy matches a season in domestic competitions and an interminable Champions League. While Mexico's coach noticed that the European teams 'have shown signs of fatigue after a long and intense season', South Korea built up their teamwork by playing 28 internationals that season. As for Japan, J League coach Steve Perryman knew that 'some ordinary players are looking like good players at the moment.'

Too many others carried injuries into the tournament. To name just a famous few: Beckham, Owen, Seaman, Fowler, Ashley Cole, Zidane, Thierry Henry, Ljungberg, Figo, Bokšić,

Ballack, Morientes, Maldini, Inzaghi, Paulo Sousa, Mboma, Wilmots and half the Irish. The USA's captain Claudio Reyna said France and Argentina were knocked out because their players were exhausted, and team doctor Jean-Marcel Ferret wasn't surprised the French were eliminated early: the players, he said, were 'mentally and physically exhausted.' FIFA announced they were to launch 'a scientific investigation' into injuries and burn-out among top players. If it's anything like their investigation into the alleged corruption of their own president, we can't wait.

FIFA were more interested in suing Phred Kaufman, an American brewer who brought out a beer named World Burp, a play on the Japanese pronunciation of 'World Cup' (*waarudo kappu* becoming *waarudo geppu*). A Tokyo court ruled in Kaufman's favour.

There were more serious issues with the ball (FIFA called it 'the roundest ever made' (!), but hardly anyone could hit a long-range shot with it) and the sale of tickets. In the first four days alone, empty seats cost organisers Kuwoc £500,000 (the Seoul government threatened legal action against Byrom, the UK firm that sold tickets for FIFA), while thousands of tickets weren't issued for a big game like England v Argentina 'because the sightlines are poor'.

But it was the heat and humidity that did the biggest damage as usual. Although football's essentially a winter game, or at least one that's played from autumn to spring, the World Cup finals have always been played at the height of the northern summer, giving the Southern Hemisphere sides an obvious advantage. This time even the linesmen were sweating.

There just wasn't enough good football to compensate for all this, no great new players coming through. A crock like Ronaldo, who'd lost his thrust and disappeared for long periods of every match, was still able to dominate the tournament.

Nothing's going to change, of course. People like the big occasion too much. And the enormous sums. But as a way of deciding the best team in the world, it's always been hit and miss. After the first round of matches, Maradona said Argentina were 'the only serious team' here. Even by the end, he had a point. But they didn't have much chance of proving it in this joke of a tournament.

Oh well, at least there was the other end of the scale. A few hours before Brazil played Germany, 'the other world final' was staged between the two lowest-ranked countries on the FIFA list. Bhutan beat Montserrat 4-0 at home, their captain Wangyel Dorji emulating Geoff Hurst by scoring a hat-trick. At least the circus left us the memory of that. And the courage of Michel Zen-Ruffinen.

2002

Timetable

Germany **2006**

All kick-off times BST. Note the usual eccentric FIFA numbering in some cases (Match C before Match B, Match 12 the day before Match 11, etc)

Group A

						Match no.
Fri 9 June	Munich	17.00	Germany	v	Costa Rica	1
Fri 9 June	Gelsenkirchen	20.00	Ecuador	v	Poland	2
Wed 14 June	Dortmund	20.00	Germany	v	Poland	17
Thu 15 June	Hamburg	14.00	Costa Rica	v	Ecuador	18
Tue 20 June	Berlin	15.00	Germany	v	Ecuador	33
Tue 20 June	Hanover	15.00	Costa Rica	v	Poland	34

Group B

Sat 10 June	Frankfurt	14.00	England	v	Paraguay	3
Sat 10 June	Dortmund	17.00	Sweden	v	Trinidad & T	4
Thu 15 June	Nuremberg	17.00	England	v	Trinidad & T	19
Thu 15 June	Berlin	20.00	Paraguay	v	Sweden	20
Tue 20 June	Cologne	20.00	England	v	Sweden	35
Tue 20 June	Kaiserslautern	20.00	Paraguay	v	Trinidad & T	36

Group C

Sat 10 June	Hamburg	20.00	Argentina	v	Ivory Coast	5
Sun 11 June	Leipzig	14.00	Holland	v	Serbia & M	6
Fri 16 June	Gelsenkirchen	14.00	Argentina	v	Serbia & M	21
Fri 16 June	Stuttgart	17.00	Holland	v	Ivory Coast	22
Wed 21 June	Frankfurt	20.00	Argentina	v	Holland	37
Wed 21 June	Munich	20.00	Ivory Coast	v	Serbia & M	38

Group D

Sun 11 June	Nuremberg	17.00	Iran	v	Mexico	7
Sun 11 June	Cologne	20.00	Angola	v	Portugal	8
Fri 16 June	Hanover	20.00	Angola	v	Mexico	23
Sat 17 June	Frankfurt	14.00	Iran	v	Portugal	24
Wed 21 June	Gelsenkirchen	15.00	Mexico	v	Portugal	39
Wed 21 June	Leipzig	15.00	Angola	v	Iran	40

Group E

Mon 12 June	Hanover	20.00	Ghana	v	Italy	9
Mon 12 June	Gelsenkirchen	17.00	Czech Republic	v	USA	10
Sat 17 June	Kaiserslautern	20.00	Italy	v	USA	25
Sat 17 June	Cologne	17.00	Czech Republic	v	Ghana	26
Thu 22 June	Hamburg	15.00	Czech Republic	v	Italy	41
Thu 22 June	Nuremberg	15.00	Ghana	v	USA	42

2006

1930
1934
1938
1950
1954
1958
1962
1966
1970
1974
1978
1982
1986
1990
1994
1998
2002

Group F

Tue 13 June	Berlin	20.00	Brazil	v	Croatia	11
Mon 12 June	Kaiserslautern	14.00	Australia	v	Japan	12
Sun 18 June	Munich	17.00	Australia	v	Brazil	27
Sun 18 June	Nuremberg	14.00	Croatia	v	Japan	28
Thu 22 June	Dortmund	20.00	Brazil	v	Japan	43
Thu 22 June	Stuttgart	20.00	Australia	v	Croatia	44

Group G

Tue 13 June	Stuttgart	17.00	France	v	Switzerland	13
Tue 13 June	Frankfurt	14.00	South Korea	v	Togo	14
Sun 18 June	Leipzig	20.00	France	v	South Korea	29
Mon 19 June	Dortmund	14.00	Switzerland	v	Togo	30
Fri 23 June	Cologne	20.00	France	v	Togo	45
Fri 23 June	Hanover	20.00	South Korea	v	Switzerland	46

Group H

Wed 14 June	Leipzig	14.00	Spain	v	Ukraine	15
Wed 14 June	Munich	17.00	Saudi Arabia	v	Tunisia	16
Mon 19 June	Stuttgart	20.00	Spain	v	Tunisia	31
Mon 19 June	Hamburg	17.00	Saudi Arabia	v	Ukraine	32
Fri 23 June	Kaiserslautern	15.00	Saudi Arabia	v	Spain	47
Fri 23 June	Berlin	15.00	Tunisia	v	Ukraine	48

2006

2nd Round

Group winners (A1 etc) v runners-up (A2 etc).

Sat 24 June	Munich	16.00	A1	v	B2	49 (1)
Sat 24 June	Leipzig	20.00	C1	v	D2	50 (3)
Sun 25 June	Stuttgart	16.00	B1	v	A2	51 (2)
Sun 25 June	Nuremberg	20.00	D1	v	C2	52 (4)
Mon 26 June	Kaiserslautern	16.00	E1	v	F2	53 (5)
Mon 26 June	Cologne	20.00	G1	v	H2	54 (7)
Tue 27 June	Dortmund	16.00	F1	v	E2	55 (6)
Tue 27 June	Hanover	20.00	H1	v	G2	56 (8)

Quarter-finals

Fri 30 June	Berlin	16.00	Winner (1)	v	Winner (3)	57 (A)
Fri 30 June	Hamburg	20.00	Winner (5)	v	Winner (7)	58 (C)
Sat 1 July	Gelsenkirchen	16.00	Winner (2)	v	Winner (4)	59 (B)
Sat 1 July	Frankfurt	20.00	Winner (6)	v	Winner (8)	60 (D)

Semi-finals

Tue 4 July	Dortmund	20.00	Winner (A)	v	Winner (C)	61
Wed 5 July	Munich	20.00	Winner (B)	v	Winner (D)	62

2006

1930
1934
1938
1950
1954
1958
1962
1966
1970
1974
1978
1982
1986
1990
1994
1998
2002
2006

3rd-Place Final

Sat 8 July Stuttgart 20.00 63

Final

Sun 9 July Berlin 19.00 64

All-time World Cup XI

Very subjective, as these things always are, but one of the perks of editorship. Here goes. I've kept to a loose 4–3–3 line-up, with a back four and a midfield ball-winner, rather than simply including as many skilful players as possible.

Sepp Maier
GER 1970–78

Víctor Rodríguez Andrade　　**Obdulio Varela**　　**Bobby Moore**　　**Nílton Santos**
URU 1950–54　　　　　　　　URU 1950–54　　　ENG 1962–70　　　BRZ 1954–62

Johan Neeskens　　　　**Diego Maradona**　　　　**Mário Zagallo**
HOL 1974–78　　　　　　ARG 1982–94　　　　　BRZ 1958–62

Garrincha　　　　　　**Gerd Müller**　　　　　**Pelé**
BRZ 1958–66　　　　GER 1970–74　　　　BRZ 1958–70

Coach: Vittorio Pozzo (ITA)

Ten best matches

1	Uruguay v Brazil	1950	6	Uruguay v Argentina	1930
2	Italy v Brazil	1982	7	Northern Ireland v Spain	1982
3	Hungary v Uruguay	1954	8	Holland v Argentina	1998
4	West Germany v Hungary (Final)	1954	9	Argentina v England	1998
5	West Germany v France	1982	10	Brazil v Sweden	1950

Bibliography

Books

5000 Goles Blancos, historia del Real Madrid, La Gran Enciclopedia Vasca, Bilbao 1969

Tony Adams, with Ian Ridley: *Addicted*, CollinsWillow, London 1998

Roger Allaway: *The International Matches of the USA*, Soccer Book Publishing, Cleethorpes 1995

Almanacco Illustrato del Calcio, Panini, Modena 1979 & 1991

Gordon Banks: *Banks of England*, Arthur Barker Ltd, London 1980

John Camkin: *World Cup 1958*, Rupert Hart-Davis Ltd, London 1959

Jean-Michel Cazal, Pierre Cazal, Michel Oreggia: *L'Équipe de France de Football*, Féderation Française de Football, 1992

Jean-Michel Cazal, Pierre Cazal, Michel Oreggia: *L'Intégrale de L'Équipe de France de Football*, Éditions Générales First, Paris 1998

Jean-Michel Cazal & Michel Oreggia: *Équipe nationale d'Israël 1948–89*, ASFS 1990

Dave Clayton & Jan Buitenga: *The International Matches series: Czechoslovakia, East Germany, Holland, Romania, Spain, Turkey, USSR, Yugoslavia*

Donal Cullen: *Ireland on the ball (1926–93)*, ELO Publications, Dublin 1993

Das Bilderbuch von der Fussballweltmeisterschaft, Vienna 1954

Lubomir David: *Rocenka Futbal 1983–84*, Bratislava 1984

Gareth Davies & Ian Garland: *Who's Who of Welsh International Soccer Players*, Bridge Books, Wrexham 1991

Arthur Ellis: *Refereeing round the world*, Hutchinson & Co, London 1954

Pedro Escartin: *Lo de Brasil fue asi*, 1950

Federação Portuguesa de Futbol: *Review 1972–73*

Rui Tovar: *Almanaque da Selecção*, Almanaxi, Lisbon 2004

FIFA News (various eds.) 1927–78

FIFA: *Official Reports* (various), 1962–94

Tom Finney: *Football round the world*, Museum Press, London 1953

Jean Norbert Fraiponts: *Belgium 1904–1940*, IFFHS

Jean Norbert Fraiponts: *Onze Rode Duivels*, Helios NV, Antwerp 1982

R Franta: *Fussballweltmeisterschaft 1938*, Agon Sportverlag, Frankfurt 1995

Bruno Govers *et al*: *De Rode Duivels. . .van A tot Z*, Euro Images Productions, Brussels 2000

Andrzej Gowarszewski: *Bialo-Czerwoni 1921–2001*, GIA, Katowice 2001

Andrzej Gowarszewski: *Encyklopedia Pilkarska: Copa América*, GIA, Katowice 1995

Andrzej Gowarszewski: *Encyklopedia Pilkarska: Herosi Mundiali*, GIA, Katowice 1993

Harry Gregg: *Wild about football*, Souvenir Press, London 1961

Hardy Grüne: *Fussballweltmeisterschaft 1934*, Agon Sportverlag, Frankfurt 2002

Eduardo Gutiérrez Cortinas: *Uruguay 1902–1940*, IFFHS

Mike Hammond (ed): *European Football Yearbook*, Sports Projects, Warley 1994, 1998 and 2002

Johnny Haynes: *It's all in the game*, Arthur Barker Ltd, London 1962

Tony Hilton & Barry Smith: *An Association with soccer*, Sporting Press, Auckland 1991

Zander Hollander (ed): *The American Encyclopedia of Soccer*, Everest House, New York 1980

Geoff Hurst: *The world game*, Stanley Paul, London 1967

Gordon Jeffery: *The report from Chile*, Souvenir Press, London 1962

Pat Jennings: *Pat Jennings An Autobiography*, Willow Books, London 1983

Nils Johansson: *Sweden 1908–1940*, IFFHS

Kicker-Almanach 1992, Copress Verlag, Munich 1991

Doug Lamming: *A Scottish Internationalists' Who's Who*, Hutton Press, Beverley 1987

Francis Lee: *Soccer round the world*, Arthur Barker Ltd, London 1970

Ally MacLeod: *The Ally MacLeod Story*, Stanley Paul, London 1979

Colin Malam: *World Cup Argentina*, Collins, London 1978

Max Marquis: *Sir Alf Ramsey: Anatomy of a football manager*, Arthur Barker Ltd, London 1970

Jimmy McIlroy: *Right inside soccer*, Nicholas Kaye Ltd, London 1960

Hugh McIlvanney (ed): World Cup '66, Eyre & Spottiswoode, London 1966

Hugh McIlvanney & Arthur Hopcraft (eds): *World Cup '70*, Eyre & Spottiswoode, London 1970

Peter McParland: *Going for goal*, Souvenir Press, London 1960

Julio Héctor Macías: *Argentina 1902–1940*, IFFHS.

David Miller: *World Cup 1970*, William Heinemann, London 1970

David Miller: *World Cup The Argentina Story*, Frederick Warne, London 1978

Mundial 1930–1982, La Gazzetta dello Sport, Milan

Jørgen Nielsen: *Denmark 1908–1940*, IFFHS

Official Report, 1934

Official Review, Brazil 1950

Franco Ossola: *I grandi del Torino*, MEB, Turin 1975

Pelé & Robert L Fish: *My life and the beautiful game*, New English Library, London 1977

Jeff Powell: *Bobby Moore*, Everest Books, London 1976

Ferenc Puskás: *Captain of Hungary*, Cassell & Co, London 1955

Alf Ramsey: *Talking football*, Stanley Paul, London 1952

George Raynor: *Football ambassador at large*, Soccer Book Club, Norwich 1960

Phil Soar & Richard Windows: *Spain '82*, STW & Hamlyn, London 1982

Phil Soar: World Cup '78, Marshall Cavendish, London 1978

Nobby Stiles: Soccer my battlefield, Stanley Paul, London 1968

Jack Taylor & David Jones: *Jack Taylor world soccer referee*, Pelham Books, London 1976

Kåre Torgrimsen: *Norway 1908–1940*, IFFHS

Martin Tyler: Boys of '66, Hamlyn, London 1981

Serge Van Hoof & Jairo Herrera Villareal: *Colombia the national teams 1938–1991*, 1991

Voetbaljaarboek 1991–92, KVBV, Belgium 1992

Billy Wright: *Captain of England*, Stanley Paul, London 1950

Newspapers and magazines

Balón (Mexico)
Il Corriere della Sera (Milan)
L'Équipe Guide 84–85
Football (France, June & July 1938)
IFFHS Fussballweltzeitschrift (1930 and 1934 finals)
Glasgow Evening News
The Guardian
Guerin Sportivo
The Independent
El Mercurio (Santiago)
La Nación (Buenos Aires)
El País (Montevideo)
Plaçar (80 Anos de Seleção Brasileiro)
La Prensa (Buenos Aires)
La Prensa (Lima)
New York Times
Official World Cup Final Programme 1966
Official World Cup Programme 1954
Soccer America
Soccer News (USA)
St Louis Post-Dispatch
Tempo (Yugoslavia)
The Times
World Soccer (various eds) 1982–2002

Videos

Esclusiva Film del Campionato Mondiale di Calcio (1934)
Coupe Du Monde De Football 1938
Mondiali di Calcio 1950–1958
Mondiali di Calcio 1962–66
Mondiali di Calcio 1970–74
Football World Championship (1954 The Official Film)
World Cup Review 1958 & 1962
World Cup Review 1966 & 1970
World Cup Review 1974 & 1978
Heading for Glory (The World Cup 1974)
All the goals of World Cup 1982
All the goals of World Cup 1994
All the goals of World Cup 1998
All the goals of World Cup 2002
The Boys from Brazil (1930–86)
Greatest Goals (The World Cup from Charlton to Maradona)
World Cup Winners (Europe)
World Cup Winners (South America)
Full-length videos of every match in the 1998 and 2002 finals

Picture credits

Integrated black and white photographs
Allsport: 109, 129, 347; **Associated Press:** 224; **Colorsport:** 84, 203; **Empics:** 178, 314, 352; **Hulton Getty:** 32; **Popperfoto:** xii, 16, 44, 64, 154, 256, 284.

Colour plate photographs
Action Images: 14(all), 15(tl); **Beejay Soccer Enterprises:** 1(all), 2(bl), 3 (t), 4(tl & tr); **Colorsport:** 2(br), 4(b), 5(b), 6(t), 7(tl & tr), 8(b), 10(tl), 13(b), 16(br); **Empics:** 14(all), 16(bl); **Getty Images:** 2(t), 7(b), 9(bl), 10(tr & b), 11(t), 12(tl, m&b), 13(tl & tr), 15(b), 16(tl); **MSI:** 3(b), 4(m), 5(tl & tr), 6(m&b), 12(tr), 15(m); **Popperfoto:** 8(t), 9(tl, tr&br), 11(b), 13(m); **Reuters/Corbis:** 15(t); **UPPA:** 16(tr).